Why Do You Need this New Edition?

If you're wondering why you should buy this new edition of *The Expanded Family Life Cycle*, here are 12 good reasons!

1. NEW Chapters on Alcohol, LGBT issues, Men, and Migration

2. NEW Chapter on Sexuality over the Life Cycle

3. NEW Chapter on Mental Illness and the Life Cycle

4. NEW Chapter on Spirituality through the Life Cycle

5. NEW Chapter on the Life Cycle Transition of Divorce and Remarriage

6. Updated! Information on race, culture, class, gender, and sexual orientation through the life cycle

7. Expanded information on increasing diversity of American families over the life cycle

8. Expanded formulation of cultural dimensions of human development (i.e., race, religion, class, sexual orientation, ethnicity, gender, and socioeconomic issues)

9. Integrated! Concept of home place as the core of meaningful life cycle assessment

10. NEW Appendix outlining multi-contextual life cycle framework for clinical assessment

11. Expanded analysis of the impact of social norms on every family

12. NEW descriptions of rapidly changing patterns in American families including: patterns of adolescence and young adulthood; marriage, divorce, and re-coupling; parenthood—two employed parents, increasing participation of fathers, cross-cultural adoption, and single parent adoption; and later life development.

Fourth Edition

THE EXPANDED FAMILY LIFE CYCLE: INDIVIDUAL, FAMILY, AND SOCIAL PERSPECTIVES

Monica McGoldrick
Director, Multicultural Family Institute,
Highland Park, New Jersey

Betty Carter
Emerita Director, Family Institute of Westchester

Nydia Garcia Preto
Associate Director, Multicultural Family Institute,
Highland Park, New Jersey

Allyn & Bacon
Boston   Columbus   Indianapolis   New York   San Francisco   Upper Saddle River
Amsterdam   Cape Town   Dubai   London   Madrid   Milan   Munich   Paris   Montreal   Toronto
Delhi   Mexico City   Sao Paulo   Sydney   Hong Kong   Seoul   Singapore   Taipei   Tokyo

Executive Editor: *Ashley Dodge*
Editorial Project Manager: *Carly Czech*
Senior Marketing Manager: *Wendy Albert*
Marketing Assistant: *Patrick M. Walsh*
Senior Production Project Editor: *Pat Torelli*
Manufacturing Buyer: *Debbie Rossi*
Cover Administrator: *Kristina Mose-Libon*
Editorial Production and Composition Service: *Prepare*
Interior Design: *Prepare*
Cover Designer: *Kristina Mose-Libon*

Library of Congress Cataloging-in-Publication Data
The expanded family life cycle : individual, family, and social perspectives / [edited by]
   Monica McGoldrick, Betty Carter, Nydia Garcia Preto. — 4th ed.
   p. cm.
Includes bibliographical references and index.
ISBN 978-0-205-74796-2
1. Life cycle, Human.   2. Family counseling—United States.   3. Family psychotherapy—United States.
I. McGoldrick, Monica.   II. Carter, Elizabeth A.   III. Garcia Preto, Nydia.
HQ536.C417 2011
306.85—dc22   2010019459

10 9 8 7 6 5 4   EBM   14 13 12

Allyn & Bacon
is an imprint of

www.pearsonhighered.com

ISBN 10:   0-205-74796-5
ISBN 13: 978-0-205-74796-2

Dedication

To Betty Carter, the bright star that brought forth this book from its first edition in 1980. She is now an emerita editor for this edition, but we have been grateful every day for the brilliance and creativity of Betty's thinking, which is at the center of this book. Her star has been a guiding light for this fourth edition, and we have felt deeply her presence as our guardian angel as we have tried to move the ideas forward to address the changing life cycle of the new millennium. She was the model, who taught us to be hands-on, in-your-face editors, though hopefully with a caring arm around the shoulder. We hope we are continuing to live up to her highly collaborative and rigorous standards even without her physical presence. This book has been very much a continuation of her creative energy, and we hope it is worthy of her.

CONTENTS

PREFACE

FOR WHOM WE ARE WRITING

The Expanded Family Life Cycle is a book for professionals and students in all areas of health care, social service, and education: psychology, social work, family therapy, nursing, and sociology, and all fields of counseling, school guidance counseling, vocational, college, addictions, and pastoral counseling. Our aim has been to lay out a perspective that has broad applicability for understanding and working with individuals and families through the evolution of their life cycle in a social and cultural context. We have divided the book into three parts: Perspectives on the Evolving Family Life Cycle, Life Cycle Transitions and Phases, and Clinical Dilemmas and Interventions and have included a separate Appendix, which offers a Multi-contextual Life Cycle Framework for Clinical Assessment.

REDEFINING HUMAN DEVELOPMENT

The book bridges the traditionally separate spheres of individual development and the family life cycle with cultural and social perspectives in a way that transforms the traditional categories and proposes a new, more comprehensive way to think about human development and the life cycle. Our expanded view of family actively includes the reciprocal impact of stresses at multiple levels of the human system: the individual, the immediate family household(s), the extended family, the community, the cultural group, and the larger society.

PUTTING THE INDIVIDUAL IN CONTEXT

Although social scientists give lip service to the notion of the individual's role in the system, there has been a tendency for mental health professionals to compartmentalize theorizing about family separately from theorizing about the individual. Theories of individual development evolved in the field of human development have espoused primarily psychodynamically oriented schemas, especially Erikson's modifications of Freudian theory, that ignore the gender, race, sexual orientation, and class norms of society that have produced deeply skewed models of "normal" child and adult development; such schemas make those who don't conform to dominant norms seem deficient. This thinking has been reinforced by the entire enterprise of diagnosis focused on universalizing individual pathology and ignoring systemic assessments as they influence human health and illness, strengths and resilience.

In our view, such splitting is not compatible with systems thinking. It leads to divergent and inconsistent definitions of the problem and its locus. Bowen's family systems theory, like Engel's bio-psycho-social model in medicine, is a notable exception to this tendency to split individual and family systems thinking. Bowen's theory places individual behavior and feelings squarely in the context of the family system, elaborating on the intricacies of the impact and the interaction between an individual and the family system of three or more generations. Bowen's theory also holds each adult individual responsible for creating change in the system.

To address these problems, we have made a continuing effort in this edition to spell out a more comprehensive framework for individual development in the context of relationships and society (Chapters 1 and 2). We also include a chapter based on Bowen's model of coaching individuals to obtain family systems change over the life cycle (Chapter 27). Other cases using the coaching method are discussed in various chapters throughout the book and in the chapter on the therapist's own life cycle (Chapter 29).

REDEFINING FAMILY: WIDENING OUR LENS

This edition celebrates diversity as we welcome the multiculturalism of the twenty-first century. We refer not only to cultural diversity, but also to the diversity of family forms. There are many ways to go through life in a caring, productive manner, and no specific family structure is ideal. Indeed, most of the criticisms of life cycle theory have actually been only about the limited focus of theoretical and research attention to the developmental stages of just one family form: the White, Anglo, middle-class, nuclear family of a once-married heterosexual couple, their children, and (occasionally) their extended family. This book expands that definition of family in ways that attempt to include everyone in our society.

We have widened our lens to deal more concretely in large and small ways with the fact that every family is a group of individuals embedded in communities and in the larger society whose impact is definitive and must be taken into account for interventions at the family level to succeed. Our choice of language symbolizes our recognition of the vast changes in family structure that are taking place. We have replaced the limited term "nuclear family," which has come to refer only to a father and mother and their children in intact first families, with the term "immediate family" referring to all household members and other primary caretakers or siblings of children, whether in a heterosexual couple, single-parent, unmarried, remarried, gay, or lesbian household. We believe "commitment to each other" more than biological or legal status to be the basic bond that defines a family.

While it may be statistically accurate to outline the widely experienced stages of the family life cycle, focusing on marriage (Chapter 13), the birth and development of children and adolescents (Chapters 14 and 15), launching (Chapter 16), young adulthood (Chapter 12), aging (Chapter 17), and death (Chapter 18), there is no single list of life stages that can be sufficiently inclusive. Throughout this edition, we have tried to recognize the vast number of families whose family life cycle varies in significant ways from the traditional stage outline. Individuals of different cultures and socioeconomic groups go through the stages at very different ages. A growing number of adults are choosing not to marry (Chapter 11) or, like gays and lesbians, are prevented from marrying (Chapter 8) or, like the poor (Chapter 6), find marriage almost impossible to afford. It thus becomes appropriate because of the increasing diversity of couples over the life cycle to speak of "couples therapy" rather than "marital therapy" (Chapter 13).

Growing numbers of women are delaying childbearing or are choosing to remain childless. The prevalence of divorce and remarriage is requiring a large proportion of our society to manage additional life cycle stages and complete restructuring of their families as they move through life. There has been a dramatic increase in the percentage of permanent single-parent households created by divorce or single-parent adoption. For clinical interventions with families at these stages we offer chapters on divorce (Chapter 19), single parents (Chapter 20), and families transformed by the divorce cycle: reconstituted, multinuclear, recoupled, and remarried families (Chapter 21). Families that experience migration must also negotiate an additional life cycle stage of adjusting to a new culture (Chapter 22).

Finally, vast differences in family life cycle patterns are caused by oppressive social forces: racism, sexism, homophobia, classism, ageism, cultural prejudices of all kinds, poverty, and immigration. We seek to include all of these elements in our thinking, while still providing clear and manageable clinical suggestions related to the family's place in its many contexts. Chapters that expand on these more inclusive perspectives include the chapters on women (Chapter 3) and on men (Chapter 4), on social class (Chapter 5), and on LGBT families (Chapter 8). Further expanding our view of family relationships, we have separate chapters on siblings through the life cycle (Chapter 10), spirituality (Chapter 9), sexuality (Chapter 7), chronic illness (Chapter 23), mental illness (Chapter 26), alcohol problems (Chapter 24), domestic violence (Chapter 25), and on creating meaningful life cycle rituals (Chapter 28).

While family patterns are changing dramatically as we enter the twenty-first century, the importance of community and connection are no less important than ever, but we must shift our paradigm to understand people's experiences of community as they move through life. Our identity is bound up in our interrelatedness to others. This is the essence of community—relationships that bridge the gap between private, personal, and family relationships, and the impersonal public sphere. We have a need for a spiritual sense of belonging to something larger than our own small, separate concerns. With our ever-greater involvement in work, time for anything "unnecessary" has been disappearing, leaving little time for church or synagogue, friends, family Sunday dinners, supporting children's school activities, political action, or advocacy. These activities often get lost in the scramble to survive, leaving little but the individual striving for power and money.

We look at the concept of home as a place of self-definition and belonging, a place where people find resilience to deal with the injustices of society or even of their families, a place where they can develop and express their values. Home reflects our need to acknowledge the forces in our history that have made us strong, but it is also a concept that we remake at every phase of life, with family, with friends, with work, with nature, with smells and sounds and tastes that nurture us, because they give us a sense of safety and connection. Clinical intervention needs to acknowledge the importance of this place of psychological and spiritual safety at each life cycle phase. We see the concept of home as at the core of a meaningful life cycle assessment. We must assess clients with regard to their sense of belonging and connection to what is familiar. Having a sense of belonging is essential to well-being. Grasping where this sense of home is for a client is an essential part of any assessment and clinicians and policy makers who do not consider our deep-seated need for continuity and belonging as we go through life, especially through traumatic transitions and disruptions, will increase the trauma of the original experience.

THE SOCIAL PERSPECTIVE

In addition to focusing down from family to the individual, we have expanded our focus up to the community and larger societal levels. This book aims to help us to include in our clinical evaluations and treatment all of the major forces that make us who we are: race, class, sexual orientation, gender, ethnicity, spirituality, politics, work, time, community, values, beliefs, and dreams. We no longer have separate chapters on culture, because we believe that consideration of culture, race, and ethnicity is so essential to every issue discussed in the book that we have urged all authors to keep cultural considerations in the forefront of their clinical descriptions. As our awareness of societal patterns of domination and privilege has grown, we have greatly expanded our analysis of the impact of social norms on every family. We have also included throughout the book cases that reflect the social forces that impinge on individual and family functioning. It is our strong belief that this expanded family life cycle context is still the best framework for clinical intervention because it deals with the development over time of individuals in their family relationships and within their communities as they struggle in this new millennium to define and implement life's meanings within a larger society that helps some more than others. To be lasting, change must encompass every level of our lives. We have summarized this multicontextual life cycle framework in our Appendix on Clinical Assessment.

MONICA MCGOLDRICK'S ACKNOWLEDGMENTS

The Fourth edition of *The Expanded Family Life Cycle* has been a labor of love with my dear friend and sister, Nydia Garcia Preto. I am extremely grateful that Nydia, who has been my collaborator in so many other efforts over many decades, has been at my side to develop this Fourth edition. We have struggled together mightily to figure out how to transform this edition to include the many changes of the past decade. I am so appreciative of her thoughtful efforts to make sense of the complex issues of the life cycle in our new century. I know I pressed her for more time than she had, and I am grateful for the many days we spent at our table trying to figure out how to express ourselves, organize our thoughts, and understand of the complex phenomenon of the life cycle and to deal with the numerous challenges of this many layered book for which we had a strong vision that demanded much rigor of our authors. This book has also been the fruition of my love for and debt to Betty Carter, with whom I shared so much for so many years. For three decades she and I wrote together, taught together, and thought together more closely than I have ever done with anyone else. I have greatly missed her collaboration on this edition. Having to proceed without her enormous good humor, creativity, energy, and willingness to stretch herself and to stretch others has been hard indeed. I have missed her at every turn. I am thankful to Nydia for having agreed to step in and work with me, and I am extremely proud of what we have accomplished together. I am very grateful as well for the contributions from so many colleagues who have delivered the best papers ever for this edition! Betty would appreciate their efforts.

This edition required a whole rethinking of the life cycle to fit the changing circumstances of the new millennium. Nydia and I have worked hard to understand the increasing complexities of families as they move through the life cycle and deal with increasingly difficult global constraints. These complexities have made it very difficult to write in as straightforward a way as we would wish. Each time we would write a sentence, we would say, "On the other hand, there is this other factor that influences that phenomenon." Space constraints were especially challenging, and we were incredibly fortunate in the efforts of our authors to write meaningful chapters in their limited space.

I thank my wonderful friends for the support they give me every day, no matter where on the globe they are. In addition to Nydia, my appreciation goes to Nollaig Byrne, Froma Walsh, Carol Anderson, John Folwarski, Imelda McCarthy, Jayne Mahboubi, Elaine Pinderhughes, Matthew Mock, Maria Root, Fernando Colon, Robert Jay Green, Michael Rohrbaugh, Doug Schoeninger, Glenn Wolff, Salome Raheim, Vanessa Jackson, Vanessa Mahmoud, Kalli Adamides, Charlotte Danielson, Jane Sufian, Roberto Font, Barbara Petkov, and Sueli Petry. I thank my friends Evelyn Lee, Michael White, and Sandy Leiblum whom I lost since the last edition of this book. I miss them greatly, and they live on in my heart every day. I hope I am doing them proud with this work.

My son grew up and was launched in the decade since our previous edition appeared. How did that happen so fast? I now wish him Godspeed for his own life cycle journey. Sophocles has kept the home fires burning, as he has done for more than 40 years now, while I was preoccupied or off working to bring this book forth. I am very grateful for his love and steadiness through all. I thank my sisters Morna and Neale for being at my side for my life cycle journey, and my nephews, Guy and Hugh, for rooting for me from their place in the next generation and I celebrate with this publication the first member of the next generation of our family, Renzo Robert Livingston, born just before this edition was published. Long may he thrive. Always I have been standing fortunately on the shoulders of my parents, my caretaker, Margaret Pfeifer Bush, my Aunt Mamie, and my godparents Elliot and Marie Mottram and Jack Mayer.

Finally I thank my sister, soulmate, friend, and longtime collaborator Betty Carter for her friendship and intellectual stimulation over so many years. I am so grateful for her life force, her humor, her intelligence, her sticking power, and the warmth of her friendship.

NYDIA GARCIA PRETO'S ACKNOWLEDGMENTS

Taking part in this project has been challenging and transformative in more ways than I expected. First I want to thank Monica for her encouragement and support throughout the years we have worked together. Our personal histories and lives are very different, yet we seem to share a strong spiritual connection and a thirst for learning about and understanding the complexities of life which for me has been essential. It has been a privilege to work with her, to share the joys and pains in our personal and professional lives during these past 35 years. When she first asked me to be a co-editor of this book, a book I have found to be fundamental in my learning about families, I was taken aback. Knowing how closely she and Betty had worked together, and how powerful and influential their thinking has been for so many of us who studied with them, I questioned the value of my contribution. My initial response was not to do it. But, in her wonderfully convincing way, Monica presented her reasons for asking me. We teach together, we stay up late trying to figure out how to continue on this journey of learning and teaching the concepts we love and find transformative. We love working with families, teaching about systems theory, strategizing about changing systems, mentoring students, building networks, and supporting each other when we are without answers. How could I not be part of rethinking and editing this wonderful book? I am thankful for her trust and for the experience. I also want to acknowledge the support of my colleagues at MFI: Barbara, Roberto, and Sueli, who were willing to read my writing and listen to my complaints, and my friends who understood my unavailability when I couldn't play with them.

And, of course, I am especially grateful for the encouragement and support I received from the many members of my family, particularly my daughter Sara and son David. They have given me the opportunity to experience the complexities of being a mother raising children while also having a career. We have gone through adolescence, and now they are both at different stages of young adulthood. I am learning about staying connected while letting go, and enjoying having two wonderful grandsons. We have survived my separation from their father and are adjusting to different configurations of family structure. I thank them for their lessons, their challenges, and their love. I thank their father, Carl, and his extended family for their understanding and friendship. I have found strength in the memories of my life with my mother, father, and brother, who are now gone, but living in my heart. And, I especially want to acknowledge my partner in life, Conrad, whose generosity and caring keep me hopeful as I become older.

JOINT ACKNOWLEDGMENTS

We both give heartfelt thanks to every author in this book. We know we have been, as Betty used to put it: "critical, hands-on, in-your-face editors, full of requirements and suggestions." It couldn't have been easy for you authors, but you came through with wonderful, thoughtful material.

And those of you who answered our cries for help very late in the process—you know who you are—we'll never forget your rescue of several important chapters! And to those who did yet one more draft when you thought you weren't up to it—and you know who you are—we are grateful for your perseverance. We love you for it and we know the readers will as well. We are also deeply grateful to Tracey Laszloffy, a genius of a collaborator, who has prepared the manual to accompany this book. She is brilliant, creative, and extraordinarily generous with her time. We greatly look forward to further collaboration with her as the book continues to evolve.

We also thank our friend and Office Manager, Roberto Font, our Administrator, Fran Snyder, and our office secretary, Agi Sanchez, for keeping our office running smoothly so that we could concentrate on the many tasks this book entailed. You helped us keep things in order, communicated with authors, and also protected us when we needed time alone to concentrate on this work.

We are more grateful than we can say to our editor at Pearson, Ashley Dodge, for her ability to keep her eye on the ball and help this book to see the light of day. She made efforts way beyond the call of duty and had a measure of personal integrity and comradeship in our work together which was extraordinary and deeply appreciated. We also offer a deep thank you to Carly Czech for her very careful and thoughtful husbanding of the manuscript. We are very appreciative of your intelligence, attention to details, your generosity and thoughtfulness about the book, and your close collaborative work with us through every aspect of its production. Many thanks!

We are extremely grateful to Pat Torelli for her efforts on a beautiful production. Finally we thank Frank Weihenig of Prepare, Inc, a new friend made in the process of this book's production. He answered every email with great promptness and good humor and took a generous and personal interest in helping to make every aspect of the manuscript come forth in the final book, and not to forget the wonderful meeting and lunch in Pompeii!

ABOUT THE EDITORS

Monica McGoldrick, M.A., M.S.W., Ph.D. (h.c.), is the Director of the Multicultural Family Institute in Highland Park, N. J., and on the Psychiatry Faculty of the Robert Wood Johnson Medical School. Her other books include: *Ethnicity and Family Therapy*, Third Edition; *Genograms: Assessment and Intervention*, Third Edition. *Living Beyond Loss,* Second Edition*; Revisioning Family Therapy: Race, Culture, and Gender in Clinical Practice*, Second Edition; and *The Genogram Journey: Reconnecting with Your Family* to be published by W. W. Norton in the Fall of 2010, which translates her ideas about family relationships for a popular audience, using examples such as Beethoven, Groucho Marx, Sigmund Freud, and the Kennedys.

She received her B.A. from Brown University, a Masters in Russian Studies from Yale University, and her M.S.W. and an Honorary Doctorate from Smith College School for Social Work. Dr. McGoldrick is known internationally for her writings and teaching on topics including culture, class, gender, loss, family patterns (genograms), remarried families, and sibling relationships. Her clinical videotape demonstrating the use of the life cycle perspective with a multicultural remarried family dealing with issues of unresolved mourning has become one of the most widely respected videotapes available in the field.

Betty Carter, M.S.W., founder and Director Emerita (1977–1997) of the Family Institute of Westchester in White Plains, New York, spent over 30 years as a family therapy clinician, supervisor, teacher, and director of a major training institute. She received awards from the American Family Therapy Academy, Hunter College School of Social Work, and the American Association of Marriage and Family Therapy Research and Education Foundation. With her colleagues Peggy Papp, Olga Silverstein, and Marianne Walters she co-founded the Women's Project in Family Therapy, which promoted a feminist revisioning of family therapy and received awards from both the Family Therapy Academy and the AAMFT. Their work culminated in a book on gender-sensitive family therapy practice: *The Invisible Web: Gender Patterns in Family Therapy Relationships*.

In 1996 Betty Carter authored a trade book on couples, *Love, Honor and Negotiate: Building Partnerships That Last a Lifetime*. She published numerous professional book chapters and journal articles, along with educational videotapes produced by Steve Lerner for Guilford Press. Married to her husband Sam, a musician, for over 50 years, Betty has two sons and three grandchildren. She has said that of all her ideas she always loved the family life cycle framework most "because it contains all the other ideas and has room for more."

Nydia Garcia Preto, M.S.W., is the Associate Director at the Multicultural Family Institute in Highland Park, N. J., where she also has a private practice. Ms. Garcia Preto was formerly a Visiting Professor at the Rutgers Graduate School of Social Work, and for many years the Director of the Adolescent Day Hospital at the University of Medicine and Dentistry of New Jersey. She received her M.S.W. from Rutgers Graduate School of Social Work and her B.A. in Sociology at Rider College. A highly respected family therapist, author, and teacher, and organizational trainer, she has publications in textbooks and journals on issues of cultural competence, Puerto Rican and Latino families, Latinas, immigration, ethnic intermarriage, and families with adolescents. She is co-editor of the most recent edition of *Ethnicity and Family Therapy*. Ms. Garcia Preto received the Frantz Fanon, M.D. Award from the Post Graduate Center for Mental Health for her work with Puerto Rican and Latino Adolescents and Families, and the Social Justice Award from The American Family Therapy Academy. She and her colleagues at MFI have developed many training for many years on multiculturalism in clinical work, and organizational consulting on cultural competence.

CONTRIBUTORS

Constance Ahrons, Ph.D., *Professor Emerita and former Director of the Marriage and Family Therapy Doctoral Program, University of Southern California, Los Angeles. Private practice in San Diego.*

Carol Anderson, M.S.W., Ph.D., *Professor Emerita, University of Pittsburgh Medical School, Pittsburgh, PA.*

Maria Anderson, M.S.W., *is a therapist in the Adolescent Division of Addiction Medicine at the Western Psychiatric Institute and Clinic, Pittsburgh Pa.*

Deidre Ashton, M.S.S.W., L.C.S.W., *Faculty, Center for Family, Community, and Social Justice, Inc. Princeton, NJ. Faculty, Ackerman Institute, NYC, and the Multicultural Family Inst., NJ. Couple and Family Therapist, Princeton Family Institute, NJ.*

Kathy Berliner, L.C.S.W., *Marriage and Family Therapist. Former faculty Family Institute of Westchester.*

Ellen Berman, M.D., *Clinical Professor of Psychiatry, University of Pennsylvania School of Medicine.*

Lynne Blacker, L.C.S.W., *is a supervisor at the Family and Youth Intervention Program, Children's Aid Society, New York, New York.*

Celia Jaes Falicov, Ph.D., *Private Practice, San Diego, CA, Clinical Professor, Department of Psychiatry, University of California, San Diego, CA.*

Richard H. Fulmer, Ph.D., *Post-doctoral Programs in Psychoanalysis and Psychotherapy, Adelphi University, Garden City, NY. Private practice, New York, NY.*

Alison Heru, M.D., *Associate Professor of Psychiatry, University of Colorado, Denver.*

Paulette Moore Hines, Ph.D., *Director, Office of Prevention Services and Research, a division of UBHC-University of Medicine and Dentistry of New Jersey, Piscataway, NJ.*

Evan Imber-Black, Ed.D., *Program Director of the Marriage and Family Therapy Masters Degree at Mercy College, Dobbs Ferry, NY; and Director of the Center for Families and Health, Ackerman Institute for the Family.*

Demaris Jacobs, Ph.D., *Former faculty Family Institute of Westchester.*

Jodie Kilman, Ph.D., *Core Faculty, Psy.D. Program, Clinical Psychology, Massachusetts School of Professional Psychology, Boston, MA; founding member Boston Inst. for Culturally Affirming Practice.*

Tracey Laszloffy, Ph.D., *Private practice, Norwich, CT.*

Steve Lerner, Ph.D., *Private Practice, Topeka, KS.*

Matthew Mock, Ph.D., *Professor of Psychology, J.F.K Univ.; Private Practice and Consulting Practice, Berkeley, CA; Former Director CIMH Center for Multicultural Dev.; Director, F. Y. C. and Multicultural Services, Berkley. CA.*

Barbara Petkov, L.M.F.T., Ed.S., *Faculty of the Multicultural Family Institute, and in private practice in Highland Park, NJ.*

Sueli Petry, Ph.D., *Faculty of the Multicultural Family Institute and in private practice, Highland Park, NJ.*

John Rolland, M.D., *Professor of Psychiatry, University of Chicago and Co-Director, Chicago Center for Family Health, Chicago, IL.*

Mary Anne Ross, B.A., *COPSA Institute for Alzheimer's Disease and Related Disorders, CMHC Piscataway University of Medicine and Dentistry of New Jersey.*

Natalie Schwartzberg, L.C.S.W., *Marriage and Family Therapist. Former faculty Family Institute of Westchester.*

Froma Walsh, M.S.W., Ph.D., *Co-Director Chicago Center for Family Health; Mose & Sylvia Firestone Professor Emerita, School of Social Service Administration. The University of Chicago.*

Marlene F. Watson, Ph.D., *Professor at Drexel University in Philadelphia, PA.*

David Wohlsifer, Ph.D., L.C.S.W., *Private Practice, Bala Psychological Resources, Bala Cynwyd, PA; Adjunct Professor, Bryn Mawr College, Graduate School of Social Work.*

Chapter 1

Overview: The Life Cycle in Its Changing Context
Individual, Family and Social Perspectives
Monica McGoldrick, Betty Carter, Nydia Garcia Preto

Introduction: The Family Life Cycle: A System Moving Through Time

We are born into families. They are the foundation of our first experiences of the world, our first relationships, our first sense of belonging to a group. We develop, grow, and hopefully die in the context of our families. Human development takes shape as it moves and evolves through the matrix of the family life cycle, embedded in the larger socio-cultural context. All human problems are framed by the formative course of our family's past, the present tasks it is trying to master, and the future to which it aspires. Thus, the family life cycle and the larger social context in which it is embedded are the natural framework within which to focus our understanding of individual identity and development. This chapter and this book offer a framework for understanding families in the U. S. in their cultural context over the life cycle. Statistics offered refer to the U.S. unless otherwise specified and are an effort to help clinicians appreciate the larger context of individuals, their families, and their larger social system, as they move through the life cycle.

Families comprise people who have a shared history and an implied shared future. They encompass the entire emotional system of at least three, and frequently four or even five, generations held together by blood, legal, and/or historical ties. Relationships with parents, siblings, and other family members go through transitions as they move through life. Boundaries shift, psychological distance among members changes, and roles within and between subsystems are constantly being redefined (Norris & Tindale, 1994; Cicirelli, 1995; Tindale, 1999; Meinhold, 2006; McKay & Caverly, 2004; Connidis, 2001, 2008). It is extremely difficult to think of the family as a whole because of the complexity involved. As a system moving through time, families are different from all other systems because they incorporate new members only by birth, adoption, commitment, or marriage, and members can leave only by death, if then. No other system is subject to these constraints. A business manager can fire members of his organization viewed as dysfunctional, and members can resign if the organization's structure and values are not to their liking. In families, by contrast, the pressures of membership with no exit available can, in the extreme, lead to severe dysfunction and even suicide. In nonfamily systems, the roles and functions are carried out in a more or less stable way, by replacement of those who leave for any reason, or else the group dissolves and people move on into other systems. Although families also have roles and functions, their main value is in the relationships, which are irreplaceable.

Until recently, therapists have paid little attention to the family life cycle and its impact on human development. Even now, psychological theories tend to relate at most to the nuclear family, ignoring the multigenerational context of family connections that pattern our lives. But our society's swiftly changing family patterns, which assume many configurations over the life span, are forcing us to take a broader view of both development and normalcy. Those milestones around which life cycle models have been oriented (birth, marriage, childbearing, and death) hold very different roles in the lives of families in the twenty-first century than they did in previous times. Even in the three decades of this book's history we have revised the definitions of life cycle stages and their meanings with each of our four editions to reflect our evolving understanding of this framework and the exciting and dramatically changing realities of the life cycle of families in the United States in our times. The tremendous life-shaping impact of one generation on those following is hard to overestimate. For one thing, the three or four different generations must adjust to life cycle transitions simultaneously. While one generation is moving toward old age, the next is contending with late middle age, caregiving or the empty nest. The next generations cope with establishing careers and intimate peer adult relationships, having and raising children, and adolescents, while the youngest generations are focused on growing up as part of the system. Naturally, there is an intermingling of the generations, and events at one level have a powerful effect on relationships at each other level. The important impact of events in the grandparental generation is routinely overlooked by therapists who focus only on the nuclear family. Painful experiences such as illness and death are particularly difficult for families to integrate and are thus most likely to have a profound, long-range impact on relationships in the next generations.

Of course, in different cultures, the ages of multigenerational transitions differ markedly. In addition, ethnicity, race, sexual orientation, gender identity, socio-economic status and health status influence the life cycle. The stages of the life cycle themselves are rather arbitrary breakdowns. The notion of childhood has been described as the invention of eighteenth-century Western society and adolescence as the invention of the nineteenth century (Aries, 1962), related to the cultural, economic, and political contexts of those eras. The notion of young adulthood as an independent phase could be thought of as an invention of the twentieth century, due to society's technological

needs. The inclusion of women as independent individuals could be said to be a construct of the late twentieth century. The lengthy phases of midlife, the empty nest, and older age have certainly been developments primarily of the late twentieth and early twenty-first centuries, brought about by the smaller number of children and the greatly increased life span of our times. Given the current changes in the family, the twenty-first century may become known for an even more expanded launching stage, influenced by the educational requirements of the post-industrial age. We certainly seem headed for a transformation in our concept of marriage and of nurturing/caretaking relationships with both children and older family members.

Just as the texture of life has become more complicated, so too our therapeutic models must evolve to reflect this complexity, appreciating both the context around the individual as a shaping environment and the evolutionary influence of time on human experience. From a family life cycle perspective, symptoms and dysfunction are examined within a systemic context. At the same time we must be extremely cautious about stereotyping people who do not fit into traditional norms for marriage, or having children, as if they were in themselves measures of maturity, which they are not. So we must consider in our clinical assessment the critical life cycle challenges of individuals and families at each point in their lives, while being careful not to marginalize those whose life courses differs from the norms of the majority. Relevant life cycle questions include how family members are managing their same-generation and intergenerational relationships at each phase for the healthy evolution of the family. Are certain family members over-functioning for others and are certain developmental or caretaking needs being neglected?

Families characteristically lack a time perspective when they are having problems. They tend to magnify the present moment, overwhelmed and immobilized by their immediate feelings. Or they become fixed on a moment in the past or the future that they dread or long for. They lose the awareness that life always means motion from the past into the future with a continual transformation of familial relationships. As the sense of motion becomes lost or distorted, therapy involves restoring a sense of life as a process and movement both from and toward.

The changing American family structure should be put in the context of similar changes occurring worldwide and at every economic level: vastly increased divorce rates, the rise of single parent families, two-income households, an increase in work time, especially for women, and high rates of unwed childbearing. Experts have expressed hope that the universality of family change will bring about new thinking on social policy and a new attention to the integrity of families in their community context.

Despite the fact that in our era nuclear families often live on their own and at great distance from extended family members, they are still part of the larger multigenerational system, intertwined in their past, present, and anticipated future relationships. We have many more options than families of the past: whether or whom to marry, where to live, how many children to have, if any, how to conduct relationships within the immediate and extended family, and how to allocate family tasks. Our society has moved from family ties that were obligatory to those that seem voluntary, with accompanying shifts in the clarity of norms for relationships. Relationships with siblings and parents are fairly readily disrupted by occupational and geographic mobility as we move through the life cycle; even couples are increasingly struggling with bi-coastal relationships (Hess & Waring, 1984; Connidis, 2001; Mckay & Caverly, 2004; Pruchno & Rosenbaum, 2003; Taylor, Clark, & Newton, 2008).

Therapeutic interventions with a life cycle framework aim at helping families to reestablish their evolutionary momentum so that they can proceed forward to foster the uniqueness of each member's development. We can, through our therapeutic efforts, validate, empower, and strengthen family ties or, by ignoring them, perpetuate the invalidation, anomie, and disconnection of the dominant value structure of our society, which privileges individualism, autonomy, competition and materialistic values, over connectedness to a whole network of kin with whom one feels "at home."

The Changing Family Life Cycle

Family life cycle patterns have changed dramatically over the past century. In 1900 the average life expectancy in the U.S. was 47 years; by the year 2000 dying before old age has become a rare event. About 75 percent of the population live beyond their 65th birthday, whereas, in 1850, only 2 percent of people lived to this birthday (Skolnick, 2009)! Two thirds of the longevity increase of all human history has taken place since 1900. At that time half of all parents experienced the death of a child; by 1976 this rate was only 6 percent. Thus, in earlier times couples had to have two children in order to have one who survived to adulthood, but this is no longer necessary. Twenty-five percent of children in 1900 had lost a parent by death before age 15; by 1976 only 5 percent of children experienced parental death by that age. In 1900 one out of 62 children had lost both parents; by 1976 this was only one out of 1800 (Skolnick, 2009).

At the same time that we are living much longer and experiencing much less untimely loss than ever in history, our couple and parent-child patterns are also changing dramatically. In terms of couples, fewer and fewer appear to be marrying. It has been speculated that the major change is the economic situation of women, who, once they can support themselves, may not want a marriage with the traditional caretaking rules. As one well-paid working wife and mother put it, "Women's expectations have changed dramatically, while men's have not changed at all. . . . Providing is not enough. I need more partnership" (Jones, 2006, p. B1). Fifty-one percent of women live without a spouse (Zernike, 2007). The marriage rate has dropped by about 50 percent since the mid-twentieth century (McManus, 2006). Marriage rates are decreasing dramatically (33 percent of men and 26 percent of women never marry) and the age of marriage has been increasing dramatically, from age 21 to age 25 for women and from age 23 to age 27 for men in the last 30 years (Cherlin, 2009; U.S. Census, 2007). Whereas in 1976 women had on average 3.2 children, current childbearing rates in the U.S. have diminished to less than 2 children per couple, although rates are higher for Latinas (2.3) (Zezima, 2008). In 1970 only 10 percent of women did not have children, while currently that rate has doubled. Even more educated professional women (27 percent) are remaining childless (Zezima, 2008). Whereas in 1950 only 4 percent of births took place outside of marriage, the current rate is 35 percent, though many of these parents are living in couple relationships, a fair percentage being same-sex parents (Cherlin, 2009). Married couples with children have shrunk from 40 percent of all households in 1970 to less than 25 percent (Saluter, 1996; www.statemaster.com, 2009).

Overall changes in family life cycle patterns have escalated dramatically, in recent decades owing especially to:

A lower birth rate

Longer life expectancy

The changing role of women

The rise in unmarried motherhood

The rise in unmarried couples

Increasing single-parent adoptions

Increasing LGBT gay and lesbian couples and families

High divorce and remarriage rates

Increasing two-paycheck marriages to the point where they are now the norm

One of the greatest changes in living patterns in the U.S. in recent years is the increase in single person households, which now represent 26 percent of U.S. households, up from 10 percent in 1950 (Francese, 2003). Another major change is that child-rearing, which used to occupy adults for their entire active life span, now occupies less than half of the adult life span prior to old age. The meaning of family is thus changing drastically, and there are no agreed-upon values, beyond child-rearing by which families define their connections. The changing role of women is central to these shifting family life cycle patterns. Sixty percent of working-age women are now in the paid workforce (U.S. Census, 2007). Even women who choose primary roles of mother and homemaker must now face an "empty nest" phase that is longer than the number of years devoted to child care.

There is also an increasing chasm between less fortunate children, who grow up in poverty with financially pressed, often single parents, and more advantaged children, who grow up in comfortable circumstances with highly educated dual-earner parents. These differences are reflected in an expanding differential in longevity between the rich and the poor. In 1980 the differential was only three years, but that difference has increased to 10 years (Pear,

2009). Education is a powerful differential in the potential for a longer, healthier life (Kolata, 2007). At age 35, even a year of more education leads to as much as a year and a half longer life expectancy. One of the big differences in marriage rates is a class difference. Those with resources are much more likely to be married (Zernike, 2007). And children from disadvantaged backgrounds are much more likely not to be raised with both parents. The proportion of children living with both parents also varies greatly by cultural group: 87 percent of Asian children, 78 percent of Whites, 68 percent of Latinos, and 38 percent of African Americans (Roberts, 2008). Jones (2006) suggests that marriage is only for White people, indicating that it may not seem like a worthwhile proposition for African American women, who may see a husband as hazardous to their health.

On the other hand, while research has generally failed to look at the value of extended family on well-being through life, it has been shown that the presence of a grandparent, most of all the maternal grandmother, can have a major positive impact on family well-being and make a tremendous difference in children's life prospects , especially in struggling families (Angier, 2002).

The size of family living units has been decreasing for centuries (Fishman, manuscript in preparation). Through most of history families lived in bands of extended families of about 40 people. By 1500 in the west, the average household had decreased to 20 people, by 1850 to 10, and by 2000 to less than 3 in the U.S. In traditional societies, when children were raised in large family groups there were usually three or more caregiving adults for each child under six, and there was little privacy. In our society, with three people or fewer in the average household, we rarely eat family meals, we spend 30 percent of available family time watching TV or on the computer, and our children are raised in age-segregated cohorts in situations where we are lucky if we have two adults for one child. We have overscheduled our children, and they have little time for spontaneous social play with peers (Perry, 2002, p 96). Our children might develop very differently, if we resolved problems of our children not with medication or court sanctions but in consultation with the community. What if children had responsibility to the community to make up for their misdeeds? Speck & Attneave (1973) recommended such intervention decades ago. If children would be accountable to the community of those who care for them our world might begin to look very different (Perry, 2002).

Human Development in Context

The search for the meaning of our individual lives has led to many theories about the process of "normal" development, most of them proposing supposedly inherent, age-related, developmental stages for the individual (Erikson, 1963, 1994; Levinson, 1978, 1996; Sheehy, 1977, 1995; Valliant, 1977; and others) and the traditional family (e.g., Duvall, 1977). From the beginning of our work, we have placed the individual in the context of the family and have indicated the importance of the impact of cultural and structural variation on life cycle tasks for individuals and families. However, we do not espouse family life cycle stages as inherent, that is, identical for all families. We do believe it is helpful to consider all clinical assessment within a life cycle framework which offers a flexible concept of predictable life stages and acknowledges the emotional tasks of individuals and family members, depending on their structure, time of life, culture and historical era. We disagree with human developmental or life span theorists who, like many feminist theorists, have ignored the family system altogether in their effort to move away from traditional notions of the family, and act as if the individual existed in society with no mediating context.

We believe, by contrast, that individual development always takes place in the context of significant emotional relationships and that the most significant are family relationships, whether by blood, adoption, marriage, or informal commitment. From our perspective it is impossible to understand individuals without assessing their current and historical cultural and family contexts. We see the family as the most immediate focus for therapeutic intervention because of its primacy in mediating both individual and social forces, bridging and mediating between the two. However, since the family is no longer organized primarily around

married heterosexual couples raising their children, but rather involves many different structures and cultures with different organizing principles, identifying family stages and emotional tasks for various clusters of family members is complex. Yet, even within the diversity, there are some unifying principles that we have used to define stages and tasks, such as the primary importance of addition and loss of family members for the family's emotional equilibrium through life's many transitions (Hadley, Jacob, Milliones, Caplan, & Spitz, 1974). We embrace this complexity and the importance of all levels of the human system: individual, family, and social. Indeed we believe that the meaning of family is deeply intertwined with a sense of "home," or belonging, and is essential to our sense of individual and social identity. Paolo Freire (2000) put it this way:

> No one goes anywhere alone . . . —not even those who arrive physically alone, unaccompanied by family, spouse, children, parents, or siblings. No one leaves his or her world without having been transfixed by its roots, or with a vacuum for a soul. We carry with us the memory of many fabrics, a self soaked in our history, our culture; a memory, sometimes scattered, sometimes sharp and clear, of the streets of our childhood, of our adolescence, the reminiscence of something distant that suddenly stands out before us, in us, a shy gesture, an open hand, a smile lost in a time of misunderstanding (p. 31).

Freire conveys the importance of the sense of our roots, our connections, and of home that we carry with us as an integral part of our identity through life. In our view this context is essential to incorporate into our clinical assessment and intervention practice.

Part of the pull that family therapists feel to revert to psychoanalytic thinking whenever the individual is under consideration comes from the fact that our models of individual development have been built on Freud's and Erikson's ideas of psychosocial development. Compared to Freud's narrow focus on body zones, Erikson's (1963, 1968) outline of eight stages of human development, by which he was referring to male development, was an effort to highlight the interaction of the developing child with society. However, Erikson's stages actually emphasize not relational connectedness of the individual, but the development of individual characteristics (mostly traits of autonomy) in response to the demands of social interaction (Erikson, 1963). Thus, trust, autonomy, industry, and the formulation of an identity separate from his family are supposed to carry a child to young adulthood, at which point he is suddenly supposed to know how to "love," go through a middle age of "caring," and develop the "wisdom" of aging. This discontinuity—a childhood and adolescence focused on developing one's own individuality and autonomy—expresses exactly what we believe is wrong with developmental norms of male socialization even today; it devalues by neglect most of the major tasks of adulthood: intimacy, caring, teamwork, mentoring, and sharing one's wisdom.

Although there has always been a "his" and "hers" version of development, until the late twentieth century only the former was ever described in the literature (Dinnerstein, 1976; Gilligan, 1982; Miller, 1976). Most theoreticians tended to subsume female development under male development, which was taken as the standard for human functioning. Separation and autonomy were considered the primary values for male development, the values of caring, interdependence, relationship, and attention to context being considered primary only for female development. However, healthy human development requires finding a balance between connectedness and separateness, belonging and individuation, interdependence and autonomy. In general, developmental theories have failed to describe the progression of individuals in relationships toward a maturity of *interdependence*. Yet human identity is inextricably bound up with one's relationship to others, and the notion of complete autonomy is a delusion. Human beings cannot exist in isolation, and the most important aspects of human experience have always been relational.

Most developmental theorists, however, even feminist theorists, have espoused psychodynamic assumptions about autonomy and separation, overfocusing on relationships with mothers as the primary factor in human development. They have assumed that masculine identity is achieved through

separation from one's mother and feminine identity through identification and attachment to her. Silverstein & Rashbaum (1994), Gilligan (1982), and Dooley & Fedele (2004) have effectively challenged the assumption that male development requires separating from one's mother. Gilligan (1991) critiqued Piaget's conception of morality as being tied to the understanding of rights and rules and suggested that for females, moral development centers on the understanding of responsibility and relationships, whereas Piaget's description fits traditional male socialization's focus on autonomy. Eleanor Maccoby (1990, 1999), the Stone Center at Wellesley (Miller, 1987; Jordan, Walker, & Hartling, 2004; Stiver & Miller, 1988; Jordan, Kaplan, Miller, Stiver, & Surrey, 1991), Barnett/Rivers (2004), and Michael Kimmel (2000, 2007) have expanded our understanding of the power dimensions in the social context of development. Their work suggests a broader conception of development for both males and females.

Developing a schema that would enhance all human development by including milestones of both autonomy and emotional connectedness for males and females from earliest childhood has drawn us to the work of those whose perspectives go beyond white male development. These include Hale-Benson (1986), who explored the multiple intelligences and other developmental features she identified in African American children; Comer and Poussaint (1992), who factored racism and its effects into their blueprint for the development of healthy Black children; Ian Canino and Jeanne Spurlock (1994), who outlined many ways in which minority ethnic groups socialize their children; and Joan Borysenko (1996), whose descriptions of the stages of female development appear to have universal applicability for both males and females from all cultural groups. Borysenko's outline reflects the human need for responsible autonomy and emphasizes the importance of understanding interdependence, a concept that girls and children of color learn early but that is ignored in traditional theories of male development.

Dilworth-Anderson et al. (1993), Burton et al. (2004) and their colleagues argue for the importance of a life cycle perspective because it is based on interdisciplinary ways of thinking, being a framework that emerged from the cross-fertilization of the sociology of aging, demographic cohort analysis, and the study of personal biography in social psychology and history. In their view the life cycle perspective represents a dynamic approach to the study of family lives by focusing on the interlocking nature of individual trajectories within kinship networks in the context of temporal motion, culture, and social change. Their position is especially important because as researchers, they are well aware of the relevant frameworks necessary for research. As they have articulated it: A life cycle framework thus "offers the conceptual flexibility to design conceptual frameworks and studies that address a variety of family forms in culturally diverse contexts" (p. 640). This is a most compelling argument, and one that we must put forward to encourage culturally meaningful research on diverse populations.

The Vertical and Horizontal Flow of Stress in the Life Cycle

To understand how individuals evolve, we must examine their lives within their individual, family, community, and the larger social and cultural contexts over time. This can be represented schematically along two time dimensions: the vertical axis reflecting influence of the historical issues that flow down the family tree, influencing families as they go through life (our biological heritage, genetic make-up, cultural, religious, psychological, and familial issues that come down through our family tree); and the horizontal axis, which represents the developmental and unpredictable influences that affect families as they go through life. Over time, the individual's inherent qualities can either become crystallized into rigid behaviors or elaborated into broader and more flexible repertoires. Certain individual stages may be more difficult to master, depending on one's innate characteristics and the influence of the environment. At the family level (Carter, 1978), the vertical axis includes the family history, the patterns of relating and functioning that are transmitted down the generations, primarily through the mechanism of emotional triangling (Bowen, 1978). It includes all the family attitudes, taboos, expectations, labels, and loaded issues with which we grow up. These

aspects of our lives make up the hand we are dealt. What we do with them is up to us. The horizontal flow describes the family as it moves through time, coping with the changes and transitions of the family's life cycle. This includes both predictable developmental stresses and unpredictable events, the "slings and arrows of outrageous fortune," that may disrupt the life cycle process, such as untimely death, birth of a handicapped child, chronic illness, or job loss.

The vertical axis includes cultural and societal history, stereotypes, patterns of power, social hierarchies, and beliefs, that have been passed down through the generations. A group's history, in particular the legacy of trauma, will have an impact on families and individuals as they go through life (e.g., the Holocaust on Jews and Germans, slavery on African Americans and on slave-owning groups, homophobic crimes on homosexuals and heterosexuals, genocide and forced incarceration in boarding schools and on reservations for American Indians and all other citizens, and colonizing exploitation for families in Latin America and for the colonizers). The horizontal axis relates to community connections, current events, and social policy as they affect a family or individual at a given time. It depicts the consequences in people's present lives of a society's inherited (vertical) norms of racism, sexism, classism, and homophobia, as well as ethnic and religious prejudices, as these are manifested in social, political, and economic structures that limit the options of some and support the power of others.

Anxiety and Symptom Development

Stress is often greatest at transition points from one stage to another in the developmental process as families rebalance, redefine, and realign their relationships. Symptom onset has been correlated significantly with the normal family developmental process of addition and loss of family members such as birth, marriage, divorce and death (Hadley et al.,1974). We found that a significant life cycle event, such as the death of a grandparent, when closely related in time to another life cycle event,

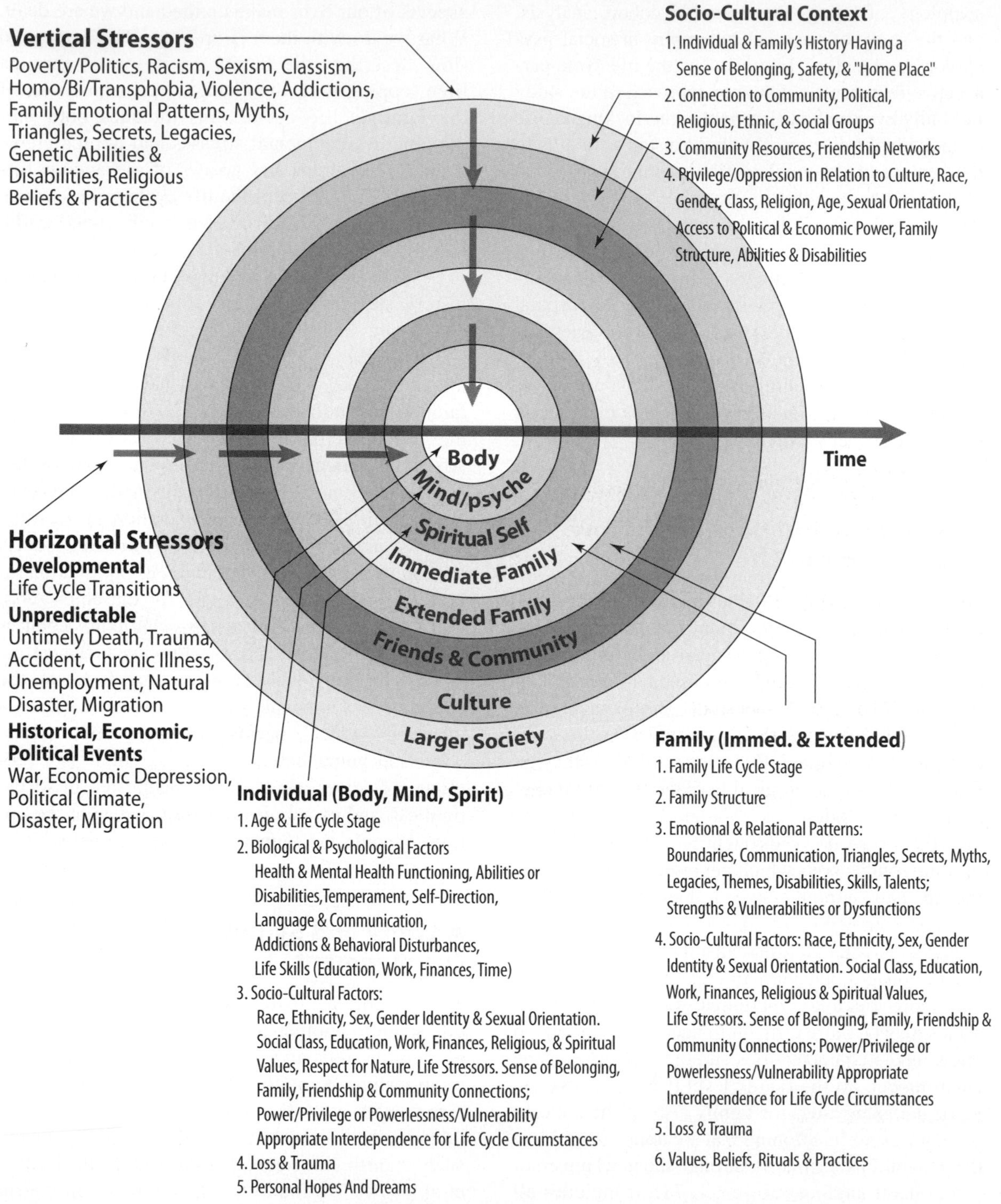

Socio-Cultural Context

1. Individual & Family's History Having a
   Sense of Belonging, Safety, & "Home Place"

2. Connection to Community, Political,
   Religious, Ethnic, & Social Groups

3. Community Resources, Friendship Networks

4. Privilege/Oppression in Relation to Culture, Race,
   Gender, Class, Religion, Age, Sexual Orientation,
   Access to Political & Economic Power, Family
   Structure, Abilities & Disabilities

Vertical Stressors

Poverty/Politics, Racism, Sexism, Classism,
Homo/Bi/Transphobia, Violence, Addictions,
Family Emotional Patterns, Myths,
Triangles, Secrets, Legacies,
Genetic Abilities &
Disabilities, Religious
Beliefs & Practices

Body
Mind/psyche
Spiritual Self
Immediate Family
Extended Family
Friends & Community
Culture
Larger Society

Time

Horizontal Stressors

Developmental
Life Cycle Transitions

Unpredictable
Untimely Death, Trauma,
Accident, Chronic Illness,
Unemployment, Natural
Disaster, Migration

**Historical, Economic,
Political Events**
War, Economic Depression,
Political Climate,
Disaster, Migration

Individual (Body, Mind, Spirit)

1. Age & Life Cycle Stage
2. Biological & Psychological Factors
   Health & Mental Health Functioning, Abilities or
   Disabilities,Temperament, Self-Direction,
   Language & Communication,
   Addictions & Behavioral Disturbances,
   Life Skills (Education, Work, Finances, Time)
3. Socio-Cultural Factors:
   Race, Ethnicity, Sex, Gender Identity & Sexual Orientation.
   Social Class, Education, Work, Finances, Religious, & Spiritual
   Values, Respect for Nature, Life Stressors. Sense of Belonging,
   Family, Friendship & Community Connections;
   Power/Privilege or Powerlessness/Vulnerability
   Appropriate Interdependence for Life Cycle Circumstances
4. Loss & Trauma
5. Personal Hopes And Dreams

Family (Immed. & Extended)

1. Family Life Cycle Stage
2. Family Structure
3. Emotional & Relational Patterns:
   Boundaries, Communication, Triangles, Secrets, Myths,
   Legacies, Themes, Disabilities, Skills, Talents;
   Strengths & Vulnerabilities or Dysfunctions
4. Socio-Cultural Factors: Race, Ethnicity, Sex, Gender
   Identity & Sexual Orientation. Social Class, Education,
   Work, Finances, Religious & Spiritual Values,
   Life Stressors. Sense of Belonging, Family, Friendship &
   Community Connections; Power/Privilege or
   Powerlessness/Vulnerability Appropriate
   Interdependence for Life Cycle Circumstances
5. Loss & Trauma
6. Values, Beliefs, Rituals & Practices

FIGURE 1.1 Multicontextual framework for assessing problems

such as the birth of a child, correlated with patterns of symptom development at a much later transition in the family life cycle, such as the launching of the next generation (Walsh, 1978; McGoldrick, 1977). Such research supports the clinical approach of Murray Bowen, which tracks patterns through the family life cycle over several generations, focusing especially on nodal events and transition points to understand dysfunction at the present moment (Bowen, 1978). The implication is that if emotional issues and developmental tasks are not resolved at the appropriate time, they will be carried along and act as hindrances in future transitions and relationships. For example, if young people do not resolve their issues with their parents, they will probably carry them into their young adult relationships and beyond. In life cycle terms, there is an expiration date on blaming your parents for your problems; at a certain point in life, maturity requires letting go of resenting your parents for what they did wrong or else you remain trapped in your family history.

Given enough stress on the horizontal, developmental axis, any individual family will appear extremely dysfunctional. Even a small horizontal stress on a family in which the vertical axis is full of intense stress will create great disruption in the system. The anxiety engendered on the vertical and horizontal axes are the key determinants of how well the family will manage its transitions through life. It becomes imperative, therefore, to assess not only the dimensions of the current life cycle stress, but also their connections to family themes and triangles coming down in the family over historical time. Although all normative change is to some degree stressful, when the horizontal (developmental) stress intersects with a vertical (transgenerational) stress, there tends to be a quantum leap in anxiety in the system. To give a global example, if one's parents were basically pleased to be parents and handled the job without too much anxiety, the birth of the first child will produce just the normal stresses of a system expanding its boundaries. On the other hand, if parenting was a problem in the family of origin of one or both spouses, and has not been dealt with, the transition to parenthood may produce heightened anxiety for the couple. Even without any outstand-

ing family of origin issues, the inclusion of a child could potentially tax a system if there is a mismatch between the child's and the parents' temperaments. Or, if a child is conceived in a time of great political upheaval that forces the family to migrate, leaving its cultural roots for another country, ordinary stresses of the child's birth may be accompanied by extra stressors. The break in cultural and family continuity created by immigration affects family relationships and family patterns throughout the life cycle for generations. (Chapter on Immigration; Sluzki, 2008).

Cohorts: When and Where in Time and Place We Are Located

In addition to the anxiety-provoking stress that is inherited from past generations and the stress experienced in moving through the family life cycle, there is, of course, the stress of living in a given place at a given time. Each group or cohort born at a given time in history, and living through various historical and sociocultural experiences at the same life cycle phase, is to an extent marked by its members' experiences. The World War II generation and the baby boomers are examples of this effect. We must also pay close attention to the enormous anxiety generated by the chronic unremitting stresses of poverty and discrimination, just as the generations that experienced the Civil Rights era were marked by the hopes of their era.

Cohorts born and living through different periods vary in fertility, mortality, acceptable gender roles, migration patterns, education, attitudes toward child-rearing, couple relationships, family interrelationships and aging. Those who lived through the Great Depression and World War II, those who experienced the Black migration to the North in the 1940s, the baby boomer generation that grew up in the 1950s, those who came of age during the Vietnam War in the 60s, and cohorts who grew up during the Reagan years, will have profoundly different orientations to life, influenced by the times in which they lived (Elder, 2002, 2006; Modell & Elder, 2002; Schaie & Elder 2005; Johnson, Foley, & Elder, 2004).

And as Malcolm Gladwell (2008) points out there are specifics of being at a certain key life cycle point when opportunities open up. For example,

19 percent of the wealthiest 75 people who were ever born anywhere in the world were born in the US between 1830 and 1840. These people made their money in the industrial manufacturing era of the 1860s and 1870s when Wall Street emerged, and the rules by which the economy had traditionally operated were transformed. Gladwell suggests that those born after the 1840s were too young to participate and those born before the 1830s were too old and fixed in their ways of doing things to become part of the new era. Thus there is a certain life cycle trajectory that influences our creativity in particular ways, assuming that we have the family and community to support the endeavor.

A similar pattern occurred with the development of computers in the 1970s. Bill Gates, Steve Jobs and a great many of the other key geniuses of the computer age were born smack in the middle of the 1950s and came of age just when they had the opportunity to work on computers during the formative years of their adolescence. These people grew up in communities and families that fostered their developing interests to allow for this creative energy. Thus, if we want to understand what creates resilient, innovative, healthy citizens, we need to look at a multiplicity of factors including the historical era, the individual, the family and its social location (in terms of class, race and ethnicity), and the community life cycle in which they were embedded.

Understanding Changing Families in Context

No single family form has ever been able to satisfy the human need for love, comfort, and security . . . We must keep our family cultures diverse, fluid, and unresolved, open to the input of everyone who has a stake in their future . . . Our rituals, myths and images must therefore be open to perpetual revision, never allowed to come under the sway of any orthodoxy or to serve the interests of any one class, gender or generation. We must recognize that families are worlds of our own making and accept responsibility for our own creations. John R. Gilles, 1996, p. 240.

The family of the past, when the extended family reigned supreme, should not be romanticized as a time when mutual respect and satisfaction existed between the generations. As Johnetta Cole (1996) put it: "No one family form—nuclear, extended, single-parent, matrilineal, patrilineal, fictive, residential, nonresidential—necessarily provides the ideal form for humans to live or raise children in" (p. 75). The traditional more stable multigenerational extended family was supported by patriarchy, sexism, classism, racism, and heterosexism. In that traditional family structure, respect for parents and obligations to care for elders were based on their control of the resources, reinforced by religious and secular sanctions against those who did not go along with the ideas of the dominant group. Now, with the increasing ability of younger family members to determine their own fate regarding marriage and work, the power of elders to demand filial piety is reduced. As women continue developing the right to have lives of their own, and are no longer willing to limit their roles to being caretakers of others as was previously expected, our social institutions will have to shift to fit with the resulting needs.

Instead of evolving values of shared caretaking, our social institutions still operate mainly on the notions of the individualism of the pioneering frontier, and the most vulnerable—the poor, the young, the old, and the infirm—suffer the consequences. Nowhere is this more readily seen than in the lonely efforts of the "sandwich" generation to provide care for both their children and their aging and dependent relatives, with woefully few resources from our society. The "typical" caregiver in the U.S. is a woman in her forties who works outside her home and spends more than 20 hours a week providing unpaid care. Caregivers often experience serious economic losses due to changes in work patterns, including lost wages, health insurance and other job benefits, lower retirement savings and no Social Security benefits for any period they spend caretaking.

Families have many forms: multigenerational extended families of three or four generations, gay or lesbian couples and children, remarried families with shifting membership of children who belong to several households, single-parent families, families of brothers and/or sisters or aunts and nieces, unmarried partners and their children and possibly a parent or an unmarried sibling of one. Yet our society still tends to think of "family" as meaning a heterosexual, legally married couple and their children. This family form is taken all too frequently as the ideal against which all other family forms are judged and found wanting (McCarthy, 1994). All other family forms, which former Irish President Mary Robinson termed "unprotected families," require our special consideration. Their history and family experience have been invalidated (McCarthy, 1994).

Backlash forces in our society have used code terms such as "family values" to imply that traditional nuclear families are the only valid families. We must resist such insidious definitions and insist on a more inclusive definition of family and family values. Most families live in more than one household. Grandparents, aunts, uncles, godparents, and other kin who are intimately involved with the immediate family may live next door or far away but still be part of the family. Immigrant families often have members living in different continents, yet stay very connected. Divorced, remarried, and unmarried families may have partners and/or children living separately with whom they are intimately connected. If two parents live apart, children are generally members of both households, regardless of the legal custody arrangements, as part of multi-nuclear families, because divorce restructures but does not end the family.

As Dilworth-Anderson, Burton, and Johnson (1993) have made clear it is impossible to understand families by using the old nuclear family model: "Important organizing, relational bonding of significant others, as well as socialization practices or socio-cultural premises are overlooked by researchers when the nuclear family structure is the unit of analysis" (p. 640). They demonstrate the important ways in which social support networks within the Black community serve as a buffer against a discriminating environment. They call for broadening ideas of what constitutes a family and its positive characteristics to allow for "culturally relevant descriptions, explanations, and interpretations of the family."

Indeed, the separation of families into generational subsystems, referred to as the "nuclear" and the "extended" family, creates artificial separation of parts of a family. Extended family may live in many different geographic locations, but they are still family. Adding or subtracting family members is always stressful, and the strain of restructuring in the extended family because of divorce, death, or remarriage adds to the normative stress for the immediate family of dealing with whatever family patterns, myths, secrets, and triangles make up the emotional legacy from the family of origin.

In our time, people often act as though membership in and responsibility for their families were optional but we have very little choice about our family ties. Children have no choice about being born into a system, nor do parents have a choice, once children are born, adopted, or fostered, as to the responsibilities of parenthood, although they may neglect these responsibilities. In fact, no family relationships except marriage are entered into by choice. Even the freedom to marry whomever one wishes is a rather recent option, and the decision is probably much less freely made than people recognize at the time. Although partners can choose not to continue a marriage relationship, they remain co-parents of their children, and the fact of having been married continues to be acknowledged with the designation "ex-spouse." Even in the divorce of a couple without children, bonds tend to linger; it is difficult to hear of an ex-spouse's death without being shaken. If a parent leaves or dies, another person can be brought in to fill a parenting function, but this person can never replace the parent in his or her personal emotional aspects (Walsh & McGoldrick, 2004).

People cannot alter whom they are related to in the complex web of family ties over all the generations. Obviously, family members frequently act as if this were not so—they cut each other off because of conflicts or the belief they have nothing in common, but when family members act as though family relationships were optional, they do so to the detriment of their own sense of identity and the richness of their emotional and social context.

Friendship Through the Life Cycle

As part of our sense of home and the importance of community, friendship is one of our most important resources through life. Indeed, dramatic research on women in the past few years has turned five decades of stress research upside down by demonstrating that women, unlike men, turn to their friends when under stress at every point in the life cycle and that is a major resource and protection. It helps when marriages are in trouble, when a spouse has died, and it even contributes to longevity (Taylor, Klein, Lewis, Gruenewald, Gurung, & Updegraff, 2000). While our society has a well developed ideology about marriage and family, we have tended to relegate friendship to the cultural attic, which has blinded us to its importance throughout the life cycle (Rubin, 1993). Friends can be crucial supports from early childhood and through adolescence and young adulthood, mitigating family trauma and dysfunction and providing encouragement, socialization, and inspiration for our development. In the phases of adulthood friends can again buffer stress as well as tell us the truth about ourselves, stimulate us to change our ways, and, in fact, keep us healthy. The loss of a close friend at any point in the life cycle can be a major stress. Friends should always be included on genograms and considered in our life cycle assessment.

The Changing Family Life Cycle of Men and Women

Perhaps the modern feminist movement was inevitable, as women have come to insist upon a personal identity. Having always had primary responsibility for home, family, and child care, women began to resist their burdens as they came to have more options for their own lives. Given their pivotal role in the family and their difficulty in maintaining concurrent functions outside the family, it is perhaps not surprising that they have been the most prone to symptom development at life cycle transitions. For men, the goals of career and family have been parallel. For women, these goals have presented a serious conflict. Surely, women's seeking help for family problems has much to do with their socialization, but it also reflects the special life cycle stresses on women, whose role has been to bear emotional responsibility for all family relationships at every stage of the life cycle (See Chapter on Women and the Life Cycle).

Men's roles in families are also beginning to change (see Chapter on Men and the Life Cycle).

They are participating more in child care (Khazan, McHale, & Decourcey, 2008; Levine, Murphy, & Wilson, 1993) and housework (Barnett & Rivers, 1996; Bureau of Labor Statistics, 2007), and many are realizing, in their minds if not always in action (Hochschild, 2001, 2003), that equality and partnership are a sensible ideal for couples (Sayer, Bianchi, & Robinson, 2004). Michael Kimmel, a sociologist and spokesman for the National Organization for Men Against Sexism, holds out to men the ideal of "democratic manhood," which "requires both private and public commitments—changing ourselves, nurturing our relationships, cherishing our families . . . but also reforming the public arena to enlarge the possibilities for other people to do the same" (1996, p. 334). Kimmel welcomes feminism, gay liberation, and multiculturalism as blueprints for the reconstruction of masculinity. He believes that men's lives will be healed only when there is full equality for everyone (Kimmel, 1996, 2007; Kimmel & Messner, 2007).

Homeplace: The Importance of Belonging Throughout the Life Cycle

When we speak of "home" we are usually referring to a place of acceptance and belonging, which is essential to our development of a solid sense of ourselves as human beings. Bell hooks (1999) refers to a sense of "homeplace," as an essential part of our cultural and individual identity. Bartlett Giamatti described it this way:

> *Home is an English word virtually impossible to translate . . . No translation catches the associations, the mixture of memory and longing, the sense of security and autonomy and accessibility, the aroma of inclusiveness, of freedom from wariness, that cling to the word home . . . Home is a concept, not a place; it is a state of mind where self-definition starts; it is origins—the mix of time and place and smell and weather wherein one first realizes one is an original . . . Home . . . remains in the mind as the place where reunion, if it ever were to occur, would happen . . . It is about restoration of the right relations among people . . . Everyone has a "hometown" back there, at*

least back in time, where stability or at least its image remains alive . . . To go home may be impossible, but it is often a driving necessity, or at least a compelling dream (1998, pp. 99-101).

Giamatti conveys powerfully the concept of home as a place of self-definition and belonging, a place where people find resilience to deal with the injustices of society or even of their families, a place where they can develop and express their values. Home reflects our need to acknowledge the forces in our history that have made us strong, but it is also a concept that we remake at every phase of life, with family, with friends, with work, with nature, with smells and sounds and tastes that nurture us because they give us a sense of safety and connection. Clinical intervention needs to acknowledge the importance of this place of psychological and spiritual safety at each life cycle phase.

Burton, Winn, Stevenson, and Clark (2004) drew attention to the concept of homeplace, described by bell hooks as that place in African American families where: "All that truly mattered in life took place-the warmth and comfort of shelter, the feeding of our bodies, the nurturing of our souls. There we learned dignity, integrity of being— there we learned to have faith" (Hooks, 1999, pp. 41-42). She spoke of it also as the site of resistance, where oppressed people resist racism and oppression, and gather their strength and do not feel invalidated. It is a place where one can mobilize a positive sense of personal and cultural identity. It is an essential concept for a life cycle framework. As Maya Angelou once put it: "The ache for home lives in all of us, the safe place where we can go as we are and not be questioned. It impels mighty ambitions and dangerous capers . . . Hoping that by doing these things home will find us acceptable, or, failing that, that we will forget our awful yearning for it" (1986, p. 196). It may be a physical location, with physical associations, but it is absolutely a spiritual location with value and deep meaning for people as they go through life. Burton and her colleagues provide important clinical examples of the value of proactively attending to our client's need for the continuity and belonging provided by the concept of "homeplace" (Burton, Winn, Stevenson, & Clark, 2004). Transferring them to a new therapist or a new home, or

ignoring their important kin connections, even where there are serious dysfunctions, may only compound their distress. We see the concept of homeplace as being at the core of a meaningful life cycle assessment. We must assess clients with regard to their sense of belonging and connection to what is familiar. Having a sense of belonging is essential to well-being.

Grasping where this sense of home is for a client is an essential part of any assessment and clinicians and policy makers who do not consider our deep seated need for continuity and belonging as we go through life, especially through traumatic transitions and disruptions, will increase the trauma of the original experience.

Community represents multiple levels of the human system, from the small face-to-face neighborhood, group, or local community to the larger cultural group, to the nation, and then to our increasingly "global" society. All these levels have an enormous impact on the individuals and families under their sway. They either offer protective safety and a sense of "home" and group identity, or of alienation, marginalization and disaffection. Many people in the U.S. do not seem to have an evolving sense of themselves as community members or participants in the developing U.S. identity or as evolving citizens of a global community.

There is an African saying, "If I don't care for you, I don't care for myself," which expresses the sense that our identity is bound up in our interrelatedness to others. This is the essence of community defined as the level of interaction that bridges the gap between the private, personal family and the great impersonal public sphere. We have a need for a spiritual sense of belonging to something larger than our own small, separate concerns. With our ever greater involvement in work, time for anything "unnecessary" has been disappearing, leaving little time for church or synagogue, friends, family Sunday dinners, supporting children's school activity, political action or advocacy. These activities get lost in the scramble to survive in a tense, high-wired time that rewards nothing but the individual acquisition of power and money.

Many traditional communities were and are repressive as well as secure, exclusionary as well as supportive of their members, and then only as long as members conform to community norms. Our social networks of friends and collective association are no longer the given they were in the past. We must find our own place in shifting social networks from neighborhoods to internet communities. Community is one of the best antidotes to the violence and anomie of our society and our best hope of an alternative to consumerism as a way of life. And the focus on clients' having a sense of home is ever more important when the network of belonging is as rapidly changing as in our society. Shaffer and Amundson (1993) defined community as a dynamic whole that emerges when a group of people participate in common practices, depend on one another; make decisions together, identify themselves as part of something larger than the sum of their individual relationships, and commit themselves for the long term to their own, one another's, and the group's well-being. Choice is the operative idea here, not nostalgia.

With our increasingly global economy, our context has increasingly become the entire earth, but we will focus primarily on the culture of the United States in the early twenty-first century. Clinicians have a meaningful role to play in encouraging clients to think about the meaning of family and community to them and asking whether they are living according to their values and ideals. To do this they must generally overcome their training to avoid topics that smack of spirituality or philosophy. In spite of thousands of years of holistic approaches to healing, our society has tended to keep physical, emotional, and spiritual healing separate.

We have also become one of the world's most class-stratified nations, with almost impenetrable walls between people of different status. The upper class lives in gated communities (where the emphasis is on security, not community), while the underclass lives behind prison bars, on the street, or in cell-like corners of the ghetto with almost no access to transportation to other parts of the community (Fullilove, 2004); and everyone in between is confused about what is going on. The poor have tended not to vote, but as we are seeing in recent times, great political victories can be won with a small percentage of eligible voters. If concerned citizens bring the poor into the system, things could change as politicians seek to respond to voters. What if we asked poor clients if they planned to vote? What if

we discussed social or political action with middle-class clients? We have to remind ourselves and our clients that if we limit our efforts to personal and family change within an unchanged larger society, we are helping to preserve the status quo.

To keep family therapy relevant to today's families, we have to learn how and when to discuss the important issues that shape and determine our lives. We have to learn to reconnect family members with their dreams and their values. We have to learn to discuss the inequalities in our society frankly —the racism, classism, sexism, and homophobia that are built into the system—and help clients join together within their families to create change for themselves and then to look outward and help bring change to the community and larger society. To be lasting, change must occur at every level of the system.

Power and Privilege Given to Some Groups over Others Because of the Hierarchical Rules and Norms Held by Religious, Social, Business, or Governmental Institutions

It is important to assess those in privileged and powerful groups regarding their awareness of their position and its responsibilities. Because most people compare themselves with those "above" them, we rarely let ourselves become aware that our privileges are at the expense of those below us in the hierarchy. But it is important to realize that sexism, classism, racism, homophobia, anti-Semitism, and other prejudices are problems of the privileged groups, not of the oppressed, who suffer from the problems. Therefore, we need to find ways, whether the issues are part of the presenting problem or not, to raise the issue of racism with Whites, sexism with men, classism with the well-to-do, homophobia with heterosexuals, and anti-Semitism or other religious prejudice with Christians. These are the groups who must change to resolve the problem.

We ask: What community groups do you belong to? Is there diversity of membership? Is that because of exclusionary policies or attitudes? What are you doing about that? Do you belong to a church or temple or other religious organization? If so, do you agree with their attitude toward people of other religions? If not, why not? Do your children have friends of other racial and religious backgrounds? How are you preparing them for the rapidly increasing multi-culturalism in our society? I notice your brother John has never married. Do you think he is gay? If he were, what would make it hard for him to tell the family? How did you and your wife decide on the al-location of household chores? How did you and your wife decide who should cut back at work to do child care? Are you ashamed of your son-in-law because he and his parents have less education and money than your family? You have much more education and money and social status than the average. Are you aware of the power that gives you? How do you use it? Do you exercise your power to make a difference in social and political issues that concern you? What would it take for you to make time to do for others?

Asking such questions is obviously not enough, since these inequities are structured into our society and our consciousness at such a profound level that those of us with privilege have extreme dif-ficulty becoming aware of this fact. We rarely be-come aware of or give up our privilege without pressure. These questions are the beginning of such challenge, because they assert that the status quo is not necessarily acceptable to us or to our clients if we are pushed to think about such issues seriously.

Life Cycle Stages: A Provisional Framework

Current definitions of life cycle stages differ from those of all other times in history. Indeed, it is becom-ing increasingly difficult to determine what family life cycle patterns are "normal," causing great stress for family members, who have few consensually agreed-upon models to guide them through life's passages. We offer **Table 1.1** as a map for considering the trans-formational nature of different stages of life and the tasks required to accomplish the tasks at each stage. Readers need to beware of such maps—as every sys-tems thinker knows, the map is not the territory, and a schema for defining stages of the family life cycle is a mere approximation of complex processes, not an af-firmation that stages really exist. The definition of stages is remarkably different in differing cultural contexts (McGoldrick, Giordano, & Garcia Preto,

2005) and historical eras (Elder & Johnson, 2002; Elder & Shanahan, 2006; Gladwell, 2008). The gener-al paradigm offered for American families is currently more or less mythological, relating to the ideal stan-dards of a romanticized past against which most fami-lies compare themselves: an intact, self-sufficient nuclear family that goes through prescribed life cycle transitions on time from birth to death. It is imperative that therapists recognize the pattern variations that are now part of changing and expanding norms. We must help families to stop comparing their structure and life cycle course with those of middle class White TV families of the 1950s. While relationship patterns and family themes may continue to sound familiar, the structure, ages, stages, and culture of families are changing dramatically.

It is high time we expanded our traditional defi-nitions of family. We know what patterns are not healthy: Wife beating, child abuse and neglect, sexual abuse, psychological terror, material deprivation, mal-nutrition, emotional abuse. These abuses, which occur in all family forms, must be eradicated. And our re-sponsibility, whether as single parents or co-parents or no parents at all, is to do all in our power to help create a healthy non-oppressive family environment for every human being, regardless of its particular structure.

We need to put a more positive conceptual frame around what exists: two-paycheck marriages; permanent single-parent households; unmarried, re-married, and GLBT couples and families; single-parent adoptions; and men and women of all ages not partnered. We must stop thinking of transitional crises as permanent traumas and to drop from our vo-cabulary words and phrases that link us to norms and negative stereotypes of the past, such as "broken" or "fatherless" homes, children of divorce, out-of-wed-lock children, and working mothers.

Community-level interventions have been rec-ognized as essential within the social work field for more than 100 years. The Community Mental Health movement of the 1960s made great strides forward in attending to the community level of services to maintain family members' health and mental health. Unfortunately, the capitalistic, me-first, "not in my backyard" dismantling of communities and commu-nity services that has been going on since the 1970s had far-reaching implications in terms of making the

Table 1.1 The Stages of the Family Life Cycle

Family Life Cycle Stage	Emotional Process of Transition: Key Principles	2nd Order Changes in Family Status Required to Proceed Developmentally
Leaving Home: Emerging Young Adults	Accepting emotional and financial responsibility for self	a. Differentiation of self in relation to family of origin b. Development of intimate peer relationships c. Establishment of self in respect to work and financial independence d. Establishment of self in community and larger society e. Spirituality?
Joining of Families Through Marriage/ Union	Commitment to new system	a. Formation of partner systems b. Realignment of relationships with extended family, friends, and larger community and social system to include new partners
Families with Young Children	Accepting new members into the system	a. Adjustment of couple system to make space for children b. Collaboration in child-rearing, financial and housekeeping tasks c. Realignment of relationships with extended family to include parenting and grandparenting roles d. Realignment of relationships with community and larger social system to include new family structure and relationships
Families with Adolescents	Increasing flexibility of family boundaries to permit children's independence and grandparents' frailties	a. Shift of parent–child relationships to permit adolescent to move into and out of system b. Refocus on midlife couple and career issues c. Begin shift toward caring for older generation d. Realignment with community and larger social system to include shifting family of emerging adolescent and parents in new formation pattern of relating

Table 1.1 The Stages of the Family Life Cycle *continued*

Family Life Cycle Stage	Emotional Process of Transition: Key Principles	2nd Order Changes in Family Status Required to Proceed Developmentally
Launching Children and Moving On at Midlife	Accepting a multitude of exits from and entries into the system	a. Renegotiation of couple system as a dyad b. Development of adult-to-adult relationships between parents and grown children c. Realignment of relationships to include in-laws and grandchildren d. Realignment of relationships with community and larger social system to include new structure and constellation of family relationships e. Exploration of new interests/career given the freedom from child care responsibilities f. Dealing with care needs, disabilities, and death of parents (grandparents)
Families in Late Middle Age	Accepting the shifting generational roles	a. Maintenance of own and/or couple functioning and interests in face of physiological decline: exploration of new familial and social role options b. Supporting more central role of middle generations c. Realignment of the system in relation to community and larger social system to acknowledge changed pattern of family relationships of this stage d. Making room in the system for the wisdom and experience of the elders e. Supporting older generation without overfunctioning for them
Families Nearing the End of Life	Accepting the realities of limitations and death and the completion of one cycle of life	a. Dealing with loss of spouse, siblings, and other peers b. Making preparations for death and legacy c. Managing reversed roles in caretaking between middle and older generations d. Realignment of relationships with larger community and social system to acknowledge changing life cycle relationships

rich richer and the poor poorer. But we do not need to lose our moral sense or our essential common sense awareness of what is obviously in the best interest of families through the life cycle just because the dominant elite are trying to blind us to the common welfare of our whole society. And in spite of our hyper-individualistic times, some creative therapists are still daring to maintain their social perspective and challenge the dominant ideology. Therapists can make a difference in large and small ways, even in our office practices.

Our assessment of families and our interventions must attend to the unequal ways that families are situated in the larger context so that we don't become part of the problem by preserving the status quo. Areas to assess include the following:

1. Current or Longstanding Social, Political, and Economic Issues

    How have these become family problems? It is helpful to make a list of issues that you think have an impact on your locale, to help keep these issues in the forefront of your mind, since there are so many forces that would obscure them. Such a list at the start of the twenty-first century might include random violence, affirmative action, de facto school and neighborhood segregation, gay and lesbian adoption or marriage, welfare reform, abortion rights, the education of all our children, prejudice against legal and illegal immigrants, health care and insurance, tax cuts, layoffs, social services to the elderly and other groups, cost and availability of infertility treatments, and physician-assisted suicide.

    It is extremely important that we not "psychologize" social problems by searching for the roots of every problem in the interior motivations and actions of the individual and/or the family. Many clinical problems can be directly connected with the social system. A lesbian couple came to therapy because of ongoing conflict between them. One partner described the other as neurotic and restless, always wanting to move to a different neighborhood, pressuring her ceaselessly. Assessment

revealed that the "neurotic" partner was a schoolteacher who feared, realistically, that she would be barred from teaching if her sexual orientation were reported to the school system. She was extremely anxious about contacts with neighbors and very sensitive to indications that neighbors were puzzled about or suspicious of their relationship.

2. Bias against Race, Ethnicity, Class, Gender, Sexual Orientation, Religion, Age, Family Structure, or Disability

    How does a person's, family's, or group's place in these hierarchies affect family relationships and limit or enhance the ability to change? Much has been written about the impact of the norms and values of the larger society on the individuals and families within it. What is most important for the clinician to grasp is that race, class, gender, and sexual orientation are not simply differences; they are categories that are arranged hierarchically with power, validation, and maximum opportunity going to those at the top: whites, the affluent, men, and heterosexuals.

We must learn to be aware of and deal with these power differences as they operate (1) in the therapy system, in which they add to the already existing power differential between therapist and client; (2) within the family system, in which social stress easily becomes family conflict; and (3) between the family and society, in which they either limit or enhance the options available for change.

Clinically, the therapist must be prepared to discuss explicitly how racism, sexism, classism, and homophobia may be behind the problems clients are taking out on each other. The goal is to help the family members to join together against the problems in society instead of letting these problems divide them. Explicit discussion and strategies will also be needed to overcome the obstacles to change, which unaware therapists may blame on the client's "resistance."

A severely injured Irish American fireman and his Italian American wife came to therapy because of the wife's complaints about her husband's drinking and depression. She also expressed great concern about family finances because his disability pay could not support them and their two young children. The therapist discovered that although the wife was a trained bookkeeper, the sexist norms of their ethnicities and class did not permit either of them to even consider one obvious solution: that the wife could get a full-time job while the husband stayed home with the children and planned or trained for whatever new work he would be able to do in the future. Not until the therapist explicitly addressed this and tracked the relevant attitudes about gender roles in their families of origin and in their friends and community network did the couple realize that they could choose a different set of beliefs about gender roles—and did so.

A middle-class African American woman and her husband entered therapy because of marital conflict, which her husband blamed on her depression. She agreed, saying that her depression was caused by her lack of progress at work, which she blamed on herself. Only after detailed questioning from the therapist did she come to realize that her supervisor's racism might be behind her poor evaluations. Encouraged by the therapist and her husband, she then discussed the issue with a higher-level manager and was transferred to a different supervisor, who subsequently promoted her. It is disconcerting to contemplate how many therapists might have suggested Prozac and explored her marriage and family of origin for the source of her depression and "poor work performance."

The multi-contextual framework first laid out by Betty Carter in 1993 and expanded in Appendix 1 is a framework to assist clinicians in assessment of all levels of the system. Our intent is to make an enormous amount of information manageable and clinically relevant without diminishing its complexity. We have been evolving this guide over the years. It is meant to be suggestive and always subject to clinical judgment for a particular case.

Conclusion

Catherine Bateson (2001) has described the need for flexibility in life cycle thinking in our time thus:

> *I believe in the need for multiple models . . . to weave something new from many different threads . . . When we speak to our children about our own lives we tend to reshape our pasts to give them an illusory look of purpose. But our children are unlikely to be able to define their goals and then live happily ever after. Instead, they will need to reinvent themselves again and again in response to a changing environment. Once you begin to see these . . . multiple commitments and multiple beginnings as an emerging pattern rather than an aberration, . . . the models for that reinvention . . . are not fixed but . . . evolve from day to day (pp. 16-17).*

This is our concept of the life cycle, that we must reinvent ourselves and our relationships as we go through life, always in relation to those in our social and family network of belonging, and in our times especially each generation must be flexible in relation to changing rules and relationships as they go through life's transitions.

What clinicians require is a framework that does not force clients to make molehills out of mountains by ignoring all aspects of their lives except their individual thoughts, feelings and behavior in clinical situations. At the same time, our family models need to articulate not a rigid, inequitable multi-generational patriarchal family, but a recognition of our connectedness in life—regardless of the particular family structure or culture—with those who went before us, those who go with us, and those who will follow after us. Exploring problems within this broad and flexible framework will help individuals and their families draw on the multiple resources of their actual kin arrangements for resilience, healing, support, and caretaking as they go through life.

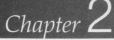

Self in Context: Human Development and the Individual Life Cycle in Systemic Perspective

Monica McGoldrick, Betty Carter, & Nydia Garcia Preto

Redefining the Dimensions of Human Development

This chapter attempts to broaden traditional Euro-American formulations of human development, which have begun with the individual as a psychological being and defined development as growth in the human capacity for autonomous functioning. It broadens this conceptualization, from discrete tasks and stages of accomplishment to an identity, which evolves over the life cycle in the context of our social and cultural world in terms of gender, class, race, spirituality, sexual orientation, and ethnicity. In African and Asian cultures, the very conception of human development begins with a definition of a person as a social being and defines development as the evolution of the human capacity for empathy and connection. We present a theory of individual development that integrates race, class, gender, sexual orientation spirituality, and culture as central factors that structure development in fundamental ways. This theory of self in context defines maturity by our ability to live in respectful relation to others and to our complex and multifaceted world. This view of maturity requires the ability to empathize, trust, communicate, collaborate, and respect others who are different and to negotiate our interdependence with our environment and with our friends, partners, families, communities, and society in ways that do not entail the exploitation of others. Maturity requires us to appreciate our interconnectedness and interdependence on others and to behave in interpersonally respectful ways, controlling our impulses and acting on the basis of our beliefs and values, even if others do not share them.

Developing a Self in Context

Gender, class, culture, race, sexual orientation, and spirituality structure our developing beliefs, values, relationships, and ways of expressing emotion. This context carries every child from birth and childhood through adulthood to death and defines his or her legacy for the next generation. Each generation or cohort is different, as cultures evolve through time, influenced by the social, economic, and political history of their era, which makes their world view different from the views of those born in other times (Cohler, Hosteler, & Boxer, 1998; Elder, 1992; Elder

& Shanahan, 2006; Elder & Johnson, 2002; Neugartcn, 1979; Gladwell, 2008). The gender, class, and cultural structure of any society profoundly influences the parameters of a child's evolving ability to empathize, share, negotiate, and communicate. They prescribe his or her way of thinking of self and of being emotionally connected to others.

Healthy development requires establishing a solid sense of our cultural, spiritual, and psychological identity in the context of our connections to others. In many ways this involves the development of a sense of belonging or "home," as we go through life. Developing an integrated sense of ourselves requires incorporating a sense of safety, belonging, and stability about who we are in relation to our closest family and social context. Researchers on African Americans and others who have been marginalized in our society have written often about a notion of "homeplace," and the need for belonging, for rootedness and connection to place and kin that is a crucible of affirmation for our sense of social and cultural identity (hooks, 1990). hooks describes homeplace as deriving from communal experiences anchored in a home where "all that truly mattered in life took place, the warmth and comfort of shelter, the feeding of our bodies, the nurturing of our souls. There we learned dignity, integrity of being . . . thcrc we learned to have faith" (hooks, 1990, 41–42). Linda Burton and her colleagues have urged us to take the concept of home into account in assessment and intervention (Burton, Winn, Stevenson, & Clark, 2004). Homeplace involves multilayered, nuanced individual and family processes that are anchored in a physical space that elicits feelings of empowerment, belonging, commitment, rootedness, ownership, safety, and renewal. This includes the ability to develop relationships that provide us with a solid sense of social and cultural identity. In the long-term ethnographic and clinical research of Burton and her colleagues with African Americans, homeplace emerges as a force that individuals and families must reckon with throughout their life course (Burton, Hurt, Eline, & Matthews, 2001; Stevenson, Winn, Coard, & Walker-Barnes, 2003; Burton et al., 2004). We believe the notion of homeplace is relevant for people of all cultures throughout the life cycle. This is especially true for immigrant groups who move away from their homes and form networks and communities that represent and celebrate their hometown rituals. Puerto Ricans in the mainland, for example, form social clubs with others from their hometown as a way to stay connected to their home. Homeplace also serves as the site of resistance against the oppressive forces of our society (Burton et al., 2004). Home provides security and safety to develop self-esteem, political consciousness, and resistance in the face of societal invalidation, racist and other oppressive stereotypes. Of course, those who are gay, lesbian, bisexual, or transgender may need special adaptive strategies to find a place where they can feel at home, because the very place that others rely on fundamentally may become a place of greatest danger. This is often true as well for children whose families suffer from mental illness, violence, addictions, and other negative or disruptive forces.

We all need to experience a sense of belonging—to feel safe and secure, especially when living in a multicultural society where connecting with others who are different from us becomes particularly challenging. Indeed, the most challenging aspect of development involves our beliefs about, and interaction with, others who are different from ourselves: men from women; young from old; Black from White; wealthy from poor; heterosexual from homosexual. Our level of maturity on this crucial dimension of tolerance and openness to difference is strongly influenced by how our families of origin, communities, cultures of origin, and our society as a whole have dealt with difference.

Because our society so quickly assigns roles and expectations based on gender, culture, class, and race, children's competences are not milestones that they reach individually, but rather accomplishments that evolve within a complex web of racial, cultural, and familial contexts. Racial, religious, and other prejudices are learned emotionally in childhood and are very hard to eradicate later, even if one's intellectual beliefs change. Children's acquisition of cognitive, communicative, physical, emotional, and social skills to succeed over the life course is circumscribed by the social context in which they grow up. Our evaluation of their abilities is meaningful only if these constraints are taken into account.

The Myths of Complete Autonomy and Self-Determination

Given the American focus on individualism and free enterprise, it is not surprising that autonomy and competitiveness have been considered desirable traits leading toward economic success in the marketplace, and qualities to be instilled in children (Dilworth-Anderson, Burton, & Johnson, 1993). While self-direction and self-motivation are excellent characteristics, they can be realized only in privileged individuals who have health and resources and are permitted to attain them and are helped to do so by their families and by society. Development requires much more than intellectual performance, analytical reasoning ability, and a focus on one's own achievements, as if they resulted from completely autonomous efforts. The people with the most privilege in our society—especially those who are White and male and who have financial and social status—tend to be systematically kept unconscious of their dependence on others (Coontz, 1992, 1998, 2006). They remain unaware of the hidden ways in which our society supports their so-called "autonomous" functioning. Thus, many White men who benefited from the GI bill to attain their education now consider it a form of welfare to provide education to minorities of the current generation. Those who are privileged develop connections amidst a web of dissociations. Their privilege maintains their buffered position and allows them the illusion of complete self-determination. Men of any class or culture who are raised to deny their emotional interdependence face a terrible awakening during divorce, illness, job loss, or other adversities of life.

Developing a Mature Interdependent Self

We believe maturity depends on seeing past myths of autonomy and self-determination. It requires that we appreciate our basic dependence on each other and on nature. Viewed from this perspective, in addition to an adequate degree of self-direction, maturity involves skills such as:

1. The ability to feel safe in the context of the familiar *and* the unfamiliar or different.

2. The ability to read emotion in others, to practice self-control, to empathize, and to engage in caring for others and in being cared for.
3. The ability to accept one's self while simultaneously accepting differences in others, to maintain one's values and beliefs, and to relate generously to others, even if one is not receiving support from them or from anyone else for one's beliefs (defined by Murray Bowen as "differentiation").
4. The ability to consider other people and future generations when evaluating sociopolitical issues such as the environment and human rights.

We believe that children are best able to develop their full potential, emotionally, intellectually, physically, and spiritually, when they are exposed in positive ways to diversity and encouraged to embrace it. Children who are least restricted by rigid gender, cultural, or class role constraints have the greatest likelihood of developing an evolved sense of a connected self.

Gendered Development

Children's sense of security evolves through their connection and identification with those who care for them—mothers, fathers, siblings, nannies, baby sitters, grandparents, aunts, uncles, teachers, and all the others who participate in their caretaking. Traditional formulations of child development have ignored this rich context and offered us a one-dimensional lens for viewing a child's development: through the mother–child relationship. In most cultures throughout history, mothers have not even been the primary caretakers of their children, usually being busy with other work. Grandparents, older siblings and other elders have, for the most part, been the primary caregivers of children. When we focus so myopically on mothers, we not only project impossible expectations on them, but we are also blinded to the richness of environments in which children grow up.

Most child development theories, even feminist theories (Chodorow, 1974; Gilligan, 1993), explain male development's focus on autonomy and independence as resulting from the child's need to separate from his mother by rejecting feminine qualities. Like Maccoby (1990, 1999), Kimmel (2008), and many others, we doubt that children's development of distinct styles of interacting has much to do with the fact that they are parented primarily by women. Their identification with the same-sexed parent is more likely a consequence than a cause of their developing sex-typed interaction styles. Maccoby thinks that processes within the nuclear family have been given too much credit and blame for sex-typing. The larger society's attitudes about gender roles, conveyed especially through peer group, appears most relevant as the setting where children discover their differential social power: boys discover the requirements of maintaining their status in the male hierarchy, and the gender of friends becomes paramount. Many of the apparent gender differences we observe are not gender differences at all but differences resulting from being in different positions in society (Kimmel, 2008).

Parents expect and reinforce different behaviors in their sons than in their daughters (Hastings, McShane, Parker, & Ladha, 2007; Clearfield & Nelson, 2006; Martin & Green, 2005). They treat boys and girls differently from earliest infancy. In general, they discuss emotions—with the exception of anger—more with their daughters than with their sons. They use more emotional words when talking to their daughters (Brody & Hall, 1993). Fathers tend to treat young boys and girls in a somewhat more gendered way than mothers do (Siegal, 1987). The "appropriateness" of these behaviors is then validated by the media as well as by teachers, pediatricians, relatives, babysitters, and by parents' own observations of children's play groups. Meanwhile, science argues about whether these are inborn differences or self-fulfilling prophecies. Only if we expand our lens to children's full environment can we properly measure the characteristics that may help them to attain their full potential and see clearly the influences that limit it. Seo (2007), for example, found that father's involvement with his young children had a long-term influence on their children's later life satisfaction.

Indeed, the traditional norms of male development (Green, 1998; Kivel, 2010) have emphasized many of these characteristics including keeping emotional distance; striving for hierarchical dominance in family relationships; toughness; competition; avoidance of dependence on others; aggression as a means of conflict resolution; avoidance of closeness and affection with other males; suppression of feelings except anger; and avoidance of "feminine" behaviors such as nurturing, tenderness, and expressions of vulnerability. Such norms make it almost impossible for boys to achieve the sense of interdependence required for mature relationships through life.

Female development was, until recently, viewed from a male perspective that saw women as adaptive helpmates to foster male development and child development. Most early male theoreticians, such as Freud, Kohlberg, and Piaget, tended to ignore female development, which has been only discussed in the literature for the past few decades (Dinnerstein, 1976; Gilligan, 1993; Miller, 1976). While separation and autonomy have been considered the primary values for male development, caring, ability to nurture others, interdependence, relationship, and attention to context have been viewed as the primary dimensions in female development. Values that were thought to be "feminine" were devalued by male theoreticians such as Erikson, Piaget, and Levinson, while values associated with men were equated with adult maturity. Concern about relationships was seen as a weakness of women (and men) rather than a human strength. George Valliant (1998, 2003; Wolf, 2009), in the largest longitudinal study ever conducted, has come after many years to the conclusion that relationships are key to male development in the long run, a surprise to him and to many others.

In fact, women have always defined themselves in the context of their changing relationships over the life span. A life cycle framework, developed as a perspective on self-in-relation, seems a much more appropriate way to think of human development for both men and women (Korin, McGoldrick, & Watson, 1996; Jordan, 1997). Erik Erikson's (1968, 1994) still widely taught eight stages of development ignored completely the evolution of our ability to communicate, "tend and befriend,"(Taylor, 2002) characteristics that most distinguish us from all other animals. Sara Lawrence-Lightfoot, recent author of a wonderful book about creativity and learning in the "third chapter" of life, tries to use Erikson's scheme, but finally admits his eighth stage model "seems too linear and predictable to match the messier, more unruly stories people were telling me" (2009, p. 43). She has to admit as well that Erikson seems to have missed entirely the reciprocity that is such a powerful part of our "giving forward" in life. Erikson's scheme makes no reference between age 2 and 20 to interpersonal issues. Identity is defined as having a sense of self *apart from* rather than *in relation to* one's family and says nothing about developing skill in relating to one's family or to others. It suggests that human connectedness is part of the first stage (Trust versus Mistrust), during the first 2 years of life (but he discusses this, as have so many since then, as attachment primarily to the mother). The complex nature of human attachments from earliest infancy has been grossly oversimplified in discussions of early attachment that focus primarily on mothers. In such individually focused schemes as Erikson's, development of interpersonal skills is not even described between infancy and adulthood, stage six (Intimacy versus Isolation). All of Erikson's other five stages from infancy to adulthood focus on individual rather than relational issues: Autonomy versus Shame and Doubt, Initiative versus Guilt, Industry versus Inferiority, and Identity versus Role Confusion. Doubt, shame, guilt, inferiority, and role confusion are all defined as counter to a healthy identity. Yet these concepts all have great significance in our understanding of our interrelationship to other human beings and to nature. We have to recognize that we need to develop skills in listening and learning, admitting our doubts and mistakes. While Erikson's own personal life story may explain his skewed perspective (for discussion of Erikson's own genogram see McGoldrick, Gerson, & Petry, 2008; Friedman, 1999; Erikson & Bloland, 2005) we must still challenge skewed perspectives on human development. In Erikson's scheme, even the concept of generativity is ignored during the time of greatest human creativity, bearing and raising children, and appears only at midlife.

Given such distorted norms for healthy development as we have been offered, it is not surprising that men so often grow up with an impaired capacity for intimacy and connectedness. Our culture's distorted ideals for male development have made it hard for men to acknowledge their vulnerability, doubt, imperfection, role confusion, and desire for connection (Kimmel, 2005). In our view, all stages of the life cycle have both individual and interpersonal aspects. We are indeed the most flexible species on earth because of our social brains, which enable us to coordinate our needs with those of people around us. Our success as a species, as Shelly Taylor says in *The Tending Instinct* (2002), has come entirely from this gregarious nature.

Developing a Self in a Nonaffirming Environment

The developmental literature, strongly influenced by the psychoanalytic tradition, has focused almost exclusively on mothers, giving extraordinary importance to mother–child attachment in the earliest years of life, to the exclusion of all other relationships in the family or to later developmental phases. This focus has the result of leading to a psychological determinism that early child experiences with one's mother are responsible for whatever happens later in the life cycle. Much of the feminist literature continued this focus on mothering while locating the mother–child dyad within a patriarchal system (Chodorow & Contratto, 1982; Dinnerstein, 1976). We urge a different perspective, which views child development in the context of multigenerational family relationships as well as within the child's social and cultural context.

The developmental literature has also largely ignored the powerful impact children have on adult development. Children's role in changing and "growing up" their parents, as parents respond to the unfolding of their children's lives, is lost in a unidirectional linear framework. It ignores also the powerful role grandchildren often play in promoting their grandparents' development, just as grandparents are often a major influence on child development (Mueller, Wilhelm, & Elder, 2002). Children are actually a major impetus for growth for older generations. Indeed, to offer a small example, a recent study of congressmen demonstrated that parenting only daughters significantly impacts their feminist sympathies and the more daughters they have the more impacted they are (Washington, 2007). Just as parents, siblings, peers, and neighbors influence us (Bertrand et al., 2000; Fernandez et al., 2004), so do our children. Far from being the one-way street that most life cycle formulations have offered us, our lives continually spiral through multigenerational and contextual connections with those who come before us, those who go with us through life, and those who come after us.

It is difficult to determine which behavioral differences between males and females are based in biology, since socialization affects people so powerfully and so early. We do know that females are more likely to survive the birth experience, less likely to have birth defects, and less vulnerable to disease throughout life. The major gender differences in early childhood are that girls develop language skills earlier, and boys tend to be more active. But because studies of infants show that parents talk and look more at girls and engage in more rough play with boys, we cannot say whether these gender differences are biological or social. Eleanor Maccoby, one of the leading researchers on sex differences, has found that the sex differences noted on various dimensions have not changed too much in the past several decades. Moderate differences continue in performance on mathematical and spatial abilities, while sex differences in verbal abilities fade. Most other aspects of intellectual performance continue to show gender equality (Maccoby, 1999), but social behavior orients boys to competition and girls to relationships. Preschool girls increasingly try to influence others by polite suggestions, and have less and less ability to influence boys, who are increasingly unresponsive to polite suggestions. Both boys and girls respond to a vocal prohibition by another boy. Maccoby thinks girls find it aversive to keep trying to interact with someone who is unresponsive and begin to avoid such partners.

As for specific problems due to gender, there is evidence that women feel at a disadvantage in mixed-sex interaction. Men are less influenced by the opinions of others in a group than are women and have more influence on group process than women do. Women are more likely to withdraw or take unilateral action to get their way in a dispute, a pat-

tern that appears to reflect their greater difficulty in influencing a male partner through direct negotiation (Maccoby, 1999). Women tend to enter into deeper levels of reciprocity with their children than men do and to communicate with them better. Extensive gender segregation continues in workplaces (Chugh & Brief, 2008; Alksnis, Desnarais, & Curtis, 2008) and in some social-class and ethnic groups, in which leisure time is still spent largely with others of the same sex even after marriage.

Kagan and Moss (1962) a generation ago traced achievement-oriented adults back to their relationships with their mothers, but did not look at their relationships with their fathers. They found that these males had very close, loving relationships with their mothers in infancy, while the females had less intense closeness with their mothers than the average. Hoffman (1972) suggested that a daughter is more likely to become achievement oriented if she does not experience the training in dependence that has generally been prescribed for girls. It appears that a mother's education and success play a larger role in the success of at least their sons.

Children in fatherless families generally experience more interaction with their mothers and perceive them as more available than do children in father-present homes (MacCallum & Golombok, 2004). Stevens, Colombok, and Beveridge (2002) found no differences in gender-role behavior of children in father-present and father-absent families. McCallum (2004) found boys appear to show more feminine gender role behavior, but no less masculine behaviors than boys in father-present families. Romer (1981) found that some boys displayed extremely "masculine" behavior, possibly because their mothers' sensitivity to the lack of a father encouraged them to emphasize such behavior. Children raised in fatherless families seem indeed to experience more collaborative, democratic relationships throughout childhood, which may be a particular strength in our competitive, hierarchical society (Hartman, 1987).

Infants and toddlers begin early to develop trust in their immediate environment, which ideally supports their safety and development. As soon as they reach the point of leaving the safety of their home environment, however, developing trust depends on how their cultural group is positioned in the larger world. It takes greater maturity for children to be able to develop their sense of self in a nonaccepting environment in which they do not receive support, than in a context in which everyone in the outside world affirms their values. Members of the dominant groups of our society receive this affirmation daily, whereas many others do not. A gay or lesbian child, a disabled child, a girl, a child of color, or a poor child is often stigmatized and vilified, and is not the one depicted in books, TV programs, and movies as the "valued" child. Thus, a nonprivileged child who does manage to develop a strong self has accomplished a developmental feat beyond that of a child who has always been affirmed both at home and in the larger society (Kunjufu, 1995). Our theories of child development must take this into account.

Actually, children of privilege may lack certain adaptive skills because they live in such an affirming, nonchallenging environment that they are sheltered to an extreme degree from ever feeling "other" or being the only one of their opinions in a group, experiences that promote growth as well as difficulty.

Children raised in poverty, of whom a much larger proportion are children of color, are incredibly disadvantaged in development, having less access to a safe home and neighborhood environments, less access to adequate education and health care, and in every way are less supported by our society. Their families experience more illness, unemployment, incarceration, disruption, and untimely death than other children, and their dreams are short circuited in every way. Additionally, as Janice Hale puts it: "Children who cannot conceptualize a future for themselves, do not have the motivation to defer the gratification found in premature sexual activity or substance abuse" (2000, p. 43). Their life cycle trajectories are stunted by their lack of support at every level: racism, class oppression, growing up in physically and psychologically dangerous environments. Everything must be done to support the resilience and nurture the development of children who are at risk. It is much more difficult to change their life course if they are not supported in early childhood (Goldstein & Brooks, 2005).

In our view, the richness of possibilities for learning and expressive styles should be celebrated, and all children should be encouraged to develop their potential and to appreciate others for their different ways of knowing and doing. Thus, girls should be allowed and encouraged to develop their individual abilities without being viewed as selfish. They should be supported in developing leadership skills and in being comfortable with their accomplishments without fearing that their success hurts others, while boys should be encouraged to develop their relational and emotional selves, currently devalued in our theories and in the dominant society, which sees these styles as "unmanly." Psychological studies reveal that when fathers are involved in child-rearing in a major way, sons become more empathic than sons raised in the traditional ways (Miedzian, 2002; Meeker, 2008). A 26-year longitudinal study of empathy found that the single factor most linked to empathic concerns was the level of paternal involvement in child care (Koestner, Franz, & Weinberger, 1990). The negative role modeling of a distant father on his children appears to be significant and should be taken into account clinically.

Peggy McIntosh (1985, 1989), in her article "On Feeling Like a Fraud," has described the ways in which women who have been socialized in the single track logic of academia can end up feeling stupid, when they have intellectual approaches that emphasize making outlines that lay out subcategories in hierarchical order. Catherine Bateson (1994) and Peter Senge (2006) likewise challenged the very ordering of education as a precursor to living life, suggesting instead that it makes more sense to thread education throughout our lives. Our ability to acknowledge our ignorance and maintain openness to learning throughout life is essential, but it is not highly valued in our culture. When political leaders hesitate or revise their views or apologize for mistakes, we take it for weakness, not strength. The implications of this are evident. People of privilege can be at the greatest disadvantage because of the smugness and inflexibility of mainstream learning styles, which may leave them unable to acknowledge their ignorance or to place themselves in the position of learner. Many adults take on the challenge of new learning only when they are desperate. We need to modify our cultural norms so that people do not feel humbled or threatened to open themselves to new learning throughout life so that there is affirmation and support for all of the ways of learning and asking for help with something they cannot do. Peter Senge (2006) has described our need to teach people to be perpetual learners, so that they have the flexibility to change with new circumstances. Constraints on our current work environment make it necessary to modify the rigid roles we have encouraged for males, without which they will not be able to succeed in our quickly changing technological global environment.

Our Multiple Intelligences

In the same way that we must expand our notions of educational development to be open to new learning throughout the life cycle, we need to expand traditional child development theories that have conveyed that intelligence is one-dimensional. The intellectual tasks that theorists such as Piaget have used as definers of maturity are extraordinarily narrow indicators of intelligence and totally inadequate for understanding the rich possibilities of a child's intellectual development (Ogbu, 1990). Many other forms of intelligence have been described, including social and emotional intelligence, interpersonal and intrapersonal intelligence, graphic, musical, and other forms of artistic and spatial intelligence, linguistic intelligence, intelligence in understanding nature, etc. (Goleman, 2006, 2007; Hale-Benson, 2001; Gardner, 2006; Staridou & Kakana, 2008; Sew, 2006.)

Traditional child development schemas reward only the development of the analytic style of processing information. This is reflected in the requirements that the children learn to sit still for longer periods of time, concentrate alone on impersonal learning stimuli, conform to rigorous time frames, and engage only in very controlled and restricted interpersonal learning experiences. How might different groups react to this?

In China studying music is all about learning to play in harmony together; there is no concept of the musical virtuoso. So the highest development involves the most accomplished ability to be in harmony with others. American Indians, as another example, raise their children to be keen observers of the world around them. Intelligence in this context involves being able to look and listen carefully to animals, birds, and trees in ways that are almost totally unknown to most other children in the United States.

Many values within African American communities are at odds with the dominant priorities for child development. Lerome Bennett has described their verbal emphasis thus:

Black culture gives rise to highly charismatic and stylistic uses of language. There is no counterpart in white culture to the oratory of a Dr. Martin Luther King, Jr., a Rev. Jesse Jackson, . . . or a Shirley Chisholm. The verbal rituals, particularly of Black male children, expressed in woofin', soundin', signifyin', chants, toasts, and playin' the dozens are examples of stylistic uses of language. These language skills of Black children are not assessed on the standard measures of verbal intelligence. (Hale-Benson, 1986, citing Lerome Bennett, p. xiii)

Black children must master two cultures to succeed (Hale-Benson, 1986). Even though they are using complex thinking skills on the street, the problem of transferring these skills to the classroom remains a problem. Our current theories of intellectual development fail to make room for people of color to look any way but deficient and pathological (Quintana, 2008; Quintana & McKown, 2008).

Black children are exposed to a high degree of stimulation from expressive performers of music and the visual arts, which permeate the Black community. Their cultural style is organized in a circular fashion, in contrast to the linear organization of European/U.S. culture (Hale-Benson, 1986). They are proficient in nonverbal communication and use considerable body language and interaction in communication. Nonverbal expression and highly physical expressiveness of emotions, such as moving close or touching others, are in general more characteristic of non-White cultures, such as Latino cultures. Latino children are spontaneously more likely to touch others when in familiar surroundings or with peers. They also learn rules for behaving respectfully especially with adults, which means to speak only when spoken to, and other rules that are learned by nonverbal teaching. By contrast, White children in the United States are born into a world where their style of communication is given priority everywhere: linear language, minimal body language, a preference for written over verbal expression, and a tendency to view the world in discrete segments rather than holistically.

Daniel Goleman (2006, 2007) has laid out clearly the extreme importance of understanding and supporting the development of emotional and social intelligence. All the skills essential for academic success are related to emotional competence: curiosity, confidence, intentionality, self-control, relatedness, cooperativeness, and communication. School success is not predicted by a child's fund of facts or a precocious ability to read, but rather by emotional and social measures: being self-assured and interested; knowing what kind of behavior is expected and being able to rein in the impulse to misbehave; being able to wait, follow directions, and ask the teacher for help; being able to express one's own needs in relationships with other children. Almost all children who do poorly in school lack one or more of these elements of emotional intelligence, regardless of other cognitive abilities or disabilities (Goleman, 2006). Social intelligence includes the ability to find solutions to social dilemmas such as how to de-escalate a fight, how to make friends in a new situation, how to defuse bullying, how to make others feel at ease, how to help rally support for a new idea, how to deal with volatile people to calm a situation, and sensing another's needs and feelings. All of these abilities are extremely important to our successful development as human beings. Without such interpersonal intelligence we will end up isolated. Yet our theories rarely emphasize the pervasive need for these abilities for adult functioning. The health value of emotional connectedness is evident from the fact that isolation is as significant a risk to health and mortality as are smoking, high blood pressure, high cholesterol, obesity, and lack of exercise. Empathy, the earliest emotion, is the root of all caring about others: intimacy, ethics, altruism, and morality itself.

Emotional and social incompetence and disconnection lead to:

1. Prejudice, lack of empathy, the inability to direct adequate attention to the needs of others
2. Aggression, poor self-control, and antisocial behavior
3. Depression and poor academic performance
4. Addictions (attempts to calm and soothe oneself with drugs and other addictive behaviors).

Goleman suggests that curing our current worldwide tendencies toward depression and crime involves helping families and schools to realize that a child's development and education must include developing essential human competencies such as self-awareness, self-control, empathy, and the arts of listening, resolving conflicts, and cooperation (Goleman, 2006, 2007; McLaughlin, 2008; Cohen & Sandy, 2007; Shin & Yoshikawa, 2008). To change our world, we must focus on child development, the critical window of opportunity for setting down the essential emotional habits that will govern our lives in adulthood. Later remedial learning and unlearning in adulthood are possible, but they are lengthy and hard.

The Connected Self

The connected self is grounded in recognition of human interdependence. Skills in mature interdependent relating include the ability to:

1. Listen with an open heart, read the feelings of others, and respond empathically
2. Participate in cooperative activities of many kinds at home, at work, and at play.
3. Relate with openness, curiosity, tolerance, and respect to people who are different from ourselves, listening to their beliefs without attacking or becoming defensive.
4. Express a full range of emotions and tolerating such emotions in others.
5. Nurture, care for, and mentor others.
6. Accept the help and mentoring of others.

Bowen's (1978) concept of differentiation describes a state of self-knowledge and self-definition that does not rely on others' acceptance for one's beliefs but encourages people to be connected to others without the need to defend themselves or attack others. Ironically, although Bowen's is the only family therapy theory that gives equal weight to autonomy and emotional connectedness as characteristics necessary for the differentiation of adult maturity, his concepts have been widely misunderstood. His term "differentiation," which he equated with "maturity," is commonly misused and misquoted as though it referred only to autonomy, separateness, or disconnectedness. Also, because Bowen emphasized the necessity of distinguishing between thinking and feeling, some feminists criticized him for elevating "male" attributes of rationality over "female" relationality. Actually, Bowen was addressing the need to train one's mind to control emotional reactivity so that, unlike other animals, we can control our behavior and think about how we want to respond, rather than being at the mercy of our fears, phobias, compulsions, instincts, and sexual and aggressive impulses. This kind of reactivity has nothing to do with authentic and appropriate emotional expressiveness, which is a primary goal of Bowen therapy. Developing a personal connection with one's family is considered the blueprint for all subsequent emotional relationships.

Goleman (2006) discusses this same process of mind over emotional reactivity, attributing to Aristotle the original challenge to manage one's emotional life with one's intelligence: "Anyone can become angry. That is easy. But to become angry with the right person, to the right degree, at the right time, for the right purpose—this is not easy" (cited in Goleman, 2006, p. ix). The question is, Goleman says, "How can we bring intelligence to our emotions, civility to our streets and caring to our communal life?" (p. xiv).

What Bowen's (1978) theory does not take into account is that women and people of color have grown up with an oppressive socialization that actually forbids the assertive, self-directed thinking and behavior essential to differentiation. Lack of acknowledgment of this prohibition blames people for their own disenfranchisement, leaving groups to blame themselves or to be blamed by others without recognition that the playing field is not level. Girls in this society are expected to put the needs of others

before their own. People of color are expected to defer to the beliefs and behaviors of White people, the poor are expected to perform as well as the privileged without their resources. A White male who tries to differentiate will generally be responded to with respect, while a woman or person of color may be sanctioned or even harmed or ostracized by the community. Our assessment of development must address societal obstacles to a person's accomplishing the tasks leading to mature functioning.

Countering Unequal Gender, Class, Cultural, and Racial Socialization

In our clinical work, we celebrate the diversity of our clients' backgrounds. To counter our society's privileging of particular skills for only certain children, we can challenge families on their distribution of chores and their role expectations, but we need to do more. We must learn basic, crucial information on a family's social style and expectations, not just with culturally diverse children, but with all children (Canino and Spurlock, 2000; Le, Ceballo, Caho, Hill, Murry, et al.):

- Is the family isolated or active in their community?

- Does their culture expect frequent and intense social interactions in an extended network or does it privilege privacy and a nuclear-family orientation?

- What kind of community is the family living in socially and culturally: a homogeneous community or a heterogeneous setting, a safe community, a community with resources?

- Who are the models and teachers of socialization skills in the family?

- Do the skills taught at home converge with those required at school, in the park, or on the playing field?

The diagnostic challenge is to "make a clinical judgment as to whether a behavioral or emotional attribute is a culturally syntonic way of manifesting distress, a behavior adopted to survive in a particular sociocultural milieu, or a universal symptom of psychiatric disorder. These judgments can be sound only if clinicians are knowledgeable about the culture of their patients" (Canino & Spurlock, 2000, p. 86).

Many guidelines and programs have been shown to be effective in fostering children's emotional competence in schools and other settings. We should do all that we can as mental health practitioners to support the establishment of such programs in clinics and schools in our communities. The most crucial factor in teaching emotional competence is timing, with infancy as the beginning point and childhood and adolescence as the crucial windows of opportunity. (McLaughlin, 2008; Salovey, 2007; Cohen & Sandy, 2007).

The "Slings and Arrows" as Individual, Family, and Community Intersect

The special and unpredictable individual life cycle problems of members of a family affect other family members at both an individual and family level. These issues, of course, also have extended family implications. Siblings, aunts, uncles, nieces, nephews, friends, godparents, and godchildren are also affected by the problems, having to decide how much each of them can or should do to help out. The problems also have community ramifications. A person's disabilities require various community resources throughout the school age and adult years. Access to community resources for help with an alcohol problem, mental illness, or a stroke and to help family members with the disabilities created by these problems will have profound implications for the whole family's negotiation of their individual and family life cycles.

The Individual Life Cycle in Context: Developing an Autonomous and Emotionally Connected Self

We have quoted or paraphrased on **Table 2.1** the relevant milestones from Borysenko's (1996) book about the development of women as we think they

might and should apply to the development of both females and males in a nonsexist, nonracist culture.

Many of us have struggled against the cultural bestowing of power on Whites and the denigrating of all others, and the splitting of males and females into half-people, one half focused on achievement and autonomy and the other on the emotional connectedness of relationship. Thanks to the women's movement, females have received compensatory help with this problem of imbalance in recent decades with many parents supporting their daughters' autonomy and the wider culture accepting it up to a point. That point is usually reached in adolescence, when dating begins, or when women marry and have children and are then expected to revert to an exclusive focus on relationships. However, the threats, epithets, and punishments visited on parents who question the culture's definition of masculinity and try to raise sons with an enhanced capacity to relate emotionally are swift and unforgiving (Kimmel, 2005, 2008; Silverstein & Rashbaum, 1994). Perhaps if we therapists expected the same development in autonomy for females and in the skill of emotional connectedness for males, we could help parents find ways to defeat the destructive gender and racial stereotyping of our children. We owe it to our children not to permit the current deterioration of relationship and of community life to continue. What more important goal than connectedness could we have for our turn to shape the future?

Evaluating problems in terms of both the individual life cycle and the family life cycle is an important part of any assessment. Human development involves the accomplishment of certain physical, intellectual, social, spiritual, and emotional life cycle tasks. Each person's individual life cycle intersects with the family life cycle at every point, causing at times conflicts of needs. A toddler's developmental needs may conflict with a grandmother's life plans, if she is the child's primary caretaker. When individual family members do not fit into normative expectations for development, there are repercussions for family development. A family's adaptation to its tasks will likewise influence how individuals negotiate their development, and the cultural, socioeconomic, racial, and gender context of the family will influence all of these developmental transitions (Quintana & McKown, 2008).

There are serious limitations to any schematic life cycle framework, such as the suggestive schema we are offering here for exploring normative individual life cycle tasks. The phases of human development have been defined in many ways in different cultures and at different points in history. This outline is a rough and suggestive guideline, not a statement of the true and fixed life stages. People vary greatly in their pathways through life. It is always important to consider the cohort to which family members belong, that is, the period in history when they grew up (Treas, 2002; Cohler, Hosteler, & Boxer, 1998; Elder, 1992, 1999; Elder & Shanahan, 2006; Elder & Johnson, 2002; Shaie & Elder, 2005; Shanahan & Elder, 2002; Gladwell, 2008; Neugarten, 1979; Brown & Lesane-Brown, 2006); it influences their worldview, their sense of possibility, and their beliefs about life cycle transitions. It may also be an important factor in intergenerational conflicts. Furthermore, accomplishing the individual tasks of a stage depends on resources available to individuals and families to help them to develop their abilities.

In addition, we must be open to considering life patterns that vary from the dominant norm and adjust our expectations for these variations. The larger social context will heavily influence how people go through various stages. For example, gay and lesbian adults are stressed at many life phases including the phase of young adulthood, because of the stigma attached to their partnering, parenting, and developing their spirituality, as well as by the frequent necessity to keep their true lives secret at work. These struggles, created by our society, have implications for negotiating the life course smoothly and for emotional development and well-being. Those who do not form couple relationships at this phase will often feel marginalized in the larger social context. Clinicians must be careful not to participate in psychologizing clients' reactions to such marginalization, but rather to help them define a life course for themselves and not be constrained by society's definitions.

THE FIRST STAGE OF LIFE MIGHT BE THOUGHT OF AS COVERING A BABY'S FIRST 2 YEARS OF LIFE During this time, babies need to learn to communicate their needs and have some sense of trust, comfort, and relationship with their caretakers and with the world around them. Their needs have to be satisfied consistently so that they can develop trust in others and a sense of security. They learn to coordinate their bodies and begin to explore the world. It is during this stage that empathy, the earliest emotion, begins to develop. From earliest infancy, babies are upset when they hear another infant cry (Goleman, 2006).

THE SECOND STAGE, THE CHILD'S PRESCHOOL YEARS FROM AGE 2 TO 6, is an era of great strides in language, motor skills, and the ability to relate to the world around. Children learn to take direction, cooperate, share, trust, explore, and be aware of themselves as different from others. As early as age $2^1/_2$, children recognize that someone else's pain is different from their own and are able to comfort others. How discipline is handled at this phase influences the development of emotional competence; for example, "Look how sad you've made her!" versus "That was naughty!" (Goleman, 2006). It is at this phase that children begin to form peer relationships. They also develop various cognitive skills with numbers, words, and objects and motor skills in relation to the world around.

During this phase, children learn where, how, and when to show aggression (Comer & Poussaint, 1992; Comer, Joyner, & Ben-Avie, 2004; Comer, 2007). They need to be taught control of their anger, aggression, distress, impulses, and excitement and to regulate their moods and delay gratification. This self-management, along with the continued development of empathy, is the basic skill in relating (Goleman, 2006). By age 3, children become actively interested in defining how they are like or different from others, including skin color and hair texture. They can start to share and be fair rather than to exclude others; they take their cues from the adults around them for how to treat others.

THE THIRD DEVELOPMENTAL PHASE MIGHT BE SAID TO COVER THE ELEMENTARY SCHOOL YEARS of childhood, from about age 6 to 12. During this time, children typically make many developmental leaps in their cognitive, motor, and

Table 2.1 The Individual Life Cycle in Context

Infancy (Birth to About 2) Development of Empathy & Emotional Attunement to Others

Our brains are wired in a way that allows emotional learning throughout the life span, as long as our caretakers are reasonably well attuned to our emotions & capable of mirroring them back to us in the 1st 18 months of life. (Borysenko. 1996, p. 19)

- Communicate frustration & happiness
- Make needs known & get them met
- Develop physical coordination to sit, stand, walk, run, manipulate objects, feed self
- Recognize self as separate person
- Trust others, primarily caretakers
- Overcome fears of new situations
- Develop beginning of empathy for others
- Begin to develop language to communicate needs, feelings, share intimacy

Early Childhood (Approximate Ages 2 to 6)
A Growing Understanding of Interdependence

The bio-psycho-spiritual basis of the . . . life cycle is wired firmly into place by the end of early childhood, conferring the gifts of empathy, relationality, interdependent perception and intuition. (Borysenko, 1996, p. 35)

- Develop language and ability to relate & communicate
- Develop motor skills, eye–hand coordination, etc.
- Develop control of bodily functions–bowels, urine
- Starting awareness of self in terms of gender & abilities
- Start to become aware of self in relation to world around
- Start to become aware of "otherness" in terms of gender, race, & disability
- Learn cooperative play, ability to share, & start to develop peer relationships
- Learn to obey rules, delay gratification, regulate & control emotion & impulses
- Increase ability to develop trusting relationships
- Develop ability to dramatize & engage in fantasy play to master own behavior & control anxieties

Middle Childhood (Approximate Ages 6 to 11 or 12) Mastery & Moral Development:
"Heart Logic" + "Mind Logic"

Developing the capacity to use linear logic while retaining the interrelational, interdependent perceptual capability developed in early childhood. (Borysenko, 1996, p. 38)

- Increase skill with language
- Begin development of morality, challenging lack of fairness, intuition, tolerance for difference
- Increase physical coordination & motor skills
- Learn reading, writing, & math
- Increase understanding of self & "otherness" in terms of gender roles, race, culture, sexual orientation, class, & abilities/disabilities
- Increase understanding of self in relation to family, peers, and community
- Develop awareness & knowledge about human beings & nature

Table 2.1 The Individual Life Cycle in Context *continued*

- Increase ability to conduct peer relationships & engage in cooperative activities
- Increase ability to conduct relationships with authorities
- Develop empathy & ability to be intimate and to express anger, fear, and pain in nondestructive ways

Pubescence (About 11–13 for Girls; 12–14 for Boys) Finding One's Own Voice: The Beginning Development of Authenticity

Where do I begin and other people end?. . . Can I take care of my own needs and still maintain relationships with others?. . . Learn the lessons of gaining affection and interdependence on which true intimacy is based. (Borysenko, 1996, pp. 71, 73).

- Cope with dramatic bodily changes of puberty
- Increase ability to assert oneself
- Increase physical skills & coordination
- Increase development of emotional competence
- Develop awareness of own & others' sexuality
- Begin to learn control of one's sexual and aggressive impulses
- Increase capacity for moral understanding, and recognizing injustices
- Increase ability to read, write, & think conceptually & mathematically
- Increase understanding of self in terms of gender, race, culture, sexual orientation, & abilities
- Increase understanding of self in relation to peers, family, & community
- Increase ability to handle social relationships & complex social situations
- Increase ability to work collaboratively & individually

Adolescence (Approximate Ages 13 to 21) Looking for an Identity: Voicing Own Opinions & Feelings in Context of Societal, Parental, & Peer Pressure to Conform to Age, Gender, & Racial Stereotypes: Learning to Balance Caring About Self & Caring About Others

Uncanny tendency to recognize instances of relational injustice and cry foul, and the development of morality of the heart . . .) By this time we can think our own thoughts we have opinions that are separable from other people, we can group concepts, and calculate probabilities, and we can stand back and reflect on ourselves. (Borysenko, 1996, pp. 59, 75).

- Continue to deal with rapid bodily changes & cultural ideals of body image
- Increase awareness & ability to deal with own and others' sexuality
- Increase emotional competence & self management, and begin to develop ability to handle intimate physical & social relationships as well as increase ability to judge & handle complex social situations
- Learn to handle one's sexual & aggressive impulses
- Develop one's sexual identity
- Increase physical skills & coordination
- Increase ability to think conceptually & mathematically & learn about the world
- Increase discipline for physical & intellectual work, sleep, sex, & social relationships
- Increase understanding of self in relation to peers, family, & community
- Begin to develop a philosophy of life & a moral & spiritual identity
- Increase ability to work collaboratively & individually

Table 2.1 The Individual Life Cycle in Context *continued*

Young Adulthood (About 21–30) New Phase in Human History Development of Committed Mutual Relationships & Financial Independence–Commitment to Both Work and Family

Development of a core self, a strong, yet pliable identity in which the previous relationality, intuition, & the logic of the heart are combined in a conscious way, bestows life's most precious gift—the ability to relate to both self & others with true intimacy. (Borysenko, 1996, p. 76)

- Increase ability to take care of one's own needs financially, emotionally, sexually, & spiritually

- Increase discipline to develop physical & intellectual work & social relationships, & tolerance for delayed gratification to meet one's goals

- Learn to focus on long-range life goals regarding work, intimate relationships, family, & community

- Develop ability to nurture others physically, emotionally, & sexually

- Evolve further in ability to respect and advocate for others less fortunate than oneself or to help oneself if socially disadvantaged

- Develop ability to negotiate evolving relationships to parents, peers, children, & community, including work relationships

Middle Adulthood (Approximate Ages 35 to 55) Emergence into Authentic Power, Becoming More Aware of the Problems of Others

Along with balancing life tasks, there is a review of one's priorities, a striving toward balance and harmony with self and others while resisting pressure to pursue traditional gender patterns. There is greater community involvement and participation in social and political action. (Borysenko, 1996, pp. 135, 181)

- Firm up & make solid all of the tasks of early adulthood

- Nurture & support one's children & partner, including caretaking of older family members

- Reassess one's work satisfaction & financial adequacy & consider possibility of changing work or career to achieve greater life balance

- Recognize one's accomplishments & accept one's limitations

- Involve oneself in improving community & society whether one is personally advantaged or disadvantaged

- Deepen & solidify friendships

- Accept the choices that made some dreams & goals attainable but precluded others

- Focus on mentoring the next generation

- Solidify one's philosophy of life & spirituality

Table 2.1 The Individual Life Cycle in Context *continued*

Late Middle Age (Approximate Ages: 55 to early 70s) Beginning Wisdom Years: Reclaiming the Wisdom of Interdependence

Intensification of the altruism and service begun in the previous phase. Helping others, serving the community and mentoring: passing along our values and experience. . . . There is a need to resist our culture's dismissal of older people, especially older women. . . . The pendulum swings away, from the active and productive principles back to the spiritual principles that value nature as well as technology, that honor cultural diversity, that foster caring for the less fortunate and that seek physical, emotional, and spiritual harmony. (Borysenko, 1996, pp. 202, 219)

- Handle some declining physical & intellectual abilities
- Deal with menopause, decreasing sexual energies, & one's changing sexuality
- Come to terms with one's failures and choices with accountability but without becoming bitter
- Plan and handle work transitions & retirement
- Define one's grandparenting and other "senior" roles in work & community
- Take steps to pass the torch & attend to one's connections & responsibilities to the next generation
- Accept one's limitations & multiple caretaking responsibilities for those above & below
- Deal with death of parents & others of older generations

Aging (Approximate Ages: From 75 on) Grief, Loss, Resiliency, Retrospection, and Growth

Time to reflect on and review one's life with appreciation of its successes and compassion for its failings, and with an effort to extract new levels of meaning that had previously been unappreciated. (Borysenko, 1996, p. 243)

- Respond to loss and change as opportunity to reevaluate life circumstances & create new fulfilling pathways
- Remain as physically, psychologically, intellectually, & spiritually active and as emotionally connected as possible
- Come to terms with death while focusing on what else one can still do for oneself & others
- Bring careful reflection, perspective, & balance to the task of life review
- Accept dependence on others and diminished control of one's life
- Affirm & work out one's financial, spiritual, & emotional legacy to the next generation
- Accept death of spouse & need to create a new life
- Accept one's own life and death

emotional skills. They expand their social world in terms of their ability to communicate and to handle relationships with an increasing range of adults and children beyond their families. Children begin to understand their identity in terms of gender, race, culture, and sexual orientation and to differentiate themselves from others (Quintana, 2008; Quintana & McKown, 2008; Bennett, 2004; Coll & Szalacha, 2004; Robbins, Szapocznik, Mayorga, Dillon, Burns, et al.). They improve in their ability to follow directions, tolerate frustration, work independently, and cooperate with others. If deprived of support for these developments, children may develop physical, emotional, or social symptoms—fears, anxieties, phobias, stomachache or headaches, and aggressive or withdrawn behaviors.

BETWEEN AGES 6 AND 8 children tend to develop a great passion to belong. They exclude others so that they can feel "in." Children of color must be taught at this age to handle racist acts in ways that are not self-destructive, while children of privilege must be taught not to commit racist acts and to be proactive in relationship to others who are experiencing oppression (Comer & Poussaint, 1992; Comer, Joyner, & Ben-Savie, 2004; Quintana & McKown, 2008; Neblett, White, Ford, Philip, Nguyen, et al., 2008; Suizo, Robinson & Pahlke, 2008). At this phase, children learn competitiveness by comparing themselves to others and cooperation to the degree their parents, caretakers, or teachers teach them. Otherwise, competitiveness remains a problem. By age 7 or 8, dreams and make-believe (e.g., Santa Claus) are no longer considered real. At this stage, children should learn the truth about slavery, colonialism, war, and the like, which can be done through the stories we tell them about our holidays such as Thanksgiving and the Fourth of July. Children start to read, watch television, and play video games independently and should be monitored by parents, especially for exposure to racial, gender, and violent content, which can have a profound influence on them. Children at this phase are deeply affected by parental and school definitions of "normal." They learn to imitate racial, gender, and other discriminatory words and actions (Thompson, Meyer, & McGinley, 2006; Thompson, 2006).

Sex segregation increases greatly, influenced by the fact that boys' behavior, unless checked, becomes characterized by competition, demands, and dominance. Girls have such difficulty having influence in play with boys that they avoid them (Maccoby, 1999). Boys tend to play more roughly in larger groups, and girls are likely to form close friendships with one or two other girls. Golman (2006) reports studies in which 50 percent of 3-year-olds, 20 percent of the 5-year-olds, and virtually no 7-year-olds, have friends of the opposite sex. (Liu, 2006).

At this time, children become chums and segregate themselves by gender and often by race, discovering that skin color is a code denoting rank and even fate (Comer & Poussaint, 1992; Ogbu, 1990; Bullard, 1997). Girls become adept at reading verbal and nonverbal emotional signals and at expressing and communicating their feelings. White children continue to express discriminatory behavior as they become older, but show increasing inhibition when there is an antiracist norm (Franca, & Rodrigues, 2009). Children raised in nonauthoritarian homes are much more likely to become antiracist as adults (Flouri, 2004). Penner and Paret (2008) found in a longitudinal study of gender differences in math education that where boys and girls start out equal, even highly educated parents are continuing the gender segregation in math and science by their attitudes toward their sons and daughters. Boys minimize the emotions connected to vulnerability, guilt, fear, and hurt (Goleman, 2006). Without specific intervention, these differences will persist into adulthood. Boys especially, in their efforts to establish their own sexual identity, may focus on their dislike of girls; they need adult validation of the other gender's interests and feelings to avoid establishing a gender role split. Friendship and conversation with friends become very important for the development of language and social skills.

At this phase also, children have a better memory, a longer attention span, and can understand more complex explanations and ask constant questions. Parents' responses are very important. They should not pretend to know everything, but rather teach the child how to look up information. Children produce creative works of art, dancing, and singing. Parental responses will encourage or discourage the development of this creativity.

Boys especially may have difficulty talking about subjects like race, sex, anger, and conflict and need adult encouragement to foster skill in this (Comer & Poussaint, 1992). Children begin to develop respect for the rights and needs of self and others. They tattle on wrongdoers, and are concerned about rule-breaking, commitments to rules, and fairness. How children learn life's "rules" will form the foundation of their morals (Kochanska, & Aksan, 2007). If they are continuously put down, they will lose faith in others; if they are not admonished for selfish or unfair acts, they will grow up with a false sense of privilege. Boys especially can be physically aggressive and need to be taught fairness and to have plenty of outlets for their physical energy. Games and hobbies can mitigate social conflicts.

BY AGE 9 TO 12 (LATER ELEMENTARY SCHOOL) children spend a lot of time discussing, arguing, and changing the rules of games. As the independence–dependence struggle intensifies, it is important to teach children to do chores and meet responsibilities for their own sake, rather than because they are told, which encourages them to begin to establish their own standards. Doing chores teaches them that their contribution to the family is valuable. They may talk in a mature way, but they are still fearful and insecure. Family rituals and celebrations are important to children at this age, who start learning how to plan and organize events if their parents do this well. It matters a great deal whether children get the message "I can" or "I can't" from their school and family experiences.

By age 9 to 12 parental support is essential for helping children cope with peer pressure. It is at this age that children become able to distinguish their own values and attitudes from those of the peer group. This is the last stage for parents to affirm their support of their children's competence and abilities before teen struggles for independence begin. It is also the last chance for parents to strongly influence a child's choice of peers and to widen the child's social circle by encouraging diversity. Children may be preoccupied with prepubertal body changes and extremely sensitive to unkind remarks from others.

They are not always cooperative or obedient and may not want to be affiliated with others who are "different." It is a very important age for children to see parents actively handling and dealing with social problems in constructive ways. It is at this stage that children become able to differentiate between what is expected of them at home and what is expected outside of home. By this stage, children's identification with the causes, problems, aspirations, and privileges of groups they belong to provides direction, limitations, and motivation to think and act in certain ways. At the same time, their ability to experience empathy deepens, and they are able to understand distress beyond an immediate situation and to feel for the plight of an entire group, such as the poor, oppressed, or outcast (Goleman, 2006). Contextual, racial, and cultural factors are especially important at this phase of development, most of all for children who are not part of the mainstream. They need resources and support to contend with discrimination, bullying, racism, and a general lack of safety in their communities and in their efforts to contend with the pressures of the dominant culture against them (Coll & Szalacha, 2004; Robbins et al., 2007).

Children may play adults off against each other to get what they want because they do not yet know how to confront adults to let them know they feel neglected or ignored (Comer & Poussaint, 1992). The quality of a child's relationships with adults is more important than the gender of the adults, for both male and female children. Children between ages 9 and 12 are aware of unfairness and hypocrisy of adults and authorities. It is important for adults to help them understand adult failings and to model doing something about it so that they don't feel powerless and cynical. Abused or neglected children may become aggressive, picking fights out of frustration, disconnection, and hopelessness.

Children who are shy need encouragement from adults to participate. They may be very sensitive to racial attitudes at this period and may hide behind race or other "differences" to excuse poor performance, so adults should be careful not to permit children's outrage to become an excuse for poor performance. Self-esteem is precarious at this age (9 to 12), and pride in race is crucial to self-esteem (Comer & Poussaint, 1992; Murry & Brody,

2002; Neblett, White, Ford, Philip, Nguyen, Hoa, Sellers, 2008).

PUBESCENCE We might consider the fourth developmental stage to be pubescence, from about age 11 to 13 for girls and age 12 to 14 or 15 for boys. At this time, children are normally ambivalent, rebellious, bored, uninterested, or difficult. They are highly critical of others who don't look or act like them, and they identify with a preferred group of friends who agree on dress, music, and even language. They now challenge morality and rules imposed by parents and society, and experiment with new rules, valuing peers' values more than those of parents (Matthias & French, 1996; Hughes, Bigler, & Levy, 2007). To prepare White children for a multicultural world, they need to experience diverse social groups. Young teens rarely turn to parents with problems, even major ones. Parents have to persevere and learn to speak of their own worries at that age rather than questioning their children. At this phase, children benefit from group experiences that encourage the expression of diverse thoughts and feelings and from volunteering for community service. Children at this age are idealistic and respond to calls for help.

For some reason, during certain phases in development, including preschool and adolescence, children seem to hold rigidly to sex-role stereotypes, even more so than their parents or teachers. It is important not to encourage this stereotyping but instead to encourage girls to develop their own opinions, values, aspirations, and interests. During the adolescent years girls often confuse identity with intimacy, defining themselves through relationships with others. Advertising and adult attitudes toward girls, which define their development in terms of their ability to attract a male, are bound to be detrimental to girls' mental health, leaving them lacking in self-esteem; fearing to appear smart, tall, assertive, or competent; and worrying about losing their chances of finding an intimate relationship with a male. It is important to raise questions about such norms, since they put the girl into an impossible bind: You are healthy only if you define your identity through your mate, not yourself. Girls are twice as likely as boys to become depressed as they enter puberty (Hankin, Mermelstein, & Roesch, 2007).

THE FIFTH PHASE, ADOLESCENCE goes from about age 13 for girls and about age 14 or 15 for boys and continues until about age 21. During this phase, young people go through major bodily, emotional, sexual, and spiritual changes; evolve their sexual and gender identities; learn to relate to intimate partners; and develop the ability to function increasingly independently. They renegotiate their identity with their parents as they mature; refine their physical, social, and intellectual skills; develop their spiritual and moral identity; and begin to define who they want to become as adults.

Erikson (1968) described the development of adolescent girls as fundamentally different from that of boys, holding their identity in abeyance in preparation to attract men by whose name they would be known and by whose status they would be defined. Feminist research has luckily challenged this patriarchal view. Gilligan (1993) in her landmark study of preadolescent and early adolescent girls attributed the girls' loss of voice and low self-esteem to their fear of appearing too smart, assertive, or competent to attract a male. This sexist requirement is now seen as cultural, not inherent in girls' development.

Families of color have special tasks to help their children negotiate the burdens and pressures of dealing with a racist world without becoming bitter, hopeless, or cynical (Nicholas, Helms, Jernigan, Sass, Skrzypek, & De Silva, 2008). Adolescents react to social hostility and are attracted to causes. Black adolescents may succumb to despair and give up hope of a productive future. Adolescents of color may have identity problems if they are completely segregated from Whites or if they live in mostly White communities. Middle- and upper-class Black adolescents may have identity problems because Black poverty is both romanticized and vilified. They may need help to find a positive Black identity and not succumb to hopelessness or rage in the face of racism and the White supremacy of the dominant society (Canino & Spurlock, 2000; Comer & Poussaint, 1992; Comer, Joyner, & Ben-Avie, 2004; Comer, 2008, 2009; Robbins et al., 2007).

Sexual issues and information should be discussed with adolescents at home and at school, building on earlier sex education. Powerful attraction to members of the opposite sex does not mean that gender segregation disappears. Young people continue to spend a good portion of their social time with same-sex partners (Maccoby, 1999). However, the higher rates of depression in females may have their onset during adolescence, because of the difficulties of cross-sex interaction. Adolescents who are not succeeding tend to form gangs and involve themselves in fighting, aggression, and violence. Adolescents who date exclusively outside of their own race probably have identity problems or are trying to provoke their parents.

Adolescents are typically searching actively for an identity. Sexual, religious, and racial issues that earlier seemed settled are reevaluated and subject to new understanding and revision. Similarities and differences, even within groups, cause the formation of in-groups and out-groups and for and against attitudes. The community climate regarding race and religion is important. Minority–majority ratios in school have great influence on the social atmosphere.

During adolescence, children begin to look beyond their own needs. They identify with community ideas and idealistic causes as a way to establish their own identity. This is an excellent age to involve them in community service programs, especially those catering to young children, or national organizations dedicated to helping their particular group socially and politically (Matthias & French, 1996). Their sense of empathy buttresses their moral conviction, which centers on wanting to alleviate misfortune and injustice (Goleman, 2006). To promote a sense of power and participation in society, 18-year-olds should be encouraged to vote.

Older teens finally understand morals and values not as impositions but as necessary for order and fairness. The media depict teens as selfish, aimless, and immoral, a picture that can become a self-fulfilling prophecy. In a disorderly and unfair society, they can stumble into drugs, alcohol, eating disorders, sexually transmitted diseases, and pregnancy. Parents must try to counteract the negative influence of the peer group and the larger society—always an uphill struggle (Matthias & French, 1996). Teens are aware of social hypocrisy. To remain credible to teens, parents must reveal their own uncertainties, beware of double messages delivered nonverbally,

speak clearly from the heart, and keep the door open for discussions.

Adolescents who display homosexual interests need their parents to understand that sexual orientation is not a mental disorder. This is a normal sexual identity for perhaps 10 percent of males and 5 percent of females, for complex biological and environmental reasons that are not yet understood. Family acceptance is very important, and parents often need help in understanding and supporting their adolescents in the coming-out process (LaSala, 2010). Although there is increased knowledge and acceptance gay, lesbian, and bisexual teens still have many concerns about feeling different from peers, and worries about being accepted by parents, family, and friends. Parents and others should be aware of signs of distress, such as withdrawal from activities and friends and lack of concentration and seek counseling if necessary. This is important because, as recent studies show, there is an increase in suicidal behavior among adolescents struggling with sexual identity (Parker, 2005).

YOUNG ADULTHOOD We might think of the sixth phase of development as covering the decades of young adulthood (from about age 21 to the mid-30s). Of course, there are great differences in the pathways at this phase, depending on a person's race, gender, class, and sexual orientation and for the latest cohorts as well, for whom it is sometimes said that we need a new phase called "adultolesence" to describe the period that is expanding at both ends in between childhood and independent adulthood (Kimmel, 2009). Adolescence has expanded downward by about 4 years in the past century to about 12 for girls and 14 for boys. Our society has created a huge dilemma with children who are physically the size of adults, and think they should be free to act like adults, but they are often unable to support themselves for as long as 20 years from age 12 into their 30s! Where it used to be possible for someone with a high school education to support a spouse and children, this is for the most part no longer the case. In general the tasks of finishing one's education, leaving home, finding a spouse, and becoming a parent all used to occur within a short period of time in the early 20s. But within the past generation these tasks have been spread out and changed so that the average marriage doesn't occur until people are in their late 20s, and education may continue until at least that late. So there may be an increasing phase of "preparation" for adulthood during which unlaunched children require ongoing parental support in a very changed life cycle process than has ever been the case before, and that was not even the case a generation ago.

In general, the first years of adulthood are a phase of generativity in terms of partnering, work, establishing one's own place in communities of friends and social groups, and of beginning to raise children. It is a time when adults are expected to move toward functioning without the physical or financial support of their parents, a time when they begin not only to care for themselves but also to take on responsibilities for the care of others, establishing themselves in work, partnering, and parenting. But there are major developmental problems in this phase for those without the educational skills to function independently in society, and this involves a growing percentage of the population. While the vast majority of the population is completing high school, many more than even a generation ago, and the percent completing college has doubled to 30 percent of the population, it has become increasingly difficult for one parent to support a family in our increasingly technological global society.

Young adults more frequently need extra support from parents, and increasingly, families have to accommodate to changing family constellations. Three generations may live together, which can create its own stresses, as the middle generation may remain more like children to their parents than partners or parents to their children.

Among African Americans, a higher percentage of young adult males are in jail than in college (Knepper, 2008; Johnson, 2007). Many who are able and ready to work find themselves increasingly shut out of meaningful jobs because they lack the necessary education. This obviously impedes their potential for marriage. This lack of stable wage earning for young Black men creates a problem for young women as well, who have a severely diminished pool of marital prospects. Taken together, the massive obstacles of racism and poverty impede the forward development of young adults of color at this phase and way too often derail potentially productive people into the underclass, from which escape becomes harder as the life cycle continues.

MIDDLE ADULTHOOD The seventh stage of the life cycle, which might be thought of as middle adulthood, lasts from about age 35 to 55 or 60. It is a time when, generally speaking, adults are still in good health, in the midst of their work life and child-rearing, if they have children. During the latter part of this phase, people often begin to do a philosophical reexamination of their lives, or even several reexaminations, and may need to reinvent themselves in their work and community to fit changing circumstances. There is often caretaking responsibility for older or ailing relatives, as well as for children, and the span of childbearing years is widening from late 20s to early 50s so the tasks of the phase are less predictable than ever before.

It is generally the last opportunity for active, hands-on parenting. In addition to the usual power struggles with teenagers pushing toward launching, it is a time to shift parental gears and start treating adolescents more like the young adults they will soon be, emphasizing the wish to trust rather than constricting or punishing them. This is the last chance to help children develop emotional competence. It is a time for parents—unmarried, married, divorced, or remarried—to realize the grave dangers and temptations facing today's adolescents and to resolve their own differences with partners or other adult family members enough to guide their adolescents as a team, united in concern and advice for them.

LATE MIDDLE ADULTHOOD The next stage of the life cycle (from about age 55 or 60 to the early 70s) might be considered later middle age blending into early aging, a time when adults are generally still in good health, have the energy for major undertakings, and often still have responsibilities for their not quite launched children. They may begin to retire and to take up new interests, Though they are generally freed from immediate child-rearing or financial responsibilities, depending on the age at which they had their own children, they are often beginning to help their grandchildren, and mentoring those who will follow them in the work world. Women go through, or have already gone through, menopause, which often frees them up to concentrate their energies on new projects as well as friends (Taylor, Klein, Lewis, Gruenewald, Gurung, & Updegraff, 2001). Freed from major caretaking, they often decide that it is their turn. It is a time when people are coming to terms with the fact that they can't do it all. They have to let go of certain dreams, recognizing their limitations so that they can concentrate on what they can do. Men often "mellow" at this phase as they become less focused on work and more involved in family relationships and domestic life.

People have to be concerned about husbanding their financial resources and preparing for future health care needs. It is a time to work out increasing supports and find ways to manage decreasing physical strength and endurance. It is also a time of facing the death of parents and losses of older friends and relatives.

THE LAST STAGE OF LIFE, AGING AND DEATH covers roughly the ages from the middle 70s to 100+ as people come to terms with their own mortality and that of their peer group. It is a time for working out one's legacy, as well as any other personal business with one's descendants, to be prepared for death. An essential task is the completion of a life review in which one assesses the pluses and minuses of one's life and comes to a relatively positive acceptance.

The longer one lives, the more losses one sustains: family members, colleagues and lifelong friends, even some younger than oneself. The death of a spouse, one of life's heaviest blows, will occur during this phase for those who are still married. This produces many mixed emotions, from relief, if the death was preceded by a lengthy period of caretaking, to guilt— for surviving and feeling relieved— to devastation, if the marriage was a long one, especially if the partners were very interdependent in emotional and other functioning. The surviving spouse then has the task, one last time, of creating a new vision of life.

This is a time of life when friendship and spirituality are important resources against depression and to tolerate one's growing dependence on others while continuing to maximize one's abilities. The following chapters in this book will focus on different stages, transitions, and discontinuities in the life cycle of families, and will offer clinical suggestions to help the therapeutic process.

Chapter 3

Women and the Family Life Cycle

Monica McGoldrick

If I imagine myself whole, active, a self, will I not cease in some profound way to be a woman? The answer must be: imagine, and the old idea of womanhood be damned. . . . When I was a girl, my father told me the story of the bumble bee. According to the science of aeronautics . . . it was impossible for a creature of the size and weight and construction of a bumble bee to fly. But the bumble bee, not having been told this, flies anyway.

—From REINVENTING WOMANHOOD by Carolyn G. Heilbrun. Copyright © 1979 by Carolyn G. Heilbrun. Used by permission of W. W. Norton & Company, Inc.

Women have always played a central role in families, but the idea that they have a life cycle apart from their roles as wife and mother is a relatively recent one and is still not fully accepted. Until very recently, "human development" referred to male development. Women's development was defined by the men in their lives, their role being defined by their position in someone else's life cycle: wife, daughter, mother, sister, grandmother. The expectation for women has been that they would take care of the needs of others, first men, then children, then the elderly. Rarely has it been accepted that they have a right to a life for themselves. Women's life cycle experiences differ depending on where they are in the larger sociopolitical structure; even as we acknowledge their common experiences, we must work to keep the lives of women of color, lesbians, transgender and bisexual, and poor women from remaining invisible. We must pay attention to their adaptive strengths as we assert the traumatic inequities they have experienced. The struggles for women of color are dramatically more complex and difficult than those of White women. Audre Lorde described a key difference between Black and White women boldly:

Some problems we share as women, some we do not. You fear your children will grow up to join the patriarchy and testify against you; we fear our children will be dragged from a car and shot down in the street, and you will turn your backs upon the reasons they are dying. (1984, p. 9)

African American and other marginalized women perceive their womanhood differently than White women and may distance themselves from feminists, seeing them as underestimating the integral role of cultural traditions and racism in their lives (Hall & Greene, 1994). Paula Gunn Allen summarizes the context of American Indian women's lives:

American Indian women struggle on every front for the survival of our children, our people, our self-respect, our value systems, and our way of life. The past five hundred years testify to our skill at waging this struggle. For all the varied weapons of extinction pointed at our heads, we endure. We . . . survive colonization, acculturation, assimilation, . . beating, rape, starvation, mutilation, sterilization, abandonment, neglect, death of our children, our loved ones, destruction of our land, our homes, our past, and our future. We . . . do more than just survive. We bond, we care, we fight, we teach, we nurse, we bear, we feed, we earn, we laugh, we love, we hang in there, no matter what. Of course many of us just give up. Many are alcoholics, many are addicts. Many abandon their children, the old ones. Many commit suicide. Many become violent, go insane, Many go "white" and are never seen or heard from again. But enough hold on to their traditions and their ways so that even after almost five hundred years, we endure. And we even write songs and poems, make paintings and drawings that say: "We walk in beauty. Let us continue." (1992, p. 43)

Overall, women lead far more complex, varied, and unpredictable lives than men do, reinventing themselves many times to meet different circumstances. While men's work life tends to follow a linear course, women's usually consists of starts, stops, meanders, interruptions, revisions, and detours as they accommodate to the others in their lives (Shapiro, 1996).

Clinical work involves helping both men and women appreciate women's courage and the odds they face and break down the patriarchal vision of women as sex objects and servers of others rather than human beings in their own right.

Women's Changing Life Cycle Roles

Women's lives have always required amazing improvisation, but never more than today. They were never about following a single thread of the evolution of the hero into the undaunted, courageous, and goal-oriented achiever, as seemed to be the life plan for European American men. As Catherine Bateson puts it: "Life . . . [is] an improvisatory art. . . . We combine familiar and unfamiliar components in response to new situations . . . my own life . . . (was) a sort of desperate improvisation in which I was constantly trying to make something coherent from conflicting elements to fit rapidly changing settings" (1989, p. 3). Women's lives have always involved a weaving together of many strands, attending to multiple tasks, sounds, and images at once. They created the "nest" that was home for everyone else; they provided the

food, the nurturance, and the care for all from the youngest to the oldest; they created the family rituals, bought the presents, made birthdays and Thanksgivings happen. They nursed the sick, washed and mourned the dead, and attended to the needs of other mourners. But women were systematically kept out of the public spheres of life—government, business, the world of power and money—all of which had to change, for women to have a life cycle of their own. As Carolyn Heilbrun discussed in her classic analysis of women's biography, *Writing a Woman's Life,* women's right to her own story, depends on her ability to act in the public domain. Heilbrun sees power as "the ability to take one's place in whatever discourse is essential to action and the right to have one's part matter" (1988, p. 18). The life cycle of women has been changing because women have been asserting the right to have their part matter in the public domain, which determines their possibilities also in the intimate, personal domain—from infant care to physical, psychological, spiritual, and financial security in old age, a phase of life that has always been for women only but which even now is still controlled by men, rather than by women themselves.

The conundrum of responsibility without power has long characterized women's lives. Women had responsibility for clothing their children, but fashion and advertising were a man's world; women were the cooks at home, but not the chefs of record; they were the artistic creators of the home, but they were not the artists of record. For centuries, women remained voiceless in the public sphere, having to stitch their lives together here and there as they could. This was a tragedy, but it has also given them an adaptive strength, making them able to weave lives out of many disparate strands. Even in the private sphere, in their homes, the pervasive private abuse, persecution, and humiliation of women has been an unacknowledged societal shame for centuries. Battering of women, date rape, marital rape, dehumanizing treatment of women as sex objects, psychological abuse, financial control, sexual harassment, and exploitation of women have only recently begun to be acknowledged as problems. Bill

Clinton spoke publicly of the problem more than a decade ago:

> *If children aren't safe in their homes, if college women aren't safe in their dorms, if mothers can't raise their children in safety, then the American Dream will never be real for them. Domestic violence is now the number one health risk for women between the ages of 15 and 44 in our country. It is a bigger threat than cancer or car accidents. (quoted in Barnett, Miller-Perrin, & Perrin, 1997, p. 15)*

The exclusion of women from public spheres of education, lawmaking, business, the arts, money, and power is gradually changing. But the issues remain. Nevertheless women's roles have been changing dramatically in the past generation. They are delaying marriage. Instead of being passed from their fathers to their husbands, they are claiming an increasing span of time to define their own lives. A much higher proportion of women than ever before is experiencing a period of independent living and work before marriage (Coontz, 2006). Now more than two-thirds of women under 25 are unmarried. The typical first-time bride in 2007 was 27, almost four years older than her counterpart of 1970. Child-bearing has fallen below replacement levels, as women are increasingly electing to postpone child-bearing. Women are refusing to stay in stifling or abusive marriages. Divorce is at 46 percent, and women with the most education and income who divorce are less likely to remarry, in contrast to men, the most wealthy and well educated of whom are the most likely to stay married or to remarry quickly. But women are also more likely to move down to poverty after divorce, while men's income actually rises after divorce. Currently, 75 percent of the poor are women or children, most of whom live in one-parent households. The number of single-parent households (86 percent headed by women) has more than doubled. For the increasing number of teenaged unmarried mothers, their mothers, aunts, are playing a major role in raising their children. For the first time, a fair number of women in their 30s and 40s are choosing to have and raise children without part-ners, a new phenomenon altogether. Lesbians, who are increasingly having children together, are broad-ening and reworking the concept of family and com-munity to include their own special relationships with friends, extended family, and ex-lovers (Slater, 1995). Many more women are living longer, having adventurous lives, and reinventing themselves well into their 70s, 80s, and 90s (Heilbrun, 1997; Lawrence-Lightfoot, 2009). Finally, the majority of people who live alone are women (11 million versus 6.8 million men), who tend to be widowed or di-vorced elderly. Between 1970 and the present, there has been a large increase in the percentage of women over age 75 who live alone.

Women and Education

Education is a key to liberation. Since 1979, more women than men have been enrolled in college. Women now make up 55 percent of college students and 65 percent of students over age 35, so they are becoming a majority of Americans with higher education (Malveaux, 2005). Indeed there is strong evidence that the Ivy League and other prestigious colleges are offering affirmative action for male students to keep the proportion of men close to 50 percent (Kivel, 2002; Britz, 2006). But for educa-tion to work for women it, like all other institutions of our society, needs to change. Within the hallowed halls of academia, women have been made to feel like frauds. Peggy McIntosh (1985, 1989), in her articles "On Feeling Like a Fraud," has described the ways women who have been socialized in the "single track logic" of academia can end up feeling stupid because they are unable to make an outline that lays out categories and subcategories in hierarchical order. McIntosh asserts that the very requirement of acting as if all ideas fit in logical and hierarchical sequence is absurd.

> *Language is an invention . . . Life doesn't come in sentences, paragraphs or arguments. For me, the outline now joined the argumentative paper as a problematical form, requiring pretenses, such as subordinating all ideas to one "main" or governing idea. . . . For me the outline is . . . a fraudulent form. My genre . . . is the list. . . . On a list everything matters; you need not rank,*

subordinate, and exclude; you can add or sub-
tract, elaborate or delete. . . . With an outline,
one must (pretend to) justify the sequence, and .
. . the relative significance of each item or idea.
One cannot be generous in an outline. . . . The
list allows me to keep everything, to expand, to
add at any time. (1989, p. 2)

We must challenge the categories we have been offered to gain better perspective on the complex threads of a woman's life cycle. McIntosh calls for developing a "double vision" regarding a woman's sense of being a "fraud." On the one hand, we need to help women to overcome their feelings of inadequacy and of not deserving a place to stand or speak out. On the other hand, we need to validate and appreciate women's acknowledgment that they do not know everything and their resistance to making pronouncements as if they held "the" truth, as men have done so often. McIntosh's intuition about lists and outlines seems particularly apt for understanding women's need to reinvent themselves continually to meet ever-changing circumstances throughout the life cycle. It helps if we keep a broad perspective on women's expanding lives in the public domain of work, school, governance, business, power, and money.

Marta Powell was a talented, highly educated artist of Irish and German background who had attended private schools and an Ivy League university where she met her husband Robert whose ancestors went back to the Mayflower. Both Marta and Robert completed masters in Fine Arts. He then became a college professor, and she became the "wife," continuing her artwork on the side and through cooking, sewing, gardening, and decorating their home. She could not work in the university's art department because of nepotism rules, but eventually she got a job as an adjunct teaching graphic design in the architecture department. By the time her sons left for college, Marta had become depressed and frustrated and wondered what had become of her own aspirations. By chance she got the opportunity to attend a summer Artists seminar when someone else dropped out and once she was away she realized how unhappy she had become in the marriage. She realized very quickly that the marriage had buried her self. She had sacrificed too much of herself for her husband's dreams and

lost sight of her own. When her husband was negative about renegotiating their relationship, she told him she wanted a divorce. The divorce left her feeling amazingly free. She had not realized until she separated how much she had come to take responsibility for whatever went wrong in her husband's world. Now she no longer had to worry about his unhappiness and could, for the first time concentrate on her own life. However, without her husband's income she quickly moved toward the poverty level. She tried to figure out how to move ahead on the academic pathway, but continuously felt inadequate in preparing the required papers for presentation and publication because her thinking went in spirals and loops, and she could not make it go in a straight line. At this point her depression and frustration led her to seek help. When she told her story, she was shocked by the therapist's response to her narrative. She had come to think of her life as a failure, but the therapist characterized her as a pioneer who had kept up her creativity through all sorts of endeavors during the years when by her station in life she had not been able to formally pursue her career, and now she was getting ready, suggested the therapist, to break forth in a new incarnation, drawing on all the work she had been doing throughout her life. Of course doing a linear outline was too constraining for someone as creative as she. And of course she was frustrated! How could she not be? With minimal coaching Marta found the way to publishing and presenting in her own voice and moved to a new university where within a few years she was a highly respected member of the senior faculty. At age 60 she achieved tenure and at age 70 became an Emerita Professor at her university.

The therapeutic input Marta required was minimal. Had she seen a therapist who focused on her depression rather than on her creativity and the life cycle dilemma of a woman in her situation, she might, of course, had a very different life trajectory. The clinical input she received helped her to see herself among the women of her generation as a true pioneer and to appreciate the accomplishments of her improvised life. Very often this is all that women need—to be helped to empower themselves and realize how much they have accomplished already, to see themselves as a woman among women, whose lives have been constrained by circumstance, and who need to gather strength from others who understand their situation. Marta had had good female friends throughout her life and close relationships with her three sisters, although these relationships had been sidelined during her marriage. At the point of her separation she reconnected with these relationships and from that point on her network of friends became her greatest resource as she developed herself over the next chapter of her life.

We must pay more attention to the family and community networks that women have always been responsible for maintaining and that are crucial to their safety and ability to have a gratifying life. We must also attend to the possibilities of equal partnership, connection, and flexibility in couple relationships, friendships, and intergenerational bonds through the life cycle. We must bear in mind that women of color experience double jeopardy and lesbians of color experience triple jeopardy in adjusting to a world in which the institutions have been defined by others. Lorraine Hansberry, author of *Raisin in the Sun,* provides an example that still has relevance:

> *She had begun her college career awkwardly and it had stayed that way. The point of things eluded her—things like classes and note-taking and lecture and lab. She found most of them unspeakably dull and irrelevant to virtually anything she had ever had on her mind or ever expected to. Worst of all was something called "Physical Geography," which required, among other things, that she spend some four hours a week knocking on rocks with a little metal hammer. (1969, p. 37)*

How many women, especially lesbian women and women of color, have been thrown into experiences in which societal assumptions had absolutely no connection to their life experience? Many have found that to survive they had to draw from inner resources and make improvisatory connections and transformations to bridge to that which was relevant in their souls. Hansberry was more than up to the task. Before she turned 30, in her play *Raisin in the Sun,* she had articulated the intergenerational relationships of African American men and women through the life cycle and became the youngest person, the only African American, and only the fifth woman ever to win the New York Drama Critics award for best play. Therapists have important work to do with women at every phase of the life cycle in encouraging their ideas, intuitions, and adaptive resourcefulness, helping them to realize that they are not "frauds" and validating their "ways of knowing" (Belenky, Clinchy, Goldberger, & Tarule, 1986).

Women and Work

The vast majority of women, even mothers of small children, are now in the paid workforce. This includes 71 percent of mothers of children under 18. The continuing differential roles of men and women in the larger context is illustrated by the fact that a large portion of women are still in sex-segregated, low-paying jobs. One quarter of all employed women are crowded into just 22 of 500 occupations distinguished by the Bureau of the Census.

Several myths have been created about women and work. The first is that traditionally mothers didn't work, which is, of course, an absurdity. Second is the myth that women only work for extra money or for selfish reasons. In fact, women's income is essential for the survival and well-being of most families in the twenty-first century. Another myth is that maternal employment is bad for children. This is demonstrably false, as maternal employment tends to improve a mother's self-esteem and well-being. Indeed, maternal depression, which is correlated with unemployed mothers, does have a negative impact on children. Generally speaking employed mothers have higher aspirations for their children, discuss and share school activities more, encourage independence skills more, have more parenting satisfaction, fewer family conflicts, and are more effective at setting limits; their children have fewer behavior problems, watch less TV, and experience greater family cohesion; in addition father involvement is significantly greater when mothers are employed, which is associated with a host of favorable affective and cognitive outcomes as well as the healthy social adjustment of children (Gottfried & Gottfried, 2008). Of course jobs with no flexibility or security, poor pay and benefits, irregular schedules, and low control may jeopardize health, whereas having high-quality roles, even if they are numerous, may help to maintain or enhance health. Even with difficult jobs, the income and ability to provide for one's children is an asset. Women with more high-powered, high-status careers obviously have more advantages. Job-related social support has particularly beneficial effects on women's health. In any case there is no evidence that children lose out when their mothers are employed, and there are many advantages to maternal employment (Marcus-Newhall, Halpern, & Tan, 2008).

Achieving equal pay for equal work is a major issue for women in the United States, one third of whom earn more than half of their family's income. Indeed two fifths of working women are the sole heads of their households. Among African American women and other women of color, the issue of undercompensation is even greater. Overall, women working is positive for them and for their children, for financial, psychological, and social reasons (Barnett & Rivers, 1996; Marcus-Newhall, Halpern, & Tan, 2008). Daughters appear to benefit most of all from having a working mother. They have been shown to be more self-confident, to get better grades, and to be more likely to pursue careers themselves than children of nonemployed mothers (Hoffman, 1989). For African American families, a mother's working has been shown to improve not only her self-esteem (Hoffman, 1989), but also her daughters' likelihood of staying in school (Wolfer & Moen, 1996). Furthermore, fascinating and little-publicized early findings suggested that the high achievement of mothers is even more predictive of high achievement of both their sons and their daughters than is the high achievement of fathers (Losoff, 1974; Padan, 1965).

The main point is that very few families can afford to have children these days unless both husband and wife have paying jobs. Still, while family and work are seen as mutually supportive and complementary for men, for women, work and family remain highly conflicting demands. Traditionally, the family has served to support and nurture the male worker for his performance on the job, whereas working women have been seen as depriving their families by working. In no sense is the family a refuge for women as it has been

for men. In fact, the high level of psychological demands in their jobs at home and often in the workplace, with little actual control or power over their situation, can put women in particularly stressful situations much of the time (Barnett & Rivers, 2004). Women have been in a double bind in this regard. Although the dominant belief has been that women belong in the home, participation in the labor force has been shown to be the most important determinant of a woman's psychological well-being. In traditional cultures, mothers always worked, and children were raised primarily by grandparents and older siblings. Yet there are many social pressures against women feeling good about working. It is not the number of activities that is burdensome to a woman's well-being, but rather the lack of support and the inability to choose one's roles and organize one's resources to meet the demands.

The major source of stress for working women appears to be sexual harassment, followed by efforts to "mommy track" mothers out of their jobs. Men's participation in household chores has risen dramatically, even in working-class families, though it still lags far behind the participation of women (Barnett & Rivers, 1996; Hochschild, 2003). Couple relationships are changing dramatically in dual-worker families. The real problem, though, is our nation's refusal to support good-quality child care for all children, as other advanced nations of the world have done, which is essential in a country that requires dual-worker families.

In any case, economic independence for women, which has profound implications for traditional family structures, is crucial for women's protection from the high risk of abuse, divorce, poverty, and powerlessness in old age. Poverty rates are higher for women than for men at every age for all races and cultures (Costello, Wight, & Stone, 2003). Both young and old women are twice as likely as men to be poor. Overall about one quarter of African American women and Latinas live in poverty and about 10 percent of White women. To accomplish this independence, massive power changes are required. Wives' economic dependence, which is the greatest factor in their returning to abusing husbands, creates a serious power imbalance that threatens marriage altogether. Unless clinicians are aware of the impact of unequal power on women, they will be unlikely to challenge the real sources of stress in male–female relationships (Hare-Mustin,1991).

Velma Jefferson, a 55-year-old African American school secretary came to therapy with a very specific agenda: She had had a heart attack the previous summer, which she believed was caused by her marital distress. She was seven years from being able to retire and wanted me to help her not have another heart attack over her husband, Carl, before retirement. At that point, she said, she'd have the resources to leave him if he didn't change his ways, but she could not afford to lose the share he gave to their income until that time. She hoped he would change, but she did not want to waste her time with marital therapy. She thought if he wanted to work on himself that would be fine, but she wanted help to keep herself healthy and not be derailed to his lies and promises. The couple had been married in their early twenties, but she had left him five years later because of his physical abuse, taking their little daughter to Chicago where she had family. Three years later he followed her there, promised to turn over a new leaf, and she remarried him. Since that time he had never been physically abusive, but she said he was a "high roller" full of lies about his relationships with other women, always letting her down financially with big promises and then gambling most of his money away or spending it on himself. She was tired of arguing with him about where he had been or with whom and about his excuses regarding money. She said that because of his financial problems the house was in her name only and if she could hold on for the next few years she would have her pension and the money from the house to retire to Georgia, which was her dream. I soon met the husband who was very keen for couples therapy to begin and could not understand why I was not trying to help them work out their "misunderstandings." We had a couple of joint sessions where Mrs. Jefferson laid out that she was tired of arguing about money and would expect her husband to pay his share of the mortgage and his contribution to food and household expenses but was no longer going to nag him about the money. He could just leave it on the table. He tried to bring up that she was always suspicious that he had a girlfriend. I asked if he did and he denied it but said she never believed what he said. She said she would not be asking about this again. When I met with Carl alone

he was very frustrated that I was not doing more to help him connect with his wife who, he was sure, was angry with him. I questioned him further about a girlfriend because he had had some hesitation when in her presence. He admitted he had someone he had been involved with for a long time that he had been trying to break up with, but she had a schizophrenic son and needed him and he was having trouble breaking the relationship off. We discussed the limits his wife seemed to be establishing regarding the finances—even though she had not said she would do anything if he didn't come through with the expected money. He said she had been a wonderful wife and he wanted my help to win her back. We discussed his drinking and spending patterns and he said he had decided the previous week to cut down on his drinking because it was costing him a lot of money.

From that point on I coached the couple separately to achieve their goals. Velma's goal was to stay healthy and follow through on her goal of not letting herself be derailed by anger and frustration with Carl which had taken up too much space in her life. His goal was to win her back, which, he gradually realized meant to get himself back from excessive drinking, spending, and involvement with other women. Over the next several years the wife developed her network of friends, worked on herself physically to stay calm, and interpersonally to avoid getting into "useless" discussions with Carl about issues where he might lie. She had had a negative attitude about organized religion since growing up with an abusive minister father and being pained by the hypocrisy of his religiosity. She now found a spiritual community, which had meaning to her and which she felt she would be able to continue when she moved to Georgia.

For Carl her behavior seemed like shock therapy. He became more aad more committed to working on himself. Perhaps he sensed that she had set herself a real bottom line, not now, when she would not be able to manage a separation, but in the future when she was definite she would if he did not change. By the time of Velma's retirement their relationship was in a very different place. He had become a caring, thoughtful, and appreciative husband. He had reconnected with a daughter he had fathered and abandoned in his earlier adulthood, and was connecting now with his grandchildren. The couple had ended therapy several years before retirement but made a reunion appointment before moving together to retirement in Georgia, where we were able to review the importance of

Velma's taking responsibility for keeping herself healthy and Carl's taking responsibility for creating the kind of trust and loving relationship he wanted with his wife.

Velma Jefferson did not think of her problems in gender terms, but my understanding was that her courage and accommodation to her husband for so many years, her going along with him even to the point of putting her own health in jeopardy before taking a stand seems like a common problem for women, who have been raised to accommodate and think of their own needs as selfish. What was remarkable was her clarity about what she needed to do to survive and her ability to seek the support she needed to get herself to a healthy place. Luckily I was able to support her in this journey. The main clinical point is not to pathologize women who are coming to an understanding of their oppression but rather to support their efforts to empower themselves as Velma Jefferson did over a several year period.

In spite of household and other strains, the more roles a woman occupies, the healthier she is likely to be. Employed married parents have the best health profile, whereas people with none of these roles have the worst profile. Employed women are healthier than nonemployed women, and lack of employment is a risk factor for women's health (Gannon, 1999). Multiple roles may provide cognitive cushioning in the face of stress. There is a significant relationship between underemployment and decreased physical and mental health. While work seems to be a stress on men, indications are that paid work actually improves the health of women. Women who are homemakers end up with a lower sense of self-esteem and personal competence, even regarding their child care and social skills, than do mothers in the paid workforce. Women who take any time off from full commitment to the paid workforce lose a great deal of ground in their power in their relationships, their work flexibility, and their financial options (Barnett & Rivers, 1996).

As more women have entered the workplace, they have become more aware of the external constraints on them in the labor force. As a result, they often become more aware of pay discrimination, job discrimination, and sexual harassment than they were in the past, and this awareness can be intensely stressful, even when it leads to change. The main clinical implication is that therapists need to be active educators in therapy, helping women to realize that they are not alone, encouraging them to network to diminish their sense of isolation, and empowering them to join forces to change the way society operates. A woman who must bring a charge of sexual harassment against her boss by herself will have great difficulty. A class action suit is enormously easier to handle, and women are more likely to win, when they operate together. Linking women to other women is one of the most important tools we have as clinicians.

Women in Families

Being part of a family and the breaking up of a family have profoundly different implications for men and women. Women in traditional marital relationships have poorer physical health, lower self-esteem, less autonomy, and poorer marital adjustment than women in more equal relationships. Indeed, being part of a family has been a serious danger for many women but rarely for men. For example, women are 10 times more likely than men to be abused by an intimate partner and 6 times more likely to be abused by an intimate partner than by a stranger. At least 29 percent of the violent crimes against women are committed by husbands or boyfriends. The number of women murdered by their intimates in the United States during the years of the Vietnam War (51,000) approximated the number of soldiers killed in the war (58,000), yet we have heard virtually nothing about these tragic losses, and there are no memorials to these women.

Yet, as problematic as traditional patterns have been for women, changing the status quo has been extremely difficult. Barnett and Rivers (2004) speak of the incomplete gender revolution. Even as women are rebelling against the burden of bearing full responsibility for making family relationships, holidays, and celebrations happen, they still feel guilty when they do not do what they have grown up expecting to do. When no one else moves in to fill the gap, they often feel blamed that family solidarity is breaking down and believe that it is their fault. Men's emotional and physical distance is still largely ignored in writings about the changing family. In earlier times, when community cohesion was greater, women often had at least a network of extended family and neighbors to help out. But now, increasingly, extended families are not easily accessible, and those networks that ease the burdens of child-rearing by providing supplementary caretakers are not available. The importance of these invisible networks has rarely been acknowledged by society, which has espoused values that have regularly and intentionally uprooted families for jobs, military duty, or corporate needs. Thus, when women have found themselves without such supports, they have often been unable to articulate what is wrong, since the need for community and family support has not been socially validated. In the absence of such acknowledgment, women often blame themselves or are blamed by society when they cannot hold things together. The argument typically moves between the use of the word "mother" and the word "parent" in such a way that mothers are blamed for abandoning their children, while fathers' traditional absence from the interior of the child's life is continuously obscured. Conservative commentators talk about the selfishness of "parents," who are spending less time with their children, by whom they mean mothers, because they fail to refer to the fact that fathers have been absent from families for a long time already.

Such backlash responses to the changes in women's roles in our times typically hark back nostalgically to that idiosyncratic period in U.S. history: the 1950s for White middle-class families, when women, at higher rates than at any other time in history, were isolated in nuclear families as homemakers with their children. As Stephanie Coontz (2006) has pointed out, the "traditional" marriages of that generation created the most drug-oriented, rebellious children of the 1960s as well as the fastest-growing divorce rate in the world, so we should think twice about our reverence for that phase of the "good old days," not to mention the suppression of women entailed in that family

arrangement. Susan Faludi (1991) detailed brilliantly the conservative backlash response to the changing roles of women, which blamed women for destroying families by their selfishness in considering their own needs.

The majority of household labor is still done by women, with other family members still thinking that their role in participating in chores is to "help her." Arlie Hochschild (2003) actually calculated a few years ago that over a year, women averaged an extra month of 24-hour work days, and over 12 years, they averaged an extra year of 24-hour work days. Recent indications are that the skew in housekeeping and child care is diminishing but that mothers of preschoolers still work 17 hours more a week than their mates, and once their children enter school, mothers still work an extra 5.6 hours a week more than their husbands (Barnett & Rivers, 1996). Blumstein & Schwartz (1983, 1991) found that money buys power in marriage. It buys the privilege to make decisions—concerning whether to stay or leave, what the family will purchase, where they will live, and how the children will be educated. In other words, money talks. In the years since this study the patterns have not changed as much as they should have.

Women in the Middle: Women and Caretaking

Unfortunately, the well-being of both children and the elderly, who are mostly women, may be gained at the expense of the quality of life of the middle generation of women who are most burdened, squeezed by overwhelming demands of caretaking for both older and younger generations. Sometimes referred to as "the sandwich generation," they are often caught in a dependency squeeze between their parents and their children and grandchildren. Older women are also often squeezed to accept work their lives had not prepared them for, since they did not expect to have to seek employment after midlife, but the current economics often require them to earn money well into their 70's. The realities of their financial future are increasingly hitting women at midlife. They are realizing how severely the inequalities of their position in the power structure limit their other options for the rest of their lives. Elderly women have much higher poverty than their male contemporaries (Costello, Wight, & Stone, 2003).

Women are exposed to higher rates of change and instability in their lives than men and are also more vulnerable to life cycle stresses, because of their greater emotional involvement in the lives of those around them. This means that they are doubly stressed, exposed to a wider network of people for whom they feel responsible and more emotionally responsive to them. Their role overload leaves them further burdened when unpredictable stresses such as illness, divorce, or unemployment occur. Women are much more emotionally affected than men by deaths and by other events in their networks. Men respond less to events at the edge of their caring networks and to the distress of neighbors and friends. They actually hear less about stress in their networks. People who need emotional support more often seek out women as confidants. Therefore, women have more demands for nurturance made on them. Daughters are more involved with and visit parents more than sons do. Grandmothers are twice as likely to have warm relationships with grandchildren as grandfathers. Indeed, grandfathers tend to be active with their grandchildren only if their wives are (Lott, 1994).

Traditionally, women have been held responsible for all family caretaking: for their husbands, their children, their parents, their husband's parents, and any other sick or dependent family members. Even now, almost one fifth of women aged 55 to 59 are providing in-home care to an elderly relative. Over half of women with one surviving parent can expect to become that parent's caretaker. Usually one daughter or a daughter-in-law has the primary responsibility for the care of elderly women. Clearly, caring for the very old (who are mostly women) is primarily a woman's issue, but increasingly younger women are in the labor force and thus unavailable for caretaking without extreme difficulty. Increasingly, with more and more four-generation families, the caregivers themselves are elderly and struggling with declining functioning. Twelve percent of caregivers are themselves over age 75.

Women's Exclusion From Power Under the Law and Societal Expectations

The overwhelming majority of lawmakers in our society are males. Their record on legislation in support of family caretaking is a travesty. This is a critical issue for divorced women, mothers of small children, women of color, the elderly (who are mostly women), and others who do not have the power to make the laws and thus get doubly burdened: with the responsibility and without the power or resources to take care of their families. The laws regulating social services do not support women. Contrary to the claim that government services sap the strength of family supports, the failure to provide public services to families exacerbates marital and intergenerational conflicts, turning family members against each other.

We must move farther and faster to tackle the hard political tasks of restructuring home and work so that women who are married and have children can also earn money or have their own voice in the decision-making mainstream of society. The guilt of less-than-perfect motherhood and less-than-perfect professional career performance is real, because it's not possible to "have it all," when jobs are still structured for men whose wives take care of the details of life, and education, transportation, and homes are still structured for women whose only responsibility is running their families (Barnett & Gareis, 2008). As Goldner put it long ago in her critique of our field:

By ignoring the complex relationship between the structure of family relations and the world of work, family therapists tacitly endorse the . . . mystification and . . . distortion that masks a fundamental organizing principle of contemporary family life. The division of labor (both affective and instrumental) and the distribution of power in families are structured not only according to generational hierarchies but also around gendered spheres of influence that derive their legitimacy precisely because of the creation of a public-private dichotomy. To rely on a theory that neither confronts, nor even ac-knowledges, this reality is to operate in the realm of illusion. (1985, pp. 43–44)

The pressures on women to lower their sights for educational or career opportunities are at times intense. They are presented with more obstacles in the work world and negative pressure from media, community, and family. Often, they have also internalized beliefs about their own limitations and the role of women as secondary to men. Clinically, it may be useful to help clients to outline all the unrecognized work that their mothers and grandmothers did to raise their families and keep a household going. This emphasizes their courage, abilities, hard work, and strength as role models for positive identification, since women are typically hidden from history. A major role in clinical work is coaching women on transforming their family relationships and redefining their own lives.

Women and Marriage

The rate of marriage has increased since 1960, but marriage now plays a less comprehensive role in defining a woman's social and personal life than it did in earlier times. Nevertheless, "his" marriage is still very different from, and a great deal less problematic than, "her" marriage. Although many men remain ambivalent about getting married, fearing ensnarement, it is women who become more symptomatic and prone to stress in the married state (Goleman, 1986; Heyn, 1997). A woman has often given up more to be married than a man (her occupation, friends, residence, family, name). She adjusts to his life. Although men are willing to spend time with women during courtship in ways that enhance the women's sense of intimacy, after marriage men tend to spend less and less time talking to their wives. Husbands often consider that doing chores around the house should be an adequate demonstration of caring and that sex should provide an adequate demonstration of intimacy; they may feel mystified about what women want when they seek more emotional contact. Women are often frustrated by the limited degree of relating that their husbands

offer. While men's and women's priorities in marriage differ (for example, regarding the place of sex and of financial security), men are generally less willing to admit to problems and to acknowledge their part in them, and tend to rate their marital communication, relationships with parents, and sexual relationships as good, while women rate all of these as problematic (Goleman, 1986). Furthermore, it seems that the double standard continues to operate, with women considering their husband's fidelity more important than men do and men being more likely to expect fidelity from their wives than from themselves. It is ironic that women, who are seen as dependent and less competent than men, have had to function without emotional support in their marriages—to be, indeed, almost totally emotionally self-sufficient (Bernard, 1982). Women have typically had to bolster their husbands' sense of self-esteem but have been seen as "nags" when they sought emotional support for themselves. In clinical practice, men's marital complaints typically center on their wives' nagging and emotional demands, while wives' complaints center on their husbands' lack of emotional responsiveness and underresponsibility for homecare and children. In any case, the general lack of political and social equality between marital partners makes the myth of marital equality a dangerous mystification for most women. The transition to marriage is an important time for helping young women (and men) look beyond the inequitable, often dysfunctional couple roles that were prominent in previous generations. Patterns that get set at this point in the life cycle may have great importance later on. Many young women resist challenging the romantic myths about marriage until later stages, when real problems emerge. Yet it is a lot easier to change patterns in the early years of marriage than later, when they have become entrenched and when women's lack of power in the social domain is likely to increase with parenting responsibilities.

Becoming Mothers

Although our society has been changing rapidly, normative expectations for men and women in families have lagged behind the realities of family life. Mothers are particularly vulnerable to blame and guilt because of societal expectations that they bear primary responsibility for the care and well-being of homes, husbands, children, and aging parents. The traditional family not only encouraged, but even required, dysfunctional patterns such as the over-responsibility of mothers for their children and the complementary underresponsibility or disengagement of men. Daughters and daughters-in-law still tend to bear responsibilities for their own and their husbands' extended families. Now that most women are combining work and family responsibilities, they are increasingly overburdened.

Even for today's dual-career couples, the transition to parenthood tends to mark a reversion to a more traditional division of roles, with women doing the lion's share of household maintenance and child care planning. Even so, having a child per se does not appear to cause women psychological distress, but leaving the labor force does (Barnett & Rivers, 1996). Our culture still leaves women with the primary responsibility for child-rearing and blames them when it goes wrong (Caplan, 1996). Seventy-three percent of mothers with children in the home work, and 60 percent of working mothers have no guaranteed maternity leave (a basic right in most industrialized countries). However, since 1980, the amount of public money that we spend on daycare has actually decreased. Thus, it is clear that mothers are by no means receiving social support for the tasks that are expected of them in parenting.

Remarried families offer a number of particularly trying situations for women. Most difficult of all family positions is undoubtedly the role of stepmother. Given our culture's high expectations of motherhood, the woman who is brought in to replace a "lost" mother enters a situation fraught with high expectations that even a saint could not meet. One of the major clinical interventions is to remove from the stepmother the burden of guilt for not being able to accomplish the impossible—taking over the parenting for children who are not her own. Our general guidelines involve putting the biological parent in charge of the children, however difficult that may be when the father works full-time and

feels that he has no experience with "mothering." The problem for the stepmother is especially poignant, since she is usually the one who is most sensitive to the needs of others, and it will be extremely difficult for her to take a back seat while her husband struggles awkwardly with an uncomfortable situation. The fact is that she has no alternative. The major problem for women in remarried families is their tendency to take responsibility for family relationships, to believe that what goes wrong is their fault and that if they just try hard enough, things will work out, since the situation carries with it built-in structural ambiguities, loyalty conflicts, guilt, and membership problems (see McGoldrick, 1996 for a videotape illustration of the problems of remarried families).

Eleanor Maccoby, who has been writing for many years about gender differences in sex-role development, has repeatedly pointed out that while innate gender differences do not appear to be major, the social context constricts girls from earliest childhood, and gender segregation is pervasive. This seems influenced primarily by boys' orientation toward competition and dominance, to which girls seem to be averse, and girls' apparent minimal ability to influence boys when they are together (1999). It seems natural that girls are averse to interacting with someone who is unresponsive and that they begin to avoid such partners. But what is it in the social context that reinforces boys for being unresponsive to girls? And what can we do to change these patterns? Obviously, there is much that we need to do as adults to ensure that girls' opinions are validated and given space in social interactions, but we must change our socialization of boys to increase their sensitivity and responsiveness to others. This is something that must be worked on from earliest childhood if girls are to achieve equity in relationships.

Questions therapists can ask to challenge the gender role status quo include the following: Do both parents equally attend children's school plays and sports events? How are your children changing your perspective on the meaning of your life? Does the father get to spend time alone with each child? (It is almost impossible to develop intimacy if he does not.) Is the time spent fairly equally divided among the daughters and sons? How are domestic responsibilities divided? How is money handled and by whom? Who makes decisions about spending? What are each parent's hopes and expectations for each child in adulthood? How do you as parents try to counter societal preferential treatment of boys and show your daughters they are valuable?

Adolescence

Adolescence is a time when traditional deferential behaviors for girls come particularly to the fore. School sports, for example, are unfortunately still too often organized to highlight boys' competitive prowess, with girls cheerleading on the sidelines. Clinically, in working with adolescents and their families, it is important to ask questions about the roles each is asked to play in the family. What are the chores and responsibilities of boys and of girls? Are girls spending too much time and money on their clothes and appearance in response to media messages that they should concentrate on being sex objects? Are sons encouraged to develop social skills, or are parents focused primarily on their achievement and sports performance? Are daughters encouraged to have high academic aspirations? Are both sexes given equal responsibility and encouragement in education, athletics, aspirations for the future, extended family relationships, buying gifts, writing, calling, or caring for relatives? Do both sexes buy and clean their own clothes? Are daughters encouraged to learn about money, science, and other traditionally "masculine" subjects? Clinicians can help by asking questions about these patterns.

We also need to help families find more positive ways of defining for their daughters the changes of the menstrual and reproductive cycle so that they do not see themselves as "unclean" or "impure." For so long, if sex was even discussed in the family, daughters were not taught to appreciate their bodies but to think sexuality was dangerous and would reflect negatively on them. Sons, by contrast, were taught to view their bodily changes, especially their sexuality, as positive, powerful, and fulfilling aspects of their identity.

Adolescence is a key time in a young woman's life. It is the time when, traditionally, she was specifically inducted into the role of sex object and when, instead, she needs to be encouraged to form her own identity and life. Although acceptance of conventional gender values is at an all-time high during adolescence, it is also during this phase that crucial life-shaping decisions are made. It is extremely important for therapists to support and encourage parents to be proactive with their daughters, to counter discriminatory messages that girls receive within the culture, and to encourage them not to short-circuit their dreams or submit to objectification in their relationships or work.

This phase may mark a time for conversion to a feminist position for fathers of daughters, as they want to support their daughters' having the same rights and privileges that men do. This awareness is important to capitalize on therapeutically. Mothers may be feeling a strain as their children pull away, particularly as they realize the limitations of their own options if they have devoted themselves primarily to child-rearing. On the other hand, mothers may feel a special sense of fulfillment in their daughters' going beyond the constrictions that limited their own lives. As Ruth Bader Ginsberg said about her mother when nominated for the supreme court: "I pray that I may be all that . . . she would have been had she lived in an age when women could aspire and achieve and daughters are cherished as much as sons" (Encyclopedia of World Biography, 2010).

Launching Children and Moving On

For women, this may be a time of special opportunity to reinvent themselves, but also a time of special stress, since women often feel very much behind in the skills to deal with the outside world. Just when their children no longer need them and they are beginning to be defined by the male world as too old to be desirable, they must reinvent themselves. The initial steps are usually the hardest. Once they have begun to move in this arena, many women experience a new confidence and pleasure in their independence—able to really claim their lives for themselves. Because of the social and management skills they have generally developed in the previous life cycle phases, women have remarkable resources for building a social network. Their lifelong skills in adapting to new situations also serve them in good stead. But the world of work still does not recognize their efforts in a way that is commensurate with their contribution, and women have generally been excluded from the financial world—and experience frequent discrimination in banks and legal and business institutions. In addition, women have typically not been socialized to expect or demand the recognition they deserve, whether they function as career women in business or are raising grandchildren at 50.

Of course, the divergence of interests for men and women, as well as the shift in focus of energies that is required at this phase, often creates marital tensions, at times leading to divorce. Far from the stereotypes, for the majority of midlife and older women who divorce, it is a catalyst for self-discovery, change, and growth (Anderson, Stewart & Dimidjian, 1994; Apter, 1995). These women tend to develop new confidence and self-esteem, despite the staggering drop in their income after divorce. However, many of them have little idea how to confront the financial realities of their lives. The financial empowerment of women deserves much more clinical attention. For women, whose options are much more limited than men's, the likelihood of remarriage after a divorce at this phase is quite slim. In part, this is due to the skew in availability of partners, and in part, to older women's having less need to be married and thus, perhaps, being less willing to "settle," particularly for a traditional marriage, which would mean a return to extensive caretaking and sacrifice of their own needs and interests.

Obviously, women who have developed an identity primarily through intimacy and adaptation to men will be vulnerable in divorce during the launching phase, when they may feel that their very self is disintegrating. Women's risks at midlife due to their embeddedness in relationships, their orientation toward interdependence, their subordination of achievement to care, and their conflicts over competitive success are a problem of our society more than a problem in women's development.

This life cycle phase has often been referred to as the "empty nest" and depicted as a time of depression for women. Menopause, which usually occurs in a woman's late 40s or early 50s, has generally been viewed negatively as a time of physical and psychological distress, especially for those whose whole lives have been devoted to home and family. However, this appears to be much more apparent than real (McQuaide, 1998). Typically, women are grateful and energized by recapturing free time and exploring new options for themselves. They are not nearly as sorry to see the child-rearing era end as has been assumed. For many women, it is a turning point that frees them sexually from worries about pregnancy and marks a new stabilization in their energies for pursuit of work and social activities.

Older Families

The final phase of life might be considered "for women only," since women tend to live longer and, unlike men, are rarely (though increasingly more often!) paired with younger partners, making the statistics for this life cycle phase extremely imbalanced. Since women are the primary caretakers of other women, these problems will affect at least two generations of women, who will be increasingly stressed as time goes along.

Women who need care and those who give it are statistically the poorest and have the least legislative power in our society. As mentioned earlier, legislators have given little consideration to services that support family caregivers. The immediate cause of nursing home admission is more likely to be the depletion of family resources than a deterioration in the health of the older relative. While the increase in remarried families might mean that a wider kinship network is available for caregiving, the increasing divorce rate probably means that fewer family members will be willing or available to provide care for elderly parents. Since both those who give care to the elderly and most of those who receive it are women, the subject tends to escape our view. As therapists, we can counter this imbalance by redefining the dilemmas of both the elderly and their caretakers as serious, significant issues.

Women and Their Friendship Networks

Friendship is an extremely important resource for women throughout the life cycle. From earliest childhood, girls concentrate more energy on working out friendships than boys do. Girls assess activities in terms of their impact on relationships, whereas boys usually subordinate relationships to the games they are playing. Throughout life, women tend to have more close friends than men do, but the relationships that women have are often not validated by the larger society (Antonucci, 1994). Schydlowsky (1983) showed that the importance of women's close female friendships diminishes from adolescence to early adulthood, as they focus on finding a mate and establishing a marriage, and then increases throughout the rest of the life cycle. Indeed indications are that marriage actually tends to isolate partners from other people in ways that pose potential long-term problems. They have fewer ties to relatives, fewer intimate talks with others, are less likely to care for aging parents, and less likely to socialize with friends (Gerstel & Sarkisian, 2006). This can be a particular problem for women, whose close friendships are a major support in life. Close female friendships appear to second only to good health in importance for satisfaction throughout the life cycle.

A major UCLA study of women's friendships has turned upside down many decades of stress research, primarily focused on men, which had concluded that under stress people's responses are either fight or flight. On the contrary, under stress women are more likely to "tend and befriend"— that is to nurture their children and seek out their friends (Taylor, Klein, Lewis, Grucnewald, Gurung, et al., 2000). Study after study has shown that social ties to friends reduces stress and health risk. Berkowitz (2002), for example found that the more friends women had, the less likely they were to develop physical impairments as they aged and the more likely to be enjoying their lives.

We urge family members to respect and nurture friendship systems and challenge in therapy societal values that would allow a husband to block his wife's friendships or invalidate their importance. In traditional heterosexual couples, women were expected to make friends with their husbands' friends' wives to facilitate their husbands' social or business contacts, rather than to form their own friendships based on common needs and interests. In such traditional arrangements, women were expected to replace friends whenever they moved for their husbands' jobs. Such arrangements do not respect friendship as a basic support throughout the life cycle and show a distorted prioritizing of career networking over friendship.

The expanded networks of many lesbian communities can provide a corrective model, emphasizing the importance of friendship and neighborhood networks, even including ex-partners in a permanent extended community network. Lesbians' careful nurturing of their networks is an excellent adaptation to a society that has been unsupportive and invalidating of their life cycle rituals and transitions, leaving them one of the most invisible of minorities. This adaptive response is one from which we could all learn.

Women and Loss

Women are often left alone to deal with the sorrow of losses in a family. Men are more likely to withdraw, take refuge in their work, and be uncomfortable with women's expressions of grief, not knowing how to respond and fearful of losing control of their own feelings. Women may perceive their husbands' emotional unavailability as abandonment when they need comfort most, thereby experiencing a double loss. When husbands are expressive and actively involved in illness, death, and the family bereavement process, the quality of the marriage and family relationships improves markedly.

Most commonly, when there is a loss, it is women who present themselves—or are sent by their husbands—for treatment of depression or other symptoms of distress concerning loss. Interventions need to be aimed at decreasing the sex-role split so that all family members can experience their grief and be supportive to one another in adapting to loss. Facilitating fuller involvement for men in the social and emotional tasks of the loss process will enrich their experience of family life as it lessens the disproportionate burden for women. A greater flexibility of allowable roles for both men and women will permit the full range of human experiences in bereavement as in other areas of family life.

The full participation of male and female family members in mourning rituals should be encouraged. One woman, at the death of her 100-year-old grandmother, expressed her desire to be a pallbearer at the funeral. A cousin replied that only males could do that; another added that they already had picked six pallbearers (who all happened to be male grandchildren). She persisted, suggesting that they simply have more than six. In the end, all twelve grandchildren, including five women, shared that important experience.

Conclusion: That the Bumble Bee Should Fly: Affirming Women Through the Life Cycle

Carolyn Heibrun's advice at the opening of this chapter to imagine ourselves and fly like the bumble bee anyway seems essential to clinical work that would free women from the oppressive structures that would tell them they cannot fly. Therapy requires recontextualizing women's history, countering societal pressures for voicelessness and invisibility, and affirming women's own life stories. Traditional therapies have probably done more harm than good, failing as they did to acknowledge women's oppression and invalidation in the larger context and psychologizing social problems that made women think they were responsible for creating problems in which they were, in fact, trapped by the social structure. Thus, it is most important, in working with women of every age, to be a force for liberation, validating the ways in which women are different and encouraging them to follow their dreams. A wise poet, Pat Parker, illustrates the power of this multigenerational perspective—one that puts us within the context of "herstory," of not

denying the problems that remain but validating the power of the women who have come before and the connectedness they have to the present generation and those who will come after:

> *It is from this past that I come, surrounded by sisters in blood and in spirit. It is this past that I bequeath, a history of work and struggle. Each generation improves the world for the next. My grandparents willed me strength, My parents will me pride. I will you rage. I give you a world incomplete, a world where women still are property and chattel, where color still shuts doors, where sexual choice still threatens, but I give you a legacy of doers, of people who take risks to chisel the crack wider. Take the strength that you may wage a long battle. Take the pride that you can never stand small. Take the rage that you can never settle for less. (Pat Parker, 1985, p. 64)*

In 1976, Jean Baker Miller's brilliant essay *Toward a New Psychology of Women* outlined a new pathway for women's relationships that would involve reorganizing all men's relationships as well. In the generation since that book appeared, we have been going through nothing less than a revolution in the pathways of the life cycle of women. We hope that our clinical interventions become a liberating force, fostering the creative and adaptive changes in human development that allow more latitude for both men and women in their ways of relating to their mates and peers, in their intergenerational connectedness, and in their relationships to work and community. We do not believe that the relational and emotionally expressive aspect of development is intrinsic to women. We see the romanticization of "feminine" values as inaccurate and unhelpful to families. It is also not enough for women to adopt the "male" values of the dominant culture or to value what have been traditionally "female" values.

We aim toward a theory of family and individual development where both instrumental and relational aspects of each individual will be fostered. The "feminine" perspective has been so devalued that it needs to be highlighted, as Harriet Lerner, the Stone Center, bell hooks, Audre Lorde, Paula Gunn Allen, Carol Gilligan, Betty Friedan, Rosalind Barnett, Caryl Rivers, and so many others have been doing. It is hoped that both men and women will be able to develop their potential without regard for the constraints of gender stereotyping that have been so constricting of human experience until now. Traditional marriage and family patterns are no longer

working for women, if they ever did, and the statistics reveal women's refusal to accept the status quo. These patterns are changing and we need to work out a new equilibrium that is not based on the patriarchal family hierarchy. We need to understand and appreciate women's potential and dilemmas and consider all women together: gay and straight, young and old, Black and White and all the hues in between.

Chapter 4

Men and the Life Cycle: Diversity and Complexity

Matthew R. Mock

Introduction

For me, writing this chapter comes with an enormous sense of responsibility. How can I, as a man who is also heterosexual, middle class, highly educated, ethnically Chinese American, even attempt to speak about the experience of all or even most men across the life cycle? Rather than present a monolithic, linear view of men across the life span, this is an opportunity to offer some perspectives of diversity and complexity. Describing men across the life course through the life cycle is not a static photograph but a moving picture. Societal influences for boys, young men, men at midlife, and as elders continue to change, though some more gradually than others. We need continuing dialogue and debate on specifics that constitute the lives of men young, old, and in between. I invite everyone, including men of all backgrounds, perspectives, and stages of the life cycle, to stay engaged in discourses about what it means to be male and what might be our convergences, divergences, and continued emergences in the future.

I puzzled about how to capture significant aspects of what it means to be a man in this society without promoting limiting stereotypes? How can I provide perspectives grounded in the research, writing, or experiences of other men, while acknowledging that others may not agree? How do I ensure that what I say is fair, not biased by my own experiences? McIntosh first wrote of "*White Privilege and Male Privilege: A Personal Account of Coming to See Correspondences Through Work in Women's Studies*" in 1988 and has continued to write about White male privilege. Influenced by McIntosh, Deutsch's (2010)

list of 46 invisible privileges of being male continues to grow. Besides the privileges I am afforded just by being born male, there are also things that are out of my consciousness but have a gendered valence to them nonetheless. An aspect of my power as a heterosexual man similar to other men is not having to think about it. However, not acknowledging my background would mean colluding in making others invisible, including those who are female or gay. My lifelong work in community mental health and private practice is dedicated to families with multiple challenges, fewer resources, lower income, and often socially marginalized. I must strive to acknowledge my privileges as a heterosexual man on an ongoing basis. I want to affirm my daily commitment to social justice, including gender and sexual equity.

The body of early research on men's life cycle—*The Seasons of a Man's Life* (Levinson et al., 1978, 1986), *Adaptation to Life* (Vaillant, 1977), and *The Myth of Masculinity* (Pleck, 1981)—added to the theory of developmental stages laid out by Piaget (1973) and Erikson (1963, 1968). Pleck suggested that men are socialized for behaviors congruent with traditional masculinity. His concept of "gender role discrepancy strain" implied that men submit to pressures to fulfill the social requirements of a traditional male. It was groundbreaking to write about the experiences of men. However, it was odd to me as an avid reader, because I could not completely relate to the men who were studied—predominantly White, middle class, heterosexual. As Kimmel and Messner (2008) state succinctly, "men are divided along the same lines that divide any other group: race, class, sexual orientation, ethnicity, age, geographic origin, and geographic region. Men's lives vary in crucial ways, and understanding these variations will take us a long way towards understanding men's experiences" (p. 1).

The responsibility of providing additional perspectives on men and the life cycle provides a freeing sense of possibilities. Discussing variations of men's lives with a wider, more inclusive lens adds to our richness of understanding and appreciation.

Men: A View of Their Relationships Across Generations

Societally, men are often seen and valued for their prowess or what they produce. Social and cultural influences play significant roles in shaping our identities throughout the life cycle. There are now opportunities for redefinitions of men in relationships and their value in being interconnected while leading productive lives. The significance of men-in-relationships can be illustrated by a favorite story:

A motivational story with wisdom— the wooden bowl (unknown author)

A frail old man went to live with his son, daughter-in-law, and four-year-old grandson. The old man's hands trembled, his eyesight was blurred, and his step faltered. The family ate together at the table. But the elderly grandfather's shaky hands and failing sight made eating difficult. Peas rolled off his spoon onto the floor. When he grasped the glass, milk spilled on the tablecloth.

"We must do something about Grandfather," said the son. "I've had enough of his spilled milk, noisy eating, and food on the floor." So Grandfather was sent to eat at a small table in the corner, alone, and since he had broken a dish or two, his food was served in a wooden bowl. When the family glanced in Grandfather's direction, sometimes he had a tear in his eye as he sat alone.

One evening before supper, the father noticed his four-year-old son playing with wood scraps on the floor. He asked, "What are you making?" Just as sweetly, the boy responded, "Oh, I am making a little bowl for you and Mama to eat your food in when you get old."

The parents were speechless. Tears started to stream down their cheeks. Though no word was spoken, that evening the husband took Grandfather's hand and gently led him back to the family table. For the remainder of his days, he ate with the family. And neither husband nor wife seemed to care any longer when a fork was dropped, milk spilled, or the tablecloth soiled.

For me, this story speaks to the impact on some men, once healthy and productive, who now need caretaking and to take on a different role in the family as they age. It reminds us that as we go on in life, we may forget what we learned in our early innocence. Was the boy showing empathy for his grandfather or only imitating what his parents modeled for him? Was the Grandfather's tear due to the pain of loneliness and shame or to remembering how he had once treated his own son when he was growing up? This is a poignant story not only describing the interactions of individuals but more importantly, addressing family relationships, treatment by others, relational acceptance and making a place for everyone, literally and figuratively, at the table.

Men in Multiple, Mutual Relationships Across the Life Span

The male self-in-relation theory and its related notions have added to the riches of understanding men and their relatedness to others (Bergman, 1991; Garcia Coll, Cook-Nobles, & Surrey, 1997). In his own personal reflections, Bergman (1991), a psychiatrist trained in the theories of Freud, Erikson, Kernberg, Kohut, and Mahler, writes:

> "After almost two decades as a therapist, in my daily work I have found myself being less and less concerned with penises and castrations and internal objects and narcissistic mirrorings, than with the healing power of mutual relationship, with men and women both. In my own early training I came to believe that theories built on images such as 'projective identification' were brilliant and crucial. . . . Theories can serve as implicit justifications for the distant and relationally unskilled therapist to maintain a self-out-of-relation context with the client. At worst, if used to justify power-over actions, they can pave the way for abuse" (p. 5).

In my clinical work with boys and men, I focus on understanding them across the life span with gender as a major construct but in multiple contexts. It is essential to account for both the internal and external contextual forces that shape them and to inquire about choices and decisions made during stages of development, individually and in the family. Simply stated, we must consider gender in context across men's life cycle.

The Intersection of Gender and Other Social Complexities

In addition to gender influences, clinicians must ask about and observe the *intersectionality* of complex social structures and influences including sexual orientation, culture, race, nationality, class and caste, resource availability, faith, spirituality and religion, physical and mental abilities, geographic location, immigration status, and more. These are all interconnected influences that construct and reinforce one another and are more useful than simple dichotomies or binaries of male versus female, and straight versus gay (Collins, 1998; Mock, 2008). Care must be taken to acknowledge the differences in men's life cycle experiences even while implying seemingly common experiences. The larger sociopolitical structure influences men's lives throughout the life span. It is the *intersectionality* of multiple forces, most of which are socially shaped, that gives the textured meaning of gender and being male in this society. In some ways, we are each like *some* men, like *all* men, and like *no other* men. This summarizes our diversity, complexity, and other challenges of the male experience across the life span.

The family systems perspective we utilize as therapists is complex and multilayered, providing us with avenues of curiosity and respectful, collaborative inquiry with our clients. We must appreciate stages of the family and individual life cycle in context. An understanding of the flow of stressors that impact families and a multicultural framework for assessing all levels of the family system are also essential to understanding families that seek our consultation.

I will further illustrate this complexity and importance of intersectionality for men through the clinical vignettes. These examples included throughout this chapter illustrate key points discussed in greater length, breadth, and depth by other authors in this book.

Gender as a Significant Matter

It is critical that we frame a perspective for including gender as a defining factor in our work with families. In the late 1970s and throughout the 1980s, feminist critiques of family and couples therapy articulated how gender played out in clients' problem presentations and behaviors, how therapists constructed problems, and the very practice of therapy. Feminists advocating for transformation in the field were often challenged. While sexism by men was generally accepted, it was still sometimes denied or protested. Gradually, the field of couple and family therapy has evolved to generally accept that gender should be considered as a salient influence (Goldner, 1988; Pasick, 1992; Rampage, 2004). Therapeutic neutrality in a situation of a man battering a woman, essentially playing out his power over her physically, abusively, and dangerously, is tantamount to the therapist's collusion. Men are often still taught to be strong and powerful, to stand up to others, not to be weak or show emotions that reveal vulnerabilities. We see this still in books, magazines, portrayals on television, movies and other broadcast media, and even in video games. Across the globe, patriarchy is often given preference. With more responsibility and control than females are afforded by the dominant society in areas of academic, physical, sexual, and employment opportunities for success, males are pressured to perform, to be productive and to show prowess. While some "glass ceilings" have been broken by women, men are still overrepresented leaders and decision makers.

An Understanding of Intersectionality and Male Power

Previously, theories about human development largely based on men did not consider context, the impact of multiple social influences, and how they intersect. The following vignette illustrates this perspective.

Nine months prior, feeling severely depressed, Bradley, age 50, had tried to commit suicide by shooting himself. The resulting brain damage left him very dependent on others. Married briefly to a woman when he was in his twenties, he was now alone and fairly isolated with few reliable relationships. His male doctor recommended that he work with a man comfortable in talking about his multicultural background. As Bradley framed his life course in our initial session, he commented, "You see doc, there is no aspect of my life where I can lift my head up as a man, a *real* man."

In addition to Bradley's gender, an assessment included his age, sexual orientation, temperament, abilities, worldview, culture, race and ethnicity, sociocultural values, class, religious or spiritual values, financial and resource availability, autonomy skills, affiliative skills, power/privilege or powerlessness/abuse, education and work, physical or psychological symptoms, addictions or behavioral disturbances, allocation of time, social participation, and personal dreams. Some of Bradley's issues included:

Coming to terms with his multiracial identity as a darker-skinned man of European, African, and Native American origin.

Early memories of being taunted and bullied as a young child because of his appearance, being short and viewed as a "sensitive child."

Fractured and fluctuating relationships with his parents since boyhood—his father was in and out of the home, and was "stern and distant."

Status as a marine veteran dishonorably discharged for unwillingness to face combat if ordered.

Bisexual ("two-spirited"), having only recently "come out" to others.

Health concerns, being recently diagnosed as HIV-positive and severe organic neurological problems due to the suicide attempt, including a seizure disorder and cognitive deficits.

Interest in attending church but having no strong affiliation or philosophical belief.

Intermittently homeless since adolescence with his single mother being in and out of jail, and not having contact with his father since age seven.

Unemployment and being on government aid.

Struggles with co-occurring alcohol and street drug use and abuse.

Throughout our work, I felt it was important to provide a place for Bradley to discuss growing up male and to share his vulnerabilities, perceived failures, and inadequacies. It was important to assess carefully his different reactions toward women and men and to understand key pressure points and traumatic situations throughout his life. According to Bradley, previous interactions with significant men in his life were often met with scorn, criticism, and even abuse. Since his mother had not always been available to care for him, Bradley had an ambivalent relationship with her and with women in general. He felt it hard to trust them with intimate feelings and feared being abandoned when most in need.

Bradley alluded to sensitive topics he had discussed with female therapists. He protested when they focused solely on his traumas and minimized the gendered parts of his story. During those times he increased his drug and alcohol abuse ("they helped me deal with the pain like my father did") and often fled therapy with female therapists. A female therapist would have to maintain a fine balance of bringing out Bradley's power and control issues without moving into what he previously experienced as "mothering," which would carry the risk of being abandoned. Coming out as a bisexual man meant probable rejection and vilification, and fear that his family, friends, and fellow marines would not accept such sexual fluidity. When Bradley eventually came to trust our relationship, he shared hopes and dreams as a writer or storyteller working with young people. "It is the closest I may get to being a father."

Clearly, Bradley struggled not only with the issue of gender but also with his multicultural, sociocultural, economic, sexual orientation and other intersecting contextual factors that shape the male psyche. It was critical for me to assess his multiple issues, taking into account how life cycle transitions and events affected Bradley in his present situation.

As gender does matter, so does power—overt and covert, earned and unearned by men. Power and influence over others plays a role throughout society that is undeniable (Pinderhughes, 1989; Mock, 2008). It also plays a role in the identity development of men throughout the life cycle, as boys, in adolescence, as adult men, as partners in relationships and in families, as fathers, and as elders. Just as gender and power have been hard to acknowledge in our field, so has the role of race, ethnicity, culture, and class.

As with Bradley, men are shaped by dominant social forces of racism, sexism, classism, and others. In *The Rice Room: Growing Up Chinese-American, from Number Two Son to Rock 'N' Roll*, Fong-Torres (1994) captures one of his earliest recollections of confronting race and gender as a kindergartner: "I was reminded of my Chineseness even in the comic books I'd escape to. I remember the Blackhawks, a paramilitary team that never fought the Nazis without their mascot, 'Chop Chop,' a round little Chinese cook wielding a Chinese knife. How I wished he— and I—didn't require a different color ink in the comics" (pp. 49–50). Discussion of such experiences is often important for men but sometimes uncomfortable for therapists.

Discomfort has led to undervaluing of other core issues in men's lives. Most writings on men's life cycle have not acknowledged cultural diversity, especially sexual orientation. This omission colludes with the idea that sexual orientation is not important in men's identity. Current nationwide debates on same-sex marriage, as highlighted by Proposition 8 in California, emphasize the challenges of the intersection of gender and sexual orientation and life cycle issues. Supporters of gay marriage contend that denial of gays' rights to marry is unconstitutional. Those opposing same-sex marriage, spearheaded by a conservative coalition called Protect Marriage, raise fundamental questions based mostly on religious beliefs about the very nature, definition, existence, and morality of being gay. This has a profound impact on gay identity and gay relationships, as well as transition and loss issues among gay elders. While traditionally Catholic nations like Mexico and Portugal have legalized gay marriage, gay males await the same right with increased concern, anger, and feelings of helplessness in the United States. Understanding the very nature of masculinity and what it means to be a man is seemingly at another crossroads of examination and deeper discourses (Good & Brooks, 2005).

In his classic work, Erikson (1963, 1968) proposed that development is comprised of "eight stages of man." Within each stage, there were polarities that determined the formation of the individual's person-

ality. Erikson's early work was critiqued as an example of gender centrism, for example, by separating the life goals of men and women into career versus intimacy, where men valued career identity over intimacy. Doyle and Paludi (1998) also critiqued Erikson as ethnocentric, because he failed to include evidence from a variety of cultures, including gay and lesbian families. While the deleterious impact of racism has still to be fully acknowledged, there must also be commitments to addressing heterosexism and homophobia.

Childhood

Young males are often born and raised with certain family and social expectations. The environments boys are raised in are influenced by their parents' values, histories, and life cycle issues.

Jamal and his mother's expectations

Jamal is an athletically gifted 9-year-old African American with twin brothers two years younger who are physically disabled, needing physical and emotional care. He carries himself with a tough façade with seemingly little care for others. Jamal is torn between taking care of his mom and brothers while being launched early as a boy with special athletic skills. "Maybe if I did well enough in football, my stepdad would like us and would stay." Jamal learned from peers that being tender and "softer"—as he was with his brothers— meant being a "mama's boy." When he could not play football, he struggled to find other ways to be accepted.

Jamal was often pressed into being "the man of the house" by his mother. He needed to come home immediately after school to help his brothers with homework. Jamal did not develop empathy or a strong understanding of the importance of interdependence. Instead, he felt thrust into being older more quickly. Early on, he learned "street smarts" and survival skills in a rough neighborhood.

His mother's background had a significant impact on how she raised Jamal. Her wariness in relationships with men was in some ways a response to her own residual trust concerns. Her father was aloof and distant as a parent; ; her memories of him were as a handsome man who often brought home gifts from his many travels but rarely spent time at home. During this time in her life, Jamal's mother expected to be married, to be provided for financially, and also to have her own business. Instead, she experiences uncertainty and the stress of having three children highly dependent on her as their primary caregiver. Understanding Jamal's mother's expectations influenced by her own life cycle experiences would prove important for our work. She expected Jamal to be highly successful and easily provide for himself.

To help Jamal develop empathy, compassion, and interconnectedness as a boy, his mother must recognize his needs for nurturance, support, and guidance. During one of our final face-to-face sessions, Jamal smiled. "It's like my coach teaching me plays in practice: when it comes to the actual game, I have to do it myself. I also have to rely on my teammates to do their part."

Like Jamal, in my own Chinese American family we were raised with a strong sense of the importance of patriarchy. Although never directly acknowledged, my parents' child-rearing practices were very much influenced by Confucianism and Buddhism. There is a Confucian saying that translates into a woman must be obedient to her father before marriage, to her husband after marriage, then to her son after her husband dies. While this certainly says a lot about the dictated role of women, it also speaks to the expectations of Chinese men in relationship to women throughout the life cycle. Family expectations based in patriarchal dominance carry strong messages of sources of approval, esteem, positive "face," and success. Not being able to live up to the expectations that culture imposes on men even as boys can lead to performance anxiety, restricted life choices, depression, and a lower sense of self-worth in relation to family and community, especially in collectivistic cultures.

There has been increased focus on what it means to be a boy in contemporary society. Leading up to and entering school, boys are immersed in a socialization process that impacts their emotional expression and behaviors. In what Levant (2005) has referred to as the "code of masculinity," boys are generally socialized to show less vulnerability than girls. In his writings on Real Boys (1999), William Pollack tackles the construct of the "Boy Code," where boys must be tough, cool, rambunctious, and obsessed with sports, cars, and sex. Research by Osherson (1986) showed that boys from ages 3 to 5 withdraw from mothers and femininity to be "more

like Daddy," thus leading to what he calls "the wounded father within," where there is an enactment of loss, injury, or even a severing of the mother–son bond for the sake of connecting with masculine ideals. By school age, boys have received innumerable messages from multiple sources to suppress shame, fear, sadness, loneliness, hurt, disappointment, and any form of neediness (Levant & Kopecky, 1995; Levant & Pollack, 1995). Osherson (1986) posits that, in order to feel empowered, men must heal this angry-sad version of themselves that is unlovable to embrace one that feels loved once more. This implies that men learn to become more distant rather than stay consistently engaged, to cut off from or avoid conflict rather than address it as part of life, and not to show strong emotion outwardly especially if it may be socially perceived as weak, needy, or frail.

Childhood is full of countless opportunities for exploration and new information. Whether at home, in the park, or at school, boys are absorbing experiences and learning their social place. Boys are told to be tough and in control by being assertive or aggressive, not backing down, making mistakes, or showing vulnerability. They are to take charge and be productive, have lots of money and sex, and be responsible. A boy's experience of the emerging definition of what it means to be masculine may be confined to behaviors that focus on competition, strength, and control, both physically and emotionally, and suppression (if not repression) of fears and overt emotional expression. As Kivel (2010) writes: "My colleagues and I have come to call this rigid set of expectations the 'Act-Like-a-Man' box because it feels like a box, a 24-hour-a-day, seven-day-a-week box that society tells boys they must fit themselves into. One reason we know it's a box is that every time a boy tries to step out he's pushed back in with names like wimp, sissy, mama's boy, girl, fag, nerd, punk, mark, bitch, or even more graphic terms. Behind those names is the threat of violence" (pg. 83).

Of course, the words used to emasculate boys—such as "sissy" or "fag"—refer to being feminine or gay. Homophobia is taught early on with shamefulness for being considered gay (Kimmel and Messner, 2001). When accused of being gay or effeminate, many may respond by attacking back in a supposed masculine manner. This is a powerful example of how gender and homophobia, or heterosexism, interact. The works by writers such as Kivel, Kimmel, and Messner certainly can be applied cross-culturally. In addition, patriarchal dominance is still prominent across cultures, even with strides made for and by women.

School-age boys are vulnerable, given their developing maturity. Boys are less able to handle the new school environment than girls. They are often slower to read and write, and they have more challenges in sitting quietly and listening to their teachers. They have greater needs for large-muscle activity, which has become an even greater challenge in schools with reduced recess time. After 10 years of research, Levant (2005) enumerated the following major beliefs placed on males from a very young age: 1) be independent and self-reliant, 2) do not express emotions (especially those that show attachment needs or vulnerability), 3) be tough and aggressive, 4) seek high social status, 5) always be ready for sex, 6) avoid all things "feminine," and 7) reject homosexuality. These beliefs can affect boys' abilities to form enduring relationships and pose significant obstacles in situations that call for more flexibility.

The experiences of boys are further complicated by issues of race, ethnicity, and culture. African American boys are often confronted by what Franklin (2004) described as race-related indignities and invisibility, or "an inner struggle with feeling one's talents, abilities, personality, and worth are not valued or recognized because of prejudice or racism." Such messages may contribute to a child's becoming confused and frustrated. Many African American boys grow up without positive African American male role models, instead receiving many negative messages from the media. Educational systems that do not effectively address issues of inequities in content and process can contribute to further uncertainty in terms of life course. A sense of personal power (Franklin, 2004), where there are elements of recognition, satisfaction, legitimacy, and validation, are important to mitigate some of the deleterious impact of invisibility experienced in childhood. Asian American boys may also be confronted for their differences and yet, due to issues of "maintaining face," they may not express this marginalization and these injuries openly. Latino Ameri-

can boys, especially those of recent immigrant parents, are taught the importance of striving to provide for their family in the United States and in their home countries. In order to cope with societal oppression, they may attempt to be more assimilated and minimize or disparage their cultural identity.

Kimmel (2008) notes two separate dimensions of masculine power: 1) of men over women and 2) of some men over other men, in particular "the distribution of those rewards among men by differential access to class, race, ethnic privileges, or privileges based on sexual orientation—that is, the power of upper-class and middle-class men over working class men; the power of White and native-born men over non-White and/or non-native born men; the power of straight men over gay men." Men with power are described as "successful, winners, admirable, virile, heroic or powerful;" those at the bottom are described as "weak, humiliated, cowardly, shameful, unproductive, ineffective, impotent" (Kupers, 1993).

Some writers and researchers have noted developmental issues for racially diverse children that impact the life cycle. Powell-Johnson (1983), who studied inner-city African American boys, observes that children become aware of skin color or race differences by age 2 or 3. African American boys are often aware by age 7 or 8 that societal treatment is not equal and that they may have to work harder. Others (Tatum, 1997; Obama, 2004; Boyd-Franklin, Franklin & Toussaint, 2000), writing about the positive raising of African American sons, support similar important differences that are societally constructed and maintained. Stereotypes still run deep and start early. Generations of young men of color, especially African American and Latino American boys, are hurt by institutional inequities. African American males are dealt with more severely than White offenders (Poe-Yamagata & Jones, 1998). Even when facing the same charges, African American youths are more likely than White youths to be formally prosecuted, tried as adults, and incarcerated. In contrast, White youths are more likely to receive probation and avoid being locked up. Inequities of young boys by race, class, and ethnicity remain apparent.

In raising young Black males, Boyd-Franklin, and Franklin and Touissaint (2000) advocate teaching them how to maintain self-dignity, responsibility, and respect for others in a world that is sometimes racist and hostile. These proactive steps and lessons contribute to a cycle of success rather than demise, enabling our young boys to become young men with bright futures. As therapists, we must reach out to those at risk.

In working with boys, clinicians should assess their values, messages about respectful interaction with others, and treatment of others who are different, whether by race, culture, sexual orientation, abilities, or other qualities. It is important to ask how conflicts are managed in the home, how differences are negotiated, how feelings are managed and expressed, and most particularly, how are they disciplined and whether there is abuse. For older boys it is important to understand their adjustment to physical changes especially in puberty. It is important to assess their judgment when interacting with peers, siblings, adults, authority figures, and their world overall.

Adolescence

Mac illustrates the multiple influences, sources, and pressures a teenager may experience on his way to becoming a young man.

Mac is a 15-year-old biracial teenager. Growing up, he was often teased as the babyfaced member of the family. Even his 12-year-old brother Sam has joined in playful taunting. His 21-year-old sister Jan is an academic scholar.

Mac acknowledges feelings of guilt. "I carry on because I'm Mac '*The Man*,' and sure, I try to score with the girls even to the point of being obnoxious sometimes. One of my best friends, a really smart girl, is mad at me. She says I have changed too much. But she just doesn't understand. If I don't act like a man is supposed to, my buddies are after me. One time they even suggested that I am still a virgin or maybe I am gay.

"I would rather be disliked by the girls than be harassed by my guy friends. Worse, there's my dad. He doesn't understand or relate for sure. He thinks I should be hooking up with more girls by now. He was smart, an achiever, and popular in school when he was my age. I have his legacy to uphold. When my mother tries to help me, I am seen as a 'mama's boy.' I feel pulled, torn between my dad's African American heritage and my mother's Jewish background.

My older sister has made it and is on her way. She has so many friends, is the 'smart one' of us three kids, and even has had several boyfriends. I can't live up to the standard she set. What choices do I have? Will I make the right one?"

In some ways, Mac's situation may reflect that of many adolescents. Postpubescent, he was aware of changes in his physique as well as interaction with peers. As a heterosexual male, he feels an attraction to teenage girls around his age but is uncertain and awkward in expressing himself. He feels external pressures to be sexually active. He has growing questions—even anxieties—about his identity and is experiencing more questions regarding with whom to affiliate. He also feels pressure to be with the popular group in school. He feels competition with his older sister, a successful college junior, and feels that he cannot live up to her standards. His struggles as an adolescent are clear in initial sessions. As a teenager, he is still reliant on his parents but also beginning to establish some independence from them. With an older sister who has launched, he is already aware of his potential trajectory in the future.

While adolescence is filled with excitement and possibilities, it can also be a period filled with unrest and challenges during a period of physical and emotional changes. For boys, adolescence may present some special challenges, which must be considered clinically. Research continues to suggest that what is considered to be "normal adolescent male behavior," while not inherent, may include aggression, social withdrawal, and emotional inexpressiveness. With otherwise limited definitions and descriptions of masculinity, adolescent boys have a tendency to hold themselves in opposition to others: nonfemale, nonhomosexual, and antiauthority.

Conventional gender values may be particularly strong during adolescence. Parents, friends, and the media—including music, television, movies, and even messages online or in video games—often perpetuate the belief that to be "buff, tough, and rough" puts adolescent males on the road to success. Social scientists, educators, policymakers, and therapists who work with individuals and families have tried to break these stereotypes, and assert that "normal masculinity" can be achieved through confronting fears perpetuated by sexism, heterosexism, and classism.

During adolescence, it is important that therapists inquire about adolescents' roles in their families and the expectations explicitly or implicitly exerted by family. Do they align with gender stereotypes? By challenging stereotypically patriarchal values as needed, the adolescent male achieves greater flexibility and understanding of roles and responsibilities.

Studies have focused on occupational aspirations comparing young men to young women, particularly in the educational system. A gender-biased educational system still exists, where male adolescents are differentially rewarded for pursuing occupations such as construction, business, athletics, or the sciences. While women have certainly made strides for greater equity in traditionally male-dominated professions, there are still gender imbalances and a certainly lack of equality in economic compensation.

Boys may need more support during adolescence. Studies show that boys are more likely than girls to have discipline or behavior problems. Boys constitute 71 percent of school suspensions. Though eighth grade boys and girls use substances at the same rate, or possibly girls use even more than boys, as they grow older, boys abuse more than girls. Boys are also more likely to be diagnosed with attention-deficit hyperactivity disorder (ADHD) but are seriously underdiagnosed for depression. More are placed in special education and involved in criminal and violent behavior. Boys are much more often diagnosed with conduct disorders or with autism spectrum disorders than girls and referred for special services. Boys of color and of lower economic status also encounter more limited alternatives for defining masculinity. African American and Latino American boys are more likely to be involved with crime and violence on school property but less likely to be diagnosed with ADHD or to receive appropriate services. This should be of concern to all, as once boys (especially Latino American and African American youth) are in the judicial system, the downward spiral is often hard to break.

In her pioneering work, *In a Different Voice* (1993), Carol Gilligan emphasized that responsiveness in relationships and emotional intelligence are critical components of mental health. During her ongoing research project Boys' Development and the Culture of Manhood," Gilligan examined ADHD and the serious increase in violence among young boys, which has led to concerns about the cultural crisis over norms and values associated with masculinity. Though boys have the ability to accurately read human emotions and to be self-reflective as well as empathic, societal influences may run counter to these innate skills. It is therefore important to set the stage early in life and nurture the development of empathy in relationships with others—male or female, gay or straight.

Young Adulthood

Crossing the bridge from adolescence into adulthood may pose particular challenges for men. Besides the continuing emergence of sexuality, intimate urges, and questions of affiliation, young men wrestle with the future—college, leaving home, relationships, work, and career. They redefine themselves in relation to their parents, siblings, and family.

Eduardo: "Taking it" or "Teaching it"

Eduardo's family brought him to therapy with concerns for his anger and expressions of aggression. He was the oldest of three children in a family with Chicano and Catholic roots. At 17, he had adequately passed all of his classes in high school but had a series of difficulties with authorities. He was recently caught cruising with friends and in possession of alcohol.

In family sessions, his father proudly and eloquently spoke of how he was able to have all of his immediate family in the United States while other less resourceful and "weaker" families stayed in Mexico. Adopting a "strong father carries his family on his shoulders" stance, the father worked two jobs. Eduardo was awed by his father's physical work but confused by his silence when co-workers made fun of him or of Chicanos. "He told me that this was the way to gain friends."

The dominant discourse in Eduardo's family was to be tough and not show signs of outward vulnerability or weakness. The neighborhood Eduardo grew up in was rough and crime-ridden. One of his ways of getting by was to learn "street language" and not show others—especially other boys and men—any vulnerability. After all, the weak would "stay behind" and "do the worst work."

I invited Eduardo's father to talk about what his experiences were in being the head of the family. Eduardo was surprised to hear his dad describe the importance of his image of being Latino in America. Being a man not only meant being strong, masculine, and the head of the family but also leading, protecting, and caring for one's family and close friends. He made it very clear to Eduardo that his mother had equal importance in the family and emotionally expressed his gratitude toward her. Subsequent acceptance by the father of Eduardo's softer, emotional experiences opened up other possibilities for improved interactions. Ensuing family conversations were more open, interactive, and mutually supportive. Eduardo commented he felt less pressured, less constrained.

Several years later, Eduardo was teaching at an independent high school. He felt drained in trying to reach out again and again to students who were at high risk of dropping out, especially the young men. He expressed great disappointment and anger toward one particular young man for not paying attention to Eduardo's cautions. His anger represented feelings of helplessness, along with a sense of urgency to influence this teenager's immediate decisions. After again understanding some of the sources of his own feelings rooted in his growing-up experience, he felt further validated and able to look to additional creative solutions. Using lessons from some of his own family circumstances, Eduardo reached out to the teenager's family, feeling more hopeful that he could help effect change.

In *Guyland*, Michael Kimmel (2008) talks about "young men, poised between adolescence and adulthood," many of whom "are more likely to feel anxious and uncertain." Most of the 400 young men interviewed were heterosexual, college educated, White, and middle-to-upper class, but some had only finished high school, some gay and bisexual, and some reflected Latino American, African American, and Asian American vantage points. When asked about their future they might say, "it's all good."

Yet the picture Kimmel draws is not so rosy and one to be viewed with caution. In previous eras, such young men stepped into the adult world to become professionals and civic leaders. Instead, these young men were more likely to live out a kind of "amorphous uncertainty." For some, college meant slipping through academic cracks and getting by rather than excelling with commitment and drive. The path to the future seems less certain or clear. Distractions like being online or playing video games, or "hooking up" every so often with a "friend with benefits" to go out drinking may be preferred over work or planning for the future. It is unclear how this "amorphous uncertainty" affects young women, if at all. The young men Kimmel interviewed seem to adopt a kind of "Guy Code," where there is a strong peer influence on attitudes and behaviors—an ongoing question of "what would the guys think of this?" Many got by easily in school, then drifted and took on a series of jobs after college. In other words, he sees patterns of remaining in "boyhood."

More young men in current times seem to be struggling to move into adulthood. Kimmel (2008) describes ages 16 to 26 as a period of "gender intensification," the most gender-influenced stage of a person's development, a period of "exaggerated notions associated with the different roles that still hold many men and women in separate spheres of endeavor." Yet the traditional markers of manhood—such as heading the household and being the "breadwinner"—are no longer clear and may even be obsolete. What used to be called "emerging adulthood" or "transition into adulthood" is no longer a clear destination, and the path to get there is more vague and diffuse. There is a pervasive attitude that getting drunk and "hooking up" are harmless fun. Gay-baiting and gay-bashing ("that's so gay") are ubiquitous.

Young adulthood is still an exciting time for many young men, as they are focusing more on life outside the immediate family. For many, this means pursuing a new period of aspirations after high school. There are many young men who are resilient, determined, and motivated to launch, similar to young men in previous times. Culture often plays an additional role in terms of support or pressures related to leaving home (Wong & Mock, 1997). Asian Americans remain influenced by a collectivistic culture rather than by individualistic ideals. They may experience additional pressures to succeed, to achieve prominence through employment and earnings. For immigrant or refugee young adult men, pre- and post-migration experiences lead to both spoken and unspoken expectations of success (Lee & Mock, 2005; Wong & Mock, 1997). Failure of the young adult male to fulfill some family expectations can lead to compounded stressors and psychological problems. In supporting young men to move successfully into adulthood, experts stress the importance of reconnecting with family (Pollack, 1999; Kimmel, 2008). They encourage reaching out to parents and caregivers as ways to assist boys, teenagers, and young men in developing authentic empathy for others, exploring their emotionally connected side, and working with them to build positive self-esteem.

Men as Partners and Husbands

Dave and Molly: Dating in the computer age

Dave is a man of German and Italian ancestry in his early thirties 30s who works as an executive in the computer industry. With long hours at work and lots of disposable income, he was more often a part of the party scene rather than in an ongoing relationship. His last two relationships with women lasted 1 to 2 years. In the first relationship, "she was more into me than I was into her." He began seeing Molly 10 months ago. In contrast to his prior relationships, he cares deeply about her.

Like his father, Dave has some ambivalence in committing to a relationship too early in life. Molly wants Dave to fully acknowledge her career and make adjustments if they further commit to being together. Mutual feelings of romance and passion seem to have passed, and she now experiences him as distant. He denies this, saying he is tired from work pressures. After many sessions, Dave revealed his concern that Molly would be hired by a big law firm and want to move away, which he realized was making him distant from her to be prepared should she leave him.

Discussions of different scenarios in their life course led to decreased anxieties and increased abilities to see a future through their own decision making together. One of the lessons from our work was that using their individual insights and abilities to be more flexible actually created more exciting possibilities together.

Dating, courtship, and establishing longer-term relationships today is different from before.

Through his extensive studies, Kimmel (2008) notes that young adults are getting married on average 8 years later than their mothers and fathers. "Hooking up, in the college students' minds is not an alternative to relationships—it's the new pathway to forming relationships" (p. 214). Hooking up may not lead to a relationship or to marriage, however.

Some sociologists observe that men (and women) of college age may be postponing marriage so they have time to consider options, both in partners and in vocation. Economic downturn and challenges have contributed to an air of uncertainty and instability of alternatives from which to choose. During the past year, stories have surfaced of young people compromising on their selection of undergraduate or graduate school or having to stay in school longer to graduate. With a more uncertain future, they may be less certain to be in a committed relationship.

Once in partnerships, there are additional challenges for men. Traditional norms of masculinity have to be examined, challenged, and redefined. This often means examining gender roles learned by each partner. As women are having more opportunities for self-development, they are less dependent on men in heterosexual relationships. This is leading to adaptive difficulties in long-term relationships. Current trends show more men than women acknowledging work–life conflict. In studies focusing on Latino American men in relationships, potential conflict areas include authority conflicts; feelings of isolation, and depression due to the need to be strong; conflicts over discrepant messages for a man's role in his family; and anxiety over sexual potency. Cultural dictums for men in patriarchal roles are often more strictly reinforced in traditional families (Sue and Sue, 2008).

Coupling is a phenomenon and life endeavor that is complex for all partners regardless of sexual orientation. The well-being and satisfaction of the couple may depend on the ability of the partners to develop and sustain authentic relationships with their families of origin (Bowen, 1978). Gay couplehood may cause conflicting joy with resurfacing questions of social acceptance (see Chapter 8 on **LGBT** families and the life cycle). Even where parents accept their son's gay identity, they may be concerned about his gay marriage if it is not legally sanctioned. In addition to being harassed or questioned about their relationship, there may not be equal protections or benefits afforded to their partners. Overall, marriage has long been known as more beneficial for men than women. Questions that we might continue to ask include: What are the societal and innate pressures on men to marry and procreate? What can be learned from men (gay or straight) who remain bachelors yet sustain satisfying lives? While there may be a conflict with the evolutionary perspective for men procreating regardless of couplehood, marriage appears tied to healthier outcomes. Why is this so?

Fatherhood

Over the past 40 years, men's roles in the overall family have changed, matured, and grown. While mothers continue to be mainly responsible for the raising of children, fathers have become more involved and assumed more responsibility (Day et al., 2004). Trends show men, particularly those under age 29, spending more time with their children. Some surveys also show them doing more housework than men in previous generations. The crucial role men play in families, and for the well-being of children, women, and men themselves, has finally been acknowledged. Supporting men in their role as parents and contributors to home life, and promoting gender equity in relationships must be encouraged if there is to be an evolution of new role models (Engle, 1997; Pittman, 1994).

Urbanization and the increase in women's employment and under- or unemployment of men have influenced the roles of men in families. Increased technological advances have also led to greater flexibility of work hours and the option of telecommuting. Economic downturns have led to reformulations of family composition and coping strategies. In a small study of stay-at-home fathers (Rochlen, Suizzo, McKelley, & Scaringi, 2008), though they were acutely aware of traditional concepts of masculinity, they consistently rejected such traditional gender-role norms. In his book *The Daddy Shift* (2009), J.A. Smith cites research that, during the Great Depression when men were unable to find work, they divorced their partners or abandoned their families.

With somewhat increased flexibility in ideas regarding gender, he predicts more men will take on roles as the primary caregiver for children. Rather than a revolution, he views this as an evolution that is one of the teachings arising from feminism.

Increased attention is being paid to gay men as parents (Erera, 2002; Laird, 1993). Heterosexism, homophobia, and other negative stereotypes have previously raised the question of gay men being suitable fathers or parents. Erera (2002) notes that there are some studies that show that gay men do not take on typically gendered roles in raising children. For gay or straight couples, role shifts and challenges that arise from couplehood changing to fatherhood must be negotiated. Open validation in couples sessions can lead to productive conversations and successful tackling of stressors. For gay and straight couples, responsible working and parenting, and "second shift" roles in doing both, may be the order of the day. Solely patriarchal arrangements may be less and less effective. Shared responsibilities among couples may be more effective and may actually be more often called into play with economic downturns and increased competition for labor. Having children later in life also tests the flexibility and adaptability of the family and role taking.

There may be additional considerations for racially diverse fathers. In the documentary *Unnatural Causes* (California Newsreel, 2008), psychologists and social scientists tracked health and mental health outcomes with social conditions. One shocking finding is that African American women disproportionately delivered premature or underweight babies, which led to additional health concerns for the children. Racism even before conception can lead to the release of stress hormones that continues while the developing fetus is in the womb. This can have a cascading effect on the fathers in their relationships and in raising their children with this additional health stressor.

Men at Midlife

Life stage, social role and biological perspectives, definitions, boundaries, and characteristics of midlife and middle age vary. Taking into account life span and expectancy, Cochran (2005) places midlife as beginning somewhere between ages 33 and 38 for men. Men's concerns at this time include responsibility, commitment, direction, identity, intimacy, and loss.

Generally by midlife, a man has made decisions and taken actions over his career, intimate partnerships, friendships, and family relationships—with his family-of-origin, extended family members, and in creating his own family. He may be raising children alone or in partnership, he may be getting ready to launch the children he has raised as a father, or he may be mentoring the next generation as godparent, uncle, or friend. This change in the family constellation often means a renegotiation of relationships with his partners, friends, co-workers, and other family members. His role of parenting and guiding his children is transformed into one where there is a letting go. There may be almost automatic reflections on what he has accomplished as a man, father, parent, and partner.

Henry: An examination of midlife accomplishments

By several accounts, Henry would be viewed as a highly successful White, middle-class man. He is 45, heterosexual, and remarried for 5 years to a woman who is also married for a second time. He has a stepson in college who is temporarily living at home. They own their house in a comfortable community, and he is a highly accomplished physician, considered an expert in his specialty.

Henry's primary area of concern is a feeling of never "doing enough" or "doing well enough." He interpreted the painful ending of his first marriage as proof of his failure as a man, husband, and potential father. One of his early recollections of his own father was that he had overcome many obstacles. Despite his father's doubts about him, Henry had also succeeded in finishing medical school.

Henry often experienced an emptiness, feeling like some of his contributions were "false wins." He has been distant from his stepson Michael. On a long drive to visit his parents, Henry shared with his second wife nightmares he often had. "I was surprised—shocked actually—that she responded with such understanding and unconditional acceptance. It was one of the best trips we have had. After that, even the usual stresses of visiting my family and seeing my father in the care home didn't really bother me."

Many men, like Henry, feel liberated after successfully engaging in more communication with their partners, family, and friends. Discussions of life cycle demands and transitions in therapy can lead to helpful normalizing of feelings of doubt, lack of confidence, soul-searching, change, and even loss.

Vaillant (2002) revised Erikson's model to six adult developmental tasks that are generally sequential: 1) *identity*, 2) *intimacy*, 3) *career consolidation*, 4) *generativity*, 5) *keeper of the meaning*, and 6) *integrity*. *Identity* is the last task of childhood. According to Vaillant, men who had not accomplished the task of solidifying an identity by age 50 often never achieved independence from family or institutions.

Intimacy entails close reciprocal emotional bonds with a mate by expanding one's sense of self to include another person. This may mean being with and even living with another person in an interdependent, reciprocal, committed, and contented relationship. While only mentioned as a footnote of sorts, the majority of all of Vaillant's (2002) cohort members were heterosexual. Only 2 percent of the college sample acknowledged being homosexual. During the phase of working on intimacy, there is a renegotiating of relationships with parents. Spouses and partners become the primary focus of relationships. Peer friendships may sometimes compete with this focus. Having children increases the emphasis on family bonds and cohesion.

The next adult task of *career consolidation* involves expanding one's personal identity to assume a social identity within the world of work or career involving other people. Vaillant (2002) comments "I believe there are four crucial developmental criteria that transform a 'job' or hobby into a 'career': contentment, compensation, competence, and commitment. Obviously, such a career can be 'wife and mother'—or in more recent times, 'husband and father.' (p. 47). Not achieving a social identity of "career" is often a blow to a man's self-esteem and self-worth. He may become jealous or resentful of his partner or peers and remain reliant on others such as his parents.

Generativity is the caring for, raising, mentoring, and guiding one's children or the next generation of young adults. A parent's control over young children must evolve into guidance and mentoring. While productivity continues, achievement may decline, and the need for community and affiliation may increase. Accomplishing these tasks in midlife can have an impact on later elder tasks of being the *keeper of meaning* and maintaining *integrity* (Erikson, 1997; Vaillant, 2002). Those unable to transition or let go can find themselves in adversarial relationships with their children. They may also be confronted with existential questions about the meaning of their lives, feeling emptiness or depression if they have not achieved intimate connections with their partners and children.

Men as Friends With Other Men, Women and Friendship Networks

When men seek friendships with other men, they are often not seeking intimacy in terms of communication at a deep or emotional level but companionship; not mutual disclosure but comfort in closeness through shared activities (Kupers, 1993). While some men may be aware that something is lacking in their relationships, it may go unexpressed. Friendships with women may still be seen as the more appropriate forum for sharing of emotions, support, and their adequacy as men.

Meth and Pasick (1990) list societal rules in male–male friendships as: 1) reciprocity, 2) trust, 3) not crossing the line of male propriety, and 4) not exposing one's raw emotional experiences if there is a chance for no response. These social rules may make it hard to open up to another man when the experience of taking a chance may actually be quite validating. Homophobia and the adherence to a stereotypical definition of masculinity are additional barriers to establishing and maintaining emotionally satisfying and enduring male–male relationships. In a collectivistic culture, such as China, cooperation does not necessarily lead to friendship (Kupers, 1993; Connell, 1987). In a society that promotes individualism, such as the United States, competition serves to further barriers in the formation of friendships. Encouragement of healthy, lasting male–male friendships where there is mutual trust,

openness, and sharing of experiences and emotions often leads to a stronger and healthier sense of self.

Men, Work, and Family Health

The 2000 Census reported that 49 percent of the population of the United States is male and 51 percent female, yet 71 percent of men 16 and older are in the labor force, compared to 58 percent of women. Women are encroaching on men's occupations, jobs, and pay rates. This seems to have an influence in how male identity gets defined; "being a man" has been so tied to the ability to be a provider. For men, jobs in jeopardy or threats to livelihood may be more closely related to the loss of identity. This is especially relevant in the face of changing economics in the United States and around the world. In contrast to prior times, men may be working harder, longer hours, and in more than one job. Technology shifts and outsourcing have contributed to increased competition and uncertainty in the job market. Given the time invested by men at work and the extent to which it defines their self-concept, it may be important to examine relationships with peers and supervisors. Meaningfulness of work, job satisfaction, and work milestones of promotion or pay raises may yield important information related to men's health and ability to multitask in private life.

Of particular concern have been reports of murder-suicides of families committed by fathers who became unemployed. Faced with the inability to support himself and his family, there may be an increased temptation for a father to take his own life and the lives of those for whom he feels financially responsible. Other workplace pressures, discrimination, and mounting tension without appropriate release may lead to drug or alcohol abuse or other forms of addictive or escapist behaviors. The experienced "indignities" can lead to rage (or outrage), ending in violence, internally or externally directed. As therapists, we can help men negotiate difficulties in their experiences of unemployment and gain self-worth not tied solely to vocational success or earning power. This speaks to the issue of men's losses and the need for therapists to help men negotiate what this means and to arrive at an understanding of the meaningfulness of life.

Elders and Older Age

The case of Neal: Coming out and going home

Neal is a 71-year-old man of Italian heritage. He has lived alone for the past 15 years, following the end of a 20-year marriage. He has three grown children and two grandchildren. With support from his small circle of male friends—mostly from his former work in transportation—he has tried to go out on some dates with women. Recounting one of these recent dates, he said the woman found him interesting, charming, and intelligent—a Renaissance man" of sorts.

Rather than feeling energized, he seemed tired. While he privately knows that he is bisexual, perhaps even gay, and longs to be in the company of other men, he fears the wrath and judgment of those closest to him. "I would be cut off from seeing my grandchildren, I am certain." He has never told this to prior therapists who sometimes prescribed medication and explored some of his "unresolved reactions" to the divorce. Neal talked proudly of one of his sons with whom he feels closest. "Perhaps he can come to a session and he can meet you. Maybe we can start with him and let him know."

Men are living longer than ever before, but data in the United States, and across the world, continue to show that women outlive men. More males are conceived and born than women but from birth onwards males overall die at a higher rate than females throughout the life cycle. Additionally, more males than females die from accidents, suicide, or homicide (Kruger & Nesse, 2006). In 2005, average male life expectancy has hit a record 75.2 years. By 2030, people 65 and older in the United States are projected to be 20 percent of the population (Cherry, Galen, & Silva, 2007). Race and social class also affect life expectancy. Individuals who are marginalized and have fewer resources may have abbreviated lives.

As a society with a growing percentage of elders, aging well is an important matter. Older adults should be valued members of society. Valiant's longitudinal of 268 Harvard men, 456 socially disadvantaged inner-city men, and 90 middle-class, intellectually gifted women, Vaillant (2002) found that:

Positive aging at 80 was predicted by a good marriage at age 50.

Alcohol abuse consistently predicted unsuccessful aging, at least in part due to the toll alcoholism has on social supports.

More than retirement income (perhaps more significant than men as traditional breadwinners), being able to create and play after retirement and gaining younger friends after losing older ones add to life's enjoyment.

Objective good physical health was not as important to successful aging as subjective good health.

Relationships with loved ones, once damaged or severed, may be repaired by the capacity for gratitude, forgiveness, and the enrichment of other loving connections.

Men as fathers or mentors may have shepherded in the next generation of young people during the midlife task of *generativity* (Vaillant, 2002). The task of being the *keeper of the meaning* relates to conservation of the culture in which one lives and its institutions. It also entails preparation of the next generation to inherit all that has been learned. A *keeper of the meaning* guides groups, organizations, and groups of people toward the preservation of past traditions. In some ways, performing this task is an extension of *generativity*, with greater shift of the man's role within the family and the larger community. As wise elders, grandfathers, and men in their 70s have a long experience from which to speak and reflect.

Integrity is "an experience that conveys some world order and spiritual sense. It is an acceptance of one's one and only life cycle" (Erikson, 1963; 1968). Despite potential decline of bodily and mental functions, a man's wisdom from life experience can help him maintain his value and place in the family. This can reinforce positive relationships, especially in cultures where family members that live longer are respected, revered, and cared for. In situations where an elder man's experiences may no longer seem relevant, there can be alienation or opposition by those who are younger. Valliant's (2002) finding that a successful marriage is a predictor of successful aging is a strong argument for focusing our efforts on men's couple relationships, as well as, of course, their exercise, drinking, friendships, and relationships with their children.

Conclusion and Areas of Future Focus

One of the goals of this chapter was to further the complex and multiple discourses regarding men's lives. While I might wish for a resounding, unanimous validation that all that was described above *does* represent the majority of men through the life cycle, this is not realistic. There is so much to be said, debated, and considered.

The majority of research and writings to date, with the exception of this book, have not done justice to addressing the cultural, racial, ethnic, sexual orientation, and overall diversity of men. I have ongoing conversations with a colleague who teaches psychology and family therapy with the intersections of race, culture, gender, social class, and social justice. As he was preparing for his course on multicultural family therapy, he was provided a classic textbook on multicultural counseling published within the past year. One of the last sections of this textbook is dedicated to therapy with "other multicultural populations." It has one chapter dedicated fully to women but does not have a chapter dedicated to men. What interpretations should one make from this? Are there no considerations to be made when working with men in therapy? Is our therapy with couples, families and their children a gendered one in which men and masculinity are considered the dominant discourse? Is there a chapter dedicated to women because they have greater psychopathology than men, so more attention needs to be dedicated to them? These are subtle messages that we must continue to challenge.

As a man, father, professor, and therapist I need to continue to examine these perspectives. Writing this chapter on men and the life cycle was done with soul searching, consulting, and repeated re-examination. Writing my thoughts came at the behest of two strong women, Monica McGoldrick and Nydia Garcia Preto, who trusted that I would do some justice to this incredibly broad topic. Being able to explore and therefore further understand what it has been like to be a man through this writing has been a special opportunity.

Chapter 5

Social Class and the Life Cycle

Jodie Kliman

Rich relations give
Crust of bread and such,
You can help yourself
But don't take too much.
Mama may have, papa may have
But God bless the child that's got his own,
That's got his own

—GOD BLESS THE CHILD written by Billie Holiday and Arthur Herzog, Jr. Used by permission of Edward B. Marks Music Company.

Introduction

Four babies, Sophie, Daniel, Ta'esha, and Miguelito, are born into families in three different class positions. Because their families have unequal access to educational and work opportunities and disparities in their health and longevity, these infants will participate in divergent family life cycle patterns with different expectations for intergenerational relationships. This chapter addresses the influences of social class on family life cycle trajectories, how families understand those trajectories, and their implications for family therapy. Social class combines with other sources of privilege and marginalization, such as race, gender, marital status, sexual orientation, religion, immigration history, and health, to shape family life through the life cycle.

Class position intensifies or softens the impact of crises on families at each family life cycle stage. It influences whether family members receive higher education or life-saving surgery, whether they turn to family or paid helpers for assistance, and whether they can immigrate together or separately. A child's serious illness, devastating in any family, can also cause job loss and even homelessness when her working-class parents lose work time to care for her. This chapter explores how families and their therapists see their lives through lenses formed by their class-based experiences, and the implications of those lenses for family therapy.

Social class shapes the developmental and meaning-making systems of all families and the relationships within and between families. It is therefore useful to explore the clinical and social implications of social class history and position in a family's life cycle and how families make sense of their journeys together from cradle to grave, in their respective social contexts.

Despite a soaring gap between the richest and poorest (U.S Census Bureau, 2007), dominant American discourse promotes mutually contradictory beliefs in a classless society (in which everyone but the richest and the invisible poorest is defined as "middle-class") *and* in nearly universal intergenerational upward mobility (Kliman & Madsen, 2005). These class narratives are challenged by current economic reality, as jobs and retirement funds disappear and downward mobility grows. Downwardly mobile families who grew up expecting upward mobility but now face global economic crisis, may feel self-doubt, helplessness, and shame. How can family therapists help people consider the economy's contributions to their difficulties without contributing to these paralyzing feelings?

Downward mobility can be incremental or sudden. When housing, health care, child care, and education costs climb incrementally, families with stagnant paychecks find themselves in trouble. People feeling ashamed of struggling financially more than their own parents did may not realize that their elders' housing and medical costs were a fraction of today's costs, or that their fathers' education and their family home were paid for through the GI Bill benefits of their time. Working-class parents, whose high school diplomas no longer ensure employment security, may be determined to get their children through college, only to find that even public colleges are beyond reach, leaving the next generation even more vulnerable.

Families can experience sudden downward mobility when a breadwinner is laid off or becomes disabled, grandparents lose retirement funds, or their credit line is frozen during a health crisis. Many women must suddenly fully support children after divorce, abandonment, or their partners' disability or death—while making 78 percent of what men do (U.S. Census Bureau, 2007a). Like slow downward mobility, sudden downturns can feel shaming. Families may turn inward, rather than toward community, as they wonder, "why was *I* (or my father) laid off and not someone else?" or "why couldn't we save more for a rainy day?"

Families in immediate crisis, or even on unsure financial footing, may reach desperately for risky solutions, as they struggle with big dilemmas: "Should we get married now, so he gets my health insurance?" "Now that our daughter's aged out of our insurance, we'll have to pay for her chemo with a credit card, but the interest rate just went up to 18 percent!" "Without any home equity, and with the credit cards maxed out, I'll just have to give up on community college and work at Wal-Mart." "Maybe I should just join the army so my wife and kids can have my salary—or at least my death benefits?" Family therapists are not financial advisors, but they can help families manage the growing stress and relational reactivity of financial hardship.

Understanding societal contributions to downward mobility can reduce family members' felt shame, depression, and violence. Externalizing questions (White, 2007) inviting them to separate the impact of their financial difficulties on them and their relationships from their individual or family identities can help families move forward. Externalizing questions can help families to appreciate and act on their values and

to build on their resilience, as well as their resistance to internalizing shaming narratives. Helping struggling families to see their troubles in social context reduces shame; multiple family groups for families coping with unemployment or underemployment can also counter shame.

Families can have internally diverse class origins and trajectories. Families of different class backgrounds may find themselves related through marriage or coupling. One sibling may veer away from the class trajectories of siblings who were born into the same class position. She may lose class privilege through disability, mental illness, cutoff, or life tragedy, or gain it through higher education or marriage. In the latter instance, Renee, encouraged by her teacher, was the first in her African American working-class family to attend college, on a full scholarship. In graduate school, she married a classmate, Jason, the son of two British-American professionals. When her sister, Marceline, a single mother, loses her job, Marceline needs their help to avoid eviction, but also feels shame and resentment toward her more fortunate sister and anger at her privileged brother-in-law, whom she sees as spoiled. Jason does not share Renee's sense of obligation to divert their investments into a crisis he sees as not his own.

When her in-laws hear about her sister's potential eviction, Renee feels ashamed and angry when they, unfamiliar with the rigors of living paycheck to paycheck, disparage Marceline and accuse Renee of enabling her "irresponsibility." When Jason neither defends his sister-in-law nor supports Renee's priorities, marital tensions also escalate. At the same time, Renee responds defensively when her parents criticize her for not sharing more, forgetting "where she comes from," and acting "better" than they are.

Family therapists can help families address the strains internal class differences can exacerbate, demystifying how class position can limit or expand families' choices, values, and possibilities, and therefore, family relationships. It is helpful to address class's intersections with race, culture, and gender. Renee and Marceline grew up valuing collectivism, since sharing resources is essential for survival in poor African American communities. In contrast, Jason and his family, steeped in individualist narratives of British-American culture and the more privileged classes, saw

Marceline's need for help as evidence of personal irresponsibility and Renee's desire to help as foolish.

Class and race, while distinct, intertwine when some are privileged and others are disempowered on the basis of both class and race. The median income (before the latest economic crisis) was about $55,000 for non-Latino White families but only $39,000 for Latinos and $34,000 for African American families (U.S. Census Bureau, 2007a). Moreover, while 8 percent of White households live under the (artificially low) poverty level, 22 percent of Latino households and a quarter of Black households live in these severe conditions (U.S. Census Bureau, 2007a).

Economically diverse communities of color have fewer medical services and sources of healthy food; they also have lower-quality education, and more violence, with direct consequences for longevity and how long family members can expect to live together. Whites live longer than Blacks (Centers for Disease Control, 2008) and wealthier Americans of all races live longer than their poor counterparts (Agency for Healthcare Research and Quality, 2003).

Immigration status also moderates income's effects on the family life cycle. Class position and understandings of class can change radically, for better or worse, on immigration, as family members leave one culture and economic system for another. The median household income for noncitizen householders is reported at 75 percent that of U.S.-born adults (U.S. Census Bureau, 2007a). (The discrepancy might be still greater if all undocumented workers reported their earnings, often below minimum wage.) As the U.S. government has tightened its own belt, immigrant families (both documented and undocumented) lose health insurance and other forms of essential assistance, plunging more families into poverty.

Children pay the highest price for poverty: Nearly a quarter of all American children and even more children of color live at just over the poverty line (U.S. Census Bureau, 2007a). Schools in poor communities with the greatest educational and social needs have fewer resources. Immigrant children miss school to translate for parents and return to classes they cannot easily follow. Poor children whose parents cannot afford younger siblings' day-care often miss school, as do children whose asthma is exacerbated by exposure to lead, bus fumes, and other toxins that abound in poor communities. Children with learning disabilities, which are often related to toxic exposure in utero and in early childhood, are harder to diagnose and help in overcrowded, underfunded schools. Family therapists should directly address these class-related issues in working with families referred by schools that, ignoring the social context in which children's difficulties emerge, may pathologize them.

Gender, marital status, and sexual orientation also moderate the effects of class on families. Because women make 78 percent as much as men, lesbian couples and their children live on less than gay or heterosexual couples. With single-mother families' median income 45 percent that of heterosexual couples' (U.S. Census Bureau, 2007a), many women stay in unhappy, even abusive marriages. A family therapist may have trouble understanding how a mother could let her children experience and witness abuse unless he knows how hard it is to support children without education or job experience. Exploring gender and economic constraints in the face of a mother's needing to feed her children can help therapists work respectfully and knowledgeably with a family in such distress.

Understanding Social Class

Class position involves one's relationship to the economic structure, which varies from country to country and region to region. This relationship includes the nature and relative self-direction of one's labor (Ehrenreich, 1989; Kliman, 1998). Class position relates not only to income, but more importantly, also to wealth and access to money, information, influence, privilege, and other resources. It is interwoven with educational level and to the intangibles of social standing in one's immediate and larger community.

Class includes educational experience and related discourses about family, work, and community life, which vary greatly with educational level and intersect with race, ethnicity, and other factors. One so-called "middle class" family sends children to overnight camps, junior year abroad, volunteer internships, and professional schools, ensuring handsome future incomes. Children in another "middle-class" family work full-time to help pay the family's rent, exhaustedly taking community college night classes; they can expect a considerably lower lifetime income (U.S. Census Bureau, 2006a). A third self-identified "middle-class" family of blue-collar and service workers cannot even dream of college because of poverty and/or immigration status; their children's high school diplomas produce far less future income.

"Social class" is often confused with "socio-economic status" (SES). The latter, a decontextualized and hierarchical formula of educational, and occupational levels, and income, divides people into upper, middle (which is further subdivided into upper-middle, middle, lower-middle), and lower SES. Yet most Americans place all but the wealthiest and the poorest in a vaguely defined middle class (or middle SES). This conflation of class position and SES obscures how one's current and historical class positions influence workplace autonomy, access to resources, information, and the intangibles of influence, privilege, and power. It also obscures how wealth (assets minus debts), education, and the intangibles of social standing matter more than income in how families live.

For example, Annie, an MBA student, reports $25,000 a year in student loans on her taxes, but drives her attorney father's SUV, vacations abroad, lives rent-free in the condo her parents bought and largely furnished for her, has a small trust fund from her grandparents, and benefits daily from her family's wealth. In contrast, her sister Laurel's undocumented child care provider, Iris, supports her baby on $25,000, without health insurance, savings, or family money and is a paycheck away from homelessness. The two families' access to social, political, and informational resources differ as starkly as the expectations with which their children are raised.

The nonrelational, decontexualized concept of SES obscures how Iris's underpaid child care work supports Laurel's and her husband's well-paid, prestigious work. It also obscures how this arrangement separates Iris from her own child, who stays with her aunt and cousins 10–12 hours a day. Class not only *affects* relationships; it *is* a relationship between those in different class positions (Kliman, 1998), such as Laurel's and Iris's families. Given this relational imbalance, families who employ household help may see their nannies and housekeepers as family members, while the latter's kin rarely feel even known by employer families.

Class position is constructed in relation to one's community, which may be economically homogeneous or mixed (Boyd-Franklin, 2003). Being employed, poor, working-class or professional class is experienced differently in different neighborhoods. For instance, the Jenkins's old neighbors once saw the couple, a hospital orderly and a cafeteria worker, as "middle class" in their urban neighborhood because they had two incomes. Since the area's gentrification, their son, Greg, won't let his school classmates, who live in beautifully rehabbed condos, meet his parents or see his tenement apartment, which would mark his family as working-class.

The Jenkins's family therapist would do well to recognize how intergenerationally divergent class experiences shape Greg's disrespect to his parents, who sacrificed to provide him an easier future, as he compares them to his classmates' privileged parents. She must also help Greg appreciate his parents' sacrifices, economic constraints, and commitments while helping his parents understand how Greg's new expectations and priorities, nurtured in his shifting class context, reflect their success in giving Gregory an easier life. How can she help this family find room for both realities? How well does she monitor herself to avoid imposing her own class-informed assumptions about parent–adolescent child relationships, or to avoid responding reactively to the family's assumptions about her own class experience?

Social class influences family life cycle options subtly, in part through participation in largely class-homogeneous social networks, as data from the Framingham Heart Study's longitudinal network analysis (2008) suggest. This study of thousands of Framingham, Massachusetts, participants' cardiac health discovered that obesity levels and smoking cessation relate to social clustering patterns; people grow obese (or do not) together and smoke (or do not) together. Better-educated people are more likely to be influenced by acquaintances' quitting smoking and to marginalize smokers than are less-educated peers. Thus, members of highly educated networks are less likely to smoke or be obese (thereby improving their longevity), than those in less educated networks. My network therapy experience suggests that the same applies to other factors affecting life cycle, such as when and if to have a first child, leave home, or binge drink.

Social class plays out differently in different countries and different economic systems. Western Europeans have higher taxes than Americans, which is outweighed by nearly free health care and higher education, subsidized daycare, and long, paid vacations, which help extend life, especially for the poor and working-class. In many developing countries, professional and business-class families usually have live-in servants; on immigrating to the United States, these educated immigrant families may do more for themselves, feel more stress, and eat less healthily.

Class position is communicated in code, through dress, manners, language use, and leisure activities. Greg Jenkins's parents' clothing, grammar, and table manners embarrass him; his friends' parents travel, eat, dress, speak, and decorate elegantly. His girlfriend, a classmate, teases him for not knowing cultural references that her family takes for granted. She can't understand why he refuses invitations to family ski trips to work during vacation. Greg's parents, in turn, judge his girlfriend for being spoiled, entitled, and unproductive.

CLASS POSITION Rather than relying on SES, this chapter categorizes families as ruling class, professional-managerial class, working class, and underclass (Ehrenreich, 1989). The tiny ruling class, the families of "big business" owners, controls over 90 percent of the nation's wealth (Domhoff, 2006). Although work is optional, parents are busy with philanthropy, social functions, and entertainment, while children are often raised primarily by household help and boarding schools. As a result, clinicians may find that intergenerational struggles between ruling-class youths and their parents, or between parents and their own aging parents, are not softened or mitigated by the strong bonds that often develop between children whose parents are their primary caretakers. Clinicians may also find themselves being treated as employees, undercutting their effectiveness.

Members of the professional-managerial class, who have at least a college education, often identify with an amorphous "middle-class" or "upper-middle-

class." Professional-managerial class families range from those who count on inheritances and parental help with mortgages and children's college, to those who expect only limited family financial help, and those who have moved "up" from the working class and get no such help. Families in this class generally expect moderate to high incomes, some autonomy and meaning at work, coupled with having to juggle expanding work hours and family responsibilities. Parents are the primary caretakers but often have some paid domestic help. Increasingly, such families have two earners or a working single parent. Historically, these families had the financial cushion to manage economic or health crises or divorce, but that cushion is disappearing as pensions, savings, and jobs disappear and costs soar. Family stress increases as parents face "proletarianization" by changes in the job market.

Families in the working class (traditionally divided into white-, blue-, and pink-collar workers) are often identified as "lower-middle-class." Children in these families rarely go beyond high school and may live with family until marriage (or beyond) as a matter of necessity. Historically, working-class high school and vocational school graduates could count on job stability, but as previously economically stable families lose pensions, savings, and health insurance, they slide into financial insecurity. Family therapists should watch for signs of new, stress-related illness, shame, depression, substance abuse, family conflict, and violence, which family members may not connect with their recent downward mobility.

The underclass includes the chronically unemployed, those on disability or welfare, in the drug, weapons, and sex trades (Ehrenreich, 1989), undocumented immigrant workers and those who transport them. Undocumented workers, often paid below minimum wage, may live with spouses and children (some of whom, born here, have citizenship); most support families in their home countries who depend on their earnings for survival (Falicov, 2005). Most underclass families, with little to no education, have little hope of supporting themselves through legitimate (or any) work. They are most likely to have children very young and to die young. Most rarely see doctors and never see family therapists; those in therapy are most often sent by child protective services, the judicial system, or schools.

Family therapists often encounter couples and families with divergent class backgrounds who do not recognize or appreciate the impact of their class differences and so bump into contradictions and misunderstandings with each other. Therapists may notice clashing expectations when, for instance, a (professional class) doctor's daughter couples with a (working-class) pipe fitter's daughter who see themselves and each other as middle-class. Words with multiple meanings in different class and cultural contexts, such as "responsibility," "support," "independence," or "respect" can get lost in translation in arguments over saving, spending, or sharing money with relatives, prioritizing children's sports, enrichment classes, and chores, and table manners. Helping families externalize the effects of class and explore its influence on meanings and expectations can move them from mutual judgment to mutual respect and understanding.

CASE EXAMPLES

SOPHIE AND DANIEL We now return to the family life cycle trajectories of the families of four newborn babies mentioned at the start of this chapter, beginning with the birth of babies whose family life cycle trajectories are strongly influenced by their class positions. Twins Sophie and Daniel were delivered by Caesarean section in a teaching hospital after Daniel went into fetal distress a month early. Their parents were Sarah, 39, a German-Jewish American lawyer, and Jeff, 44, a Scots-Irish American advertising executive. Insurance paid all hospital expenses and most of the fertility treatments. Jeff's parents promise to add to each twin's college fund yearly, as they do for Jeff's older son, Max. (See **Genogram 5.1** for their genogram at the time of the twins' birth.)

Seven years later, Daniel has reading, sensory integration, and attentional difficulties, to his achievement-oriented family's disappointment, but benefited from early intervention. Sophie's sensory

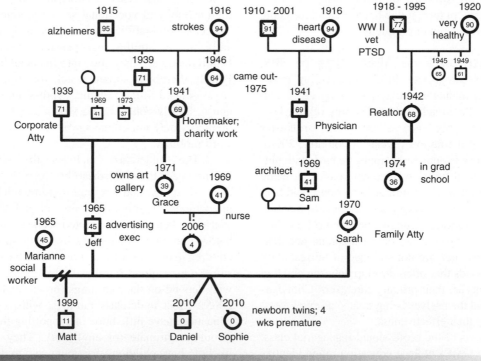

GENOGRAM 5.1 Sophie and Daniel's Family

integration problems are mild and she learns easily, but her asthma preoccupies her and she gets anxious leaving home for school or play dates. Their parents, grandparents, and nanny push the children to "live up to their potential like Max," despite their prematurity-related challenges; they get tears and tantrums in return.

Their private family therapist helps the family accept Daniel's learning difficulties in a community expecting high achievement, while helping to scaffold his learning process in a private school without individualized education plans. He encourages Sophie to find strategies to soothe herself—and encourages her family to give this child with chronic illness room to develop socially a bit more slowly than her brothers. He encourages Sarah and Jeff to find activities that pull for the children's areas of strength and strengthen areas of relative weakness.

TA'ESHA (GENOGRAM 5.2) Ta'esha was born 6 weeks early, in a Louisiana public hospital. Ta'esha's mother, Ronita, 16, started bleeding and was hospitalized until delivering. The doctor blamed formaldehyde in her family's FEMA-funded trailer, their home since Hurricane Katrina displaced them from New Orleans. He also sternly said that had Ronita stopped smoking, waited a few years, and gotten prenatal care, Ta'esha would be bigger and healthier.

Ronita's grandmother, who has obesity, diabetes, and heart problems, supports the family with her disability insurance; Ronita's youngest brother, Donnell, has cerebral palsy and frequent seizures, and also receives disability. Her mother and older brother are unemployed, like most FEMA trailer park residents (Henderson, 2009; Parks, 2009). Her father, a day laborer, was murdered 5 years earlier. The family's phone was disconnected, so Ronita could not reach her family when she went into early labor.

Ronita had returned to school, 2 years after Katrina, when she went into labor. The local schools, overwhelmed by thousands of children displaced from New Orleans (Rabina, 2009), did not welcome more students, especially with babies, and her help with her youngest brother was needed at home. She liked high school and had hoped to graduate, baby and all, but worried her mother and grandmother could not manage without her.

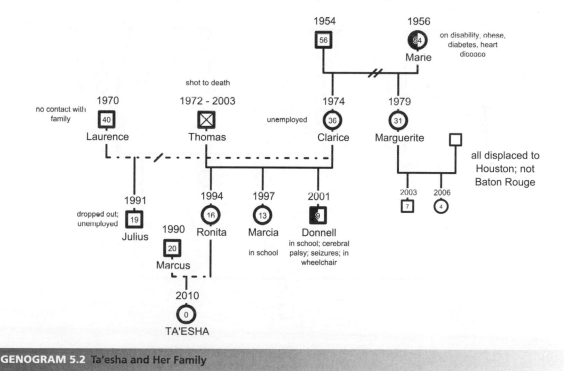

GENOGRAM 5.2 Ta'esha and Her Family

Ronita wanted Ta'esha, whom she thought would always love her best. She assumed her mother and grandmother would help with Ta'esha, as her grandmother had helped with her. But holding a 4-pound, intubated, un-cuddly preemie in the NICU scared her. She wished her mother could leave Donnell for a while, and that her grandmother's angina was better, so they could come and comfort the baby—and her.

Ronita's mother, Clarice, prays that Ronita gets free care and that the hospital will arrange medical and educational services for Donnell, who has been out of school since Katrina. Then Ronita's grandmother could stay home with just the baby, rather than caring for both a baby and a boy in a wheelchair. She hopes to find work and help Ronita stay in school. She is less optimistic about her oldest, Julius, who is drifting toward gang membership.

A NICU nurse, concerned about the lack of family visitors and Ronita's tearful anxiety about holding Ta'esha despite urgings about skin-to-skin contact, alerted a hospital social worker, who contacted a visiting nurses' program and a home-based family therapy agency. The family therapist, a young social work student, is stunned by the number of challenges this multi-stressed family faces. She must support them through illness in grandmother, Donnell, and Ta'esha, a depressed teen mother, and an at-risk young man, bereavement, and displacement to a cramped, toxic FEMA trailer. She must address the tension among three generations over authority and responsibility for the baby that comes with teen pregnancy. Getting this family early intervention to help Ta'esha develop cognitively would help a year from now—but the therapist will have graduated and left by then. In the meantime, can this White, well-educated therapist appreciate how hard this overburdened family works to stay together and survive in terrible circumstances, rather than pathologizing or judging them (Madsen, 2007)?

MIGUELITO (GENOGRAM 5.3) Miguelito was born 6 months after his father, Manny, an Army Reservist, had deployed to Iraq. Sonia, who came from Mexico at age 2, gave birth in a community hospital with her

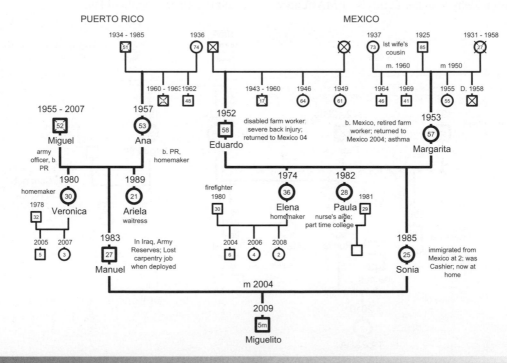

GENOGRAM 5.3 Miguelito and His Family

sister Elena, who lives out of state, and her mother-in-law, Ana. Manny saw his big, healthy boy delivered, thanks to the Army's video hook-up. When the doctor held Miguelito up to the camera, Manny cried, promising to hold him soon. The women wept too, praying he could keep his promise.

Manny's parents, Puerto Rican migrants, raised their children on military bases where his father, Miguel, served; fellow army families sustained the family during his peacetime deployments. Manny joined the Reserves after his father died, to honor him and for the educational opportunity. As a Reservist who usually worked as a carpenter, he and Sonia had lived far from a military community. Both of their families felt that Sonia should not manage pregnancy and motherhood alone while dealing with Manny's combat deployments and increasingly difficult returns. Manny was more angry and upset after each deployment (Gorbaty, 2008), and both families wanted to support the young parents and their new son. Sonia's parents, retired from farm work due to disability, were back in Mexico. Her sisters were not in a position to take her in, so Sonia left her sales job in New Mexico to live in Texas with Manny's mother and sister, near Miguel's last army base.

Manny had lost his job and family health benefits with this third deployment; the military gave him (but not Sonia) health insurance. Relatives on both sides emptied their credit cards, Christmas accounts, and equity lines to pay for Sonia's hospital costs—a year before the economy tanked. Sonia's gynecologist suggested therapy for Sonia after diagnosing postpartum depression. The extended family decided on family therapy, since Ana (herself depressed since being widowed) and Sonia argued over Miguelito's care and what to tell Manny about Sonia's state of mind on his calls home.

They found a bilingual family therapist, the brother of a career officer, who understood the issues families face with military deployment, reunification, and combat-related stress. Unmarried, childless, and unversed in the challenges related to newborns, postpartum depression, or three-generation households, he knew to rely on the family's own experience and his supervisor to work constructively with this extended family.

He was working with the family when Manny returned, when Miguelito was 6 months old, with clear signs of PTSD and worked with the extended family to integrate Manny back into his mother's household. He helped the extended family to understand and respond helpfully to Manny's hypervigilance and outbursts of anger and to ensure that Manny's wife, mother, and sister felt empowered to get the help they needed.

Social Class and Families With Young Children

The birth of these four newborns shifts each of their respective families' developmental journeys, rerouting the ongoing, multigenerational life courses of their siblings, parents, and relatives. Each family's life cycle is shaped by social class location, which in turn influences the particulars of each child's birth and health. Their class position, in turn, is influenced by the age, ethnicity, citizenship, health, and location of family members, and by the effects of disaster and war (which in turn, affect members of different classes differently), among other factors.

Sophie, Daniel, and Ta'esha were all premature, but their family life cycle trajectories look very different. Multiple birth babies like Sophie and Daniel are often premature, as are babies born, like Ta'esha, to African Americans, teenagers, smokers, and mothers with little or no prenatal care (Centers for Disease Control, 2007). Ta'esha and the twins got medical care of contrasting quality and their families' resources for helping vulnerable children thrive differed.

The implications of these differences are great; 28 multiple birth infants per 1,000 die, while 53 per 1,000 of Black infants die (Matthews, Menacker, & MacDorman, 2002). A quarter of neonatal deaths are premature and low-birthweight babies (Centers for Disease Control, 2007), one of the starkest of family life cycle derailments. Premature infants who survive have high rates of attentional and other learning disabilities and chronic medical difficulties (National Library of Medicine & National Institutes of Health, n.d.). Many fragile preemies who survive these difficulties today would have died decades ago, but their chronic illnesses and learning disabilities can decelerate and derail their family life cycle.

The life-long challenges of prematurity and low birth weight are greatest for poor, young families of preemies. Young and poor parents are less developmentally or financially prepared to care for chronically sick or disabled children, without the resources, information, or quality medical, educational, and psychological help that older, more affluent parents like Sarah and Jeff rely on to help their premature children thrive.

Ta'esha was born into three generations of poor, Black teen mothers. Very young mothers and their families often must spend much of their limited time, energy, and money on their children's health needs; this often means giving up the educations that could improve their economic circumstances. Furstenberg (2007) reports, however, that teen parenthood itself contributes less to the intergenerational transmission of poverty than does living in poor neighborhoods, without access to resources and information available elsewhere. Poverty and racism had already ravaged Ta'esha's family's New Orleans neighborhood when Hurricane Katrina dealt it a final blow. Schools, health centers, and social service agencies in neighborhoods like hers were permanently boarded up, their residents scattered nationwide.

Attending school takes a back seat to Ronita's trips to the ER when her grandmother has angina, her brother has a seizure, or her infant gets the respiratory infections common to preemies and babies in FEMA trailers. Ta'esha, like Ronita and her siblings, does not have the benefits of having a mother with enough education to support them. Unlike Daniel and Sophie, they do not get early intervention or preventive medical care to help children with learning disabilities or chronic illness live full lives. Without such intervention, Ta'esha may stay sick and do poorly in underperforming schools; her disabled young uncle Donnell, though only 14, is not even in school.

Race and educational level interact in seeking prenatal care. More educated and affluent women get prenatal care, which they see as important and affordable. Only 6 per 1,000 of infants of all races whose mothers received first-trimester prenatal care die in infancy, as compared to 34 per 1,000 without prenatal care. Yet even African American babies whose mothers do get first trimester prenatal care still die at double that rate; Black infants without prenatal care die at the stunning rate of 50 per 1,000 (Matthews et al., 2002).

Miguelito started life as the healthiest of the newborns, but several factors counter the advantages of his full-term birth. His father, an Army Reservist in Iraq, returns from deployment with an exacerbated PTSD; worse yet, in future deployments, a traumatic brain injury might leave him unemployable (Gorbaty, 2008). He could be killed, leaving Sonia, a Mexican citizen, without the legal residency that marriage to an American citizen provides, restricting her ability to get a job remunerative enough to support her son.

Miguelito is an only child. Sophie and Daniel have a 10-year-old half-brother. Ta'esha's grandmother and great-grandmother have parental responsibilities for children spanning 19 years, including baby Ta'esha, her adolescent, quasi-sibling mother (16), and her aunt (12) and uncles (19 and 9). Their experience of raising children across such an age range differs greatly from the twins' parents, whose financial and household resources and 10-year span make their family's complex developmental needs more manageable.

Before antibiotics and modern obstetric and surgical practices, big sibling age ranges were common across classes because many parents, widowed while young, remarried quickly to ensure their children's care and support. This often meant joining stepsiblings of varying ages, and children from the new union (Coontz, 1992). Before birth control was widely available, even nuclear families had wide ranges, and still do in some religious groups and in agrarian societies where children's labor is essential to family welfare. In my own extended family, the 14 siblings in my stepchildren's mother's underclass family were 28 years apart (see **Genogram 5.4**) . In her family, as in most large families, older children cared for younger ones, since one parent (or even two) could not possibly care for so many children. The next, mostly high school–educated next generation in her family had much smaller families; she herself had only two children.

In the more privileged classes today, big age ranges result from divorce and remarriage more than death. My spouse and I (Genogram 5.4) adopted our newborn son when my stepchildren were 13

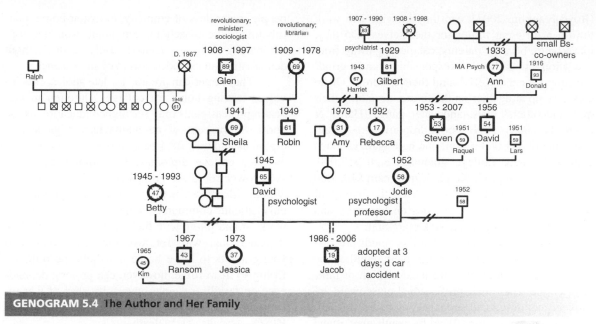

GENOGRAM 5.4 The Author and Her Family

and nearly 20 (see in Genogram 5.4), simultane-ously raising an infant and a young teenager, while paying college tuition for my stepson, who lived with us. As great as the developmental and financial challenges were, as professionals in our 30s and 40s, we had resources unavailable to Ronita and her mother, a grandmother in her 30s. Our higher in-come and some help from family, friends, and paid sitters made a difference. In our baby's first year, our careers as psychologists allowed my spouse and me the flexibility to work half-time, which most parents can neither afford nor arrange with employ-ers. In contrast, our son's 22-year-old working-class birth mother knew that keeping him, her second baby, as a single mother would mean losing her restaurant job and stark poverty for her family.

Because both adoption and reproductive tech-nology are so costly, social class affects whether single, gay, lesbian, and/or infertile would-be parents can even start new generations. When private adop-tion is arranged, exploitative private adoption rela-tionships can develop, with wealthier adoptive parents supporting and sometimes controlling the younger and poorer women who bear the children they adopt. Similar patterns are common with non-kin surrogacy. Children adopted privately, through child protective services, or internationally generally

grow up in families with more class (and sometimes more racial) privilege than their birth families, which sometimes creates identity challenges in adolescence.

Social Class and Families With Older Children and Adolescents

Class-specific narratives prevail in families' social networks regarding the rights, responsibilities, and developmental tasks of older children and adolescents. Is adolescence a time to explore one's options and iden-tities, with family financial and emotional support, or to take on financial and domestic responsibility for one's family? Do teens attend college, work, join gangs, volunteer, enter the military, or take time to "find" themselves? In the professional-managerial class and upper segments of the working class, older children and teens are generally seen as needing guid-ance, care, and protection. In contrast, most working-class and underclass young people are often needed to help parents with major domestic responsibilities like laundromat trips, cooking, and watching younger chil-dren. Some children and teens may navigate social systems for parents who speak little English or are disabled.

If youths in poor communities see few educat-ed adults outside of school with legal, well-paid jobs

(Boyd-Franklin, 2003), can they imagine and work toward a different future for themselves? Do they, like Ronita, become parents, catapulting away from education into early adult responsibility and a grinding future for themselves and their children? Or do they give up altogether on the future, devaluing their own and others' lives, and enter gangs (Hardy & Laszloffy, 2005)? High school dropouts earn, on average, about $21,000 a year, and half again as much with a diploma. College graduates earn $57,000, while those with professional degrees earn $103,000 (U.S Census Bureau, 2006b). Given the impact of education and income disparities on longevity and health, the family life cycle stakes are high.

Working-class and underclass youth are disproportionately separated from their families by juvenile detention or parental incarceration or military service when their professional-class peers are actively monitored and supported by parents, teachers, coaches, and tutors. Wealthy youth may attend boarding schools, joining their families only for holidays and vacations. What are the implications of these differences for family therapists, who may tend to apply their class-informed experiences of their own or their children's adolescence?

Social Class and Families With Late Adolescents and Young Adults

How long do parents and children expect to live together? Do children leave home in their teens or 20s for college, work, military service, marriage, or prison, or do they never leave? Do adolescents with children stay at home with their own parents? How much contact do young adults have with their parents? What determines adulthood? Is it the first "real" job, marriage, the first child, or high school graduation? Turning 18? Joining the army? Joining a gang? Graduating from college? Renting one's own apartment? Buying a home? Finishing graduate school?

Dominant cultural narratives normalize leaving home by the early 20s, except in ethnic groups that value collective family well-being over individual preferences. The more class privilege (and generations in the United States) a family has, the more they expect young adults (of any ethnicity) to live separately. Economic necessity requires poorer young people, regardless of ethnicity, to live at home, contributing to the household. Immigrants from developing nations may see teens as fully adult, without demarcating an extended period of adolescence.

The "American dream" for late adolescents involves leaving home for college. Although mental health professionals may see higher education as the norm, 85 percent of all adults have high school diplomas and only 28.4 percent of people aged 25 to 34 have college diplomas; Educational levels are even lower for older groups (U.S. Census Bureau, 2006a). Moreover, many working-class youths can only attend community college part-time, while working and living with their families. One reliable, if dangerous, way for working-class youth and young adults to leave home is to join the military. Doing so in wartime, however, can prolong dependence on family (or government) because of war-related injuries (especially traumatic brain injuries) or PTSD—or cause early death.

Young people planning to attend college usually delay having children into their 20s and 30s. Doing otherwise presents major child care and social challenges. But if youth see neighbors and classmates dying young from violence, addiction, preventable illness, or war, and if their only acquaintances with college educations or stable careers are their teachers, why wait to have children? If your parents and other elders had their children young, that seems simply, "the way it is." Similarly, if everyone you know has finished at least college and starts having children in their 30s, that is equally "the way it is."

The consequences of compressing or elongating the interval between the generations are great. So is the danger of living in a poor community of color, where there is both more crime and a greater judicial readiness to arrest (sometimes violently), detain, and jail youth for behaviors that would get more privileged youth a stiff warning. A prep school student who gets into a fight is expelled and gets a fresh start at a new private school; his poor counterpart of color is incarcerated for the same behavior. The Department of Justice (2006) reports that in 2005, 12 percent of all African American men in their late 20s were incarcerated, as compared to 3.7 percent of Latino young men and only 1.7 percent of their White, non-Hispanic peers.

My own son, Jacob, died in a car accident at age 19. His death stunned our family, our suburban neighbors, friends, and colleagues. Many people told us, "It's not natural. Parents don't bury their children." But, alas, parents do bury their children and always have. It's just that, since the advent of antibiotics and the end of the military draft, class-privileged people no longer *expect* to lose their children. I certainly did not. But poor families of color bury their children with heart-breaking regularity in neighborhoods best described as war zones, only a mile from me. Most inner-city Boston teens know at least one murder victim and many survivors and perpetrators of assault; their parents live in dread for them (Lazar, 2008). And families in official war zones around the world lose their young continually.

What is the effect on the family life cycle, when survival into adulthood is so uncertain, as it is in American inner cities and in war zones worldwide? Family therapists whose class privilege buffers them against chronic danger must enter full-heartedly into the realities of families whose lives are so precarious, remembering that, "there but for the grace of God go I."

Social Class and Families With Adults in Mid- and Later Life

How long do people expect to live, and how long do they expect their parents, siblings, partners, and children to live? How do these expectations influence individual and family choices, throughout their lives? Whether you expect to live a long life in good health—or believe you may not live to see your 50th year—will inform life-shaping decisions from early on. Do family members plan to work (or count on their relatives working) until their 60s? Do they foresee a comfortable retirement or scraping by on social security and Medicare? Or do they expect to work until they drop or until disability stops them, as it did Miguelito's grandfather, and Ta'esha's great-grandmother?

What do middle age and old age even mean, in class context? My father, 80, a psychiatrist, works full-time, because he loves it *and* because he will send my 17-year-old half-sister to college soon (see Genogram 5.4). This obligation marks his upward class mobility.

He could afford to adopt a baby at 62, long after raising 3 children and a stepchild. His labor is not punishing, as is stooping over strawberries (like Miguelito's maternal grandparents, whose back injury and asthma and lack of health insurance—see Genogram 5.3—necessitated their return to Mexico). (Family disposition might trump class in my own case; my working-class great-grandfather worked until 89, making paper pads in his basement). One significant downside of this class-specific parental age flexibility is that my half-sister, when she is my age, will surely have lost her parents and much-older siblings.

In contrast, my stepchildren's maternal grandfather, a poor African American/Native American father of 14, died before many of his 40 grandchildren were born; his exhausted ex-wife lived only into my older stepchild's infancy. They clearly led much harder lives than my stepchildren's White, professional-class paternal grandparents and step-grandparents.

Consider the different experiences of grandparenthood for Sophie and Dan's robust grandparents (ages 67–70), Miguelito's disabled maternal grandfather and caretaking paternal grandmother (ages 57 and 52), and Ta'esha's grandmother, age 30. What does it mean to be a grandparent at 70 or at 30, and what does it mean to have grandparents of those ages? Ta'esha's disabled *great* grandmother, at 53 (see Genogram 5.2), is close in age to the other infants' grandparents (and to me, who has no grandchildren). If infirmity can come in the 50s, having children young means that you can help raise grandchildren while still vigorous (Stack & Burton, 1993) and that older children can care for the young ones when your own energies prematurely flag.

An 80-ish wealthy widow needing full-time nursing care can pay for home health care or a well-appointed assisted living residence; her children can comfortably delegate her care to staff. Her working-class counterpart enters an understaffed Medicare-funded nursing home, leaving her unemployed daughter and grandson (who had moved into her small, subsidized senior housing unit after fleeing domestic violence) homeless and unable to monitor her care.

As people live longer, elders increasingly serve as regular caretakers to grandchildren, ailing spouses and siblings, their own old-old parents and/or ailing late middle-age children, sometimes simultaneously. Privileged families, whose members live longer, can meet this responsibility by coordinating paid help for loved ones. Working-class families, especially women, do the hard work of caretaking themselves, often at expense to health and income.

Affluent families can afford to plan on getting old; their home equity, retirement plans, disability insurance, life, health, and long-term care insurance policies ensure that they and their loved ones will be well cared for. Less affluent families try to do at least some of the same, but often find they have already gotten old, while growing housing, health care, child care, and college costs eroded their hopes for a "good" retirement.

In contrast, Americans in the underclass, without any economic "cushion," spend more than they earn, leaving little for old age. Many undocumented immigrant workers spend every extra penny on remittances to their families back home so their children and aging parents have enough to eat. These workers have often watched their elders die young and poor. Without the luxury to plan ahead, they work to the point of disabling injuries or chronic illness. Finally, in some violent inner-city neighborhoods, poor and working-class elders (and previously "middle-class" elders living in homes that used to be good places to live) may not see all their children or grandchildren live to see 30, let alone retirement age (Stack & Burton, 1993).

Less affluent and less educated people have shorter life spans. Access to healthy food, safe exercise, and regular medical care correlates with neighborhoods' median income; thus, the poor are beset by high rates of chronic illnesses, some relating to factors like obesity and smoking. Poorer families are more vulnerable to work-related injuries, pollution, violence, and the damaging health consequences of worry about violence to self and family (Lazar, 2008). Even when medical care is available, significant health care delivery and outcome disparities exist based on income and education (Agency for Healthcare Research and Quality, 2003).

Conclusions: Implications for Family Therapy

The family life cycle of family therapists, like those of their client families, are shaped by class history and current class position. Their social locations influence their cultural narratives about a "healthy" family life cycle and about their clients. Lisa, a middle-aged family therapist and mother of two, was the first to attend college in her family. She is seeing a college student, Julia, and her parents, Will, a cardiologist, and Becca, a homemaker and volunteer. Will is upset at Julia's "entitlement" and at Becca's enabling Julia's "profligate spending."

Lisa finds herself siding with Will without knowing why until, exploring the family's class history, she finds that like her, Will grew up financially struggling and put himself through college. He wants to spare his daughter his struggles, but also wants her to be appreciative and wise with money. Becca takes comfort for granted. Had Lisa instead grown up privileged like Becca, especially if she were younger or childless, she might have seen Will as withholding and judgmental. That is, unless she explored his family class history and compared it to her own.

Of course, family therapists do best when they avoid judging or taking sides—this can be done by attending to how their assumptions about family life are informed by their own class and other social experiences, and attending to those of their client families (Kliman, 2010; McGoldrick & Hardy, 2008). This attention is especially important when clinicians are more class privileged than their client families. It is easy to pathologize class-bound life decisions and their impact on the family life cycle when therapists know nothing of the constricting realities of class oppression, or of the invisible benefits their own class privilege has bestowed on them.

Chapter 6

The Life Cycle of African American Families Living in Poverty

Paulette Moore Hines

Well, you were born . . . and though your father and mother and grandmother, looking about the streets through which they were carrying you, staring at the walls into which they were carrying you, had every reason to be heavy hearted, yet they were not. For here you were: Big James, named for me—to be loved. To be loved, Baby, hard, at once, and forever, to strengthen you against a loveless world. Remember that. I know how black it looks today for you. It looked bad that day too. Yes, we were trembling. We have not stopped trembling yet. But if we had not loved each other, none of us would have survived. And now you must survive, because we love you, and for the sake of your children and your children's children.

—Letter from James Baldwin to his 15-year-old nephew

This piece was originally written for *The Progressive* magazine, 409 East Main Street, Madison, WI 53703. www.progressivemediaproject.org.

James Baldwin's touching letter to his nephew evokes the importance of our kinship network, of hope in the face of so little, of remembering our history and our connectedness and our strength to survive—all that African American families living at or below the poverty threshold need so desperately in our times. Nowhere is the need for a life cycle framework more urgent than in work with African American families who struggle to live without adequate resources. Nowhere is it more crucial that we attend to the importance of people's connections to their history, communities, and hope for a future.

About 12.3 percent (37 million people) of the total U.S. population is African American (U.S. Census Bureau, 2006–2008 American Community Survey). The dominant discourse is that African Americans are responsible for their position in society and have equal opportunities to achieve the American Dream. But the truth is this group's struggle for basic freedoms and opportunities has continually been thwarted by the pernicious and pervasive effects of racism at every level of our society. Poverty adds its own pain. Families who are poor and African American (approximately 8.7 million or almost 24 percent) must contend with systematic efforts to disconnect, invalidate, and crush dreams on a daily basis. Single-parent Black households face the highest poverty rates and, overall, the lowest median income ($12,500). Low income Black families are 2.4 times (24.7 versus 10.5 percent) as likely as non-Hispanic Whites to live in poverty (U.S. Census Bureau, 2006–2008 American Community Survey). About 44 percent of these families have a family member working full-time. Nevertheless, 50 percent of those living in poverty live in deep poverty (i.e. less than 50 percent of the poverty level). Racial differences are not erased with increased education; low-income Blacks are poorer than non-Hispanic Whites even when they have a high school diploma or college degree (Simms, Fortuny, & Henderson, 2009).

Over the recent decades, a growing number of family theorists, researchers, and practitioners have countered deficit-focused perspectives about families living in poverty and have brought much-needed attention to their strengths. These include M. Akinyela (2008), Harry Aponte (1994), Andrew Billingsley (1992), Nancy Boyd-Franklin (2003), Linda Burton (1995, 1996a, 1996b), Ken Hardy and Tracy Laszloffy (2008), McAdoo, (2007), Robert Hill (1999), Hines and Boyd-Franklin (2005), Elaine Pinderhughes (1982, 1989), and many others. The common thread across this expanding body of work is that the lives of this sub-group of African Americans can only be understood within a framework that acknowledges the far-reaching interactive effects of African culture, slavery, racism, and its residuals (e.g., internalized racism), and social, economic, and political disenfranchisement.

What is essential to our efforts as therapists is to focus on African Americans' resourcefulness and ability to survive and even thrive under oppressive circumstances throughout history in this country. It is a true testament to the resilience of the human spirit and nothing short of a miracle that African Americans have survived and made such significant gains in the educational, economic, political, and many other arenas (McKinnon, 2003). Despite their economic challenges, countless uncelebrated African Americans lead invisible lives within a context of poverty but are still distinguished by a defiant spirit of hope, an exceptional capacity for problem solving, and a commitment to transcending the odds (Hines, 2008).

The purpose of this chapter is to dispel the notion that family therapy is a futile endeavor with African American families living in poverty and reinforce the value of working from a framework that situates families within their cultural and life cycle context and links them with the rich resources of their heritage.

Factors Influencing Diversity, Functioning, and Resilience Through the Life Cycle

In recent years, the economic downturn in the United States has drastically reduced the resources (e.g. training programs) that were previously available to the poor of all backgrounds. Technology advances have contributed to an increasing gap between the haves and have-nots. In 2008, the unemployment rate for African American men was 13.4, compared to 9 for

African American women, 6.5 for White men, and 5.4 for White females (U.S. Dept. of Labor, 2009.) Some estimate that unemployment in major inner cities is an appalling 40 to 50 percent for Black males. There is strong evidence that once work disappears from a community and people grow up without even the hope of working, drug use and crime intensify dramatically, and the disorganization of the social community becomes overwhelming (Wilson, 1997).

These circumstances have extensive consequences for adolescents and young adults, in particular, who have had limited opportunity to develop a job history or skills. Far too many youths graduate from schools that leave them ill-prepared to compete in society.

The media and professional literature construct and reinforce a negative identity for African Americans and perpetuate the inaccurate notion that the poor are a homogenous population, doomed to be dysfunctional. The focus on negative elements in the lives of poor African Americans leaves many therapists inclined to overlook the fact that living without an adequate income (i.e. being "poor") simply does not equate with family functioning. Economically vulnerable families vary in structure, coping styles, and levels of resilience. Some live in single-family units; others reside with members of their kin network. Some are working poor; some are temporarily unemployed. Some are downwardly mobile; others are slowly improving their economic status. Some 38 percent of Black families live in families in which the only source of income is government assistance (i.e., Temporary Assistance for needy families, General Assistance, food stamps, nutrition program, housing assistance); others (25 percent) make do with what they can generate through their meager earnings and by exchanging resources within their family support system (Dye, 2008).

Numerous factors mediate the effects of adverse economic, environmental, and social conditions on family functioning, including the number of generations families have been embedded in poverty, the level of their connection with their larger family systems, level of acculturation, their spirituality and religiosity, and the extent to which they avoid self-defeating responses to oppression (Pinderhughes, 1982).

Characteristics of the Family Life Cycle

Despite their heterogeneity, African American families living in poverty are uniformly apt to face innumerable barriers to transcending their concrete circumstances on a daily basis. Their life cycle is distinguished by at least four characteristics.

Condensed life cycle

Progression through the various life cycle phases is generally more accelerated for African Americans living in poverty than for their working- and middle-class counterparts. Individuals have children and become grandparents at far earlier ages (Burton, 1996a). When families have a condensed, overlapping intergenerational structure, family roles are chronologically and developmentally out of sync with generational position (Burton, 1996b). Acceleration for one person creates acceleration for others throughout the family system. For example, the adolescent mother, by giving birth, is launched into young adult status (parenthood), and her young adult mother becomes a grandmother, often being forced to assume the role responsibilities of surrogate parent. The potential for role overload in such life cycle patterns is tremendous. The abrupt assumption of new roles and responsibilities often means that they have inadequate time to resolve their developmental tasks. Facing so many pressures, adults may be overwhelmed, inconsistent, or too busy to pay sufficient attention to their own or their children's needs. Outcomes depend on the extent to which transitions are anticipated, the level of support available from extended family, and the extent to which the development of caretakers is stalled (Burton, 1996a, 1996b). Families adapt better when there is clarity about the logistical, emotional, behavioral, and relational shifts that must be made at all levels of the system to support the family and its members' progress through the life cycle.

Female-headed households

Out-of-wedlock births in the United States have climbed to an all-time high in all racial groups and among all age groups except youngsters ages 10 to 17 (MSNBC, 2006). Between 1970 and 2000, the percentage of African Americans who had never married increased from 36 percent to 45 percent among men and from 28 percent to 42 percent among women and now exceeds the proportion currently married. Black women were more likely than women of other racial/ethnic groups to experience disruption of their first marriages, whether by divorce (11.6 percent) or separation (4.7 percent) (U.S. Census, American Community Survey 2006–2008). In 2007, 39.6 percent of Black families living in poverty were headed by women with no spouse present (U.S. Census Bureau, Income Poverty, and Health Insurance Coverage in the United States, 2007). The trend toward motherhood without marriage reflects not a cultural devaluation of marriage (Chapman, 2007; Staples, 2007), but rather an adaptation to circumstances that limit the availability of mates who have employment and the perception that they can realize their life dreams. Young girls may come to think of pregnancy and motherhood as offering the hope of love and increased status in their families.

Chronic stress and untimely losses

Unrelenting stress is normative in low-income families and the potential exists for distress that can impact the quality of individual functioning and family relationships. Still there is great diversity of functioning within low-income families as a group, just like there is diversity within their more economically advantaged counterparts. There are innumerable examples of economically challenged individuals and families from whom we can learn much about resilience. More research is needed to identify the factors that can successfully mediate negative outcomes. However, environmental context undoubtedly renders low-income families vulnerable to adverse outcomes. Frequently embedded in large, extended family networks that span the life cycle continuum, African American families living below the poverty threshold frequently experience shifts in household membership as a result of job loss, illness, death, imprisonment, and alcohol and drug addiction. It is not uncommon for families to move several times a year, and children may experience many different family constellations. The contrast of living in a society of plenty in which they must struggle constantly to meet basic needs can breed frustration. Their capacity to work around obstacles and to be hopeful about life is stretched continuously. Ordinary problems—such as transportation, health care, child care, or a sick child—can easily become crises because of a lack of resources to solve them. A high rate of relocation and high rates of crime in urban neighborhoods hamper social connectedness and activity outside the house and a sense of community. Neighbors may not know one another and, in these instances, lack the benefit of long-term and trusting relationships and the social support that might otherwise be afforded. Men and women, young and old, sometimes assume an outward facade of apathy that is merely armor intended to protect themselves from disappointment, pain, and degradation. Persistent stress is likely to adversely affect their physical as well as spiritual and emotional health (Williams, Neighbors, & Jackson, 2003).

Reliance on institutional supports

Approximately 62 percent of African American mothers with a birth in the last year were recipients of public assistance (U.S. Census Bureau, May, 2008). Stigmatization and the need to comply with numerous regulations, which barely allow them to survive, can push an already stressed emotional system over the edge. Many survive only because of their participation in mutual aid, a prominent feature of African American culture. The strongest institution in the natural support system has been churches. Many other civic organizations, such as Urban Leagues, also provide a critically needed help (e.g., energy assistance) for families whose needs far surpass their resources.

Stages of the Family Life Cycle

The life cycle of low-income African Americans who are marginalized both because of race and their economic circumstances can be loosely divided into three basic life cycle phases, which are frequently overlapping. It is common for families to be in several stages simultaneously, given their extended kin and intergenerational context.

Stage 1: Adolescence and unattached young adulthood

African American youths who are members of economically challenged families are at risk for many life difficulties given the combined effects of racism, poverty, and the general vulnerabilities of adolescence. In addition to the ordinary tasks of adolescence, they have the added burden of developing a sense of efficacy in the face of persistent racism and other oppression. Their environment is full of minefields, and there is little room for error; actions such as dropping out of school or being argumentative when stopped by the police may have lifelong consequences. The jobless rate of Black teenagers age 16 to 19 increased from 30.9 percent to 41.3 percent between October 2008 and October 2009 (U.S. Depart of Labor, 2009). Pregnancy is usually high on parents' worry list especially for their adolescent daughters. AIDS is the fourth leading cause of death in African American females aged 15 to 24 (Herron, 2007). For sons, parents fear for their safety and lives, knowing that authorities are more quick to arrest them for minor offenses, book, remand them for trials, and give them harsh dispositions (U.S. Bureau of the Census, 2006–2008 American Community Survey). Their neighborhoods are too often drug- and crime-ridden, and there are constant pulls to engage in illegal activity. In fact, homicide is now the leading cause of death for African Americans of both genders between the ages of 15 and 44 (National Vital Statistics Reports, 2009). Many youths feel compelled to carry weapons for self-protection.

At every life cycle phase, families need to provide family members with a balance of separateness and attachment that will promote their success. During adolescence, this balance becomes especially difficult to work out. While yearning for independence, acknowledgment, and respect, many youths from low-income families learn to protect themselves emotionally by tuning out the rules of the dominant society that devalues and excludes them. The infiltration of "street values" into youth culture and the media's preoccupation with this subculture has heightened negative sentiments about youths everywhere they turn. Most African American youths learn to project an external demeanor that masks the disappointment, hopelessness, and helplessness that flow from their economic, racial, gender, and age-based oppression. Their creative and distinctive use of nonstandard language and attraction to nontraditional clothes, music, and hairstyles might be viewed as an effort to reject rejection and to exercise some power in their lives (Franklin, 2004). The schism between societal expectations and what they are able to achieve puts these youths at high risk for depression, anxiety, physical problems, rage, and a host of other problems. Staying connected with their dreams and not compromising their priorities require extreme determination.

Kunjufu (2005) contends that there are several critical periods in Black youths' development: fourth and fifth grade when Black children, especially boys, seem to experience a slump in their achievement; adolescence, which appears particularly turbulent; and the young adult years, which offer critical opportunities that may determine the quality of later life.

Some youths try to fend for themselves in spite of their difficulties making financial ends meet; others remain in their families' household, whatever inner or interpersonal conflict this entails. Some deal with pressure to strike out on their own by breaking away in anger; others get married and/or have children with the assumption that this new status will force others to acknowledge them as adults. Some try to resolve the dilemma by relocating to another geographic area but can afford to do so only if they live with relatives, which may create other relationship problems.

Learning to cope with racism and other oppression is an unenviable challenge. It is most difficult for parents to help their children approach school and the world of work with optimism. Even a high school degree now carries little guarantee that a person will find work, and training beyond high school costs money that youths do not have and may lack the guidance to pursue. Even more than their elders, they need the skills to operate in a bicultural context. Young adults encounter far more subtle racism than their parents and grandparents experienced growing up. The curricula that they are taught on a daily basis remain largely Eurocentric in focus. Parents have the complex task of teaching their children to cope with racism without overfocusing or underfocusing on the issue, a challenge at any life cycle phase but especially so at this time when rebelliousness and the value teens place on the opinions of their peers interfere with their receptiveness to

learning from their parents anyway. Obviously, youths are particularly vulnerable if their parents are absent or dysfunctional and if other adults are not available to provide positive role modeling and active guidance. The best protection is having parents or caretakers and mentors who acknowledge and openly communicate regarding the harsh realities of their world while conveying clear principles for living and high expectations and also monitoring the youths' activities without being overprotective.

Financial limitations and family obligations can make it difficult for young adults to fulfill key tasks of this stage: to establish intimate relationships and a work identity and to self-differentiate.

KEY THERAPEUTIC TASKS Therapists often need to conduct both separate and joint sessions with parents and youths to help them sort out their beliefs, feelings, and concerns. Therapists should assess whether there is a need to coach parents and caretakers to: 1) communicate clear, specific conduct guidelines to their children, 2) acknowledge situations that are unfair and perhaps even oppressive, and 3) still hold the youths accountable to themselves, their families, and their community for their *conduct*—i.e., whether they choose to use constructive or destructive strategies to cope with adversity.

Given the time and energy that are dedicated to surviving each day, we should not underestimate the value of simply creating a forum where family members allow each other to have a voice. Therapists must be able to sift through family members' expression of their pain, disillusionment, and rage while reminding them of the values they hold, which may be different from the choices they are making daily. Therapists must also be willing to label destructive behaviors, even while acknowledging their positive intent. It may be useful to facilitate discussion between parents and adolescents about differences in the challenges that they have faced. Getting adults to tell relevant stories is an excellent strategy for (re)connecting everyone with the legacies that can serve as road maps for coping with current struggles. (This is part of the principle of *connecting*, described in the list of African-centered principles.)

Parents may become immobilized in their ability to set limits on their children out of frustration or hopelessness about their children's chances of finding a meaningful place in society. Therapists can be of great service in getting parents and other caretakers to come up with a clear position or to at least avoid sabotaging each other in setting limits. Anxieties need to be channeled into activities that do not exacerbate the youth's inclination to invalidate parental feedback. Respected older male relatives and community members may be brought in to help young men reexamine their definitions of manhood and free themselves of the limitations that their peers and larger society may impose. Videotapes can be a powerful stimulus for conversations about courage and conduct and help family members to make emotional as well as cognitive shifts.

It is critical for the executives in families to impress on their adolescents the necessity of having a plan of action to accompany their dreams. Young adults require knowledge and a toolbox of life skills, including anger and stress management, conflict resolution, safer sex negotiation, and time-management skills to effectively negotiate the demands they will face in life. Therapists should not assume that parents or adolescents possess these skills or the confidence to apply them.

Stage 2: Coupling and bearing and raising children

Forty-four percent of low-income, Black families have at least one adult working full-time, full year, and 19 percent of these families have a member working full-time, part year and part-time, full year. Even so, there is a gap between the income they earn and what is required for self-sufficiency (Simms, Fortuny, & Henderson, 2009). A related and significant factor, influencing male–female relationships and, hence, family life is that for the Black population age 15 and over, Black females outnumber African American men and likewise outnumber them in the civilian labor force (U.S Bureau of the Census, 2006–2008 American Community Survey).

COUPLE RELATIONSHIPS Couple relationships can be extremely difficult to develop and sustain in the context of poverty and racism. Stress is persistent,

and conflicts arise easily. In this context, 30.4 percent of the Black or African American population is married; 11.6 percent are divorced; 4.7 percent are separated, and 47.0 percent were never married. The divorce rate for Blacks was 1.5 times the rate for Whites, and this statistic did not include those who have ended their relationship without legal divorce (U.S. Bureau of the Census, ACS 2006–2008). The media provides a constant inducement for couples to compare their lives and relationships to those of the rich and famous, whose resources are dramatically better than their own. Housing tends to be substandard and overcrowded, with no physical space or money for recreation or cooling off when conflicts arise. There is a tendency for the many frustrations of living in a context of insufficient resources to get misdirected into male-female relationships. As in most other cultures, women are socialized to be the nurturers in their families and are particularly inclined to ignore or sacrifice their own needs. Within the culture, individuals are seen as having intrinsic worth irrespective of their level of academic achievements or economic success in life. Related, there is widespread recognition of the special oppression that impedes Black men's capacity to live up to their role demands. These combined realities increase the risk that women will accept role overload as a way of life.

Young African American males, who are the most direct focus of the larger society's racism, may be reluctant to make a commitment to a relationship when they are unable to meet their financial obligations.

TAKING ON PARENTAL ROLES While some African American mothers are mature, working women, many are unmarried teenagers (Burton, 1996a). When adolescent sexual experimentation leads to pregnancy, young women frequently reject abortion and adoption, choosing to have and keep their babies. They may quickly feel overburdened and depressed. Particularly if their education is interrupted, their role can become constricted to that of caretaker. If they attempt to enter the job market, child care and transportation costs can be prohibitive. Many are forced to obtain public assistance to ensure housing, food, and medical benefits.

The role of young fathers with children born outside of marriage is often vaguely defined (Paschal, 2006). If they still identify with their adolescent peer group, they may be slow to accept shared responsibility for their children. Mothers may actually restrict fathers' involvement to protect their children from the possibility of broken promises. In time, children may expect their fathers' absence, though it may bother them. Boys, in particular, are handicapped by this concept of maleness, but there has been a concerted effort to reverse this trend. An increasing number of young men are getting involved in parenting education and support programs.

Parents can easily become overburdened with too many responsibilities and too few resources and emotional reserves. Research indicates that the prevalence of depression is high among teen mothers (Barnet, Liu, & DeVoe, 2008). Frequently, children are close in age, and it is not uncommon for children to span the range from infancy through adolescence. An older child may take on responsibility for helping to reduce the parental load, helping with child or elder care, household maintenance, or working to contribute to the family's meager cash resources. Parents tend to be authoritarian and use physical punishment to ensure that children quickly learn and abide by lessons that are intended to protect them from dangers in their harsh surroundings.

REALIGNING RELATIONSHIPS WITH EXTENDED FAMILY The birth of children hastens couples' need to integrate new spouses or mates into extended-family networks. An estimated 30.3 percent of Black children below the poverty level lived with their mother and a grandparent in the household; another 15.3 percent of Black children lived with both parents and a grandparent present in the household (Kreider, 2007). Households may also include other relatives of one or both partners (6 percent of all Black households without regard to income), creating the challenge of fitting together disparate and changing relationships (U.S. Census, American Community Survey 2006–2008). Younger mothers, in particular, may rely on their own mothers or older family members for assistance with help with child care. While the extended-family network is likely to provide a much-needed cushion of emotional if not

financial support, a high level of connection leaves room for some predictable problems. Couples may struggle with issues of loyalty between their newly created family and one or both extended-family systems. Furthermore, poverty tends to mean an extremely high family mobility, so parents and children must continually adjust to relatives moving in and out, and they themselves tend to change living quarters and schools very frequently.

Single-parent family structures are not inherently dysfunctional, but they are particularly vulnerable because of poverty, task overload, and a lack of resources. More relevant than the structure of the single-parent family are the availability of essential resources and the family's patterns of functioning. Family adaptive strategies, when pushed too far, can be vulnerable.

EMPLOYMENT McLoyd & Enchautegui-de-Jesús (2005, p. 136) assert that African Americans' work experience is organized around four themes that represent the legacies of racism: "1) higher labor force participation among women and mothers; 2) increased difficulty in finding and maintaining employment; 3) less favorable employment conditions, circumstances, and experiences (i.e., longer work hours, increased likelihood of working nonstandard hours, decreased likelihood of having a flexible work schedule and other family-friendly employee benefits, lower wages) among African Americans; and 4) prejudice and discrimination against African Americans." Those who essentially drop out of the labor market out of frustration and hopelessness in finding employment or because they lack the means to negotiate work with child care, transportation, their own poor health, ill family members, and other barriers to working must contend with the assumption of many in the larger society that they devalue work and that they are lazy and without ambition. Unemployment has obvious, far-reaching implications for individual functioning and all aspects of family life for adults in their roles as spouses and partners, parents, and family members concerned with the welfare of elderly relatives and other extended family.

KEY THERAPEUTIC TASKS Given the likelihood of role overload and isolation at this phase, helping parents and other caretakers to maintain supportive, reciprocal connections with family, fictive kin, friends, and community supports is extremely important. This is even more critical when aging grandparents assume parental responsibilities, especially when children have special needs stemming from parental drug addiction and AIDS. Sibling relationships, which are especially important in African American culture, should be validated and nurtured as an extremely important part of the relationship network (Watson, 1998). It is important to maximize the involvement of noncustodial fathers and the paternal extended family if these connections have not been developed. Therapists can help to strengthen family systems by linking them with community organizations that can provide concrete resources and supporting their capacities to advocate on their own behalf. Schools often do not validate or reward children who have relational cognitive styles as African Americans typically do as a result of growing up in fluid, shared-function families. Therapists need to advocate for financially struggling families with school systems and to empower parents to take an active role in their children's education because of the likelihood of racist disempowerment of children, which contributes to their acting-out behavior.

Many parents and caretakers require assistance to increase their focus on caring for self and reducing the level of their overfunctioning. This is likely to involve setting limits on relationships in which there has been little or no reciprocity in terms of emotional or concrete support. For others, it will involve reducing their role overload by negotiating to share family tasks. Therapists may need to structure discussions that help families to see the dangers of overdependence on one person. Also, by assisting families to learn about their heritage, families may gain a sense of hope and connectedness to something larger than themselves.

Parents may need coaching about how to provide children with age-appropriate details regarding imminent changes in the living situation and family member absences as well as how to avoid placing children in the middle of adult conflicts.

Most are socialized to understand that their lives will involve ongoing struggle and sacrifice. Adults will generally be more comfortable making changes for the sake of the children than for themselves. Therapists must be willing to acknowledge the obstacles that families face even when the intention is to challenge some of the premises that lead clients to give up on their dreams. Reference to sayings or proverbs (Hines, 2008) that have evolved in the African American community over the generations may have a richness of reverberation with which families can connect.

Stage 3: Families in later life

African Americans continue to have a lower life expectancy rate than the overall population, 73.2 years compared to an average of 78.2 years for all population groups (National Vital Statistics Reports, 2009). In contrast to middle-class families, this phase of the life cycle does not signify retirement or a lessening of daily responsibilities for low-income African Americans. Many continue working to make ends meet in spite of poor health. Even when they do retire, it is unlikely they will have "empty nests." Instead, they are likely to be active members of expanding households and family systems, frequently providing care and assistance to grandchildren, adult children, and other elderly kin (Kreider, 2007). It is not usual for the elderly to hold the belief that "idleness hastens aging-related symptoms." Coupled with financial stressors, illness is too frequently disregarded by the elderly until their functioning is seriously impaired.

Elderly family members are great sources of human wisdom and strength by virtue of their survival. They serve as family advisors, mediators, and transmitters of the family history and culture. Grandparents often have relationships with their grandchildren that are as close as, if not closer than, the relationships they have with their own adult children. They may spend more time nurturing their grandchildren, nieces, nephews, and other kin than they were able to devote to their own children. Their homes are usually the gathering place for the kin system.

Life for African Americans living at or below the poverty threshold typically involves repeated loss both because of the size of their kinship system and the impact of their socioeconomic realities on their well-being. Given the cultural emphasis on being strong and the common interpretation that this means "keep on keeping on," family members are challenged to grant themselves time to rebound from physical and emotional depletion, not to mention interests and dreams they set aside or never explored.

KEY THERAPEUTIC TASKS The assistance that aging family members are able to provide to others, particularly in later life, can help them to retain a sense of purpose. However, one area for clinical assessment is whether they can do so without compromising their own physical and emotional well-being.

Denial about a decline in functioning, illness, or ultimately death may result in delayed family communication around issues that are critical to maintaining family stability. Family members may benefit from coaching to confront an elderly family member about the need for medical treatment, restrictions on his or her activity, or the need for institutionalized care. Elderly family members, themselves, may serve as the catalysts for gathering family members to address the need for a changing of guards so that continuity of family functioning is maintained. When family members are ambivalent about or closed to participation in therapy sessions, it can help to appeal to their concern that their elderly family members experience greater peace of mind from knowing that all is in order. In return, therapists can motivate the elderly to participate in sessions by emphasizing the need for family members to access the wisdom of their elders and avoid unhealthy dependency that will leave them unprepared to function effectively when the elderly person can no longer participate in caretaking.

Older family members are sometimes ambivalent about discussing certain topics (e.g., drugs, illicit sex, or criminal behavior) with younger family members if they have not resolved their own guilt and/or confusion about choices made when they were younger. But their advice may be even more credible because of their life experience and it may be helpful for them to speak openly about information they may have long avoided or kept secret. Exploring individual and family legacies often results in reconnecting with stories, images, and the fortitude of ancestors and mobilizes family members to move forward with tasks they have magnified to the status of undoable.

Assessment and Treatment Considerations

A family life cycle framework is totally congruent with African values, the most widely held being a deep sense of family or kinship, including both the vertical (the living, the dead, and those yet unborn) and the horizontal, encompassing all persons living in the tribe (Mbiti, 1970). A life cycle approach counters the pervasive narrow, individualist focus that characterizes so much of the social science literature, promoting a deficit approach, which has amounted to blaming the victim. For example, most discussions of teen mothers and their children still focus narrowly on the maternal grandmother and the young teenage mother as they provide for the child. This myopic focus ignores the caregiving responsibilities and practices of the young father, grandfather, great-grandparents, siblings, and other kin in such situations who influence the quality of life for a teenage mother and her child as well as others in the family (Burton, 1995).

The family life cycle approach becomes even more powerful when linked with principles of living and adaptation that have promoted African American survival and transcendence through many generations of slavery and oppression. A growing number of theorists and practitioners have formulated prevention and treatment approaches based on Africentric values (e.g., Phillips,1990; Rowe & Grills, 1993; Mazama, 2003; Nobles, 2004; Williams, 1992, and many others). Undergirding these perspectives is the premise that healthy functioning of African Americans is closely linked to principles drawn from African culture that define what one stands for and how one behaves within a bicultural and oppressive context. There is also a common belief that transformative healing involves understanding and resolving the problems of today, drawing upon the solutions of the past.

Drawing on these scholars' body of work, the author conceptualized an approach to preventive intervention (Hines & Sutton, 1998) that incorporates seven traditional African principles that can enrich therapeutic intervention with African Americans:

1. *Consciousness* pertains to having a clear awareness of one's feelings, thoughts, beliefs,

principles, purpose, family, cultural heritage, and potential, as well as obstacles to self-actualization and group actualization, including racism.

2. *Connectedness* pertains to unity or sticking together, a sense of belonging. It is reflected in the African adage "I am because we are" and reflects the idea that our self-definition depends on our fundamental interrelationships with our family as well as mutually supportive links within our kin network and community (Rowe & Grills, 1993).

3. *Caring* pertains to the ability to nurture, protect, support, and show concern for the safety of our family and the larger group and a belief in giving back (Nobles, 2004). Caring reflects the essential interdependence of African Americans, the belief that "If I don't care for you, I don't care for myself" (Rowe & Grills, 1993).

4. *Competence toward our purpose* pertains to self- and group actualization, developing ourselves to our fullest potential; achieving the skills to cope with and even modify or transcend our circumstances (Rowe & Grills, 1993).

5. *Conduct* pertains to accepting our reciprocal responsibility to engage in right behavior and to teach others how to do so. It involves the ability to forgive and resolve past injustices with one another.

6. *Creativity* involves using originality, inventiveness, imagination, intuition, and artistic abilities to transform pain into meaning and hope and to leave the world better than it was when we inherited it (Karenga, 1988).

7. *Courage* pertains to demonstrating the spiritual strength to withstand adversity and to achieve one's goals; to live up to the examples of one's ancestors (Karenga, 1988).

Incorporation of these Africentric principles into a life cycle framework allows therapists to assess families' competence in fulfilling life cycle tasks within the context of values drawn from their heritage. Therapists can assess individual and families' functioning in relation to the seven principles.

The power of engaging families in this dialogue is linked to the growing need for African American families to critically examine the myriad messages they receive about how to survive in a rapidly changing society. The Africentric life cycle framework also promotes awareness of the relationship between the behavior of family members across generations (vertically) in relationship to socio-political and economic conditions (horizontally). Family members can be empowered to participate in their own healing and to search for wisdom in their own cultural and family heritage.

The task of understanding the presenting problem(s) within the context of the family's life cycle phase, family functioning consistent with traditional values, and the larger ecology must be undertaken with care. Genograms (McGoldrick, Gerson, & Petry, 2008) have obvious value in helping a therapist keep track of who's who in the family and social network, as well as key facts. Taking a genogram history requires diplomacy, and details should be gathered gradually as the family comes to trust that the therapist has the goal of understanding what has happened to the family up to this point and identifying family resources.

Work with African American families who struggle daily to make ends meet requires creativity, and validation of their potential, regardless of where they are in the family life cycle. Most families will benefit from an orientation to therapy and knowing the nature of the therapist's connection to other service agencies. Convening family members to communicate and problem solve without their usual distractions can be invaluable in and of itself. It is important to clarify reality constraints (e.g., conflicting work schedules) that may hamper family members' participation in therapy (Hines & Boyd-Franklin, 2005) and to leave families with some hope even in the first session that therapy will make a difference. There is nothing sacred about the typical one- or even two-hour session; half- and full-day sessions may be more effective and may enable therapists to mobilize key family members who may not otherwise be available for appointments. Extended sessions also make it easier to engage and mobilize families before they are distracted by new stresses.

Therapists must strive to empower family members by helping them to understand the ways in which the social system may undermine their functioning as individuals and a family, sorting out the factors in their predicament that are influenced by the larger society and external systems and those that belong to them. In doing so, therapists help family members avoid assuming blame for systemic influences while taking responsibility for ways in which they may collude in reinforcing their own powerlessness (Pinderhughes, 1982). The author recommends incorporating and prescribing culturally congruent strategies—such as asking clients to conduct oral history interviews, read relevant scriptures or meditations, watch relevant videos, and read teaching fables or popular books based on the lives of African Americans—to help families connect with their family and group history, their potential, and their hope for overcoming their current challenges (Hines, 2008).

CASE ILLUSTRATION

A brief case vignette illustrates the use of an Africentric-oriented life cycle framework with a family whose status might be aptly described as having spiraled from "working to nonworking poor." Their story exemplifies the reality that resilience may be strained in the midst of living "under fire" but neither poverty of spirit—loss of hope, dreams, and human potential—nor dysfunction is inevitable nor irreversible.

The Long family was referred for treatment by school authorities to address the excessive school absences and growing anger and moodiness of 15-year-old Raheem. The immediate family consisted of Raheem's parents, Isabella (age 46) and Ralph (age 48), and a 13-year-old sister, Rachel. The previous year, the oldest son, Lashan, at age 19 had been accidentally run over by a police car that had been chasing someone else, as he was walking to evening classes at a local college. Lashan had resided in a rehabilitation center since his release from the hospital; while there was an experimental treatment that might reverse his comatose condition, the family was without insurance to cover the recommended procedures. The paternal grandmother, 65-year-old Caroline, lived several blocks away

with her 29-year-old son, Larry, and her 12-year-old grandson, Andre, who had lived with her since he was a toddler. Andre's father (Caroline's son), 31-year-old Michael, had been incarcerated for the last 4 years. Larry worked as a mechanic and spent much of his free time with his girlfriend. Caroline was suffering from diabetes and high blood pressure. Her husband, Joe, had died from a stroke 2 years ago while at his second, evening job. Most of Raheem's maternal family lived in his mother's hometown, several states away. The Longs had regular telephone contact with them.

Raheem's problematic behavior had begun after his brother's accident. Lashan had been the first in his immediate family to attend college. Throughout Raheem's life, Ralph had worked two jobs to make ends meet, but shortly after Lashan's accident, Ralph lost his primary job as a painter because of new regulations that blocked the employment of those without union credentials. Since then, Ralph could find only occasional odd jobs, which offered neither him nor his family health benefits. Isabella had reluctantly given up her job as a school crossing guard during the last year because of a painful back condition. Both Ralph and Isabelle had exhausted their unemployment benefits. Isabella had been denied disability but was awaiting a decision from her appeal. Six months ago, Ralph reluctantly had decided to "disappear" from the household so that his family would qualify for medical benefits and food stamps, and he was now staying with his mother. Ralph had noticeably become less involved at church where he had formerly volunteered with the parking and security team, a group of men with whom he had formerly much enjoyed meeting. Isabella and Caroline suspected that Ralph was hiding the fact that he had begun to drink alone. Recently, Rachel had started to violate her curfew and angrily accused her mother of being overprotective with her but permissive with Raheem.

Over time, the therapist focused the therapeutic interventions at several levels of the family system. The therapist invited all family members; only Larry refused to attend. While the family members seemed anxious and unsure about what was expected of them, they quickly labeled the problem as Raheim "being out of control." The therapist attempted to expand the family's consciousness that each of them had coped in his or her own way and that all of them had avoided talking about their sense of being overwhelmed for fear they would further burden the others and the common perception that talking wouldn't change their reality. The therapist normalized their dilemma and shared his hypothesis that the family had been pushed to their limit by the continuing threat of losing Lashan, the dramatic decline in the family's meager financial underpinnings, and the deterioration of Isabella's and Caroline's health. Using easel paper to visually dramatize his point, the therapist further outlined the various stressors that were beyond the family's control (e.g., escalating crime in the neighborhood, illness, unanticipated job loss, negative peer pressure, housing, and school problems). Each family member had handled the feelings of loss, anger, hopelessness, and helplessness with behaviors that were not helpful to their individual and family functioning.

The members of the executive system of the Long family, connected in their concerns, emotional pain, and hope, were divided in their awareness of each other's needs, and ideas about how best to counter the circumstances that threatened their family. The therapist conveyed his belief that the family was *strong enough* to connect with and walk through their pain to a place of healing.

To connect them with a sense of their own potential to act on their own behalf, the therapist encouraged the grandmother, father, and mother to talk about their family history during the session with Raheem, Rachel, and Andre. They told stories of the extraordinary challenges that members of the Long family had overcome over the generations and the creative ways that their ancestors and elders had found to address their anger associated with injustices. Themes of family togetherness, faith, perseverance, and leadership were clearly threaded in these empowering memories. Returning to the list of stressors on the family, the therapist facilitated what grew into a lively conversation about which of the stressors were within the family's capacity to exert any influence. In a separate session, the therapist met with Ralph, Isabella, and Caroline to discuss their expectations and the messages they were giving to the children in the family. The therapist discussed with them how to hold the youths in the family and

each other accountable and helped the parents and grandmother to define what shifts were necessary in their co-parenting to maximize their success with their common child-rearing goals. At the therapist's urging, Ralph subsequently took Raheem and Andre with him to see Michael at the prison for the first time in 9 years. Michael was able to penetrate Raheem's armor and impressed upon him the inaccuracy of Raheem's peers' visions of prison life. He spoke candidly to Raheem and Andre about the devastating ways in which drugs had affected not only him but also his son and mother.

In subsequent individual sessions with Ralph, the therapist urged him to call upon the courage that had brought him through the Vietnam War and the wisdom passed on by his father to confront his feelings of being "down and out," his children's need for a positive role model, and his own desire to be responsible as a father and husband. Ralph was reluctant to attend AA meetings but agreed and initiated a supportive relationship with a man in his church group who was in recovery and an active member of a church-sponsored support group. Isabella was coached to communicate her distress to her husband without resorting to yelling, which typically resulted in angry exchanges and distancing by Ralph. Ralph was able to articulate his disappointment that his wife seemed less than appreciative of his effort to be a good husband and father. Isabella acknowledged the contributions that Ralph had historically made and, more important, the contributions that he could continue to make on behalf of his wife and family in spite of his joblessness. The therapist coached the couple to effectively renegotiate their roles in their home. Similarly, Raheem and Rachel rehearsed ways to negotiate for privileges with their parents. Ralph began to take a more active role in the family and coordinated meetings to help Raheem reestablish his academic standing.

The therapist then turned his attention to the grandmother's health. Caroline spoke to her family about her belief in not giving in to her aches and pains. Discussion ensued about how she could acknowledge her illness by taking her medication and continue to support herself and her grandchild but give up the overtime cleaning and home health care jobs she regularly accepted. In turn, she insisted that the family join her in attending church services on Lashan's birthday, which all anticipated would be a difficult anniversary for the family. The family was pleased to have the church community surround them with a special prayer during the service. Acknowledging the innumerable demands and circumstances that impeded their social activity, the therapist asked the executives in the family system to explore the down-side of allowing themselves to become totally depleted. The themes of courage, caring, and doing the right thing by each other reverberated for the adults and youth in the family system.

The therapist verbally acknowledged the family's unspoken concern that these efforts, without new opportunities, would still fall short of helping the family reduce their level of dependence on government assistance. With the coaching of the therapist, Mr. Long made a connection with a cousin who owned a small business and was able to secure a part-time position, which had the potential of becoming full-time. The therapist devoted one session to a discussion with Mr. and Mrs. Long about depression. The therapist patiently explored the ambivalence that Mr. and Mrs. Long had about taking medication and enlisted them in a conversation about the warning signs that they should heed if overcoming his depression proved more difficult than Ralph envisioned. The therapist encouraged the family to utilize the resources available at their church, which included mentor and tutor for Andre and cultural and social opportunities that the three teens could more actively explore. Isabella and Ralph, acknowledging that they needed all the support they could get for themselves and their children given the multiple stressors they were besieged with, decided to make a road trip to Isabella's upcoming family reunion at her parent's birthplace.

Avoiding Therapist Burn-Out

Work with African American families who live in poverty requires significant time, creativity, energy, and clarity. These are families whose daily experiences include ongoing challenges in terms of concrete resources and related emotional, relational, spiritual, and physical health concerns. Most therapists who work with families living in poverty have a genuine commitment to assisting the population and often ignore the need to retreat and replenish their own energy. A key process, essential to refueling our own tanks, is staying connected with our respective wellsprings of energy and spiritual renewal.

Further, we as therapists need to explore where we fall on the continuum of privilege and assess our personal beliefs about poverty and coping with adversity. It also is helpful to stay in regular, active consultation with colleagues who can help us stay out of the minefield of guilt or do-gooder behavior that does not benefit our clients or ourselves. Humility and active commitment to collaboration are essential therapist skills. The value of our work does not reside in our ability to provide answers to our clients' problems, but rather in helping them to define their options, however limited; take responsibility to reduce the stressors that are affecting them negatively; improve their handling of circumstances beyond their control; and define ways to advocate for a change of oppressive conditions.

Family therapists are also constantly challenged to redefine the roles and boundaries we were taught to observe during our training. Families may request assistance with issues that are not related to the presenting problem or planned session goals. Families may leave treatment without termination interviews, only to reappear after another crisis. This revolving-door phenomenon is typically perceived as treatment failure but potentially represents an opportunity to help families reach higher levels of functioning as they progress through the family life cycle. Larger service systems must be challenged to remove barriers to effective engagement and intervention, e.g. caseload assignment policies and scheduling flexibility (Hines, Richman, Hays, Maxim, 1989).

Conclusion

Stress in the lives of those living below the poverty threshold is unrelenting, and the likelihood is great that these families confront situations that are outside the experience of the professionals who attempt to serve as their life coaches. Admittedly, there is much for us to learn about how to assist families living in the context of poverty and racial discrimination *and* there is so much that could be done, given sufficient public and political will, to reduce the likelihood that families experience living with inadequate means. Even so, it is this author's contention that our current knowledge is sufficient to use family therapy as a tool that can help families. An Africentric-oriented family life cycle perspective, in particular, provides a useful framework for assessment and intervention, since it does not focus solely on the impact of context and external stresses but rather permits an understanding of how these exacerbate the stress of normal developmental needs and unresolved family issues. It encourages therapists to validate clients' experiences within a context of societal oppression while empowering them, in the spirit of their ancestors, to take whatever steps they can to counter the forces that would undo them.

While most attention has been given in the literature to families living in poverty who succumb to the related stressors with individual and family dysfunction, we would do well to turn more of our attention in family research to families who could be described as "bruised but not broken." It is these families who can give each other and therapists the hope that families living in poverty are not hopeless. They inform us about what is possible. It is they who remind us that "healing" for those who appear and feel defeated as well as those who carry invisible wounds must involve addressing their "poverty of spirit." It is they who remind us of a lesson consistent with African values: People are not defined by the situations they confront but by how they respond to the situation.

Chapter 7

Sexuality and the Life Cycle

Ellen Berman & David Wohlsifer

S exuality and gender are embedded in every aspect of human society and the family life cycle. Sexuality encompasses more than behavior in bed. It is part of our fundamental selves, brain and body, cognitions and beliefs, and our relationships with others. It is a critical part of couples' connection and bonding. Sexual/reproductive body changes mark the major points of adult development—puberty as part of the entry into adulthood, shared sexuality and pregnancy as the beginning of the new family, and menopause/shifting desire as a mark of aging. The interaction between the body's changes, and the individual and family's knowledge, experience, relationship, and culture make sexuality a highly complex and variable phenomenon. Because sexuality is at the root of marital bonding and reproduction, all cultures have a strong interest in patterning and controlling its expression to fit cultural norms.

The Biology of Sexuality

While sexuality is governed in many ways by feelings and beliefs, its basis is structured by biology. Three interconnected biobehavioral systems–sexual drive/desire, romantic love, and attachment, form the underpinnings of adult relational sexuality. These systems can be separated; for example, sexual drive is foremost in the one-night stand and attachment in the long married couple who have stopped sexual behavior. When romantic love, sexuality and attachment occur together they form one of the most deeply satisfying connections in life. The *experience of desire, romantic love, and attachment can occur at any point in the adult life cycle,* with both heterosexual and same-sex attachment bonds. Sexual desire and attachment behavior are seen in many mammals and birds, and our sexual biology has its underpinnings in mammalian bonding systems (Driscoll, 2008).

Drive/Desire

People vary enormously in their focus on and desire for sexual experience in the same way they vary in other appetites. Sexual drive is directly mediated by gonadal estrogens and androgens (for a review, see Regan & Berscheid, 1999) and at the physiological level can be altered by aging, medications, illness, and other body events. While biology forms the basis of drive, the willingness to feel and behave sexually is to a large extent under the control of psychological forces and influenced by cultural values.

It is possible to have high sex drive without acting on it, and it is possible to behave sexually in the absence of drive, especially for women. (We define "sexual behavior" as behavior in which one or both partners experience the behavior as arousing or erotically charged; orgasms usually occur but not always.) The crucial variables that shape tendencies to *behave* sexually are social situation, age, gender, and health (Laumann & Michael, 2001). While sexual wishes and fantasies may be impulsive and transgressive, sexual behaviors are highly controllable in the absence of alcohol, drugs, or certain forms of mental illness such as mania.

Sexual drive, and sexual pleasure, can occur with or without emotional connection for both men and women. Men have a higher involvement with nonrelational sexuality (as their use of sex workers and pornography indicate).

Romantic love

Romantic love is an intense focus on a specific other person, which usually includes desire. The experience of idealization of the other, intense, obsessional focus on that person, and deep wish for constant physical closeness, involve parts of the brain that determine pleasure and goal-directed activity, and involve endorphin release in the brain. (An excellent review of this research is Fishbane, 2007). Sexual chemistry is a complex blend of biology and belief systems and emotional responses (Leiblum & Brezsnyak, 2006). Choice of a romantic partner seems to involve a combination of pheromones, rational choice (partly influenced by cultural norms), and sexual scripts.

Romantic love is seen across all cultures and throughout history. Western culture demands it as a prerequisite for marriage. Some societies have tried to suppress it in favor of arranged marriages or family alliances (Hatfield & Rapson, 2006). It can occur at any point throughout the life cycle, from the 13-year-old's crush to the 80-year-old's love affair.

Romantic love accompanied by desire is one of the strongest emotional experiences known; one that can lead to acts of great bravery, but also, when it occurs outside of "acceptable" boundaries, to destroying a life structure or a family. To some extent it can be culturally repressed or encouraged, but its power remains a "wild card," which neither culture nor religion has been able to completely control.

Attachment

If a sexually active couple remains together, most commonly after a year or two the intensity of romantic love recedes. It alters to a more comfortable and less obsessional experience of an attachment bond, which is critical to long-term love relationships. This calmer experience is mediated by a biological shift in neurotransmitters in the brain and is usually referred to as companionate love (Fisher, 2004). Its characteristics are a deep friendship and sense of security, continued sexual interest, anxiety when the loved one is "off the radar," and long-term grief when the relationship ends. Within this bond, sex continues, but the quality of the sexual experience begins to depend on the emotional tone of the relational bond between the partners as much as biological drive. Sexual interest and desire with a long-term partner normally wax and wane over the life cycle depending on both family and individual transitions and stresses.

Attachment bonds are physical as well as psychological. In evolutionary theory, a biologically based adult attachment bond promotes family life by keeping parents together to raise children and pro- motes physical health by reducing stress. A break in the bond, from a loss or a death, deeply affects body processes, including immune system function.

Sexuality and Gender Across the Life Cycle

All societies structure and attempt to control sexual behavior, but there are large variations in what behavior is normative for each gender at each life stage. Sexuality is embedded in an almost universal cultural pattern that privileges men, and male sexuality, over women and female sexuality. The double standard stating that men need and should have sex, while women should not be sexual except in monogamous relationships, is still part of many cultures. When patriarchal thinking dominates a culture, virginity before marriage, and faithfulness after can determine a woman's worth in society. Men are expected to be sexually aggressive and experienced. The level of intimacy within the sexual experience, and expectation of women's pleasure, varies with the culture. For example in historical (and patriarchal) Chinese culture, men were expected to know how to please women sexually, while in Victorian U.S. culture, also patriarchal, a virtuous woman was not expected to experience pleasure. Past reproductive age, women may be ignored, in many cultures, and seen as wise (although asexual) in others.

In almost all cultures men have power over women, which is often expressed in sexual ways. Sexual harassment of women, rape, and violent pornography are still common. In more patriarchal cultures, women are often reduced to objects or property.

Nevertheless, women's ability to arouse desire and reject a man's advances, which is experienced as sexual power over men, is a powerful force in both men and women's lives. Fear of this power is one of the drivers of men's desire to control women. Men's shame and fear over being seen as inadequate, coupled with socialized entitlement, may produce anything from sexual dysfunction to violence. Women are mostly deeply confused about issues of gender and power, whether sexual power is acceptable to use, and whether any sexuality is safe to acknowledge.

In cultures where women cannot support themselves through work, sexuality is one, sometimes the only, possible source of financial safety. For young women, granting sexual favors for gifts or money, or "marrying up" have been ways of using sexual power. For older women this becomes less possible; remaining in marriage may be their only option. Older men may gain more sexual favors as they acquire money or status.

In societies where sexual desire is seen as acceptable for women, it is clear that women can have as much interest in and capacity for sexuality as men. (For an excellent review of gendered sexuality, see Kimmel, 2000). In the last 30 years, in the Western world, women have caught up with men in level of enjoyment, and to some extent in number of partners. A recent international study (Laumann et al., 2006) indicates that both men and women report the highest levels of sexual satisfaction in countries where men and women are considered equal. However, men reported higher levels of sexual satisfaction than women across cultures. There is some evidence that women's sexual arousal patterns are quite different from men's: less connected to drive and more to complex social motivation (Basson, 2000).

Sexuality, religion, class and culture, and family life interact in complex ways. While one may describe a culture in general terms as patriarchal or not, and sex-positive or not, careful exploration of religion, class, and multigenerational family background is required to understand an individual's specific sexual feelings and preferences. Historical and generational context are also important. For example, sexual norms in the United States were quite different in 1880 and 1930 from what they are in 2010, and people from the same family born in different generations may have very different beliefs, concerns, and backgrounds.

Sexuality Through the Life Cycle

The unattached young adult

Older adolescence and young adulthood, in this culture, are a time for exploring and developing one's sexuality. For most, sexual experience is a mark of finally becoming an adult. Some parents may attempt to avoid knowledge of their child's behavior or become overly invested in it. Early sexual patterns may be informed by three generational family sexual

scripts such as number of sexual partners, or the timing of romantic connections. In U.S. mainstream culture, with the average age of marriage 27 years old, most young adults have a variety of premarital sexual experiences (Kinsey Institute, n.d.). The broad media culture has become increasingly sexualized in recent years. The expectation of premarital chastity common in previous centuries has all but disappeared. However, the double standard still prevails, with men being admired and women censured for multiple sexual experiences.

Sexual experimentation often starts with concerns about the self (am I adequate? desirable? functional?), but over time it usually develops into a more relational experience. Relational sex involves elements of taking and giving, fusion and separateness, emotional vulnerability, and primitive wishes to be overwhelmed or to control. The experience of giving up control to another may be highly pleasurable, frightening, or both. The same sexual act may be perceived quite differently depending on personality and context. For example, one woman may experience a sense of power because her partner is highly aroused, while another, particularly if she has been sexually harassed or subjected to sexual abuse, may feel used or frightened. For some people, masturbation remains an easier choice than bringing one's vulnerable self to another person. For women, letting go of old beliefs and fears, and accepting and taking responsibility for one's pleasure so that sexuality may be freely enjoyed, may take many years. For many young men, sexuality is bound up with conquest rather than intimacy through much of young adulthood.

Women are still supposed to be the gatekeepers of sexuality, so men are seen as getting something or taking something when they have sex, and women as giving something up. Within this context, however, many private scenarios are possible. For example, a man who is powerful in the world may want to be dominant in bed, or may be a caring and nurturing lover, or may wish to be dominated or babied as a retreat from the outside world.

The issue of whether sex is acceptable when separate from affection in unmarried people of either gender is highly variable culturally. Alcohol or drug use, common during young adulthood, decreases intimacy, may increase sexually risky behavior with strangers in both sexes, and increases the chance of date rape or sexual abuse for women.

For some young adults, sexual experimentation can be difficult. Particularly for those who are socially anxious or have abuse histories or sexual dysfunction, dating can cause a series of painful experiences interspersed with long celibate periods. Unattached adults have less sex than monogamous couples, as it is not always easy to find willing partners.

Same-sex-oriented young adults face the additional life transition of coming out, along with the complexity of dealing with stigma and locating an appropriate community in which to find partners. Coming out to the family is stressful and may lead to a loss of some or all family ties. The fear of HIV has increased the anxiety around having casual sex for both same- and opposite-sex couples.

Conservative cultures and fundamentalist religious groups tend to strongly oppose premarital sex; some may encourage arranged marriages. Unmarried adults living within those groups have sex later and marry earlier. Young adults from these cultures, especially recent immigrants to Western countries that are more open sexually, are likely to have considerable intra-psychic and familial conflict if they adopt the sexual norms of their new culture. In sexually conservative cultures where men are supposed to be sexually experienced but women should remain virginal, there is usually a separate subculture of female sex workers, or women from a different social context,with whom sex is acceptable. These women tend to be powerless in the wider culture, and are often abused.

The new couple

Most unattached young people eventually fall in love and marry, or form committed relationships. For most, sexuality is a critical part of the choice to marry. Chastity prior to marriage is no guarantee of either sexual problems or bliss afterwards. The early years, particularly if there are no children, are often sexually intense. Sexual drive and sexual frequency is often high. Couples have enough time for experimenting and comfort touch to make sexuality easy. For many coupled people, self-pleasure remains an additional source of sexual stimulation.

The young couple's sexual life is not always functional or satisfactory. Many enter marriage with ongoing sexual problems, hoping that the situation will improve, or knowingly accepting an unsatisfactory sexual life for the sake of security. Some couples who had a well-functioning sexual relationship prior to marriage, find the idea of commitment frightening and begin shutting down or seeking extramarital affairs. Couples who have been living together may already find themselves past the intense romantic sexuality of the early relationship and into a calmer but less exciting experience. Couples may discover that they have differing preferences for types of sexual behaviors, or sexual frequency. Even happily married couples describe fairly frequent disagreements, with women having more complaints than men (Laumann, Michael, Gagnon, 1994). Issues may develop around who initiates sex, how much non-erotic contact is needed, and whether conflict inhibits sexuality. Relational difficulties may occur when a man wishes to be sexual in order to feel intimate, when his wife only wishes for sex when she already feels intimate from talking or nonsexual contact. Sexual dysfunctions, such as impotence or desire disorders, may develop around these issues and bring couples for treatment.

Same-sex partners may experience similar issues, based on differing levels of libido and intimacy needs. Lesbian couples may experience a lull in sexual activity as each waits for the other to initiate sex. Gay male couples are more likely to use a negotiated nonmonogamy contract as one possible solution to differing sexual needs.

Marriage and monogamy

Both sexual boredom and affairs can occur even in early marriage, seriously affecting the developmental tasks of this stage of family building. The earlier the affair, the more likely the marriage itself is problematic. The difficulties of maintaining desire and erotic sexuality within a long-term commitment, once the initial endorphin rush has worn off, has been the subject of recent books (Perel, 2006; Mitchell, 2002). They point out that for most people desire thrives on novelty and excitement, while security and attachment come from ritual, constancy, and a sense of safety. They suggest that while security is necessary, recognizing its fragility, and accepting that much of the partner is unknowable, allow the erotic back into life.

The tension between security and adventurousness in sexuality is a constant theme in couples, in individuals, and in cultural/religious strictures on sexual behavior. Romantic love and/or sexual behavior outside the pair bond carries the risks of seriously eroding the relationship. However, as the life span increases and marriages become longer, it becomes more likely that at least one partner will have a brief extracurricular experience, either emotional or sexual, at some point. A review of several studies indicates that somewhere between 30 and 60 percent of marriages in the United States will experience at least one affair (Atkins, Jacobson, & Baucom, 2001). This does not imply that such relationships are good for the marriage (although some do no harm, and some, in the short run, provide a kind of stabilization).

The attempt to mainstream "open marriage" in the 1970s was a failure, with most couples divorcing or closing the boundaries again within 5 years. Except for the rather small number of couples in swinging or polyamory subcultures, most heterosexual and lesbian couples will strive for sexual (and emotional) monogamy, although the tension of the forbidden will always be present. In some cultures, monogamy is only the obligation of the female partner.

Pornography use or cybersex is viewed by many partners to be an affair and an occasion for serious arguments over the definition of monogamy (Bergner and Bridges, 2002). However, viewing of pornographic material is acceptable to some partners, and occasional shared viewing may become part of their sexual experience.

The family with children at home

THE FAMILY WITH YOUNG CHILDREN The birth of the first child represents tremendous changes for the system. Several studies done in the United States indicate that marital happiness decreases after the birth of the first child, even if other forms of happiness do not (von Sydow, 1999). A baby greatly alters the experience of coupledom (Bitzer & Alder, 2000). Sleep deprivation, hormonal changes, emotional focus on the child, and redistribution of household tasks temporarily decrease sexual interest in most cases.

Pregnancy often changes the experience of sexuality. Sexual activity drops, particularly in the last trimester. Bitzer and Adler (2000) quoting

Ryding (1984) found that 3 months after birth, 40 percent of women still had little or no desire for sexual intercourse. If the mother is breastfeeding, she will generally experience vaginal dryness and loss of desire. Fathers may feel angry, depressed and sexually deprived. Particularly if the father is resentful or unhelpful, long-term sexual problems may begin at this time, as well as cross-generational alliances between mother and child.

Most commonly, sexual activity resumes within a few months. The experience of sexuality often deepens with the sense of connection that parenthood brings. However, as the child grows, and as additional children enter the family, parents must find time for sexual pleasure while dealing with the demands of small people who need constant physical and emotional care (**Genogram 7.1**).

Jen a 38-year-old-Jewish dental hygienist of Eastern European descent, and Bill, a 40-year-old small businessman of Anglo Episcopalian background, began therapy after 8 years of marriage. Prior to having their son Ian, now 3, both agreed they had a very happy sexual and marital relationship. After 4 years of marriage, they decided to have a family. The pregnancy was somewhat difficult and Jen's interest in sex decreased.

Following Ian's birth, Bill felt frustrated and jealous. When Jen's OBGYN said that sex was possible after 6 weeks, Bill hoped that things would finally get back to normal. However, Jen was preoccupied with Ian, and nursing, and felt that her body "had enough contact" by the time she saw Bill. He began pushing her for sex and feeling angry at being rejected.

Jen was highly sensitive to anger and had married Bill because he felt "so calm and mellow." She withdrew emotionally in the face of his anger, and was less willing to be sexual because she felt coerced instead of loved. Bill's response was to become more irritable; after a while, he withdrew into work. Three years later sex was still infrequent and unsatisfactory, and he began flirting with a coworker. Finally they decided to see a therapist.

The therapist began with a genogram that reviewed issues of gender, sex, parenting, and love, done with both partners present. Jen's mother, Reah, and her father, Harry, had an angry and difficult relationship. Both had grown up poor, and their frustrations about money led to bitter quarrels, which eroded their connection with each other. Reah

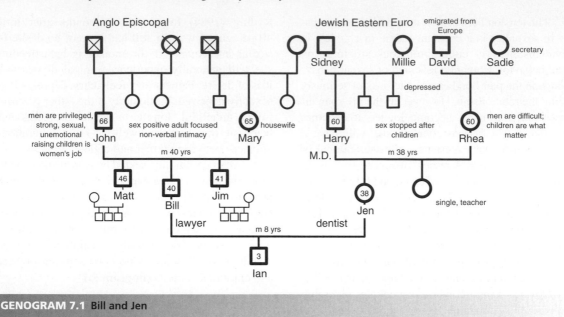

GENOGRAM 7.1 Bill and Jen

had been frightened of her own father, David, and between her anger at her father and her husband, passed on to Jen a fear of closeness. Jen saw little affection between her parents, who were sleeping in separate rooms by the time she left home for college. Marrying Bill, who was "other" in so many ways, allowed Jen to separate from her family experiences and enjoy her own sexuality.

Bill's home was very male centric. He was one of three brothers, and his father dominated the home. Bill felt that he had little emotional contact with his mother, although she was physically present. He had little sense of his parents' sexual life but assumed their relationship was positive. Children were expected to accommodate to the adults. As his father had paid attention to the boys only as they grew older, he had no idea how to enter the tight bond between mother and baby or to easily parent his infant son.

Bill's background made it hard for him to talk about negative feelings when he felt vulnerable, and also made him feel entitled to sex as a prerogative of marriage. His wife's changed response to his sexual overtures frightened and confused him, but he had little experience in talking about such feelings. His increasingly coercive requests for sex were, at base, an attempt to regain the intimacy they had had; when this failed, he gave up.

The therapist reminded them that their experience during pregnancy and the early months of child-rearing were normal, and that many couples did not resume much sexual contact until nursing ended. However she used the genogram to help them see that the transition to a triad had reactivated old family patterns of male–female distancing, so that they had developed a pattern of mutual avoidance and distrust. As they talked through their differences, Bill was able to find ways to feel like a man that still allowed for child care, attention to feelings, and acceptance that Jen might not always want an erotic experience. He was able to be loving and seductive instead of angry. Jen realized that she did not have to follow her mother's path or give up her sexuality. Their sexual life resumed over time, as they developed ways to find couple time in their new triad and pushed themselves to keep talking.

Couples with children have to adjust to a dyad becoming a triad, probably the major family life cycle transition of adulthood. The meaning of the shifts is altered by expectations of family and cultural background. Typically in Jewish families the children are the focus of family life, a pattern exacerbated in Jen's family by parental conflict. In Bill's background the children are less the focus of the family. His expectation that things should not change between him and Jen, and his inability to participate happily in the increased work of child care, frustrated and confused Jen. As Bill's anger over sex had been the flashpoint of the arguments, sex was the hardest area to regain as they began to reconnect. In more patriarchal cultures the couple might simply assume that sex would decrease, and the man might seek sex elsewhere; or the man might insist on sex without worrying about whether his wife was interested or not. In a culture that expects high intimacy and an egalitarian approach to family life, the changes required are large indeed.

Childhood development of the sexual self in a family context The child's sexual development begins within the family system. Body awareness develops early in childhood from the touch of parents and other caretakers, self-stimulation, and internal drive. Early experiences with comfort touch, prohibition or acceptance of behaviors such as masturbation, and comments overheard about gender and sexuality from parents and others form much of the basis for children's relationship to their bodies. Parental comfort or anxiety about sexuality, sometimes handed down from the grandparent generation, is absorbed early in life.

Children's direct engagement with their bodies and interest in sexuality forces parents to examine their own sexual values, feelings, beliefs, and practices. When these values conflict with those of grandparents or other relatives or with school or the religious community, problems can develop.

Children may experience romantic crushes as early as 6 or 7, although they are not sexual in any adult sense. Interest in sexuality continues through school age and increases just before puberty. As the child grows, more information about the details of sexuality (both accurate and not) and the cultural norms surrounding it are learned from peers and the media.

People develop "erotic tastes" before puberty, which influence what acts as well as what partners are arousing to them; this may evolve with age. While to some extent they are determined by parental influence, a variety of biological and learned influences are in play. The term *lovemaps* coined by psychologist/sexologist Jon Money (1986) refers to the concept that we have a template in the mind and brain of the ideal lover, as well as an ideal script

of sexual and erotic activity. Lovemaps are deeply embedded in a person's early dynamics, which may be at odds with their cultural scripts.

Questions about issues such as sexual orientation and gender identity often arise before puberty. Children who experience a first crush on a person of the same sex may experience a sense of "difference" and shame. Children who have difficulty conforming to culturally prescribed gender roles may face bullying and harassment from peers and adults.

Although it is advisable for parents to begin discussing sexual issues with their children prior to puberty, many avoid the subject until after the young person has obtained information from peers or the Internet, and adolescent embarrassment makes it impossible to talk. Parents should look for teachable moments and age-appropriate information as the child is developing. *www.familiesaretalking.org/resources/rsrc0005.html* suggests resources for parents on this topic.

It is also necessary for parents to develop and promote sexual boundaries in the home and family while establishing supportive communication lines about sexual issues. Boundaries around adult sexual behavior and eroticism are necessary so that children do not become overwhelmed by adult sexuality. Keeping the bedroom door closed for privacy (literally and figuratively) helps to keep a separate place and time for adult sexuality. When parents expose children to sexually inappropriate behavior either by flaunting their own sexuality, constant sexual talk, or showing excessive interest in the child's body, the children may develop either sexual avoidance or promiscuous sexuality.

Parents must face their children's sexual vulnerability to both strangers and family members and teach them about sexual boundaries, for example by instructing them on "good touch, bad touch." Children are vulnerable to sexual abuse; recent statistics indicate that child sexual abuse affects 10 to 25 percent of girls and 5 to 10 percent of boys worldwide (The Kinsey Institute, n.d.). However, since the majority of incidences of sexual abuse go unreported, it can be assumed that these figures are significantly higher. Sexual abuse of both male and female children is generally perpetrated by males, sometimes family members, at any point in the life cycle—older brothers, fathers or uncles, grandfathers. Scars from child sex abuse are commonly carried throughout life, impacting the way in which survivors function sexually and generally in life (Teicher, 2002). Girls and boys with abuse histories may later develop sexual avoidance or dysfunction, or, alternatively, become hypersexual without regard to their own welfare. Many, however, later find kind partners and develop comfort with sexuality. Boys may question their sexual orientation, particularly if the experience was arousing. Both may experience symptoms of post traumatic stress during adult sexuality if certain sexual activities trigger abuse memories.

Internet pornography viewing is both a parenting and a couple issue. Preadolescent children have a strong interest in sexuality and can easily find pornography on the Internet. The average age of exposure to Internet pornography is now 11 years old (Maltz, 2009).

The couple also may be in conflict about pornography. While in small doses it can increase sexual interest, very frequent use, especially in secret, tends to negatively impact close sexual relationships. Between 8 and 15 percent of regular Internet pornography users admit to developing compulsive sexual behaviors (Maltz, 2009). In adulthood, 75 to 85 percent of Internet porn site users are male; almost 50 percent are married (Maltz, 2009).

Given the differences of gender, birth order, temperament, biology, and family stress faced by sibs in the same family, no two siblings are likely to arrive at adulthood with exactly the same set of sexual preferences and issues. It is reasonable to say, however, that sex-positive attitudes in the family are more likely to produce adults comfortable with their sexuality, while experiences of shaming, abuse, violence, avoidance of touch in the family, and inappropriate boundaries are more likely to produce problems, sometimes severe. General cultural patterns of sexual repression or avoidance will not always produce sexual dysfunction but are likely to increase the incidence of shame and ignorance.

THE FAMILY WITH ADOLESCENT CHILDREN The hormone shift of puberty covers a period of about 2 years during which both bodies and brains change dramatically. By that time, sexual scripts, beliefs about sexuality, and a sense of comfort or discomfort with the body are already partly in place.

The emerging sexuality of the adolescent is often difficult for parents and is complicated by an age gap in sexual knowledge and beliefs as well as the complexity of current adolescent culture. Even the basic discussion of "what is sex" can be confusing. For example, the term "virginity" appears to be continually morphing in the United States among adolescents. One study of late teens in the United States indicated that while most (99.5 percent) considered penile–vaginal intercourse to be "having sex," more than half of them (60 percent) did not think oral–genital contact constituted having sex (Bersamin, Fisher, Walker, Hill, & Grube, 2007). Parents may disagree with each other strongly on issues of permissiveness around such sexually charged issues as curfew, clothing, and dating practices. These may form the basis of serious parental or parent–child power struggles. If parents had major struggles with their own parents, or a history of alcoholism, sexual acting out, pregnancy, or rape, they are likely to become increasingly anxious as their adolescents reach the age when they themselves had problems. Pregnancy, or the coming out of a gay child, may throw the family's three-generational system into an uproar.

Adolescent sexual development itself goes through stages. Puberty in girls typically begins between 9 and 13 years of age, and for boys between 10 and 14 (Mass General Children's Hospital, n.d.). Early maturation is socially advantageous for boys, who become more popular with peers. It is generally a disadvantage for girls, who may be treated as sexual beings far in advance of their emotional maturation (Lamb, 2006). Early adolescent sexual experience is often about proving the self. Older adolescents are more likely to see sexuality as a relational process.

As the sexual hormones increase, teenagers often develop intense romantic feelings for others, which may remain private or develop into relationships. While they are often brief, and are usually called crushes or infatuations, these are some of the most powerful emotions remembered later in life.

Gender and culture have the strongest influence on first sexual experiences (Upchurch, Levy-Storms, Sucoff, & Aneshensel, 1998). Adolescents from ethnic and religious groups with a strong emphasis on virginity tend to have their first inter-course at a later age (Bearman & Brueckner, 2001). Culturally based rules and restrictions around sexu-ality and actual sexual behavior among adolescents are often in conflict. In Latino families, adolescents, and girls in particular, have strong social control placed on sexual behaviors, but the combined im-pact of poverty and racism still may produce early sexual experimentation (Falicov, 1999). Asian cul-tures in general are patriarchal and encourage later experimentation, but younger Asians who are more Westernized may have a different point of view. African American adolescents in urban, poor areas may have a strong peer culture of early sexuality coupled with hopelessness about the future, which often results in early pregnancy, while adolescents in other African American communities are more likely to wait. Teens living in single-parent house-holds are likely to begin sexual intercourse before those living in two-parent families (Bearman & Brueckner, 2001).

The context and meaning of the sexual experi-ence is the key to understanding adolescent sexual behavior. Although good research data are not avail-able, it appears that sexual experience after the age of 16 or 17 years of age, if it develops in the context of a loving relationship, does not interfere with fur-ther sexual development. Throughout history, in many countries, marriage and pregnancy by 17 or 18 has been considered normative and acceptable. Unfortunately, teen sexual experiences can also re-sult in pregnancy, exploitation, or abandonment. Traumatic sexual experiences, especially rape, may leave lifelong scars that reverberate into the next generation. This is particularly true if parents, also traumatized and not knowing how to handle the situ-ation, do not support their child.

A rural Mexican family legally emigrated to the United States, moving into a poor urban neighborhood. A year later, their 12-year-old daughter, Lena, was raped by neigh-borhood adolescents. Not yet fluent in English, distrustful of the police, and ashamed that this had happened, the parents refused to talk to anyone about the rape, including their daughter. Both sets of grandparents were Catholic, and sex-uality was something that was not discussed in either family, so her parents felt they could not turn to them for help.

Lena grew up feeling bad about her body, responsi-ble for the rape, ashamed of her sexuality, and very angry with her parents. She became increasingly rebellious, skip-ping school, and acting out sexually, against her family and community norms. She became pregnant at 15, and chose to keep the baby, believing that "who wants to have sex with a pregnant lady or someone's mom, I am finally safe." Lena married at 23. She was able to have satisfactory sex with her husband, but she still experienced anxiety and occasional flashbacks to the rape if he would touch her "too quickly." Her husband adopted her daughter, Maria, but was never told about the rape.

When Maria turned 12, Lena became extremely anxious about her child's developing sexuality and refused to talk about sex, allow her to wear makeup, or go any-place that might be unsafe. This increased tension between mother and daughter. At 12, Maria understood this to mean that sex was dangerous and should be avoided. She had a sense that there was a sexual secret but was unable to discuss it. At 15 she rebelled, and became sexually active, although she had little desire and found it anxiety produc-ing. A tradition of silence plus sexual trauma resulted in sexual difficulties in two generations.

Issues of culture, religion, familial back-ground, and ethnicity have a great impact on how families discuss and approach sexual issues (McGoldrick, Loonan, & Wohlsifer 2005). Parents of adolescents should, but do not always, discuss issues such as the need for respect and trust in sexu-al relationships, birth control, abortion, sexually transmitted diseases and sexual assault, and appro-priate sexual conduct. This can be especially chal-lenging for couples if they disagree on these issues. Parents are more likely to warn girls of danger but not discuss sexual pleasure.

Many heterosexually oriented young people experiment with gender-bending presentation or same-sex sexual contact or during adolescence. Those with a bisexual or homosexual orientation need to develop a positive identity over time. When the family and school culture are more inclusive, the process may occur earlier and with less stress.

The Internet is a particularly confusing issue for adolescents and parents. Almost impossible to escape, it allows access to information, including sexual information, that can be beneficial. However, adolescents are vulnerable to an array of sexual media, partners, discussions, and perpetrators, of which parents are often unaware. Because of a major generation gap, it is critical for parents to seek support from peers, schools, and therapists in dealing with this rapidly changing phenomenon.

Parents of adolescents are often in a parallel process of change themselves, evaluating their bodies, their relationships, and what they want for the future (Garcia Preto, 2005). For many couples, sexuality is improved by having more private couple time as children become involved in their own lives and activities. For other couples, sexual boredom and emptiness may lead to affairs, divorce, or a determination to improve their relationship. Some parents reexamine their sexual and/or gender orientation and come out as lesbian, gay, bisexual, and/or transgender when they believe the children are old enough to understand or deal with it.

Single parents may be particularly aware of the contrast between their own and their adolescent child's sexuality. It may be a reminder of what they are missing, or a message that they will soon be alone. For those who are dating, other difficulties arise, particularly if they are dating while their children are not.

Marilyn is a 40-year-old African American, divorced teacher who entered therapy wondering if she was depressed. Marilyn's mother, who she had depended on, had died recently, and she was only close to one sister; her relationships with her father and her ex- were friendly but distant.

Marilyn's family had been comfortable with sexuality, but there had been multiple divorces in the immediate family, including her own parents.

Marilyn and her husband John divorced when their son Steven was 10. The marriage had been good sexually but was stressed in other ways. After the divorce Marilyn decided that sex did more harm than good, and deliberately shut down her sense of desire and her sexual self. She had primary custody of Steven, now a well-behaved 16-year-old sophomore in high school.

At the second session she reported that while doing laundry, she had found an opened condom wrapper in the pocket of Steven's pants. She phoned John who laughed and said, "It's about time."

Marilyn saw that they were in a new part of the family life cycle. Her son would be leaving in 2 years, her mother had died, and she would be living alone. She need-

ed to talk to Steven more about his life and to prepare for the next phase of hers.

Steven had been sexually active for a few months with a steady girlfriend his own age. He had begun the later adolescent task of discovering sex as part of an ongoing romantic relationship, and was feeling competent as a man.

Marilyn and her therapist reviewed her family's views about men, commitment, and sexuality, using the genogram as a starting point. She decided to allow herself to be sexual again, even if the relationships were not permanent.

Steven felt protective of her but was uncomfortable with meeting her dates and asked her not to bring them home. Marilyn and Steven were able to talk about sexual values, birth control, and respect for the partner and also respect for their own relationship as mother and son. Eventually she found a man with whom she experienced both romantic feelings and desire. They are discussing moving in together when Steven leaves home.

Couples from 40 to 65—with or without children at home

The couple issues of midlife sexuality are in many ways separate from the child-focused life cycle. For the later phases of midlife, both married and single people usually live without children at home, unless they have started families late in the life stage. Sexuality in midlife is part of an individual's rethinking of the self as a person who is no longer young but not yet old. Internally, sexuality is experienced as a youthful activity, and the need to see oneself as vital sexually may prompt marital changes or an affair.

This life stage has changed dramatically in the past 30 years, at least for the middle class, as exercise, nutrition, and improved medical care have produced a generation of fit, energetic adults. Divorce, remarriage, medications to treat erectile dysfunction, and new reproductive technologies have also drastically altered the sexual landscape for midlife couples.

PHYSICAL ISSUES OF MIDLIFE Sexual function commonly continues throughout midlife, in individuals and in couples not exhausted by circumstance or a difficult marriage. A multiethnic study of midlife women indicated that 79 percent had had sexual contact in the preceding 6 months and that most considered sex very important (Cain, et al., 2003). For long-married couples there may be a sense of sexual freedom and enjoyment missing earlier in life. The sexuality of midlife couples is patterned and driven by their history as much as by their biological drive. However, desire slowly decreases over time, and physical changes still occur in midlife and beyond that alter sexual functioning in significant ways. Accepting the changes of midlife and finding pleasure in sexuality that may lack some of the intensity of earlier years is integral to this phase of the life cycle.

In long married couples, affairs may occur in early midlife as a response to fear of aging, as a way of regaining sexual intensity. Newly married couples may find themselves alive to sex in a way they have not been previously. Some couples discontinue active sexual behavior without obvious marital problems in later midlife.

FEMALE SEXUAL FUNCTIONING The average age at menopause (defined as a year since the last period) is 52, although changes in the menstrual cycle begin years earlier. The end of reproductive life is a complex experience of relabeling the self and rethinking what it means to be female and sexual. As the body's cycling becomes more irregular, sexual desire may vary. In the postmenopausal period, decreased lubrication may produce painful intercourse. Psychologically changes also occur due to the end of the possibility of pregnancy. Some women become sexually freer; others experience a shutting down and lack of interest in sexual experience.

MALE SEXUAL FUNCTIONING For most men, the ability to develop an erection regardless of circumstances begins to decrease with age. Approximately 40 percent of middle-aged men experience some degree of periodic erectile dysfunction (ED). By age 70 approximately 67 percent experience mild to severe ED (Hillman, 2008). Most erectile dysfunction in older men is caused by decreased blood flow to the penis, due to physical problems such as hypertension, diabetes, or early heart disease. Fatigue, performance anxiety, or relationship problems also cause ED and are more likely to do so in physiologically vulnerable men. Since 1998, medications have been available to enhance erectile functioning.

Viagra™, Cialis™, and Levitra™ all increase blood flow in the penis in response to sexual stimulation, resulting in a stronger erection. Men have always sought solutions to erectile difficulties (and paid well for them), and these drugs are widely prescribed and used both for treatment of ED and for recreational sex. They do not increase desire, although frequently the decrease in performance anxiety increases desire. A drug has not yet been found that will consistently increase female sexual desire or orgasm.

These medications have solved some problems (Rosen, 2006), but caused others. Many men are given these medications by their doctors without consultation with wives or partners. Their partners may believe the use of such medications means "he is less attracted to me," or may be unhappy with their husbands' regained sexuality. The medication clearly does not solve relationship problems—even if it does work, an angry or withdrawn husband may stop using it, or a wife may turn away.

NEWLY SINGLE AT MIDLIFE Developing a sexual life when newly single at midlife is different for men and women. Men have a larger "pool" of available women, both younger and older, to date. Men remarry more quickly and often to women considerably younger (Goode, 1993). Many men do not leave a marriage until they are already in another relationship, and for them, there is very little "single" time. Cultural expectations that women tend to date same age or older men, produce a smaller dating pool, although women have a broader friendship network. Women over 40 who remarry typically do so more slowly, and have a lower rate of remarriage. Both men and women may discover their sexual selves for the first time in midlife dating. Some women find themselves without sexual partners for long periods; some turn off their sexuality.

Sexuality in later life

People are living longer, healthier lives and are doing so as sexual beings. As we age the need for approval and comfort touch does not decrease. While energy and sexuality tend to slowly wane over time, many people are still highly physically active at 80 and sexual into their 80s and 90s (Hillman, 2008). In older age sexual behavior is likely to be less intercourse focused, but a majority of people still enjoy touching, embracing, and kissing (Ginsberg, Pomerantz, & Kramer-Feely, 2005). Sexual behavior provides a sense of aliveness and connection.

As parents and grandparents, older adults send powerful messages down the generations about whether sexuality is acceptable and joyful or dangerous and bad. Grandparents who are able to model respect for, and pleasure in, sexuality provide a powerful buffer against parental anxiety as the grandchildren begin to experiment sexually.

There is still a great deal of stigma in the United States against sexuality in older people, who are expected to retire quietly and are not seen as worthy of respect.

John and Mary, a conflict-avoiding Quaker couple in their 70s, entered treatment because Mary was still furious over John's multiple affairs in midlife, and her anger had been retriggered by his recent behavior flirting with a colleague at work. In response, she refused to have sex with him, although they both felt desire and were deeply attached to each other. The therapist reviewed their life history, encouraged Mary to express her feelings, discussed what John might do to make amends, and wondered with them if they wished to reconnect physically. John was able to listen without defensiveness, agreed he had been flirting, and said that it made him feel attractive and "less old," but his heart was with his wife and his marriage. Eventually they resumed sexual activity, including intercourse. The therapist, who was in her early 40s, noted that she frequently found herself surprised and uncomfortable discussing affairs and sexuality with a couple "that old."

Significant disability and/or illness and death of a partner are the primary reasons people stop having sex in old age. Because women on average live longer than men, the over-70 population is primarily a society of women. However therapists should not assume that just because a person reaches a certain age, has lost a life partner, or has decreased physical and even cognitive abilities, he or she is no longer feels sexual. As one 87-year-old, homebound, widowed African American woman told her social worker, "I think I miss the company of a man. I might be old but I still got the hunger for men, always had it, always will."

Long-term care facilities are making efforts in their policies and practices across the country to ensure the privacy and space for residents to be sexual and are providing training to decrease the stigma that staff and families may have around issues of sexuality and the elderly (Sisk, 2006).

Conclusion

Sexuality is a highly complex mix of biology, culture, psychology, and system functioning, which is one of the key dimensions of family life throughout the life cycle. Sexual interest, behavior, and physical abilities change in many ways over a lifetime, and it is not possible to treat sexual problems without an understanding of the person's point in the life cycle. Whether or not people present with sexual problems, it is critical to routinely inquire into the issues of gender, love and sexuality at all ages, in order to understand the families that we treat.

Chapter 8

Lesbian, Gay, Bisexual, and Transgender Individuals and the Family Life Cycle

Deidre Ashton

Introduction

Lesbian, Gay, Bisexual, and Transgender (LGBT) people have been members of families of origin, families of choice, and families of creation throughout history. Prior to the spread of homophobia through Western colonialism, same-sex relationships were socially accepted and well-integrated into family structures in many cultures throughout the world (Williams, 1998). The contemporary LGBT civil rights movement marked by the Stonewall rebellion of 1969 has vigorously fought for the legal rights of LGBT people as individuals entitled to fair and just treatment in all areas of life including employment, housing, education, health care, marriage equality, and creation of family. Prior to the efforts of the LGBT civil rights movement, LGBT people were frequently portrayed as single adults, ostracized from their families of origin, incapable of establishing lasting partnerships, unfit to raise children, and relegated to residing in the "gay ghettos" of major urban cities. Although there is still much work to be done, the LGBT civil rights movement has made significant strides in establishing and protecting the rights of LGBT people to couple, have children, and be recognized as healthy, productive, moral, and lawful members of families, communities, and society.

This chapter focuses on how people who are LGBT move through the family life cycle as members of families of origin, families of choice, and heads of families. It builds on the excellent framework and insights of Tom Johnson and Pat Colucci's chapter "Lesbians, Gay Men, and the Family Life Cycle" (2005) in the previous edition of this book. The reader will be oriented to the life cycle discussion through clarification of language and terminology, a review of the current legal status of LGBT families, conceptualization of LGBT individuals and families as multicultural people, and a review of models of LGBT identity formation.

After clarifying language and terms, I will discuss the decision to present LGBT people in the family life cycle in one chapter. The need for clarification of language is related to the generally accepted rigid, narrow, and erroneous construction of gender and sexual identity as biologically determined. The dominant culture holds the belief that biological sex determines gender identity, gender identity determines gender role, and gender role determines sexual orientation (Lev, 2004). Lesbian, gay, and bisexual are categories of sexual orientation or identity (Lev, 2004; Mallon, 2008a; Savin-Williams, 1996). LGB may be the self-selected terms that represent the individual's sexual orientation, the direction of sexual, affectional, and emotional attraction (Lev, 2004; Mallon, 2008a; Savin-Williams, 1996). Thus, individuals of LGB orientation may have various sexual identities, gender identities, or gender role expressions. For others, LGB may also be the self-selected terms that reflect sexual identity or the individual's sense of sexuality that integrates biological sex, gender identity, gender role expression, and sexual orientation (Lev, 2004). Among individuals who claim their sexual identity as LGB there may be variation in biological sex, gender identity, and gender role expression. Transgender or gender-variant may be the self-selected

115

terms that reflect experiences of gender identity that fall outside of the dominant culture, biologically determined bipolar gender system (Lev, 2004). Among transgender or gender-variant individuals there may be variation in sexual orientation, sexual identity, and gender role expression. In this chapter, the terms lesbian, gay, and bisexual reflect sexual orientation or identity and the terms gender-variant and transgender reflect gender identity.

If "LGB" references sexual identity or orientation, and "T" references gender identity, it may seem that we are conflating aspects of identity that are simultaneously related and different by discussing LGBT people as one group in the family life cycle. The reasons for presenting LGBT people in one chapter are fourfold: 1) although separate constructs, sexual identity, sexual orientation, gender identity, and gender role are interrelated; 2) LGBT people share in common the experience of transcending the limiting dominant social construction of sexuality and gender identity and thus share histories of marginalization; 3) LGBT people have all been marginalized in the discussion of families, and 4) bisexual and transgender people are often made invisible in the literature and in the LGBT communities. However, it is critical to acknowledge that while similarities exist, the experiences of these four groups are not identical, and thus there will be variations in family life cycle issues. This chapter serves as an overview introducing the reader to LGBT experiences in the family life cycle. The reader is encouraged to study each group seperately to cultivate a more nuanced understanding of LGBT people and their families.

Current Status of LGBT Families in the United States

Because marrying, coupling, having biological children, and adopting or fostering children are the ways in which families are created, examination of the laws relating to LGBT families is part of understanding the climate in which LGBT-headed families develop and thrive. The LGBT civil rights movement has made great strides in legitimizing and legalizing the created families of LGBT communities by advancing and pursuing the legalization of gay

marriage and adoption of children by LG individuals and couples. However, while gains have been made there is still a long way to go.

Access to marriage

According to the National Gay and Lesbian Task Force ([NGLTF], 2009a), as of this writing, the states of Iowa, Vermont, New Hampshire, Massachusetts, and Connecticut have legalized gay marriage granting full marriage equality to same-sex couples. Washington, Oregon, California, Nevada, New Jersey, and the District of Columbia (DC) have broad relationship laws that recognize civil unions and domestic partnerships between same-sex couples. Hawaii, Colorado, Wisconsin, and Maryland have limited relationship recognition laws, and New York and DC recognize same-sex marriages performed in other states. The federal government and the majority of states have either outlawed same-sex marriage or have other legal prohibitions against same-sex commitments (NGLTF, 2009b). Additionally, the federal government does not recognize same-sex marriages performed in states where it is legal and denies to these couples the more than 1,000 federal benefits afforded to heterosexual married couples (NGLTF, 2009a). Bisexual people seeking to marry a same-sex partner will be subject to laws applicable to LG couples, and bisexual people seeking to marry the opposite sex will be subject to the laws that regulate opposite-sex marriage.

According to the American Civil Liberties Union Lesbian, Gay, Bisexual, Transgender and AIDS Project ([ACLU-LGBT], 2009), the marriage of an individual who transitions from one sex to another via hormone therapy and sex reassignment surgery remains valid. However, because of transphobia and discrimination, the couple may experience difficulties when attempting to access or utilize federal, employer, health care, and other benefits granted by marriage. In California, New Jersey, and Maryland access to marriage is based on the postsurgical sex of the transitioning partner (e.g., a male to female (MTF) transsexual can marry a natal male). Courts in Florida, Kansas, New York, Ohio, and Texas have ruled that access to marriage is granted based on the natal sex of each partner. Therefore an MTF transsexual can only marry a natal female, and a female to male (FTM) transsexual can only marry a natal male. The question of access to marriage for gender-variant individuals appears irrelevant in states where both opposite-sex and same-sex marriage are legal.

Family creation

LGBT individuals and couples seek to create family by having, formally or informally adopting, or fostering children. Some individuals or couples may have children from prior relationships. When a couple decides to have a biological child, the nonblood-related parent must establish parental rights through adoption or parentage judgment (The National Center for Lesbian Rights [NCLR], 2009). California, Colorado, Connecticut, DC, Illinois, Indiana, Iowa, Maine, Massachusetts, New Hampshire, New Jersey, New York, Oregon, Pennsylvania, and Vermont allow same-sex couples to adopt through civil union, domestic partner, or second-parent adoption. Alabama, Alaska, Delaware, Hawaii, Louisiana, Maryland, Michigan, Minnesota, Nevada, New Mexico, Rhode Island, Texas, Washington, and West Virginia allow local counties and jurisdictions to make adoption decisions. Florida prohibits adoption by LG individuals or couples. Mississippi prohibits adoption by same-sex couples, and Utah prohibits adoption by all co-habiting, unmarried people. Arkansas goes one step further than Utah's law and also prohibits co-habiting unmarried individuals from acting as foster parents. Courts in Kentucky, Nebraska, Ohio, and Wisconsin have ruled that current adoptions statutes do not permit second-parent adoptions by unmarried heterosexual or same-sex couples (NCLR, 2009). The federal government appears far more protective of parent–child relationships than couple relationships as federal law mandates that all states and jurisdictions recognize second-parent adoptions regardless of local law (NCLR, 2009).

Currently, there are no laws protecting parenting rights of gender-variant individuals (ACLU-LGBT, 2009). In some divorce and custody proceedings, courts have ruled against gender-variant parents regarding custody because of their transgender identity (ACLU-LGBT, 2009). In contrast, courts in Colorado, Minnesota, and Nevada have found that

transgender identity is not harmful to child development; but this ruling falls short of acknowledging that gender identity is not relevant to parenting ability as evidenced by emerging research (Mallon, 2008b).

Despite limited legal recognition and legal protection, LGBT families continue to grow and thrive even at the margins. On a daily basis, LGBT individuals, families, and communities demonstrate their resilience in the face of legally sanctioned oppression and defy myth and rhetoric that they are antithetical to family values. Acceptance of LGBT individuals and their families is increasing as evidenced by changing laws as well as increasing visibility in scholarly literature and more realistic representation in the popular media (e.g., cable network programs increasingly reflect the experiences of LGBT communities).

Diversity Among LGBT Families

LG individuals have been characterized as bicultural because they have been raised in the heterocentrism of the dominant culture (Laird 1993; Lukes and Land, 1990), but, in fact, LGBT individuals are multicultural as they are also members of various racial, ethnic, and religious groups, as well as social classes. Cole (2009, p. 179) states that

> . . . . *gender, race, class, and sexuality simultaneously affect the perceptions, experiences, and opportunities of everyone living in a society stratified along these dimensions. To understand any one of these dimensions, psychologists must address them in combination . . . To focus on a single dimension in the service of parsimony is a kind of false dimension.*

The intersection of multiple aspects of identity creates richness and texture in one's life and in the world. Occupation of multiple marginalized identities also means that LGBT people will experience the powerful interactive effects of other forms of oppression along with heterosexism, homo-, bi-, and transphobias (Walters and Old Person, 2008). The interactive effects of multiple forms of oppression are greater than the additive effects as the whole is greater than the sum of its parts (Bowleg, 2008).

Multiculturalism and intersectionality are the lenses through which LGBT people in the family life cycle will be viewed.

Although integration of the multiple aspects of identity and active participation in each reference group may be optimal, many LGBT people of color are challenged to choose allegiance to either the White, eurocentric LGBT community or their hetero-centric racial/ethnic community. They must decide whether to seek protection from the heterosexism and homo-, trans- and biphobia of the dominant culture and their racial/ethnic group or to seek sanctuary from the racism of the dominant culture and the White, eu-rocentric LGBT communities. Audre Lorde (as cited in Walters and Old Person, 2008) attributes this dilem-ma to "a colonized mentality." Choosing allegiance to the White LGBT community could result in the loss of support of the racial or ethnic community that has been present throughout the life course. Choosing al-legiance to the heterocentric ethnic/racial community could result in the loss of the burgeoning support of the White LGBT communities. Walters and Old Per-son (2008) make it clear that the racism of White LGBT communities goes further in maintaining white-skin, heterosexual, male privilege, and that the heterosexism of communities of color has no benefit for those communities. The heterosexism of commu-nities of color is understood as a survival strategy, as homosexuality can be mistakenly seen as a challenge to the survival of the race (Greene, 1998; Walters and Old Person, 2008). Bisexuality and transgenderism appear to be seen similarly within communities of color. These loyalty binds can intensify identity devel-opment tasks and add more complexity to the process-es and tasks of each stage of the family life cycle for individuals and their families. However, membership in multiple reference groups can also be a source of support, strength, and creativity in overcoming adver-sity and leading a rich and fulfilling life.

Models of LGBT Identity Development

Familiarity with LGBT identity development models is beneficial to a discussion of the family life cycle as the family is the context in which identity devel-opment takes place and the tasks and processes of

LGBT identity development interact with those of the family life cycle. LGBT identity development can begin at any age and at any stage of individual or family life cycle development. It occurs along with, or in the context of, other aspects of identity development such as race or ethnicity (Bowleg, Burkholder, Teti, & Craig 2008; Lev, 2004; Walters and Old Person, 2008). Some people become aware of their LGBT identity at an early age; for others awareness emerges at later stages in life (Connolly 2004a; Herdt and Beeler, 1998; Sanders and Kroll, 2000). Regardless of when LGBT identity develop-ment begins, there is variation in experience. People move around and through the stages at various rates and times, in varying order, and sometimes skip stages without indicating pathology or arrested devel-opment (Lev, 2004; Savin-Williams, 1996; Walters and Old Person, 2008).

Lesbian and Gay Identity Development

Although there are several, the Cass model is the most widely accepted model of LG identity develop-ment. However, Cass (1998) acknowledges the limi-tations of the model as it was developed based on a White, Western population. The stages of the model are identity confusion, comparison, tolerance, ac-ceptance, pride, and synthesis and reflect movement from uncertainty to integration (Cass, 1979). The in-dividual moves from coming out to self and then to others, potentially including family members. The model has been criticized because it equates sexual behavior with sexual identity (Lev, 2004), and for its failure to attend to cultural and historical contexts.

Morales (1989) developed a model specifically for LG people of color that is more relationally focused. The five stages of the model are: 1) denial of conflicts in allegiances, 2) coming out as bisexual versus gay or lesbian, 3) acknowledging conflicts of allegiances, 4) establishing priorities in allegiances, and 5) integration of identity. The inclusion of refer-ence groups in the model is more congruent with the values and norms of collectivist cultures. It should be noted that in this model, coming out as bisexual does not imply that bisexuality cannot be a complete identity for people of color. For some people of color bisexuality may be an expression of allegiance conflict as the LG person strives to hold on to the more culturally accepted heterosexual identity.

Bisexual Identity Development

Oftentimes it is erroneously assumed that bisexual identity formation follows the same trajectory as LG identity development; that it is a step in moving toward an LG identity; or that it is a denial of homosexuality. These false assumptions about bisexuality may be reflective of the ways in which bisexual people are marginalized within the dominant culture and the LG communities. Weinberg, Williams, and Pryor (1994) propose a four-stage model that consists of initial confusion, finding and applying the label, settling into an identity, and continued uncertainty. The individual moves from emerging awareness of attraction to men and women in the context of a binary system of sexuality to maintaining a sense of integrated identity to conceptualizing identity as fluid (Lev, 2004). Bisexual people may experience oppression by both heterosexual and LG communities and may cope with feelings of invisibility and the stress of passing as either heterosexual or homosexual (Weber & Heffern, 2008).

Transgender Identity Development

In her hallmark text, Lev (2004) proposes a six-stage model of transgender emergence. The six stages are: 1) awareness, 2) seeking information/reaching out, 3) disclosure to significant others, 4) exploration: identity and self-labeling, 5) exploration: transition issues/possible body modification, and 6) integration. In the awareness stage, the individual is realizing that his or her sense of gender does not conform to dominant culture definitions or that his or her body does not reflect the internal sense of self. The seeking information stage focuses on acquisition of knowledge and support for gender variance. Disclosure is the stage in which gender-variant individuals come out to friends and family. In exploring identity and self-labeling, individuals are figuring out how they want to name and express themselves, who they want to be in the world. Exploring transition issues is a continuation of the prior stage and also includes consideration

of body modifications. The final stage, integration and pride, focuses on integration of the past and present selves and moving forward.

It is noted that there is a dearth of literature and research on bisexual and transgender people of color in general and specifically concerning identity development.

Coming Out

Just as identity development can begin at any stage of the family life cycle so can disclosure or coming out (Mallon, 2008a). Disclosure or coming out is an individual and relational process in which LGBT individuals become aware of their sexual identity or orientation or their gender variance and inform others. Many people conceptualize coming out as a one-time event, but because the world is heterocentric and organized by a biologically determined binary gender system, coming out is a lifelong process (Mallon, 2008a). All of the previously reviewed identity models are inclusive of coming out as part of the identity formation process as these are often recursive processes in that disclosure "redefines" self and self-labeling "drives" disclosure (Savin-Williams, 1996).

Coming out is a process that can take place in multiple ways and may vary according to familial and cultural norms. Methods of disclosure include both verbal and nonverbal expressions that can be voluntary or involuntary. Among people of color, nonverbal signifiers and processes may be privileged over verbal disclosure (Walters & Old Person, 2008). In fact, being LGBT may be more acceptable in families and communities of color if unseen or not openly discussed because in many collectivist cultures calling attention to self, and privileging individual expression over group norms violates cultural norms (Walters & Old Person, 2008). Salience of identity may be related to the coming out processes for LGBT people of color. Bowleg et al. (2008) found that among Black lesbians and bisexual women, those who found their sexual identity to be more salient were more likely to be out and that those who found their racial identity to be more salient were less likely to be out.

The families of LGBT individuals also go through a coming out process similar to that of the

LGB family member as they decide to whom to be out. The family processes may include grieving expectations and the existing sense of family identity, facing their own attitudes regarding sexual and gender nonconformance, working through feelings of guilt and shame, accepting (or rejecting) the LGBT family member, integrating the LGBT member's newly disclosed identity, and assessing the potential costs and benefits of coming out as a relative of an LGBT individual. These processes will be shaped by the values and beliefs of the family and existing dynamics and coping strategies, as well as heterosexism, homo-, bi-, and transphobia (Connolly 2004a). LaSala (in press) frames coming out during adolescence as a five-stage developmental process for youth and their families: 1) family sensitization, 2) family discovery: youth come out, 3) family discovery: parents react, 4) family recovery, and 5) family renewal. In this process, adolescents and their families move from awareness of the child's differentness, to disclosure/discovery, in which the child may experience relief from anxiety and parents assume the anxiety, to acceptance and celebration. LaSala's model focuses on the ways in which family relationships shift and grow as the adolescents and their families discover and accept their LG identity.

Lev (2004) outlines a four-stage process for families of transgender individuals: 1) discovery and disclosure, 2) turmoil, 3) negotiation, and 4) finding balance. In this model, families move from a sense of betrayal and confusion to integration of the family member back into the system. Like individual coming out, the family process is not a one-time event, but is rather a process that will be repeated across the life span. The family coming out process takes place in the context of the family life cycle just as individual identity development and coming out processes do. Family life cycle, identity development, and coming out are not linear processes that occur in order. They are circular processes that interact and inform one another.

The Family Life Cycle

The family life cycle discussion will focus on the ways in which multigenerational LGBT families complete the tasks and processes of each life cycle stage in the context of multicultural identities, sexual and gender identity development, coming out, heterosexism, homo-, bi-, and transphobia, and a biologically determined binary gender identity system. The unique challenges and opportunities of being "other" at each stage of the life cycle will be examined with the understanding that these challenges are not related to sexual or gender identity but rather to the experiences of marginalization and multiple oppressions (Lev, 2004; Mallon, 2008a; Walters & Old Person, 2008). For a more detailed review of cultural differences at each life cycle phase, the reader is referred to other chapters in this text. Although the following discussion will address voluntary coming out for the individual and family, it is acknowledged that in many situations, the coming out process is an outing, or an unplanned discovery that can heighten stress and anxiety for the individual and for the family system.

Regardless of life cycle stage, there are unique challenges that LGBT families will commonly experience. Because of social and familial expectations that all people are heterosexual, the belief that gender identity is biologically determined, and the lack of accurate information, individuals and families must renegotiate how they fit together and cope with the shifting identity of the system as a whole. In turn, families must grieve their expectations and assumptions about the LGBT family member and determine to whom to disclose, how, and when (Connolly, 2004a; Lev, 2004; Mallon, 2008a). LGBT individuals who are growing up, or who have been raised in heterosexual families in which all members are gender conforming and adherent to traditional gender roles, lack role models to inform sexual and gender identity formation, the coming out process, and the development of survival strategies in the face of sexual and gender oppression (Connolly 2004a). Families that have experienced racial oppression may see the individual's LGBT status in opposition to strategies taught to combat racism (Greene, 1998; Walters & Old Person, 2008) and may not be able to see that these strategies may be helpful in combating heterosexism. Both dominant culture and marginalized families may support and operate from heterosexist, homo-, bi-, and transphobic ideologies, and therefore may unintentionally participate in oppressive systems that harm and dehumanize their family members (Connolly 2004a).

Along with challenges come benefits, or at least opportunities, that will be present across all stages of the life cycle. Because of the lack of family role models, LGBT people and their families have unique opportunities to name themselves and to create family structure and roles based on needs and preferences instead of existing prescriptions. The creation of the family of choice demonstrates positive adaptation to a rejecting family of origin experience. It also demonstrates an innovative approach for transmitting norms, knowledge, rituals, and survival skills unique to the LGBT experience to the next generation. Although some LGBT families choose to adopt gender roles associated with patriarchal, heterosexual paradigms, many families transcend traditional roles and define roles based on equality, interests, and talents (Mallon, 2008b). For example, research suggests that among lesbian couples, family responsibilities, chores, and tasks tend to be more evenly distributed between partners (Patterson, 1996) and that gay fathers tend to be less concerned with traditional gender roles, specifically the role of financial provider, and more concerned with the nurturing and expressive roles than their heterosexual counterparts (Mallon, 2004).

Many communities of color define family in a broad manner including both blood and nonblood kin in varying functional roles (Boyd-Franklin, 2003a; Watts-Jones, 1997; Walters and Old Person, 2008). It appears that LGBT communities have adopted this same practice forming families of choice (Weston, 1991). In doing so, LGBT families are finding ways to provide instrumental and emotional support in the face of adversity and a mechanism for transmitting values, norms, rituals, and survival skills.

Family rituals are helpful in transitioning through the life cycle, as rituals demarcate important life events, both joyful and painful (Imber-Black & Roberts, 1998). Slater (1995) observed a lack of ritual among LGBT individuals and their families and found the lack of ritual to be problematic. However, LGBT communities, along with families of choice and origin, have developed rituals that celebrate and

recognize transitions in the lives of LGBT individuals and families. The development of family rituals may have been accelerated by the marriage equality movement and the advancement of information-sharing technology.

Throughout the discussion of life cycle stages, there is an implicit assumption that every adult wants to couple and raise children and will do so. Many healthy, well-adjusted individuals may not partner or parent by choice or circumstance. Remaining single or childless does not represent pathology or exclude individuals from the family life cycle process. Single adults, and those who do not parent, have membership, roles, tasks, and meaningful relationships within the contexts of their families of origin, their families of choice, and their communities.

Leaving Home and Staying Connected: Launching and Single Adulthood

These two stages have been combined because launching reflects exit from the family of origin, and single adulthood reflects entry into a life that is simultaneously independent of and connected to the family of origin. Processes focus on accepting movement in and out of the family system, shifts and renegotiations in the parental (couple) system, developing adult relationships with the younger generation, adjusting to changing abilities, and integrating illness and eventually loss of the older generation. For the single adult, tasks include starting career/work life, forming adult-to-adult relationships with parents and other adult family members, cultivating intimate relationships with peers, and assuming financial and emotional responsibility for self.

When young adults come out as LGBT to their families at this stage, the process can feel risky as they may be early in their independence and still experience a heightened need for the support of their families of origin. Yet, they are not as vulnerable as adolescents and children because they are no longer fully dependent on the family, may be beyond familial control, and may be aware of their ability to survive without family of origin support. Furthermore, LGBT young adults may be aware that family of origin support may be replaced or augmented by a developing family of choice or peer network. If the young adult has not come out to the family of origin, being single may allow the system to assume heterosexuality and gender conformance. If the young adult has come out, then being single may create space for the family to view the nonheterosexual or nonconforming gender identity as a phase to be grown out of upon meeting the "right" person. The family of the bisexual single adult child may particularly see bisexuality as a phase and push for opposite-sex dating in an effort to promote heterosexuality.

Because entry into single adulthood is a time of restructuring in the family of origin, the young person and the family may struggle with the role and place of the LGBT person in the family as the young adult may be failing to meet family expectations. If the family experiences conflict regarding the young person's sexual or gender identity, there is a chance that they will overfocus on the young adult and neglect the other tasks of this stage, such as renegotiating the parental couple relationship or other important relationships, or changing roles and relationships with older family members.

As young adults establish their work lives or careers and strengthen their peer support networks, they must constantly decide to whom they can safely disclose (Connolly 2004a), and consider how disclosure may impact their relationships and careers. LGBT young adults of color who are forming more intimate bonds with peer groups may begin to experience conflicts in allegiance to the respective reference groups. As at other stages, some young adults may choose to lead separate or split lives (participating in LGBT communities while allowing people in the rest of their lives including family to assume heterosexuality and gender conformity). If the gender-variant individual is transitioning and the transition includes body modification therapies, leading a split life may not be an option.

Unlike heterosexual young adults, LGBT young adults are more likely to learn about the norms and rules of dating from their families of choice rather than their families of origin. If they have yet to cultivate a family of choice, they are left to figure out dating rules on their own. Fortunately, many urban areas have LGBT community centers that can help to convey the norms of LGBT culture.

The challenges of dating may be further complicated by variation in stage of development regarding sexual and gender identity development as well as other identity statuses (e.g., race), adding another layer of complexity to this life cycle stage.

When a parent, grandparent, or other adult family member comes out while the young adult is moving into single adulthood, there may be reverberations felt throughout the system. The family may shift attention from supporting the single young adult's renegotiation of role in the family to coming to terms with the newly announced identity of the other family member. Young adults may neglect their tasks to support the newly out member, or if conflict emerges, to help the family cope with the conflict. If the disclosing parent or other adult family member is partnered, the couple relationship will need to be renegotiated, and the young person may become involved in or triangulated into this process. If there are children or adolescents in the familial home, the single young adult may focus on helping these younger siblings understand and adjust to this transition in the family.

Regardless of who is coming out, the single young adult or the parent of the single young adult, families will have to come to terms with their attitudes and beliefs about homosexuality, bisexuality, and gender variance. Even the most open-minded, progressive families that may embrace LGBT friends must face their internalized heterosexism, bi-, trans-, and homophobia. Families of color may worry that the young adult now has another layer of oppression with which to cope. Dominant culture families who have not had or are unaware of experiences of oppression may feel unprepared to help their child cope with the newly declared devalued status.

At first glance it may appear that an LGBT identity is burdensome to single young adults and their families. However, this perceived burden affords the family the opportunity to consciously examine its values, beliefs, and ways of being and relating to one another, as well as the opportunity to create a stronger, more open, and communicative family structure. Because of existing patterns and habits of responding to change, or difference, some families may break apart. However, many families often successfully complete this life cycle stage and continue to thrive and move forward (Benshorn, 2008; Cramer & Roach, 1988; Griffin, Wirth, & Wirth, 1986; Johnson, 1992; Robinson, Walters, & Skeen, 1989).

Randy, a 23-year-old African American man, who is close to his multigenerational family of origin, was raised and remains a member of a historically Black, fundamentalist Christian church. He was born, raised, and continues to reside in an urban northeast area, in a predominantly African American community. During his formative years, the family viewed Randy as "soft" and "girly." Throughout high school, Randy found himself drawn to activities traditionally reserved for girls and experienced himself as neither man nor woman but transgendered. Randy's family saw his behavior as sinful and pushed Randy to seek healing and forgiveness through prayer and worship. Randy found his family's urgings to be intolerable and longed to openly explore his gender nonconformance freely, to date men, and strengthen his connection to LGBT communities of color. Despite limited income, Randy moved out of the family home, into an LGBT neighborhood, and started dating a new acquaintance. After dating for 3 weeks, Randy invited his new acquaintance to move in with him because he could not afford rent on his own. The acquaintance sold stolen property out of the apartment to earn his share of the rent. The two were caught, arrested, and convicted. Because it was Randy's first offense, and the court viewed transgenderism as pathological, Randy was referred to a community-based social service agency for mental health treatment. The agency's worker supported Randy to explore his gender variance and to identify and negotiate the conflicts he felt regarding his gender identity, religious beliefs, and family norms. The worker helped Randy to connect to an LGBT faith community that had its roots in African American spirituality and traditions. Randy and the worker also met several times with his family of origin. Although the family held that Randy's behavior was sinful, they were willing to provide emotional support and guidance so that he could successfully live on his own with the understanding that they would silently pray for him and that Randy would refrain from discussing his gender identity in their presence. Randy accepted these terms for now, and invited his family to continue to participate in the therapeutic process. Living independently and connecting to an affirming, culturally relevant faith community allowed him to grow in his identity as an African American, Christian, gender-variant man who is closely connected to his family of origin in an authentic manner.

Coupling

The focus of the coupling stage is the joining of two adults to form a committed union or subsystem while blending their respective families and realigning their relationships with families of origin, families of choice, and friends.

The primary functions of coupling are to solidify intimate bonds with a desired emotional and sexual companion, to build a shared life, pursue common goals that may include creating a family, supporting the individual goals of the partner, and formalizing the status of the relationship as permanent or committed. Coupling may also have several unintended or intended outcomes for LGBT people. Coupling may serve as a declaration of sexuality to the LGB individual's family of origin and friends. This may be particularly so in cultures where nonverbal cues are valued over verbal declarations. Same-sex coupling may also be a signal to the family that being LGB is not just a phase. For many individuals, coupling does not inform coming out, as individuals may already be out or because, as a couple, they will decide whether or not to live as an openly LGBT couple (Connolly, 2004b; Goldenberg & Goldenberg, 1998). If a bisexual person couples with a person of the opposite sex, the family may continue its heterocentric assumptions or see the bisexual person as emerging from a developmental phase. These assumptions may be a source of conflict and frustration for the bisexual person (Weber and Heffern, 2008). As mentioned, individuals may be at varying stages of sexual and other identity development, and these variations may complicate the decision of whether or not to live as an out couple.

Most individuals learn and adopt their ideas about coupling from what they have observed in their families of origin, as well as in popular culture and media. From these sources they learn values, norms, create the definition of a couple, and develop expectations. Some LGB couples will apply a heterosexual paradigm to their relationship and seek to live by these norms and roles. Others will create their own way of enacting couplehood. However, as Bowen prescribed, creating a separate unit while maintaining authentic ties with the family of origin is the task of all couples. Bowen's prescription is culturally bound in that individuation and personal satisfaction may be less important than maintaining familial norms, beliefs, membership, and identity for some cultural groups. Thus, in order to maintain family norms, membership, identity, and authentic connections, individuals may choose to be silent about the LGBT aspect of identity including commitment to a partner.

Tunnell and Greenan (2004) describe the three basic tasks of all couples as 1) creating a couple identity and boundary around the unit, 2) regulating closeness and distance, and 3) accommodating difference. These tasks can be complex for heterosexual couples but are further complicated by heterosexual privilege and traditional gender role socialization for LGBT couples. Identity and boundary formation are interactive processes that occur between the couple, their families, communities, and society. Just as there is recursive relationship between disclosure and identity formation (Savin-Williams, 1996), there is a recursive relationship between recognition as a couple and couple identity and boundary formation. Recognition strengthens identity and boundary formation, and couple identity and boundary formation drive the desire for social recognition (Tunnell and Greenan, 2004). Families of origin and creation, as well as society in general, serve as sources of recognition. Social recognition includes legal recognition and helps to draw the boundary around the couple as a subsystem functioning within larger contexts. If families, communities, and society do not validate the couple identity and boundaries around the subsystem, then couple identity formation may be hampered and can become a source of stress and conflict for the couple. LGBT couples may choose to physically and or emotionally move away from invalidating sources and move toward affirming sources such as the family of choice. LGBT couples still have an uphill climb in obtaining social recognition. Although there is growing legal recognition of same-sex couples, in most instances that recognition is the second-class status domestic partnership or civil union and is only at the state level.

Regulation of closeness and distance within their relationship may be more difficult for same-sex couples because of socialization (Tunnell and Greenan, 2004). In United States culture, men tend to be socialized to be independent and to seek separateness and often have experiences of being shamed for expressing the desire for connection. Women tend to be socialized to be interdependent and to seek emotional connection and may have been shamed for displays of independence and the desire to be separate. To their same-sex relationships, men may bring greater expertise in creating distance, while women may bring greater expertise in creating closeness. Each same-sex couple will need to find a way to cultivate expertise in creating both closeness and distance, and each individual will have to give up participation in socially sanctioned shaming in response to out-of-traditional-gender-role behaviors. Some literature suggests that lesbian couples are fused or enmeshed and that this fusion is problematic (Krestan and Bepko, 1980). However, current, feminist-informed clinical literature suggests that lesbian couples desire more intimacy and closeness and do not report what may be seen as fusion as problematic. Lesbian couples may actually find what is described as enmeshment to be self-affirming, satisfying relational needs and providing protection against homophobia, heterosexism, and sexism (Biaggio, Coin, and Adams, 2002).

Just as closeness may be a protective factor in same-sex relationships in coping with oppression, difference may be experienced as a threat. Additionally, gender role socialization plays a role in this threat perception as men have likely been trained in competition and dominance while women have likely been trained in accommodation. Therefore, when difference emerges men may address through competition and combat while women may erase difference by silencing their own opinions and needs. In same-sex unions, male partners may have to work harder at resolving difference through negotiation and accommodation (Tunnell and Greenan, 2004) while women may have to work harder to assert their separate needs and interests.

Obviously the process of joining the respective families and gaining familial support will be influenced by whether or not the couple is out. For couples who are out, the degree of family support may be informed by whether or not the individuals are accepted within their families of origin, whether or not the couple expresses their status in a culturally acceptable manner, the individual family's attitudes toward gender variance and nonconforming sexuality, and the effects of internalized oppression (single or multiple forms). In order to join, each family must be willing to come out, at least amongst themselves and to the partner's family.

While there are tasks that are common to all couples, LGBT couples face unique challenges. Lack of legal recognition and protection means that as they are forming, LGBT couples will need to enlist the aid of an attorney to draw up legal documents (e.g., power of attorney, health care proxy, and will) to establish many of the rights that are automatically granted to heterosexual married couples. However these legal contracts can be costly and are somewhat limited as there is variation in validity across states, and they cannot grant all of the 1,000+ benefits bestowed upon married heterosexual couples. LGBT couples who are members of the dominant racial/ethnic group will have to cope with the effects of heterosexism and homophobia on their relationship (Connolly, 2004b), while LGBT couples of color will face the interactive effects of multiple forms of oppression. Couples may be affected by, and will need to work through, their own internalized homo-, bi-, and transphobia and heterosexism (Connolly 2004b). Family members who seem supportive may engage in unintentional invalidating actions such as introducing the partner as a friend, expecting the adult child to privilege the family of origin over the partner, providing separate sleeping accommodations when visiting, or failing to recognize the couple's anniversary.

Couples in which one or both partners are bisexual may have additional tasks and challenges. First, because the dominant culture frequently understands sexuality and sexual orientation as binary categories, sexuality is assumed to be either hetero- or homosexual. Unlike lesbian and gay individuals, bisexual individuals must decide whether or not to disclose their sexual identity to their partner. Bisexual people may enter a committed relationship without disclosing their bisexuality (Bradford, 2004b). If they choose to come out to their partners,

the couple will deal with the relational fallout, which may include mistrust, a sense of betrayal, and an erroneous assumption that the bisexual partner will be unfaithful (Bradford, 2004b). Often bisexuality is not accepted as complete identity and so both same-sex and opposite-sex partners may be waiting for the bisexual partner to clarify his or her identity (Bradford 2004a, 2004b). When partnered with an opposite-sex person, the bisexual partner may experience invisibility while also benefitting from heterosexual privilege, generating feelings of shame and guilt (Weber & Heffner, 2008).

When transgender individuals disclose their gender variance as a member of an existing lesbian, gay, or heterosexual couple, it may be falsely assumed that he or she wants to terminate the relationship (Israel, 2004). Coming out may send the committed relationship into a crisis as partners often feel betrayed and experience the disclosure in ways that are similar to learning of infidelity or illness (Lev, 2004). As the couple faces the crisis and moves through the emergence process, both people will address the viability of the relationship, negotiate the rules of the relationship, and address their sexual identity as a couple (Lev, 2004; Malpas, 2006). Like bisexual individuals, gender-variant people must determine when and if to come out to a potential partner when dating or when the two individuals are solidifying their couple status. Many couples in which there is a gender variant partner find ways of negotiating this transition, relinquishing their fear, shame, and ignorance about gender variance, and are able to move forward in their lives with the transgender member fully integrated into the family system (Lev, 2004).

Some of the benefits and opportunities for LGBT couples are freedom from the limitations of traditional gender role expectations, freedom to create their own unique way of being a couple, and freedom to define the terms of their relationship including who will work, how money will be handled, how decisions will be made, and how issues concerning sexual exclusivity will be addressed. LGBT couples may turn to their families of choice to determine how to be a couple and they may also borrow that which is most appealing from their families of origin, while abandoning that which is most unappealing. Through the use of legal contracting, LGBT couples can find creative ways to use existing laws to protect their relationship.

After dating for more than 3 years, and living together for 2 years, Deborah who is Jewish American, and Sabrina, who is Irish American, decided that they wanted to mark the beginning of their life as a committed couple by having a commitment ceremony. Their families of choice instantly celebrated the decision. Sabrina wanted to include their families of origin in the ceremony, while Deborah did not want to include her family of origin because she was not out to them. Sabrina believed that the ceremony presented the opportunity to tell Deborah's family that they were not just roommates. This difference erupted into intense conflict that prompted the couple to postpone the ceremony and seek therapy. During the course of the LGBT affirming therapy, it became apparent that each partner was at a different stage of LGBT identity development, and that there were differences concerning their expectations regarding family of origin involvement in their lives. Sabrina and Deborah worked to resolve their differences by clarifying and working through relationship expectations. The couple came to a mutual understanding regarding the role of Deborah's family in their relationship and Sabrina came to respect the boundary that Deborah had already created. The couple resumed planning their ceremony and had legal contracts drawn up to protect their relationship. Deborah and Sabrina created their ceremony by borrowing from their respective cultural traditions and incorporating suggestions from their families of choice. The ceremony was officiated by a well-respected, long-time lesbian couple from their community, and Sabrina's family of origin was prominently featured throughout the ceremony. Many of the ceremony guests commented that it was one of the most thoughtful and authentic marriage rituals they had ever attended. Sabrina and Deborah recently celebrated their fourth anniversary and continue to thrive as a couple, in part due to the continued support of their families of choice and Sabrina's family of origin, and the couple's clarification and negotiation of their relational expectations.

Parenting: Families With Young Children

The primary process of families with young children is bringing and integrating new members into the family system. Couples assume responsibility for their children while maintaining responsibility for,

and to, each other and adjusting their relationship to create space for the child. Additionally, they make changes in their relationships to family members and help those family members adjust to their new roles as grandparents, aunts, etc.

Deciding to become a parent brings a host of questions and issues to be addressed. The decision itself is one that is a significantly more conscious and aware process for LGBT couples and single adults. They must determine the method by which they will become parents. Methods include donor insemination using a known or anonymous sperm donor, surrogacy, shared custody of children from a prior relationship or encounter, adoption, or fostering. Some lesbian and gay couples opt to conceive a child together, act as donors or surrogates for one another, and may choose to parent together. If a known donor or surrogacy is chosen, couples must decide if the donor or surrogate will be in the child's life, whether the child will have knowledge of that individual's status, and at what age such information will be shared. Lesbian couples who opt to give birth to biological children must decide which partner, or if both partners, will become pregnant. Gay men must decide which partner's sperm or both will be used to impregnate the surrogate. Despite supportive adoption laws, couples seeking to become parents through adoption may face obstacles because of heterosexist beliefs and bi-, trans-, and homophobia of agency workers. LGBT individuals and their partners may experience difficulties in gaining custody and visitation of biological children from prior heterosexual relationships. Once the method of having children has been selected, parental rights must be established. While married heterosexual couples are automatically granted parenting rights, LG couples must figure out how to establish the legal connection of both parents to the child through second-parent adoption or parentage judgment based on the availability of these options where they live. The decisions regarding how to become parents and how to protect parental rights may be informed by financial resources, access to medical care, community and familial support, and cultural norms of the LG couple.

Once the couple or single adult makes the aforementioned decisions, and engages in the process of becoming a parent, he or she must also determine what and when to disclose to the families of origin. Regardless of the existing degree of acceptance in the families of origin, having a grandchild, or niece, or nephew, etc., not only increases the visibility of the LGBT family member, but it also further increases the visibility of the families of origin as parents, or siblings, etc., of LGBT people. Conflict may arise within LGBT families where silence or invisibility is the term for acceptance of an LGBT identity. If a couple has been presenting to their families of origin as friends or roommates, or if the family has been denying the true nature of the relationship, having a child may act as a nonverbal cue to the family, pushing the couple to disclose or forcing the family to come to terms with the true nature of the relationship.

In order to integrate children into the family system, LGBT couples must make adjustments in their own relationships. They need to renegotiate the boundaries that define their identity as a couple, their roles, responsibilities, expectations regarding closeness and distance, connections to friends, and work or career. The parenting couple will also need to develop or refine their decision-making system as they collaborate together on behalf of their children. New parents must reorganize priorities, making the care and nurturing of their children paramount. Issues that existed within the parenting couple, or between them and their respective families of origin, may intensify (Mallon, 2008b). LGBT couples must help integrate their new child into their families of origin. They may follow family of origin norms regarding the relationships between the child and other family members or they may create their own standards. The way that family members respond to the new children and integrate them into the family may be informed by heterosexism or homo-, trans-, and biphobia, and thus families of choice may take up that life cycle task either in place of, or in addition to, the families of origin.

Individuals who have children from prior relationships have additional tasks to complete in their coming out process. They must negotiate being their authentic selves while maintaining family ties and bonds with children from the prior union as well as with their former partners with whom they may co-parent. This process has been described as a simultaneous "rebirth and loss" (Mallon, 2008b).

Although it is a complex and often painful process, being true to self and disclosing provides children with a model for how to be one's authentic self in the face of challenges (Mallon 2008b).

When a parent comes out as LGBT, co-parents, children (Mallon, 2008b), and other family members may react with shock. The co-parent may be confused about the meaning of the couple relationship, both past and present in the context of the partner's newly disclosed identity. How children respond may be related to their stage of development. For young children, the disclosure may be meaningless, but for adolescents it can be unsettling as they are dealing with their own emerging sexuality. Parents may feel concerned about how the disclosure will affect their legal rights related to custody and or visitation (Mallon, 2008b).

The research and literature about transgender parents and the effects of growing up with a gender-variant parent are extremely limited (Lev, 2004; Mallon, 2008b). Despite the fact that there is no evidence that being raised by an LGBT parent increases the likelihood of nonconforming gender or sexual identities or struggles in these areas, concerns run rampant about the impact of the parent's gender identity on the gender or sexual identity of the children. Although it is recognized that children raised in families where a parent is transitioning may have difficulty, the expectation is that they will cope in a manner similar to other normative life cycle transitions (Lev, 2004).

Families with young children who express gender nonconformity will have the additional tasks of grieving their expectations for them and developing coping and advocacy skills to respond to their other children, relatives, friends, schools, and other social institutions, and for incorporating the needs of the gender variant child into family life (Lev, 2004). Some young children grow up feeling different but are unable to name the nature of the difference. During adolescence, or later in life, they may come to understand that difference as being related to their emerging sexual identity, orientation, or gender identity (Lev, 2004; Savin-Williams, 1996). It is the role of the family to provide nurturance, unconditional support, and acceptance as their children discover who they are in the world, and how to name and present themselves.

LGBT parents experience unique challenges in relationship to their own sexual or gender identity or in relationship to the nonconforming sexual and gender identities of their young children. Becoming a parent is a much more complex and more costly process. Through legal contracting, parents must explicitly establish the rights of the nonblood parent or the parent who is not the primary adoptive parent. Once they become parents, they must learn to cope with the stress related to witnessing their child's experience of heterosexism, homo-, trans-, and biphobia, and they must teach their children to cope with and survive oppression. They may worry about their children being teased either about their parents' sexual or gender identity, or about the child's gender nonconformance. However, the same skills used to cope with bullying for other reasons, or in response to other forms of oppression, can be taught and applied to these situations (Mallon, 2008a, 2008b). Additionally, the provision of a nurturing, supportive, and loving home is a powerful buffer against all types of bullying and oppression.

LGBT families with young children also experience unique benefits and opportunities that include transcending the limitations of gender roles and the opportunity to create alternative family structures that are more consistent with the concept that "it takes a village" to raise a child. LGBT families of color may be particularly adept at taking advantage of the support offered by families of choice due to a cultural tendency to define family broadly. There is a significant body of research demonstrating that relationships among family members and the quality of care provided by parents are much more critical and important to the healthy development of children than the sexual or gender identity of parents or family structure (Mallon, 2008b).

When Esther, a Korean American woman, and Julia, a Jamaican woman, celebrated their 10th anniversary, they decided to have a child. They elected to use an anonymous sperm donor and decided that Esther, who was older, would be the first to carry and deliver their child, and in a few years Julia would become pregnant using the same donor. After locating a fertility clinic that would service a lesbian couple, the two proceeded with their plan. They

had a healthy baby girl and named her Ayana. The baby suffered from severe colic prompting Julia's mother to stay with the couple for several months to help out. Sleep deprivation, worries about Ayana, the lack of privacy, and concerns about their ability to parent disrupted the plan to have a second child and created tension between them. The tension heightened to a point that Esther and the baby went to stay with a close sister-friend. Although supportive on the surface, Julia's mother told her that she was not surprised by their failure as everyone in their family agreed that these two women needed a man to make a family. Julia sent her mother home and asked that she and other family members think about how they could be a supportive kinship network to Ayana. She pleaded with Esther to return home, sought the support of their family of choice, and suggested that they begin couple's therapy. Esther agreed, Ayana's colic improved, the couple adjusted to their parenting roles, renegotiated their relationship, confronted the heterosexism in Julia's family, and had their second child 4 years later.

Parenting: Families With Adolescent Children

Families with adolescents are focused on revising boundaries to allow for the increasing independence of children, the increasing frailty of the older generation, and movement in and out of the family system. During this stage, the adolescent is separating from the family, identifying more with the peer group, and locating individual uniqueness. Parents are refocusing attention on themselves as a couple (or for single adults, their peer relationships/dating), their own life's work, and caring for the older generation.

During adolescence, coming out to oneself and others is often a complex process that can be filled with joy, excitement, pain, fear, loneliness, conflict, acceptance, and rejection. Becoming aware of one's sexual identity or orientation at this stage may be helpful to the young person as it may clarify feelings of differentness or feelings that previously may have been confusing (Savin-Williams, 1996). This clarification of misunderstood feelings may also hold true for gender-variant youth. While teens are often seeking independence from parents, disclosure to the family of origin may be motivated by a desire to be closer to family, to be one's authentic self with family members, and to enlist family support (Savin-Williams, 1996; LaSala, in press). Whether families ultimately accept or reject their LGBT adolescents, the initial parental response is often unpredictable and the coming out process is likely to be stressful. Following the initial shock, familial responses may range from acceptance to rejection and may include abuse or expulsion. Responses tend to be informed by existing familial values, norms, familial tolerance of difference, existing family dynamics, the quality of the existing relationship between the youth and the parents, and attitudes and beliefs about homosexuality, bisexuality, and gender variance (Connolly 2004a; LaSala, in press; Savin-Williams, 1996).

LGBT youth are challenged by the same developmental tasks as heterosexual, gender conforming youth. If they are aware of their attraction to both sexes or the same sex, or are aware that their natal sex is not congruent with their gender identity, they have a much more tumultuous journey ahead of them (Hunter & Mallon, 2000; Lev, 2004). The development of positive sexual or gender identities may be the most challenging tasks for LGBT youth (Durby, 1994). Their identities are forming in what may be openly hostile or subtly rejecting families, schools, and communities. Because increasing independence is a task of adolescence, it is appropriate for youth to seek distance from the family of origin. That distance may be widened by the emergence of an LGBT identity as the youth moves away from the family's way of being in the world and into a way of being that may be unfamiliar to the family of origin. As noted in single adulthood, when adolescents disclose during this life cycle stage, families may overfocus on the youth's sexual identity and neglect the tasks of renegotiating the parental couple relationship, attending to careers or other interests, meeting the needs of younger children in the family, and supporting older family members to adjust to changes in abilities.

Although there is a dearth of research concerning the experiences of LGBT youth of color, a few speculations can be made. LGBT youth of color are more likely to be members of collectivist ethnicities, and as noted the family is more likely to be inclusive of blood and nonblood kin, community members, and ancestors (Boyd-Franklin, 2003a; Walters and Old Person, 2008; Watts-Jones, 1997). Thus, coming out to the family of origin becomes a more complex process as the adolescent must give consideration to the responses of a broader, more complex family network that has played a pivotal role in protecting and supporting the youth in a world that is organized by White-skin privilege. Sadly, it can be expected that LGBT youth of color will not only contend with racism or heterosexism, but also with the interactive effects of multiple forms of oppression. They will face racism within White LGBT communities and heterosexism/homophobia within racial/ethnic communities leaving them with conflicting allegiances at a time when they most need to locate reference groups in which they feel welcomed, validated, and at home.

During the stage of parenting adolescents, the nonconforming gender or sexual identity of an LGBT parent may create additional tasks for the adolescent regardless of whether the parental identity is a new disclosure or whether the young person was raised in this context. The social stigma of having an LGBT parent may increase stress and anxiety as the adolescent strives to integrate the parent's identity with his or her own and to fit in with peer groups (Welsh, 2008). Although moving away from parents during adolescence is normative, distancing may increase family conflict if it is motivated by negative feelings about the parent's sexual identity or gender variance. During teen years, as youth become increasingly aware of negative social attitudes toward homosexuality, bisexuality, and gender variance, concern for the well-being of the family, fear of oppression, and conflicted feelings about wanting to pass as a heterosexual family may emerge (Welsh, 2008). It is imperative that the parent support the adolescent to cope with these feelings, or locate a member of the family of origin or of choice, a mutual support group, or a helping professional to do so.

LGBT youth and the adolescent children of LGBT parents face a multitude of challenges during this most taxing life cycle stage. LGBT youth may struggle silently with gender and sexual identity issues because they fear hurting or disappointing their families (Savin-Williams, 1996). Parents may not take their child's disclosure and identity seriously as they may view it as an adolescent phase. Even if parents are accepting, their anxiety will most likely increase knowing that their child will probably face oppression, hatred, and discrimination. This may result in decreased willingness to allow the child much freedom and independence. Where there is pathologizing of LGBT identities, parents may engage in self-blame for what they see as their child's dysfunction. Rejection or abuse by the family of origin in response to their LGBT teen may trigger anxiety, depression, suicidality, other mental health symptoms, substance use, or running away from home (Mallon, 2008a; Savin-Williams, 1996).

Families of choice may provide mentorship and role modeling to assist the family through this period of transition. Parents, especially, are in a position to shape the lives of their LGBT adolescents in a positive way, as studies have demonstrated that parental acceptance has positive impact on self-acceptance among LGBT youth (Savin-Williams, 1996). As more families, schools, and communities become LGBT affirmative, positive social and psychological outcomes for adolescents will be enhanced, and they will be better equipped to launch and move into young adulthood.

Sonia's parents were called to school by their daughter's high school counselor. The counselor had been seeing Sonia for a few weeks out of concern for her declining grades, her withdrawal from school activities, and her overall sadness. On this day, Sonia told the counselor that she thought that her family would be better off if she were dead. The parents, a Latino couple that had been married for 20 years, arrived to the school angry with Sonia because they had to take time from work in response to what they described as a ridiculous statement. Sonia was taken to the local hospital where she was diagnosed with major depressive disorder and referred for psychotherapy. The therapist began meeting with Sonia individually and at times with the entire family. During family meetings, the therapist worked with the family to make room for their daughter's feelings, to understand the changes in her behavior, and to explore how processes in the family system related to

Sonia's behaviors. During an individual meeting with the therapist, Sonia shared her attraction to both boys and girls and asked the therapist to refrain from disclosing this information to the rest of the family because she feared rejection. The therapist agreed, and as they continued talking the therapist sought to understand Sonia's concerns while listening for potential sources of support within Sonia's life. During a family meeting, it was discovered that Sonia's 19-year-old brother, Roberto, had many gay male friends and that Roberto saw nonconforming sexual and gender identities as normative. When meeting alone with the therapist, Sonia began to consider sharing her attraction to girls and boys with Roberto and eventually, with the support of the therapist, did so. Roberto initially responded with surprise, and then offered his unconditional love and support to his sister while agreeing to keep her confidence. As the sibling alliance strengthened, Sonia enlisted Roberto's help in coping with other family issues. Although she chose not to discuss her sexuality with her parents, Sonia was able to address other concerns with her parents. Subsequently, her mood and grades improved, and Sonia was able to use the therapy to explore her emerging sexuality and to decide when and how to come out to her parents.

Families in Later Life

During this stage, families will focus on adjusting to shifting generational roles. The middle generation may be caring for the older generation and supporting the fullest functioning of older members, while also benefitting from their wisdom and experience. Tasks for older family members include supporting the middle generation, maintaining their highest level of functioning, cultivating their own interests, and attending to their couple relationship. Older members may also be coping with the loss of loved ones, partners, siblings, peers, etc., and preparing for death. Prior to addressing the ways in which LGBT individuals and their families negotiate this stage, it should be noted that there is limited contemporary research about later life LG individuals and their families (Ritter & Terndrup, 2002; Herdt & Beeler,1998) and even less about bisexual and transgender older adults and their families.

No matter at what life cycle stage individuals become aware of, or disclose, their sexual or gender identity, the process can be challenging because familial responses are unpredictable, relationships can be at risk, and being LGBT is a stigmatized status. Some individuals, who disclose their LGBT status after raising families as single adults, or in the context of heterosexual or same-sex unions, will have to contend with the responses of partners, adult children, grandchildren, and families of origin. However, they may find the process less stressful as they are often wiser, more experienced, better resourced, more financially stable, and more independent than those who come out earlier in life (Connolly, 2004a). Older adults who are less financially independent, or whose health is failing, may face similar challenges as adolescents when disclosing due to their dependence on family support to survive.

Prior to the contemporary LGBT civil rights movement and the depathologizing of sexual and gender nonconformance, it was far more risky and dangerous to disclose an LGBT identity to anyone. Thus, prior to the 1969 Stonewall rebellion, individuals may have been more likely to refrain from living as out LGBT individuals. They also may have been more likely to lead double lives, allowing their families of origin and the rest of mainstream society to assume their heterosexuality or gender conformance while living a secret LGBT life. Other LGBT individuals may have been rejected by their families or may have chosen to cut off from their families in order to live more authentically. Some LGBT individuals who came out to their families may have found acceptance (Herdt & Beeler, 1998). In situations where cut offs occurred, the family of choice may have emerged as more salient and relevant. The family of choice may have been established over the life course, thereby playing a significant role in providing material or emotional support (Friend, 1991; Kehoe, 1989; Kimmel & Sang, 1995; Reid 1995; Tully, 1989). Thus, among LGBT people, the tasks and processes of later life may occur in the context of the families of choice, either in addition to or in place of families of origin.

Many LGBT individuals will assume the roles of the senior generation, such as forming adult relationships with adult children, grandparenting, and

focusing on their relationships with partners in a smooth manner, while others will contend with disapproval and rejection. Some assume the roles of mentors and elders in their families of choice and in return receive needed care. LGBT-headed families might have an easier time accomplishing the tasks of later life than families where family heads disclosed sexual or gender nonconformance during the lives of their children or grandchildren. In LGBT-headed families, by this stage, the sexual or gender identity may be a nonissue as the younger generations have been raised in this context. As LGBT couples and individuals grow older, they may require care or assistance from their own children, siblings, or other family of origin members. If there have been cut-offs in these relationships, old conflicts may resurface: older LGBT adults may be more inclined to seek out families of choice. While conflict may bring up stress and painful emotion, reconnection provides opportunities for repair. If the family of origin never recognized a partner, the family of creation or choice, they may be unnecessarily concerned about the well-being of their later life LGBT relatives. As LGBT couples age, they may also contend with illness and the loss of a partner. If the relationships were not accepted by families of origin or creation, there may be a lack of support in providing care, for grieving, and rebuilding life as bereft partners. Finally, if wills and other legal documents were not created, a partner may be denied the right to make health care and other end of life decisions, as well as the right to claim their partner's belongings or shared property by families of origin or creation.

During later life, LGBT adults and their families have the opportunity to act as models for disclosure, living authentically, and thriving and surviving in the face of oppression for younger generations of LGBT individuals and families. Older adults may also act as mentors, parents, grandparents, etc., to members of their families of creation and their families of choice.

Janice and Marva met as young 20 somethings working together as nurses in their city's local hospital. They were both married to men and were raising young families. Although they were already best friends, when Marva's husband died suddenly, the friendship between her and Janice deepened and the two families became inseparable. As time passed, Janice and Marva grew to understand their relationship as more than friendship. They were soul mates who were deeply in love with one another. However, because they feared that their children would reject them, and because Janice did not want to hurt her husband, they continued to represent themselves as friends over the next 20 years. When Marva's adult children moved out of state, she went with them to be closer to her grandchildren. Janice could not tolerate the separation so she divorced her husband and relocated to be near Marva. Marva and Janice created a life together without formally coming out to their families. Their adult children and their grandchildren liked and respected them both and viewed each woman as their "other" mother/grandmother. This living arrangement worked until Marva became gravely ill. When Marva's adult children attempted to exclude Janice from participating in health care and other decisions about Marva's future, the two women disclosed the full nature of their relationship to their families. Both families were distressed. Janice's family distanced themselves and blamed the relationship with Marva for their parent's divorce. After initial upset, Marva's family came to accept and respect Marva and Janice as a couple and helped them establish legal documents to protect their rights as a couple. Janice and Marva's children cared for Marva together until her death 5 years later.

Conclusion

As stated at the opening, lesbian, gay, bisexual, and transgender individuals have always been members of families and always will be. The commitment to family bonds and lasting relationships is evidenced by the fierceness, innovativeness, and creativity with which LGBT individuals create and expand their families. The United States is slowly recognizing and legitimizing LGBT families and creating structures that will nurture their survival, but there is still a long way to go before LGBT-headed families are afforded the rights and benefits that are identical to those granted to heterosexual-headed families. LGBT individuals and their families face the same life cycle processes and tasks as dominant culture families and draw from their experiences as multicultural people to transact these processes and complete these tasks. The additional tasks and challenges that emerge for LGBT individuals and their families do not emerge because there is something wrong with being LGBT. They emerge because of heterosexism, homo-, bi-, and transphobia, rigid adherence to a biologically determined binary gender system, and the interactive effects of multiple forms of subjugation. As discussed, LGBT individuals and their families are resourceful in negotiating these additional tasks and often turn challenges into opportunities for self-determination.

Chapter 9

Spirituality and the Family Life Cycle

Sueli Petry

For much of history, and across cultures, we humans have tried to understand our world and the reason for being here through spirituality or religion. Spirituality has been a healing force through countless generations, embedded in culture and religious traditions. For many people, spiritual beliefs influence how to deal with life's stressful events and pain, and it can offer hope and resilience in times of adversity. Spiritual beliefs can be a powerful resource for people who have lost their way, are feeling despair, or are suffering from oppression, racism, poverty, and trauma (Aponte, 1994, 2009; Barrett, 2009; Boyd-Franklin, 2003a; Hines, 2008; Kamya, 2005, 2009; Walsh, 2008, 2009). It can be a resource in all phases of the life cycle and may become even more important in later age as a means of reviewing one's accomplishments, life's meaning, and coming to terms with the end of life.

Yet, very few mental health professionals explore spirituality as a source of strength. There have been attempts to remedy this situation, especially in the area of substance abuse. The Joint Commission on the Accreditation of Healthcare Organizations requires that a spiritual assessment be conducted with mental health and substance abuse patients (JCAHO, 2008). Psychiatry includes a category of "religious or spiritual problem" in the *Diagnostic and Statistical Manual of Mental Disorders, IV-TR* (American Psychiatric Association, 2000), and Professional Codes of Ethics for social workers and psychologists direct professionals to respect religious diversity (NASW, 2008; APA, 2002). These directives are inadequate, however, because they do not emphasize spirituality as a resource from which clinicians can draw to help people overcome adversity.

In this chapter we address spirituality in clinical work, within the religious diversity present in the United States, exploring the ways in which spirituality may be used in therapy as a resource throughout the family life cycle. We offer guidelines for including spirituality in any clinical assessment and discuss implications for treatment. Various models have been proposed for assessing spirituality (Birkenmaier, Behrman, & Berg-Weger, 2005; Hodge, 2004; McGoldrick, Gerson, & Petry, 2008), exploring spirituality over the life cycle (Kelcourse, 2004), and exploring the influence of cultural experiences on spirituality using a genogram or ecomap (Hodge, 2004). Here, we provide a framework for a systemic assessment, which places the presenting problem in the context of spiritual development, culture, and life cycle stage, using genograms and family chronologies. Understanding context provides alternative views of why a problem exists and helps clinicians and clients see opportunities for new ways of being and relating. Genograms help the clinician and the client to consider family members' spiritual beliefs, how the family has survived and dealt with problems in the past, and to identify people in the family network who might be available as resources for spiritual and emotional support. Family chronologies used in conjunction with genograms facilitate tracking family patterns through time and space (McGoldrick, Gerson & Petry, 2008). Together, these tools help clinicians track the ways in which spiritual beliefs may change over time and as families encounter different experiences. The emphasis on fluidity and change over time and space creates a sense of hope and helps people to see the various ways their families have transformed suffering and adapted to difficult circumstances, through understanding, forgiveness, and growth.

Spirituality and Religion in America

Accurate statistics on practices of spirituality and religion are difficult to confirm, however, according to recent Gallup polls (a widely cited source) approximately 50 percent of Americans describe themselves as "religious," and another 33 percent say they are "spiritual but not religious" (Gallup, 2002). In recent years the Internet has created opportunities for "virtual faith communities," where people may communicate with each other and find inspiration. A Google© search of the word "spirituality" resulted in dozens of spiritual Web Sites, one of the largest, "Beliefnet" (www.beliefnet.org), offers a variety of spiritual resources including message boards and prayer circles for multiple faiths. The religions represented in the United States have changed significantly in the last 3 decades. Whereas Christianity has remained dominant, the non-Christian population has been increasing steadily. Islamic centers or mosques and Hindu and Buddhist centers can be found in nearly every major city in the United States. Americans identify as Jewish, Muslim, Hindu, Buddhist, Baha'i, Jain, Pagan, Zoroastrianist, and more (Pew Forum on Religion and Public Life, 2008). This finding suggests that many times the therapist and client may have differing views or experiences regarding spirituality, which may affect the way in which they relate to each other and the ways in which spirituality may be a part of treatment. Understanding how to proceed with a spiritual assessment and how to integrate it into treatment will help therapists to raise the topic confidently.

Family Life Cycle Theory and Application to Context of Spirituality

Children and spirituality

In the first stages of life, until adolescence (Infancy, Early Childhood, Middle Childhood, and Pubescence) children are dependent on their parents and are the beneficiaries of their parents' spiritual beliefs. They learn values and social behavior and conform to expectations guided by the family's spiritual or religious practices. Often, they derive comfort from religious rituals and beliefs. For instance, a prayer before bedtime can allay a child's anxiety about the darkness or sleeping alone and can help the child feel safe when he or she believes that God, Spirit, or some higher power loves and cares for him or her. Moreover, children develop and grow spiritually just as they do physically and emotionally (Roehlkepartain, King, Wagener, and Benson, 2006). They develop increasing spiritual capacities and experiences as they mature, and their innate sense of wonder leads to exploration and speculation about spirituality (Hart, 2006). When working with traumatized children of varying cultures and religions, asking about spiritual beliefs will likely open up avenues to help them to transform pain and to heal (Kamya, 2009). For those who lost a parent or sibling spiritual beliefs can help them to grieve, as all religions have rituals or beliefs for dealing with death and bereavement. Spirituality can be a tremendous resource in working with children, just as it is in later stages of the life cycle.

Yet, at times their spiritual beliefs may cause children discomfort when they believe they have not lived up to what is expected of them. Parents may not be aware that their children are agonizing over some small infraction that is inflated in their child's mind. Children may worry about what will happen to a family member, friend or others who do not conform to the spiritual practices they have been taught or who do not follow a prescribed code of behavior. In clinical work with children, assessing a child's spiritual beliefs in the context of their family's beliefs may uncover areas of concern for the child. In my experience, children's spiritual beliefs have been relevant in working with children in foster care, those who had parents who were struggling with substance abuse, children who had been sexually abused and were dealing with their feelings about the abuse, and even children with less severe problems such as impulsivity and behavioral difficulties. Some children believe God is watching them and will punish them for their bad behavior.

Understanding the child's beliefs, as well as the family and cultural beliefs, will allow the clinician to address areas of concern for the child and parent and will provide a means to draw on those beliefs to foster healing.

CASE STUDY

Anthony and Angelina: Children's Spiritual Beliefs May Comfort or Cause Anxiety

This case illustrates how a spiritual assessment helped the parents in this Brazilian-American Evangelical family church to comfort and support their children, and fostered the family's healing. At this stage of the life cycle Anthony (10 years old) and Angelina (8 years old) were the recipient of their parents' beliefs. They feared repercussions and experienced feelings of guilt based on what they had learned about religion from their parents and their pastor, but their parents had the power to allay the children's fears.

Anthony and Angelina were living with their father (Hugo) after their parents separated (see **Genogram 9.1**) because their mother (Mariza) was abusing drugs. When they started therapy, Mariza was in treatment for substance abuse and had weekly

GENOGRAM 9.1 Anthony and Angelina

supervised visits with the children. To assess this family it was important to meet with each parent separately and to meet with the children alone in order to allow everyone to speak frankly, and to limit the children's exposure to any of the parents' negative reports about the other. Although children are often exposed to parents fighting at home, it is best to protect children from such scenes in the therapeutic setting.

In the parent sessions, both Hugo and Mariza said they had drifted away from their religious beliefs and experimented with drugs before getting married. Later they stopped using drugs and returned to their religious practice in the Evangelical Church. The couple remained active in the Church until the separation; Hugo and the children continued their religious practices, but Mariza stopped attending services. The reason for the parents' separation seemed to be related to Mariza's substance abuse, but would need further exploration.

When I met with the son, Anthony, alone, I asked him about his spiritual beliefs, and he hesitantly said that using drugs was a sin and he was worried that God would punish his mother because she had used drugs. His loyalty to his mother prevented him from discussing this with his father or anyone else. In a later session with both children, I asked if they had any fears about God and learned they were afraid that God would punish them because they were sometimes angry with their mother. The children's spiritual beliefs caused them feelings of anxiety and guilt. However, as I continued with the spiritual assessment I discovered that their spiritual belief also gave this family something to believe in that was larger than themselves, a belief that could be drawn on to comfort the children and help them to heal.

In separate sessions with each parent, Hugo said he believed in the guidelines of his religion, but having lived through many experiences including abusing drugs himself, he concluded that God was forgiving and provided guidance rather than punishment. Mariza was ambivalent about her beliefs. She believed God would help her find the strength to overcome her addiction and be reunited with her children, but she was struggling with feelings of anxiety and guilt over her behavior, and anger because she felt judged by some members of her congregation. Mariza would not be helpful in allaying the children's fears until she resolved her mixed emotions. Hugo, on the other hand, was in a better position to do so. After coaching Hugo on how to encourage the children to share their feelings and their fears with him, Hugo comforted the children and told them that God loved them and their mother. He told his children that God would look after their family and would help them to get through their troubles.

Hugo's spiritual belief gave the children hope. If Hugo had taken a different position it would have been harder for the children to reconcile their feelings of anxiety. Anthony, because he was older, would be more likely to begin to question his parents' beliefs at this age and to start to form his own views in order to reconcile his religious beliefs and his love for his mother. However, at this stage of the life cycle, both children would have been vulnerable to increasing feelings of anxiety had it not been for their father's reassurance.

When parents have stricter religious views it may be more difficult for children to reconcile religious beliefs when they or their loved ones do not live up to prescribed codes of behavior or when they encounter people with different beliefs. In that scenario spirituality and religion can become a source of struggle, rather than strength. At such times the clinician will need to accept the parents' beliefs and look to other avenues for intervention. The best intervention may simply be to make the parents aware of the child's struggles and to normalize them as something to be expected at this developmental stage. Often children feel guilty when they misbehave. Once they are aware of the problem, most parents can usually figure out a way to help their children reconcile their spiritual beliefs with the realities of the world. Parents want their children to feel safe and loved. We as clinicians can help by respecting the parents' beliefs and coaching them to talk to their children in a way that invites children to ask questions, rather than suffer silently. Children in families who practice a religion that is marginalized

in our society are vulnerable to teasing and prejudice from other children or even adults. Clinicians can intervene by raising these topics and coaching parents so they can in turn raise the issue with their children. Children feel protected and buffered from the cruelty of the outside world when families provide such a safe haven.

When treating children whose parents have left, died, or are otherwise not available, asking about children's beliefs and enlarging the genogram to include beliefs of family, friends, relatives, teachers, and mentors will help children to draw on spiritual strengths. We should not overlook this resource just because a client is young. Children of all ages have the capacity for spiritual thoughts and beliefs, and very often their spirituality can help them to heal.

Adolescence: Identity Development and Spirituality

As children enter the stage of adolescence they can be more autonomous, seek out experiences on their own, and challenge the system as they search for meaning and form opinions about their family's spiritual beliefs. This is the stage of looking for an identity and voicing authentic opinions and feelings in the context of societal, parental, and peer pressure to conform to age, gender, and racial stereotypes. At this phase of the life cycle, some adolescents will question their families' spiritual beliefs as they try to develop an independent sense of identity. While others, particularly those in marginalized groups, may embrace their families' beliefs as they try to affirm their sense of identity within a dominant culture that marginalizes them, for example, Muslim teens growing up in a predominantly Christian community (Chaudhury and Miller, 2008). African American adolescents tend to draw on spiritual strengths to foster a positive racial identity and to overcome the insults of living in a racist society (Moore-Thomas & Day-Vines, 2008), and research indicates that in marginalized communities where spirituality is emphasized adolescents are better adjusted because spirituality increases their sense of belonging, pride, and self worth (Aponte, 1994; Boyd-Franklin, 2003a; Marsiglia,

Parsai, Kulis, & Nieri, 2005; Roehlkepartain, King, Wagener, & Benson, 2006). Still some adolescents in nondominant religious groups may rebel against their family's traditions in order to "fit" with the dominant group.

Given all that we know about spirituality as a resource for helping adolescents in therapy, clinicians need to ask questions about adolescents' beliefs. However, adolescents with a religious affiliation different from the clinician's, or no religion, may be uncomfortable with this topic. First acknowledging that you have different religious beliefs and then asking an open-ended question such as "Will you tell me about your belief?" is one way to communicate that you are comfortable with your differences and that you honor the adolescents' beliefs.

CASE STUDY

Joshua: Adolescents Challenge Family Beliefs

The following case illustrates how an adolescent may shake up the family system and challenge adult beliefs, leading adults to reconsider their own views on religion and spirituality. The case evolved over many months and the treatment is reported here in four phases:

Joshua (18) and his parents Michael (52) and Marcy (50) sought family therapy when Joshua stopped attending high school in his senior year. The crisis occurred when Joshua told his parents he was gay. Joshua felt accepted in his circle of friends, and he wanted the same acceptance from his family. Michael and Marcy were anguished by their son's coming out and their religious belief that homosexuality was a sin, as it is considered in nearly all organized religions due to the rigid constructs of sexuality created by patriarchy.

Phase 1) The genogram (Genogram 9.2) set the context for examining the challenges to spiritual beliefs.

In the initial stage of treatment we explored what Joshua's coming out meant for the family. I asked to meet with the parents alone first to allow them to speak freely without hurting their son. I met Joshua alone once, and later we moved to sessions including all of them, with short meetings alone with each of them to check in on how they were feeling. As shown on the genogram, both Michael and Marcy came from religious families where homosexuality was not accepted, and both had suffered family losses related to religious beliefs.

Phase 2) The chronology (Chronology 9.1) highlighted how earlier generations either turned away from religion or turned toward religion in response to loss, and ultimately transformed the pain of loss and found ways to remain connected through their beliefs.

I asked about the family's history of religious beliefs and practices and wrote down the dates of various

CHRONOLOGY 9.1

Case of Joshua	
1940 Michael's uncle, Joseph, married a Christian woman, left Jewish faith, and was cut-off from family for 20 years.	1960 Joseph's son, Jared, returned to study Jewish religion and the cut-off between Joseph and Morris was repaired.
1940 Michael's father, David, was very close to Joseph and the brothers secretly remained in contact through letters.	1992– Marcy's sister and her husband (Lauren 1999 and Alan) suffered several miscarriages. They consoled themselves through their faith, and by doting on Joshua.
1945 Marcy's paternal grandparents' family was killed in the Holocaust, her father was the sole survivor. He immigrated to New York in 1945 and joined a Jewish community.	2009 Family sought therapy when Joshua told his parents that he was gay.

events they reported. Michael's uncle Joseph was cut off from his family in 1940 when he married a Christian woman; this was a difficult loss for Michael's father (David) who had been very close to Joseph. The brothers remained connected through correspondence. The cut off lasted 20 years and was repaired when David's son, Jared, returned to the Jewish religion in his adolescence. As we tracked these dates related to the challenges to the family's religious beliefs and created a chronology of the family history, a pattern of loss of family, loss of faith, and return to faith emerged. Michael saw that his family had survived challenges of faith and family cut offs in the past. The family became hopeful that they would survive this new challenge.

Marcy's paternal grandparents, uncles, and aunt were all killed in the Holocaust in 1943, a tragic loss for her father, Irving, who was the sole survivor. In 1945, Irving moved to New York and found a Jewish community where he felt welcomed, and he

began to heal from the loss of his family. From 1992 through 1999, Marcy's sister Lauren suffered several miscarriages and was very distraught. Her faith carried her through those difficult years, and when she celebrated the birth of her son, in 1999, the religious ceremony was especially meaningful for the family. Tracking these events and writing them down on the chronology reinforced for Marcy that her family had already suffered too many losses, and that being Jewish was very important for her. She could not lose her son nor her religion.

Phase 3) Therapy enlarged the context to explore religious beliefs about homosexuality within the societal constructs of patriarchy and oppression.

We discussed the implications of Joshua's coming out in light of patriarchy, homophobia, and society's constructs about love and marriage. Enlarging

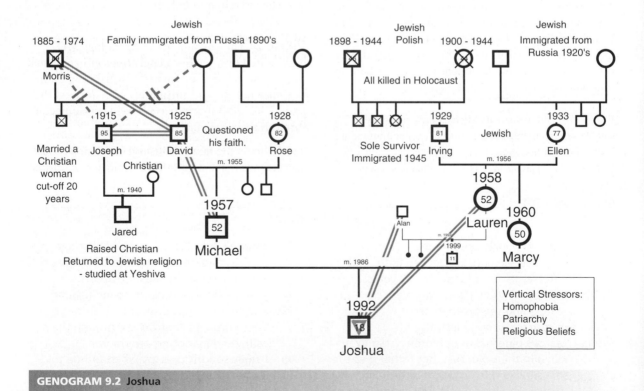

GENOGRAM 9.2 Joshua

the context brought to light how rigid constructs of sexuality were created by patriarchy and oppression so that nearly all of the world's major religions and governments colluded in dictating sexual behavior and marginalizing homosexuality. These conversations helped to alleviate feelings of shame and opened up multiple possibilities for spirituality, religion, and sexuality. As a result the family moved to a more liberal congregation that allowed gay and lesbian rabbis. Joshua had challenged his parents' beliefs. Their determination to remain connected to their son made the parents reconsider their own views on religion and find an alternative they could live with.

Phase 4) The genogram identified family members who would be good resources of support for the family in coming out to their extended family and friends.

Using the genogram, we identified Marcy's sister and her husband, Lauren and Alan, as "good resources" who would be supportive. They chose to tell them first and then to gradually tell the others. The systemic spiritual assessment enlarged the context and created a space where Joshua felt like a fully accepted member of his nuclear family, which they then extended to their relatives and larger community.

This treatment evolved over many months and many families do not have such a successful outcome. However, this family was very committed to each other, as they realized all the more through the exploration of their struggles with religion and spirituality over several generations.

Early Adulthood: Time to Explore and Make Choices About Spiritual Beliefs

As young adults differentiate from their families of origin they may move away from their religion, especially as they come in contact with a wider social network in our diverse society, as they go to college, or enter the workforce. They may become less involved in their family's religious practices and many explore other spiritual paths. Some may wish to distance from practices they felt were oppressive; however, more often this is simply a result of exposure to others' beliefs intersecting with the developmental task of differentiation. Young adults who grew up with no religion may become more religious or may engage in "shopping" for religion or searching for a community. Young people are more likely to engage in varying religious practices and alternative spiritual beliefs (Pew Forum on Religion and Public Life, 2009). Others may need to let go of religion, and say they don't believe, in order to feel freer. At some point individuals have to make a choice about where they stand in relation to their family's beliefs. Often this happens when they move away from home or when they engage in intimate relationships. For many, a crucial time when they need to take a position about their beliefs occurs as they form relationships and make decisions about marriage ceremonies.

Approximately one forth of American adults who are married or living with a partner are in religiously mixed relationships, and the number would be much higher if families with different Protestant denominations were included (Pew Forum on Religion and Public Life, 2008). Jewish communities in particular are concerned about the high rate of intermarriage, and Jewish families may react with disappointment or disapproval (Walsh, 2009). Historically many religions prohibited interfaith marriages, but as society has become more open interfaith marriages have become more prevalent. This is a relevant issue in marriage and family therapy. Spouses with similar beliefs and religious practices report greater personal well-being, more relationship satisfaction, and lower likelihood of divorce (Myers, 2006). Some questions that are helpful in gathering data for the spiritual genogram when working with couples are: What are their spiritual beliefs? What is the history of their family's religious beliefs and practices, including changes in belief? What has been the impact of intrafamily religious differences or those between the family and the surrounding community? Have any family members changed religion? How did other family members react to this change? (McGoldrick, Gerson,

& Petry, 2008). These questions will help the clinician immediately assess the complexities of the spiritual resources available to the couple.

CASE STUDY

Lorraine and Richard: Interfaith Couple's Counseling

Lorraine sought couple's counseling before marriage. One major point of contention was that Richard had not told his family that they did not want a religious wedding ceremony. Lorraine felt that Richard was behaving in a cowardly manner. She wondered whether this was going to be a pattern in their relationship and wanted to address it now before they married.

Getting the family and spiritual history for the genogram helped me to learn that Lorraine was an atheist, she was the eldest of three girls, and her ethnicity was Norwegian. Her grandparents were Protestant but not very religious and her parents were atheists. Richard was Catholic but had not attended services since he moved away from home in his first year of college. He was the only son of an Irish-Catholic father and Italian-Catholic mother. When he was 10, his mother died in a car accident when his father had been driving. The father

went into a depression and never remarried. All four grandparents helped raise Richard after his mother died.

I asked the couple to tell me more about their spiritual beliefs. Lorraine said she believed in science, nature, and charity and she had high moral values. She felt that Richard should be proud of her. Instead he was behaving as if he were ashamed of her and afraid of his family.

Richard said he was not religious but he was not sure what he believed. I wondered if his indecision was related to loss and asked Richard how his family had grieved the death of his mother. Richard said that he and his grandmother lit a candle in church every day for his mother, for many years. He said that thinking about it now, he still envisioned his mother in Heaven. Encouraging the couple to talk about their spiritual beliefs in the context of their family history through the use of the genogram helped Richard realize that he was more religious than he thought.

In future sessions I encouraged Lorraine and Richard to consider how they would raise their children, celebrate holidays, and commemorate other occasions in the future. They were thoughtful young people who loved and respected each other. They had a lot to talk about, now that Richard was finally talking.

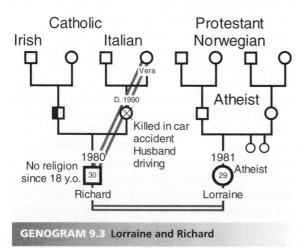

GENOGRAM 9.3 Lorraine and Richard

Even when couples of different faiths have made the adjustments with their families and each other, spiritual and religious beliefs may become a source of conflict as they decide how they wish to raise their children. Most parents want their children to have some religious upbringing (Gallup & Lindsay, 1999), and often couples who viewed religion as unimportant find that the birth of a child changes their perspective and they feel strongly about providing religious instruction for their children (Walsh, 2009). As young adults move from coupling to starting a family they consider what they want their children to learn and believe about religion and spirituality. This may become a source of conflict as couples try to decide how they wish to raise their children, as illustrated in the case of Ana and Luis.

In this case, questions about their spiritual beliefs, in conjunction with the genogram, quickly identified complex issues related to spirituality, class, gender, and oppression.

CASE STUDY

Ana and Luis: Spirituality Overcomes Oppression

Ana called for the appointment for marriage counseling—she said she was feeling sad and lonely because Luis spent many hours out of the home working and studying while she stayed home with young children. She felt they had been growing apart lately. The initial genogram questions revealed that Ana and Luis were married in 2001, they immigrated from Peru 3 years later and they had two children,

Miguel (age 4) and Anita (age 2). In response to questions about their spiritual beliefs Ana and Luis said their family was Catholic. This was a vague answer and it gave me a hint that there might be a problem in this area. I asked, "Your family is Catholic, but what is *your* belief?" Luis said he was agnostic and uncertain about religion. He disagreed with many of the conservative tenets of Catholicism and he did not want to teach his children such conservative beliefs. Ana said she believed in God, and before the birth of their children she had not given much thought to religion, but now felt strongly that she wanted her children to be baptized. She said that since she and her husband disagreed, they had put off making a decision about baptizing their children rather than arguing about it. My hypothesis that they had a problem regarding spiritual beliefs was confirmed. Clinicians may feel uncomfortable pushing

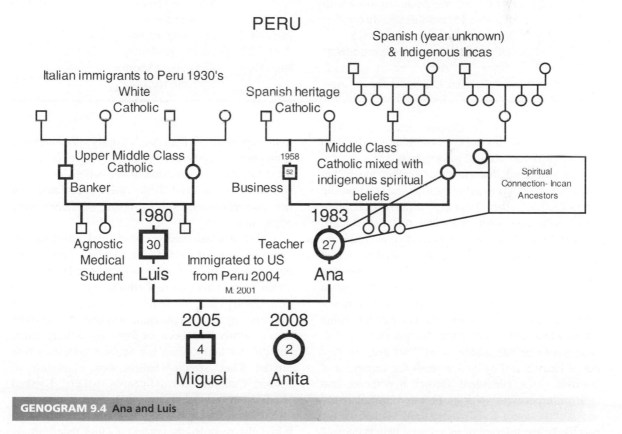

GENOGRAM 9.4 Ana and Luis

CHRONOLOGY 9.2

Case of Ana and Luis

Relevant historical context relating to spiritual beliefs: Religion in Peru was influenced by the Spanish conquest in the 16th century and currently more than 75% of the population is Catholic. Historically, Catholicism was mixed with expressions of the indigenous and African religions.

Pre-1800s Yr Unknown	Ana did not know when her White ancestors arrived in Peru. Her family was mixed racially: White from Spain and the indigenous Incas. Religion was a mixture of Catholicism and indigenous beliefs.		and honoring a "huaca" (holy space), along with the Catholic rituals.
1930s	Luis' family migrated to Peru from Italy. They were White and Catholic.	1984	Ana's father was promoted and the family moved to Lima. Family began to attend Catholic Church in Lima, where most parishioners were upper middle class.
1980	Luis was born in Peru, 3rd of 4 children—family was of upper middle class socioeconomic status, they practiced traditional Catholic beliefs.	2001	Luis and Ana married.
		2004	Luis and Ana immigrated to the U.S. from Peru (the only ones in family to travel to the U.S.). Luis was a medical student in NJ and Ana was a teacher by profession, but did not work in the U.S.
1983	Ana was born, 1st of 4 children. Her family was poor but moved up in status to middle class through father's education. They were Catholic and practiced a modified version of their ancestors' spiritual beliefs, such as respect for nature	2/15/2005	Son, *Miguel*, was born.
		5/1/2008	Daughter, Anita, was born.
		July 2009	The couple sought marriage counseling.

for an answer in this area, but probing gently often reveals important clinical information.

I suspected that Ana was feeling lonely because in their effort to avoid conflict she and Luis did not talk to each other about their differences of opinion. I wondered whether gender role expectations made it difficult for Ana to be assertive with Luis regarding her religious beliefs, and I asked her to tell me about her feelings about baptizing her children. She said she was embarrassed to say that she worried that the children might suffer harm if they were not baptized. She said she knew that she was just being superstitious, but at times she thought that her children would be vulnerable to an "evil eye," or kept out of Heaven if they died without the sacrament of Baptism. This generated further hypotheses that their differences in spiritual beliefs were related to social class status. Luis's upper-middle-class family was likely less tolerant of indigenous beliefs deemed

to be superstitious, than Ana's family who had risen from poor to middle class and had indigenous ancestry. Also, Ana's description of her beliefs as "superstitious" marginalized them, and I speculated that her embarrassment was a result of internalized oppression.

We tracked family history and religious beliefs, and related them to social class, power, and oppression. Luis' family immigrated to Peru in the 1930s from Italy where Catholicism had a 2000-year history, and the family continued to practice Catholicism in much the same way they had in Italy. Ana's family had been in Peru for a long time; she did not know when her Spanish ancestors first arrived. Their spiritual beliefs were a mixture of Roman Catholic and indigenous beliefs. I asked about the timing and changes in spiritual practices and tracked them on the chronology (**Chronology 9.2**). I also recorded the context of class, race, culture, and spiritual beliefs on the genogram, which I showed to the couple. It helped Luis and Ana to see the influence of class and colonization on their beliefs. The upper social classes in Peru were less likely to include indigenous people, and indigenous beliefs were devalued as a consequence of the oppression of colonization. Ana's family moved in socioeconomic status from poor to middle class through her father's education and employment, and they had combined Catholic and Incan rituals for many years. But after 1984 her parents abandoned those rituals when they moved from their village to the capital city of Lima.

I talked about the concept of internalized oppression and asked Ana whether she believed it had influenced her parents' decision to abandon the indigenous rituals in order to be accepted among their new cosmopolitan friends in the corporate world of Lima. The question enlarged the context for Ana and Luis. Ana thought her family felt slightly ashamed of their indigenous ways. She wondered whether her mother had felt as lonely after they moved to Lima as she herself was feeling now. Luis began to consider whether his disillusionment with Catholicism was in response to subtle but similar societal pressures he might be feeling to fit into the scientific community, as a medical student in the United States.

The changes in spiritual beliefs over time were tracked through the chronology, and genogram questions facilitated discussions of the contexts of ethnicity, social class, gender role expectations, power, and oppression. Ana and Luis saw their marital problems in a larger context. They knew that spiritual beliefs had sustained their ancestors. They began to see the loss of spiritual beliefs in their family as a result of internalized oppression and disconnection from their community. As educated young professionals they were interested in the benefits of spiritual beliefs and community as protective factors and wanted them for their children and themselves. They made plans to join a church and to visit Peru more often.

Spirituality can be a source of strength as well as difficulty for couples. Luis and Ana were alone and far from their home and family. As young adults who were busy working and establishing a career and family in a new country they had not been overly concerned about spiritual matters. The birth of their children brought spirituality to the forefront, and it became a source of conflict. Ana avoided the conflict and became sad and lonely as a result. Talking about the historical, political, and familial context of their spiritual beliefs helped the couple draw on their spiritual resources and the strength of their community to reconnect with each other.

Middle-Age: Beliefs Reaffirmed

As in any stage of the life cycle, under particularly difficult circumstances middle-aged people will draw on their spiritual beliefs to sustain them. However, for most, middle age is not a time of deep spiritual change because generally people have already made decisions about their spiritual beliefs earlier in life, usually in early adulthood. Midlife is roughly between ages 45 and 65—the age of launching children and/or caring for elderly parents or aging relatives, in some cultures more than others. By this age most people have had a number of losses and other negative experiences. Some people may turn deeper into spirituality or renew their faith in their religion to make meaning of their losses and disappointments (Wink & Dillon, 2002), or as they deal with other challenging issues. For example, adult children caring for their aging parents with chronic illness may experience a deeper intimacy and spiritual bond with them (Walsh, 2009), and they may find that spiritual resources are especially important at this time (Smith & Harkness, 2002). The importance of spirituality may increase as middle-age adults become older, or have health problems, and face their own mortality. People who had put aside spiritual beliefs may find a need to reconsider their beliefs especially as they try to make sense of loss, trauma, disillusionment, and lost dreams.

CASE STUDY

Lucy: Spirituality, Spirits, and Resiliency in the Face of Untimely Loss

This case illustrates the need for clinicians to be open to multiple possibilities regarding spiritual beliefs. It is not enough to be sensitive to other beliefs. We must be ready to embrace spiritual and cultural resources we may not understand and that may make us uncomfortable, in order to provide good clinical care.

Lucy, a 53-year-old Cuban American woman, who had been diagnosed with chronic major depressive disorder with psychotic features, was grieving the recent death of her 33-year-old daughter from brain cancer (see **Genogram, 9.5**). After her daughter died Lucy became withdrawn, tearful, restless, and unable to sleep. Although spirituality can be a resource in many circumstances, it is particularly appropriate for bereavement issues because all religions have rituals or beliefs for dealing with death, and this comforts many people. When asked about her spiritual belief, Lucy said she converted to Catholicism when she married into a very religious Catholic family. I asked about her spiritual belief before marriage, and she hesitantly told me that her own family of origin had practiced *espiritismo* (the belief in spirits), not unusual in Cuba and other Latino cultures (Petry, 2004; Korin & Petry, 2005). She seemed conflicted about her belief in spirits and needed encouragement. I acknowledged that I was aware of the practice of *espiritismo* and said I would like to know more about her belief. Still hesitant, Lucy told me that she saw her daughter's spirit.

I suspected Lucy was having a psychotic hallucination and asked about conversations she may have had with her daughter to assess for psychosis and suicidal ideation. Other than telling me she saw her daughter's spirit, all of Lucy's answers, as well as her mood and affect, were appropriate. She denied suicidal ideation. She was tearful but said she felt comforted by her daughter's presence and that she needed to be well to help raise her grandchildren. Although my hypothesis needed more testing, I felt

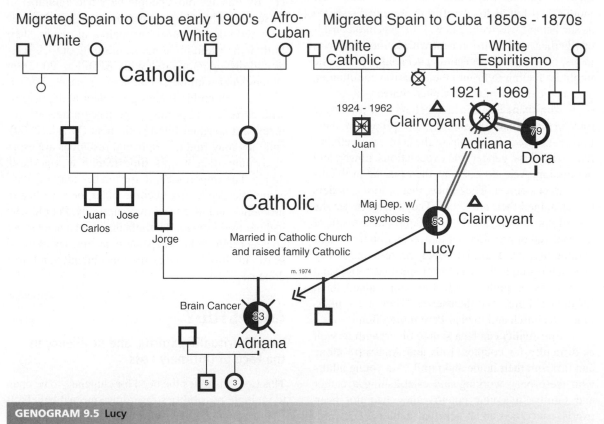

GENOGRAM 9.5 Lucy

reasonably sure that she was safe at this point, and Lucy seemed to be more at ease. I felt I had established rapport with her.

We were at the end of our first session and Lucy asked me if she might take the risk of telling me something. I nodded and said, "Yes, certainly." She told me the spirit of a man named Francisco was standing near and guarding me. She caught me off-guard and I was visibly surprised. Lucy said, "I know you recognize his name by the look on your face," and she described his appearance, a White man with gray hair and a receding hairline descending in a V-shaped point known as a widow's peak. She was describing my grandfather, Francisco Separovich, who died in 1973. This was the first time I met Lucy; she could not have known about my grandfather. Lucy had the ability to see the dead. She saw my grandfather. Now I had to reconsider my hypothesis. Was Lucy clairvoyant? Was her long-term depression caused by a lifetime of being misunderstood? I had joined with Lucy and encouraged her to talk to me about her belief by telling I knew of *espiritismo*. Yet, I had not expected this. I had tried to be sensitive to Lucy's beliefs, but I had not believed in her. Now I had to accept that Lucy had abilities I did not understand! And I had to be comfortable with not understanding in order to do a better assessment.

In subsequent sessions, we worked on her genogram and discussed her family's spiritual beliefs. Lucy spoke about a family myth that her Aunt Adriana was clairvoyant and that she had inherited her aunt's abilities. As a child Lucy had been close to this aunt, but as a young adult she distanced from her family and from her belief in *espiritismo* when she met her husband. Even though many people in Cuba believed in *espiritismo* it was nonetheless an unconventional belief. Lucy described a typical progression of spiritual development over the life cycle: she questioned her spiritual beliefs as a young adult and then abandoned her old beliefs and adopted Catholicism, which she thought was a more acceptable religion. Having struggled with her beliefs in young adulthood and having made her choice, Lucy probably would not have given too much thought to her spiritual beliefs in middle age. However, the loss of her daughter compelled her to reconsider her decision. She derived little comfort from her adopted religion, and perhaps her chronic depression was caused, at least in part, by the denial of her earlier beliefs and her abilities.

Using the genogram to explore spiritual, cultural, and family themes helped Lucy to reconnect with her family's history and beliefs. She began to feel better as she acknowledged that she had felt lost when she denied her belief to practice a more conventional religion. She decided that she could indeed hold both beliefs. She could be Catholic and also believe in spirits. Eventually she told me that her daughter's spirit had gone on its journey, which she understood to mean that her daughter was at peace. From a clinical perspective, I understood this as progress in the process of grief, and believed that Lucy was feeling stronger and therefore could let her daughter go.

My systemic assessment brought out Lucy's strengths, derived from her spirituality and culture. Spiritual beliefs that had been denied because they were unconventional were revived, and they transformed pain and suffering for Lucy. She was still reluctant to talk about her belief in spirits outside of our therapy sessions, but remembering her Aunt Adriana and talking about her spiritual beliefs and childhood experiences in Cuba helped Lucy to find a more inclusive spirituality. Feeling that her spiritual beliefs were validated helped Lucy begin to heal from grief and depression.

No doubt, I was more comfortable than others may have been with Lucy's story because we have similar cultural backgrounds, and her beliefs were familiar to me. However, clinicians can be prepared to hear about uncommon spiritual beliefs by doing the work of self-exploration, which leaves one centered and better able to listen. Sometimes, we do not need to understand or share the belief. Simply listening, with an open heart, can be validating and empowering for the client.

Older Adults: Aging and Facing Mortality

The developmental task at this stage of the life cycle, reviewing a lifetime's relationships and accomplishments and coming to terms with aging and mortality, is spiritual. People who are lucky enough to reach old age in relatively good health and have the time and energy to contemplate death usually want to prepare to dispense of worldly goods, repair relationships, and review their life's work. People do not necessarily become more religious or spiritual as they age, but the process of making sense of life is spiritual. Those who are religious may turn toward the rituals and community of their religious practice to accomplish this task. Those who are not particularly religious or spiritual nonetheless often engage in this spiritual process as they approach the end of life. We all want to believe that our life has meaning and love. This is the essence of spirituality.

Spirituality can be a powerful resource especially for the elderly who are poor, disadvantaged, and disempowered. Poverty and oppression leaves people with diminished power over their destiny. It contributes to the loss of a sense of identity and self-worth, making the task of reviewing one's life particularly painful. Spirituality can give meaning to people's struggles and help them transcend the deprivation of poverty and oppression (Aponte, 2009; Boyd-Franklin & Lockwood, 2009). It can be the light that gives purpose and value to life.

CASE STUDY

Pearl: Spirituality Promotes Dignity in the Face of Poverty and Oppression

Pearl was a 76-year-old African American great-grandmother raising her 15-year-old great-grandson, Jerome. Pearl was diagnosed with terminal cancer and was referred by her primary care physician for therapy. I began with the family history using the genogram and asked Pearl about her spiritual belief. Pearl told me that her faith in God and her church community had always pulled her through. She said she had struggled all her life, but she was a survivor. She had raised three children and helped to raise nine grandchildren. She had no fear of dying as she

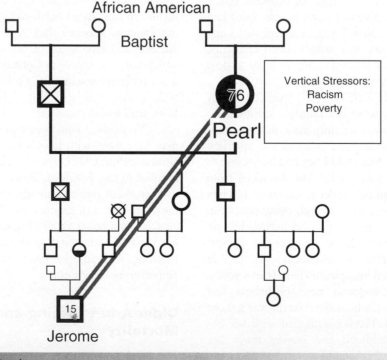

GENOGRAM 9.6 Pearl

was at peace with God, but she wanted to work on a plan for someone to care for Jerome after she died.

Pearl had had more than her share of troubles. She had endured the stresses of poverty and discrimination, but she did not feel defeated. She drew strength from her faith. She was facing a terminal illness and nearing the end of her life, but her spiritual beliefs gave her strength to carry on with dignity and grace.

Unfortunately medical advances and our Western beliefs have made acceptance of death more difficult with the emphasis on mastery over destiny. Some older adults believe that good health and the belief that one is in control of one's life is more important than spirituality (Lowis et al., 2009), but as physical health declines, a focus on psychological and spiritual well-being will help older adults deal with losses related to health issues, diminishing physical stamina and productivity, deaths of loved ones, and their own mortality. Therapists can encourage the elderly to share their life story and assess for spiritual resources to help them avoid depression, disillusionment, or fear of illness and death.

At the same time, while spirituality can be a significant source of strength, unresolved spiritual struggles, such as conflicts over religious beliefs, can cause difficulties leading to declines in health, stress, anxiety, depression, and even death (Ano & Vasconcelles, 2005; McConnell, Pargament, Ellison, & Flanell, 2006). A systemic assessment will help clinicians probe beyond the surface and evaluate for spiritual resources as well as areas for concern.

Good questions to ask at this stage of the life cycle are: Have your beliefs changed over the years? Do your beliefs bring you comfort? Do you consider spirituality to be a source of strength? Whether the answer is "yes" or "no," follow up each question by asking, How? and Why? or Why not? and Are you at peace?

CASE STUDY
Eleanor: Unresolved Spiritual Issues and Depression

This case illustrates how unresolved struggles with religious beliefs made it difficult for Eleanor to find peace. In order for her to move forward, the therapy had to address her spiritual conflict.

Eleanor, an 86-year-old widow of Polish descent, was referred for treatment of depression. She had completed treatment for colon cancer, which was in remission, yet she was sad, withdrawn, and isolated. Before this illness Eleanor had been perky and energetic. After retiring from her position as a secretary in a manufacturing company she had remained active for many years. Until recently she had volunteered at a hospital, taken classes at the local community college, and taken care of herself and her apartment. Now she had to force herself to get out of bed before noon; she had lost interest in everything, and she was afraid to leave home.

In exploring her history, Eleanor told me she was Polish Catholic, the eldest of four children, but had not attended church for many years. I asked if her beliefs had changed over the years, and she told me that she became disillusioned with the Catholic Church a few years ago when she learned that a priest had sexually abused her brothers when they were boys. Eleanor had been married to Joe, who was also Polish Catholic, and they had raised their children, Joe Jr. and Karen, in the Catholic religion.

She believed in God but was disillusioned with the Catholic Church and organized religion. She said that she was afraid to die. She enjoyed good relationships with family members, and was especially close to her sister, but she could not talk to them about her fear of dying. As Eleanor spoke about her family history I wondered whether her unresolved issues with the Catholic Church were exacerbating her stress, anxiety, and depression. At this stage in the life cycle, Eleanor's developmental tasks included dealing with chronic illness and making meaning of her life. My hypothesis was that she needed to resolve her conflicts with the Catholic religion in order to manage those tasks and be at peace.

I encouraged her to bring her sister, Caroline, to therapy because they were close. I asked about their belief in God and an afterlife. Eleanor's conversations with Caroline helped her realize that she could believe in God and pray at home. She concluded that her decision not to attend church was the right one for her, but she could still honor her spiritual and religious beliefs in her own way.

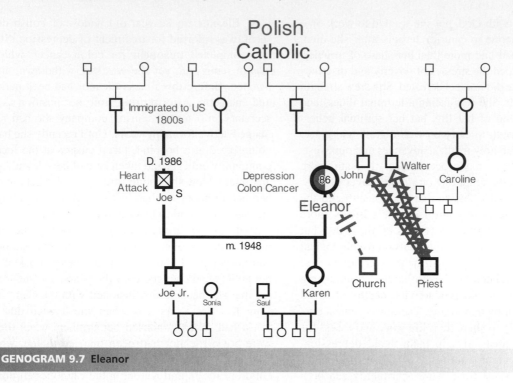

GENOGRAM 9.7 Eleanor

The systemic assessment including questions about spirituality helped Eleanor to see her problem in the context of her family's history with the Catholic religion. She found spiritual peace by speaking directly to God and sharing her thoughts with her family. Finding peace allowed her to work on her life cycle tasks of dealing with chronic illness and facing death.

Conclusion

Throughout history and across cultures people around the world have relied on religion and spirituality to promote emotional well-being during times of celebration and times of loss or trauma. Spiritual awareness and growth are possible throughout all life cycle stages, and spirituality becomes especially significant when facing times of stress. The case illustrations presented highlight how to do a systemic assessment that takes into account spiritual resources and family strengths across the life cycle, tracking changes over time and looking for opportunities to enlarge the context in order to transform pain into healing.

Chapter 10

Siblings and the Life Cycle

Monica McGoldrick & Marlene F. Watson

My dearest friend and bitterest rival, my mirror and opposite, my confidante and betrayer, my student and teacher, my reference point and counterpoint, my support and dependent, my daughter and mother, my subordinate, my superior and scariest still, my equal.

ELIZABETH FISHEL (1979, P. 16)

The Importance of Sibling Relationships Through the Life Cycle

Sibling relationships are the longest that most of us have in life. Indeed, from a life cycle perspective, the sibling bond may be second only to the parent–child bond in importance. In our modern world, spouses may come and go, parents die, and children grow up and leave, but if we are lucky, siblings are always there. During the middle phases of the life cycle siblings may be preoccupied with partners, children, and work, but as people move through the life cycle, sibling relationships show increasing prominence (Cicarelli, 1995; White & Riedman, 1992a; Meinhold, 2006; McKay, Cryer & Caverly, 2004; Friedman, 2003). Our parents usually die a generation before we do, and our children live on for a generation after us. It is rare that our spouses are closely acquainted with our first 20 or 30 years or for friendships to last from earliest childhood until the end of our lives. Our siblings thus share more of our lives genetically and contextually than anyone else, particularly sisters, since sisters tend to be emotionally more connected and are likely to live longer than brothers. In fact, we can divorce a spouse much more finally than a sibling (McGoldrick, 1989b).

Yet sibling relationships have been largely neglected in the family therapy literature and in the mental health field in general. Children spend more of their out-of-school time in childhood with siblings than with anyone else in their lives (McHale &

Crouter, 2005) and are more likely to grow up in households with siblings than with fathers. In later life, once parents are gone, the sibling bond can become our primary attachment, though at that point sibling relationships also become optional and many times break (Gold, 1989; Norris & Tindale, 1994). Especially in recent times as parents are living longer and often need long-term caretaking, conflicts among siblings can become painfully intensified in late middle age (Friedman, 2003; Connidis & Kemp, 2008). It is a great wonder that family scholars and developmental psychologists so often overlook this area of study, given the primary reciprocity of siblings to well, being throughout life (McHale & Crouter, 2005).

Apart from Adler's (1959, 1979) early formulations, followed up by Walter Toman's *Family Constellation* (1976), hardly any attention has been paid to siblings in the psychological literature. Luckily, a number of excellent works in the past few years have begun to counter this neglect, such as Bank and Kahn's *The Sibling Bond* (2008), Kahn and Lewis's *Siblings in Therapy* (1988), Barbara Mathias's *Between Sisters* (1992), Marianne Sandmaier's *Original Kin* (1994), Susan Scarf Merrell's *The Accidental Bond* (1995), Frank Sulloway's *Born to Rebel* (1996), and Victor Cicirelli's *Sibling Relationships across the Life Span* (1995). In our view, the neglect of siblings in the literature reflects cultural attitudes that overvalue the individual and nuclear family experience and neglect the lifelong connections that we have to our extended family members throughout the life cycle.

We hope that this chapter will encourage therapists to ask more questions about sibling relationships for people of every age, affirm the importance of sibling connections through the life cycle in all clinical assessments, and validate sibling relationships through therapeutic interventions that support and strengthen these bonds. We encourage therapists to hold specific sibling sessions when appropriate.

Perhaps our therapeutic approach would be facilitated if we worked on the basic assumption of including siblings unless there is a reason not to. That is, in doing an assessment, we could start with the question "Why *not* have a sibling session to understand or help clients in this situation?" rather than starting with the negative and including siblings only if there is a specific sibling conflict.

In some families, relationships with siblings remain the most important. In others, sibling rivalry and conflict cause families to break apart. Siblings can become the models for future relationships with friends, lovers, and other contemporaries, and for a significant portion of the population, their strongest and most intimate relationships (Wellman, 1979).

In today's world of frequent divorce and remarriage, there may be a combination of siblings, stepsiblings, and half-siblings who live in different households and come together only on special occasions. There are also more only children, whose closest sibling-like relationships will be with their friends or cousins. There are more two-child families as well, in which the relationship between the children tends to be more intense for the lack of other siblings, especially if their parents divorce. Thus, sibling relationships may become more salient for the current generation because of all the factors that are diminishing the size of the family and community network. Clearly, the more time siblings spend with one another and the fewer siblings there are, the more intense their relationships are likely to be. Furthermore, siblings who have little contact with outsiders grow to rely on each other, especially when parents are absent, unavailable, or inadequate.

Though there has been extremely little research on longitudinal aspects of sibling relationships, siblings generally seem to have a commitment to maintaining their relationships throughout life, and it is rare for them to break off their relationship or lose touch with each other completely (Cicirelli, 1985). Among the few findings that we have are data showing that siblings of the handicapped, especially sisters, are particularly likely to become drawn into emotional caretaking demands from their families. Involving siblings in planning and treatment obviously benefits the whole family. Yet very few programs for the disabled include work with siblings (whether children or adults) as a focus of their intervention.

The evidence is that sibling relationships matter a great deal. According to one important longitudinal study of successful, well-educated men (the Harvard classes of 1938–1944) the single best predictor of emotional health at age 65 was having had a close relationship with one's sibling in college. This was more predictive than childhood closeness to parents, emotional problems in childhood, or parental divorce, more predictive even than having had a successful marriage or career (Valliant, 1977)!

Age Spacing

Sibling experiences vary greatly. An important factor is the amount of time brothers and sisters spend together when they are young. Two children who are close in age, particularly if they are of the same gender, generally spend a lot of time together, must share their parents' attention, and are usually raised under similar conditions. Siblings who are born far apart spend less time with each other and have fewer shared experiences; they grow up at very different points in their family's evolution and are in many ways more like only children.

Sulloway (1996) maintains that children who are closest in age have the greatest competition and rivalry for their parents' care; therefore, the second sibling has the greatest need to differentiate from the older to find a niche for him- or herself.

The ultimate shared sibling experience is that of identical twins. They have a special relationship that is exclusive of the rest of the family. Twins have been known to develop their own language and maintain an uncanny, almost telepathic sense of each other. Even fraternal twins often have remarkable similarities because of their shared life experiences.

The major challenge for twins is to develop individual identities. Since they do not have their own unique sibling position, there is a tendency to lump twins together. This becomes a problem especially when, as adolescents, they are trying to develop their separate identities. Sometimes twins have to go to extremes to distinguish themselves from each other.

Gender Differences

Sister pairs tend to have the closest relationships. Sisters generally have been treated differently from brothers in families, given the pivotal caretaking role that sisters typically have in a family. Both brothers and sisters report feeling more positive about sisters (Troll & Smith, 1976) and indicate that a sister was the sibling to whom they felt closest (Cicirelli, 1982, 1995; White & Riedman, 1992a). According to a survey by Cicirelli (1983), the more sisters a man has, the happier he is and the less worried about family, job, or money matters. Sisters seem to provide a basic feeling of emotional security. The more sisters a woman has, the more she is concerned with keeping up social relationships and helping others (Cicirelli, 1985). Siblings can provide role models for successful aging, widowhood, bereavement, and retirement. They act as caretakers and exert pressures on each other to maintain values.

With rare exceptions, fewer expectations for intellectual and worldly achievement are placed on, or allowed to, sisters than brothers. It is interesting that in Hennig and Jardin's classic study (1977) of highly successful women in business, not a single woman in the sample had had a brother. Research indicates that while the preference for sons is diminishing (Entwistle & Doering, 1981; Washington, 2007), there is still a greater likelihood that a family with only female children will continue to try for a boy. We have come a long way from the infanticide that other cultures have resorted to when they had daughters instead of sons, but the remnants of those attitudes still exist. Families are more likely to divorce if they only have daughters, and divorced fathers are more likely to lose contact with children if they are daughters. On the other hand, recent research has shown that parenting daughters increases feminist sympathies. Fathers of daughters vote significantly more liberally than fathers who have sons only, and the more daughters a father has, the higher his propensity to vote liberally, particularly on reproductive rights issues (Washington, 2007).

Unlike oldest sons, who typically have a clear feeling of entitlement, oldest daughters often have feelings of ambivalence and guilt about the responsibilities of their role. Whatever they do, they feel that it is not quite enough, and they can never let up in their efforts to take care of people and make the family work right. They are the ones who maintain the networks; who make Thanksgiving, Christmas, and Passover happen; who care for the sick; and who carry on the primary mourning when family members die. They are central in family process, more often taking responsibility for maintaining family relationships than their brothers. Sisters not only do the majority of the caretaking, but they tend to share more intimacy and have more intense relationships than brothers, although they typically get less glory than brothers do. From childhood on, most sibling caretaking is delegated to older sisters, with brothers freed for play or other tasks (Cicirelli, 1985). Brother-to-brother relationships appear to be characterized by more rivalry, competitiveness, ambivalence, and jealousy (Adams, 1968; Cicirelli, 1985), while sister relationships are characterized by more support and caretaking.

Sister relationships, like those of women friends, are more often devalued than peer relationships involving men. A woman who wants to avoid a move for her husband's job to be near her sister is considered strange indeed. She will probably be labeled "enmeshed" or "undifferentiated." Yet it is the sister who was there at the beginning, before the husband, and who will most likely be there at the end, after he is dead and gone. A strong sense of sisterhood seems to strengthen a woman's sense of self (Cicirelli, 1982, 1985; Noberini, Brady, & Mosatche, in press).

With the best of intentions, parents may convey very different messages to their sons than to their daughters. In certain cultures, such as Italian and Latino, daughters are more likely to be raised to take care of others, including their brothers. Some cultural groups, such as Irish and African American families, may, for various historical reasons, overprotect sons and underprotect daughters (McGoldrick, 1989a; McGoldrick, Giordano, & Garcia Preto, 2005). Other cultural groups have less specific expectations. Anglos, for example, are more likely to believe in brothers and sisters having equal chores. But, in general, it is important to notice how gender roles influence sibling patterns in understanding a family (McGoldrick, 1989b).

Birth-Order Effects in Sibling Relationships

Although birth order can profoundly influence later experiences with spouses, friends, and colleagues, many other factors also influence sibling roles, such as temperament, disability, class, culture, looks, intelligence, talent, gender, and the timing of each birth in relation to other family experiences—deaths, moves, illnesses, changes in financial status, and so on.

Parents may have a particular agenda for a specific child, such as expecting him or her to be the responsible one or the baby, regardless of that child's position in the family. Children who resemble a certain family member may be expected to be like that person or to take on that person's role. Children's temperaments may also be at odds with their sibling positions. This may explain why some children struggle so valiantly against family expectations—the oldest who refuses to take on the responsibility of the caretaker or family standard bearer or the youngest who strives to be a leader. In some families, it will be the child who is most comfortable with the responsibility —not necessarily the oldest child—who becomes the leader. Parents' own sibling experiences will affect their children as well. But certain typical patterns often occur that reflect each child's birth order.

In general, oldest children are likely to be the overresponsible and conscientious ones in the family. They make good leaders, because they have experienced authority over and responsibility for younger siblings. Often serious in disposition, they may believe that they have a mission in life. In identifying with their parents and being especially favored by them, oldest children tend to be conservative even while leading others into new worlds; and though they may be self-critical, they do not necessarily handle criticism from others well.

The oldest daughter often has the same sense of responsibility, conscientiousness, and ability to care for and lead others as her male counterpart. However, daughters generally do not receive the same privileges, nor are there generally the same expectations for them to excel. Thus, they may be saddled with the responsibilities of the oldest child without the privileges or enhanced self-esteem.

The middle child in a family is in between, having neither the position of the first as the standard bearer nor the last as the baby. Middle children thus run the risk of getting lost in the family, especially if all the siblings are of the same sex. On the other hand, middle children may develop into the best negotiators, more even-tempered and mellow than their more driven older siblings and less self-indulgent than the youngest. They may even relish their invisibility.

Frank Sulloway (1996) argues on the basis of a large sample of historical figures that later-born children, both middle and youngest children, are very much more likely to be rebels than are oldest or only children because of the Darwinian imperative for survival. The niche of following in the parental footsteps has already been taken by the oldest, and they need to find a different niche to survive. They therefore tend to be less parent identified, less conscientious, and more sociable. Traditionally, in many European cultures, younger children, sons in particular, had to be disposed of, since the oldest took over the family farm or business from the father; younger sons tended to become warriors or priests or fulfilled other less conventional roles in society.

A middle sister is under less pressure to take responsibility, but she needs to try harder to make her mark in general because she has no special role. She remembers running to catch up with the older sister from childhood and running frantically from the younger one, who seemed to be gaining on her every minute (Fishel, 1979).

The youngest child often has a sense of specialness that allows self-indulgence without the overburdening sense of responsibility of oldest children. This pattern may increase in intensity with the number of siblings there are in a family. The younger of two children probably has more a sense of pairing and twinship—unless there is a considerable age differential—than the youngest of 10. Freed from convention and determined to do things his or her own way, the youngest child can sometimes make remarkable creative leaps leading to inventions and innovations.

Youngest children can also be spoiled and self-absorbed, and their sense of entitlement may lead at times to frustration and disappointment. In addition, the youngest often has a period as an only child after the older siblings have left home. This can be an opportunity to enjoy the sole attention of parents but can also lead to feelings of abandonment by the siblings.

A younger sister tends to be protected, showered with affection, and handed a blueprint for life. She may either be spoiled (especially if there are older brothers) and have special privileges or, if she is from a large family, frustrated by always having to wait her turn. Her parents may have run out of energy with her. She may feel resentful about being bossed around and never taken quite seriously. If she is the only girl, the youngest may be more like the princess, yet the servant to elders, becoming, perhaps, the confidante of her brothers in adult life and the one to replace the parents in holding the family together at later life cycle phases.

Like middle children, only children show characteristics of both oldest and youngest children. In fact, they may show the extremes of both at the same time. They may have the seriousness and sense of responsibility of the oldest and the conviction of specialness and entitlement of the youngest. Not having siblings, only children tend to be more oriented toward adults, seeking their love and approval and in return expecting their undivided attention. The major challenge for only children is to learn how to get along with others their own age. Only children often maintain very close attachments to their parents throughout their lives but find it more difficult to relate to friends and spouses.

The number of children in a family is also a determining factor in siblings' life course. The more siblings there are, the less likely success appears to be as a function of having to compete for resources (Conley, 2005).

Life Cycle Issues in Families With Disabled Siblings

We need to plan therapeutically for the lifelong implications that a handicapped child has for all family members, especially for the adjustment and caretaking responsibilities of the siblings. Siblings respond not only to the disabled child but also to parents' distress and/or preoccupation with the needs of the disabled child. Parents may also shift their hopes and dreams onto their other child, which can create burden and sibling strains (Cicirelli, 1995). Older children tend to make a better adjustment to disability than do younger ones because older children are better able to put the situation in perspective. Relative birth order is also important. A younger sibling may have difficulties associated with needing to assume a crossover leadership role (Boyce & Barnett, 1993). Siblings become especially stressed when parents expect them to be preoccupied with the needs of the disabled sibling or to treat him or her as "normal." During adolescence, siblings may feel particular embarrassment about a disabled sibling. On the other hand, if they have developed greater maturity through sibling caretaking experiences, they may feel out of step with peers (Cicirelli, 1995).

Oldest sisters of disabled siblings are at greatest risk because of increased parental demands on them. Brothers of the disabled tend to spend more time away from the family (Cicirelli, 1995). This is something that clinicians can help families to change. Parental expectations need to be questioned as we help parents to include brothers in caretaking and prevent sisters from becoming overburdened. Otherwise, in later life, brothers may become completely disengaged from the disabled sibling, while sisters are left with total responsibility for them.

Small families tend to experience more pressure when there is a disabled child because there are fewer siblings to share the responsibility. The pressure seems increased when the disabled sibling is a brother, probably because of parents', especially fathers', reactions of personal hurt to pride in having a disabled son. Sisters seem more ready to accept the role of caretaker for a brother and to have more sibling rivalry or competition with a disabled sister. In a study of siblings of children with intellectual disabilities, older sisters were more affected than older brothers, because they generally got the lion's share of the caretaking responsibility for the sibling. Their career and family decisions were also the most influenced by the disabled sibling. Sisters tended to be closer to the impaired child than brothers, to be given more responsibilities as well more information about the sibling's disability than brothers were. Older sisters were found to enter the helping professions more often than other siblings (Cicirelli, 1995).

The following is an illustration of the life cycle implications of the imbalance in caretaking responsibilities between an older sister and younger brothers in providing care for a disabled brother (**Genogram 10.1**). It provides a classic portrayal of the findings in the literature.

The Donnellys (Genogram 10.1) are a family of Irish-German and Roman Catholic background. Both parents had died in the past few years of chronic illnesses, leaving behind an oldest daughter, Mary Ann, a younger brother, Jim, and youngest fraternal twin brothers, Michael and Charles. Charles had been born with cerebral palsy. Mary Ann had been reared for a caretaker's role since childhood;

she had also taken care of her chronically ill father for 2 years before his death. And then she cared for her chronically ill mother until her death 2 years after the father. Although she had attended college and had a successful career as a computer analyst, she was never free to take even an overnight vacation from her brother.

When her other brothers distanced themselves from her and Charles in the wake of the mother's death, Mary Ann began to have unexplained stomach pains, and her family physician referred the family for therapy. The family therapist initially addressed the family's problems as unresolved mourning and attempted to involve the reluctant brothers in taking some responsibility for the disabled brother in an attempt to reconnect the family by helping them to mourn the death of their mother. Many attempts were made to assemble all family members together.

Charles's twin brother Michael was easier to involve in therapy than the older brother, Jim. Michael had almost cut off from the family when he married his Italian

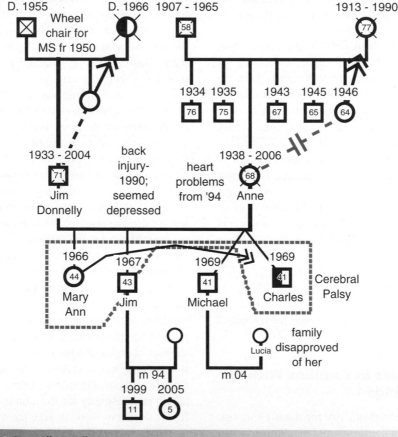

GENOGRAM 10.1 Donnelly Family

wife, Lucia, of whom the family disapproved. The marriage had occurred shortly after the father had died, and the mother had felt doubly bereft by the loss of her husband and her son, who, she said, chose to leave the family in their time of need. Michael almost seemed to have been waiting for the chance to sort out issues he had with the family. Within 2 months, he sought help for his own marital problems and continued working hard on his connections to his brother and sister.

The older brother, Jim, was much harder to involve in the therapy. He made one excuse after another for not attending sessions and then said that his wife's feelings were hurt because Mary Ann had not attended his daughter's christening. He assumed unquestioningly that it was the sister's responsibility to care for Charles, a role Mary Ann herself seemed to accept as hers alone. She presented as guilt ridden and depressed, having pledged undying loyalty to her mother's dying wish that she care for Charles, despite the fact that her personal and social life had been sacrificed by this commitment.

To understand this better, we inquired about the sibling relationships of both parents and discovered that the father, also named Jim, also an oldest son, had been virtually cut off from his sole sister, who had cared for their widowed mother, who was wheelchair-bound with multiple sclerosis for many years. We were able to explore with the other siblings the father's longstanding depression, which they believed resulted from his own unhappy cut off from his parents. We discovered that the sibling overfunctioning and underfunctioning in the current generation and the imminent cut offs reflected similar imbalances in both parents' families that had led to sibling cut offs at midlife. Mary Ann and Charles initially wanted to ignore Jim and his family, but the therapist challenged them to try to overcome the family legacy of sibling cut off. The therapist also challenged Mary Ann and the others with her "duty" and the long-held family and cultural beliefs about sisters' obligations in caretaking. She has recently been successful in asserting herself with Charles's doctors regarding their assumptions about Charles's need for her continual monitoring. She took her first vacation in many years, while Charles went to stay with Michael and his wife.

Sibling Positions and Parenting

If you have struggled in your own sibling position, as a parent you may overidentify with a child of the same sex and sibling position as yourself. One father who was an oldest of five felt that he had been burdened with too much responsibility while his younger brothers and sister "got away with murder." When his own children came along, he spoiled the oldest and tried to make the younger ones toe the line. A mother may find it difficult to sympathize with a youngest daughter if she always felt envious of her younger sister. Parents may also identify with one particular child because of a resemblance to another family member. Whether these identifications are conscious or unconscious, they are normal. It is a myth that parents can feel the same toward all their children. Problems develop when a parent's need for the child to play a certain role interferes with the child's abilities or with two siblings' relationship to each other or to outsiders. A parent's identification with a child may be so strong that he or she perpetuates old family patterns in the next generation. On the other hand, if their own experience has been different, parents may misread their own children. A parent who was an only child may assume that normal sibling fights are an indication of trouble.

Siblings and Adolescent Relationships

At least by adolescence, siblings provide important models and alter egos. One sibling may begin to live out a life path for the other, so that they become alternate selves. Sisters in particular also often share secrets, clothes, and sensitivities about their parents' problems.

Gay and lesbian adolescents may have a particularly difficult time at this phase of their budding sexuality, in dealing with peers, parents, and institutions. Having a supportive sibling network can be an extremely important cushion against these rejections, while the lack of sibling support can add to the sense of isolation and rejection of children at this time.

Obviously, not all siblings are close. Childhood rivalries and hurts carry over into adolescence and adulthood. At family get-togethers, everyone tries, at least at first, to be friendly and cordial, but beneath the surface old conflicts may simmer. By adolescence sibling dysfunction may require one child to grieve the loss of dreams for another and for their relationship, if the other is seriously dysfunctional, suffering from autism, mental illness, or addiction.

Sibling Relationships in Young Adulthood

Closeness to siblings has been found to be strong just before they leave their parental home (Bowerman & Dobash, 1974; Troll, 1994). This closeness is followed by a distancing during the early and middle years of adulthood, but at later life cycle phases people rate affectional closeness with siblings higher and conflict lower than do middle-aged siblings (Brady & Noberini, 1987). As they reach young adulthood, sisters often grow farther apart, each focusing on her own friends, work, and relationships and on developing her own family. Siblings may get together during holidays at the parental home, but often the focus is primarily on the relationship of each to the parents or spouses rather than on their relationships with each other. Support may be weakest at this phase, and competition may be strongest: Who went to the better school? Whose husband or children are more successful? Whose life is happier? The images that each develops of the other are often colored less by their personal interchanges than by the rivalries carried over from childhood or the parental images, which get transmitted to each other as they each hear from parents about the other's life. A younger sister who felt dominated or abused by her older brother may feel uncomfortable even sitting at the same table with him. All the unpleasant memories flood back. Two brothers who spent their childhoods competing in sports, in school, and for parental attention may find themselves subtly competing in the holiday dinner table conversation. Even if there are no major flare-ups, family members may leave the dinner feeling bored or vaguely dissatisfied, glad that such occasions occur only a few times a year.

Whether deliberately or inadvertently, parents can perpetuate such old sibling patterns. A mother may compare one child with another, perhaps chiding one for not calling as often as another does. A father might talk repeatedly about how proud he is of his son, not realizing that he is ignoring his daughter. A parent may elicit the support of one sibling in an effort to "shape up" another. Clinically, therapists can do much to challenge such values on behalf of all siblings.

It is at this phase also that sisters may move into different social classes as they marry and move, according to the culture's expectations, to adapt to their husband's socioeconomic context. They themselves are often not able to define this context, which has traditionally been defined by the husband's education, work, and financial status. Although some cultures, such as African American and Irish, emphasize friendship between siblings more than other groups, such as Scandinavian or Jewish culture (Woehrer, 1982), the sister bond is generally continued through a mutual sense of shared understanding and responsibility for the family, more than through common interests, especially when class differences between the siblings have developed.

Sibling Positions and Marital Relationships

Sibling relationships can often pave the way for couple relationships—for sharing, interdependence, and mutuality—just as they can predispose partners to jealousy, power struggles, and rivalry. Since siblings are generally our earliest peer relationships, we are likely to be most comfortable in other relationships that reproduce the familiar sibling patterns of birth order and gender. Generally speaking, marriage seems easiest for partners who fit their original sibling pattern, for example, if an oldest marries a youngest, rather than two oldests marrying each other. If a wife has grown up as the oldest of many siblings and the caretaker, she might be attracted to a dominant oldest, who offers to take over management of responsibilities. But as time goes along, she may come to resent his assertion of authority, because, by experience, she is more comfortable making decisions for herself.

All things being equal (and they seldom are in life!), the ideal marriage based on sibling position would be a complementary one in which, for example, the husband was the older brother of a younger sister and the wife was the younger sister of an older brother. However, the complementarity of caretaker and someone who needs caretaking or leader and follower does not guarantee intimacy or a happy marriage.

In addition to complementary birth order, it seems to help in marriage if one has had siblings of the opposite sex. The most difficult pairing might be that of the youngest sister of many sisters who marries the youngest brother of many brothers, since neither would have much experience of the opposite sex in a close way, and they might both play the spoiled child waiting for a caretaker.

There are, of course, many other possible sibling pairings in marriage. The marriage of two only children might be particularly difficult, because neither has the experience of the intimate sharing that one does with a brother or sister. Middle children may be the most flexible, since they have experiences with a number of different roles.

Coupling and marriage tend to increase the distance between siblings. Sisters may be pressured by their spouses to decrease their intimacy with each other, and that pressure may create sibling distance that lasts until later life. Maya Angelou (1981) has described the efforts siblings must make to remain connected in spite of spousal pressure:

> I don't believe that the accident of birth makes people sisters and brothers. It makes them siblings. Gives them mutuality of parentage. Sisterhood and brotherhood are conditions people have to work at. It's a serious matter. You compromise, you give, you take, you stand firm, and you're relentless. . . . And it is an investment. Sisterhood means if you happen to be in Burma and I happen to be in San Diego and I'm married to someone who's very jealous and you're married to somebody who's very possessive, if you call me in the middle of the night, I have to come. (p.62)

In-Laws, Step- and Half-Siblings

The relationship of half- and stepsiblings through life depends on many factors including the distance in age, gender, presence of full siblings in the household, gender of stepparent and continuity of stepparent experience, length of time living together during childhood, marital status, race, social class, religion, parental divorce, proximity and emotional closeness to parents and to each other, and the overall cultural values of family connectedness (White & Riedman, 1992b). Generally speaking they are not as close as full siblings except where circumstances have drawn them into special connection as where a parent or another sibling has been impaired or lost. Nevertheless, the interesting point is that people generally define step- and half-siblings as "real" kin, even though the connections are overall weaker than for full siblings.

In similar ways, sister-in-law and brother-in-law relationships can have some of the positives of sibling relationships without the tensions, but things only sometimes work out this way. Sisters-in-law share a future but not a biological or childhood history. As Bernikow (1980) put it:

> At the border of family and friends stands my sister-in-law Marlene. We do not share a mother, do not worry about the pull of likeness and the need for separation. Much of the conflict and tension between sisters is missing for us. Still, as sister-in-law, it is possible that she might be my sister in spirit. The things that arise between us are things that arise between other women, touched by our family affiliation. (p. 105)

The interesting aspect of in-law patterns is the extent to which the structure of the family tends to determine in-law relationships in a family, even though family members are sure that it is just personality characteristics that they are reacting against in rejecting an in-law.

Sisters-in-law who marry into families that have only brothers probably have the greatest likelihood of developing positive connections to the new family. The wife of a youngest brother of older sisters is probably in the most difficult position, since this brother may have been treated like a prince. He may be resented though protected by his sisters, whom he probably tried to avoid for their "bossiness." When he finds a wife, his choice is likely to reflect in part his need for some protection against other powerful females, and his wife may then become the villain, supposedly keeping him from having a closer relationship with his sisters. Nevertheless, family relationships of those who have been raised as kin and peers, such as half- or step-siblings, and often also cousins or those who live through adulthood as kin and peers such as sisters- and brothers-in-law have real clinical importance. They may be significant resources and supports to family connectedness. On the other hand, when their connections are negative, they can be a source of great difficulty.

Sibling Relationships in Midlife

Often, it is not until midlife that siblings reconnect with each other, through the shared experiences of caring for a failing or dying parent, a divorce in the family, or perhaps a personal health problem, which inspires them to clarify their priorities and to redefine which relationships in life really matter to them. Sometimes, at this point, relationships that have been maintained at a superficial level may break under the strain of caretaking or under the pain of the distance that has grown between them. On the other hand, siblings may now be brought closer to each other. Their relationships may solidify through the realization that their parents will not always be there and that they themselves must begin to put the effort into maintaining their own relationship.

In our culture, sisters are generally the caretakers of parents and other unattached older relatives or the managers who have responsibility to arrange for their caretaking. In other cultures, such as in Japan, this role goes to the wife of the oldest son. In our culture, if sisters do not do the primary caretaking, they often feel guilty about it because the cultural pressure is so strong and they are often held responsible by others.

Sibling relationships can be a most important connection in adult life, especially in the later years. However, if negative feelings persist, the care of an aging parent may bring on particular difficulty. At such a time, siblings may have been apart for years. They may have to work together in new and unfamiliar ways. The child who has remained closest to the parents, usually a daughter, often gets most of these caretaking responsibilities, which may cause long-buried jealousies and resentments to surface.

While the final caretaking of parents may increase a child's commitment and closeness to them (Bass & Bowman, 1990), it may either draw siblings together or arouse conflicts over who did more and who felt loved less. It is at the death of the last parent that sibling relationships become voluntary for the first time in life. While parents are alive, siblings may have contact with and hear news about each other primarily as a function of their relationships with their parents. If there are unresolved problematic issues in a family, they are likely to surface at this time in conflicts over the final caretaking, the funeral, or the will. Once the parents die, siblings must decide for the first time whether to maintain contact with each other.

Because it is women who tend to be central in maintaining the emotional relationships in a family, sisters may focus their disappointments on each other or on their sisters-in-law more than on their brothers, who are often treated with kid gloves and not expected to give much in the way of emotional or physical support when caretaking is required. Brothers may provide financial support, but the usual excuse for their lack of involvement is that they don't have the time—they are busy with their work—as if sisters were not equally busy with their own work.

Sibling Relationships After the Death of Parents

Once both parents have died, sibling relationships become truly independent for the first time. From here on, whether they see each other will be their own choice. This is the time when estrangement can become complete, particularly if old rivalries continue. The focus may be on concrete disagreements: Who should have helped in the care of their ailing parent? Who took all the responsibility? Who was more loved? Strong feelings can be fueled by old unresolved issues. In general, the better relationships siblings have, the less likely it is that later traumatic family events will lead to a parting of the ways.

At the end of the life cycle, sisters are especially likely to be a major support for each other or even to live together. Older women are especially likely to rely on their sisters, as well as their daughters and even their nieces for support (Anderson, 1984; Lopata, 1979; Townsend, 1957). Anderson (1984) found that sisters were the ones to whom older widows most often turned, more often than to children, even though they were not more available geographically.

She speculated that the reasons might include sisters' shared history of experiences and life transitions. She concludes that siblings, especially sisters, take on added significance as confidants and emotional resources for women after they have been widowed.

Because siblings share a unique history, reminiscing about earlier times together is an activity in which they engage at many points in the life cycle. Such reminiscing tends to become even more important late in life. It helps all siblings to validate and clarify events and relationships that took place in earlier years and to place them in mature perspective, and it can become an important source of pride and comfort (Cicirelli, 1985). This seems especially meaningful for sisters who tend anyway to define themselves more in terms of context and to place a high value on the quality of human relationships. Cicirelli (1982) found that having a relationship with a sister stimulates elderly women to remain socially engaged with others as well. Although the relationships of sisters, like all female relationships, tend to be invisible in the value structure of the culture at large, sisters tend to sustain one another in time of need throughout life. In old age, they become indispensable. As Margaret Mead (1972) described it:

> Sisters draw closer together and often, in old age, they become each other's chosen and most happy companions. In addition to their shared memories of childhood and their relationships to each other's children, they share memories of the same house, the same homemaking style, and the same small prejudices about housekeeping.

Mead's comment is interesting in its focus on the details of life. Especially as we grow older, it is the details—of our memories, or of our housekeeping, or of our relationships with each other's children—that may hold us together.

We are coming to appreciate more the importance of adult sibling relationships as researchers have observed that family support for caregivers correlates with the presence of siblings (Bedford, 1989). As we age, some sibling relationships lose the competitive quality of childhood and become more like friendships (McGhee, 1985; Norris & Tindale, 1994). As personal resources may become overtaxed by the demands of frail or demented aging parents, sibling bonds may either become overtaxed or provide the extra energy for caretaking. Sibling relationships may also become closer with aging, as activities and preoccupations of earlier life cycle phases diminish. The loss of a spouse who may have interfered with sibling closeness leaves siblings with more time and need for the comfort and sharing of the sibling bond. Cicirelli (1989) found that attachment is more likely to characterize sibling ties when sisters are involved. It does appear that sibling rivalries generally diminish in later life. Generational solidarity increases and sibling bonds appear to have greater salience for siblings as they age (Norris & Tindale, 1994).

Other Factors That Intersect With Sibling Patterns: Culture, Class, and Race

In addition to early parental loss, temperament, the child's physical attributes, family traumas, and major life changes related to politics, economics, and emotional factors affecting families, class, culture, and race also powerfully influence sibling patterns. Cultures and classes differ in the expected roles and relationships of siblings (Leder, 1991; McGoldrick et al., 2005; Nuckolls, 1993; Sandmeier, 1994; Sulloway, 1996; Zukow, 1989).

A family's ethnic identity may determine whether siblings are close, distant, or created equal (Leder, 1991) and the meaning of the siblinghood. Some ethnic groups, such as Asians, may show a greater preference for male children; some, such as African Americans, value the family unit over individual members; others, such as Anglos, give priority to autonomy and self-reliance. Even the concept of sibling rivalry is culture-bound, being largely a Western phenomenon that stems from a focus on individual achievement, competition, and status. In contrast, a huge segment of the world's population dissuades children from assuming the stance of sibling-as-rival by instilling in them a sense of "we-ness" rather than "I" (Sandmeier, 1994). In cultures that train their children to view each other as necessary, siblings are more likely to have lifelong, enduring ties.

In some oppressed cultures, the closely knit sibling bond is also influenced by historical needs for survival. Family members rely on mutual support and aid to fulfill basic material and emotional needs. In African American families, the tradition of tightly woven sibships that was passed down from African culture is combined with the family's need to function as a unit to deal with the forces of racism (Watson, 1998). Thus, strong sibling bonds may be more necessary for African Americans than for people in cultures that are not affected by oppression and in which siblings can live independently of each other. In cultures in which sibling caretaking is a major form of caretaking, as it is for African Americans, strong emotional attachment, positive or negative, may have a profound effect on siblinghood throughout the life cycle (Watson, 1998). Although large sibships such as those that may be found in Irish Catholic families may also produce older sibling caretakers, this role will probably end with childhood. Among African Americans, however, sibling caretakers tend to continue their role into adulthood. Childhood sibling caretaking helps to prepare them for their lifelong role as each other's keeper (Watson, 1998). Hence, the expectations of African American siblings have implications for individual and family development throughout the life cycle.

Some cultures use the term "brother" or "sister" to convey the depth of a cherished relationship. The Vietnamese, for example, address lovers and spouses as "big brother" or "little sister," and African Americans may greet one another with the term "Brother" or "Sister" to convey their sense of kinship (Sandmaier, 1994). Such terms of endearment express the particular culture's valuing of sibling relationships.

The family's emotional map is governed by its cultural roots. Families of Northern European and Anglo backgrounds may discourage strong displays of feeling or affection and will probably view themselves, their siblings, and their parents as a related collection of individuals. German brothers and sisters would also be likely to refrain from showing strong or open affection toward one another because of the cultural prescription to maintain a stiff upper lip (Sandmaier, 1994). In Italian culture, in which the family supercedes the individual, sibling relationships tend to be close, especially between same-sex pairs. In a study conducted by Colleen Leahy

Johnson (1982), 63 percent of middle-aged Italian women saw a sibling daily, in contrast to 12 percent of their Anglo counterparts. Among college-educated older Americans, African American siblings were three times as likely as Whites to focus on themes of loyalty, solidarity, and enduring affection. Hence, the cultural message that African Americans receive to stay together and help each other does not disappear as family members move up the class ladder or move toward old age.

In Greek and Jewish cultures, conflicting messages about family loyalty and individual success and competition may add to sibling tensions. Siblings may be fierce rivals at the same time that family cohesion is expected (Sandmaier, 1994). Irish siblings also seem to have ambivalent feelings toward one another. Irish culture's emphasis on dichotomies and labels may spark sibling rivalry while simultaneously inducing guilt in the sibling for having bad thoughts. Thus, buried resentments that enable siblings to appear connected while the parents are alive may lead to sibling cut offs in the wake of parental death.

Culturally influenced family rules and scripts set the stage for sibling relationships (Sandmaier, 1994; Watson, 1998). As more Americans face longer lives without partners or children, sibling relationships must be revisited. Our brothers and sisters are potentially emotional and physical resources at all points of the life cycle, but individual needs for attachment and belonging are apt to be more critical at later junctures of the life cycle.

In cultures that prize individuality over family unity, siblings' life cycle patterns may remain distinct and separate as brothers and sisters keep their families of procreation apart. In cultures that demand family cohesion or enmeshment, siblings' life cycle patterns may become fused, making it difficult for families of procreation to establish their own traditions and ways of relating.

Understanding the cultural context of sibling relationships provides a larger framework for addressing individual issues of self-esteem and identity, unresolved issues of childhood, and sibling relationships through the life cycle. A sister from a culture that prefers sons may stop blaming her brother and have greater compassion for her parents once she realizes the cultural script in which they all played a part.

Class differences are likely to have a major impact on adult siblings from oppressed cultures or poor families. Unacknowledged or overt resentments may characterize adult sibling relationships for siblings who end up in different socioeconomic groups. Lower-class African American siblings may hold their resentment of middle-class or professional brothers and sisters in check because of cultural expectations of familyhood and their need for physical support. Middle-class brothers and sisters may resent lower-class siblings for relying on them but not feel free to express such resentment because of the sense of family obligation.

In Jewish families, sibling resentment or cut offs may result from intense feelings around the success or lack of success of one's brother or sister. Parental reactions to successful and non-successful children may exacerbate sibling fissures related to class differences. The need to prove oneself intellectually superior and successful for Jewish siblings may be related to their cultural history and oppression. Class differences between Jewish siblings might adversely affect their relationship, especially if one perceives the other as having had an unfair advantage.

Class differences in Anglo families may result in sibling antagonism, but the cultural pattern of individuality and autonomy may obscure such resentments or conflicts. Since these siblings tend not to mingle except for formal family occasions, sibling tensions would go virtually unnoticed and probably would not be dealt with by the siblings themselves. Lower-class family members at family events may be treated like poor relations, or they may be closed out of family events altogether. Although lower-class family members could be treated negatively by middle-class African Americans, it would not go unnoticed, and the mother would probably intervene on behalf of the lower-class sibling. Regardless of the ethnic or cultural group, class tensions are likely to surface when aging or ill parents require care from children.

Class may influence the way rebellion intersects with sibling position. Just as oldest sisters may be more rebellious than oldest brothers because the gender inequities impinge on an oldest sister's "right" to be the leader, oldest siblings in minority families may become more rebellious than oldest siblings

from the dominant groups because of the interaction of social privilege and status with sibling status. Sibling position may exaggerate the class effects of oppression, which lead people to resist the status quo (for example, making a younger sibling of a poor family even more rebellious), Sulloway (1996) found that, as with the interaction of gender and birth order, the oldest child in a poor family may use a strategy of rebellion against the status quo as the best way to achieve eminence. Radical reformers have tended to come from racial minorities and lower classes, and to be later-borns. In Sulloway's research, abolitionism attracted the highest proportion of later-borns of any reform movement he surveyed. Still, because Sulloway's research focused primarily on Europeans who became involved in scientific revolutions, we need further research on culture, class, gender, and sibling patterns from other countries where lives include other spheres of activity and interest. Sulloway suggests that the early parental loss in the upper classes diminishes sibling differences based on birth order, as nannies and other caretakers come in to replace the lost parent, and siblings become more supportive of each other as they share their loss. In middle- and lower-class families, the opposite may happen. The oldest child is drawn into the burden of parenting younger siblings and becomes even more conservative, leading the younger siblings to become even more rebellious than otherwise. Large sibships reinforce the first-born's duties as surrogate parent.

Rules of Thumb for Sibling Relationships Through the Life Cycle

1. Take a proactive stance about including siblings in assessment, whatever the presenting problem. Say to yourself, "Why not have a sibling session?" rather than thinking of including a sibling only when the client presents a sibling problem directly.
2. When one sibling is bearing the weight of sibling caretaking for a parent or a disabled sibling, work to improve the balance of sibling relationships so that the siblings can be more collaborative.
3. Assess and carefully challenge inequities in family roles and emotional and caretaking

functioning of brothers and sisters. In general, sisters tend to be seriously overburdened and brothers to seriously underfunction in terms of meeting the emotional needs of the broader family.

4. Validate the importance of sibling relationships and encourage resolution of sibling conflicts whenever possible.

Conclusions

Throughout the family life cycle, relationships are constantly changing. Our relationships with our parents are the first and, perhaps, foremost in reminding us of our family lineage—where we come from. Without knowledge of our uncles, aunts, grandparents, and great-grandparents, how can we know who we are? Just as important in shaping our personality development are our relationships with our siblings (Adler, 1959, 1979; Sulloway, 1996; Sutton-Smith & Rosenberg, 1970). Unlike our relationships with our parents, our friends, and our spouses, our sibling relationships are lifelong. However, the gender differences are pronounced in sibling relationships. Sibships of sisters tend to differ from sibships of brothers. Whereas brother relationships are often more competitive and superficial, sisters tend to be more connected and deeply involved in each other's lives and the lives of other family members throughout the family life cycle. Although less honored or glorified, sisters are often the designated caretaker of disabled family members. They are confidantes and healers of the family. Their lifelong friendships become even more significant and stronger after parents

die and as they themselves enter old age. Given the importance of these bonds, which are always present in the family therapy context, therapists should become more aware of their influence, initiate more clinical research, and integrate these observations in their interventions. Including siblings in therapy at any point of the life cycle can validate the importance of their relationships, help them to resolve their conflicts, whether recent or deep seated from unresolved childhood conflicts, and strengthen them for their future. Sibling sessions can unlock a client's stuckness, provide richness to an understanding of a client's history, and provide relief for dealing with current stresses. A single sibling session may become a pivotal experience in an adult's therapy. One isolated research scientist who sought therapy because of his wife's frustration with his emotional distance held a session with his three brothers who came from all, over the country for the meeting. All three brothers who were in their 40s, discussed their different responses to their mother's mental illness in their childhood and learned that each had become isolated in his own way. Each brother thought his problems were unique and individual, but they discovered as they reviewed their life experiences how profoundly connected they had always been and would always be. This session shifted the client's basic relationship with his wife. He now saw himself as a man among brothers, going through life together, and felt strengthened in his ability to be open with his wife. As was described earlier, sibling sessions can encourage under-involved siblings to share caretaking burdens, modify gender imbalances, resolve longstanding conflicts, and increase collaboration.

Chapter 11

Single Adults and the Life Cycle
Kathy Berliner, Demaris Jacob, & Natalie Schwartzberg

The Single Adult and the Family Life Cycle

Although most people marry at some point in their lives, the numbers of those who are single are increasing. In the 1970 adult (over age 18) population in the United States, 19 percent of men and 14 percent of women had never been married. By 2006, 33 percent of men and 26 percent of women had not married (U.S. Census data). Even when marriage does occur, factors such as delayed marriages, increased birth rate for single mothers, a 40 to 50 percent divorce rate, and longer life expectancy mean that more people than ever live single during the course of their life. The 2007 census update showed that, for the third consecutive year, the majority of households in America are headed by unmarried people. (U.S. Census data.)

It is much more common, therefore, to be single in the twenty-first century. As it has become more common for people to live alone, societal tolerance has broadened to include many more "acceptable" forms in which adults may live, thereby increasing options for adult life. There has been a mushrooming of singles organizations, advocacy groups, and blogs not aimed at achieving marriage, but at addressing the needs of the unmarried. At the same time, our society continues to have a bias toward marriage and a form of adult life (i.e., two married parents and children) that no longer represents the norm. In 2008, the U.S. Government launched a $5 million media campaign aimed at 18 to 30 year olds extolling the benefits of marriage . . . just like health campaigns to stop smoking or wear seat belts (Jayson, 2007). The research on the benefits of marriage is as yet inconclusive with some studies indicating married people are healthier and some indicating no difference between married people and singles on measures of emotional maturity and physical health (DePaulo, 2006). Apart from the institution of marriage, what research does show is that affiliation reduces stress (Taylor 2000), and marriage has been the traditional way to engage in a social context, particularly for men. While marriage may be less of a requirement of adulthood, it still represents for many the desired if not idealized state. As a result single people continue to be viewed and may view themselves as flawed or vulnerable.

Single people are likely to experience ambivalence about their single status. One therapeutic focus may well be to help the single person view the single life as an authentic way to live, even in the context of societal messages that denigrate them or relegate them to the margins of the "mainstream." At the same time, singlehood presents certain practical challenges. In addition to managing social and familial stigma, the single person must address the human need to seek and maintain emotional ties to others. Married or single, the capacity to develop secure attachments is critical for one's well-being. The pursuit of romantic relationships and the expression of sexuality, establishment of friendships that endure within continual shifts in mutual emotional availability, and attachment to other forms of "family" within religious, political, or other communities are more crucial for the single.

Singleness has been regarded as simply a transitional period between families or, if prolonged, as a sign of failure to achieve an essential adult task. While marriage is one of life's big milestones, problems arise when people regard marriage as *the* next step necessary for the unfolding of adult life. The single person may become frozen, waiting for marriage, not moving forward with the business of life. We all will, in all likelihood, spend some part of our adult life singly. In this chapter, we hope to articulate the issues and the pressures contributing to emotional and developmental growth in the single person's life cycle, without marriage and children as the driving factors.

We have tried to grasp the experience of living life singly, without children or a live-in romantic partner, and validate the experiences of those who may marry in the future, those who choose to be single, those who may rear children without partners, and those who simply happen to find themselves single at a time in their lives when they had not imagined they would be. Much of the material in this chapter is derived from our book *Single in a Married World* (Schwartzberg, Berliner, & Jacob 1995), which contains a more comprehensive discussion of the clinical issues and the context (ethnic, class and cultural, and sexual orientation and identity) of the single person. While some of what we present is relevant to gay and lesbian single people, the experience of living in the intense homophobia of our society, and the denial of the legal sanction of marriage, until recently, wields a profound impact. Additional issues overlay those that heterosexual single people deal with and are beyond the scope of this chapter. (see Chapter 9 for a discussion of the impact of marginalization on gays and lesbians).

Setting the Clinical Stage

Clients often come to therapy distressed about their single status, and in working with these clients therapists must recognize the impact of messages from the culture, the family, and from the therapist that imply that single people are not mature adults. The therapist needs to understand the meanings *each individual client* has taken from 1) the larger society, 2) multigenerational themes in the family, 3) class and culture, and 4) gender.

Marriage as social empowerment

Marriage is an empowering institution that creates an automatic status change for both men and women in the family of origin, in religious and societal organizations, and in the perception of self. It provides public acknowledgment of movement to responsible adulthood and participation in the ongoing history of family and society. As one 50-year-old divorced Jewish woman put it, "I became a second-class citizen overnight."

The importance of marriage, and conversely societal discomfort with singlehood, varies with

political climate. The emotional power of the code phrase "family values" gives the clear message that those who live outside a heterosexual marriage are outside the accepted fabric of American life itself. The struggle in the gay community to be able to achieve the status of "married" may well be taken as evidence of the sense of empowerment and legitimacy that marriage provides (Cherlin, 2005). We haven't changed all that much; this is reminiscent of life in the 1950s, when the postwar culture also elevated marriage, the family, and family consumerism (Coontz, 1992).

Furthermore, community and religious life is structured to a great degree around passages of life created by marriage and parenthood. A Christening, a Bar or Bat Mitzvah, Confirmation, graduation . . . these are the events that are celebrated. Single people participate, but the main story is always about someone else's children.

Marriage and the family of origin

Marriage has important functions in the structure of the family of origin. It is the way to perpetuate names, rituals, and family lineage. In the ongoing life of the family, marriage often initiates the realignment of relationships between parent and child. It can signal a "successful" end to the rearing of children and defines new boundaries between generations. When marriage doesn't occur in the expected time frame, a gridlock can occur in the unfolding of family life, leaving parents and the single adult struggling to find other ways to mark adulthood. This process has historically been more difficult for daughters, who only recently are being raised to have an adult role outside of marriage.

Multigenerational themes

The meaning of marriage and singlehood in each family is best viewed from the perspective of at least three generations. The highly conflictual or abusive marriage of an emotionally important ancestor, for example, may continue to ripple its "marriage meaning" through time. Marital events such as divorce are also pertinent. Parents may worry that their divorce is influencing their child's ability to wed, or unresolved issues from the divorce may perpetuate a reactivity that either romanticizes or damns marriage. The view of single people in the family will also be an influence. Identifying roles models who have led satisfying single lives may provide a counterpoint to the importance of marriage.

When reactivity around marriage/singlehood interlocks with other generational legacies, the impact will be even more powerful. Family sensitivity to a theme of underresponsibility in men, for example, may greatly intensify pressure on sons to demonstrate responsible manhood through marriage.

Class and culture

The single client's vision of the roadmap of single life, the alternatives available and the shape of the life itself, are highly impacted by class (the amount of money available) and culture (the converging threads of religious, racial, ethnic, and immigration history). As therapists, we tend to make fewer inquiries about money than we do about emotional and multigenerational legacies; this omission does a disservice to working-class (or lower-income) people. Economic status not only impacts alternatives such as the viability of establishing a residence outside the parental home but also the issue of "marriageability" itself (particularly for men). The decline in blue collar jobs since the 1970s, for example, has made men without a college education less desirable as marriage partners (Cherlin, 2005) In the American Black community, racism, high mortality and incarceration rates, and economic disadvantage in obtaining skills necessary for upward mobility have also decreased the pool of marriageable men. (Lane et al., 2004). As the rate of Black women entering college and graduate school has increased, the disparity in achievement has made it harder for Black women to find equal status partners; high achieving Black women have a lower marriage rate than their White counterparts (Nitsche and Brueckner, 2009). According to 2000 data, Black Americans had the lowest rate of marriage of any cultural group. Forty-three percent of adult Black men and 42 percent of Black women reported themselves never married. (U.S. Census Data), representing a drastic change in the Black community's historical embrace of marriage as a way to join mainstream society (Heiss, 1988).

Living in a time of economic fluctuation or depression can also seriously disrupt people's vision of what they "should" be doing to be successful as single adults. There are wide cultural variations in patterns of launching young adults into the world beyond family of origin. For example, those of Anglo American heritage traditionally expect their children to establish independence early and with less parental involvement than those of Italian or Brazilian heritage. (McGoldrick, Giordano, & Garcia Preto, 2005) In times of economic growth, the expected early launching can be accomplished; in hard economic times, single adults and their parents may feel they have failed and have no well-known pathways of incorporating independent adults into daily family life.

A deep ethnic thread impacting "acceptable" alternatives for single people is the experience of genocide in the family multigenerational religious or ethnic history (Rosen & Weltman, 2005). Jews and Armenians, among others in our very recent past, have been peoples whose liquidation has been systematically attempted. Thus, the emotional imperative to procreate is strong, with marriage the prescribed precursor. Choosing to remain single in this context becomes not just an individual decision; it impacts the continuance of the entire culture.

There are also wide cultural variations in who is considered "family" and in the presence (or absence) of valued roles available to the single person throughout the life cycle within family, religious, and cultural contexts. Family may mean just immediate relatives, several generations as in Italian families, or one's ancestors as in Asian families. In working with single clients it is important to gain as complete a picture as possible of their understanding of what singlehood means in their own context. For example, many Black Americans have grown up within an expansive notion of family, including blood and nonblood kin, which makes more room for valued functional roles for single people than in cultures that place emphasis on nuclear family units. (Boyd-Franklin, 2003a). The Irish have had a greater tolerance for singlehood than almost any other group (McGoldrick, 1996). Marriage was viewed not as a framework for self-fulfillment but rather for parenting, often bringing economic hardship in the wake of increasing numbers of children (Diner, 1983). For women, the Church—not the family—had histori-cally been the center of community life (McGoldrick, 2005).

These provide only a few examples of the complexity of the interweaving of cultural and class threads that impact your single client. Understanding these legacies is essential so that therapists will be less likely to impose their own cultural biases, and clients can approach family of origin issues in new ways. Clients who are fixated on marriage may see these explorations as digressions; therapeutic finesse lies in respecting client's perceptions while making larger perspectives relevant.

The Single Person's Life Cycle

Single people often have difficulty locating themselves in the flow of "normal life"; they (and their families) are unclear as to what the next step is when marriage and/or childbirth don't occur. Our life cycle phases and tasks are based on life's chronological milestones as well as other drivers of adult development.

At each phase of adulthood, single people still need to confront the expectation of marriage, cope with having an unrealized goal if marriage is desired, and understand the impact of living a life that is different from the expected norm. While we have broken the life cycle into phases, we recognize that there will be considerable variation as to when issues emerge as well as overlap from stage to stage. What is consistent is the ongoing need for emotional support and attachments. Creating support systems and accommodating their ebb and flow over the life span demands more effort and thought for single people, whereas married people, especially with children, can fall back on those social structures that accompany marriage. At the same time, it is easy to idealize the amount of support, nurturance, and affiliation that marriage provides. Single people should therefore, in anticipation of marriage, not neglect this work.

Although the stages of the single adult life cycle form a progression through nodal points of the aging process (which trigger the need for growth), the specific ages associated with each life cycle stage are meant to be viewed as relatively elastic guidelines.

The Stages

The Twenties: Establishing Adulthood
Restructuring interaction and boundaries with family from dependent to independent orientation.

Finding a place for oneself in the world outside the family—in work, friendships, and love.

The Thirties: The Single Crises
Facing single status.

Expanding life goals to embrace possibilities in addition to marriage, including child-rearing.

Midlife: Developing Alternative Scripts
Addressing the "ideal family" fantasy to accept the possibility of never marrying and the probability of never having biological children.

Redefining the meaning of work.

Defining an authentic life that can be established within single status.

Establishing an adult role within the family of origin.

Later years: Putting It All Together
Consolidating decisions in work life.

Enjoying the freedom and autonomy of singlehood.

Acknowledging and planning for the future diminishment of physical abilities.

Facing increasing illness and death of loved ones.

The Twenties: Establishing adulthood

The complex emotional work of the young adult is launching from the family of origin and finding a place for herself or himself in the world. During the past 2 decades, with the trend toward marriage at a later age, this stage may include a period of living on one's own or with a partner (Cherlin, 2005), with early marriage playing less of a role in defining boundaries and bestowing adult status. Anxiety about single status for most will be at its lowest in the 20s, when developing a career or job skills for men and women is at the forefront. The backdrop for the 20s, however, continues to be the assumption that marriage will eventually take place and that finding a mate is part of the "work." The young adult's gender, class, ethnicity, and sexual orientation will shape the vision each young adult has of how and when this will be accomplished.

When the central emphasis of the young adult period is preparing for a career and developing a sense of self, concern about finding a mate will be lower. In cultures in which universal and early marriage is expected, however, or when career opportunities are limited and/or young people do not have the money for prolonged career preparation, a focus on marriage or child-rearing as the next step will arise earlier.

GENDER DIFFERENCES While both men and women of all educational levels are postponing marriage, there are gender differences in the perception of the impact of achievement on marriageability. Men know that increased status through education and earning power will only be an enhancement, while women worry that achievement may diminish their chances for marriage. (Faludi, 1991). The perception is that men also have more time to become marriageable while women's marriageability decreases with age. Over the last decade, however, better educated and achieving women are marrying in greater numbers than less educated women, and two-income couples are the largest growing demographic of married people (Zernike, 2007). Yet, popular culture portrays higher achieving women at best as missing their moment to find a mate or at worst lacking in the ability to form relationships. The pressure on men to achieve and accept responsibility, perhaps in the face of high achieving women and uncertain economic times, has spawned what has been coined the "bro" culture for middle-class White young men described by Kimmel in his book *Guyland*, in which 18- to 26-year-old men are embracing a prolonged adolescence and buddy substitute family that is both homophobic and anti-woman, in the service of avoiding adult responsibility (Kimmel, 2009). Women's anxiety about postponing marriage or men's anxiety about being able to provide for wife and family reflect our continued belief in a marriage gradient in which men should marry women of equal or less economic status and women should marry equal or up.

For women, when messages from society and family equate concentrating on career with lowering one's marriageability, singlehood anxiety and conflict about the next life step can become intense by the late 20s. These feelings are illustrated in Betsy Israel's article in *Mirabella* (1996), in which she writes:

> *My symptoms (loss of purpose in life, loss of interest in career, crying continuously) could have indicated any number of depressive states. Yet I came to view them all in one highly particular way: I had failed completely to become a couple. (p. 69)*

Black women may feel less in a bind; while White parents (especially working-class ones) continue to view marriage for daughters as a route to financial stability, Black parents place much more emphasis on preparing daughters to work (Higginbotham & Weber, 1995) and tend not to see marriage as a replacement for the need to earn money (Staples & Johnson, 1993).

MARRIAGE AS A PREMATURE SOLUTION Although less frequently than in previous generations, young adults may enter marriage as a premature solution to the central emotional work of negotiating an adult self within the family of origin or as a way to escape intense intergenerational conflict in the home. When children cannot afford to leave and establish their own territory, or when parents expect their children to live at home until marriage, the conflict between generations can escalate greatly.

Therapy may involve helping the young client and his or her family to postpone a precipitous marriage that would only detour or triangulate the emotional work of negotiating an adult self. Renegotiating new boundaries without marriage is difficult work, however, when positions are rigid and conflict is intense.

ESTABLISHING RELATIONSHIPS OUTSIDE THE FAMILY Friendships and love relationships outside the family supply the emotional foundation for emerging independence and the development of an adult self. When friendships are taken seriously, as they should be—not viewed as transitional to marriage—there is less of a tendency to invest all of one's emotional energy in finding "Mr(s). Right." We need to inquire about the meaning, depth, and extent of friendships in all people's lives, but particularly for single people. Finding a path that places equal emphasis on the development of work skills and the capacity for close relationships is important for the healthy growth of both sexes. The treatment of Bob illustrates the problems a man may have with investing in friendships

Bob, a White, middle-class, 28-year-old man of British, Dutch, and German background, entered therapy depressed and demoralized because he had been unable to find a new girlfriend after the breakup of a 3-year relationship. Bob was very successful at work but was lonely and isolated. He had trouble making friends on his own and counted on girlfriends to provide emotional anchorage. His neediness was pushing women away.

Rather than focusing exclusively on his difficulties in romantic relationships, the therapy addressed the crucial task of creating social networks. For Bob, looking at multigenerational themes was particularly relevant. He came from a Midwestern Protestant family. The older of two boys, he described his mother as emotionally distant and his father as warm but weak. His mother, to whom he looked for the moral leadership of the family, had never sought friends. She thought the need for friends indicated a weakness of character. When Bob was coached to find out more about his mother's family, it emerged that her own mother had been orphaned at birth. Although Bob's grandmother had been raised by a caring relative, she had feared becoming emotionally attached. The lesson she taught her daughter, Bob's mother, was that one should act as if one didn't need people.

Tracking the generational messages about the meaning of friends was key for Bob in opening up awareness of his needs for affiliation. Having friends would make for a more enjoyable life and take the intensity off finding a mate. Bob's work in exploring his parents' history allowed him to approach his family differently. He now

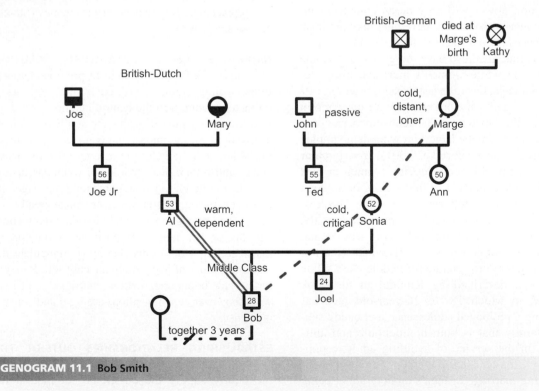

GENOGRAM 11.1 Bob Smith

began to have more personally revealing conversations with his mother, broaching previously taboo subjects such as her "self-sufficiency" compared to his own neediness.

If the young adult can keep anxiety about finding a spouse low enough, the process of dating can be helpful in learning about the self in relationships and in experimenting with adult gender and social roles. Dating that is fraught with intensity about latching onto a mate can only become draining and painful.

Owning an adult self also includes finding ways to validate one's sexuality. This means either dealing with the complexities of being sexual outside of marriage (including the specter of AIDS in each encounter) or, if celibacy is valued, acknowledging the absence of sex as a healthy choice.

The Thirties: The single crisis

At 30, there is typically an urgency to getting one's act together; the age of experimentation is supposed to be over (Levinson et al., 1978; Stein, 1981). The realization that many of one's peers are now married propels many single people to intensify their search for a mate. Seeing others proceed with the "real" business of life (having children and juggling childrearing and work), single people begin to feel out of sync. Anxiety around getting married can intensify so greatly at this age that one's experience of self and one's development can be almost totally eclipsed. Women usually experience this "singlehood panic" at a younger age than men, partly because of the pressure of the biological clock and partly because of the societal judgment that says that men may choose to remain single but women do so only involuntarily.

This increased anxiety means that requests for therapy often focus on enhancing marriageability. Rather than trying to move clients off this goal, it's better to stay relevant to the client's vision of the purpose of treatment, since the desire to be married is an important adult goal. Getting married is a legitimate—but incomplete—frame for therapy. An initial dilemma is how to honor a client's desire for marriage and still address issues in a context that doesn't make marriage the end product of successful treatment. Moving ahead with work on the developmental tasks of this phase can lower anxiety and increase self-respect. But moving too exclusively—not acknowledging the validity of a desire for marriage or the real problems a single client might have with intimacy—can be experienced by the client as the therapist's judgment that the client really *is* "unmarriageable."

To remain open to the possibilities for marriage yet not be taken over by this pursuit, the single person and his or her family need to make a major shift: attaining the belief that there is more than one way to lead a healthy life. This shift is fundamental to the emotional work of this period and sets the stage for later years, should the client remain single.

Working on life cycle tasks does not rule out marriage but simply facilitates the experience of growing as an adult. It takes into account the reality that the client is now single, whatever the future brings. Coming to grips with singlehood means looking at the ways the single person may be putting his or her life on hold, such as postponing financial planning, setting up a home, even buying kitchen utensils. Not doing these things helps to maintain the presumption that important aspects of life proceed only after marriage.

What are put on hold are usually the things that the institution of marriage has typically assigned to a heterosexual mate. Traditional gender training does not lend itself well to single status, and members of each sex need to develop skills in areas that are assumed to be the province of the other. For a woman, this means that work has to be taken seriously to provide both financial stability and a sense of identity—something that women (particularly lower-middle-class White women) have not been socialized to consider. For a man, it means learning how to develop networks and friendships (Kimmel, 2008; Meth & Pasick, 1990). For both, it means making one's home feel like a home.

Friendships need to accommodate what Peter Stein (1981) called their "patchwork" quality. This is a time when friends move into and out of romantic relationships or marry and therefore are not consistently available. A large circle of friends to share celebrations and life together can help to decrease the sense of abandonment when good friends shift their primary emotional loyalty to an other.

Helping single clients to articulate aspects of an adult self in the family of origin is a key aspect of coaching in this phase. Acknowledging sexual maturity outside marriage can be one of the most anxiety-provoking areas for both client and parents.

Young Soon, a Korean-American woman in her mid-30s, was the youngest of seven children and the only single person in the family. Though she had a very successful career in television she had never considered moving out of the parental home. She felt a strong obligation to her widowed mother and, in the context of her Korean cultural heritage, took meaning and validation in fulfilling what was a necessary and important "job" in not leaving her mother to live alone. Her single status was not a major concern for her, but she did feel restricted in terms of her activities away from home. She also wanted more privacy when at home, to have "alone time," and also have friends over.

Being a single woman and still achieving independence while living at home was not a common pathway in her culture, and she was at a loss about how to manage these adult needs without previous role models. People may feel there is something lacking or wrong with them when they experience needs and feelings that have little place for expression in traditional cultural models, particularly when two cultures "collide" such as the Korean model with the American emphasis on individual achievement and fulfillment. It takes a delicate therapeutic touch to validate these "disloyal" needs and feelings while at the same time respecting the client's attachment to the values with which they have been raised and which they believe. Young Soon decided a first step would be to establish one room in their home as "hers" and, being artistic, was able to create a space that felt to her as a Parisian boudoir would, in which she could feel herself. Her own decoration, it goes without saying, was very different from the rest of the home. After feeling more comfortable with the whole spectrum of her feelings, Young Soon next spoke to her siblings about needing their cooperation so she could go out on her own and sometimes stay away from home. The siblings were amenable and agreed to spend more time at their mother's house, which allowed Young Soon the opportunity to stay away a few days on her own and at the same time know that her mother was cared for in the traditional family way.

In Korean families each relationship involves reciprocal obligations and responsibilities. (Kim and Ryu, 2005). Young Soon was being responsive to what she saw as her cultural role of caring for her mother. At the same time she found a way to lead a more satisfying life as a singe person without eliminating the contexts of family and culture that gave meaning to her life.

Toward their mid-30s, most women and some men (and their families) experience heightened concern over potential childlessness. The thought of missing out on one of life's most profound experiences surfaces and may keep reverberating for years. When combined with parental distress over not having grandchildren, this sadness can develop into a dense web of reactivity. It is important to truly hear this concern without trying to change or fix it.

The painful intensity of these feelings can lead to closing off discussion about marriage or childlessness to maintain pseudo-calm in the family. When family colludes to deny important realities, however, relationships and personal growth suffer.

Susan, a 39-year-old Jewish woman, and an only child, no longer discusses her childlessness with her parents. When she had divorced 10 years earlier, she had apologized to her mother about not giving her a grandchild. Her mother then had been very reassuring, telling her that parenthood wasn't all it was cracked up to be and not to worry. She was totally taken aback when now, 10 years later, her mother relayed an anecdote of meeting a friend who had recently become a grandmother. Susan asked the name of the baby, to which her mother replied, "I didn't ask. It made my heart ache."

Susan's own pain about her lack of children, which she had hidden from her family, and her high reactivity to her mother's similar feelings, led her to close off this toxic issue, thereby freezing the development of their mother–daughter relationship. While the realization that there will be no future generation is generally painful for any family and family member, there are occasions when familial, racial, and religious themes form a dense web of emotional reactivity that is very difficult to work with. In Susan's case, her relationship with her mother had always been characterized by a mutual unspoken protection agreement: Susan was not to cause her mother pain but was to achieve and be happy. Susan's mother, on the other hand, was to remove any pain that Susan was experiencing so as to "make her happy." In the context of the Jewish race, with the recent history of the Holocaust, not producing children to ensure the overall survival of its people took on not only a familial but an entire cultural sadness and guilt. Susan's age made apparent to both mother and daughter that children would probably not be coming. Susan, therefore, was causing her mother pain and her mother had difficulty pretending it didn't matter. They had developed no way for negotiating this "betrayal" to each other. "Failing" family, race, and religion, all core cornerstones of defining who we are, created, of course, deep and difficult feelings.

Exploring these familial, racial, and religious themes is often helpful in lowering the intensity of emotional reactivity, so that people can widen their view beyond their own feelings of guilt, failure and anger. Susan no doubt would have benefited from examining the intersection of her unique family dynamics with the cultural and religious issues as well as her own sense of loss. She might then have been able to make a more sympathetic bridge to her mother, allowing the relationship to evolve.

Midlife: Developing alternative scripts

A fortieth birthday ushers in the realization that time is running out. The emotional weight of closing options falls most heavily on women. Women have a procreative time limit and usually continue to feel social and personal pressure to marry "up" (taller, richer, older). Men can have children much later in life and many continue to have a wide range of acceptable partners from which to choose. However, for both men and women at this age there is the probability of never achieving the family they might have expected to have. If marriage does happen, it will likely be with a divorced or widowed spouse. If child-rearing is in the picture, it will likely be with someone else's children or as a single parent.

A drift toward segregation between single and married people, begun in earlier years, is typically firmly in place by midlife. There are powerful reasons for this divide, among them differing demands for time and commitment, perceptions of single people as a threat to married life, and single people's avoidance of married life and child-focused celebrations to bypass painful feelings of loss. This segregation contributes greatly to feelings of isolation from mainstream life as well as to idealized fantasies of married life. Work on diminishing this gap can help a great deal.

Helping clients to disentangle the main loss—spouse, child, or "package"—is important. It opens up consideration of alternatives. Those whose primary distress centers on child-rearing, for example, can explore other options for bringing children into their lives, including the difficult step of single parenthood, rather than remaining mired, awaiting a spouse. The pain of these losses around expected family and particularly around childlessness may wax and wane throughout life, getting retriggered by changes in circumstance and priorities.

GENDER DIFFERENCES Connecting with a viable social network becomes increasingly difficult yet more important for single men as they get older. While the percentages of never married men has grown at this age, from only 6 percent in 1980 to 16.5 percent in 2004 (U.S. Census Data), the divide between single and married men in income and educational levels also becomes greater. In addition, by the end of the 40s, unmarried men's health status deteriorates much faster than that of married men, with the difference long attributed to the positive benefits of marriage and having a wife. Interestingly, this health gap has been closing according to recent reports, raising the question as to whether it is marriage that makes the difference or access to social resources and support, historically found in a spouse, now developing to service a growing single population (Liu & Umberson, 2008).

On the other hand, Anderson, Stewart, and Dimidjian (1994) in their book *Flying Solo* recount the stories of midlife women who feel happy about their lives in part because they have worked on their social networks and taken their economic lives seriously. Based on in-depth interviews of 90 women—unmarried, divorced, and/or single mothers—these stories reflect the sense of competence, satisfaction, and pleasure in life that these women feel—contrary to continuing stereotypes.

DEFINING AN AUTHENTIC LIFE AS A SINGLE ADULT Societal emphasis placed on marriage and children as the primary vehicles for mature love may leave some single adults feeling that their relationships and loves are less valuable. This is a notion that must be challenged. Holland (1992) writes,

We need to stay open to the simple possibilities of loving. We were told in youth that the whole point and purpose of love, the only possible excuse for it, was to set up a traditional household that becomes a working part of the social machine. Just maybe, though, love comes in other shapes usable by us, the non-traditional unfamilied legion. (p. 252)

Disentangling love from marriage allows single people to legitimize their loving experiences, whatever their form, and not feel that they are, as Anderson et al. (1994) put it, "make do" substitutes for the real thing.

Another aspect of feeling authentic involves forging a connection with future generations. This connection helps people to feel a sense of continuity with history and meaning beyond individual achievement and personal satisfaction. Single people will need to create their own connections; they are not automatically provided by marriage and the family package. Single people often don't realize that connection to the future is important. One woman who chose to become a Big Sister said, "I don't know why I waited so long to bring a child into my life."

Feeling authentic also means accepting that friends are family, not a poor substitute. Being aware of the quality and breadth of these friendships circles is critical to clinical work because feeling attached to others provides stability and satisfaction in the lives of single people. Strong friendships, according to several recent studies, are positively correlated with longevity and healthier living (Parker-Pope, 2009). The availability of friendships may vary throughout the life cycle for single people as it does for everyone. People can move in and out of relationships; they may move to different areas of the country, or may become ill and die. Therefore single people have to be aware that they need to work at keeping an emotional support system alive. Women have an easier time of this because they have been socialized to express the need for connection to others that we all have (Taylor, 2000). If single men have not worked at this in earlier stages they are at more of a disadvantage by this age as their single cohort is vastly diminished.

REDEFINING THE MEANING OF WORK The workplace is usually the central organizing hub of daily life for single people, and the connection of work life to personal satisfaction cannot be overestimated. Work is more than earning money; skills and talents must be used in a meaningful way in one's job or in other arenas. Clients themselves may not realize the importance of work to their feelings, continuing to view their job as a means to pay the rent while waiting for their "real" life to begin. For Lorraine, however, the needed redefinition revolved around the meaning of the fruits of her labor.

Lorraine Sampson, a 48-year-old Black American woman, came for a consultation around recent feelings of apathy and emptiness about her life. Usually she had a "zest for life" and took pride and pleasure in her work (she was partner in a law firm), her family, and her friends. Lorraine had relationships with men on and off all her adult life, but "men have never been the center of (her) life."

Lorraine came from South Carolina and was a middle child of four. Her family, of working-class background, was well known and respected in their town, having lived there for three generations. She had two sisters, both of whom were married with children, and a brother who had died in his 20s of a drug overdose. When Lorraine thought of family, however, it included more than just her nuclear family. In keeping with the Black American notion of family, Lorraine kept in close touch with not only aunts, uncles, and grandparents but also with many members of her church who had been with her in growing up.

With her expanded notion of family came an enhanced sense of responsibility and interconnectedness. She had benefited from this family sense as a young woman, when the "family" had sacrificed considerably to send her . . . the "studious one" . . . to college and law school. As soon as Lorraine got her first job, she began helping the next generation. First she sent money home to be used for education, and later she had nieces, nephews, and cousins live with her while they attended college.

She had been "mothering" in this way for over 20 years, and now she believed the younger generation was at the point where they could take over. Lorraine had been looking forward to using her money on deferred personal pleasure, when her sister, together with her two grandchildren, came North to live. Again Lorraine felt she had to take Alva and the children under her wing, as they were strangers to the city. This was the beginning of her depression.

Lorraine, while single, had an integral place in her extended family, as well as opportunities and obligations to be a close, involved, active aunt and second mother to the younger generation. Childlessness or lack of a legitimate role was not an issue for her in her singleness. In addition, her success was highly valued by the family. However, because she had neither nuclear family nor children of her own, and was financially self-reliant, the implied reciprocity in the mutual support system (Boyd-Franklin, 1989) was not enacted. Her desire to lead a more "selfish" life put her at odds with her family's expectations of her.

For many Black families, as well as others with limited economic resources, the answer to the question "When does the caretaking stop?" may be "Never." It is particularly important that therapists coming from different backgrounds respect the resiliency and the interconnections of extended family networks, and not view Lorraine's dilemma, for example, as a lack of differentiation or as a problem in learning how to disappoint others; i.e., just say "No." Lorraine, an intelligent person, readily grasped the value of exploring the issue of what being selfish meant in her family, of the fates and lives of other "selfish" women, of the women who had "turned their back" on their family. In the course of these conversations, Lorraine was able to more deeply connect with the women in her family, and to find that none viewed the issue (self versus family) in the unilateral way in which Lorraine was seeing it (i.e., you cannot quit until someone else takes over from you).

Taking work seriously goes hand in hand with taking responsibility for one's financial future. This is a necessity in the 40s and 50s. Men may have anxiety about how they are managing their money, but they don't usually doubt their need to do it. Women, on the other hand, may have been brought up to believe that this is man's territory and might also need to learn about finance along with the therapy. This endeavor can be filled with anxiety; many women associate it with giving up on the possibility of ever being taken care of through marriage.

FAMILY WORK   Feelings of anxiety or failure as parents can resurface at this time, as it sinks in that their "child" really may never marry. When parental emotionality meshes with the single person's reactivity

around the same issues, the potential for misunderstanding and possible cut off is high. Work with the single person may need to begin with relationships with siblings, in which emotionality is usually less intense. Building separate relationships with nieces and nephews, and hosting events rather than being the perennial guest, are some ways in which the single person can decrease distance in the family of origin.

Later Life: Putting it all together

This phase may extend 2 decades or more, encompassing "second life" goals and plans, job shifts, retirement, and the death of parents, until failed health signals the last years. Two factors that greatly impact the single person's perspective during this time are economic class and health status. If money is limited so then are the choices of life style; people may envision having to live with a relative or a friend, thereby limiting the independence to which they may have been accustomed. Likewise early brushes with disease or illness will shape what choices are seen as emotionally and physically viable. A large number of single people in these later years, however, will have enough income and be in good enough health to be emotionally positioned to reap the fruits of single status: freedom and autonomy. Less encumbered by financial and/or emotional responsibility toward adult children than their married counterparts, single people can devote more time and energy to shaping personally meaningful work, "second life" goals and plans, job shifts, and retirement.

Later years signal an increasingly greater gender difference in overall health indices between single men and women. Research data continue to report that the health of older men (aged 50 or more) who are unmarried deteriorates statistically much faster than the health of those who are married (Rand, 1998). The National Center for Health Statistics (Gorina, 2005) found that elderly White men (65 years and older) have a suicide rate triple that of the overall U.S. rate, and are eight times more likely to kill themselves than women of their same age. The suicide rate for divorced White men according to a study done in 2000 was twice that of married or single White men (Kpowsoa, 2000). Marriage apparently continues to serve an integrative and supportive function, particularly for men. While there has been very little research on older single gay men and the impact of social networks, the process of developing "chosen families" at earlier stages may be a health advantage for gay men (Shippy et al., 2004).

By age 65, only 53 percent of women are living with a spouse, compared to 77 percent of men (U.S. Census Data). Unmarried women moving through the later years, then, find themselves to be less statistically deviant than do unmarried men, when the great majority of single men's peers are still married.

The overarching emotional tasks of this phase are 1) Maintaining Connectedness, 2) Consolidating Decisions about Money and Work, and 3) Planning for the Future.

MAINTAINING CONNECTEDNESS Attachments to others are not only crucial for emotional well-being, they are crucial for the continued development of the brain overall, according to Siegel (1999). ". . . emotionally meaningful events can enable continued learning from experience throughout the lifespan." The continued growth and complexity of neural connections, Siegel suggests, may well be the foundation of the "development of wisdom with age . . . the capacity to see patterns over time and across situations." (pp. 307–308). "Emotionally meaningful" to Siegel is being grounded in social connectedness and interactions with other people.

Maintaining connectedness becomes increasingly difficult as people move through their later years: Friends and family members die or move away to retirement communities or easier climates; the arrival of retirement (even when sought) may present a serious disruption on one's network; and the onset of waning physical strength makes it harder for people to travel distances to visit friends and family. People at all life phases may not recognize the long-term impact of shifts and losses in their network, but careful inquiry needs to be made about losses at this phase, when the extent is usually greater than at any prior time.

Family relationships often need realignment as parents age and become infirm. Parental anxiety around single status may resurface after years of dormancy as parents struggle to feel their child is "settled" before they die. Family of origin work with parents is particularly poignant now, since this may be the last opportunity for the adult child to resolve feelings about single life and communicate some reassurance to aged parents.

The need to care for aged parents often puts strains on sibling relationships, which may have stayed frozen in time at the point when each child left home. Research done on marriage and social ties has shown that the unmarried siblings are more apt to care for aging parents than their married siblings (Gerstal and Sarkisian, 2007a) and that unmarried women are called upon to be primary caretakers significantly more often than widowed daughters (Connidis, 2001). Implicit in this selection is the judgment that the lives of single women are more flexible than those of people with children. Family of origin work with siblings is made more difficult when there is little emotional glue other than the connection to the aging parents. The cost of nonresolution, however, may be the dissolution of family connections after the parents' death.

CONSOLIDATING DECISIONS ABOUT MONEY AND WORK, PLANNING FOR THE FUTURE Emotional intensity about using one's life fully tends to increase as that inner voice says, "If I don't do it now, I never will." Single people may have an advantage in making major shifts because they do not have to adjust plans around spouses and children. Exploring options for even partial realization of goals and dreams that have been put on the shelf is always useful. Even if money is limited and jobs cannot be changed, life can include these dreams. One 55-year-old factory worker saved for 10 years for a trip to a distant country. Accomplishing this enabled her to feel like an adventurous woman instead of a factory drudge.

Planning for the future is critical at this juncture. It includes thinking about a home base that feels financially and physically secure and may mean considering joining forces with others to pool resources. If a client strongly resists addressing these issues, examining multigenerational themes may help.

Lauren, a 54-year-old never-married Jewish woman had derived a lot of satisfaction from her work and great enjoyment in her life. Both her brothers had married and both had children, and Lauren enjoyed being Auntie to them. Unusually for a Jewish woman, Lauren had not been too bothered by either her single status or her childlessness. She was a cherished only daughter who was raised to feel she was indeed very special in her talents and very special in her amount of intelligence. She felt that developing her talents was exactly what her parents would have wanted for her. Now, however, she found herself almost paralyzed with anxiety about her future. She had put no money aside and was frightened about the coming years. At the same time, she strongly resisted saving money. She hosted expensive dinners and took lavish vacations, which only increased her panic.

When multigenerational themes were explored, it emerged that both her mother and grandmother had died before the age of 60. Both had had lives of hard work and little luxury. Her paralysis about planning for a future was fueled by her unconscious belief that she wasn't going to have one. Her vision of life's cycle included death within the next 5 years. Bringing this powerful template into conscious awareness was crucial in freeing Lauren from her "inexplicable" terror.

A final piece of planning is the making of one's will. This is more than a duty; it is a profound emotional experience. Looking at possessions and deciding how and with whom you want them to be valued after your death can change a client's entire perspective. People retrieve memories that have been pushed aside and rediscover priorities and attachments that have faded. Communicating decisions -directly to the people involved can shift relationships in one's current life:

John, who was raised in a working-class Italian Catholic family, had always had an affectionate and fun-filled relationship with his nieces; he was the one who took them to concerts, the theater, and dinner. When John decided to tell them about their inheritance from him, his lawyers and his own family tried to talk him out of it. They felt he might "make them lazy" and not feel they needed to get education or get a job. He decided to tell them anyway, He went ahead, on the grounds that his nieces should have this information in planning their own futures. For the first time, his nieces realized the depth of his love for them and came to see him as a second parent.

ENJOYING THE FREEDOM Personal freedom is one of the great benefits of singlehood, and using it well gives richness to the single experience. We all experience life differently as we age, married or single. Some accept old age like Prospero in the "Tempest," and some like Woody Allen and Clint Eastwood continue working (Scott, 2009). As we grow older, however, there are more similarities than differences between being single and married. What is critical for all of us is a supportive network. Researchers are now coming to realize that friendship has a bigger impact on the sense of well-being than family relationships, finding that good friendships can make the difference between sickness and health (Parker-Pope, 2009). Successful aging, married or single, therefore lies in maintaining friendships and emotional connections for as long as possible.

Chapter 12

Becoming an Adult: Finding Ways to Love and Work

Richard H. Fulmer

Adam and Eve were the first young adults. Their story in Genesis of how a family system reproduces itself is one of the oldest in Western culture. God's role in that Bible chapter demonstrates how parenting becomes more distant, the better to foster the adolescent children's independence. Adam and Eve loosen the bond with their parent, establish an intimate relationship with each other, and develop the ability to create a new home (Fulmer, 2006).

Young Adulthood(s) in the New Century

While young adulthood is expanding as an area of academic investigation (see The Society for the Study of Emerging Adulthood, 2008) the length of the stage itself seems to be growing. In the middle class (the largest single population segment in the United States) the beginning of the phase is still marked by older adolescents leaving home after graduating from high school. This group is not, however, reaching the usual markers of the end of the period—finishing postsecondary education, continuing to live separately from parents, marrying, and having a child—until later in life. (Furstenberg, et al, 2003). In his early work, J. J. Arnett, founder of SSEA, saw the period as lasting from ages 18 to 25 (Arnett, 2000), but he now sees it as stretching from ages 18 to 29 or even longer (Arnett, 2007).

Popular culture often disparages this change, referring to elders who extend their advocacy or guidance into the lives of college-age children, as "helicopter parents," and postcollege students who temporarily return home as "boomerang kids." Some young authors (Draut, 2007; Kamenetz, 2007) have protested what they experience as an unfair denigration of their generation, seeing the primary cause of lengthening young adulthood as financial.

Other scholars differ on the meaning of extending this period. Those who see it as a necessary time for self-discovery and identity development consider it advantageous to have a longer time to accomplish this task (Arnett, 2007). Those less sanguine consider the prolongation as a developmental arrest or a self-indulgent refusal to accept the responsibilities of adulthood (Cote, 2000 p. 57; Kimmel, 2008 pp. 3–13).

How family therapists regard this period will certainly influence how we treat it: as an artifact of difficult financial conditions, as an opportunity for creative maturation for both the parental and young adult generations, or as a potentially malignant interaction of parental overinvolvement and adult child overdependence. The field itself has moved from the "breaking ties" model of the 1970s and 1980s (Haley, 1980; Stierlin, 1977) that overemphasized separation, to a model that blends separation and attachment by recognizing the need for individuation while retaining cross-generational relationships. This shift was embedded in the larger realization that human sciences had unwittingly been framing a story of male development as universal human development. This new understanding enabled workers to describe male needs for relatedness (Silverstein and Rashbaum, 1994; Miller, 1976; Benjamin, 1988; and Bergman, 1991) and female needs for individuation and separateness (Gilligan, 1982, 1991; Coontz, 1992). This family tension (for the children, between being free of parental control versus prematurely losing parental support; for the parents, between offering protective guidance versus overindulging a developmental delay) is often still the central clinical problem of treating families in this stage.

The ways to pass through this developmental stage vary with gender, socioeconomic status, race, culture, sexual orientation, and time in history. It is misleading to see one such path as "normal" and all others as "deviant." This chapter proposes a developmental model that is meant to describe some themes and tasks for the period and then suggests how environmental conditions create many different young adulthoods for different groups in society. It will also divide young adulthood into two phases, early and late, which entail different developmental tasks and objectives. I have come to appreciate, however, how my attempts at "themes" are embedded in my value system—Modern (as opposed to Postmodern) and Enlightenment-based in its assumptions. Falicov (2009), for instance, shows how alien even the seemingly familiar young adult goal of "independence" may be to parents in a Latino culture when she offers an example of culturally attuned therapy: "If Latino parents value a family orientation for their adolescents instead of supporting a launching phase of the life cycle, a culturally attuned therapist helps the immigrant family bridge their internal differences when faced with new societal demands for adolescent autonomy" (p. 303)"

Early Young Adulthood: Developmental Tasks

Erik Erikson (1963) wrote that Sigmund Freud's goal for therapy was to enable patients to work and to love. The young adult must negotiate a path between these activities. For the middle and upper classes, one path focuses on the development of a highly valued profession. Most adults in the Western middle and upper-middle classes begin young adulthood by working hard to develop their careers and subordinating relationships to work. In later emerging adulthood, this path divides into two. The second path finds meaning in human relationships in addition to work, eventually resulting in the building of a new family. Both roles are essential to society. Religious, political, and military leaders, as well as artists, scientists, and cultural innovators, all continue to find such primary meaning in their work that they may not develop a strongly invested family life. A larger number find as much or more meaning in

relationships and become "householders," physically reproducing society.

Work Tasks: Preparation Without Pay or Earning out of Necessity?

Young adults of all social classes hope to depend on their families for tangible and emotional support as they develop themselves as workers. Ideally, the work for which they prepare will express some meaning about themselves as well as supplying a wage that permits financial independence. The way in which such a wage can be earned "has transformed radically in the past thirty years," becoming "postindustrial, nonunion, service-oriented, highly competitive, highly flexible, and technology-dependent" (Kamenetz, 2007 p. 98–99). This job market requires more skills to be acquired through some form of postsecondary education. Today nearly 75 percent of high school graduates enroll in some type of college after high school (Draut, 2007 p. 29). The middle-class culture grants a moratorium on cash-producing work during this period, but only to those able to pay (or borrow enough) for such a delay. For lower-income groups, even a short pause in wage earning is extremely difficult or impossible, and borrowing may be out of the question.

The average rate of freshmen graduating from public high school in 4 years in our 50 largest cities is 53 percent, compared with 71 percent in the suburbs (Dillon, 2009), so a very substantial proportion of our population does not enjoy this moratorium. "Postsecondary education" for dropouts consists of unskilled labor, temporary jobs, on-the-job training by employers, or "training" in criminal activities and temporary incarceration.

Relationship Tasks: Trying to Find Love in Lust

In the realm of relationships, the young adults' task is not only to loosen ties with their families of origin, but is also to expand and transfer their deep family attachments to others of both sexes. The quality of the intimate relationships that young adults form will be influenced by the parental, marital, and sibling relationships they have experienced.

To correct the usual split between concern for autonomy in male development and emotional connectedness in female development, I emphasize the importance of relatedness in male development and the need for a period of self-focus and separateness during young adulthood in female development.

For both sexes, early young adulthood is a period when the development of work skill and (if possible) professional identity takes precedence over the development of relationships. Arnett calls this "the self-focused age" and contends that it is "normal, healthy, and temporary" (Arnett, 2006, pp. 12–14). If relationship and work opportunities conflict (such as admission to a desirable college that does not offer a spot to a romantic partner) the young adult will usually choose the college. These priorities tend to change in later young adulthood. For lower-income groups, however, when college or some other extended educational preparation is not available, family relationships (including a new baby) may become (or remain) a much more important source of meaning and satisfaction than a job.

Early Young Adulthood: Ages 18 to 21

Learning to work: Blending meaning with remuneration

Young men have always been expected to work at cash-producing jobs to support first themselves and then their families. Since the 1960s, women of all social classes feel more entitled to find meaning in work and many want to increase their future independence from men. They also realize that real wages have declined so much since the 1960s that it is only the most affluent families that can survive on the husband's income alone. Since 2005, women have become more numerous (58 percent) than men as postsecondary students at every level (Lewin, 2006). Many colleges practice "affirmative action" toward men by admitting some males with lower qualifications than some females to keep the proportion of men on campus from falling too low (Delahunty-Britz, 2006).

Perhaps it is harder for young men's talents, interests, and attitudes toward authority than for young women's to be developed into a job or career in this current service economy. Adolescents' enthusiasms (eg., fashion, films, friendships, sports, music, video games) must often be considerably transformed to become a job or a career. If young people cannot find an interest (or lack the talent or training in that area), they risk having to do work that remunerates but does not express meaning about themselves. This process may involve many false starts and lead to conflicts with parents or adults who are expecting them to move toward financial independence.

If they are motivated, young adults are capable of very intense focus and hard work during this period, renouncing physical comforts, remuneration, and social contact to develop the physical and/or intellectual skills necessary for a deeply valued professional identity.

Learning to love: Hooking up

In the 1950s and early 1960s, high school and college students got to know each other by observing the conventions of pair dating. Kathleen Bogle (2008) reports, however, that in the later 1960s, college students began socializing in groups and meeting at large parties at which alcohol and marijuana were consumed. These parties "became the setting for casual sexual encounters" known as "hookups" (pp. 20–21), in which men and women had sexual contact that did not necessarily imply an ongoing relationship.

Kimmel (2008) writes, "Young people in college—and this seems to hold true for both women and men—seem generally wary of committed or monogamous relationships" (p. 201). Although "hooking up" seems to have brought increased extramarital sexual activity for some decades now, neither Bogle nor Kimmel reports higher rates of out-of-wedlock pregnancies or abortions for the college women they describe, suggesting rigorous birth control. Worried parents might be able to comfort themselves with Kimmel's eventual reassurance about "hooking up" as a developmental stage, not a new lifestyle: "The truth is, hooking up is not the end of the world—it's a time-out, like college" (p. 213).

For low-income young adults, a similar pattern of nonpermanent, nonexclusive, pleasure-oriented sexual relationships is reported, but with less fear of pregnancy. Nathan Fosse (2010) interviewed 38

African American men from poor urban neighborhoods, 20 of whom reported being "faithful" to their current partners, while 18 practiced nonmonagamy (p. 128). These men distinguished between women they considered "stunts" who were "often considered only a means for immediate sexual gratification" and "wifeys," who were "considered to be partners for social and emotional connection." Fosse reports that many of his respondents "valued these latter relationships more highly" and yearned to consider them reliable, thus suggesting affiliative needs even in these notoriously (by their own proclamation) "single" men. Pregnancies, "not planned but not accidental" help to cement the interpersonal bond and raise the status of both mother and father without marriage. (LeBlanc, 2004; Edin and Kefalas, 2005).

Idealism

Not having much life experience, many young adults try to use values to guide themselves. They feel that problems can be solved by living in accordance with ideals rather than by acting in their own immediate self-interest. They are also often grandiose, feeling they can easily avoid the mistakes their elders have made. Although not fully mature, this arrogance may still be a necessary maturational stage on the way to developing true personal authority, something that we often do not even hope for until middle adulthood.

Explicit grandiosity and arrogance may be characteristic primarily of White middle-class young adults. Perhaps, even if such feelings were harbored by immigrant Latino youth, respect for generational hierarchy (respeto) would inhibit their expression. The conflict between Latino adolescents being drawn into the majority North American culture while their parents represent the more hierarchical values of their Hispanic homeland may make this developmental friction even more intense.

Young adults' consciously (and sometimes righteously) held values may often differ, at least superficially, from those of their parents. If they are still accepting their parents' financial support, they may have to tolerate the moral dilemma of holding a benefactor in contempt. This may pose conflicts with parents, depending on how the adults handle the contempt.

Alcohol and drugs

Early young adulthood is the period when consciousness-altering drugs—such as alcohol, marijuana, the neuroenhancers Ritalin or Adderall, hallucinogens, cocaine, and heroin—are most enthusiastically used. There must be multiple reasons for this—the exercise of freedom from parental supervision, a social lubricant for the many anxiety-filled social contacts of the period, or an aid to ecstatic, sometimes sexual celebration at parties. While most will grow out of this phase eventually, often in later emerging adulthood, young people whose family members are or have been addicted to some substance are at serious risk of becoming entangled in a similar addiction.

Poor urban groups have easier access to stronger drugs in their neighborhoods than do college students. Some families are financially supported by dealers (Venkatesh, 2006, p. 45). They are at risk for developing serious addictions in their young adulthoods or, if selling, may suffer incarceration or death. Drug use that might be "recreational" for a college student could be lethal for a poor young man.

Learning disabilities

Changes in environmental demands and increases in emotional maturity during young adulthood may have an ameliorating effect on learning disabilities during young adulthood. While success in high school requires good performance in many different academic tasks, the specialization of a college "major" permits students to concentrate on their strengths. As students become more mature, they may deny less and feel less shame, and slower pacing is possible.

These advantages allow the young adult to manage the ill effects of disabilities, but the structure of college (less class time, more homework) also introduces some dangers. One of these is the loss of organizational support provided by parents, especially in the management of time. Instead of direct supervision, parents can assist in engaging college services (securing and funding the necessary testing to certify the disability, for instance) to replace such structure.

For those with learning disabilities who do not attend college (probably the majority), Marshak, Seligman, and Prezant (1999) make the important point that "At the completion of formal schooling, (youths with disabilities) are no longer protected by a comprehensive entitlement system of educational services but are thrust into an adult service system governed by different guidelines and funding streams" (p. 153). Clinicians may be able to help secure adult services for these clients, but finding such help in the adult world after formal schooling is uncharted territory.

It may be necessary to coach parents through launching their young adult child when learning problems require extra adult supports at this phase.

In one family I had coached the successful lawyer parents, Roy and Arlene, several times during the high school years of Judy, their bright but somewhat learning disabled daughter. Judy had been diagnosed with mild attention deficit disorder. Her comprehension was good, but processing was slow. She had good SAT scores and with support from both parents and her teachers, she completed high school well, being admitted to several good colleges. However, her parents thought she needed an extra year before college, and I concurred. She enrolled at a school for learning disabled students and with some fits and starts managed fairly well until the spring she turned 19. Although she liked the school, Judy had difficulties with the organizational aspects of college. She slept late, missed classes, and didn't turn in work she had finished.

At that point she dropped out, and the parents brought her into sessions for the first time. With Judy sitting between them, first one parent would remonstrate, then the other. I could see that her slow processing (combined, of course, with her guilt and anxiety) interfered with her ability to respond. Judy would fall behind in listening to her loving, anxious, emphatic parents, becoming ever more silent. I made the rule that if one parent addressed Judy, the second parent could not add anything until Judy had responded to the first. They all accepted this very willingly, the parents having been frustrated by Judy's increasing silence, and Judy feeling she had lost her voice. The parents began to pause, and Judy began to fill the silences with her own ideas, albeit haltingly.

After this shaky performance, the parents decided to again defer admission to a mainstream college and reenrolled her at the learning disability college. Her mother, Arlene, began to assist with homework by phone, by email, and during her visits home but worried about overinvolvement, "I'm addicted to meddling. It's a problem of mine." With Judy's permission, her parents monitored her attendance on the school Web site. Continued coaching and several family sessions to help parents and daughter work on the boundaries of their support and her initiative enabled Judy to complete the learning disability college. This experience caused Judy and her parents to understand, however, that she could only manage two courses at a time. She enrolled in a mainstream college with these more realistic expectations. With increased parental assistance and vigilance, the next term Judy received one A and one C+. She also made what her mother called a "real friend." Although gratified with this improvement, both parents worried about Judy's apparent passivity. Arlene said, "I feel I carried her across the finish line." Roy argued, "She can work on things when she is motivated, but she just isn't motivated about subjects in which she has no interest." Judy, however, was happy to still be in school and proud to have a B average in a mainstream college. I reassured the parents about their efforts. Arlene vowed she would never work this hard with Judy again. Roy agreed, in fact insisted, that she not do so. Judy now acknowledged: "If mom takes control, I sit back. I need less push from her. I learned two things: First: I need someone to help me work. Second: It can't be Mom." The family felt it had developed a realistic formula to enable them all to accomplish the developmental tasks of young adulthood.

I saw Judy's problems as compounded by the pressures of a popular attitude, which sees disability as a result of low motivation and feels parents should adopt a "sink or swim" strategy (Levine, 2003). I reassured them that it was due in large part to their active intervention that their daughter was moving along well. I continued to meet with them occasionally to coach them on providing structure and helping their daughter manage the extra supports she needed to develop her many talents.

Mentors

While this is a time of more or less polite contempt toward parents and their allies, the moral simplicity of young adults permits them to idealize a mentor who can serve as a bridge between immersion in family and greater self-definition. This worshipful relationship holds dangers, however, if either participant uses the relationship in an exploitive way. Lower-income youth who are not in college may use members of their extended family, employers, superiors in the armed forces, athletic coaches, senior street acquaintances, gang leaders, or older prisoners. Geoffrey Canada in *Fist Stick Knife Gun (1996)* and James McBride in *The Color of Water* (1996) tell of disreputable characters that they did not emulate, but from whom they received practical guidance about how to read street situations and protect themselves.

The same-sex gang affects love

A group of same-sex peers can form an important transition for the young adult between the family of origin and the pair-bond that is the basis for the family of procreation. Membership, structure of shared rules, hierarchy, and mutual caring and loyalty in gangs feed this need for both sexes (Taffel & Blau, 2001). At the beginning of young adulthood, it can enable separation by creating an alternative home place. Gay men and lesbians usually "come out" to peers before they do to their families, fearing their families' disapproval (Chandler, 1997 p. 130). As a result, the peer group may take on extra importance for them. A few years later, however, the emerging adult may find the gang has a conservative aspect, pulling against further progression into the erotic/romantic couple that forms the nucleus for a new family. Many young people yearn for such close relationships, but the depth of emotional investment required by exclusive partnerships and the fear of being jilted (an inevitability) inspires young people to seek security in their peer groups. This group versus pair conflict of the same-sex group can be seen at every socioeconomic level, for both men and women. Kimmel (2008) describes fraternity boys enforcing homophobic and sexist norms as standards for masculinity in his "*Guyland.*" In his *Code of the Street*, Elijah Anderson (2000) sees it in "The Baby Club," in which young, poor African American mothers become more bonded to other young mothers than to the fathers of their children. African American male rap singers (and the middle-class young White men who feel represented by their songs) look to their "Dawgs" for cautionary tales about faithless women who would ensnare them, using mottos like "Bros before Hos" (Fulmer, 2008). Powerful middle-class sisterhoods make unflattering comparisons between men and their own sex with remarks like, "Do you notice how a really great guy would only be an ordinary girlfriend?" and (in remarkable agreement with the rappers) "Men are dogs!"

The same-sex gang affects work

The gang also influences the work of young adults. Military leaders and athletic coaches customarily use loyalty to buddies to inspire compatriots to risk life and limb for the success of the group. Leaving this intense context of team-related meaning can be difficult when, later in young adulthood, individual initiative becomes necessary for success in work. Often a new work group can be found, but this is a perilous transition. Sometimes adults try to retain their membership in the old group. Sudhir Venkatesh, in his study of urban underground economy, *Off the Books* (2006), reaches back to Eliot Liebow's seminal study of poor streetcorner men, *Tally's Corner* (1967), to describe the group's conservative pull (pp. 100–102). The risks of entrepreneurship that might permit exit from poverty, like the risks of love in the couple bond, are assessed "by the . . . opinions of their peers. . . . (T)he notable achievers gradually separate off. For the rest, the group becomes . . . a tie that binds and that depresses motivation . . ." (Venkatesh, 2006, p. 101).

Later Young Adulthood, Ages 22 to 30: Trying to Consolidate Work and Family

Beginning to form a pair bond

Bogle reports that as college students graduate and begin the transition to late young adulthood, they return to a pair dating culture (2008, pp. 128–157). The loss of the relatively familiar population of fellow students and the "safe haven" of the college campus make women more cautious about the male strangers they are meeting. A second major reason for beginning to date is "a change in their relationship goals for both men and women" (p. 137).

Perfect love

Individuals from all social classes and sexual orientations begin to seek relationships with a new ambition: finding a relationship that is exclusive, intimate both erotically and emotionally, and expressive of deeply held personal values and ideas about the self. Eventually this becomes a search for a life partner, but it often takes an early form as a search for a perfect love. This search for perfection in relationship is often an important transaction between the young adult and his or her family of origin. It is a heady experience to be discovered by someone whose love is not based on role obligations and who is different in some important way from one's parents.

Rescue wishes

The hope of being able to rescue someone may be a seductive lure for both young women and men (Fulmer, 2008). It promises an increase in status (from being taken care of to taking care), an affirmation of a grandiose self-image, a chance to surpass parents at parenting, and an enactment of personal idealism. The helped partner must necessarily have some problems (drug abuse, low social status, financial or academic difficulties, or emotional disturbance) for the lover to ameliorate. That their child becomes so intensely involved with an underfunctioning partner is usually agony for parents. Efforts to break up the relationship may be surreptitiously accepted by the daughters or sons if they are already looking for a way out, or reflexive opposition to parental disapproval may hold the couple together, sometimes at considerable risk to the partners.

Random Family (2004), Adrian Nicole LeBlanc's powerful piece of immersion journalism, is a 10-year study of two Puerto Rican families in the South Bronx. Early in the book, the brilliant (and cruel) heroin dealer Boy George rescues the 16-year-old Jessica's entire family with a huge donation of much-needed food and household supplies as a way of beginning a romance with Jessica. Later he complains (p. 19) that Lourdes, Jessica's mother, did not

protect Jessica as a parent should: "She just sold her to me for a thousand dollars!"

When the transition from adolescent-in-family to adult-between-families has progressed somewhat, the need for such love diminishes, and its imperfections can be evaluated realistically. The wounded lovers may approach their next relationship (or the same one) with more grounded idealism.

Young adulthood and the Internet

Another important phenomenon in young adulthood is use of the Internet. This age group is intensely involved in video games, texting, chat rooms, dating Web sites, MySpace, Facebook, Instant Messaging, Twitter, and blogging. In his book *Childhood and Society*, Erik Erikson writes, "To a considerable extent adolescent love is an attempt to arrive at a definition of one's identity. . . . This is why so much of young love is conversation" (1963, p. 262). Internet use is surely a modern form of conversation, and young adults may pursue it as obsessively as they have falling in love for countless generations. The Web pages young people create to present themselves to their fellows on, say, Facebook, registering its 200 millionth user as this chapter is written (Stone, 2009), require introspection and selection to define the self they wish to present as a basis for their relationship to others. This identity is usually peer-oriented. Parents or future employers are not the target audience when male students include pictures of themselves drunk and female students show themselves sexily clad, for instance. These self-presentations are tested and refined according to the feedback they receive.

Rosario, et al. (2006) note that the Internet is a new source of relief for the social isolation lesbian, gay, and bisexual young adults experience when living in intolerant communities. It is relatively easy for persons of similar sexual orientations to find each other, at least for online conversation, with some degree of privacy and safety.

From self-involvement to beginning to think like a householder

The grandiosity and asceticism of early young adulthood is gradually replaced by a more realistic view of what can be accomplished: a more complex, situation-based morality, disillusionment, a focusing of work interests, and a wish for a home. Interest shifts from the difficult task of definition of the self to the even more complex project of definition of a family and self-in-a-family. As realism replaces grandiosity, young adults may enjoy actually making some of their dreams come true. They may also have a sense of disappointment in that the fantasy of many possibilities is reduced to just a few realities. This may be an early version of what Celia Falicov is describing in Latina women when she writes, "Quiet acceptance or resignation may represent a form of humble realism that contrasts sharply with the cultural mastery orientation of Western therapies" (2009, p. 304).

Mentors–disillusionment

Later young adulthood may be a time when individuals become disillusioned with their mentors. This experience can be depressing, however, as the heady feeling of "having the answer" begins to erode. Young adults may feel that their mentors have deceived them and end their relationships in a storm of bitter disappointment. Or they may simply grow away from the mentors, losing interest in their charisma. As they do, they sometimes view their own fervent, grandiose young adulthoods with some rueful embarrassment.

Alcohol and drugs in later young adulthood

After age 25, many individuals gradually back away from intense drug and alcohol use as social anxieties lessen and adult obligations increase. The exceptions, of course, are people who have become addicted. In later emerging adulthood, substance abuse can now be seen more clearly as a compulsion and addressed as such clinically.

These experiences—the acquisition of real satisfactions, the need to consider the needs of at least one other as well as one's own, the realization that many fantasies cannot be pursued, sobriety itself—are the beginnings of the householder identity.

Family dynamics

If the departing young adult is a first-born, parents may then turn their attention more fully to younger siblings who remain at home. Those siblings may grow into the space vacated by the older, with mixed consequences. A formerly crowded living situation may be relieved if a sibling can move into the now-empty bedroom. The older child may feel dispossessed, however, and that he or she has lost a home base, demanding full reinstatement when returning for holidays.

In one family, we discovered that an 8-year-old boy who was having difficulties had recently begun sleeping with his mother. His adult sister had returned home to recover from a crack episode and took back the couch he usually slept on, which had been hers as an adolescent.

Parents' relationship

As children move on, parents may turn back to each other as a couple. If reviving the couple relationship is successful, it can fill in the loss of day-to-day parental activities and contact with children. If parental activities have been a welcome distraction from marital discord, these problems may reemerge with disruptive effect. If a marriage that was held together for the sake of child-rearing is now dissolved, young adults may feel that their loyalties must be divided and the continuity of their family is interrupted, leaving them to fend for themselves.

In a lower-income family, the mother may never have married, so there is no couple relationship to revive. The executive pair may have been grandmother and mother. If the young adults all move out, grandmother may get a welcome rest and mother may be free to pursue postsecondary training to improve her employment opportunities. It is also possible, however, that mother's now teenage daughters will become pregnant and mother (now a grandmother) will take care of the newborn while daughter (now a young adult mother) tries to finish high school, enroll in college, or enter the labor force.

How financial support affects the relationship

Many middle-class parents expect to pay for tuition and college residence for 4 years, but do not plan to pay for schooling or living expenses after their children graduate. The beginning of late young adulthood thus coincides with some shouldering of financial obligation by the now older emerging adult. This may involve not only paying current expenses, but also beginning to pay already accumulated student loans. The Project on Student Debt (2009) reports that the average debt for graduating college students in the Class of 2007 rose 6 percent over that of the Class of 2006 to $18,482 for public college graduates and $23,065 for those from private colleges. For families without the means to save for college, loans or scholarships are a much more difficult option nowadays because college tuition has risen so fast and available aid decreased or stayed the same. For instance, the federal government's most generous program for low-income students—Pell Grants—covered nearly three quarters of the expense of a 4-year college in the 1970s. Today the grants cover only about 40 percent of those costs (Draut, 2007 p. 8). Graduates must either find a rental with roommates or continue to live with parents. Such temporary support is seen in every social class (one in four of all young adults will return at least once) and should be considered adaptive until proven otherwise. Low-income families heroically make their boundaries permeable according to need (Venkatesh, 2006, pp. 43–53) more often than White middle-class families do. Because of their willingness to "double up," such families are our country's greatest single bulwark against homelessness. Permeability and the consequent shifting membership of the family challenge the need for order and hierarchy, however, particularly with young adults who are developmentally programmed to resist authority and who may not be emotionally attached to the authority hierarchy of the family. Sometimes a returning young adult can add stability as a new authority and model for self-improvement, but sometimes he or she may undermine established rules and increase disorder. Clinicians might want to keep tabs on the shifting membership of any family they are seeing and ask how boundaries around and within it are managed with each change. It may help to coach mothers to have discussion with their teenage daughters about dressing more modestly when a brother's young adult male friend is staying for a while. On a more difficult level, Le Blanc (2004) tells us about poor mothers' efforts to prevent the sexual abuse of young females with the rule: "Don't ever leave your girls with a man

who's not blood" (p. 250). Clinicians would do well to assist mothers to enforce this rule, but they should also note that LeBlanc feels the vicissitudes of running a financially impoverished household render it unrealistic. It comes under extra pressure when friends of brothers are in and out, and it is important (and sometimes effective) to support mothers in their vigilance and planning for backup when they are out and the young men are not.

Young adulthood "off the books"

Venkatesh's (2006) description of the "underground economy" suggests roles in poor communities for young adults that are becoming neither taxpaying job-holders nor incarcerated criminals. He describes a society of mutual aid in which most income is not declared and in which small-scale entrepreneurs exchange goods and services in a system governed by personal relationships rather than bureaucratic procedures. Because of its small scale it can work quickly and efficiently without waiting for official wheels to grind, but because it relies on face-to-face relationships, it cannot expand much beyond the neighborhoods of lower middle class or working poor. To learn the intricate mechanisms of this "shady" (that is, illegal in a petty sense) underground society would be a useful task for young adults who could not get the credentials to move into the world of jobs, paychecks, banks and taxes. No one grows up aspiring to live in such a community. But Venkatesh (2006) contends that many who find themselves members of one do work to maintain its order (p. 182), to rely on it (p. 181), and even to take moral pride in it (p. 188). Such communities are similar in scale and style to the informal societies of mutual aid that spring up spontaneously and without government assistance after disasters. Communities of this type are described by Rebecca Solnit in her book, *A Paradise Built in Hell* (2009). Young adults acquire these skills and values by doing, not by schooling. They learn the scale of a problem that can be solved within the community, how to balance the needs of various stakeholders (including the police), how to respond to change, and how to be effective while being discreet. An adult who develops these skills can serve the neighborhood and become one of its influential and respected members without taking any of the unavailable paths to middle-class adult-hood or the catastrophic routes to prison.

Young adulthood for individuals with same-sex attractions

Some studies of gay people do not differentiate between men and women, so I report them here. When they do differentiate, I have included them in my sections about men and women. Tolerance of same-sex relationships has increased markedly in some locations and cultures in the United States over the last decade. Same-sex marriage was legalized in Massachusetts in 2003 and in five other states since. In 1997, there were approximately 100 Gay-Straight Alliances (clubs for gay and gay-friendly students) in U.S. high schools. Now there are more than 4,000 (GLSN, 2009). Where such acceptance has increased, it has changed the shape of gay young adulthood. Savin-Williams (2005) reports that he finds the new generation of gay youth to be far less suicidal, to feel less rejected by society, and even to be less likely to define themselves by their gayness. As recently as a decade ago, gays feared both family and high school community disapproval and so wait-ed until they had left home to "come out." Now the mean age of gays "coming out" to others has decreased from age 23 (D'Augelli, Hershberger, & Pilkington, 2001) to 18 (Savin-Williams, 2005) or even 16 (D'Augelli, Grossman, & Starks, 2006), an age when they are still living in their childhood households. This earlier time for self-disclosure sug-gests less fear of negative family response, more community support for the families, more cohesion within families, and more support for the gay mem-ber from the family (Denizet-Lewis, B., 2009).

However, considerable intolerance remains. In a strong backlash to some states allowing same-sex marriage, "forty-one states have passed statutes ban-ning recognition of (them)" (Cole, 2009). Anti-gay hate crimes have not decreased over the last decade (FBI, 2008). A developmental goal for LGB young adults (one that heterosexuals do not have to face) is still to reduce the "internalized negative evaluations of gays, lesbians and bisexuals that are made by the majority culture" (Rosario, Scrimshaw, Hunter, & Braun, 2006, p. 46).

In line with the differences within the popula-tion just reported, Diamond & Butterworth (2008) conclude from their review that when family rejection does occur, it remains a powerful negative force in gay young adulthood. They found that White and Latino LGB (their research does not include transgen-dered) youth who reported high levels of family rejec-tion were far more likely to be depressed, to use illegal drugs, and to attempt suicide. Non-Latino White women reported the lowest levels of family re-jection, while Latino men reported the highest (Ryan, Huebner; Diaz, & Sanchez, 2009). Clinicians should note that some researchers question whether disclo-sure to family is always beneficial as a therapeutic goal. They suggest that therapists working with gay clients contemplating disclosure should "carefully evaluate their goals . . . and realistically assess whether –given their own particular family dynam-ics—these expectations are likely to be met" (Dia-mond & Butterworth, 2008, p. 366). LaSala (in press) interviewed 65 gay and lesbian youth and their parents, discovering a *family* "adjustment process" (p. xv)" in reaction to gay children coming out to their parents. This study is especially useful to systems cli-nicians in that it does not describe gay self-acceptance as a solely *individual* process but as a "reciprocal parent-child interaction pattern." While LaSala considers the news that a child is gay to be an "earth-quake" (p. xiii), he also notes that all the families attracted to his study had recovered "at least some-what" from that news. His work emphasizes the mech-anisms of "the adjustment that is possible," but he cautions that his sample did not include families who did not recover or were persistently estranged (p. xvi).

Young Adulthood for Men

Many writers (Badinter, 1996; Gilmore, 1990) be-lieve that heterosexual manhood must be achieved or proven, leaving masculine identity in doubt until it is. Vandello, et al. (2008) refer to this as "Precarious Manhood." Michael Kimmel deplored this pressure in *Manhood in America* (1996) when he asserted that heterosexual manhood is negatively defined in three main ways: A man is not a boy, not a woman, and not a homosexual. The narrowness of adult male heterosexual sex-role expectations may make men feel that they can never gain adult status without renouncing important parts of themselves (Kilmartin, 1994, p. 100).

In his most recent book, *Guyland* (2008), Kimmel sees this narrow definition of heterosexual masculinity as stimulated by homophobia (p. 50), enforced by the same-sex gang (pp. 13, 47–55), and permitted by parents who abdicate guiding responsibility of the elder generation after the middle-class young men he is describing enter college (pp. 18, 101).

To some degree, men are expected to eventually prove love *by* work, that is, by financially supporting those they love, their families. The anticipation of being able to do this permits the proud, antiauthoritarian young middle-class man to accept the ordinary humiliations of learning a skill, temporarily enduring financial deprivation, or of having to do a low-status job to gain access to a higher-status one. But if young men must prove themselves in love and work, what if there is no work? If, as in lower-income neighborhoods, even entry-level jobs are not available, or, because of racism, young men cannot see the senior men of the neighborhood ascending through and beyond such jobs, they have little reason to expect to prove themselves or gain status or attract and support a wife through work (Franklin, 2004).

William Julius Wilson reports in his most recent book, *More Than Just Race* (2009) that African American workers' participation in manufacturing jobs and in unions has dropped considerably between the mid 1980s and 2007 (pp. 70–71). He also notes that the computer revolution has put even many entry level service jobs out of reach for someone without computer skills (p. 8). Wilson details other structural causes for young Black male underemployment: the geographical concentration of poverty (Appendix A in Wilson, 1997; Wilson, 2009), "job spatial mismatch"—the fact that many poor people live in inner-city ghettos, but the greatest employment growth has occurred in suburban areas that they lack information about and cannot easily reach (Wilson, 2009, p. 10), negative employer perceptions, poor educational preparation for "hard skills" such as literacy and numeracy (Wilson, 2009, p. 136), little practice afforded by the "harsh ghetto environment" of "soft skills" such as maintaining eye contact with a customer, tolerating

unreasonable complaints , or working cooperatively in groups (Wilson, 2009).

Joblessness makes crime seem like a reasonable alternative to such men (Wilson, 1997), often leading to incarceration: "Among [Black] male high school dropouts the risk of imprisonment has increased to 60 percent, establishing incarceration as a normal stopping point on the route to midlife" (Western, 2006, cited in Wilson, 2009, p. 72).

Not surprisingly, straight young adult men of all races are the age group and sex that commit the largest number of violent crimes. Of persons arrested for murder and manslaughter, 90 percent are males and 40 percent are between the ages of 18 and 24 (U.S. Department of Justice, 2006). Being responsible for such a disproportionate share of violent crime, straight young men are understandably the most feared group in any society. Every culture must struggle with the problem of what to do with this highly energetic, highly dangerous group. One strategy is to imprison them, which our society does increasingly every year with a huge bias toward poor men of color. Another strategy is to harness their idealism and daring by giving them the opportunity to kill and be killed in war.

Anticipation of Death

Young adult men of all races and socioeconomic classes engage in risky behaviors, exposing themselves to serious, sometimes lethal dangers. The leading cause of death for young White men is automobile accidents (Barker, 2005). The leading cause of death for young Black men is murder (Kelley & Fitzsimons, 2000). Nearly every poor young Black man knows peers who are incarcerated, have died of a drug overdose, were beaten up badly either by peers, strangers, or police, or were killed. Fosse reports that for the nonmonagamous men in his sample, ". . . longer-term goals lose their meaning in an environment characterized by the threat of violence, death and prison" while monoganous men envision longer-term goals and eschew their own infidelity as interfering with them (p. 138). They may think of their young adulthoods as their only adulthoods, that is, they see a much shorter life horizon than more affluent males. In LeBlanc's *Random Family*, as the young men grow older (ages 21 to 25), they also wish to impregnate particular women to whom they are emotionally attached, and are especially eager to have sons. These young women also begin to deliberately wish for children and expect to be valued more highly (and for a longer time) if they can bear a man his first son. Perhaps these strong wishes for sons are also an artifact of the young men's anticipated short life horizon—that they do not expect (or perhaps even want) to live long, but they do want a son to be a legacy (I am indebted to Stephanie Sorrentino, LCSW, for this last idea).

Barriers to Affiliation for Men

Although Wilson strongly emphasizes that structural causes are the most important determinants of Black male unemployment (Wilson, 2009), he believes that such unemployment is also abetted by a poor job referral network in the culture. He reports a study by Sandra Smith (2007) that found "a culture of distrust and a discourse of individualism" in the Black community in which because of mistrust and shame, Black men do not as often seek work by using informal personal referrals from friends and relatives as do other ethnic groups (such as Mexicans). They consequently develop a defensive, individualistic, "go-it-alone" value system (Wilson, 2009). Wilson emphasizes that this culture is not a "Black" culture, but that it is a characteristic of the Black lower class and quite different from the Black middle class (Wilson, 2009).

While mistrust within the population of lower-income Black men may contribute to the extreme unemployment seen there, it also seems to extend into the other domain in which a young man might prove himself—the realm of love. In his chapter entitled "The Fragmentation of the Poor Black Family," Wilson also notes the lack of trust between men and women in the poor Black population (Wilson, 2009). He reports that men protest that women are attracted to material resources that their meager employment prospects cannot supply. Such mistrust is hardly confined to lower-income Black males, however. The White, very middle-class rock group, Good Charlotte (2002), sings, "Girls don't like boys, girls like cars and money." This is a classic plaint

stimulated by all young males' fears of inadequacy and consequent rejection by females, but in the case of low-income men, it is also literally true that they lack material resources, whatever the attitudes of women are. Wilson contends that for all the structural causes that make marriage a less viable arrangement in the poor Black community, cultural variables also may explain some differences in attitudes between poor Black and other poor groups. He cites higher marriage rates among equally poor, undereducated and socially concentrated Mexican immigrants (Wilson, 2009). Fosse also reports that the high levels of mistrust in his poor Black population cause unfaithful men to practice infidelity preemptively to "protect" themselves from being hurt by women. Fosse reports, however, that his monogamous interviewees (53%) are able to "suspend doubt" and consider current partners trustworthy when the relationship is tested over a long trial period of six months to one year (p. 132).

Clinicians who are able to engage these young men may wish to plot their informal job referral networks, just as they would do a genogram, beginning by asking if they know anyone who has a job. His family may be able to help the young man identify personal strengths as well as resources in the extended family and community to decrease the young adult's feeling of alienation from the world of work.

Young gay men may not be driven by the same anxiety about "proving" their masculinity, nor are they responsible for nearly the amount of crime as straight men. But Pachankis (2009) makes it clear that gay men also measure themselves by the standards of "precarious manhood," often leading to an experience of deep inauthenticity. For instance, boys who show behavior described as "effeminate" (not all of whom who eventually identify as gay men) often still receive negative reactions to those gender nonconforming styles from peers and parents, particularly fathers. Gay males may internalize this disapproval and learn to "increasingly downplay their outward displays of effeminacy as they grow older" (D'Augelli, et al., 2006). The display of such behavior may become more of a choice in young adulthood and may be turned on and off according to social context. But the internalized years of societal censure may be associated with "attachment difficulties and depressive symptoms" in young adult life (Josephson and Whiffen, 2007). Self-acceptance and the ability to withstand the blatant, explicit, and gratuitous disapproval by a substantial portion of our society without shame can be a major issue in young adulthood for gay men. "LGB individuals are often raised in communities that are either ignorant of or openly hostile toward Homosexuality" (Rosario, Scrimshaw, Hunter, & Braun, 2006).

LaSala writes about how this self-acceptance can be enhanced by the parents' adjustment to a child's gayness. Parents can sometimes be comforted by contact with other nonjudgmental parents who have had similar experiences. They also report being helped by seeing their child's relief and happiness at being more open and their (sometimes consequent) developmental success in education, work, or finding a steady partner. They report their adjustment to be "impeded" if children appear "obviously gay," are involved in risky behaviors, or are showing psychological distress (whether it appears to be related to being gay or not). Some parents laughed at their own inconsistent limits, saying, "It is OK if he is gay—Just don't really *act* gay" (p. 245).

If leaving the home town after high school for a more gay-friendly environment increases the social opportunities for gay young adults, the "hook-up" culture of college described above for heterosexuals may be a natural fit for college-aged gay men. Diamond & Butterworth (2008) report that researchers have investigated "whether *combining* two men or two women in the same relationship magnifies (typical gender–related patterns)," thus "providing a 'double dose' of male-typical behavior in male-male relationships. . . ." Their review confirms that "gay men's relationship scripts are more likely to involve the establishment of sexual intimacy prior to the development of emotional intimacy" (p. 355).

Affiliation: Can Fathers Help?

Silverstein and Rashbaum (1994) and Miller (1976) argued strongly that separation-based theories of development underestimate how much men "long for an affiliative mode of living" (Miller, 1976, p. 88). In their book *The Courage to Raise Good Men* (1994), Silverstein and Rashbaum present many convincing cases of premature or too extreme separations between mothers and sons leaving sons with feelings of depression and longing that endure well into adult life. Attachment to fantasies of an ideal love that will fill up their feelings of emptiness may interfere with attachment to a real, possible woman, prolonging some of the unrealistic idealism of young adulthood. Silverstein's clinical approach is first to interpret and acknowledge these sometimes as yet unnamed yearnings. She encourages appropriate delays in physical separations and advocates reconciliation between too-distant mothers and sons. She does not say so, but her examples—personal, literary, and clinical—make it clear she is writing for middle- and upper-middle-class White women in particular.

Although she states that "(family) life with a man is better than it is without," Silverstein vehemently opposes the idea that boys need a "male role model" to develop a "masculine identity," calling it a "myth" and asserting that a woman who reclaims devalued parts of herself ("gentleness, firmness, and caring") can supply the necessary nutrients for male identity (p. 88).

Some of the books written by African Americans about African American sons approach men's affiliative needs from a different perspective. In *Boys into Men* (2000), Boyd-Franklin and Franklin also address mothers first but urge them to ask more of their sons in terms of responsibility for schoolwork, child care, and household chores, thereby "raising" them as they do their daughters, rather than only "loving" them. It is very likely true that mothers train their daughters more in household chores and child care in all races; the authors seem to also be talking about imparting a more rigorous sense of responsibility to provide for and lead a family in the future. They do not say so, but this demand implies that fathers might model child care and performance of household chores themselves. They also make a special point of addressing fathers and strongly encourage them as "role models." They say of sons, "They need their father's active involvement in their lives! The value of a father's (and other males') input and love cannot be overestimated" (p. 21). In the absence of an appropriate man, they feel it is sometimes necessary to reach outside the family to find a male mentor for a son.

In Geoffrey Canada's *Reaching Up for Manhood* (1998), bonds are formed by adults training children how to do chores, but he also notes that such training is given more to daughters than to sons, leaving poor males of color ill-prepared to work for bosses in the outside world. Canada also encourages relationships in which boys' affiliative needs are met by male mentors' nurturing behavior. He emphasizes the need for training mentors to guard against their offering developmentally inappropriate advice. As an example of naïve advice, he tells of his boyhood friendship group being warned in harsh detail by a street group of ex-convicts about how to avoid anal rape in prison, terrifying the boys and making them suspicious of later mentors. The mistrust Canada describes in this community is also described by William Julius Wilson and Nathan Fosse, and the fear among straight Black males of homosexuality is the same fear that Kimmel finds so prevalent in the straight White male collegians he studied.

In *From Brotherhood to Manhood* (2004), A. J. Franklin contends that young Black men are treated as "invisible" by society. He describes how low expectations from the majority culture, blatant discrimination, and relentless racial microaggressions cause them to search for ways to maintain pride. This self-protective reaction makes the development of pride in gender and race a major task of young adulthood for Black males. Preventing dishonor can lead them to value male social contact over classroom striving, reject jobs in which they feel treated unfairly, and court women for their trophy qualities rather than expectation of partnership. When exercised with discipline (as in male groups in African American churches) Franklin sees the development of dignity as enabling affiliation with other Black men, with Black women, and in practicing fatherhood with children.

Another difference between Silverstein and the aforementioned books written for African American readers is that the latter three have portions or entire chapters describing religious faith as a source of self-support, a helpful community, or an opportunity for male affiliation and the Silverstein book does not. I have often found churches in communi-

ties of color to be very positive forces in the social life of their parishioners. A personal collaboration on practical, concrete matters between therapist and pastor (best face-to-face, but even a phone call makes a difference) is very powerful and comforting to the client.

Young Adulthood for Women

Women's lives have been lived more "in relationship" than men's at every stage. For many decades, women married out of one household and into another. In recent years, however, middle- and upper-class women, like men, often leave home and live alone before marrying. For this reason, young adulthood for these women can be the era of their lives that is least centered on relationships.

Young adult women have not been as expected to be financially independent and to live in a domicile separate from their parents as men. They are also not expected to prove their adult gender identity. They are permitted and expected to maintain relatedness, especially in the middle, lower-middle, and low-income classes where they are often drafted into positions of child-care service to their extended families, either paying off debts of service or "loaning" service to "call in" in the future. Even if such service is not requested, they are more subject to a feeling of continued obligation to family and friends. When they can afford it, however, young women attempt to create a relatively self-involved period in which to develop their skills and their knowledge of themselves.

Kerr (1994) distills from the biographies of eminent women some common characteristics that enabled them to succeed, including the opportunity to have time alone, the chance to be connected to others without losing "separateness," and the ability to know their own feelings. I have encountered many women in midlife who are quite willingly involved in a network of relationships to family of origin, family of procreation, friends, and career. These highly related women look back with relish, however, to a period in their young adulthoods during which, with fewer commitments, they traveled, had lovers, worked hard, or sowed wild oats. They generally felt free to enact or postpone relationships.

Some women regret missing such a period, saying, "I never lived alone" or "I never did anything just for myself." This theme is present in the young adulthoods of lower-income women as well. In *Random Family*, Jessica's mother, Lourdes, had always wanted to be a singer, and, when a young woman, had even received an offer to join a touring singing group. She was bitter, however, that she could not do so because her mother had a job outside the home and needed her to care for her siblings (LeBlanc, 2004).

Anticipation of Birth

Young women are more thoughtful about the timing of their giving birth and subsequent child care than are young men. Aspiring professional women once anticipated that they could "have it all," by using a strategy of developing their careers first and adding a husband and children later. Some women who are currently middle-aged look back at these expectations when they were young adults and now consider them naïve, particularly if they were disappointed by age-related infertility. In *Creating a Life: Professional Women and the Quest for Children*, Sylvia Ann Hewlett (2002) describes the unplanned childlessness of many successful professional women as a "creeping non-choice." Clinicians may have to introduce the topic of fertility to young middle-class adult women (and men) who are developing their careers to make sure they are really deciding to risk not being able to have children. Not realizing they might be disappointed is consistent with the ascetic, work-oriented, immortal grandiosity of young adulthood.

If they have not already had children as adolescents, most lower-income African American women have children in this life cycle phase. They may even feel that it is dangerous to delay having children. This fear stems from Geronimus' "weathering hypothesis," the idea that "the health of African American women may begin to deteriorate in early adulthood as a physical consequence of cumulative socioeconomic disadvantage" (Geronimus, 1992). This hypothesis is an attempt to explain the finding that "unlike non-Hispanic White infants, African American infants with teen mothers experience a survival advantage relative to infants whose mothers

are older." It should be noted, however, that Nigel Thomas (2006) has questioned Geronimus' finding, citing the "paradox" that Black women live longer than both White and Black men. At any rate, this perception may be the female version of the fears of mortality— the expected short life (or in this case, fertility) horizon—that Fosse described for young men of this class.

Edin and Kefalas interviewed a group of 162 poor single mothers who were equally divided among Whites, Latinas, and African Americans to understand why low-income women tend to have children before they marry, thus reversing the middle-class sequence. Their subjects "revered . . . marriage as a luxury, something they aspired to but feared they might never achieve." However, "they judge children to be a *necessity* [emphasis mine], an absolutely essential part of a young woman's life, the chief source of identity and meaning" (2005, p. 6). They report that "poor women often say they don't want to marry until they are 'set' economically and established in a career." The young woman feels that marriage "will mean loss of control . . . to "an authoritarian head of the house" (p. 9). Money of her own ensures her "freedom from a man's attempts to control her behavior." The authors feel that socioeconomic class (rather than race) drives the cultural differences in timing of pregnancy during young adulthood between these women and those in the middle class.

Young adult mothers have a more clearly defined role in their extended families (as caregivers to their children) than do jobless young men. By entering this economy of mutual obligation, they gain adult status and respect, but they are rarely free to pursue solitary postsecondary education that would permit an exit from poverty and allow financial self-sufficiency. Physical separation or even financial self-sufficiency may not be a realistic or even desirable goal for young adult mothers. Because of the variety and changing nature of these family structures, discovering the executive subsystem is not always a straightforward task. A very useful question for young adult mothers is, "Who helps you?" The answer begins to reveal whom she can or must count on. A follow-up question that addresses the emotional climate of this network is, "Who gets to express their opinion on how you are raising your kids?" This group may include some additional individuals who do not supply care directly, but who affect the morale of the mother with their criticisms.

Researchers are beginning to differentiate some of the unique stresses of young adulthood for lesbians. Rosario, Scrimshaw, & Hunter (2008) report that within the lesbian population, those with a more "masculine" self-presentation, whom the authors refer to as "butch" are reported to consume more cigarettes, marijuana, and alcohol than young heterosexual women and other lesbians with a more "feminine" presentation ("femmes"). Rosario and her colleagues surmise that lesbian "butches" are more visible and so experience more homophobia and "gay-related stressors" than lesbians with a "femme" presentation.

Lesbians tend to bond earlier in young adulthood into stable couples than gay men do. Researchers find that the "dose" of gender identity that is "doubled" in lesbian couples is the female interest in and propensity for the emotional relationship. They see a contrast with the "sexual intimacy script" more prevalent in the gay male culture. Diamond & Butterworth (2008) summarize research to conclude that, more often than gay men, lesbians follow a "friendship script" in which couples begin as friends, cultivate their emotional compatibility and communication first, and later form an erotic/romantic bond.

Because their identity is then partially expressed as a member of a partnership, they (like married heterosexuals) want to present themselves as couples to their families. Their appearing as a couple makes their homosexuality much more difficult for their families to deny, however. They may wish to visit or attend family rituals with their partners, forcing themselves, their partners, and their families to decide how "out" they want to be. If the partner isn't welcome, both the young adult and family have a hard choice. I generally have seen the parents and lesbian daughters separately at the beginning of such cases, giving them a chance to discuss their strong emotions out of the others' hearing. I find that hearing feelings such as disgust, contempt, shame, and hate from a close family member in a too-soon, uncontrolled session can have an indelibly destructive effect. Such emotional states

are usually temporary and are incompatible with the rational processes of negotiation and compromise that are necessary to resolve disagreements such as attendance at family rituals. I also try not to be stampeded by the urgency of an impending date for the ritual. Whatever happens on that day does not have to be a permanent statement. I have found that family attitudes about homosexuality and the intensity of members' reactivity can change a great deal over time. Parents get used to the idea, find that their friends' children are also gay, or find that other loyal family members aren't as bothered by it. This long-term change is more important to the happiness of the family than a premature pretense on either side.

There are fewer physical barriers for lesbian women to have children than for gay men, and they may be more inclined in that direction as well, so they do so more often (33 percent to 23 percent). For this reason, when choosing a partner, they may think not only of who would be a good spouse but who would be a good parent as well. The fact that both parents are likely to have reproductive capacity leads to symmetries (two children, each with a different biological mother and still in the same family, for instance) the effects of which are uncharted by heterosexual marriage.

Conclusion: Young Adulthood as a Transition for Three Generations

Few young adults present for family therapy, but their parents do. If their children have gone to college, some psychoeducation about the ordinary vicissitudes of college life (the need for the organization of time, uncertainty about choosing an academic focus, sexual freedom, and substance use) may diminish parental anxiety. I also ask how they passed this developmental period themselves and what their relationship was to *their* parents during it. I wonder how their experiences (good and bad) as young adults influenced their ambitions for how their children should pass the same stage. While normalizing some of the shocking parts of college life, clinicians must also name the red flags that should command the parents' attention. These may include missing classes, failing to turn in work, or debilitating use of drugs or alcohol. Any grades of C or below deserve a careful inquiry, and more than one at that level requires a conference between parents and student, perhaps face-to-face. This is assuming, of course, that the student permits the parents to view his or her transcript. I try to lift the stigma of "helicopter parents" that is sometimes encouraged by colleges themselves. Coaching parents to use a light touch focused on inquiry and problem solving rather than reprimand and exhortation can be useful, as is coaching parental follow-through.

If the young adult is not attending college and still lives at home or has been to college and returned, the parents usually present with some conflict about how the child wants to demonstrate adult status while living under their roof. The young adult may expect to be free of curfew, to occasionally sleep elsewhere without enduring an inquiry, or to sleep at home with a girl- or-boyfriend without explanation. Parents may feel obliged to enact some stereotype of thwarting dependency. They may want to continue a high school tradition of respectful ges-

tures toward the parent and enforce the safety of their home by monitoring guests. A clinician may help frame these good-faith but contradictory goals as developmentally appropriate for both generations. The solution must recognize the young adult's growth and the parents' representation of structure and continuity. Young adults can prove their case by working (school or job) outside the home and being considerate (rather than entitled) in their behavior. Parents can aid growth by increasingly recognizing their children's rights and responsibilities as partners.

As this is the developmental period when family members are meant to be least in relationship with each other, seeing individuals or coaching subsystems is often a necessity and sometimes the first choice of therapies. Keeping in mind the differences between groups described in this chapter, family therapists are well equipped to combine systemic and developmental approaches to this exciting and productive phase of life.

Chapter 13

Becoming a Couple

Monica McGoldrick

For most of history it was inconceivable that people would choose their mates on the basis of something as fragile and irrational as love and then focus all their sexual, intimate, and altruistic desires on the resulting marriage.

—STEPHANIE COONTZ (2005, P. 15)

Marriage in Our Times

Of all dilemmas of the life cycle, the existential dilemma of coupling is probably the most difficult interpersonally. Marriage is the only family relationship we swear is both exclusive and forever, and it is the family relationship least likely to be either. Just as society has defined "family" as a legally married heterosexual couple with children, "couple" has meant a married heterosexual couple, in which the man is taller, older, smarter, possessing more income-generating power, and in charge of supporting his wife and any children they may have. Meanwhile the wife was expected to be physically attractive and ever supportive of her husband in the fulfillment of his dreams, while taking care of all other family members: their children, her parents, his parents, and anyone else in the family who became ill or needed help. Those who didn't fit into this ideal were generally found wanting. Yet couples come in many varieties: gay and straight, married and unmarried, ambitious tall wives and short, nurturing homebody husbands. The ideal itself costs us all a tremendous amount in terms of our ability to be ourselves and find harmony in our relationships with each other and support the tasks of family life. Thus a major role for therapists is to normalize the patterns of those who do not fit into traditional stereotypes and to educate couples about the pitfalls of those mythical images.

The meaning of marriage in our time is profoundly different from its meaning throughout all previous human history, when it was tightly embedded in the economic and social fabric of society, often more about getting good in-laws, increasing one's family labor force, and solidifying political

and economic power in the community than finding a life companion (Coontz, 2005, p. 6). The changing role of women and the dramatic effects of widely available contraceptives, along with our increasing longevity and the mobility of our culture, have contributed to a major redefinition of marriage in our society. While at its best marriage has become more fair and fulfilling for both couples and their children than ever before, when marriage depends on love, flexibility, and equity it becomes more fragile and optional than ever before (Coontz, 2005).

The place of marriage in the life cycle has also been changing dramatically. Men and women are having sex earlier, but marrying later and less often than ever before. More people are living together before marriage, living with several partners before deciding to marry, or not marrying at all. At any time about 51 percent of adult women are living without a spouse, married couples are becoming for the first time a minority of American Households (Schultz, 2007). Indeed, so many African Americans are not marrying that some are saying marriage is only for White people (Jones, 2006). These changes are thought to reflect cultural shifts that mean "sex, love, and childbearing have become a la carte choices rather than a package deal that comes with marriage" (Jones, 2006, p. 2). Whereas in the past marriage was primarily a business and cultural arrangement between families, it has become a choice for self-sufficient individuals who no longer require a spouse for survival. Indeed if the man is not "the good provider" and hasn't moved toward equitable partnership in the administrative and relationship tasks of a family, women often think marriage is not worth undertaking.

Andrew Cherlin, one of the premier trackers of U.S. marriage patterns for many years, says that as a nation we still seem to believe in marriage more than other Western societies, and yet we have the highest divorce rate in the Western world and the greatest number of co-habiting relationships that break up more rapidly than those in other Western countries. (Cherlin, 2009). Cherlin attributes this paradoxical pattern of believing in marriage while practicing divorce to reflect our conflicting values about marriage. We view it as a cultural ideal, but it conflicts with our belief in free choice, which becomes reflected in our high rate of marital breakups. It is also a paradox that we even having governmental programs to promote marriage yet we fight same-sex marriage more than other countries (Cherlin, 2009). Cherlin points out that these patterns create great turbulence in American family life, where the coming and going of partners occurs more than elsewhere and may be very difficult for children, particularly because of the lack of stable community networks.

Marriage used to be the major marker of transition to the adult world, because it symbolized the transition to parenthood; now it often reflects a greater continuity with the phase of young adulthood or even adolescence, since childbearing, especially for the middle and upper classes, is increasingly postponed for a number of years after marriage. And indeed, increasing numbers of women (20 percent as of 2006) are not having children, double the percent of only 30 years ago (Zezima, 2008).

As a multigenerational, communal event, marriage symbolizes a change in status among all family members and generations and requires that the couple negotiate new relationships as a twosome with many other subsystems: parents, siblings, grandparents, nieces, nephews, and friends. In fact, the status changes of marriage may not be fully appreciated by the family until the next phase, the transition to parenthood, which challenges traditional sex roles and multigenerational family patterns even more. Increasingly, women want to have their own careers and are resistant to having the primary responsibility for the household and childcare as well as to husbands who are absent from family life. Men's participation in childcare is increasing, but more slowly.

In traditional societies to talk of the choice to marry or not would be about as relevant as to talk of the choice to grow old or not; it was considered the only route to full adult status. To marry was simply part of the "natural" progression through life, unless catastrophe intervened. Only recently have society's norms on this been modified, as more of the population do not fit into traditional patterns and raise questions about their viability.

Another paradox is the stereotype that men are polygamous and women are monogamous, yet if this is so, why is there so much effort throughout history to control women's sexuality with veils, genital mutilation, chastity belts, purdah, etc. (Barnett & Rivers, 2004).

A major problem in coupling is that patriarchal rules of male domination in marriage get obfuscated and mystified by the mythology of coupling as a love story of two equals. The patriarchal courtship ideal of Cinderella and Prince Charming gets mystified with a myth of a partnership of two lovers whose souls and bodies mingle, such that they will think and act as one until death does them part. The contradiction in these two propositions makes marriage a problem for both men and women, but especially for women, a fact which has only very recently begun to come to our national and international consciousness. Carolyn Heilbrun (1988) has asked: "Was marriage always in such danger of becoming unappealing to women that the whole society had to contrive to keep the fiction of its desirability alive and intact?"(p. 88). When women have options and resources, traditional marriage is increasingly viewed as a bad bargain.

Couple relationships have many dimensions:

- **Economic** (family support and finances equally earned and shared or controlled by one)
- **Emotional** (a continuum from communication and intimacy to mind control and dependence)
- **Power** (a continuum from male privilege, dominance, intimidation, and abuse to partnership, equity, and respect for each partner)
- **Boundaries** (a continuum around the couple in relation to all other connections:

friends, extended family, work, children, and religion—may be tight and controlled by one partner, or flexible in each area)

- **Sexuality** (involves a continuum from sexual intimacy to sexual objectification, rape, and exploitation)
- **Child-rearing** (involves a continuum from parenting as shared to it being women's responsibility)
- **Chores and Leisure Activities** (involves a continuum of decision making and tasks from home care, food preparation, administration of health care, education, work, transportation, vacation, and leisure time)

The complexity of these dimensions conveys how difficult this life cycle phase is. However, along with the transition to parenthood, which marriage has long symbolized, society has skewed us toward a romanticized view of this transition as the easiest and most joyous, which adds greatly to its difficulty, since everyone—from the couple to the family and friends—wants to see only its happiness. The emotional and sexual dimensions are the ones given priority in the dominant framework, and the issues of power are subtly kept invisible. Even now with marriage rates going down and divorce rates high, weddings are becoming ever more expensive and elaborate, even for those who cannot afford them, probably reflecting the ongoing idealization of marriage. The problems entailed in forming a couple may thus be obscured and pushed underground, only to intensify and surface later on.

Furthermore, as Michael Lerner has pointed out (1995) finding a partner, which used to be a community affair, has become an individual decision often made in terms of what the partner can do to satisfy our needs:

In the past relationships were embedded in larger communities of meaning and purpose. The relationship was not about itself, but about some larger shared goal. But today, with those communities of meaning in decline, people increasingly look to their primary sexual relationship to become a compensation for the meaninglessness surrounding them. Yet judged against such standards, very few relationships feel adequate (Lerner, 1995, p. 10).

More than any other life transition, marriage is viewed as the solution to life's problems of loneliness, work or career uncertainty, or extended-family difficulties. The wedding itself is seen as the end of a process: "And they lived happily ever after," but it is really only the beginning. Marriage requires that two people renegotiate a great many issues they have previously defined individually or through their culture and family of origin, such as money, space, time, and when and how to eat, sleep, talk, have sex, fight, work, and relax. The power aspect of negotiating these dimensions often remains invisible, since power inequities in most heterosexual couples are highly likely to be obscured by the couple, the extended family, and others in society (Carter & Peters, 1996). Decisions must be made about which family traditions and rituals to retain from each side of the family and which ones partners will develop for themselves. Partners have to renegotiate relationships with parents, siblings, friends, extended family, and co-workers once they marry; it is extremely important, especially for women, that they not curtail these relationships, which would leave them vulnerable to isolation and too frequently to abuse in the marriage.

The joke that there are six in the marital bed is really an understatement. It has been said that what distinguishes human beings from all other animals is the fact of having in-laws. In the animal kingdom, mating involves only the two partners, who usually mature, separate from their families, and mate on their own. For humans it is the joining of two enormously complex systems. If couples could fully appreciate the emotional complexity of negotiating marriage from the start, they might not dare to undertake it.

Contrary to the widespread cultural stereotypes that marriage is something men should dread and fear, the research supports the opposite—marriage improves men's mental health, sex lives, and financial success and leads them to lower rates of drug and alcohol abuse and depression (Barnett & Rivers, 2004, p. 62). At the same time, studies indicate that women get fewer tangible benefits from marriage. They often suffer a wage loss, especially after children, and tend to be burdened with more housework, and their sexual satisfaction does not appear to improve with marriage (Steinhauer, 1995; Apter, 1985). Contrary to the stereotypes of the frustrated old maid and the free unencumbered bachelor, so-called "spinsters" may do better than bachelors, although bachelors are doing better than they used to, perhaps because they are increasingly finding ways to have a meaningful social network.

Socioeconomics are a major factor in marriage patterns. Educated women among both Whites and African Americans are more likely to marry and less inclined to divorce (Zernike, 2007). The most likely to marry are those with a college education, although they are marrying later. They are most likely to marry each other and less likely to marry up or down. The divorce rate for college-educated women is about half the rate of those without a college education. These couples tend to have higher incomes as well. The income of married couples living with their own children has increased 59 percent over the past 30 years compared with 44 percent for all households (Harden, 2007). The percent of men who are married has decreased from 69 percent in 1960 to 55 percent now, while for women it has gone from 66 percent to 52 percent. In earlier times people often married as part of launching, but now it is increasingly not undertaken until people are financially stable. An increasing percentage of African Americans are not married, more than 40 percent of men and women, compared to 27 percent of White men and 20 percent of White women (Jones, 2006). Between 1970 and 2001 the overall U.S. rate of marriage declined by 17 percent, but for Blacks it fell by 34 percent in this time (Jones, 2006). Women appear to be no longer content with the thought of the "good provider" husband. Currently even where both spouses work, one in four wives earns more than her husband (Falk, 2009). They are questioning the value of marriage unless the husband is a real partner (Jones, 2006). Couples are also marrying more often for health benefits, which are becoming increasingly expensive and hard to hold on to. There are, of course, also societal constraints on who can marry whom. Gays and lesbians are still denied federal and most religious recognition of their relationships. Only a few states so far allow same-sex marriages. Interracial marriages have only been legal since the Supreme Court decision in Loving vs. Virginia in 1967. Prior to that interracial couples could be sent to prison.

More and more couples are passing through a stage of living with one or several partners before marriage, making the transition to marriage much less of a turning point in the family life cycle than it was in the past. Obviously, the meaning of a wedding changes when a couple has been living together for several years and participating jointly in extended-family experiences. Nevertheless, the transition to marriage can create great turmoil, more so if the partners have not yet dealt with their extended family as a couple. Indeed, the parents may have been hoping the couple would break up and now have to acknowledge the centrality of the relationship for their child. It places no small stress on a family to open itself to an outsider who is now an official member of its inner circle. Frequently no new member has been added to the system for many years. Parents must now deal with their child and the partner as a twosome, which can radically change the dynamics of interaction. The tendency of members to polarize and see villains and victims under the stress of these changes can be very strong.

In any case, there seem to be a timing to the phase of coupling. People who marry before 20 often have more difficulty adjusting to the tasks of coupling and are much more likely to divorce. Those who marry after 30 (about 20 percent of women) are less likely to divorce. Marrying later appears better than marrying early. Early marriage may also reflect cultural patterns (e.g., Latinos) or class norms (e.g., working-class couples), but those who marry early may also be running away from their families of origin or seeking a family they never had. They may leave home by fusing with a mate in an attempt to gain strength from each other. They may have more difficulties later on as a result of their failure to develop an independent identity first. Women who marry late may be ambivalent about losing their independence and identity in marriage. An increasing number of men also seem to be avoiding commitment. Some who marry late have seen a negative image of marriage at home. They may have been enmeshed in their families and find it hard to leave home, form outside relationships, or develop a secure work situation.

In spite of the trend toward delaying marriage and pregnancy, most people do marry and have children before age 35. Naturally those who have children shortly after marriage have relatively little time to adjust to the status changes of marriage and its accompanying stresses before moving on. What is amazing, considering the long-range implications of marriage, is that so many couples spend so little time thinking about the decision. The timing of marital decisions often appears to be influenced by events in the extended family, although most couples are unaware of the correlation of these events and the process that underlies their decision to marry. People often seem to meet or make the decision to marry shortly after the retirement, illness, move, or even untimely death of a parent or after other traumatic family loss. The sense of loss or loneliness can be a strong contributing factor in the desire to build a close relationship. A person in need of being "completed" may be blind to the less-than-ideal aspects of a prospective spouse This desire for completion is likely to lead to difficulty accepting the spouse's differentness in the course of the relationship. As one woman put it

> My husband and I have always been afraid of the stranger in each other. We keep wanting to believe that the other thought the same as we thought they were thinking. We just couldn't appreciate that here was a new and different person, with his or her own thoughts and feelings, who would make life more interesting.

Fusion and Intimacy

The basic dilemma in coupling is the confusion of intimacy with fusion. There is a profound difference between forming an intimate relationship and using a couple relationship to complete one's self. Poets have long talked about the difference. Rilke wrote: "Love is at first not anything that means merging, giving over, and uniting with another (for what would a union be of something unclarified and unfinished, still subordinate); it is a high inducement to the individual to ripen. . . . It is a great exacting claim"(1954, p. 54).

There are, of course, sex differences in the way fusion is experienced, since women have traditionally been raised to consider "losing themselves" in a relationship as normal, and men have been raised to see intimacy as "unmanly." Thus men more often express their fusion by maintaining a pseudo-differentiated distant position in relationships, or by possessive demands that their partner conform to their wishes, and women by giving themselves, their dreams, and their opinions up to the relationship.

The romantic mythology about couples has led to much confusion in notions of closeness, enmeshment, and fusion, on one side and differentiation, autonomy, disengagement, and distance on the other, The categories offered by Green, Bettinger, and Zacks (1996) provide a useful and demystifying framework for understanding the individual and collaborative aspects of intimate couple relationships:

- **Closeness-Caregiving** (made up of warmth, time together, nurturance, physical intimacy, and consistency)
- **Openness of Communication** (made up of openness, self-disclosure, and the ability to face conflict and differences without avoidance)
- **Lack of Intrusiveness** made up of:
  1. Lack of Separation Anxiety
  2. Respecting the Other's Need for Privacy and Time Alone
  3. Lack of Possessiveness and Jealousy
  4. Lack of Emotional Over-Reactivity to the other's life problems
  5. Lack of Mindreading of the Other
  6. Lack of Thinking One Knows the Other's Wishes Better than s/he Does
  7. Lack of Aggressive Criticism, Hurtful Attacks or Attempts to Diminish the Other
  8. Lack of Attempt to Dominate the Other in Disagreements

Both lesbian and gay couples tend to have more intimate, cohesive relationships than do heterosexual couples, lesbians the most so. Gottman found that the expression of negativity appears as necessary as positivity in a marriage, though to be successful couples need to have more positivity than negativity (Gottman, 1993; Carstensen, Gottman, &

Levenson, 1995) and relationships of heterosexual couples tend to be defined along power and status lines. That is, the partner who makes more money and has more status (usually the man) tends to control the relationship decisions, right down to where they will go on vacation and who will clean the toilet. There have been indications from early research that lesbian couples may be freer to develop their roles and relationships on a basis other than money, power, and status (Blumstein & Schwartz, 1983).

Frequently others expect a couple to fuse and view the wife as somehow joined to the identity of her husband, increasing the difficulties for women in differentiating and maintaining their separate identities. Men's fear of intimacy and the social expectations of his "independence" along with women's adaptiveness inhibit men from developing intimate relationships. Forming an intimate relationship requires men to learn a new model of human development, within which they can develop interdependence and interpersonal relationships (see Chapter 2).

Bowen Theory (1978) suggests that the tendency to seek fusion with a partner is related to a person's incomplete differentiation or maturity in relation to her or his family of origin. In other words, couples seek to complete themselves in each other to the degree that they have failed to resolve their relationships with their parents, which would enable them to build new relationships based on each person's freedom to be him- or herself and to appreciate the other as he or she is. When people seek to enhance their self-esteem in marriage, they deny their "differentness" from their spouse and may develop severe distortions in communication to maintain the myth of agreement.

During courtship couples are usually most aware of the romantic aspects of their relationship. Marriage shifts the relationship from a private coupling to a formal joining of two families. Issues that the partners have not resolved with their own families tend to be factors in marital choice and are likely to interfere with establishing a workable marital balance.

Our experience of romantic love may be largely determined by our family. From this perspective Romeo and Juliet might have felt intensely attracted to each other precisely because their families prohibited their relationship. Such obstacles may lead to an idealization of the forbidden person. Like so many romantic heroes, Romeo and Juliet were conveniently spared a deeper view of their relationship by their untimely deaths, preserving the romance and perhaps obscuring the more pedestrian underlying family dramas that probably fostered their attraction in the first place. In everyday life the outcome of such love affairs is often not so romantic, as the following case illustrates

Susan, (**Genogram 13.1**: Joe and Susan) the older of two children of a middle-class Jewish family, met her future husband, Joe, the summer of her first year of college. Her parents had been unhappily married and had invested all

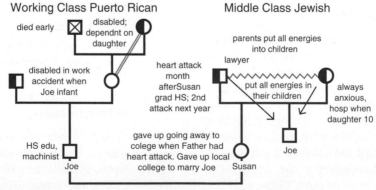

Working Class Puerto Rican

Middle Class Jewish

GENOGRAM 13.1 Joe and Susan

their energies in their children's success. Susan planned to go away to college as did her "computer genius" younger brother, Joe. A month after her high school graduation, Susan's lawyer father had a heart attack. Her mother, who had always been anxious, had been hospitalized for depression when Susan was 10. Ever since then the mother was viewed as fragile and now seemed quite close to the edge, criticizing her husband continuously, now that he was so dependent. Susan gave up her plans for going away to college and enrolled in a local college. Over the next year her father recovered, but then he had a second heart attack and had to stop work. Shortly afterwards Susan began dating Joe, a machinist whom she met at her summer job as a secretary. Joe was an only child from a working-class Puerto Rican family. Joe hoped to improve his parents' situation by marrying Susan, whose family represented for him social and financial stability. These were important to him because of his own family's poverty, related to his father's disability in a work accident when Joe was a child. Joe's mother had cared for her husband, as well as her own mother. Joe had always felt responsible for his parents but powerless to make them happy. He was delighted when Susan gave up college and began pushing to marry him. He had felt threatened by her college pursuits anyway. For Susan he represented the only way she knew to get away from her family's expectations. She had been conflicted about school, having felt inadequate in comparison to her brother whose accomplishments were so much the focus of family attention. She had received mixed messages from her family about continuing her education. She had grown up not believing she was really smart and had felt under great pressures about schoolwork. Joe would free her from these pressures, and would not push her to achieve. He accepted her as she was. He had a steady income, which would mean she would not have to worry about her inability to concentrate or her fears of failure. She could be Joe's wife, raise a family, and her worries about her own identity would be over.

Both Joe and Susan found the other attractive and thought their relationship made them feel better than they ever remembered feeling before. Joe's parents disapproved of Susan's not being Catholic and suggested strongly that they wait. Susan's father disapproved of her marrying someone without a college education and thought she should finish school herself. He also disapproved of her marrying someone who was not Jewish, though the family was not religious. In quiet moments, Susan herself wondered if she might want someone more educated, but her parents' disapproval pushed her to defend her choice and to reject their "snobbery." Prior to marriage, Susan and Joe had little chance to be alone together. What time they did have was filled with wedding arrangements and discussion of the families' pressures on them. Almost immediately after the wedding, Susan felt restless. Things with her family had quieted down; they had no more reason to protest. Susan quickly became bored and began to pressure Joe to get a better job. He felt guilty for having "abandoned" his parents, something he hadn't let surface during courtship. To improve their financial situation and to deal with his guilt, he suggested they move into his parents' apartment, while the parents would move to a smaller apartment upstairs. It would save on expenses and be a good investment. Susan agreed because it meant they would have much nicer living quarters. Almost immediately she began to feel pressure from Joe's parents to socialize with them and to have children for them. Having married to escape her own parents, she now felt saddled with Joe's parents, with the added burden of not knowing them well. Suddenly Joe's personality irritated her. Where initially she had liked him for his easy-going style and his acceptance of her, she now saw him as lacking ambition. She was embarrassed to have him spend time with her friends, because of his manners and lack of education, so she began to avoid her friends, which left her even more isolated. She tried pressuring Joe to fulfill her dreams and satisfy all her relationship needs. He felt increasingly inadequate and unable to respond to her pressure. She felt he was a good lover but began to be more attracted to other men at work and to turn him away. His sense of inadequacy led him to retreat further and he took to going out in the evening with his own friends, with whom he felt more accepted.

Susan's resistance to parental expectations had now been transferred into the marriage. Joe's hopes for moving beyond his parents' disappointing lives had now been transformed into pressure from Susan for him to succeed, and he resented it. Neither partner had worked out individually what each wanted in life. Each had turned to the other to fulfill unmet needs and now each was disappointed.

What began to happen between Susan and Joe is what happens to many couples when the hope that the partner will solve their problems proves unrealistic. There is a tendency to personalize stress and place blame for what goes wrong with oneself on one's spouse. Given enough stress, couples tend to define their problems solely within the relationship. Once this personalizing process begins, it is difficult to keep the relationship open. Susan began to lay the blame for her disappointments in life on Joe, and he saw himself as responsible for her unhappiness. One major factor that tightens couple relationships over time is their tendency to interpret more and more facets of their lives within the marriage, which is often promoted by the wider social context, which also supports this narrow focus. During courtship, if one partner becomes depressed the other is not likely to take it too personally, assuming that there are many reasons one might get depressed in life and this may have nothing to do with him or her. The assumption that one is not responsible for the other's feelings permits an empathic response. After several years of marriage, however, partners have a greater tendency to view the other's emotional reactions as a reflection of their input and to feel responsible for getting the partner out of the depression. Once a partner begins taking responsibility for the other's feelings, more and more areas in the relationship may become tension-filled. The more one spouse defines him or herself by the other, the less flexibility there will be in the relationship and the more their communication will become constricted in areas that are emotionally charged.

These responses are profoundly "gendered" as well. Because women are socialized to take responsibility for others' lives, feelings, and behavior and to consider it selfish to have a life of their own, they are more likely to internalize their problems and feel overresponsible for the marriage. Because men are socialized to define themselves primarily by their ability to provide for their families financially, perform sexually, and handle their emotions without overt emotional dependence, these dimensions will tend to define their feelings of success. Beyond this they may externalize blame when things go wrong.

In the case of Susan and Joe, neither of them probably had any awareness that she was bringing into the relationship a lifetime of feeling like a second-class citizen in relation to her brother. Nor did she realize that her mother's depression, anxiety, and frustration may have related to her having lived a life that disallowed any personal fulfillment, while she was supposed to devote herself to caring for the needs of others. The mother had been a brilliant student herself and had wanted to go to medical school, but she was told by her parents that this goal was inappropriate for a woman and would mean she would "never find a man." So she found a man, but probably lost herself in the process. Now Susan was perhaps repeating her mother's mistake. Joe could not see that the very "life force" that attracted him to Susan soon became the rub. He felt "inadequate" in relation to her intelligence and drive. If he hadn't had to measure himself by a yardstick that said men should be smarter and more successful, he could have enjoyed her strength and intensity. Instead he saw it as a measure of his failure and tried to stifle or avoid it. Had Susan felt freer from the gender inequities and constraints of our society, she might have appreciated Joe for his sweetness and commitment to his family and used the marriage as a security base from which to evolve her own life and develop her confidence and skills.

Courtship is probably the least likely time of all phases of the life cycle for couples to seek therapy. This is not because coupling is easy, but rather because of the tendency to idealize each other and avoid looking at the enormous and long-range difficulties of establishing an intimate relationship. While the first years of marriage are the time of greatest overall marital satisfaction for many, they are also a time of likely divorce. The degree of mutual disappointment will usually match the degree of idealization of the relationship during courtship, as in the case of Susan and Joe. The pull during courtship may be to ignore potential difficulties, which are then avoided until further down the road. On the one hand, as Bowen observed, most spouses have their closest and most open relationship during this period. It is common for living-together relationships to be harmonious and for symptoms of fusion not to develop until after marriage. It is as if the fusion does not become problematic as long as there is still an option to terminate the relationship easily (Bowen, 1978, p. 377). While the demands of marriage frequently tighten a relationship, fusion may start during courtship if couples begin a pattern of pseudomutuality, saying they like everything about each other, want to share all their free time together, and keep their negative reactions hidden.

On the other hand, it is not uncommon for two people who have been living happily together to find that things change when they do get married, because they and society have now added to the situation the burdensome definitions of "husband" and "wife." These concepts often bring with them a heavy responsibility *for* rather than *to* each other, which living together did not engender and the feeling of no exit imposed by most religions. There may also be the burden of having passed definitively beyond youth into "serious" adulthood. Couples may also have the misperception that marriage will automatically fulfill them regardless of other aspects of their lives. Family attitudes and social myths about marriage filter down from generation to generation, making such transitions smoother or more difficult.

Couples can become bound in a web of evasiveness and ambiguity, neither daring to be honest with the other for fear of hurting the other's feelings, if their families of origin had tenuous or negative relationships. Communication may become more and more covert, the more they define their own worth by the relationship. The concept of "marriage" may have taken on a meaning far beyond the fact of two people sharing their lives with each other. Very often couples fall into stereotypical roles where she can think of nothing but marriage, which is the one thing he cannot think about. These patterns reflect the gendered opposite sides of the same lack of differentiation from their families of origin. Men who are not comfortable with their level of differentiation typically fear commitment, whereas women typically fear being alone. More recently women want the freedom to develop their own lives and relationships while men may want them to stay at their side.

Gay and Lesbian Couples

The patterns described here for heterosexual couples may be both simpler and more difficult for gay and lesbian couples (Green & Mitchell, 2008). It appears to be an advantage for gays and lesbians that they are less bound by the constricting rigidities of traditional gender roles, which may leave them freer to develop intimate relationships (Green et al., 1996). On the other hand, the stigmatizing of homosexual couples by our society means that their relationships are often not validated by their families or communities and they must cope with prejudice on a daily basis. The AIDS crisis produced a terrible trauma for the gay community, and its impact on a whole generation of gay men at the point of forming couple relationships cannot be underestimated. On the other hand, both partners being of the same gender may increase the couple's understanding of each other. Although some therapists have thought that being of the same gender might increase the likelihood of fusion, research indicates both gay and lesbian couples seem to have more cohesive relationships than heterosexual couples, lesbians tending to have the greatest level of closeness (Green et al., 1996). On the other hand, the lack of acceptance that many gay couples experience from their families and from society at large throughout the life cycle is a serious issue and one clinicians are often in a position to help families modify. The price of the secrecy forced on many gay and lesbian couples by society's disapproval is one we need to change. Related to this familial and societal negativity, clinicians can help couples and their families develop life cycle rituals to celebrate and affirm their relationships. Special effort is often required on the couple's part to receive adequate recognition of their relationship transitions.

Katherine Moore, (**Genogram 13.2**: Rita and Katherine) a 27-year-old journalist, and Rita Hidalgo, a 30-year-old graphic artist, had been living together for almost 2 years when they sought help for their relationship problems. Katherine was not sleeping, and Rita was concerned that she was depressed, anxious, and drinking too much. Katherine had been withdrawing from Rita, feeling she was becoming intrusive and bossy. Katherine had struggled since her midteens with her lesbianism. In college she dated men occasionally, hoping this would release her from her homosexual feelings and the disruption she felt a homosexual lifestyle would create for her and her family of origin. In fact, after college she kept a great distance from her parents, with whom she had always had a stormy relationship. She had been known in her family as the problem child since elementary school. Her conservative Anglo-Irish family operated on the basis of keeping up appearances. Her older sister was the "good girl" and never went beyond the limits accepted by the family. Katherine was the outspoken one, seen as the rebel. She argued politics with her father, and when she became involved in women's rights he became particularly incensed. Katherine felt that her mother covertly sided with her at times but never dared to disagree openly with her father.

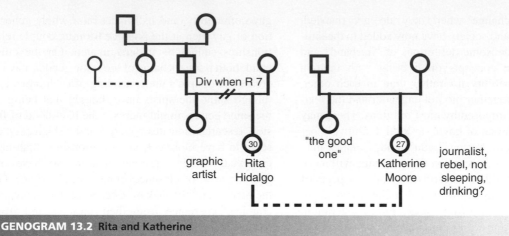

GENOGRAM 13.2 Rita and Katherine

After she became involved in women's rights, Katherine had several lesbian relationships, but Rita was her first live-in relationship. Four months earlier they had decided to commit to their relationship permanently, at which point Katherine's symptoms increased.

Rita, who came from a Puerto Rican family, had known clearly since high school that she was a lesbian and had socialized with a gay social group from the time she began college. She had not seen her father for years but felt close to her mother and sister. She had never directly spoken of her sexual orientation at home, but she had occasionally brought home female friends and sensed that her mother, who had never remarried after divorcing her father when Rita was seven, might be lesbian herself without knowing it. She suspected that a paternal aunt who had lived for years with another woman was lesbian also.

What precipitated Katherine's turmoil was her announcement to her parents during a visit, which she always made without Rita, that she was lesbian. She had decided to tell her parents about this because she was tired of keeping her life a secret, and the decision to have a commitment ceremony was part of this decision. Her mother initially seemed not unsupportive, but her father became extremely angry and told her this was just the last in a series of her "bad judgments" over many years. In several phone calls to her parents over the next weeks she was greeted with stony silence by both parents. Rita tried to be supportive, but she had disapproved of Katherine's telling her parents about her homosexuality, believing that "parents never understand and there's no point getting into all that." Katherine's symptoms had begun just after this. Rita became increasingly resentful of Katherine's preoccupa-

tion with her parents, feeling it was destroying their relationship. Katherine had spoken to a number of her lesbian friends who also advised her to forget about her parents, because her father sounded like "an insensitive redneck" and why bother.

As Katherine described her relationship with her parents, it became clear that she was seeking not only greater closeness with them but also their approval for her lesbian choice. Rita had trouble appreciating that she had to let Katherine work out her own relationship with her parents, whatever happened, but after a few discussions she agreed to back off and let Katherine figure things out for herself.

The initial therapy sessions focused on helping Katherine sort out her feelings and desires. She struggled to distinguish between her wish that her parents would approve of her lesbianism, her desire to be closer to them in general, and her wish for their approval of her behavior. How could she remain connected to her parents even if they disapproved of her lesbianism, and how could she let go of her need for their approval? She was coached to write a series of letters to each parent about her years of distancing and rebellion, her criticism of them (for which she now apologized), and her appreciation of how difficult her lesbian choice must be for them. She spoke of her earlier fears that they would cut her off completely and her relief that they had not.

Katherine's letters helped her clarify that her lesbianism was not a matter for her parents' approval or disapproval. She came to see that discussing her lifestyle with them came from a deep need to solidify her identity as an adult and end the secrecy of her life that had kept her distant from them. Luckily, through her motivation to understand herself and her respect for her parents' limitations, she was able to keep her couplehood with Rita from being overburdened by her hurt. After 6 months of therapy Rita decided it was time to speak directly with her own mother, realizing through Katherine's efforts, how much could be gained by ending the secrecy, even when, as with Katherine, the response had not been particularly positive. Rita's mother said she had known for years and was just waiting for Rita to feel comfortable telling her. When, a few months later, they had their marriage ceremony, Rita's mother, sister, and paternal aunt came (though the aunt left her partner at home), but only Katherine's sister attended from her family. While this was not what they both might have hoped, Katherine felt reassured that her "good girl" sister had come. Perhaps in the future, when they hoped to have a baby, Katherine's sister would be able to assist the parents in moving toward more acceptance, now that the "sisterhood" was solidified.

As can be seen from this example, the systemic problems around couple formation are generally similar, regardless of the content of the problems. However, certain patterns are quite predictable for gay and lesbian couples, as they are for religious, class, ethnic, or racial intermarriages. When the extended family is extremely negative toward the couple, for whatever reason, we encourage couples to take a long view, not trying to turn the acceptance of their relationship into a yes-or-no event, but working gradually over time to build bridges for family closeness. Other life cycle transitions, particularly births and deaths, often create shifts in family equilibrium that may allow the couple to further redefine their family status.

The Wedding

Whether weddings involve jumping the broom, as in African American tradition, standing under a huppa and crushing a wine glass, as in Jewish tradition, feasting for many days, as in Polish tradition, or other customs, they are among the most interesting family rituals to observe and among the best times for preventive intervention in family process. As family events, weddings are generally the largest ceremonies organized by families themselves. The organization of the wedding, who makes which arrangements, who gets invited, who comes, who pays, how much emotional energy goes into the preparations, who gets upset and over which issues, are all highly reflective of family process. In general, those who marry in unconventional ways, in civil ceremonies, or without family or friends present, have their reasons. Most often family disapproval is because of race, religion, class, money or ethnicity, premarital pregnancy, an impulsive decision to marry, a previous divorce, or the inability or unwillingness of the parents to meet the costs of the wedding. From a clinical point of view, the emotional charge of such situations, when it leads to downplaying the marriage as a family event, may well indicate that family members are unable to make the status changes required to adapt to this new life cycle stage and will have difficulty with future stages. As rituals, weddings are meant to facilitate family transition to a new constellation. As such, they can be extremely important in marking the change in status of family members and shifts in family organization.

Some families overfocus on the wedding, putting all their energy into the event, spending more than they can afford, and losing sight of the marriage as a process of joining two families. According to a recent survey, the average wedding costs about $30,000, not including the ring or honeymoon (Wong, 2005). Such spending reflects the distorted social mythology that makes it difficult for couples and families to attend to the true meaning of marriage. Today, with the changing mores, this focus on the wedding may be less intense, but there is still a large overlap of myth associated with marital bliss, which gets displaced onto wedding celebrations in a way that may be counterproductive. Indeed, researcher John Gottman made a strong case for marital success depending on the mundane "mindless moments" of everyday life that create the emotional climate that will make a marriage work in the long run (Gottman, 1994). In addition, marriage may become a toxic issue in a family because of their particular history.

One couple, Ted and Andrea (**Genogram 13.3**), had toxic issues on both sides of their extended family. Through premarital coaching, they were able to field stormy reactions in their families and probably prevent years of simmering

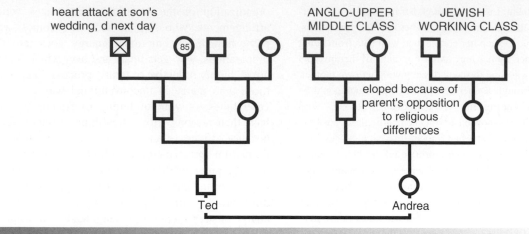

GENOGRAM 13.3 Ted and Andrea

conflicts that had hampered both extended families over several generations. When they sought help they said they were planning to marry in their apartment with only a few friends present unless they could bring their families around to accepting them as they were. Andrea's parents had eloped after her grandparents opposed their marriage because of religious differences and they had hardly seen their families since. Ted's paternal grandfather had had a heart attack at his son's (Ted's father's) wedding reception and died the next day. Thus, weddings had become dreaded events for both extended families.

Ted and Andrea began their work by contacting extended family members to invite them personally to their wedding. They used these conversations to mention in a casual way the pain of the wedding history for the family, for example, when Ted called his paternal grandmother, who was 85, and who his parents had assured him would never come to the wedding. He told her his parents were sure she couldn't make it, but that it would mean a great deal to him to have her there, especially since he feared his father might have a heart attack and he would need her support. The grandmother not only made her own arrangements to have a cousin fly with her, but also arranged to stay with her son, Ted's father, for the week after the wedding. At the reception both bride and groom made toasts in verse to their families, in which they ticked off the charged issues with humor and sensitivity and made a special point of spending time with family members.

Surprisingly, few couples ever seek premarital counseling, in spite of the obvious difficulties in ne-

gotiating this transition, and in spite of the fact that preventive intervention in relation to the extended families might be a great deal easier than dealing with issues later in the life cycle. The most that can be said is that it is extremely useful if one has access to any member of a family at the time of a wedding to encourage him or her to facilitate the resolution of family relationships through this nodal event. For example, it is often fruitful to convey to the couple that in-law struggles are predictable and need not be taken too personally. It is important for couples to recognize that the heightened parental tension probably relates to their sense of loss regarding the marriage. When families argue about wedding arrangements, the issues under dispute often cover up underlying systemic issues. Family members often view others as capable of "ruining" the event. A useful guideline is for each person to take his or her own responsibility for having a good time at the wedding. It is also useful for the couple to recognize that marriage is a family event and not just for the two of them. From this perspective, parents' feelings about the service need to be taken into consideration in whatever meaningful ways are possible. The more responsibility a couple can take for arranging a wedding that reflects their shifting position in their families and the joining of the two systems, the more auspicious for their future relationship.

Jim Marcus (**Genogram 13.4**: Jim and Joan) spent 6 months in "coaching" for his wedding, at which he wanted

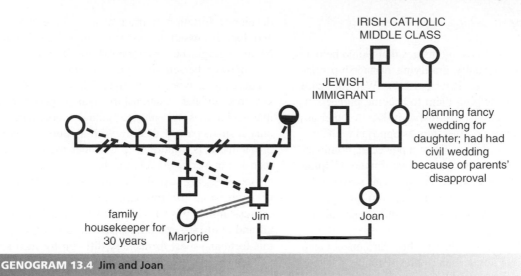

IRISH CATHOLIC
MIDDLE CLASS

JEWISH
IMMIGRANT

planning fancy
wedding for
daughter; had had
civil wedding
because of parents'
disapproval

family
housekeeper for
30 years

Marjorie

Jim

Joan

GENOGRAM 13.4 Jim and Joan

the participation of his actively alcoholic mother and the three other mothering figures who had played important roles in his life. His parents had divorced when he was 5. His father remarried for 6 years when Jim was 8 and again when he was 15. He had grown up in his father's custody, with a family housekeeper involved between his father's marriages. Jim had distanced from his alcoholic mother and had been alienated from both stepmothers for many years. Through coaching he was able to reverse the process of cut off for the wedding. He called his stepmothers and his childhood housekeeper to invite them especially to his wedding, discussing with each her importance in his life and how much it would mean to him to have her present at his wedding celebration. He wrote to his own mother and similarly reviewed the moments in their lives that were most meaningful to him. He arranged with his older brother to be on duty on the day of the wedding and escort the mother out if that became necessary.

The next problem was the parents of his fiancée, Joan, who were planning an elaborate celebration and wanted everything to go according to the book. This would have made Jim's less affluent family very uncomfortable. Initially Joan became quite reactive to her mother's fancy plans and her way of making decisions without discussion. At the suggestion of the therapist, she arranged to spend a day with her mother, during which time she could discuss her feelings about her upcoming marriage and approach her mother as a resource on how to handle things. She discovered for the first time that her mother had been married in a small civil wedding, because her Catholic parents dis-

approved of her marriage to a Jewish immigrant with no college education. Joan learned how her mother had yearned for a "proper wedding." She realized that her mother's wishes to do everything in a fancy way had grown out of her own unrealized dreams and were an attempt to give Joan something she had missed. With this realization, Joan could share her own wish for a simple celebration to make Jim feel comfortable, especially because of all the problems in his family, which she had never mentioned to her mother before. She asked her mother for advice on how to handle the situation. She told her how uncomfortable she was about the divorces in Jim's family and her fears that her own relatives would disapprove of him, especially if all his mothering figures attended the wedding. Suddenly her mother's attitude changed from dictating how things had to be done to a helpful and much more casual attitude. A week later, Joan's mother told Jim that if there was any way she could facilitate things with his mother, stepmothers, or other guests, she would be glad to do it.

It frequently happens that friendship systems and extended family relationships change after the wedding. Many couples have difficulty maintaining individual friendships and move, at least in the first years, toward having only "couple friends." We encourage spouses to keep their individual friendship networks as well, since "couple friends" typically reinforce fusion and may not allow the spouses their individual interests and preferences.

Sexuality

Our society has almost no images that would help us in developing sexually gratifying partnership relationships (Carter & Peters, 1996). Working with couples means helping them to become pioneers in their sexual relationships, just as it does in other aspects of forming a partnership, as opposed to the traditional couple relationship of a powerful, dominant male and a submissive, responsive female. Helping couples establish flexible and intimate sexual relationships involves freeing them from the gender stereotypes that are part of their familial and cultural heritage (Schnarch, 2010).

From earliest childhood boys are encouraged to feel positive about their bodies sexually, whereas girls are rarely encouraged even to be familiar with their genitalia, let alone to enjoy their sexuality. Boys typically begin to masturbate from earliest childhood, girls not till mid-adolescence, if then. Women generally have to bear the burden of the repercussions of sexuality in terms of contraception, and in many groups they are prohibited from using contraception or refusing sex, subjecting them to all the consequences of sexuality, from pregnancy to sexually transmitted diseases, but not to being proud of being sexual or even knowing how their bodies work. What is surprising is not that sex so often becomes a problem for a couple, but that it works out as often as it does.

The current generation has much more sexual experience and knowledge than previous generations. While the age at marriage has been increasing, the age at sexual maturation and first intercourse have decreased. Males and especially females are having sex with more partners at younger ages than ever before. The vast majority of young adults (approximately 90 percent) are sexually experienced, and most have sex regularly. At the same time, anxieties about AIDS, herpes, and other sexual transmitted diseases are continuous issues for young couples today.

In the past, if a husband lost interest in sex, we assumed he was having an affair. Now we ask about recent changes in the wife's income and status, since sexuality seems so clearly linked with power issues in marriage for both partners. Even where a woman develops a flirtation or affair, as in the case of Susan and Joe, discussed earlier, we explore whether her behavior might be an attempt (however misguided) to empower herself through a sexual relationship, because as a woman she has felt overall disempowered in the relationship. Our experience is that techniques to enhance sexual enjoyment are only a small part of dealing with a couple's sexual problems. It is important to consider the power dimension in a couple's relationship when the partners are experiencing sexual difficulty. Sex is at the heart of expressions of intimacy, and the inability to express intimacy is very likely to be related to familial and cultural factors that have made intimacy in this form and most forms very difficult for men and women in our society. In addition to exploring sexuality in the extended family in order to understand the specific messages that partners have been given about their bodies, their own sexuality, and their expectations about what is "sexy" with a partner, therapists need to pay much more attention to the larger cultural dimensions within which our sexual relationships evolve (Schnarch, 2010). We must pay attention to the implicit power dimensions influencing this aspect and all other aspects of a couple's relationship. Given the very high levels of violence against wives in marriage and the trouble our nation is still having acknowledging the concept of marital rape, we must be very careful not to limit our work with a couple to the interior of their intimate relationship or to ignore the power dimensions of couple relationships (see Chapter 25 on Violence and the Life Cycle).

Patterns With Extended Family

Women tend to move closer to their families of origin after marriage, while men may become more distant, shifting their primary tie to the new nuclear family. In any case, spouses' ways of dealing with their families may differ. Many find marriage the only way to separate from their families of origin, but their underlying enmeshment in the family continues even after marriage. Patterns of guilt, intrusiveness, and unclear boundaries are typical of such systems. Other couples may cut off their families emotionally even before marriage, some going to the extreme of not inviting them to the wedding. Parents are seen as withholding and rejecting and the couple decides to do without them. Others push ongoing conflicts or tension under the rug. In such families there is usually involvement of the extended family in the marriage plans, but often with fights, hurt feelings, and "scenes" around the wedding. This pattern of conflicts indicates that the family is at least struggling with separating and is not forcing it underground as in enmeshed or cut-off families. The ideal situation is where the partners have become independent of their families before marriage and at the same time maintain close, caring ties. In such instances, the wedding can serve for all the family as a sharing celebration of the new couple's shift in status.

Where couples cut off family relationships, their restrictive couple patterns may work until later developmental stages destabilize them. Where conflicts are submerged, marriage may be an excellent opportunity to reopen closed relationships, for example, inviting to the wedding relatives with whom parents are out of touch. It is a good chance to detoxify emotional issues, reviewing marital and family ties over several generations as part of redefining the system. Otherwise underlying tensions may surface in emotional scenes or arguments around wedding plans, only to go underground again as family members try to act happy and friendly so as not to "create unpleasantness." The attempt to smooth things over in itself may increase the likelihood of future relationship eruptions. The fact is that all change disrupts the system and needs to be dealt with if the developmental processes are to proceed. It may be easier for the family to move on if they are in touch with their sense of loss at the time of the wedding and if they are a bit confused and uneasy about how to manage the new relationships. Whatever the patterns of difficulty with extended family—conflict, enmeshment, distance, or cut off— the lack of resolution of these relationships is the major problem in negotiating this phase of the family life cycle. The more the triangles in the extended family are dealt with by an emotional cut off, the greater the likelihood that the spouse will come to represent more than who he or she is. If the husband's relationship with his wife is his only meaningful relationship, he is likely be so sensitive to her

every reaction, and especially to any hint of rejection, that he may overreact to signs of differentness by pulling her to agree with him or blaming her for not accepting him, jamming the circuits in time. The intensity may eventually make the relationship untenable. Our culture's social mobility and overfocus on the nuclear family to the neglect of all other relationships contributes to this tendency to place more emotional demand on a marriage than it can bear. Indeed the indications are that marriage actually tends to isolate partners from other people in ways that pose potential long-term problems: They have fewer ties to relatives, fewer intimate talks with others, are less likely to care for aging parents, and are less likely to socialize with friends (Gerstel & Sarkisian, 2006). Once a spouse becomes overly involved in the other's response, both become bound up in a web of fusion and unable to function for themselves.

Some couples transfer parental struggles to the spouse directly. Others choose a spouse who handles the family for them. A man may choose a wife totally unacceptable to his parents and then let her fight his battles with his parents, while he becomes the "innocent bystander." The price everyone pays in such situations is the failure to achieve any real connection, since issues can never be resolved when other members are brought in to handle one's relationships. Similar problems arise when a person has served a central function in his or her parents' lives or in the preservation of the parents' marital balance and does not feel entitled to marry.

In-Laws

Among the problematic triangles for the couple, the one involving husband, wife, and mother-in-law is probably the most renowned. In laws are easy scapegoats for family tensions. It is always easier to hate your daughter-in-law for keeping your son from showing his love than to admit that your son doesn't respond to you the way you wish he would. It may be easier for a daughter-in-law to hate her mother-in-law for "intrusiveness" than to confront her husband directly for not committing himself fully to the marriage and defining a boundary in relation to outsiders. In-law relationships are a natural arena for displacing tensions in the couple or in the family of origin of each spouse. The converse of this is the spouse who has cut off his or her own family and seeks to adopt the spouse's family, forming a warm, enmeshed fusion with the in-laws, based on defining his or her own family as cold, rejecting, uninteresting, and so on.

Our society generally focuses blame on the mother-in-law rather than on the father-in-law, who is usually seen as playing a more benign role. Just as mothers get blamed for what goes wrong in families because they are given primary responsibility for family relationships, so do mothers-in-law get primary blame by extension. Many factors contribute to this process. Just as wives are given responsibility for handling a husband's emotional problems, so are they often put in the position of expressing issues for all other family members and then being blamed when things go wrong.

Sibling Issues in Couple Formation

Siblings may also displace their problems in dealing with each other onto the new spouse. Predictable triangles are especially likely between a husband and his wife's brothers or between the wife and her husband's sisters. Sisters may see their brother's wife as having "no taste," infusing the brother with superficial values, and so forth. What is missed by the system in such instances is that the brother probably chose his wife as a protection from his sisters, perhaps to set the limits he never dared set alone or to allow him to distance without the guilt of doing so directly. Often the brother will get his wife to take over dealing with his family altogether, which usually succeeds only in escalating the tension.

Good clues about a couple can be found in the marital relationships of each partner's parents, the primary models for what marriage is about. The other basic model for spouses is their relationship with their siblings, their earliest and closest peers. Couples who marry mates from complementary sibling positions tend to enjoy the greatest marital stability (Toman, 1976). In other words, the older brother of a younger sister will tend to get along best with a younger sister of an older brother. They will

tend to have fewer power conflicts, since he will be comfortable as the leader and she as the follower. In addition, they will tend to be comfortable with the opposite sex, since they have grown up with opposite-sexed siblings as well. Those who marry spouses not from complementary sibling positions may have more marital adjustments to make in this regard. An extreme case would be the oldest of many brothers who marries the oldest of many sisters. Both would expect to be the leader and would probably have difficulty understanding why the other does not acknowledge their leadership, since they are used to having this at home. In addition, they will be less comfortable with the opposite sex, having grown up in strongly single-sexed environments.

Cultural Differences

Another arena that becomes problematic in a marriage under stress is the cultural or family style difference. This may be more of a problem in the United States where people from so many diverse cultural backgrounds marry and find themselves in conflict because each starts out with such different basic assumptions (McGoldrick & Preto, 1984; Crohn, 1995; McGoldrick, Giordano, & Garcia Preto, 2005).

Jack and Maria (**Genogram 13.5**: Jack and Maria) applied for therapy after a year of marriage because Maria said she was convinced Jack did not love her and that he had changed after they got married. The wife was the fifth of seven children from a Brooklyn family of Italian extraction. She had met her husband in college and was extremely attracted to his quiet strength and strong life ambitions. He was from a midwestern Protestant family of British, German, and Dutch heritage where, as an only child, he was strongly encouraged by his parents to work hard and have a morally upright life. He had found her vivacious and charming and had also been attracted to her family, because of their open affection and because, in contrast to his own "uptight" parents, they always seemed to have a good time.

Under stress the couple found that the very qualities that had attracted them to each other became the problem. Jack became for Maria "an unfeeling stone." She complained: "He doesn't care about my feelings at all and ig-

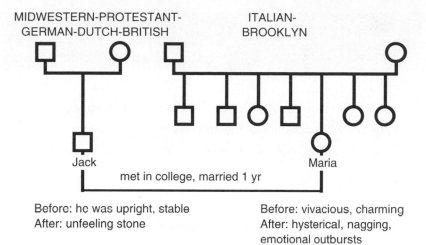

MIDWESTERN-PROTESTANT-
GERMAN-DUTCH-BRITISH

ITALIAN-
BROOKLYN

Jack

Maria

met in college, married 1 yr

Before: he was upright, stable
After: unfeeling stone

Before: vivacious, charming
After: hysterical, nagging,
emotional outbursts

GENOGRAM 13.5 Jack and Maria

nores me completely." For Jack, Maria's vivaciousness now became "hysteria" and he found her "nagging, emotional outbursts, and screaming" unbearable.

As we discussed in therapy their very different family styles of coping with stress and their opposing assumptions became obvious. In Jack's family the rule was that you should keep your problems to yourself and think them out: With enough effort and thought, most problems could be worked out. Maria's family dealt with stress by getting together and ventilating. The family related intensely at all times, but especially when they were upset. These styles had been turned inward in the marriage and were tightening things even more. The more Maria felt isolated and needed contact, the louder she sought attention and the more Jack withdrew to get some space and to maintain his balance. The more he withdrew, the more frustrated and alone Maria felt. Both had turned their differences, initially labeled as the source of attraction, into the problem and had begun to see the other's behavior as a sure sign of not caring. Neither had been able to see that their family styles were just different. They were compounding the difficulty by blaming each other for the other's response.

Once the family patterns could be clarified in the context of the extended family and ethnic backgrounds, Maria and Jack were able to temper their responses and to see their differences as neutral, rather than as signs of psychopathology or rejection.

Adjustment to marriage is being profoundly affected by the changing role of women, the increase in unmarried couples living together, the changing definitions of marriage, the diversity of marriage partners, the increasing physical distance from families of origin, the frequency of changing partners, and the diminishing role of community in supporting families. Couples are increasingly isolated and expected to manage their lives and families without the community supports that in the past were a primary resource in raising children and meeting family needs. Couples are less bound by family traditions and are freer than ever before to develop male-female relationships unlike those people have experienced in their families of origin. Couples are required to think out for themselves many things that in the past would have been taken for granted. This applies also to the enormous gap that often exists between parents and children in education and social status. Although these differences can cause strain, we also live at a time when the possibilities of couples to have creative and equitable partnerships are great. Cultural differences can add flexibility to the system and stretch the family to become adaptive over the life cycle in new ways. The marriage cycle of couples choosing to marry in the twenty-first century will surely require this creative adaptation, and we have probably only begun to imagine how couple relationships in the future may evolve.

Table 13.1 Issues that Make Marital Adjustment More Difficult

- Contextual Factors
  - Couple do not have jobs or resources to support themselves adequately.
  - The wedding occurs without family or friends present.
  - Either spouse started but did not complete either high school or college.

- Partners differ in
  - Religious, Racial, Ethnic, or Class Background.
  - Financial Power, Socioeconomic Status, Education, Career Options or Skills.

- Issues with Family of Origin
  - Either partner has a different level of success or social location from his or her own parents, especially a lower success and social location.
  - The couple resides either extremely close to or at a great distance from either family of origin.
  - The couple is dependent on the family of origin financially.
  - The couple are from incompatible sibling constellations.
  - Either spouse has a poor relationship with siblings or parents, or the parents had poor or unstable relationships themselves.
  - Either spouse considers his or her childhood or adolescence to have been an unhappy time.

- The husband believes that men's rights, needs, or privilege should predominate in marriage and that women should serve the needs of others over their own needs. The danger increases if he tries to
  - Dominate the wife
  - Isolate her from work, friends, or family
  - Control her financially or
  - Intimidate her physically

- Timing of the Relationship
  - The couple meets or marries shortly after a significant loss.
  - The couple marries early (before age 20) or late (after age 40).
  - The couple marries after an acquaintanceship of less than 6 months or more than 5 years of engagement.
  - The wife becomes pregnant before or within the first year of marriage.

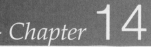

Chapter 14

Becoming Parents: The Family With Young Children

Betty Carter, Monica McGoldrick, & Barbara Petkov

Making the decision to have a child—it's momentous. It is to decide forever to have your heart walking around outside your body.

—ANONYMOUS

No other society has ever asked the nuclear family to try to raise children while living all by itself in a box the way we do, with no relatives around, no childcare supports and almost no community resources available.

—PARAPHRASE OF MARGARET MEAD,
COURTESY OF THE AMERICAN ANTHROPOLOGICAL ASSOCIATION.

Introduction

Half a century ago, the conventional wisdom was that having a child was the surest way to build a happy marriage. The decision to have a child is momentous. Becoming a parent is one of the most definitive stages of life, a crossing of the Rubicon. The transition to parenthood is characterized by changes of dramatic proportion. Once there is a child, life will never be the same again. It is certainly true that most parents fall passionately in love with their new babies and consider them fascinating, delightful, and unique additions to the family. However, the roller coaster of the early months and years of parenthood still comes as a shock to almost all new parents: sleep deprivation, shredded schedules, endless chores, worry about the baby's development or one's own competence, and the need for ceaseless

vigilance. This sudden threat of chaos puts enormous stress on new parents and on their relationship, since no amount of doing ever seems enough to get the job done before it needs to be done again. At this stage, the tremendous rewards of parenthood, expressed in all cultures across the ages, can seem largely theoretical.

The timing and patterns of this stage have changed dramatically within the past generation, largely because of the availability of birth control and shifts in gender relationships toward more equitable relationships between men and women. Families are having fewer children, and the timing of parenthood has changed dramatically. Such changes have for the first time in history made having a child a more or less conscious choice, which will probably have profound importance as time goes along. As people become parents, they assume new roles, redefine old ones, and face new challenges and questions that they never even imagined. But still, there is much more mythology and romantic fantasy attached to this transition than there are realistic expectations. Most of the mythology paints a glowing picture, especially of mother and child, a central icon in cultures and religions from time immemorial. This basic assumption that motherhood and, by extension, parenthood, is an automatic leap ahead in status, joy, and fulfillment seems not to have been much questioned in the past, though the step is now increasingly being delayed by educational and career goals and by the difficulty of supporting a family in our times.

It is hard for young couples to make a realistic decision about whether or when to have children because of the tremendous role played by the emotions and by social pressures. A person who remembers a happy childhood and good parents may want to repeat that experience, while someone escaping a terrible childhood often seems impelled to try to do it differently. Women especially seldom escape the culture's view that a childless woman is not a "real" woman. For both sexes, parenthood seems to provide the final ticket for acceptance into adulthood: the woman mothering, and the man "providing."

Expectations Versus Reality

The transition to parenthood and the care of young children has become even more difficult than it used to be, a situation that is often not appreciated by childless adults or by older parents who raised their children in a less complicated (though not necessarily better) time. The transition from couplehood to parenthood is the most romanticized of life transitions because it creates a plethora of false expectations. It appears that those who enter parenthood with fewer romantic expectations are more likely to emerge from the transition happier about their marriages and their spouses than those who enter parenthood wearing rose-colored glasses (Belsky & Kelly, 1994). Society relates only to the pleasure of life with a baby, and there has been relentless social criticism of departures from the view of the happy traditional family with the happy couple creating happy children, who grow up in a happy nuclear family of good provider father and homemaker mother, a characterization of less than 3 percent of

families in the United States, and yet the image for which the entire educational and work structures of our society are organized to accommodate. There is still lack of accommodation and wide societal disapproval for nontraditional couples, women who choose or need to go to work, and spouses with children who believe that divorce is their best or only option. The impact of these social and economic forces on couples is often outside of the couple's awareness. Over the past 2 decades, many researchers have concluded that three's a crowd when it comes to marital satisfaction. Marital quality drops, often quite steeply, after the transition to parenthood, especially when parents backslide into more traditional gender roles. Once a child arrives, lack of paid parental leave often leads the wife to quit her job and the husband to work more. This produces discontent on both sides. The wife may resent her husband's lack of involvement in child care and housework. The husband may resent his wife's ingratitude for the long hours he works to support the family (Coontz, 2005). If parents could learn that this stress is typical during family formation, the stress could be normalized and made more manageable, allowing parents to pull together as a couple to make their lives fit their own and their baby's needs (Cowan, Cowan, Heming, and Miller, 1991).

There is a very strong tendency for parents of young children to relegate their own needs as individuals and as couples to the "back burner" while they cope with the extraordinary demands of a helpless and demanding infant, one or two jobs outside the family, and all of the increased tasks to maintain an increasingly complex household. Nevertheless, parents today spend much more time with their children than they did 40 years ago. Married mothers in 2000 spent 20 percent more time with their children than in 1985. Married fathers spent more than twice as much time as they used to (Coontz, 2005).

The New Demographics of Families in the Parenting Phase

Each family brings to the transition to parenthood its own cultural history and values about intergenerational relationships, gender roles, and values for child and parent, grandparent, and aunt and uncle behavior. Failure to look at families inclusively will result in the perpetuation of a devalued status for those families who do not match the current stereotype of what the American family looks like, a family that as we know does not really exist.

Family demographics and patterns of child-rearing are changing rapidly. Our society is becoming more diverse. The parenting cycle now extends from early teen years to as late as age 50 for women and 60 for men, and couple and parenting arrangements are diverse as well. Changing trends in American families for child-rearing include the following:

At least one half of all children in the next generation will live in female-headed households (Webb, 2005).

Economic conditions affecting employment, the rising costs of child care, health care, and education will be an ever-increasing factor in how well families can negotiate the stage of parenting children. These stressors create much more severe hardships for families at the margin: those who are poor, those who are of color, immigrant families, and those whose children or other family members have special needs or experience social stigma.

Many immigrant families will include a semi-extended family form made up of fictive kin with some ties to the family members' original homelands.

Many will more than likely live in households that have two primary languages for at least two generations.

An increasing proportion of families will involve sexually variant relatives and/or parents.

An increasing proportion of families raising children will consist primarily of people of color and multiracial families.

The Emotional System

The new baby is born or adopted into an extended family system that must now make emotional and relationship shifts to make a place for the new member. Many families celebrate the event with a religious ritual: a christening, bris, or naming ceremony, usually followed by a party for family and friends. As with other family transition rituals issues about how and where the event is celebrated and who gets invited reflect the ongoing extended-family process. Whether there is a ritual or a party or not, the new member of the system is greeted with many differing emotional reactions, depending on its sex, its health, how it is named, how long it was awaited, what kind of relationship its parents have with various family members, whether grandparents approved of the marriage, and whether they're all doing their part to shift to adult-to-adult relationships in the parent–grandparent generations.

A first grandchild also creates new grandparents, who often jump into their new role without much planning or discussion with their children, not realizing that there are as many ways to grandparent as to parent. No way is "right," but some ways fit their lives and their children's lives better than others, and it is best when the issue is discussed early on. Complaints about intrusive or indifferent grandparents, or demanding or neglectful adult children, are signs of the need for such discussion.

Whether parents maintain close or distant extended family relationships, they can expect to inherit major unresolved extended family issues and patterns. Multigenerational patterns, triangles, ghosts, and taboo issues are best examined by the parents and dealt with at this time, lest they engulf the new family in emotional problems that they may think they can ignore or evade. On the positive side, this is a good stage of the family life cycle to engage parents in doing family of origin work, even if they have previously resisted or ignored opportunities for emotional differentiation. Parents will do many things for their children's sake that they will not do for themselves, and this fact provides therapeutic leverage for the coaching process. It is also a good time for grandparents to give up old grievances and make new efforts to relate positively to their adult children and the children's spouses. Grandparents may need reminding that in a society with such a high divorce rate, it is wise to be good friends with your daughter-in-law.

Child Care and the Work–Family Dilemma

Child care is the number one practical concern and problem at this phase of the life cycle, and the United States is the only industrialized nation in the world that leaves it to individual families to arrange and pay for child care themselves. The fact is that only 24 percent of children have stay-at-home mothers. All other families must arrange child care. The mothers who do stay home tend to be younger, are more likely to be foreign born and specifically Latinas (Edwards, U.S. Census Bureau, 2009).

Poor families spend almost three times as much of their income on child care as middle class families. Among the poor, almost half the children under 5 whose mothers work are cared for primarily by relatives, which is more common also among Black and Latino families. Children of single parents are more likely to be cared for by grandparents than are children of married couples. Relatives provide a great deal of child care for preschoolers in poor families because of the expense of organized facilities. Child care is more expensive in metropolitan areas and especially in the Northeast.

Social class is a primary determinant of children's well-being. Economic distress contributes to family instability, inadequate health care, a high degree of mobility, and elevated levels of stress and depression (Mintz, 2010). Working-class and poor parents are more likely to believe that child development occurs naturally and spontaneously and that there is no need to stimulate it with organized leisure activities, music lessons, or supervised homework. Their children spend more time in free, unstructured play and socializing with and being supervised by extended family. On the other hand, middle-class parents try to protect their children from harm by baby-proofing everything. They try to give their children a competitive advantage through enrichment activities with well-qualified adults to pass their social status on to their children. Poor and working-class parents are more likely to use directives rather than reasoning with their children and the children generally negotiate institutional life including day-to-day school experiences on their own, the parents being often fearful and distrustful of schools and health-care facilities (Lareau, 2010).

Clinically, family therapists should assume that most working mothers feel guilty or anxious about the welfare of their babies and toddlers, whether they are financially required to work or not. Fueling the guilt and anxiety are the steady stream of media reports decrying the poor quality of American child care. Articles frequently criticize care by relatives as less good than care by high-quality child care centers. This has serious implications for the poor and working-class families who rely on child care by relatives. It is a challenge for everyone to do their best and get the support they need.

As a nation we are not doing an adequate job of providing quality care and early education for our children. The U.S. government devotes almost 10 times as much of its budget to defense as to education (Chantrill, 2009). This, of course, has more serious implications for poor and working-class families who most often rely on child care by relatives and have little or no other choice. A further source of anxiety is that a baby's intellectual development depends on being spoken to regularly by an attentive, engaged human being during the first year of life. Even the affluent, paying for expensive live-in nanny care in their own homes, are not free from worry about what actually transpires in their absence. Their anxiety peaks during the occasional, but highly publicized, cases of nanny abuse of children.

Lost in all of this highly charged debate is the fact that most studies find that children who attend high-quality daycare centers are found to have better intellectual and social skills than children who have not been to daycare. The obvious solution to the problem is public funding that will guarantee that *all* American child care centers are high quality. The most important move that clinicians can make regarding this issue is to ensure that it is discussed as a *parental* problem, not a *mothering* problem.

The primary unresolved problems of the work–family dilemma for the parenting phase of the life cycle remain:

1. The unequal participation of men in the work at home,
2. The inflexibility of the workplace, and
3. The growing number of work hours in the lives of both men and women.

Because the two-paycheck family is now the U.S. norm, some parental adjustment in work schedule is necessary when children are born. Seventy percent of U.S. women of working age are currently in the full-time workforce, including more than half of mothers with children under the age of 6. However, it is still assumed in the workplace and by the couple themselves that the dilemma of juggling work and family is primarily the responsibility of the mother. Depending largely on their economic situation and the mother's career aspirations, she may quit work altogether, cut back to part time, or make whatever child care arrangements she can to keep working full time. If these alternatives are not what she expected to face or don't work out satisfactorily, she may become increasingly resentful and exhausted, probably blaming her husband and envying his single-track pursuit of work.

Current job insecurity at all economic levels only adds to the pressure men already feel not to "rock the boat" at work by asking for any special consideration because of family matters. This rigidity of the work system most severely affects working mothers, who are passed over for promotion or raises on the so-called "mommy track." Young women who remain childless now earn 98 percent of what men of the same age earn, whereas the average pay for all women, which includes working mothers, is only 77 percent of men's pay (U.S. Gov, Inst. For Women's Policy Research, 2008).

Following the landmark study by sociologist Arlie Hochschild (1997, 2003), which instantly gave new meaning to the phrase "second shift," family therapists became more alert to the unfair share of housework done by women even when both parents worked outside the home. It is important to realize that even with the unequal division of labor for parents in the second shift, two-income couples tend to be healthier and happier in every way, in spite of long work hours (Barrett & Rivers, 1996).

Unfortunately, home at this life cycle phase at times becomes such a time-deprived hassle for working parents that women as well as men sometimes seek escape from those pressures by willingly spending more time at the office or the factory, where they have found friends, helping networks, and community (Hochschild, 1997). Women and members of

minorities who succeed at work also value the respect and heightened self-esteem that come with their paychecks. Major involvement at work may also contribute to what is being called the "third shift," where parents try, through treats, toys, and "quality time," to do damage control on the emotional consequences for children of compressed family life, although as mentioned, families generally are spending more time together during this phase than they did in the past (Coontz, 2009).

Social scientists know in remarkable detail what goes on in the average heterosexual American home. They have calculated with great precision how little has changed in the roles of men and women. Any way you measure it, they say, women do about twice as much around the house as men. (Belkin, 2008). The average wife/mother does 31 hours of housework a week while the average husband/father does 14, a ratio of slightly more than two to one.

There is one segment of American parenting in which equality is the norm or, at least, the mutually agreed-upon goal. Belkin reports that same-sex couples cannot default to gender when deciding who does what at home, while straight parents get into the blame game about who is shirking responsibility. Lesbian couples tend to have more equal division of housework (Gartrell, 2008). Both partners seem to make equal sacrifices in exchange for this equality. "It is commonly seen that both women in the couple typically work shorter hours or have declined career opportunities so they can be more available at home. However, stress and conflict surfaces in 64 percent of lesbian couples who are new parents, around issues of feeling jealousy and competitiveness concerning bonding and child-rearing (Gartrell, 2008). A birth mother who breast feeds may feel possessive toward her child, leaving the co mother feeling left out and excluded.

Where the housework ratio is two to one, the wife-to-husband ratio for child care in the United States is close to five to one. As with housework, that ratio does not change as much as you would expect when you account for who brings home a paycheck. Clinically, it is very important that family therapists label the work–family problem as a social problem, to be dealt with by the couple, not a "woman's problem" for her to struggle with alone.

Gender Issues in Parenting: The Power Imbalance

It is not surprising that at this phase of the family life cycle there is often, even for couples with more equal sharing, a shifting back to more traditional gender roles of the breadwinner dad and the domestic mother. Suddenly or insidiously, the husband is earning and managing all or most of the money. He may feel entitled to cast the deciding vote or veto on expenditures, and his wife may not feel entitled to contest his position or to demand equal access to their money and equal voice in decisions. She may become increasingly resentful while he might feel unappreciated. In the absence of an understanding of the failure of current social policy and lack of workplace support for their equal partnership, they may blame each other, and their conflict and dissatisfaction with each other rises. Many couples in this predicament contemplate divorce and/or go to couples therapy.

An exception to the tendency of couples to shift back to traditional roles after children are born is when the wife earns more money than her husband (now one third of couples). However, wives who earn more than their husbands tend not to use that as power over the husband, but rather minimize or deny the importance of their earnings and often continue to do or manage most of the housework. They do, however, use their earnings as self-empowerment, being more willing than lower-earning wives to negotiate assertively with their husbands in decisionmaking.

In light of the severity of the role conflict and socioeconomic squeeze on families with young children, it is not surprising that this is the phase of the family life cycle with the highest divorce rate and that poorer couples have twice the divorce rate of financially comfortable ones (Ford & Van Dyk, 2009). In addition to money, the issues of time, isolation, sexual dissatisfaction, and problems with distribution of chores arise out of the power shift that pushes the couple back toward traditional roles (Ault-Riche, 1994; Carter & Peters, 1997). These are often the complaints that resound endlessly in therapy sessions, tempting the therapist to work on practical solutions to specific issues instead of on the power imbalance itself, which, when righted, will enable the couple to negotiate fair resolutions of their own.

The sexual problems that appear at this stage, often arguments over frequency, may be a result of the new mother's exhaustion, especially if she is nursing, but also may become an arena in which to conduct their power struggle. The first is transient and will pass; the second is an ominous threat to the couple's relationship and, if not dealt with at this stage, will do much to corrode their subsequent life together.

Time now becomes a rare commodity, and as the new father buckles down to work and the need for more money, and as the new mother becomes absorbed in the care of her infant, in addition to continuing to work outside the home, their time alone may virtually disappear. Recreational activities for new parents tend to drop dramatically. Shared couple time is an important intervention to keep couples in balance during this task-overloaded phase of the life cycle.

In the United States, as in most of the world, the idea of shared parenting is not new. Until relatively recently, whichever female relatives were around the farm, ranch, or urban development did much of the child care, while mothers worked at their many chores—farming, laundry, sewing cooking, etc.—all of which were much more time consuming than they are today. Nobody worried about the mother–child bond. What is new is the idea that fathers should be active, hands-on parents fully participating with their wives in the task that had fallen to mothers alone when the isolated nuclear family replaced the extended family household in the second half of last century.

In the last generation men have gotten more involved in household work and child care than in any previous American generation. Although their participation doesn't approach 50 percent, many men feel that it does because they are consciously so much more involved than their fathers were. In all surveys on the subject, American men of all ages say that family is the most important facet of their lives and fatherhood their most satisfying accomplishment.

However, while the traditional definitions of male success (career achievement, money, and power) are being challenged, they still hold sway in most men's lives. And the new rules for "man the provider" are still very slippery. Is his wife fully committed to being a co-provider for life, or will she suddenly decide that she has to stay home with the children? Will he be penalized at work if he curtails his overtime or travel or takes family leave? In addition, the male socialization process that few men escape has probably left men cut off from their deepest feelings and somewhat fearful of emotional intimacy. So most men are still just "helping" at home, even though their wives work outside the home too, many of them at full-time jobs.

Although mothers often ask their husbands for more help, they are usually reluctant to really share the role and decisions of parenting equally. Both men and women are still socialized to believe that mothers have special inborn or intuitive skills related to child care and that all young children need a mother as primary parent. In spite of all of the actual changes in our lives and in our beliefs, the two sacred cows—a "real" man's career and a "real" woman's mothering—maintain a stubborn hold on our emotions. The consequences of this paradigm, as family therapist Ron Taffel with Israeloff (1994) has said, are that the mother feels central but overburdened and the father feels one-down and somewhat defensive. The children turn to mother as the "real" parent-expert and are likely eventually to pass along this paradigm to the next generation. Worst of all, Taffel concluded, mothers and fathers are in danger of leading parallel rather than intersecting lives.

When mothers work evenings, fathers "act like mothers" moving in to the parenting role and housework roles (Barnett & Gareis, 2007, p. 401). It is interesting that this is spoken of as acting like mothers, which perpetuates the stereotype that caring for children and the home is "mothering" behavior. Indeed, when fathers spend more time caretaking their homes and their children it is not only good for their own health and stress levels, and improves their relationships with their children, but it increases their children's ability to express the full range of emotions, for girls to be assertive and boys to express more interpersonal affiliation and warmth (Barnett & Rivers, 2004; Brody & Hall, 1993).

Rhona Mahony (1995) argued that women will never achieve equality with men as long as they insist on, or fall into, primary parenting. To change their part of this ingrained pattern, women must actively resist the pull of tradition and insist on a plan of joint child care from the earliest days. Otherwise, the head

start of mother's prenatal bonding leads to her gate-keeping on all matters involving the baby, tipping the system back to familiar, but unequal, mommy-daddy roles. When men's capacity for nurturing is activated early in their children's lives, men are competent and deeply involved with their children (Pruett, 2001; Gerson, 1993; Barnett & Rivers, 2004). So, it is not nature that keeps us locked in this dilemma, but rather the powerful grip of centuries-old economic and social arrangements acting on our emotions.

Child-Rearing

The minute a child is born and often before, the nuclear family triangle (parents and child) is ready for potential activation. One of the biggest surprises for new parents may be the degree to which they discover passionate feelings about child-rearing, a subject to which they may have given little previous thought. However, the imprint of their own childhoods, their levels of maturity, and their internalized ideas about their own roles as parents make this a potentially hot issue for many couples. Gender socialization, leading to unequal participation in child care only makes matters worse. Fathers are cast as "idealists," responsible for preparing the child for the outside world, and mothers as "pragmatists," doing whatever works to get them and the children through each day's "endless list" (Taffel, 1994). These prescribed roles lead inevitably to the many destructive triangles of family life, especially those which polarize the parents in "too strict" or "too lenient" positions. "Father knows best" and "angry mommy and the naughty kids" are familiar, unhappy scenarios of family life in which one parent treats the other like one of the children.

Family therapists should help parents to develop age-appropriate, practical approaches to discipline on which both parents can agree. If they can't agree, we should help them to negotiate ways not to interfere with each other's methods, assuming, of course, that the particular methods are not harsh or harmful. Unless there is actual danger, one parent should not intervene at the time the other parent is disciplining a child. If there is disagreement, parents should discuss it in private and then either agree to disagree or shift parental responsibilities so that the parent who cares more about an issue (e.g., table manners) assumes responsibility for dealing with that issue. If the issue has already become a toxic one for parent and child, it will be more helpful to shift responsibility to the less concerned parent. The suggestion of shifting responsibility will usually unmask the underlying problem of the parents' unequal involvement in the role and work of parenting. Clinical approaches that don't address this imbalance will usually not end the disputes over child-rearing and discipline.

Underlying conflicts over discipline reflect parental marital problems. If they are engaged in intense power struggles in other areas of their relationship, these will probably spill over into their approaches to child-rearing. When a particular child arouses parental anxiety, for emotional reasons or because of the child's physical or mental problems, parents may triangulate with this particular child. In such cases, usually referred to in the literature as "child-focused families," the issue is not really discipline and has little or nothing to do with the child. Instead, issues with the family of origin or problems in the marital relationship may have created the intense triangle that then displaces the anxiety onto discipline concerns. None of this is to suggest that all or even most child-rearing arguments are a sign of basic marital problems, apart from the common gender imbalance, or to suggest that such arguments will disappear automatically if parents work on their marital relationship or their families of origin. Even when marital or family problems are primary, it is necessary first to address the problem that brought the family to therapy. As the therapist and couple work on the child-rearing or discipline problems, it will usually become clear whether extensive work on the marital relationship and/or families of origin is essential to changing the presenting problems and maintaining the change.

Many parental arguments are about disciplining children, and these will spill over into therapists' offices, where we will be called upon to say who's "right." This is the time to have reading material for parents, or to recommend a book for them to buy, rather than to step into that triangle ourselves. Harriet Lerner's book, *The Mother Dance* (1998), is particularly effective against all of the pitfalls

that precipitate discipline problems: parental guilt, anxiety, over-responsibility, and uncertainty.

Ron Taffel's book *Childhood Unbound* (2009) considers this generation of children to be the freest generation because they know no bounds, due to Internet exposure, the media, and our fast-paced world. However, according to Taffel, children are also "freer from the constraints of history—the stories of generations past are missing. . . . (Children) feel less guilt and connection to the everyday job or career sacrifices of their parents" (pp. 12–13). Children's new freedoms bring with them anxiety, infused by endless access to adult media. They get to make very early decisions about high-risk behavior. Parents are left with fear and frustration about their children's safety. Kids know parents feel helpless, and they lose confidence in adults' ability to "contain and protect" them. What is desperately needed is for parents and children to reconnect and engage, for families to share their personal journeys and their family and cultural history, which are essential to creating deeper tolerance, empathy, and a solid sense of self. What is needed is for families to spend time together and for parents to give undivided personal attention to their children (Taffel, 2009).

It is important to remember that ethnicity and class play a strong role in determining what parents have learned is appropriate discipline, and we should ask clients about their experience and ideas. Comer and Poussaint (1992) remind us that Black parents have often been strict disciplinarians because they felt that they had to force their children to obey so that they wouldn't violate racial rules and come to harm. While agreeing with many Black parents who find White middle-class parents too permissive, the authors come out strongly against spanking or shaming and provide useful alternatives by age.

Problems: Poor and teenage mothers and children

Poor children in the United States are worse off than poor children in all other industrialized Western nations. U.S. spending on children under 6, which is key to children's future well-being, lags far behind that of other countries, only two thirds of what other major developed countries pay for children's health and education (CBS News, 2009). Child poverty rates in the United States are nearly double the OECD average! This is because the gap between rich and poor is so wide in the United States. Of all the many risks for children in postindustrial societies, poverty puts children more at risk than any other single factor.

Although there is much general condemnation of single-parent families, especially the majority that are headed by women, it is important to realize that the structure itself is not the problem and that single-parent families range across the whole spectrum from highly functional to highly dysfunctional, depending on economics and emotional, family, and community connectedness (see Chapter 6, on Poor Black Families, and Chapter 20 on Single-Parent Families). Too often, problems resulting from poverty or emotional and social isolation are attributed solely to family structure. Thus, the isolation of the children of overworked, harried two-parent families may be overlooked while we approach every single-parent family from a deficit viewpoint. A useful clinical approach would be to investigate the status of the mother's family and friendship relationships and the degree to which she is connected to a supportive community, neighborhood, church, or temple. Obviously, poverty will exacerbate all of the usual problems of parents, as well as causing many new problems. If the mother is unmarried, she is facing the struggle alone, unless she is rooted in her family, friends, and community.

Single-parenthood is a growing world phenomenon, and we need to develop helpful attitudes toward it. Clearly, the children of a financially stable woman, who is emotionally connected to family, friends, and community should be expected to thrive whether their mother is married or unmarried.

Currently about 24 percent of births in the United States are to unmarried women living without a partner. Of those, the most problematic are of course, the unmarried teens, who account for about 9 percent of all pregnancies in the United States Latinas have the highest rate of teen pregnancy, almost twice as high as the overall birthrate (81 per 1,000 Latinas, 64 pregnancies per 1,000 Black teen girls, and 27 pregnancies per 1,000 White teen girls) (Basu, 2009).

In our society a teenager is, by definition, not ready to be a parent. In any social or economic bracket, a teenager is a child, regardless of intelligence, sophistication, or street smarts. This child/parent needs further time to develop emotionally and intellectually before taking on the adult tasks of parenting and earning a living. Family therapy in this crisis should be aimed at protecting the young mother's development, as well as the baby's. Family therapy should help the teenager and her family come to a joint decision about abortion, relinquishing the baby for adoption, or keeping and nurturing the baby. Plans should be made to continue the teenager's education and, if the decision is to keep the baby, for housing with mature family members who can provide assistance with baby care. Involvement of the baby's father, of course, depends on what kind of relationship he has had with the mother, whether they plan to remain a couple, and whether he can provide financial support. Up to 70 percent of these fathers are adult males. These babies are too often a result of forcible rape, statutory rape, or incest, criminal actions that are seldom prosecuted.

Since a solid majority of American teenagers have had sex by the time they graduate from high school, it is important for the therapist to investigate the level of sex education attained by the teenage mother. The dissemination of birth control and disease control information to teenagers is a sensitive area with some families, and therapists need to approach this discussion diplomatically. The controversial welfare bill of 1996 did provide funds to combat teen pregnancy but, unfortunately, only for programs promoting abstinence from sexual contact.

Homeless families with children

Of all the families our society neglects, homeless families with children are among the most desperate. They represent 10 percent of poor families (National Coalition for the Homeless, 2006). They are much less likely to attend school, a fact that is not surprising when we examine the Catch-22 residency regulations in many school districts that bar homeless children from both the school nearest their former home and the school in the neighborhood where they are temporarily residing.

Twaite and Lampert (1997) examined factors predicting favorable outcomes for homeless families and found that parental attendance, intensity of involvement in treatment, and the parent's understanding of the child's problem significantly influenced positive outcomes. Needless to say, this is important confirmation of the importance of parental and caretaker involvement in helping children overcome their problems.

Children with disabilities

So many hopes and dreams are projected by parents onto their children that a serious illness or disability in the child wreaks havoc on the family. When a child has a chronic or serious disability (see Chapter 23 on Chronic Illness), it is important for the clinician to help the parents share their grief and sadness with each other and with other family members and friends. It often happens that their perceived need to cope and to "stay strong" for each other makes them fearful of "letting down." It is also essential that very specific plans be made to give respite and encourage other activities for the chief caregiver, usually the mother. She may need help to give herself permission to go to work, go on vacation, or just pursue individual interests and hobbies. The gender imbalances so common at this life cycle phase in general tend to be greatly exacerbated by having a child with disabilities. Probably it is both the burden of caretaking and the emotional stress that contribute to this problem, but in any case it is worth a great deal to try to engage fathers and keep parents on the same page in managing their child and their family.

When parents express worry over a young child's functioning, a good first question is whether the child's caregiver or nursery school or other teacher has brought any problem to the parents' attention. Teachers and professional caregivers are used to a wide range of normal functioning and are quick to spot deviations from the norm. Spotting an apparent deviation and correctly diagnosing it, however, are two different things, and family therapists need to watch out for the "diagnosis of the year," in which new diagnoses are defined for children and then found everywhere. ADD (attention deficit disorder), ADHD (attention deficit and hyperactivity disorder) and MBD (minimum brain dysfunction), unspecified "learning disabilities," and plain old "hyperactivity" are common examples. Since most, if not all, such disabilities of children now come with recommended medications, it is important to help the parents obtain good assessment. Once a diagnosis and treatment plan have been made, possibly including special education, therapists can help the parents not to slip into an adversarial relationship with the school. Such a triangle, fueled by the parents' anxiety, will severely complicate the school's work with the child.

Child abuse

For a discussion of the dynamics and statistics on physical and sexual abuse of children, see Chapter 25 on Violence. This is a problem at every socioeconomic level in our society, and because so many of the assaults on children are perpetrated by their parents, relatives, caretakers, and family friends, they are all the more shocking. Therapists should be as alert to the signs or hints of child abuse as they are to indications of wife battering. Any suggestion of child abuse is a reason to stop whatever therapy-as-usual we are doing and explore in minutest detail the child's level of risk.

In most states, it is now possible to have the suspected perpetrator (rather than the child) removed from the home and denied access to the child. However, vigilant follow-up by the therapist is often necessary. Under no circumstances should a known child-abusing parent be included in family sessions until he or she has acknowledged the problem, agreed to whatever individual treatment and medication are recommended, and is ready to apologize in a meaningful way to the abused child and other family members. Under no circumstances should it be assumed that abuse will cease as a result of couples or family therapy alone.

Infertility

A client once said: "The only thing worse than having a child with problems is not being able to have a child at all." The trauma of infertility generates grief and mourning, which is reactivated with every attempt and failure to conceive, whether through natural means or infertility treatments. The intensity of the experience is often overlooked by the couple's family, friends, or even therapist, and there is danger that the couple will identify themselves as damaged or stigmatized, isolating themselves socially, creating stress, depression, and paralysis. This is especially likely when couples belong to ethnicities that particularly focus on the importance of children or to fundamentalist religions that expect couples to produce many children. In some cultural groups infertility is even an accepted premise for divorce. About 1 out of 12 married couples in the United States is infertile. The causes are 40 percent female, 40 percent male, 10 percent interactive, and 10 percent unknown (Meyers et al., 1995). However, regardless of cause, women generally exhibit greater emotional distress, probably because of their socialization to become mothers and also because women receive the major portion of medical procedures for infertility.

Although White professional couples may form the largest consumer contingent of infertility services (which are extremely expensive), poor people of color with little formal education are more likely to be infertile (Meyers et al., 1995). Adding to the problem, there has been a great deal of controversy about Medicaid programs that might help poor women overcome fertility problems (Beck, 1994). Almost invisible among infertility sufferers are lesbian women who try endless cycles of alternative insemination before giving up the cherished goals of pregnancy and giving birth.

Although reproductive technology has created some dazzling new techniques to help Mother Nature along, most infertility treatments are not covered by insurance. Fertility treatments can also raise the agonizing dilemmas of multiple births following fertility drugs: "selective reduction" (abortion of some fetuses to save the others) or risks of serious birth defects that are much higher in multiple births. Obviously, all protracted infertility treatments place enormous stress on the couple. Family therapists need to keep informed of the cutting-edge developments and problems of infertility treatments so that we can help couples to determine when it is time to stop such treatments and seek other ways of becoming parents.

Alternate Pathways to Parenthood

Although infertility treatments such as surgery, drug treatment, alternative insemination, in vitro fertilization, sperm injection, and surrogacy all provide a pathway to parenthood for a small percentage of infertile couples, their current relatively low rate of success and very high cost have kept this new technology from replacing the age-old alternative method of attaining parenthood: adoption.

Adoption

More than 1.6 million families in the United States include at least one adopted child under 18 (U.S. Census Bureau, 2004). Another half million people or more—grandparents, siblings, and other relatives—are touched by this process (McKelvey & Stevens, 1994). But the process and the prospects for successful adoption have become more complicated. This is due partially to the scarcity of White infants because of contraception and legal abortion, partially to the fact that more single mothers now feel free to raise their own children, and partially to the problems of the foster care system that was supposed to be part of the solution.

The most revolutionary development in the adoption process is the growing interest in—and controversy over—open adoption, where birth parents and adoptive parents meet one another, share identifying and genetic information, and communicate directly over the years. Some may get together regularly and view each other as extended kin; others stick to written or mediated communication until the adoptees are in their late teens. While advocates list many obvious advantages in direct contact, which can break the negative power of the adoption triangle with its cut offs, fantasies, and loyalty conflicts, critics most fear an invasion of adoptive family boundaries and the possibility that the birth parents may be inconsistent or even drop out of the children's lives (Gilman, 1992). Open adoption has been the norm in most countries and other times. Outcomes in our society will be known only by researching a generation of adopted children who grew up knowing their birth parents (Hartman, 1993). It is important for family therapists to pay close attention to the individual situation rather then seeking a universal "solution." We need to help our clients think this through carefully to decide which route they choose to follow, and then help them with its particular challenges. In the end, studies conclude, four out of five of all adoptions are successful.

Informal adoption is common among families of color. Nancy Boyd-Franklin has taught us the importance of understanding the reciprocity among kin that has been one of the most important survival mechanisms of African Americans (Boyd-Franklin, 2003a). This sharing, she tells us, has produced permeable boundaries around the Black family household that contrast sharply with the rigid boundaries around most White nuclear families. These flexible boundaries have been an integral part of Black community life since the days of slavery, permitting adult relatives or friends of the family to take in children whose parents are unable to care for them for whatever reason. Since original adoption agencies were not designed to meet the needs of Black children, this informal network provided—and still provides—unofficial social services to poor Black families and children.

While the advantages of such sharing of scarce resources are clear, many early family therapists ignored the difference in poor Black family structure (see Chapter 6) or automatically considered it dysfunctional. Since Black clients understand all too well how their family structure may be judged by White therapists, they may be extremely uneasy if White clinicians do formal genograms early in treatment. It is probably wise for the clinician to simply make mental notes of family and household relationships as they arise naturally in the therapeutic conversation and write these down later. Most important to remember is the simple fact that while some of these structures are dysfunctional, with role and boundary blurring, many are extremely functional (Boyd-Franklin, 2003a), as are extended family networks in other cultures. The competent clinician can assess which is which in the usual way: by closely exploring all relationships in each particular family system.

Although international adoptions are costly, the costs can often be compared favorably to the high costs of infertility treatments. Thus, increasing numbers of Americans, fearful of or burnt out by lengthy treatments and the cost and difficulties of domestic adoption, have turned their sights abroad.

This is especially so since the fall of communism added the countries of Eastern Europe to the list of the poor countries of Central and South America and Asia that permitted foreign adoption. Paperwork and bureaucracy abound, and it is important to find a U.S. agency that can help with red tape. Prospective parents should be prepared to make a commitment to embrace the culture of their child and be able to teach the child his or her country's history and culture. In pursuit of this goal, adoptive parents often join American organizations such as Families with Children from China, which offer support and the opportunity to become involved with families with similar intercultural membership.

Some international adoptions are also interracial. Domestic interracial adoptions usually consist of White parents adopting African American children. Some of the issues are similar, especially the need for parental commitment to teaching the child about his or her history and culture and help in developing a positive identity in both the birth and adoptive cultures (Zuniga, 1991). Comer and Poussaint (1992) emphasize other issues: the importance of White adoptive parents' examining their motives carefully; the need to discuss racial difference calmly with the child from time to time along with the adoption story; and the need to protect children from racism without overprotecting them. Comer and Poussaint warn against continual brooding or outraged reactions to racism, lest these transmit negative messages to the child about being Black. At the same time, it is important to provide a model of constructive ways to fight racism.

These authors also caution against middle-class or upper-middle-class parents' failing to find ways to expose their children to African Americans of their class. Children need to hear from their parents early and often that they must persist in spite of racism and that they *can* "climb every mountain" (Comer and Poussaint, 1992). They will also learn from the lives of their parents and peers.

Jerome and Karen sought consultation about the acting out of their 12-year-old daughter, Susan. The parents were a White professional couple in their forties; Susan was their African American daughter, adopted in infancy. The family lived in an affluent, all-White community, where the only people of color were maids, nannies, handymen, and delivery people. Jerome and Karen, idealistic ex-hippies, complained about Susan's growing rebelliousness and recent behavioral and academic problems in school. They were puzzled because Susan had previously done excellent schoolwork, was cooperative at home, and had many close friends.

Through conversations with Susan, alone, and the parents, I (BC) learned that the parents had lost touch with Black friends they had known previously and had not found new ones in their White suburb. Susan's friends were also all White, both in the neighborhood and at school, and they were now starting to talk endlessly about the boys, dates, dances, clothes, and romance that awaited them in high school. Although she didn't want to discuss it, it was clear that Susan was afraid of what her standing would be, once the dating game commenced. The therapist told the parents the problem seemed to be that they were raising Susan as if she were White, which she wasn't, or as if it didn't matter that she was Black, which it did.

During the next 6 months, the parents were encouraged to locate activities both for themselves and for Susan in adjoining towns where there was ethnic, religious, class, and racial diversity. After a short period of defensiveness, they did so enthusiastically, joining a bicycling club, volunteering as parent chaperones at the neighboring town's school events, and joining in PTA discussions and town meetings. As they got to know Black parents whom they liked, they invited them home, along with their usual friends. Susan joined after-school sports and recreation groups at the neighboring town's YWCA. She was encouraged to invite her new friends, Black and White, to their home. Susan's difficulties at her own school diminished as she socialized with the new group of friends. Jerome and Karen reported their enjoyment at breaking out of their own self-imposed segregation. After 6 months, Karen announced, while Jerome beamed, "We don't know how we fell into this trap, but we did; this isn't 'success,' it's isolation. And now, as soon as Susan graduates from elementary school, we're getting out of it. We're going to move to the next town so that she can go to high school in the 'real world,' and we can pursue our new friendships and activities without all the driving back and forth." We joked that this was "the community cure," and it was.

Because single parents do not have partners to share responsibility, the support of family, friends, and community becomes all the more important.

Indications are that children adopted by single parents are as well adjusted as children adopted into two-parent homes. In fact, single-parent homes may be the placement of choice for some children.

It is extremely important for family therapists to keep an open mind about the strengths of single-parent families (see Chapter 20). Until there is greater flexibility in the adoption-approval process and more understanding and respect for alternative family structures, however, some single-parent adoptions will continue to be unidentified lesbians and gay individuals who are not eligible to adopt as openly gay couples. A more promising situation for them is the right—recognized by the highest courts in only a few states so far—of a person to adopt his or her unmarried partner's child. This then bestows legal parental rights on unmarried heterosexual partners and gay and lesbian partners.

Lesbian and Gay Parenting

The variables that predict a positive transition to parenthood for lesbian and gay couples are the same as those for heterosexual couples.

- Having realistic expectations.
- Having good couple communication.
- The adaptability of each partner to change.
- The ability to tolerate chaos, noise, sleep deprivation, and lack of solitude.

The pitfalls in the parental triangle are also the same: First, there is the possibility that one parent is the primary caretaker; he or she will be closer to the child, and the other parent will feel left out. Because this would tend to be exacerbated if the primary parent were also the biological parent, lesbian couples are often especially careful to divide child care equally or, if that is not possible, to shift roles and have the nonbiological parent do the primary caretaking. When children are older and try to use the usual "divide and conquer" strategies on their parents, gay and lesbian parents are somewhat less vulnerable than heterosexual parents because both have received the same gender programming about parenting and are more likely to see eye to eye on childrearing (Martin, 1993).

What is not the same, of course, is the level of stress caused by social stigma and lack of social, and sometimes familial, support. While it is true in some cases that contact with a child softens negative attitudes in the family of origin toward gay or lesbian offspring, the news of an impending child also brings all the coming-out issues to the fore again and may bring forth a new level of homophobia as parents who have privately accepted their child's sexual orientation feel threatened by how public a grandchild will be. Questions from family and others center on fears that a child will be hurt psychologically by the social stigma and/or by having parents of only one gender (Martin, 1993). It is hard for heterosexuals to fully own and try to correct the problem of social stigma as their own problem, not that of the gay or lesbian family. Straight people also tend to overlook the benefits such as flexibility, group pride, and multicultural awareness that can accrue to children who have been raised with the tools to fight discrimination, as children of color are, as children of gay and lesbian families are, as children with disabilities are, and as Jewish children and children of other stigmatized ethnic groups are. It is also important for family therapists to remember that although many families reject their gay and lesbian children, most do not (Laird, 1996).

In the past 4 decades there has been a dramatic increase in the number and visibility of lesbian and gay couples raising children. In spite of the discrimination that keeps many gay parents from acknowledging their sexual orientation in surveys, estimates of lesbian mothers run up to 5 million, gay fathers up to 3 million, and children of these parents up to 14 million. The largest number of these children were born in previous heterosexual relationships; the second largest to single and coupled lesbians giving birth through known or unknown donor insemination and to surrogates bearing children for gay couples. The third largest group of children comes through supposedly single-parent adoptions by lesbians or gay men, most of whom are actually coupled.

In spite of efforts by social conservatives to discredit such families, not a single study has found children of gay or lesbian parents to be disadvantaged in any significant respect relative to children of heterosexual parents (Patterson, 1992; Kuvalanka, McClintock-Comeaux & Leslie, 2004). When conservative groups in Hawaii tried to forestall giving gay and lesbian couples the right to legally marry, they tried to do so by a focus on parenting and the best interests of children. This produced the most ringing endorsement by a court of gay and lesbian parenting with the judge declaring that the evidence produced established that the single most important factor in the development of a happy, healthy, and well-adjusted child is the nurturing relationship between parent and child (Goldberg, 1996).

Since gay and lesbian couples have few role models of specifically gay families, they tend to give much more thought to every step of the way than heterosexuals do: the decision to become a parent, the conscious evolution of support networks to counteract social stigma, the creation of family rituals to celebrate family life cycle transitions, the division of chores and child care, inheritance, arrangements in case of death or breakup of the relationship (important because these relationships are not as protected by law as they are for heterosexual couples).

In all clinical work with gay and lesbian families, it is essential to keep the following caveats in mind:

Stay carefully informed about the social policy context these families face in all aspects of their lives: They are excluded from the U.S. Census Bureau's definition of family; their civil rights are protected in only 8 states; their sexual contact is criminalized in over 20 states (and, of course, in the U.S. military); and in spite of many recent efforts to change state laws, they still lack the overall legal protection our government grants to heterosexuals by marriage, divorce, custody, and inheritance laws, including Medicaid and Social Security (Kuvalanka, McClintock-Comeaux, & Leslie, 2004; Hartman, 1996).

Gay and lesbian couples are both similar to and different from heterosexual couples and from each other. Only accurate personal information will help us to avoid overgeneralizing about their parenting issues.

The planned lesbian family is a living laboratory of the partnership model that heterosexuals keep striving to achieve: Both parents are heads of household, each is a primary parent, each is a breadwinner, household chores are divided fairly, and decision making is joint. Participants in one study of planned lesbian families described their families as providing more parental involvement, concern, attention, nurturance, physical affection, expression of feelings, talking, sensitivity, love, caring, and warmth (Mitchell, 1995).

Foster Care

While many parents spend fortunes and travel across the world to adopt children, almost half a million U.S. children are in foster care. Sixty-seven percent of them are Black or of mixed race; two thirds are male; some have learning disabilities or emotional problems; most are between the ages of 5 and 11 (McKelvey & Stevens, 1994). These are the children called "hard to place," and by the time the foster care system has moved, traumatized, and ignored them for years, many become even harder to place. The challenge for foster parents is to temporarily parent children from troubled families, knowing that their input is time-limited. The situation has become serious enough that Congress approved a tax credit for adopting a hard-to-place child (North American Council on Adoptable Children, 2009).

Our society's neglect of poor children remains an outrage. The welfare bill in the 1990s dismantled 6 decades of antipoverty policy, including welfare for poor children. Scant notice was given to the deletion in the bill of the one word "nonprofit," which opened the way for profit-making businesses such as managed mental health care corporations and youth care chains that are traded on Wall Street to compete for Federal welfare payments. The availability of this money guarantees an increase in foster care institutions, even though they have been shown to be detrimental to children's development over the long run. Children's advocacy groups, of course, have decried the use of poor children as a market commodity. This would seem to be an area begging for political action by mental health and child welfare workers, as well as parents of more fortunate children in this, the most affluent country in the world.

Clinical Guidelines

Whatever the presenting problem is, the entire three- or four-generation family system should be carefully evaluated at three levels:

1. **Individual:** Each individual's development and functioning (see Chapter 2).
2. **Family:**
   2.A. **Immediate Family:** The couple's relationship and interactions: communication, decision making, time, money, power, intimacy. This includes the nuclear family's handling of life cycle tasks (see Table 1.1: The Stages of the Family Life Cycle, in Chapter 1), emotional triangles, and issues.
   2.B. **Extended Family:** The extended family's current and past patterns of relating and handling loss, secrets, myths, emotional triangles, and toxic issues.

3. **Sociocultural Context:**
   3.A. **Friends and Community:** The family members' involvement in the community: neighborhood, school, clubs, sports, church, temple, or other community organization. This involves parents' values and beliefs about life, spirituality, social or political action, etc.
   3.B. **Larger Society:** The applicable rules, norms, and options available in the larger social system depending on the family members' race, ethnicity, class, gender, and sexual orientation.

For a fuller elaboration of these levels, see Chapter 1.

Sharon (Genogram 14.1 Gary and Sharon) sought therapy because of her anger about her husband Gary's long work hours and distant fathering style. In the first session, I (BC) learned that Gary—a lawyer—and Sharon—a social worker with a small private practice, lived in an affluent suburb, employed a live-in nanny, and were contributing to the support of Sharon's parents in Florida. Gary commuted an hour each way to work and worked 65 to 70 hours a week, including most Saturdays. He brought work home for Sunday and rarely arrived home on weekdays before 8:00

or 9:00 p.m. Sharon worked about 20 hours a week spread over 4 half-days and 2 evenings. Gary saw the two young children, Danielle, aged 6, and Sophie, aged 4, briefly in the mornings and tried to spend Sunday afternoon with Sharon and the kids. As a couple, they had "no time." Gary vetoed all of Sharon's efforts to get him to cut back his work hours on the grounds of their high expenses and his career goal of becoming a partner in his law firm.

The evaluation

1. EACH INDIVIDUAL:

All four immediate family members appeared to be physically healthy and functioning satisfactorily. Description of extended family members did not indicate any major physical or psychological problems. Emotionally, Gary talked about work in a somewhat compulsive, distant way, and Sharon sometimes sounded like the parent, rather than daughter or sibling, in her family of origin.

2. THE FAMILY:

The Couple: There was no couple time; sex was infrequent. The formerly equal couple was imbalanced, with Gary now ignoring or vetoing suggestions he didn't agree with. They had no effective method of discussing or negotiating differences. Family tasks were polarized, with Sharon doing or supervising all domestic tasks and Gary earning most of the income. Sharon complained of Gary's lack of emotional expressiveness, and he, of her excessive emotionality. These descriptions seemed consistent with their gender and ethnic differences: she was more emotionally expressive and he more self-contained and understated.

The Family Emotional System: In the nuclear family, father and children spent too little time together; Gary was completely uninvolved in the household schedules and tasks; Sharon was the only hands-on parent.

Main Triangle: Sharon and the children were close and Gary distant.

Relations with the Families of Origin: Relations with the families of origin were not powerful.

Gary's Family: Gary was extremely distant from his parents, who hardly saw him or Sharon. They were minimally involved as grandparents. Gary called his father "an uncaring workaholic" but was shocked that Sharon said Gary was just like his father. Gary's mother had never complained about his father's work focus and, in fact, had delivered emotionally laden messages to him about the importance of work.

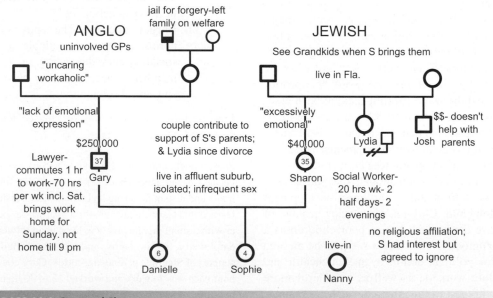

GENOGRAM 14.1 Gary and Sharon

Sharon's Family: Sharon was a typical over-responsible oldest daughter who felt obligated to take care of everyone in her family of origin. She contributed money to her sister so that she wouldn't have to move after her divorce; she shrugged off her affluent younger brother's refusal to contribute financially to their parents; and she never objected to family members' impositions on her time or money.

Significant Extended Family Intergenerational Triangles:

Gary, his father, and mother

Gary's father, Gary, Gary's children

Gary's family, Gary, Sharon

Sharon, her mother, and father

Sharon, her parents, her sister Lydia

Sharon, her parents, her brother Josh

Sharon's family, Sharon, Gary

Major Emotional Issues: Time, work, money, fathering, caretaking, lack of intimacy, lack of negotiating skills, not living according to their own values.

Major Emotional Threats:

1. Growing distance and resentment between the couple
2. Emotional distance between father and children

3. THE SOCIOCULTURAL CONTEXT:

Community and Friends: This family is extremely isolated. Gary and Sharon's schedules had no time for involvement in any community organization whatsoever, except for a half-day once a month that Sharon volunteered at Sophie's nursery school—"so they don't think I'm a bad mother," she said.

They had no religious affiliation, each having rejected the parents' religion—his Protestant, hers Jewish. Gary felt no interest in religious involvement. For Sharon, this was not true. She had thought about joining a synagogue, but Gary always reminded her of their earlier agreement to leave religious affiliation out of their lives.

Occasionally, when Sharon pleaded for weeks, they would go to dinner and the theater, but neither of them felt there was time for any other social event.

When Sharon's parents or sister insisted, Sharon took the kids to visit them without Gary.

The Family's Place in the Larger Social System: This is a White, heterosexual, affluent, educated professional couple. Gary is an Anglo American. By these measures, the family belongs to the most powerful groups in our society. Thus, if they can get psychologically free enough to avail themselves of their options, they have more power to change their situation than the members of any other group would have. The norms of the social system that militate against their getting psychologically free enough to use their options are as follows:

- The socially approved male focus on career and money, reinforced by Gary's parents' example and messages about the "work ethic."
- Gary and Sharon's affluent, consumerist, time-starved life style, called "success," and envied by their peers.
- The rigidity of the fast-track career path for corporate lawyers.
- Sharon's belief, socially approved and ethnically reinforced, that it is a daughter's "duty" to respond to the wishes and needs of her family of origin regardless of strain on her own emotional and financial resources.
- Gary's belief, consistent with decades of social practice, that young children are fine as long as their mother is available, and fathers need only "provide."

The therapy

In therapy, Gary and Sharon accomplished the following:

Gary agreed to come home "early" (by 7:00 P.M.) at least one night a week.

Sharon stopped giving her sister money (and her sister moved to a house in a town that she could afford). Sharon remained in close contact with her sister.

Gary's talks with his mother revealed a secret about the issue of work: his maternal grandfather had been an alcoholic with a checkered work history who had once spent several years in jail for forgery, leaving his family on welfare. This had led Gary's mother to preach the value of working hard ever after. Now Gary could see the emotionally programmed aspects of his own work habits. He agreed to come home before 7:00 P.M. two nights a week.

Sharon worked to restore a relationship with her brother by mail and by phone and eventually requested that he start contributing his share of support to their parents. He agreed and resumed regular contact with them.

Gary had brief, difficult, but useful talks with his father about work. His father finally acknowledged that he regretted missing Gary's youth. Gary urged him not to miss his grandchildren's youth as well. The number of visits to and from Gary's parents increased from one a year to four, interspersed with calls and gifts, and Gary took off time from work during their stay to manage their visits.

Gary and Sharon spent many weeks going over their budget. Sharon said that she would agree to sell their vacation house if Gary would get a less-demanding job. He said that he would think about it, and he eventually did, moving to a slower-paced suburban firm at a lower salary. They then sold their vacation house, causing Sharon's family to make other summer arrangements to see them.

Sharon joined a synagogue after a long discussion of their religious and ethnic differences, and she participated in the temple's discussion groups and in a social program to help the homeless. Gary joined the men's group I referred him to and became politically active at the urging of other group members.

After much discussion of "mother guilt," Sharon cut out one evening of work and gave the night off to their nanny so that she and Gary could parent together and then spend a quiet evening alone.

Gary and Sharon celebrated these dramatic moves as the crowning proof that they could now negotiate very difficult issues. They attributed their agreement to downshift to our discussions, which contrasted their early dreams, values, and ideals with the reality of what their life had become.

Gary and Sharon joined a group that met monthly for dinner and theater.

Gary said that as "daddy time" with his kids got more frequent, it got more enjoyable. "Like sex with Sharon," he added with a smile.

On making the many profound changes that they did, Gary and Sharon had three major advantages: They had an earlier strong, passionate bond and dreams to return to; their families of origin, although problematic in many ways, were essentially free of major dysfunctional patterns; and their privileged positions in the social hierarchies gave them maximum flexibility for change once they decided to go for it. Of course, being in a privileged position does not motivate people to change. In fact, the contrary is often true, depending on the degree of importance assigned by the client to maintaining maximum money and power regardless of emotional consequences.

Shifting Focus Among Levels of the System

Our clinical work does not lend itself to moving in an orderly way from one level of the system to the next, any more than real life does. So, although therapy usually begins with the presenting problem—at this phase, often a child problem—the therapist's work will address the marriage, the family of origin, the community, and the constraints of the larger social system in any given session. To get a sustained focus and eventual resolution of key issues, it is important to keep mental track of the issues at each level. Be aware of a client's repeated shift away from an uncomfortable area—maybe the marriage—back to a more "comfortable" problem—maybe the child. It is important to address the parents' preferred focus before shifting with some question about the marriage. Or one might work on the marriage indirectly through discussions of parenting roles.

Similarly, if a task to change behavior with a grandparent gets followed in the next session with a child or marital crisis, as sometimes happened with

Gary and Sharon, it is important to make mental note of this even if the opportunity to ask about the grandparent is postponed until later, or even until the next session. The important point is that the therapist should track the process.

On the macro level, it is important to help a couple achieve some small initial resolution of their presenting problems before introducing the idea of actual work in the family of origin. The first move with Gary and Sharon was to get Gary to agree to come home early one evening a week. However, in any session, one might openly refer to extended family information gathered in the evaluation and connect it to the presenting problem to show that family of origin is a relevant focus. Thus, questions about Gary's parents and work made it clear that this was an intergenerational issue as well as a couple problem.

Questions and comments about community and the rules and norms of the larger social system are usually quite easy to introduce into the discussion, since there is often not as much resistance to talking about these areas as there is to personal and family issues. Of course, it is all connected in the end, as Gary and Sharon discovered when questions about community led to their deeply personal exchange about their religious and ethnic differences.

There is still debate in family therapy about when or whether to include young children in sessions. We believe that changes in children up to adolescence depend on parental intervention on their behalf or on changes in parental attitudes and behaviors. Also, children are too powerless to change the system but sometimes feel responsible if included in problem-focused discussion and complaints. However, we ask detailed questions about their development and work with them always and only in the context of work with their families.

Transition Groups

In Cowan and Cowan (1992), a landmark 10-year study of the transition to parenthood, they developed an intervention focused on the life cycle transition to parenthood: They ran a 6-month group for couples in the 7th month of pregnancy. The couple exchanged expectations for the 3 months before the birth and for the 3 months afterward, and they discussed and negotiated problems of the first months of parenthood. Focusing on the expectations and then experience of the transition appeared to have positive effects of stress reduction, which lasted for years. On follow-up none of the couples in this group divorced, although 10 percent of couples in their study as a whole did.

Helping Fathers to Be More Involved

Ron Taffel (1994) has a lot to say about how he helps men to move more toward child care. I also have such discussions routinely with fathers and find them very productive (Carter, 1993). It is important for the therapist to take a nonblaming stance in talking with men frankly about their fear of incompetence, fear of their own angry reactions, fear of losing out in their career, and a general sense that they lack the requisite access to their own emotions. After all, we and our clients are up against 5,000 years of more distant fathering, and such a pattern can't be changed overnight. But that's no reason not to start somewhere. Levine, Murphy, and Wilson (1993) describe many strategies for involving men in early childhood programs. Many of these techniques are generally applicable to encouraging men's participation in family therapy and family life; for example, expect them to be involved, find out what they want, recognize hidden resistance in yourself as a clinician or in the wife, reach out, and recognize men's hidden fears of emotional arenas.

Helping Parents Prepare Sons as Well as Daughters to Develop into Caring Adults

Much has been said about the dangers of mothers being too close to their sons, though a much larger problem is fathers being too distant from all their children. As therapists we must be proactive in countering the cultural rules that promote a "boys will be boys" mentality, which allows boys to grow up focusing on getting ahead, even at the expense of others. All development occurs in the context of relationships, and it is essential for both parents to stay connected to their sons and inhibit the superhero tendencies that showing feelings or caring for others is for girls or wimps. In the dominant culture boys grow up with a desensitization to violence and mistreating others. Dooley and Fedele (2004) have suggested a list of rules to help families break through the "gender straitjacket," from which the following suggestions have been culled:

• Encourage boys and girls to interact, and expect them to develop friendships.

• Avoid normalizing "boys will be boys" and stereotyped girl behaviors.

• Recognize "dangerous" edges such as rough-and-tumble play for boys because they can't say when it hurts, and dieting and external body focus, which is a dangerous edge for girls.

• Raise expectations for boys regarding not participating in bullying, showing care when others are hurt, and speaking up when someone is mistreated.

• Name emotional and relational interactions with peers as courageous.

• Structure leadership opportunities for girls and relational opportunities for boys.

It is essential for parents to socialize their children about the larger societal structures that inhibit the full development of either sons or daughters. Clinicians play an important role whenever they are in the position of inquiring about children's behavior and parenting patterns to help them explore their deeper values and challenge male–female dominance/oppression structures of our society.

Helping White Parents to Prepare Their Children for a Multicultural World

In about 50 years, this country will have no single majority race or ethnic group. The White population will have to accommodate itself to loss of majority status and learn how to live, work, and relate to people of other races. In some communities, of course, this is already happening, especially in larger cities. However, mostly, it is not happening. But those who are not prepared to embrace or at least accept diversity will be at a severe disadvantage in years to come. There are many White parents who would not

wish their children to be among those die-hards, although with the obliviousness of privilege, they may not realize that they need to act now to prevent a later scenario of confusion, disorder, or even violence.

Matthias and French (1996) in *Forty Ways to Raise a Non-Racist Child* explore the many ways in which parents can help their children in this regard: Make acquaintances across color lines yourself, trace your family's history of prejudice, begin the lessons early, don't pretend that discrimination doesn't exist, tell the whole story behind the holidays (e.g., Columbus Day, Thanksgiving), choose children's schools carefully to ensure diversity, expand their circle of playmates to include children of other races and cultures, and monitor carefully what they read and watch on TV to check what messages they are receiving on this subject.

Most White parents are surprised to learn that by age 3, a child is aware of and concerned about similarities and differences in skin color and hair (Comer & Poussaint, 1992). This whole subject of multiculturalism is a topic that usually needs to be raised by the therapist, since White parents are likely to be unaware of its importance to them personally.

Helping Minority-Group Parents to Protect Their Children in an Oppressive Society

Unlike many White heterosexual parents, parents in current minority groups are only too aware of the potential harm to their children of being part of a socially stigmatized group such as people of color and gay and lesbian families. And although all of the items mentioned above also apply here, there are a few in addition: Pay close attention to the child's level of self-esteem, feelings of competence, and positive group identification; and make extra efforts to belong to communities of families like yours both for support and to counteract the negative effects of feeling stigmatized and alienated from the larger society. Therapists having such discussions with minority group parents, if they are not members of the same group, should prepare themselves by reading and discussions with colleagues and be prepared to encourage parents similarly to inform themselves about their social context.

Talking to Parents About Values

It is the essence of a parent's job to teach their children what they themselves have learned about how to live a meaningful life. If parents don't think about and articulate their own values, children will infer them from the way their parents live. It is better for us to think about what we want to teach.

Dr. Benjamin Spock declared in 1997 that "parental hesitancy" had become the most common problem in child-rearing (p. 123). Dr. Spock strongly emphasized the importance of parental discussion of their principles about crucial topics such as human relations and personal values. He supported the idea of encouraging children to ask questions about everything, including sex, and suggested that parents convey its connection to relationship. He also stated that children need to develop spiritual values and a sense of idealism such as the importance of kindliness, loyalty, and helping others. Children need to see their own parents involved at school, in the community, and in the political process if they are to learn to care about others.

This stage of life is a crucial one at which to help parents look hard at how they are living and ask themselves if this is what they want. In the scramble to make enough money, raise children, and pursue their own careers, parents often fall into one accommodation or another without really meaning to. Because of the complexity of family life at this stage and the paucity of meaningful support from our society, parents deserve an opportunity in family therapy to explore all options and possibilities for a more meaningful family life. Such discussions may lead them to redesign their own roles and relationship regardless of gender imperatives, and/or to realign their relationship to the larger society by redefining "success" in the world to suit themselves (Saltzman, 1991).

Conclusion

In spite of all the complexities and difficulties of contemporary family life, we have never actually met any parent who regretted being a parent. Whenever we have done life cycle exercises with trainees, grouping people by life cycle stage and having them discuss the issues, one of the childless participants always says something like, "It's too hard. Why does anyone have children?" At this point, the parents laugh in astonishment trying to describe the joys, pleasures, and transcendence of parenthood. Maybe it's like talking about sex to a virgin—the problematic aspects of it may be clear, but it's almost impossible to fully articulate the physical, sensory, intellectual, emotional, and spiritual experience of connectedness to another human being through love.

Chapter 15

Transformation of the Family System During Adolescence

Nydia Garcia Preto

The adaptations in family structure and organization that are required to handle the tasks of adolescence are so basic that the family itself is transformed from a unit that protects and nurtures young children to one that is a preparation center for the adolescent's entrance into the world of adult responsibilities and commitments. This family metamorphosis involves profound shifts in relationship patterns across the generations, and while it may be signaled initially by the adolescent's physical maturity, it often parallels and coincides with changes in parents as they enter midlife and with major transformations by grandparents facing later life and death.

In the twenty-first century, families in the United States are more than ever challenged by the risks of living in an increasingly endangered environment and in a society in which, largely for economic reasons, parents choose or are forced to work longer and longer hours, limiting the time they can spend at home with their children. Diminished connections to extended family and community have left parents struggling alone and more dependent on external systems for teaching children and for setting limits on them. At the same time, teenagers are turning more and more to their peers for emotional support, to the pop culture promoted by the media, and especially to the Internet for values and ideas about life. As a result, the family's function as an emotional support system is threatened. The threat is greater for families that are economically disadvantaged and living in poor urban and rural neighborhoods.

This chapter focuses on the overall transformation that families experience as they try to master the tasks of adolescence, keeping in mind that perceptions about adolescent roles and behaviors vary depending on socioeconomic and cultural context. Most families, after a certain degree of confusion and disruption, are able to change the rules and limits and reorganize themselves to allow adolescents more autonomy and independence. However, certain universal problems are associated with this transition and can result in the development of symptoms in the adolescent or in other family members. Clinical cases will illustrate some blocks that families experience during this phase and factors that may contribute to family disorganization or symptomatic behavior, as well as therapeutic interventions that may be effective with these families.

The Sociocultural Context

The experiences we have during adolescence in our families, community, and society greatly affect the way in which we teach and guide adolescents later in life. Our cultural values, attitudes about gender, and beliefs about life and death are central factors influencing the formation of their identities. However, the culture in which we live has a tremendous impact on that process as well.

In the United States, patriarchal values and racism shape relationship patterns between men and women. Men have more political and economic power than women. Whites have more privilege than people of color. Sexism and racism are sources of social oppression that affect all men and women in this culture and that marginalize and abuse women, people of color, and those who are nonconforming in gender or sexual roles. The media promote and reinforce these values on a daily basis. Adolescents, particularly, are vulnerable to media exploitation. Their values and beliefs about life, their views of gender relationships, and the way they dress, talk, and walk are all greatly influenced by what they see on TV and in films, the music they hear, and by the Internet.

The music they listen to, especially, reflects the attitudes of the peer group with which they identify. In most schools and communities in the United States, adolescents, like adults, segregate along racial, cultural, and class lines. Their identity as female, male, lesbian, gay, White, Black, Asian, Latino, rich, poor, smart, or learning disabled is partly shaped by how the media portray those roles.

Yet many adolescents cannot identify with the images promoted by the media, nor do they have access to the products being sold. They feel marginalized by society and invisible, and some don't even experience the process of adolescence because they go from childhood directly into adulthood. In White, middle-class mainstream America, turning 13 "normally" means becoming a legitimate teenager, an adolescent, and symbolizes growth toward physical and emotional maturity, responsibility, and independence. But turning 13 doesn't necessarily have the same meaning for poor African Americans or for Latino and Asian immigrants who are marginalized in this society and have little access to economic resources. Adolescence, for many in these groups, means assuming adult responsibilities as soon as possible. Many have children at age 14, quit school, and go to work as soon as they can be hired. Others stay home to take care of brothers, sisters, or parents who are unable to take care of themselves (Burton, Obeidallah, & Allison, 1996). Some cultures may encourage adolescents to fulfill adult responsibilities, such as caretaking duties, or to contribute financially to the home, yet still expect them to remain obedient to and respectful of parents. Becoming independent or living on one's own, such an important goal in the United States, may not have the same value in other cultures, in which interdependence is preferred (McGoldrick, Giordano, & Garcia Preto, 2005).

What is similar for parents and adolescents during this stage of life, regardless of variations, is their increased worry about their children's safety as they mature sexually, and they have good reason to worry. Their children's bodies and emotions are all changing rapidly, but their brains are not catching up fast enough to process all that is going on. The risk for adolescents using poor judgment and making disastrous decisions is real, and the consequences are often the reasons they and their families come for treatment.

In therapy, sharing some information about adolescent development with families helps to engage them in conversations about their own values and reactions to the changes in their children. The following sections provide a brief overview of different perspectives on adolescent development and consider some of the questions that challenge traditional views and assumptions. The intent is for these ideas to expand your understanding of adolescents and to widen your lens for assessment of the problems that they and their families bring to therapy.

Developing a Gender Identity

Substantial research has been conducted on how children develop their identity as boys and girls and how they learn gender roles. A central and ongoing debate among those who study this phenomenon has been the controversy over nature versus nurture. We think that the development of gender identity is both biological and constructed by society and culture.

Most of us have learned from courses in human development that by the age of 2, children are able to distinguish girls from boys and by age 4, they begin to identify tasks according to gender. It is common sense that boys and girls are different! But how and why does it happen? There are widely held theories that try to explain the process. Some place much emphasis on the intrinsic biological nature of boys and girls. Others believe that sex type determines their sexual roles, which are primarily learned from same-sex peers. Another explanation has been that parents, but especially mothers, are central in teaching boys to be boys, and girls to be girls. These perspectives continue to carry much weight in the field of human development, despite their obvious flaws. Certainly their focus on binary constructions of gender doesn't consider the variations in gender identity and sexual orientation that pervade society, and they give little attention to the fluid and constant intersections of gender identity with race, social class, and culture. These views have been challenged by carefully conducted studies of well-respected social scientists. Yet, they continue to influence and reinforce the sexual stereotypes that keep both males and females from developing their full human potential.

The theory that mothers are all-important in shaping gender identity and behavior was greatly promoted by psychologists, and especially by the work of Nancy Chodrow (1978), a feminist who attempted to correct Freud's assumption that fathers were very powerful forces in shaping the early development of children, by promoting the belief that mothers were as influential, if not more so than fathers. She observed that mothers raised their daughters differently from their sons, keeping them close and teaching them to be nurturing, while pushing sons away to help them become men, to individuate, and be independent. These patterns of raising children, she concluded, led girls to grow up to be nurturing and to want connection, and boys to become emotionally distant from the family, behaviors that are ingrained for the rest of our lives.

Chodrow's ideas, which were meant to address the lack of importance given to the contributions of women, have instead served to reinforce the insidious "mother blaming" trend in our male dominated culture. Her theory has been seriously challenged by Barnett and Rivers (2004), who through careful analysis of her work found no systematic data on which she based her generalizations about all men and all women. Furthermore they found in their own research on young couples, the same results that other national studies such as the one conducted by Scott Coltrane (1996) in California, that when placed in situations where they need to nurture, most men are capable of doing the "mothering" that children need. Chodrow's ideas were based on her observation of private patients in her psychoanalytic practice, who, we might speculate represented only a particular sample of women, of a certain race, class, and access to privilege. However, her work continues to be respected in the psychological field and has been used as the basis for the work of theorists like Carol Gilligan et. al. (1990) and writers such as Mary Pipher (1994).

Another important assumption about the development of gender identity has been that children learn different sex roles from their peers; researchers like Maccoby (1990) describe a culture of childhood where sex segregation takes place. She believes in "a universal tendency for this polarization that has its origin in our evolutionary past" (Barrett and Rivers 2004, p. 219). She summarizes that as girls and boys develop physically, emotionally, spiritually, and intellectually there are distinct differences in their patterns of interaction. For instance, boys have been observed to be rougher in their play than girls and more inclined toward dominance. Also, boys are less likely to be influenced by girls, who, on the other hand, tend to adopt a style of making polite suggestions. These different patterns, she reports, continue as boys and girls grow older, leading to an increased emphasis on the separation of genders. She goes on to say that, "this gender segregation is a widespread phenomenon found in all the cultural settings in which children are in social groups large enough to permit choice" (Maccoby, 1990, p. 41). Her work seems to reinforce the idea that "boys will be boys, and girls will be girls."

This view that differences in behavior between boys and girls are "natural" has been challenged by researchers such as Barrie Thorne (1994), who found that when she studied children by following them from one social context to another rather than by only observing them in the schoolyard, their behavior differed depending on the setting and situation. She reports that most of the research about sex roles in children has been conducted in school settings and believes that rather than the children segregating themselves by sex, it is the structure of the playground that imposes sex segregation on children. She bases this idea on her observation of boys and girls playing comfortably with each other in cross-sex situations where segregation was not part of the settings.

Others such as Kimmel (1996, 2004, 2008), and Mintz, (2010), have also contradicted the notion of essential differences between the genders. For instance, in *Manhood in America,* Kimmel (1996) wrote that "manhood is not the manifestation of an inner essence; it's socially constructed. Manhood does not bubble up to consciousness from our biological constitution; it is created in our culture" (p. 5). He goes on to say in *The Gendered Society* (2008), "It turns out that many of the differences between women and men that we observe in our every day lives are actually not gender differences at all, but rather differences that are the result of being in different positions or in different arenas" (p. 11).

Barnett and Rivers (2004), in their book *Same Difference: How Gender Myths are Hurting Our Relationships, Our Children, and Our Jobs*, explore the gender myths that have been promoted by the work of not only Chodrow and Maccoby but by the popular theories of Gilligan and Pipher, who have influenced many of us working with adolescents and their families. I was very excited by their work, their focus on adolescent girls, and on the effect that living in a sexist society with constant media bombardment reinforcing sexual stereotypes was having on their self-esteem. It was information we could talk about with parents and adolescents.

Sixteen years later, I read Barnett and Rivers' (2004) thorough analysis of the data on which these works was based and remembered that even back then some of us were questioning Gilligan's study. It was based on such a small number of mostly White, upper, and middle-class girls, certainly not representative of the girls I was working with in my practice, or at the day hospital for emotionally disturbed adolescents I directed. There was a similar concern about Mary Pipher's work. There were no girls of color in her study, and these girls were all in therapy. She was making generalizations about all adolescent girls based on her observations of girls she saw in therapy, some with very serious problems. Their works were thought-provoking, but had the tendency to make general assumptions about adolescent behavior based on studies with clinical populations, and without considering the implications of race, class, and culture.

It is important for us as clinicians working with adolescents to recognize the types of theories that inform our views about the development of gender identity and how they influence our practice. Where do we stand on the debate about nature versus nurture? Do we believe that adolescent girls are losing their voice and are on the verge of losing their sense of self because they are not equipped to compete in a society where males dominate? What do we think about the belief that boys need men to teach them how to be men and that mothers have to let go? I agree with the idea that "It is not nurture versus

nature. It is both. We are all the product of many interacting forces, including our genes, our personalities, our environment, and chance" (Barrett & Rivers, 2004, p. 12.) This view, I believe has much to offer clinicians working with adolescents and their families because it provides a framework for helping them think about themselves in more liberating ways, rather than trying to fit into the stereotypical straitjackets of what it means to be male or female in our society.

Gender Identity: A Social and Cultural Construct

Most of us have grown up in a social context where as children we learned that there were different sets of expectations for males and females. In this country the evolution of separate spheres for males and females can be traced back to the mid-1800s (Kimmel, 1996). To become "real men" in the new land, boys had to gain independence from the family as soon as possible. Girls, on the other hand, lost their independence once they matured and married. Being in control was essential for men to compete and be successful, and the presence of women in the workplace threatened that goal. Women became increasingly bound to the home, and their worth was largely measured by their ability to raise children and by their domestic talents. These patterns are intrinsic in patriarchal societies and are not unique to the United States. By observing the adults in their lives and through exposure to the popular culture promoted by television and the media, children learn that men have more power and privilege than women. Unless children live with adults whose behavior challenges these beliefs, by adolescence they have incorporated into their identities the stereotypes about gender that our culture promotes (Mann, 1996).

When women try to break out and be like one of the guys, they often find themselves in a bind since in this culture "the attributes of femininity such a kindness, patience, and nurturance, are antithetical to the definition of 'success' in the public sphere— competency, assertiveness, ambition. For women it means that when they are seen as competent and assertive, they are not seen as feminine, and when they are seen as kind, and caring they are not seen as competent" (Kimmel, 2008, p. 251). Although they might want to be smart and pretty, and feminine and successful, the pressure of having to conform to two different and opposing sets of standards simultaneously can be extremely oppressive, especially because complaining in the patriarchal society means failure.

For boys fitting into the expectations of patriarchal masculinity means that they have to reject everything feminine, mainly giving up their freedom to express feelings. There is increased pressure for boys to show their masculinity, especially during late adolescence as they move toward early adulthood and into the stage that Kimmel (2008) describes as *Guyland*. He speaks about a code of behavior that is expected from young men in a culture that normalizes a lack of connection with their emotions and a restrictive expression of feeling. Distance from parents, especially from mothers, is encouraged as part of their becoming independent. Many parents, particularly mothers, react to this change in the relationship by feeling rejected and pulling away from their sons. One of the detriments of this shift is that the more boys become disconnected from their feelings, the less opportunity they have to benefit from having intimate relationships that can enrich their lives. This emotional disconnection "denies them powerful inner resources for coping with stress, fear, and loss" (Johnson, 1997, p. 193). They are at greater risk for acting-out behavior such as drinking and drugs, when they don't feel free to talk about problems and conflicts (Dooley, & Fedele, 2001).

For boys, acknowledging their emotions and expressing their feelings puts into question their masculinity, and threatens their privileges as men. "Men cannot both take their place as the dominant gender and honor and develop those aspects of themselves most associated with women and with their childhood connection to women" (Johnson, 1997, p. 193). Giving up the sense of entitlement that being male engenders is difficult even for men who in other situations in their lives feel powerless. For more information regarding this see Chapter 4 on Men.

A discussion about developing a gender identity during adolescence cannot be complete without considering the influence of race, class, and ethnicity.

Developing Racial and Ethnic Identity

For African Americans, Latinos, Asians, and other adolescents of color, forming an identity goes beyond values and beliefs about gender, since they have to first cope with how society defines them, marginalizes, and oppresses them. For African Americans, forming a positive identity as a Black male or Black female in a racist society in which being Black has been demeaned for centuries poses a grave challenge for adolescents and their parents. (Hardy & Laszloffy, 2005; Boyd-Franklin & Franklin, 2000). Viewing blackness as positively valued and desired is necessary for Black adolescents to form a positive identity. Living among Whites and facing daily situations based on skin color that is hurtful, humiliating, and devaluing at school and in the street is never an easy experience. The darker their skin, the more difficult it is. Although there has been an increased visibility of African Americans in the popular culture, even more so since the election of Barak Obama as president the insidious effects of racism on the everyday lives of Blacks in this country hasn't gone away.

For African American parents the fears about the welfare and future of their children go well beyond worrying that their adolescents won't have good judgment and will put themselves in dangerous situations by abusing substances or having unprotected sex, or that predators will abuse them. They have to worry about the effects that racism will have on them, especially when they are poor and have little access to resources. There is good reason to worry if we consider that the jobless rate of Black teenagers age 16 to 19 increased from 30.9 percent to 41.3 percent between October., 2008 and October, 2009 (U.S. Dept. of Labor, 2009.) They fear especially for their sons' safety and lives, knowing that authorities are more quick to arrest them for minor offenses, book and remand them for trials, and give them harsh dispositions (U.S. Census Bureau,

2006–2008, American Community Survey). Living in neighborhoods where drugs and crime are rampant, these adolescents are constantly at risk of being pulled into the world of illegal activity and by the alluring experience of feeling powerful that making fast money can bring. Carrying weapons for self-defense is not uncommon for adolescents in these situations. In fact, homicide is now the leading cause of death for African Americans of both genders between the ages of 15 and 44 (National Vital Statistics, 2009). Considering these statistics it is no wonder many African American parents fear that their sons will be killed, and young men don't have the expectation to live a long, prosperous life.

Pregnancy is usually high on parents' worry list for their adolescent daughters regardless of race or ethnicity. Although the rate of teen pregnancy has gone down for African American teens in the past 14 years, as a group Black girls are still considered at risk (National Vital Statistics, 2009). AIDS is the fourth leading cause of death in African American females aged 15 to 24 (Heron, 2007). We can say that being Black and female means having two strikes against you. Not only are they oppressed because they are female, but also because they are Black.

Forming a positive ethnic identity is crucial for all adolescents, and even more so when they belong to groups that are marginalized in the dominant culture. A positive cultural identity is necessary to feel whole, to belong, to have a feeling of home place (McGoldrick & Hardy, 2008; McGoldrick, Giordano, Garcia Preto, 2006; Burton, Lawson, and Clark, 1996). Many adolescents in this country live in two worlds. They live with their families in communities that are ethnic enclaves where immigrants settle to support each other or at least feel connected to their motherlands. They may eat different food, listen to different music, and dress and behave according to their culture's expectations. They also have to negotiate living in a dominant culture that is patriarchal and racist, where they are seen as, and feel, different and marginal. They often feel powerless in the larger society, isolated, uncomfortable, and afraid that they will not be accepted for who they are.

When cultural differences interfere with their increased need to fit in with peers (highest during adolescence) some adolescents reject their own culture and disconnect from their families. The schism between societal expectations and what they are able to achieve puts these youths at high risk for depression, anxiety, physical problems, rage, and a host of other problems, (see Chapter 6). Latina adolescents, for instance, have the highest percentage of teen pregnancy in this country (National Vital Statistics, 2009), as well as an alarming rate of attempted suicide (Zayas & Pilat, 2008).

Developing a positive racial and ethnic identity is paramount for the well-being of adolescents and is a major task for families at this stage of the life cycle. However, this is no easy task, and it is particularly difficult when parents and families are themselves struggling to make it and are feeling oppressed by the social institutions that affect their lives. Finding legacies of hope and of spiritual strength that have been passed down by their ancestors through history is crucial for the survival of many groups. It is important that we as family therapists help adolescents and their families have conversations about their histories, stories of immigration, and people who have overcome the forces of oppression by resisting the pull to lose themselves and their purpose. Staying connected with their dreams and not compromising their priorities require extreme determination (see chapter 9x-ref).

Physical Changes

Our little kids begin to turn into adult-looking people. Their features change as their faces become more elongated, and their legs and arms dangle from a trunk that is too small to carry them, especially during early adolescence. Parents are constantly buying new clothes and shoes with mixed feelings of excitement and sadness as they try to keep up with the growth spurts.

The physical growth makes adolescents eat more and sleep longer. Following the growth spurt, their chests expand, their trunks lengthen, and their voices deepen; additionally, shoulders develop in boys and hips in girls. They also seem to have spurts of physical energy, followed by periods of lethargy. Recently there has been new research showing that there are changes in their brain that explain some of the erratic behavior and poor judgment that characterizes many adolescents and that exasperates adults (Yurgelun-Todd & Killgore, 2006). These changes lead to conflicts between parents and adolescents in most families. Parents become nags in the eyes of their children, and children become inconsiderate, lazy, and disobedient in the eyes of parents.

Outside the home, adolescents have to deal with the pressures of fitting into a peer group. These pressures are, for the most part, gender specific. For example, although the emphasis on physical attractiveness is strong for both boys and girls, the pressure to be beautiful is enormous for girls. For boys, being physically strong and athletic has more importance. Although being slight in weight and short in stature may cause boys to feel insecurities, girls who don't fit the social ideal of beauty seem to be at greater risk. One reason is that in our culture being beautiful also has negative connotations, as demonstrated by the jokes and caricatures about the "dumb blonde," creating a dilemma for girls. Another is that physical attractiveness means being thin; at an age when their bodies are changing and getting softer and fuller, girls may begin to see themselves as fat.

For many girls, dieting becomes a way to control weight. Eating disorders such as anorexia nervosa, bulimia, and compulsive eating frequently appear in adolescence, are more common in females, and affect all socioeconomic levels and all races. The wish to be thin for women in this culture starts as early as when they are 9 or 10. Based on a NIMH (2009a) report, up to 10 million females and 1 million males struggle with eating disorders such as anorexia and bulimia. More than 90 percent of those who have eating disorders are women between the ages of 12 and 25. Between 1 and 5 percent of adolescent women meet the criteria for an eating disorder diagnosis. Only about 5 to 15 percent of individuals diagnosed with anorexia or bulimia are male. The high rate of suicide in this population is cause for families with adolescents and for clinicians working with them to worry. Females with anorexia nervosa have a higher suicide rate than those with any other mental health disorder and the general population (Hudson, Hiripi, Pope, & Kessler, 2007),

up to 60 times higher according to one study (Keel, Dorer, Eddy, & Franko, 2003). Individuals with anorexia are up to 10 times more likely to die because of their illness (Hudson, Hiripi, Pope, & Kessler, 2007).

As clinicians we often think that eating disorders are behavioral manifestations of complex family dysfunction or believe that out-of-control eating is associated with out-of-control emotions. But, to understand this behavior we must also look at how our popular culture as represented by the media contributes to the problem by setting dangerous standards of beauty and thinness to which girls aspire. Some of these standards for thinness are very close to the standards for anorexia (Mann, 1996). An important point here is that although the detection of eating disorders in African Americans and Latinos seems to be increasing, the group that seems to be more affected by this problem continues to be White middle- and upper-class girls.

Sexual Changes and Sexual Orientation

The trend toward earlier sexual maturation, especially for girls, seems to be continuing in the United States. The normal age range for puberty in girls is 9 to 16, and 13 to 15 for boys, with recent studies showing that African American girls mature earlier as a group than White girls (Herman-Giddens, Slora, & Wasserman, 2007). For girls, this is usually marked by menarche, and for boys by the experience of ejaculation. Both experience sexual feelings coming to the surface, which is unavoidable because of the biological changes their bodies undergo, and most also feel somewhat awkward and self-conscious about their sexually maturing bodies. This rapid growth elicits reactions of confusion both in them and in their parents.

For boys and girls whose gender identity is nonconforming according to patriarchal standards, and who are conflicted about their sexual orientation, the onset of puberty can exacerbate this sense of awkwardness. However, the changes that have taken place during the past decade in the way GLBT people and the their lives are portrayed in society have made it possible for adolescents to feel freer about coming out to themselves, their peers, and their parents earlier. That's not to say that gay teenagers don't still suffer harassment at school or rejection at home. Parents' reactions vary depending on their own constructions of gender and sexual identity and on their homophobia. Actually, the more gay youth are perceived as nonconforming to adolescent gender norms the more at risk they are for harassment and physical abuse. Girls who come out as bisexual but are still considered "feminine" seem to be less prone to harassment, as are some gay boys, who come out but are still considered "masculine."

Overall, the increasingly accurate and positive portrayals of gays and lesbians in popular culture have lessened the fears, for adolescents and their families, that they will never find happiness. The ability to communicate online has broken through the isolation that had been so detrimental to GLBT youth and has allowed gay teenagers to find information to refute what their families or churches sometimes still tell them. In *"The New Gay Teenager"* Savin-Williams (2005) writes that being young and gay is no longer an automatic prescription for a traumatic childhood. He also says that this is the first generation of gay kids who have the great joy of being able to argue with their parents about dating, just like their straight peers do.

Although there seems to be more openness about gender variance and sexual orientation, heterosexual parents, teachers, and counselors are likely to question adolescents about the validity of their feelings when they come out. The younger they are the more we ask questions about their same-sex attractions in ways that we would never question straight youth when they talk about attractions to the opposite sex. Most of us working with adolescents have been trained to caution youth who identify as GLB that sexual identity is a fluid process and that they should wait until they are older to determine how they really feel and what they want to do about it. We also coach parents to not be too reactive and to wait to see what happens as their children mature. The down side of this approach is that we deny their feelings and miss opportunities for connection and to encourage healthy sexual behavior.

Lack of support at home, or from other adults in their community, puts GLBT youth at greater risk and is a predictor for emerging emotional problems. In these cases, there is a high risk of suicide. Generally, gay and lesbian adolescents are more likely to disclose to mothers, fearing more the reaction from fathers. Sometimes the reaction at home is dangerous and violent, yet most LGBT adolescents want their parents to know. However, for many, like Horace, a 16-year-old White male of German ancestry, the situation at school and home can lead to suicidal behavior. In therapy he talked about the loneliness and fear that he experienced.

My attraction to men is not something I chose. I tried for the longest time to push it out of my mind and do all the things that boys are supposed to do, but I can't change myself. Sometimes I get scared, especially when I hear about all the gay men who are dying of AIDS. I feel bad for my parents. They love me but don't understand why this is happening and are ashamed of me. They also fear for my life. No one else knows in the family, and I hate pretending in front of my grandparents. At school I'm constantly on the lookout, worried that they'll find me out and lynch me. I'd be better off dead. I don't see another way out.

Lesbian, gay, bisexual, transgender and questioning youth are up to four times more likely to attempt suicide than their heterosexual peers, according to the Massachusetts 2006 Youth Risk Survey. A 2009 study, *"Family Rejection as a Predictor of Negative Health Outcomes,"* led by Dr. Caitlin Ryan and conducted as part of the Family Acceptance Project at San Francisco State University, shows that adolescents who were rejected by their families for being LGBT were eight times more likely to report having attempted suicide. One of the major findings of Ryan's research is that Latino males reported the highest number of negative family reactions to their sexual orientation in adolescence. Such a response could take the form of religious beliefs that being gay is sinful or a belief that their child's homosexuality is a medical or psychological condition that can be cured. However,

Savin-Williams (2005) and LaSala (in press) both seem to point out that most families of LGBT adolescents eventually move toward acceptance after a period of anxiety and sometimes rejection. For more discussion about the development of a GLBT identity during adolescence, please refer to Chapter 8 in this book.

Regardless of their children's gender variance or sexual orientation parents worry when their adolescents begin to demand more freedom, and they no longer can supervise and protect them in the same way as when they were younger. There are so many alarming news items about teen violence, including gang fights, shootings, rapes, gay bashings, and suicide, that, as said earlier, parents have good reasons to worry. In the United States teen violence, and particularly suicide, are among the highest causes of death for teenagers (CDC, 2008; NIMH, 2009?). The use of alcohol and drugs is more often than not linked to risky behaviors. Of additional concern is the high percentage of teen pregnancy in this country; although it has gone down somewhat in the past few years, there has been an increase for African Americans and Latinas, who also tend to keep their babies. Adolescents are having sex younger, and many are not using protection, which puts them at risk for sexual transmitted diseases, such as AIDS.

Not only are parents less able to supervise and protect their adolescents when they are out of the house, but the risks to which they are exposed at home "online," which has become so much a part of their world, are sometimes even more alarming. As Ron Taffel (2005) suggests "online" they can try on different personas and experiment with establishing relationships without experiencing the same type of pressure caused by being in the same physical space. Where parents used to at least hear some of the conversations their children were having on the phone, now with texting and online conversations they are more in the dark than ever about their children's lives. For some parents becoming their children's "friend" on Facebook is a way of taking a peek into their world.

Emotional Changes

As adolescents mature emotionally, they feel compelled to turn away from their childish ways and move toward independence. Implicit in this task is the need to transform the relationship with their parents. This is complicated because along with wanting to venture out and become more independent, there is also a part of them that pulls toward wanting parents to take care of them. Adolescents want the nurturance without the fuss (Wolf, 2002).

It is not that adolescents want to break the emotional bond with their parents, but rather they want a different balance in the relationship. As with sexual changes, this is a process that cannot be avoided. It is difficult for parents who are often shocked and hurt by the intense moods and unpredictable behavior that their teens expect them to validate. The more controlled teens feel by their parents, the more turbulent this process will be. The less accepted they feel by parents the more important validation from peers becomes. For a period of time peers become a "second family," (Taffel, 2005) a community in which adolescents can begin to act mature and responsible, while at home they want to be left alone with no demands and no expectations.

Changes in the Family Structure

The adolescent's demands for greater independence tend to precipitate structural shifts and renegotiation of roles in families involving at least three generations of relatives. It is not uncommon for parents and grandparents to redefine their relationships during this period, as well as for spouses to renegotiate their marriage and siblings to question their position in the family. Because these demands are so strong, they also serve as catalysts for reactivating unresolved conflicts between parents and grandparents or between the parents themselves and to set triangles in motion. For instance, efforts to resolve conflicts between adolescents and parents often repeat earlier patterns of relating in the parents' families of origin. Parents who have made a conscious effort to raise their children differently by avoiding the same "mistakes" their parents made often have a particularly rude awakening. When their children reach adolescence, they are often surprised to observe similarities in personality between their children and their own parents. Parents in this situation may react with extreme confusion, anger, or resentment or may themselves get in touch with similar needs and, in turn, make the same requests of their own parents or of each other.

Families during this period are also responding and adjusting to the new demands of other family members, who themselves are entering new stages in the life cycle. For example, most parents with adolescents in the dominant culture are at midlife. Their focus is on major tasks such as reevaluating their marriage and careers. The marriage emerging from the heavy caretaking responsibilities of young children may be threatened as parents review personal satisfaction in light of the militant idealism of their adolescent children. For many women, this may actually be the first opportunity to work outside the home without the restrictions they faced when the children were young. For many men this is a time when they might be facing much anxiety about being stuck in a dead end at work or losing a job.

The normal stress and tension posed to the family by an adolescent are exacerbated when the parents experience acute personal dissatisfaction and feel compelled to make changes in their lives. For instance, divorce or coming out as LGBT can increase the potential for severe emotional disturbance in the family. At the same time grandparents may be facing retirement and possible moves, illness, and death. These stressful events call for a renegotiation of relationships, and parents may be called upon to be caretakers of their own parents or to assist them in integrating the losses of old age. What often forms is a field of conflicting demands, in which the stress seems to be transmitted both up and down the generations. For example, if there is conflict between parents and grandparents, it may have a negative effect on the marital relationship that filters down into the relationship between the parents and the adolescent. Or the conflict may travel in the opposite direction. A conflict between the parents and adolescent may affect the marital relationship, which ultimately affects the relationship between the parents and grandparents. And, if there is an untimely death, or serious illness of a parent or child, the family may not be able to offer the validation and connection the adolescent needs to make a safe journey into adulthood.

These patterns may differ depending on factors such as race, class, and ethnicity. For instance, Burton et al. (1996) conducted a study of poor inner-city African American teens and found that in many of the families, there was a narrow age difference between the generations, which tended to blur developmental boundaries and roles of family members. The blurring of intergenerational boundaries in these age-condensed families affected the authority that parents had over children as well as the adolescents' perceptions of appropriate behavior. Consider, for example, a family where the

child generation included both a young mother (age 15) and her child (age one), a young-adult generation, which is comprised of a 29-year-old grandmother, and a middle-age generation, which includes a 43-year-old great-grandmother.

The adolescent mother, as a function of giving birth, is launched into the young-adult role status; however, she remains legally and developmentally a member of the child generation. Similarly, the young-adult female has moved to the status of grandmother, a stage typically embodied by middle-aged or older women. Further, the middle-aged woman has been propelled to the status of great-grandmother, a role usually occupied by women in their later years. (Burton et al., 1996, p. 406)

This example illustrates the point that as a result of the closeness in generations, chronological and developmental challenges often become inconsistent with generational roles. The result may be that parents and children behave more like siblings, making it difficult for parents to discipline their children. Families may also have difficulty identifying adolescence as a specific life stage.

There are also remarkable differences in the rituals that ethnic groups use to handle adolescence. For instance, Anglo Americans (McGil, & Pierce, 2005) do not strive to keep their children close to home, as do Italians, Jews, and Latinos. Historically they have promoted early separation of adolescents and the development of an individualistic, self-defined, adult identity. Sometimes as McGill and Pearce (2005) observe, "if contemporary parents try to promote independence by withdrawing physical, financial, or emotional support too soon, the Anglo American adolescent will probably feel abandoned. The result may be a kind of false adulthood with premature identity foreclosure" (p. 526).

In contrast, Latinos tend to prolong adolescence by keeping very close boundaries around the family. The cultural patterns of mutual obligation for caretaking in Latino families can offer support and connection at home, but the oppression they experience outside in the dominant culture poses challenges that the family may not be equipped to handle. If adolescents break out and become more "Americanized" parents may try to tighten the boundaries, or sometimes they give up angrily. Latina adolescents, as stated earlier in this chapter, have the highest percentage of attempted suicides of any other group of adolescents in the United States. According to Luis Zayas and Pilat (2008), a finding in a 10-year study with Latina adolescents who have attempted suicide, is that they often feel lonely, disconnected from their parents, and that they don't fit in. Most of their parents, including many single mothers, are themselves struggling with similar issues, having to work very hard to support the family. The girls feel trapped, and their parents feel desperate.

Renegotiating rules and limits is key during this stage of development for most families. "You can't treat me like a baby anymore" may be said in the middle of a "childish tantrum," but the message must be heard and taken seriously. Parents must be ready to let go and yet stay connected to guide and protect them when necessary. This is much easier said than done. It is true that, adolescents are not babies or little children, but as discussed earlier in this chapter, neither are they adults. Even when they fulfill adult roles during early adolescence, such as having children themselves or taking care of ill parents, their brains have not matured sufficiently for them to make adult decisions. The family must be strong and yet be able to make its boundaries more flexible. This is usually easier with each successive child but is particularly difficult when parents are unable to support each other because they differ and argue about values and rules, whether they are together, separated, or divorced. The pressure is worse if they don't have the support of extended family or a supportive community.

Therapeutic Interventions

Fifteen years ago, The Carnegie Council on Adolescent Development (1995), a 10-year national study of adolescence, reported that rates of teen drug and alcohol use, unprotected sexual activity, violent victimization, delinquency, eating disorders, and depression were then sufficiently widespread that nearly half of American adolescents were at high or moderate risk of seriously damaging their life chances. This was true of adolescents across all demographic lines. Today some of those adolescents are almost 30 years old and might even be parents of young teenagers themselves. I'm sure they would agree with parents and professionals working with adolescents that the alarm about the dangerous consequences of risky behavior has not lessened. Instead, with the advent of the Internet and all the opportunities it offers to connect with peers from all over the world, the potential for engaging in dangerous behavior has escalated exponentially. Without very close parental supervision, which is difficult or impossible for most parents to provide, they can easily be exposed to exploitation.

Most parents bring their adolescents into therapy when they have reached a high point of desperation about not being able to control their child's behavior. Some are mandated by the court or referred by schools, hospitals, residential facilities, or rehabilitation programs. Many of the parents feel angry and resentful or defeated and frightened by their children's behavior. Often they are overworked, overcommitted, and tired, with few resources and little outside support. Many are single parents, mothers in most cases (Sandmaier, 1996). They tend to feel inadequate, see their families as dysfunctional, and in response to their children's rebellion, they distance themselves emotionally. Viewing these families as dysfunctional is also a widespread tendency among mental health professionals that limits our ability to intervene from a perspective that considers their strengths and takes into account how the social and cultural context in which they live might be affecting their situation.

Helping parents stay connected with their adolescents is probably the most important clinical intervention we can make with families at this stage of the life cycle. Living in a society where the dominant culture reinforces the idea that to be independent one must separate from parents doesn't make the work easy. Yet, we all need encouragement to hang in there, listen differently, confront our own limits, and take the necessary measures to earn our child's trust (Taffel, 2005). Recent studies find that teenagers who feel close to their families were the least likely to engage in any of the risky behaviors that were studied, which included smoking marijuana or cigarettes, drinking, and having sex and that high expectations from parents for their teenagers' school performance were nearly as important (Gilbert, 1997). In my clinical practice, I am constantly trying to maintain a balance that respects the parents' responsibility to protect adolescents, yet encourages the adolescents' need for independence.

Renegotiating Relationships Between Parents and Adolescents

What also happens as parents and adolescents try to redefine relationships is that parents often experience a resurfacing of emotions related to unresolved issues with their own parents. In therapy, paying attention to the triangles that operated in the parents' families of origin and coaching them to do some work with their own parents can be very helpful in furthering their ability to listen and feel less reactive to their children's behavior. Such was the case with Clara and her mother:

Clara, 15, lived with her 39-year-old mother, Mrs. Callahan, her 12-year-old sister, Sonia, and her mother's paternal aunt. Her parents had been divorced since she was 10. Her mother was Puerto Rican, and her father was Irish. He was remarried to an Asian woman. Mrs. Callahan had remained unmarried. She was a professional woman who kept herself isolated from peers and focused her energy on being a good mother. Clara, who had always been very

close to her mother, had begun to pull away, stay out late, and show interest in boys. Mrs. Callahan, afraid of the dangers in the street and worried that Clara would become pregnant, restricted her outings. The more Clara challenged the limits, the stricter her mother became. Clara threatened to run away and kill herself. After she spoke to a teacher at school, the referral for therapy was made.

Mrs. Callahan was angry with Clara and unwilling to listen to her daughter's criticisms. She felt rejected by her daughter, for whom she had sacrificed so much. Clara felt bad about hurting her mother but was angry at what she thought was her mother's unfairness. Supporting Mrs. C.'s intention to protect her daughter by validating the dangers that girls are exposed to in this society made it easier for the mother to listen to Clara's position. Inviting Clara's great-aunt, who lived with them, to the sessions clarified how Clara's adolescence had activated a triangle similar to one that had operated in the previous generation. The triangle, triggered by discipline issues, involved Clara, Mrs. C., and the great-aunt. Clara thought her great-aunt was too old-fashioned and resented her attempts to discipline. Both would complain to Mrs. C., who would try to mediate by explaining cultural differences but was confused about which values to keep and would end up feeling powerless. The aunt would react by moving in to support Mrs. C., and Clara would distance herself, feeling rejected by both.

During her adolescence, Mrs. C. had been involved in a triangle with her mother and this aunt, who was her father's youngest sister. The aunt would try to mediate between Mrs. C. and her mother when they had arguments but would usually end up defending her niece. The mother would then get angry and distance herself from Mrs. C., who in turn would feel rejected.

I was able to help shift the triangle by telling them that Clara needed support from both of them but primarily from her mother. I suggested that Clara was as confused as they by the different ways in which the two cultures dealt with adolescence.

Asking them to identify which Puerto Rican values were creating the greatest conflict at home led them to thinking about a compromise. They agreed that dating was the greatest source of conflict, since in Puerto Rico this practice has very different rules and connotations. Dating does not start until much later, and it is usually in the company of family or friends. I pointed out that for Clara to live in this culture and feel comfortable with her peers, they needed to adapt to some of the values of this culture. As a compromise, they agreed to let Clara go on double dates, but only with people they knew, and to negotiate a curfew with Clara's input.

To make additional changes in the relationship between Clara and her mother, work had to be done with Mrs. Callahan and her mother, who lived in Puerto Rico. Coaching Mrs. C. to share some of her conflicts with her mother through letters and on a visit to Puerto Rico and to ask her advice about disciplining Clara was a way to lessen the emotional distance between them. Mrs. C. became more accepting of her mother's limitations and began to appreciate the attention she gave. This helped her to listen more attentively to her daughter.

In retrospect, I could have further helped strengthen the connections between Clara, her mother, and great-aunt by exploring with them intergenerational values about gender role socialization and expression that may have been contributing to their problem by asking questions such as: How was your mother's gender role different from your grandmother's? Why do you think that grandmothers may be more permissive than mothers? How have expectations, freedoms, and obligations changed over time in your country of origin? How do you think immigration to this country has affected your expectations, freedoms, or obligations as women? How do the extended family, community, culture, and society create pressure to conform to certain rules for boys? for girls?

Another issue that this case raises is the considerable impact that the lack of extended family or other supports has on how families manage adolescence. Some ethnic groups, such as Puerto Ricans, rely heavily on extended family members to help with the discipline of adolescents and the clarification of boundaries. It is common for Puerto Rican parents to send a rebellious adolescent to live with an uncle or godparent who can be more objective about setting limits. This move also provides time for parents and adolescents to obtain enough emotional distance from each other to regain control and reestablish a more balanced relationship. Relying solely on the nuclear family to provide control, support, and guidance for adolescents can overload the circuits and escalate conflicts.

Strengthening the Parental Bond

Whether parents are living together or apart, it is critical that they agree on basic rules for keeping adolescents safe. Adolescents need nurturing, clear expectations, and appreciation as well as a feeling of belonging from both parents (Taffel, 2005). They benefit when parents recognize that their own personal dissatisfactions about work, marriage, or failed relationships with partners, family, or friends may be affecting their ability to connect with their children and guide them through this stage. When parents are at opposite ends, and engage in explosive fights with each other, or become silent enemies whether in the same house or in separate homes, the risk for adolescents to engage in dangerous behavior increases. It is also important for parents to resist the impulse to focus entirely on the adolescent's problems and to not pay attention to themselves and their own relationship (Carter & Peters, 1996). When parents disagree and one becomes involved in alliances with the children against the other, the problems presented by adolescents escalate. The case of 17-year-old Tom Murphy illustrates some of the shifts that may occur during adolescence when the child is in a triangle with parents who are in a struggle:

Tom no longer wanted to be an engineer, as his parents were planning for him, but had become interested in lighting and theater. His father disapproved vehemently of his interest, while his mother seemed to be more supportive. Although she agreed with her husband that Tom should go to college, she strongly disagreed with the way he approached their son. Afraid to cause arguments, he avoided conversations with his parents and refused to go places with them, especially with his mother, to whom he had been a constant companion. At school, he gave up, failing to do assignments that were required for graduation and dropping courses he did not want. His behavior alarmed the teachers enough to ask the psychologist to see him. When his parents were told, they reacted with fear and anger, confused by his behavior, which they experienced as a rejection of their values and efforts to give him a good future.

In therapy, it became clear that Tom was caught in a classic triangle, trying to please his parents and feeling responsible for their arguments. Marital problems and arguments in this family had gone on for years. Mrs. Murphy was very dissatisfied with the marital relationship and claimed that Tom, their only child, was the only reason she stayed in it. Mr. Murphy was resentful and tried to minimize the problems, claiming that she and Tom were against him. Mr. Murphy was also involved in a midlife reevaluation of his own work life, which meant coming to terms with disappointments and letting go of unfulfilled dreams. Overwhelmed by conflicts in their marriage and their own midlife struggles, Mr. and Mrs. Murphy had been unable to be objective and supportive of Tom's moves toward independence. Instead they experienced his behavior as Tom's collusive alliance with one parent against the other. His move toward independence represented a threat to the system, especially to the parent's relationship.

The initial focus in therapy was to help the family make decisions about handling the present problem. Mr. and Mrs. Murphy were asked to take a break from making plans for Tom's future, to back off and let him take responsibility for negotiating at school. Instead, they were to make a plan clarifying their expectations of Tom if he did not go to college. Working on this task strengthened their bond as parents and helped Tom to gain confidence about his own choices. As they reviewed their own adolescence and patterns of relationships in their families of origin, they became more objective about each other and were able to make connections between the past and present. Asking them to talk about their plans for the future as a couple enabled them to focus on their relationship and begin to face their problems directly. Tom began to make more responsible decisions about his future.

Building Community

"It takes a village to raise a child" may sound trite, but it is a concept that has deep meaning for any parent who experiences the loneliness and shame of raising adolescents who are troubled. I sit in my office with parents and adolescents and feel their pain as they tell me their stories, sharing their fear as they worry about their children's futures. I worry about my children and grandchildren and pray that the world will heal itself. I don't want them exposed to racism, sexism, violence, and apathy, and yet they are. I see their smiles and know that they have dreams and feel hopeful. I want to extend my heart and give them hope, confidence, strength, and love. In my practice of therapy these have become my most powerful tools.

There is no reason for blame; it accomplishes nothing. It does not heal adolescents or parents. Making connections with other families, other adults, and other adolescents and opening our minds and hearts to others who are also struggling are healing acts. What I can do in my office is limited. I can help them look beyond themselves, at the pressures that affect their lives—our lives. We are in it together. Their children are also mine. I can help parents think about protecting their children yet be aware of the limits that bound us. I can encourage mothers to defy society by not buying into the belief that boys need to separate from mothers to become "real men." I have become much softer with my son, letting him know that I love him and think that he is a sensitive, caring, and funny young man. I encourage fathers to look inside and outside and get in touch with how sexism limits and isolates them. I try to keep the real self in my daughter alive and look for it in every adolescent girl I meet. Sometimes it is difficult to look beyond the pain I see in their eyes as they tell me stories of sexual abuse, violence, addictions, and self-mutilation and to consider what there is that is positive in their lives to help them feel strong. I have learned from them that sometimes their only salvation lies in their spiritual beliefs or in their connections to others.

Tanya, a 14-year-old African American who came in to therapy after reporting at school that her mother's boyfriend had tried to rape her found support and strength in her church. Her mother was angry with her for reporting the boyfriend and blamed Tanya for seducing him. Tanya felt rejected and hurt but knew that she was not responsible for his behavior. She wanted her mother to believe her but had given up hope. In the church, she had found other adults who believed her and encouraged her to ask God's help to forgive her mother. I worked with her mother to help her see her daughter as a 14-year-old girl who did the right thing by reporting an adult man who abused her. I wanted her to feel angry at him and protective of her daughter; instead, she was angry about losing him. I encouraged her to go to church with Tanya, hoping that she would hear God's message and make connections with the adults who supported her daughter. She was not ready, and I had to accept it. Tanya had learned through her faith that there is strength in forgiving, and I was reminded of my limitations and felt grateful to the 14-year-old girl who was teaching me a lesson.

Conclusion

Establishing support networks with other professionals and within systems that may be part of the community, such as schools, churches, and legal authorities, is crucial. Connecting parents with teachers at schools and with other parents is an essential type of intervention that works toward strengthening natural support systems and lessening the isolation that families experience in our present-day communities. Interventions that take into account the sociopolitical context in which we live, and the effect on families with adolescents, are critical.

Chapter 16

Families at Midlife: Launching Children and Moving On

Nydia Garcia Preto & Lynn Blacker

Overview

As the last of the baby boomers turn 40, those who are launching children are doing so at a time when changes in the global economy—high unemployment and rising health costs, among many other factors—limit the choices that adults can make about their own futures and the help they can offer their children. They themselves are very different from the images we conjure up when thinking about baby boomers. This last group of children, born between 1946 and 1964, are a diverse group of people whose experiences differ not only from those of previous generations, but also from each other. They are no longer the suburban White kids who grew up watching "Mickey Mouse" or "American Bandstand," who protested the Vietnam War and were part of the "sexual revolution." Instead, they are a racially and culturally diverse group, many of whom came here as children from Asia, Latin America, and other countries. They grew up during the Reagan years and experienced economic and social changes that have tended to move this country toward a more conservative political climate, in addition to fighting two wars.

That this generation of baby boomers is not a homogenous group was supported by the findings of a study Hughes and O'Rand (2004) conducted at Duke University based on data from the 2000 census. They found a striking increase in ethnic minorities, especially Asians and Latino/as, and of more significance they found that greater diversity has not led to equality. Instead, the study showed that although baby boomers are the first generation after the Civil Rights era, differences in incomes continue to be quite entrenched according to race, ethnicity, and country of origin. For example, Blacks in the baby boomer generation are no better off relative to Whites than their parents and grandparents. Educa-

tional levels are also unequal among the baby boomers, even though this cohort is considered to be the best-educated generation in history. In reality, many boomers live in poverty, and at midlife they have the highest wage inequality of any recent generation. This inequality continues into old age and has great implications for how families negotiate transitions in the life cycle. Its effect is especially felt and reflected in the way adults and children negotiate necessary economic and emotional changes in their relationships during the launching stage of the family life cycle.

Launching

In the United States, launching is defined as that phase in the life cycle of families when parents or guardians help their late adolescents move on in life. The dominant culture views this stage as a time when most adults going through this process are themselves at midlife, making decisions about their own futures and looking forward to a less-pressured life once their children become independent and leave home. However, as the previous study shows, this is not true for all families. Race, social class, culture, gender, religious beliefs, sexual orientation, and physical and mental disabilities influence the choices young people make, as well as how parents or adults guide and support them while redefining their own lives. This is especially true in poor, marginalized groups where, for example, parents may be looking forward to their adolescents' going to work and contributing to the household, instead of urging them to leave home and live independently.

While it is true that more than half of late adolescents are still leaving home to go to college or other professional schools, many remain at home, and more return home from college and have difficulty making enough money to live in their own home (Arnett, 2004; Kimmel, 2008). There also seems to be an increase in children moving back after marriage with their own new families after losing jobs and losing their homes. What used to be more common in working-class and poor families is now true for many middle- and upper-class families. In particular, young people from the dominant culture are taking longer after adolescence, whether by pursuing higher education or working to explore identities and possibilities, before making the traditional commitments that have marked adulthood.

Cultural and ethnic identification are important considerations for understanding the way families approach the tasks of this stage. For example, in Anglo American or Polish American families, children are expected to establish their independence with less parental assistance or involvement than in Italian or Brazilian families. African American, Asian, and Latino families tend to have greater acceptance of adult children continuing to reside in the home than German families do. A study by Arnett and Galambos (2003) showed that there are also differences between young people in how they define reaching adulthood depending on whether they are members of the dominant culture or an ethnic minority. For instance, they found that youth from ethnic minorities were more likely than Whites to view criteria for adulthood that reflect obligations to others such as, "becoming capable of supporting a family financially, keeping a family physically safe, and caring for children" (p. 71). However, although these expectations fit with these groups' cultural values, the results were not gender specific. Both males and females felt that assuming these obligations was necessary for reaching adulthood. Many also seemed to have a bicultural conception of the transition to adulthood combining the individualistic transitions of the majority culture with a greater emphasis on obligations toward others drawn from the values of their ethnic minority cultures. However, regardless of differences, what most families expect at this stage of life is for the younger generation to move on and assume more responsibility for their own lives. Assessment of these factors and differences is crucial when helping families negotiate impasses at this stage of life.

Our assessment of an overly controlling, anxious parent having difficulty letting a child grow, or of an anxious, dependent, and insecure young person afraid to leave home may change as we consider their social and cultural context. Of course, we clinicians need to pay attention to how our own context and trajectory in life inform our clinical views and interventions. Most important to understand is that most men and women launching children are themselves at midlife, and are dealing with other tasks of that stage. Other midlife tasks include a significant realignment of family roles, such as: becoming a couple again, for parents who are still married or in committed relationships; developing adult-to-adult relationships with children; accepting new family members through marriage and birth; and resolving issues with, providing care for, and finally burying their parents. This is also a time to reassess work choices; nurture friendships; and for some, to have the opportunity to "come out" and give expression to aspects of their gender or sexual identity that they had felt forced to keep secret at earlier stages of life.

A key impetus for this reassessment is the realization that time is running out. As Bernice Neugarten (1968) notes, individuals at midlife begin to measure their position in the life cycle in terms of time left to live rather than time since birth. With this new perspective, priorities change. People may choose to no longer put aspirations and dreams on hold. The loss of some hopes and plans may also need to be mourned. As clinicians, we cannot lose sight of those for whom their social location limits their possibilities. However, as will be seen throughout this chapter, the majority of men and women tend to experience midlife not as an end, but as a time of great potential. This chapter will concentrate on men and women at midlife with a particular focus on the task of launching children as a catalyst for change in the family system.

Middle Age: The Longest Life Cycle Stage

Until recent studies proclaimed emerging adulthood a new life stage (Arnett, 2004), "middle age" was the most recently identified phase of the life cycle. It was first described in 1978 by Levinson (Dowling, 1996). The newness of the construct reflected the fact that we are living longer; therefore, life cycle tasks have a new normative timetable. In 1900, when people died by age 49 (Pogrebin, 1996), life cycle tasks were compressed. Launching and marrying off children, burying parents, becoming grandparents, and losing partners commonly occurred concurrently in 1 decade. But now, this phase may last 20 years or more and is currently the longest phase in the life cycle. Midlife is commonly defined as spanning the ages of roughly 45 to 65, encompassing the period from launching the first child to retirement. Because of better health and increasing longevity for a majority of the population, it may get expanded even more in the future. Of course, a significant number of men and women are beginning new or second families at midlife rather than launching them, and many are not having children either by choice or other circumstances. For more information about the varied life style options available to men and women at midlife, the effects of poverty, illness, and immigration, see related chapters in this book.

Although men and women can be single, never married, in committed relationships, divorced and single, remarried, widowed or separated, the associations of midlife with "midlife crisis" or with the "empty nest syndrome" are almost taken for granted in our culture. All we need to do is look up information about midlife on the Internet and "midlife crisis" pops up immediately. The popular view of midlife has been characterized by negative stereotypes and misconceptions. However, rather than worrying about declining health, diminished energy, and feeling generally demoralized about the idea of impending mortality, most people at this stage are in excellent health, feel young and vigorous, and are excited by the many choices they have before them (Bergquist et al., 1993). Nevertheless, this rosy picture applies mainly to the middle and upper socioeconomic classes (Gallagher, 1993; Mitchell & Helson, 1990.) For the less economically secure, the outlook is very different. The lower socioeconomic classes can anticipate decreasing job opportunities, especially with the massive downsizings and closings of industrial sites in the last decade and the increasingly technological work environment.

Working-class and poor women typically anticipate being both homemakers and employees throughout their adult lives, working in jobs that may not be particularly fulfilling (Bergquist et al., 1993.) Working-class men, who often depend on physical strength for their jobs, may be considered middle aged in their 30s, and with their poor access to health care, they may not expect to live beyond retirement. This is particularly true of African American men, who have high mortality rates due to heart disease. For these men and women, having little economic autonomy, the midlife tasks of reevaluating the life course and developing new plans and dreams are not realistic. In fact, it has been suggested that the very idea of a midlife crisis is a cultural construct that is relevant only to the middle and upper classes (Gallagher, 1993).

In poor African American, Latino, and other immigrant families where dependence on the larger family system is essential to survival, there is usually high value placed on interconnectedness between family members. In these families, there may never actually be an "empty nest," as elderly family members are likely to be active members of their expanding households and family systems (McGoldrick, Giordano, & Pearce, 2006). Especially in families where addictions and AIDS have led to parents being unable to take care of their children, grandparents may continue to be caretakers way past midlife. These social and cultural emotionally transmitted influences contribute to the family's ease or difficulty in moving through this phase.

Men and Women at Midlife

Although every generation must go through approximately the same life cycle transitions and accomplish the same tasks, each cohort brings a unique historical experience. As stated earlier, those who are now at midlife are the last of the baby boomers, and although their individual experiences may have been different, they were greatly influenced by the generation born just after World War II and were raised in the 1950s and 1960s. Many grew up with traditional values and gender role expectations, namely, to be heterosexual, find a spouse, marry early, and, if female, stay home. Male entitlement strongly permeated their socialization. However, many were also exposed to a changing social climate as the earlier baby boomers transitioned between postwar traditional values and the new changing social climate that, to a large extent, was spearheaded by the Women's Movement, the Civil Rights Movement, and more recently, by the Gay Liberation Movement.

For the first time a greater number of women attended college, entered the full-time workforce, and got divorced. This change in women has had an effect on men and their social roles. Although men and women have attempted to create more egalitarian marriages, many still struggle with two conflicting sets of values, and even the most "liberated" couples tend to revert to traditional gender roles after their children are born. Traditional gender role expectations determined by patriarchy continue to pose enormous challenges as men and women negotiate and redefine their roles at midlife with each other, within the family, and in society. Added to this, the realities of racism, heterosexism, bi-, trans-, and homophobia combine to make this transition especially difficult for marginalized groups. Nonetheless, the values of individual entitlement, self-fulfillment, and gender equality that oriented this group to the massive social changes at the end of the last century continue to be relevant as they face the challenges and demands of midlife (Kimmel, 2008).

Women at Midlife

Women experience midlife in different ways depending on their social location. A woman who is poor, without support, or seriously ill may feel a lot older and have a much bleaker outlook of her life than someone who has social and economic resources and is healthy. For example, "midlife is the most tumultuous time of life for low-income African American women, and midlife women in ill health may have a particularly tough time" (Hunter, Ski, Sundel, Sandra, Martin, 2002). However, most women at midlife feel grounded, competent, and satisfied with their accomplishments. Those who have launched children may feel some sadness when their children leave home, but more than not they are

pleased with the job they have done and freer than ever to explore and take on new challenges. This defies the assumption that all women get depressed and feel lost when their children leave home, what has been termed the "empty nest syndrome." (Hunter, Ski, Sundel, Sandra, Martin, 2002).

Another assumption questioned is that menopause has a crippling effect on women. Actually, although many women do experience some of the physical changes associated with menopause, such as hot flashes, sleep problems, vaginal dryness, weight gain, increased vulnerability to osteoporosis, and changes in cognitive function, the psychological effects of these symptoms are found to be culture bound (Hunter, Ski, Sundel, Sandra, Martin, 2002). In a longitudinal study of menopausal women Woods and Mitchell (2006) found that the majority of women at midlife do not report significant changes in anger, anxiety, depression, or self-consciousness related to menopause. For those with severe menopausal symptoms, clinicians can help by providing psychoeducational information about the natural aspects of these changes and by encouraging these women to consult their physicians about hormone replacement therapy and other health alternatives.

However, for many women aging means that they no longer feel desirable or valuable. In this society, and particularly in the dominant culture, beauty equals youth. Especially unmarried women may lose hope in finding a partner with whom to share life. If they have children, launching them might be more problematic due to their personal fears and anxiety about aging alone. Engaging women in reassessing their lives, their accomplishments, and what they still want to do, rather than buying into the negative stereotypes associated with this stage of life, can be beneficial. After all, we can all benefit from Margaret Mead's definition of the phenomenon she dubbed as "postmenopausal zest," which she described as "that creativity and energy released when we no longer have to care for children" (Bateson, 2001).

Gail, a 49-year-old, African American, single parent came to therapy because she was feeling extremely anxious and depressed since her daughter, Cheryl, 18, had left for college. She was having difficulty doing her job as an LPN at a hospital where she had worked for years, calling and texting her daughter frequently during the day. She worried about Cheryl not waking up early enough to go to class, not eating properly, not going to classes, drinking, and putting herself at risk with boys. In other words, that Cheryl could not be responsible without Gail guiding her, as she had always done. She also worried about not having enough money to pay all the expenses for college and continue to take care of her own needs. As a solution, she was not spending money on herself, and she stopped going out with friends. She stayed home crying frequently, and sometimes drank too much. In therapy, we spoke about her dreams for her daughter and for herself, and about other women in her family, especially her mother. We spoke about her own launching and the differences in how she left home and how Cheryl was leaving now. Looking at how proud she felt that her daughter, unlike herself, was going to college, that she as a single mother had been able to accomplish what her parents could not do for her, was a changing point in the treatment. She began to get in touch with her sense of competence again, acknowledge her confidence, and think about her daughter's strengths. She agreed to set some limits on her calling and texting Cheryl, who later related that the reduced communication had been a big relief. Gail's financial situation continued to be very burdensome, but in therapy we noted that it did not have to prevent her from seeking companionship and support from family and friends. Sharing food with friends or family at home provided her with some of the social connection she needed. Gail was adept at relationship skills, and she responded well to this intervention. She also found keeping a journal to be a useful tool for identifying neglected and new interests, not to be used as time fillers but as expressions of her own authentic self, which she now had the freedom to explore.

For midlife lesbians, this transition may be somewhat different, since women in general tend to focus more on the emotional than the physical aspects of intimacy. Generally, lesbians are much less prone to equate desirability and beauty with youth, thinness, or any of the other usual male criteria of female beauty (Hunter, 2005; Cole & Rothblum, 1990). But, when in partnerships with other women the transition of menopause may be more problematic than for heterosexual women. As human sexuality researcher Sandra Leiblum (2003)

suggests, the couple's adjustment to the physical and psychological effects of menopause may be exacerbated by both partners experiencing these changes together, as their sexual interest and performance may decline at the same time. Menopause also signifies the cessation of fertility, which may compound the experience of loss for lesbians who feel that their attempt to have children through insemination or adoption was prevented by social prejudice (Slater, 1995).

Men at Midlife

As with women, men at midlife can be single, married, divorced, or remarried and differ in how old they feel depending on health issues and work conditions. For men as for women, the popular conceptualization of midlife is that this process of reassessment is traumatic. The stereotype suggests that men, regardless of race, culture, education, or social class, generally begin to get in touch with their mortality during this period, and, feeling that they have squandered their dreams and have nothing to live for, suddenly quit their jobs, dash out of their marriages, and begin a spending spree on high-ticket items to bolster their self-esteem. However, research indicates that the overwhelming majority of men accomplish the developmental tasks of reevaluation and regrouping through a long, introspective process rather than an acute acting-out crisis. Although they will be making adjustments in their relationships and in their work lives, relatively few men experience the process as catastrophic (Gallagher, 1993).

Men who have challenged the traditional social codes for masculinity may find themselves in a different place at midlife. They may be missing their almost grown children and renegotiating their relationships with their adult children, their parents, and their partners. Work may take a different type of priority in their lives, as they find different meaning in their lives. It is not that the questions they ask are so different from women's, but they tend to do their thinking alone, a consequence of their socialization. A family life cycle approach can help them normalize some of the anxiety and depression they often feel by helping them realize that most men at this stage of life have similar questions.

Jerry, a 55-year-old, White professor of Dutch ancestry, came to therapy feeling very depressed about not being able to concentrate enough to prepare lectures and teach his courses or to contribute to a research project that he had initiated with other colleagues in his department. He had been divorced for 3 years and, in his judgment, was adjusting well to his single life. However, he was now blaming his absence as a father for his 19-year-old son's recent decisions not to go to college and to marry an older woman. His work had always been a priority for him, and this, he stated, had caused the end of his marriage. Now he was feeling very anxious about his son's life and about losing the connection with him. In therapy, Jerry began to review his life growing up in a Midwest farming community and to see how his values about masculinity had been heavily influenced by Dutch culture and religious beliefs. The emphasis on work and fierce determination to succeed that he learned from men in his family had prevented him from being the type of partner and father he would have wanted to be. Helping him see that there was a present and future in the relationship with his son, and that making time for the two of them to enjoy common interests or meals might begin to change the relationship, gave him hope. They loved fishing, and in time they established rituals for spending time doing that, which led to talking and getting to know each other not only as father and son, but also as men. Their relationship grew closer, and the two were able to joke about how in the future Jerry could take his grandchildren fishing.

Coming to terms with aging is a key developmental task of midlife. As they approach midlife, men begin to experience a gradual series of physical changes. They do not really bring them below their maximal level of functioning, but these changes are significant enough to notice, such as baldness, paunchiness, and wrinkles. As they get older, their physical stamina may continue to diminish, and they may no longer be able to do certain types of work, possibly putting their livelihood in question.

Among gay men, concern about body image is particularly strong, as they fear that signs of aging will mean that they are less sexually desirable. The critical midlife task of accepting one's own mortality is also drastically heightened among gay men. A large proportion of men living with HIV/AIDS are now in midlife; some of these men have been HIV-positive for 10 years or more. In addition to their acute personal awareness of mortality, gay men have buried and grieved for numerous friends and partners. Therefore, rather than just beginning to confront mortality at midlife as heterosexuals typically do, gay men have been living with a heightened awareness of death on a daily basis for many years.

Another experience that can be extremely disconcerting for men is becoming suddenly aware that they are no longer at the top of their game at work, especially if they lose their jobs. As one client expressed in great distress, "I went to the journalist's circle at the Giants Stadium and suddenly realized that no one was greeting me by my name, and that I didn't know their names either." He felt that his social status had changed in that arena, and that his future career was in question. Helping him look at his identity in terms of his relationship with his children and partner led him to think about a different type of social status, one where he could have a more lasting influence.

Other Midlife Tasks

Renegotiating couple relationships

It has been said that during midlife, men and women are sometimes moving past each other in different directions and at different paces, "like two ships passing each other in the night." Especially, if they are married, these gender contradictions are often confusing and unsettling to the partners and may lead to significant shifts in the marriage, including a redefinition of what constitutes a "good" husband or wife. As women develop autonomy and move toward outside commitments, men want more time for leisure and/or travel and expect their wives to be free to join them (Carter & Peters, 1996). As women become more independent, there may be a change in the balance of power in the marriage and a renegotiation of marital expectations, plans, and dreams—or the viability of the marriage itself. But it is important to note that this shift in expectations between men and women may be primarily a White middle- and upper-class pattern. Economic and cultural factors, as well as the stresses of immigration, may not allow for much change in gender role expectations in more marginalized groups. Adapting and integrating dominant culture values, such as women wanting more independence or searching for autonomy at middle age, may cause difficulties when men and women are at different positions in the process of immigration and acculturation.

However, for the most part launching children has been found to be good for marriages and good for each partner's general feeling of well-being. In fact, the presence of children in the home has not been found to correlate with marital happiness in any age group (White & Edwards, 1993). The removal of stress and the simplification of household routines are certainly key factors. Partners are no longer so focused on their children and can think more about and spend more energy on their marriages, and with the awareness that time is moving on partners expect more from their relationships. By midlife the very nature of marriage tends to change for couples. Relationships are increasingly characterized by friendship, companionship, equality, tolerance, and shared interests (Dowling, 1996). For many this renewed focus on the relationship enhances their sexuality, although it is common for sexual activity to decrease as couples move through midlife.

As with midlife heterosexuals, midlife GLBT couples are more companionable and less passionate. At this stage of life, both gays and lesbians report that while they remain sexually active, sex does not have the urgency it had in their youth. This is particularly true of lesbians, who are typically less sexually active (though not less affectionate or expressive) than either gay male or heterosexual couples (Green, Bettinger, & Zacks, 1996; Leiblum, 1990). However, while sex may be less frequent, gays and lesbians report sex to be more satisfying in midlife (McWhirter & Mattison, 1984; Tully, 1989). Johnson and Keren (1996) note that gay couples are much less likely than heterosexual couples to view infrequent sex with their partners as an indicator of a relationship problem.

However, the contradiction at this stage is that launching children doesn't always lead to greater marital happiness (White and Edwards, 1993). Often marital issues and conflicts are buried during the tumult of the child-rearing years and resurface after the children leave. Sometimes women or men come to the painful realization that the marriage is empty and make a decision to divorce.

Divorce at midlife

While divorce is increasingly prevalent in all age groups, it is particularly noticeable in midlife. For instance in 1979 the most-divorced age groups were men 30 to 34 and women 35 to 44. Now for both men and women it's 45 to 54 year olds. In 2000, the most recent year for which good data is available, almost 15 percent of men and 18 percent of women in that age group were divorced. About another 2.4 percent of men and 3.1 percent of women were separated (U.S. Census, 2000).

Sometimes the empty nest does not lead to the solidification of the marriage or to the acceptance of a familiar relationship. After many years of not dealing with differences, but instead burying feelings or distancing from each other or turning elsewhere, some couples realize that what is empty is the marriage. Some marriages simply cannot survive without the children present. Some couples hold onto their children as buffers; others decide to divorce. Two significant factors contribute to the timing of these midlife divorces. First, there is a change in the structure of the family and a freedom that comes with the end of the day-to-day responsibility for children. The couple has a newly available ration of time, finances, and emotional focus, which provide the opportunity and resources for change. Second, one or both of the spouses is motivated to seek a divorce by the unpleasant prospect of being left alone with a stranger or an adversary for the remainder of life. Both of these factors are magnified by the realization that time is running out.

Interestingly, 85 percent of divorces are initiated by women (Apter, 1995; Walsh, 2007). Because women today are better educated than they were in the past, they are more marketable for employment. Sometimes, as women begin to experience their independence and develop their competence, they are less willing to remain in a relationship that they recognize as dead. The sense of empowerment that comes with making the decision to end an unsatisfying relationship helps to enhance women's self-confidence and their capacity for assertiveness. Though some women may be terrified of being alone and of handling finances, the emotion that most often accompanies the decision to divorce is relief (Apter, 1995). Despite their fears, women rarely regret their decision to divorce (Dowling, 1996).

When women turn outward, men take notice. They may experience a sense of confusion, vulnerability, and abandonment. Some men, as they go through the midlife process of reassessment, develop a renewed appreciation for their marital relationship, or at least they decide that remaining in the marriage is preferable to leaving, while some men respond to the questioning of an unhappy marriage by seeking a new, exciting romance. Their developing awareness of mortality and a desire for that last chance for happiness may fuel this decision. However, a decision to end a long marriage is usually a protracted and painful one. Most people, regardless of ethnic or religious backgrounds, are likely to experience their divorces as personal failures. This is especially true for women, since they tend to assume that it is their responsibility to make relationships work.

After 25 years of marriage, Tina (age 47) and Ed (age 49), both Jewish and upper-middle-class launched their second child from the home. Tina had returned to graduate school 2 years before this event and was deeply absorbed in her studies, while Ed was focused on his legal career. Despite these distractions, Tina found the silence between them to be a painful indicator of their long-term estrangement. She told Ed that if they did not enter marital therapy, she did not want to remain in the marriage. Ed then agreed to enter treatment. After completing the initial assessment, the couple's therapist suggested a 9-month plan: Both Tina and Ed would agree to put their maximum effort into being the best partners they could be for the next 9 months; after that, they would reevaluate their relationship. During that period, in addition to couples work, both partners were individually coached to strengthen their own support systems and to identify and pursue their individual interests and needs. Despite this work, Ed and Tina remained disconnected. After 5 months, Ed disclosed that he was involved in a longstanding affair. With what she described as relief, Tina stated that she had had enough—the mar-

riage was over. Both Tina and Ed agreed to remain in treatment for 3 months to handle the separation process as constructively as possible. They were given the names of local divorce mediators so that the separation and divorce process would be collaborative rather than adversarial. Individual therapeutic work with Tina focused primarily on her learning to manage her finances, while work with Ed primarily addressed developing plans to maintain contact with his children. Tina returned to treatment several months later to address the feelings of loss and failure that followed the initial sense of relief and hopeful expectation. Exploring with Tina how traditional Jewish cultural values that emphasize keeping the family together had influenced her avoidance of divorce for so long helped her see how those cultural legacies were contributing to her difficulty in moving on with her life.

Midlife is often a time when men and women who have kept their sexual orientation secret choose to leave their marriages to live openly as homosexuals. Many LGBT parents wait to come out until their children reach young adulthood, thinking that the children will then be more able to accept their sexual orientation. However, delaying such a decision also has much to do with the ongoing homophobia that exists in the court system and the possibility of losing visitation rights with their children during divorce proceedings (Bigner, 1996). Another important factor affecting this decision is that coming out means losing the privileges that heterosexuals have in this society, especially when they are married.

Karen, 46, of White and mixed European ancestry had been married for 18 years to Stan, 49, a successful businessman of similar ancestry, and had a daughter Jill (17) who was starting to plan for college. Karen had given up a teaching career to be a stay-at-home mom and was involved in several volunteer activities in her upper-middle-class community. Before her marriage, she had experienced romantic feelings for women but never acted on them. When she married Stan, she immersed herself in her roles as wife and mother and put those feelings out of mind. Then, after 15 years of marriage, she met Elaine (age 42) at a tennis game and felt drawn to her. The two women developed a close friendship and eventually became romantically involved. Because of Stan's frequent business trips, Karen was able to keep the relationship a secret. As devoted as she came to feel to Elaine, Karen felt equally committed to her family's stability and could not leave her marriage. Feeling torn between two lives and becoming increasingly depressed about her struggle to maintain the pretense of stability, she entered therapy. Karen stated that she had no intention of leaving her family, but she needed help with her depression. Treatment initially addressed the stress of managing the logistics of her situation, but as she became more engaged she began to look at how her own homophobia was contributing to her feelings of shame and the need to keep her relationship with Elaine secret. Karen was then encouraged to look at her social network to identify those friends who would accept her as a gay woman. She was coached to firm up those relationships and then to slowly share her dilemma. She was also assisted in moving closer to her daughter, as that relationship was most important to her. Eventually with much coaching she was able to come out to her daughter and her husband. The road has not been easy, but with the help of therapy Karen continues to develop more honest relationships with her family, friends, and community.

The process of simultaneously launching children, divorcing, and coming out complicates three major life transitions that, when experienced separately, are in themselves extremely complex. Each requires major role shifts and life style changes, with feelings that range from liberation to loss. While engaged in developing more adult-to-adult relationships with their children, LGBT parents are also dealing with their own developmental lag. Bigner (1996, 2005) notes that gay men who come out at midlife are out of sync in terms of their development of a stable, positive homosexual identity compared with gays who come out earlier in life. These men may prematurely seek to replicate the exclusive, committed relationship model of heterosexual marriages, which may complicate their integration into gay culture.

Redefining relationships with adult children and boomerang kids

It is one thing to have children move out of the home. It is another to view them as adults and relate to them accordingly, and still another for young adults to see their parents as people with a history, life, and concerns of their own. Usually parents and children stay closely connected after launching, often speaking several times a week (White & Edwards, 1993). This eases the process of launching and validates their connection for both parents and children. When they see their children becoming more and more independent as young adults both inside and outside the family, parents feel that their job was well done and are able to relinquish some of their parental oversight. Unless there are major unresolved issues, or cut offs in their relationships at this stage, parents and children are increasingly able to interact on an adult, mutually supportive basis. In fact, parent–child relationships have been found to become more affectionate and close after the children leave home (Troll, 1994), and parents often come to view their children as close friends (Shapiro, 1996), especially after the children marry and have children of their own.

The above description of how parents and children negotiate relationships at midlife gives a broad scope of a process that is becoming more and more complex as this stage in the life cycle continues to lengthen. To understand this expansion, we need to consider how the changing social and economic cultural context in this country is affecting individual development in families. More and more frequently, young adult children remain at home, or return home after college or after a brief period on their own. Additionally, financial concerns, lengthened years of education, delayed marriage plans, or marital breakups may all lead to the boomerang effect.

Having adult children in the home produces stress for most parents, especially for middle-class parents who usually anticipate the freedom that comes after children leave. For them the frustration of their expectations not being met produces stress, but for most parents the household is simply more complicated with children present. How parents cope with the stress has much to do with how they interpret the children's presence. Parents may view the situation more negatively if their children are unemployed or move back after a marital breakup than if children remain home while working or going to school or if they have never married. The more autonomous and less dependent their children are the better the parents feel about having adult children in the home. Here again, class and ethnicity influence the family's responses. For example, in the following case:

Bert, 60 and of German Catholic background, and May, 59, of Irish Catholic descent, came to therapy because they were having many problems with Sue Ann, their biracial 22-year-old adopted daughter, who had returned home after a brief period at college. They had adopted her as an infant after trying to have children for several years. They had little information about her biological parents, except that the mother was African American, and the father was probably Puerto Rican. According to them, Sue Ann had been a happy child until adolescence when she began to be defiant and show difficulties at school. They had gone to family therapy for a short time, and the problems had subsided enough for her to go away to college. However, her adjustment at college became problematic, and during the second semester she became extremely depressed and unable to function. She saw a counselor at college and was referred to a psychiatrist who diagnosed her as bipolar, prescribed medication, and recommended testing for learning disabilities. Her parents brought her home, followed up with psychiatric care, and had her tested. She did have special needs and was able to get the needed supports at a local college, but she continued to have difficulties and problems at home escalated.

In therapy, several issues surfaced that contributed to the family's turmoil and stuckness. Both Bert and May were disappointed and frustrated about what they saw as their daughter's failure to move on in life. Sue Ann was trying to understand what was going on with her psychiatrically and emotionally and felt confused about her racial identity. "I am a Black woman with White parents who don't understand what it's like for me out there. They don't like my Black friends and think they are "low lifes," and I hate the fact that I have to take medicine and that because of my learning problems, I might not be able to make it in school and take care of myself." Bert and May worried about not being able to retire and move to North Carolina as they had planned, and Sue Ann felt stuck at home with parents who did not understand what it was like to be a woman of color in the world, with no money, only working a few hours a week, and no car.

Having conversations about their attitudes on racism and psychiatric illness and how they thought these issues were affecting their family has helped to lower the intensity of conflict at home. Sue Ann's struggles interrupted her parents' plans for their future. Their White, upper-middle-class values and their experience of privilege did not equip them to help their daughter cope with the challenges a woman of color with a psychiatric illness encounters. The therapeutic goal continues to be helping Bert and May find ways to move through this stage by focusing on their daughter's strengths and by supporting the positive steps she takes toward moving on. In turn, Sue Ann is taking more responsibility in exploring options for work and school. The more her parents are able to listen when she shares her struggles without telling her how to fix it, the less controlled she feels, which has lessened her angry, out-of-control reactions. I (NGP) am careful with my interventions, realizing that being a woman of color myself and having a biracial daughter influences my reactions, such as trying to explain to Bert and May how Sue Ann might be feeling and not really understanding their struggles as White parents. This continues to be a work in progress.

Redefining parent–child relationships as adult-to-adult personal relationships does not happen automatically when grown children leave home or even when they marry and have children. It is quite common for unresolved emotional issues or differences to create situations of polite, dutiful distance instead of a warm and eager sharing of lives between generations. Resolving old issues is the central emotional task of the younger generation, but parents can help or hinder the process. Their shift from hands-on direction of adolescents to on-call consultant to young adults may not be easy. Some parents also find it difficult to be more open and personal with "children" whom they have always shielded from "adult" problems. For specific interventions in helping either generation change their relationship at this juncture, see Chapters on Coaching and on Young Adulthood in this book.

Renegotiating relationships with parents

Contrary to the image of aging parents being packed off to the nursing home, most elderly people are healthy enough and financially stable enough to live independently throughout their lives. Their children care for most of those who develop infirmities or illness. Because people are living longer, the period of providing care for aging parents has moved from the 40s to the 50s. Also, because child-bearing has been delayed and children are older when they leave home, people at this stage of life may be caring simultaneously for aging parents and young adults—and perhaps for returning children and grandchildren as well. The group of adults caught in this competition of roles is called the "sandwich generation."

Typically, the caregivers are midlife daughters and daughters-in-law, not sons. Women tend to provide the day-to-day care for their aging parents and sometimes their in-laws, while their husbands and brothers provide financial support and supervise property and other assets. It is not that men do not care, but rather that the tasks of caregiving have traditionally been distributed differentially between the sexes. This difference, however, has led to enormous inequities for women, especially for those in the workforce. Working full-time jobs while care taking for family members can become overwhelming, especially for poor women who lack access to resources. Feeling pressured they often leave their jobs to do full-time caretaking. These breaks from work can have serious financial consequences for women because they often limit their ability to advance and limit their earning potential.

Fortunately, this system overload occurs when adults are at their peak of competence, control, and ability to handle stress (Gallagher, 1993). If the family views caregiving as normal rather than burdensome, the phase will be less stressful. These caregiving expectations are strongly influenced by ethnic values. For example, Latino, Asian American, African American, and Native American families tend to normalize the caregiving role, while Irish and Czech families are less likely to do so. Anglo Americans, who value independence and self-sufficiency to the extreme, tend to find provision of care to the elderly particularly problematic for both generations (McGoldrick et al., 2006). However, even in families in which caregiving is culturally supported, women caregivers are at high risk for stress-related illnesses and are sometimes called the hidden patients in the health care system. Sometimes it is only when their physicians diagnose depression that they seek therapy, as in the following case.

Delia, 48, a recently divorced Dominican woman, came to therapy with symptoms of depression and anxiety. She had decided to end the relationship with her husband after 30 years of an unhappy and unsatisfactory marriage, and after learning that he was being unfaithful. He had left and she had stayed home with her two younger daughters who were in college and living at home. The oldest daughter was 24 and had married after graduating college. Delia had been ridden with guilt and confusion about her decision to separate, but after the divorce had felt a sense of liberation and was enjoying having control of her life. Then her father came to visit from Florida and asked to live with her. She did not want to give up her freedom now that her daughters were almost launched, but as his daughter she felt obligated to take care of him. After a few months she began to feel resentful, trapped, and angry at her family, especially because her father began to complain that he felt lonely during the day when she was out working. He missed his community in Florida and regretted the decision to come to New Jersey.

Delia's father had been living alone in Florida for several years after her mother's death but in close proximity to his other three daughters. He had enjoyed his independence, but prior to his visit to New Jersey had begun to question his living alone. They worried about him and were relieved when he asked Delia to live with her. They agreed that because Delia was divorced and her daughters were more independent, she would be freer to take on the obligation. There was also a cultural assumption that as the oldest she would assume the responsibility of caretaker for her parents.

In therapy, Delia was able to talk about her conflict. She was feeling very pressured by her family's expectations and caught in a cultural dilemma. Although she felt close to her culture, unlike her siblings she had gone to college, had a graduate degree in social work, and had become more acculturated to the dominant culture. She wanted to be a good Dominican daughter but did not want to give up her freedom at this point in her life. With coaching she was able to engage her sisters in creating a different plan, one that took into account her personal needs, rather than simply going along with their cultural assumptions that as a single woman and oldest daughter she would be the caretaker. She was also able to talk to her father about his needs and with her sisters they found an assisted living situation in Florida where he felt more connected to a community. They all took turns visiting him, and he visited them.

As a result of these pressures and the potential for burnout, caregivers may need assistance with identifying their own needs and setting appropriate limits. This is particularly true for single midlife women, who are frequently the most isolated members of the family but who are assumed to be free of other responsibilities and are therefore the most overwhelmed. More resilient caregivers are able to view this period as an opportunity to resolve old issues with parents. For those who had managed their intergenerational issues as they occurred and moved more smoothly through earlier life cycle transitions, the postlaunch phase provides an opportunity for both generations to continue to adjust their relationship in ways that are mutually satisfying.

Just as people at this stage of life have the opportunity to redefine their relationships with their parents, they may also feel able to establish a more comfortable relationship with in-laws if they are not caught up in old conflicts with them. Recognizing their own mortality, they may now see themselves as peers with in-laws. Feeling on a more equal footing, the constraints of surface politeness or resentment may drop away, and they might be better able to express their own wishes.

The death of parents

Dealing with the death of parents is now considered a normative task of midlife. However, normative does not mean easy. The death of a parent at any time is a major loss, but at midlife there are special developmental tasks that are related to, and may have an impact on, the resolution of their grief. As described by Scharlach and Fredricksen (1993), these tasks include the following:

• *Acceptance of one's own mortality:* This is seen as the critical task of this life cycle phase. People are aware that they are now the executive generation and can no longer look to their parents for guidance. They may become more attentive to their own health, draft their wills, and make their own funeral arrangements. Along with freedom from child care, this awareness of mortality is a prime trigger for the life reassessment process.

• *Redefinition of family roles and responsibilities:* They are now the heads of the family. The role of maintaining family contacts, continuing family rituals and values, and guiding the next generation now falls to them. This redefinition also includes attending to unresolved issues with siblings without the impetus of the older generation to prod them.

• *Change in self-perception:* Those who experience the death of a parent may become more self-reliant and autonomous and at the same time more responsible toward others. This flowering of autonomy and emotional connectedness is viewed as an indicator of midlife maturity.

Unresolved grief following the death of a parent is usually related to longstanding unresolved issues, such as feelings of dependency, criticism, guilt, or ambivalence. For immigrants, especially if they are undocumented or have few resources, not being able to return to their countries of origin when their parents die often results in unresolved grief. In therapy helping clients talk about their experience of the death, and encouraging them to engage in mourning rituals, may provide an opportunity to work through some of these issues, even after the parents' death. As with all unresolved issues, if they are not addressed now, they will find ways of resurfacing later in life.

Accepting the expansion of family through marriage and grandchildren

While midlife is a period of family contraction because of the launching of children and the illness or death of aged parents, it is also a time of expansion and regeneration through marriage and the birth of grandchildren. Families must change their usual relationships with their grown children and also learn to incorporate their children's new spouses and their families. Although some families experience antagonism with in-laws, parents often form close relationships with sons-in-laws and/or daughters-in-law (Bergquist et al., 1993). This process is facilitated if children have chosen spouses who are compatible with their parents' ethnic, class, and religious values or, alternately, if the family is flexible and open to differences. Family of origin traditions and beliefs regarding the appropriate degree of inclusion of in-laws also govern the melding process. On the other hand, if the choice of a marriage partner is seen as a reactive challenge to the parents or if the spouse is selected as a way for the child to distance from the parents, the blending of the two families will be more problematic.

Conflicts may develop around such issues as holiday plans or acceptable terms of address. Parents may feel unwanted and attempt to be either over-involved or under-involved with the young couple or, in extreme cases, cut them off. In general, these difficulties are actually displacements for unresolved family issues that are reenacted through the children's marriage. Because women are typically assigned the role of being responsible for the family's emotional life, the most difficult of these problems usually involve the women in the family: sisters-in-law, mothers with their sons or daughters, and mothers-in-law with daughters-in-law. Betty Carter and Joan Peters (1996) note that the target of mother-in-law jokes is invariably the husband's mother. In this drama, the son is caught in the middle as family history is repeated. Carter and Peters advise that the players who are responsible for handling the problem be the family members, not the in-laws.

One of the supreme rewards of midlife is grandparenthood. Grandparents say that the pleasure of seeing their own children parent the next generation is a joy that defies description. Family identity is solidified as the family reenacts meaningful life cycle rituals and ceremonies. Grandparents have an opportunity to revisit and perhaps redo their experience as parents without the day-to-day responsibility of child care. On the other hand, if the adult children are incapacitated by drug abuse or illness, grandparents may be recruited to raise their grandchildren. This can be an incredible source of pressure for grandparents, especially if they are poor or have ill health.

Renegotiating relationships with other family members and friends

Relationships with siblings and other family members as well as with friends take on new importance at midlife. Midlife siblings tend to draw together as aunts and uncles, parents, and grandparents become ill and die, leaving them to assume their place as the older generation. They also face the stressor of distributing the tasks of providing care to their aging parents. After a parent's death, the primary caregiver may feel resentment with her siblings for their lesser involvement. There also may be other issues that have been chronic sources of conflict through other life phases. After the parents' deaths, if there is no outside help, siblings may distance themselves or cut off rather than work at resolving these conflicts. If the discord persists, the siblings risk losing a significant source of practical and emotional support that they may need in later life.

During the child-raising years, friendships are often diluted by the omnipresence of children at most social gatherings, but at midlife, they matter again in a profound and personal way. Midlifers are reinventing themselves. Their families look different. They may be suddenly single or come out as LGBT. For all the special concerns of midlife, long-term friends are there to provide a sense of belonging and continuity, while new friends are needed to address new interests and realities. With their heightened awareness of life's fragility, they consciously value and appreciate their friends.

Conclusion

Midlife, the longest phase of the life cycle, is a time of major family restructuring. The family shrinks when children are launched from the home or when parents are lost through the death. Additionally, many families experience loss through midlife divorce or the death of a spouse. Women also "leave" voluntarily by joining the workforce or other outside involvement, while midlife men may suddenly experience the loss of employment if their company is restructured. On the other hand, the family expands through the marriage of adult children and the birth of grandchildren. Families may also expand when launched children return home, some with their own children, or if aged parents join the household. Any one of these events is a stress point that might motivate families to seek a family therapist for help.

With or without treatment, families will need to adjust to the realignments and redefinitions of roles that result from these restructurings. While women typically lead the way toward change, men frequently join the process by being jolted into an awareness that they are at risk of losing relationships they had taken for granted. Making a decision about working on or ending unsatisfying relationships or reconnecting with estranged family members becomes more urgent when an individual is aware of being closer to death than birth. Accomplishing these shifts requires men and women to reexamine and alter the rigid role definitions that have defined their relationships during the child-rearing years. Admittedly, this is a tough job in a culture that still supports traditional gender roles, but at this stage people know that it is "now or never." Therefore, they may be more accessible to clinical intervention than at earlier stages in their life cycle. Thus, rather than being a time of winding down, midlife is a long life cycle stage that can be a fertile time for new options, growth, and change.

Chapter 17

Families in Later Life: Challenges, Opportunities, and Resilience

Froma Walsh

For age is opportunity no less than youth itself, though in another dress, and as the evening twilight fades away, the sky is filled with stars invisible by day.

—LONGFELLOW

Our elders never became senile because they were needed right to the end. Aunts and uncles taught you the philosophies and principles that you lived and worked by.

— LAVINA WHITE—HAIDA NATION, ALASKA.

From the book SIMPLY LIVING. Copyright © 1999 by Shirley Ann Jones. Reprinted with permission of New World Library, Novato, CA. www.newworldlibrary.com,

<http://www.newworldlibrary.com>

As societies worldwide are rapidly aging, families are also aging and becoming more diverse. This chapter examines the emerging challenges, opportunities, and resilience of individuals, couples, and families in later life. Most Americans, with increasing longevity and years of good health, are revisioning their later life possibilities for meaning and satisfaction. Salient issues concern retirement and financial security, grandparenthood, chronic illness and caregiving, end-of-life issues, and loss of loved ones. Clinical guidelines and case illustrations are offered to address common problems and to encourage the potential for personal and relational integrity and positive growth in intimate, companionate, and intergenerational bonds.

The Graying of the Family

Declining birth rates, health care advances, and increasing longevity are contributing to the unprecedented rise in the number and proportion of older people in societies worldwide (Kinsella & He, 2009). Our aging population is also becoming more racially and ethnically diverse. In the United States, life expectancy has increased from 47 years in 1900 to 78 years (over 75 years for men; over 80 years for women) (National Center on Health Statistics, 2009). However, health care disparities in prevention and treatment take a heavy toll on low-income families in blighted communities. Life expectancy for African Americans (73.2 years) is significantly lower than for Whites (78.2 years), particularly for Black men. Of note, among persons who survive to age 65—and eligibility for Medicare—the differences in remaining life expectancy diminish (18.6 years for Whites and 17.1 years for Blacks); and even more so at age 75 (11. 5 and 11.1 years, respectively).

According to recent U.S. census reports (www.census.gov), among those aged 65 to 74, the ratio is 83 men for every 100 women. For those 85 and over, it drops to 44 men per 100 women. Of all women age 65 and over, 44 percent are widowed—more than those who are married and living with their spouse. Women 65 and older are three times more likely to be widowed than their male counterparts. Among men in the same age group, 71 percent are married and living with their spouses and only 14 percent are widowed.

The baby boom generation will soon swell the over-65 population to record levels: up from 8 percent in 1950 to 12 percent in 2008. By 2030, more than one in five Americans will be over 65. With medical advances and healthier lifestyles, increasing numbers are living into their 80s, 90s, and even past 100. For most Americans, older adulthood is being redefined as two life periods: persons aged 65 to 84 who are mostly healthy and vibrant, and the very old, over 85, the fastest-growing segment of the older population and the group most vulnerable to serious illness and disabling conditions. Although research and clinical approaches tend to be individually oriented, family bonds are central in later life.

The Varying and Extended Family Life Course

The family life course is becoming ever more lengthened and varied (Walsh, 2003a, b, or c?). Four- and five-generation families add both opportunity and complexity in balancing members' needs and family resources (Bengtson, 2001; Bengtson & Lowenstein, 2003). Increasingly, adult children past retirement age, with limited resources, are involved in caring for their elders. Multigenerational relational networks are becoming smaller and top-heavy, with a declining proportion of younger people. Greater insecurity and intergenerational tensions are likely, with global economic downturns and uncertainty in employment and benefits affecting both young and old. The trend toward having few or no children will leave aging persons with fewer intergenerational connections and strain family resources for financial and caretaking support. Recent findings that 20 percent of women 40 to 44 had no biologic children intensify concern about the provision of care as this group reaches advanced age (Kinsella & He, 2009).

Pathways through middle and later life are increasingly varied. With greater life expectancy, couples raising children may have 30 to 40 years ahead after launching them. It's challenging for one relationship to meet changing developmental priorities of both partners over a lengthened life course. While divorce rates, just under 50 percent, are in the spotlight, it is perhaps more remarkable that over 50 percent of first marriages last a lifetime. Increasingly, couples are celebrating 50 and 60 years of marriage. Also,

many single, divorced, and widowed older adults are finding happiness in new relationships.

Over a long lifetime, two or three marriages, with periods of co-habitation and single living, are becoming increasingly common, creating complex kin networks in later life (Walsh, 2003a). Single older adults and couples who are unmarried or without children forge a variety of significant bonds with siblings, cousins, nephews and nieces, godchildren, close friends, and social networks. In our mobile world, many relationships are carried on at a distance and sustained through frequent cellphone and Internet contact.

The family and social time clocks associated with aging are also more fluid. As many become grandparents and great-grandparents, others are beginning or extending parenthood. With varied fertility options, women in middle age are bearing children. Remarriage brings new stepparent relationships. Men, who commonly remarry younger women, often raise second families in later years.

The dramatic societal transformations over recent decades have increased intergenerational differences between traditional and contemporary roles and relationships. For instance, elders may expect daughters to be readily available to provide care when most women at midlife are now in the workforce, with stressful conflicting demands (Brody, 2004). Tensions are particularly likely between older immigrants, who carry more traditional values from their cultures of origin, and younger generations raised in our society. For instance, traditional Eastern Asian families value harmony and filial piety and expect that elders will be honored and obeyed. Cultural dissonance arises when younger generations depart from those norms. Family therapy can facilitate family harmony with new mutual understanding by empowering family members to draw on personal strengths, recognizing, negotiating, and incorporating multiple worldviews and values (Lee & Mjelde-Mossey, 2004).

Aging gay men and lesbian women meet needs for meaning and intimacy in varied ways, influenced by their past experiences, present life circumstances, and social environment (Cohler & Galatzer-Levy, 2000; Neustifter, 2008). Many who built life structures with their sexual orientation closeted before the gay rights movement find greater authenticity and freedom of expression in open committed relationships in later years. Many older gay men who survived the HIV/AIDs epidemic, which ravaged the gay community, confronted both their mortality and loss of partners and friends earlier in life passage.

To be responsive to the growing diversity of relationships and households in society, our view of "family" must be expanded to fit the lengthened and varied life course. Therapeutic objectives must be attuned to the challenges and preferences that make each individual, couple, and family unique. We will need to learn how to help family members live successfully in complex and changing relationship systems, to buffer stressful transitions, and to make the most of their later life experiences.

From Ageism and Gerophobia to a Larger Vision of Later Life

As a society, we have not readily confronted the challenges of later life or seen the opportunities that can come with maturity. Our gerophobic culture holds a fearful, pessimistic view of aging as decay. The elderly have been stereotyped as old-fashioned, rigid, boring, useless, demented, and burdensome. Institutionalized forms of ageism perpetuate workplace discrimination. In a culture that glorifies youth, we cling to youth and strive to recapture it, facing our own aging with dread or denial.

A grim picture of aging has been portrayed in the trajectory view of progressive deterioration, decline, and loss, ending in death. Biomedical and mental health fields have tended to pathologize later life, focusing on disorders and disability and discounting functional difficulties as an irreversible part of aging. Negative stereotypes of older persons have fostered pessimistic assumptions by clinicians that they are less interesting than younger clients, a poor investment for therapy, and too resistant to change. They are often treated custodially, with a pat on the hand and a medication refill.

A larger vision of later life is required, recognizing the potential change, growth, and new learning that can occur. Scholars are reformulating conceptions of later years. Some e.g., Lawrence-Lightfoot, 2009) propose three distinct periods: extended middle age (to age 75); old age (75 to 85); and very old age (85 and over). Extended middle age is a dynamic, new cultural shift for most people in their 60s and early 70s, who are healthy, active, and productive. Lawrence-Lightfoot calls this period "the third chapter" of adulthood, when traditional norms, rules, and rituals of careers seem less encompassing and restrictive; when many women and men embrace new challenges and search for greater meaning in life. In her interviews, individuals across races and social classes related stories involving both loss and liberation, vulnerability and resilience, looking back and giving forward to others. Their vital engagement in life, while appreciating its unpredictable course, involves the need for grieving losses and reinventing themselves and their future, the need for new structure, purpose, and leisure for new learning and experimentation in uncharted postcareer years. As assisted living and more extended care are needed, new possibilities for living arrangements and community involvement are being envisioned for more satisfying and meaningful later years.

The Vital Importance of Family Bonds

Stereotypes of American families have held that adult children don't care about their elders, have infrequent, obligatory contact, and dump them in institutions. Many presume that older adults are too set in their ways to change longstanding interaction patterns. In fact, family bonds and intergenerational relations for most Americans are mutually beneficial, dynamic, and co-evolving throughout adult life (Bengston, 2001). Families provide most social interaction, caregiving assistance, and psychological support for elderly loved ones. The vast majority of older adults live with spouses, children, or other relatives, including siblings and very aged parents.

Couples who weather the inevitable storms in longlasting relationships and child-rearing report high relationship satisfaction in their postlaunching years, with more time and resources for individual and shared pursuits. Priorities for companionship and caregiving come to the fore in couple bonds. Although sexual contact may be less frequent, intimacy can deepen with a sense of shared history. New satisfactions are found in shared activities, such as travel, and in bonds with grandchildren.

The importance of sibling relationships commonly increases over adulthood (Cicirelli, 1995).

The centenarian Delany sisters, born into a southern African American family, pursued careers and lived together most of their lives, crediting their remarkable resilience to their enduring bond. They shared enjoyment in conversation and laughter, watched over each other, and saw their differences as balancing each other out (Delany & Delany, 1993).

Most older Americans in good health prefer to maintain a separate household from children, yet they sustain frequent contact, reciprocal emotional ties, and mutual support in a pattern aptly termed "intimacy at a distance" (Blenkner, 1965). The proximity of family members and contact by phone and the Internet are especially important to those who live alone. Adult children and grandchildren also benefit in many ways from frequent contact with elders. However, in our mobile society, uprooting for jobs or retirement can strain the ability to provide direct caregiving and support in times of crisis.

In an ageist social context and a clinical focus on family child-rearing phases, family literature over the past 2 decades has given scant attention to the family in later life, other than caregiving challenges, and has rarely addressed the priorities and assets of older adult members. A life course perspective on family development and aging is required, emphasizing both continuity and change.

Later-Life Transitions and Challenges

The family as a system, along with its elder members, confronts major adaptational challenges in later life. Changes with retirement, grandparenthood, illness, death, and widowhood alter complex relationship patterns, often requiring family support, adjustment to loss, reorientation, and reorganization. Many disturbances are associated with difficulties in family adaptation. Yet such challenges also present opportunities for relational transformation and growth.

A family's approach to later-life challenges evolves from its earlier patterns and cultural worldview. Systemic processes that develop over the years influence the ability of family members to adapt to losses and flexibly meet new demands. Certain established patterns, once functional, may no longer fit changing priorities and constraints. For families who have raised children, their launching from home sets the stage for relationships in later life. With the structural contraction of the family from a two-generational household to the couple or single parent, relationships with young adult children are redefined and parental involvement refocuses on individual and couple life pursuits. Most parents adjust well to this "empty nest" transition and welcome their increased freedom from child-rearing responsibilities (Neugarten, 1996). Yet, many parents continue to provide financial and emotional support, through college and beyond, and many adult children, for economic reasons, return to the nest.

Retirement

Retirement represents a significant milestone and adjustment for individuals and couples. Most who are healthy and financially secure are revisioning postretirement life, from the stereotyped retreat in a comfortable rocking chair, to new structure and purpose, with time for leisure, learning, and new pursuits. Indeed, family therapist Lorraine Wright has relabeled retirement as "preferment," a transition offering the opportunity to refocus energies to fit emerging needs and preferences. Many take on meaningful projects or new careers; some start riding Harleys and join motorcycle clubs.

For most, retirement involves the loss of job roles, status, productivity, and co-workers, which have been central to our culture's (male) standards for identity, success, and self-esteem throughout adult life. Whether retirement was desired or forced will affect adjustment. Even when early retirement or a job layoff is due to the economy or a company's relocation, self-doubts can linger, as well as anxiety and bitterness at the loss of benefits and security. Loss of income and one's role as financial provider can significantly strain relationships. Residential change, common at retirement, adds further dislocation and loss of connections with nearby family and social networks, as well as familiar services and trusted health care providers. Losses are felt in giving up the home in which children were raised and many milestones experienced.

A successful transition involves a reorientation of values and goals and a redirection of energies and relationships. The trend for older adults to move away to age-segregated retirement developments has been changing, as most prefer to remain in their communities. Many downsize from homes to apartments close to shopping, restaurants, cultural opportunities, and young people. Many parents are waiting for adult children to settle and then moving to be near them and their grandchildren. With job mobility so common, some elders experience subsequent uprooting to follow their children yet again. Often, adult children live in different regions, and grandparents shuttle around to spend time with all.

Retirement can be financially devastating for those who lack—or have lost—retirement pensions. In the current economic downturn, many must continue working long past retirement age. Those who have lost jobs and benefits must find new work. Such pressures force a major shift in expectations and later-life plans. Because of the stigma of dependency in our dominant culture, with its ethos of self-reliance, most older adults are reluctant to ask for or accept financial assistance from their adult children; issues of pride and shame keep many from even telling their children that they are financially strapped.

In traditional marriages, couples may have difficulty with the husband's retirement, accompanied by losses of his job-related status and social network, especially if they have repeatedly been uprooted from kin and social networks to accommodate career moves. Another challenge involves the retired husband's incorporation inside the home, with a change in role expectations, time together, and the quality of interaction. If a retired husband feels that he has earned full leisure while expecting his wife to continue to shoulder household responsibilities, her resentment likely will build. Dual-earner couples may get out of sync if one continues working past the other's retirement. For successful adaptation to retirement, couples need to renegotiate their relationship to achieve a new balance. With priorities and concerns shared through open communication, relational resilience can be strengthened as partners pull together to reshape their lives, plan financial security, and explore new interests to provide meaning and satisfaction.

When a child has filled a void in a marriage, it can complicate a couple's subsequent adjustment to retirement, as in the following case of a Mexican American family:

Maria, 63, brought her husband Luis, 67, for treatment of alcohol abuse since his retirement. Living with the couple was their 42-year-old son Raul, who had returned home after a divorce. Longstanding close attachment between the mother and son had stabilized a chronically conflictual marriage over the years, when Luis had worked long hours outside the home. Retirement shifted the balance as Luis, now home all day, felt like an unwanted intruder. Lacking job and breadwinning status as sources of self-esteem, he felt like an unworthy rival to his son for his wife's affection at a time in his life when he longed for more companionship with her. Competitive struggles fueled Luis's drinking, erupting into angry confrontations, as Maria sided protectively with their son.

In Latino families, as in many ethnic groups, parent–child bonds are commonly stronger than the marital dyad (see Falicov, Chapter 22 this volume). However, in this family, a pattern that was functional over many years became a conflictual triangle when retirement disrupted the relationship system.

Grandparenthood

As people live longer, increasing numbers are becoming grandparents and great-grandparents (Drew & Silverstein, 2004). The experience can hold great significance, as Margaret Mead (1972) remarked on becoming a grandparent: "I had never thought how strange it was to be involved at a distance in the birth of a biological descendant . . . the extraordinary sense of having been transformed not by any act of one's own but by the act of one's child" (p. 302). Grandparenthood can offer a new lease on life in numerous ways. First, it fulfills needs for generativity through one's descendents, easing the acceptance of mortality. As Mead experienced, "In the presence of grandparent and grandchild, past and future merge in the present" (p. 311). Grandparenthood also stimulates reminiscence of one's own earlier child-rearing and childhood experiences. Such perspectives can be valuable in gaining appreciation of one's life and parenting satisfactions despite regrets one may have.

Grandparenthood is a systemic transition that alters intergenerational relationships (Spark, 1974). When adult children become parents, it presents an opportunity for reconnection and healing of old intergenerational wounds, as they begin to identify with the challenges inherent in child-rearing and develop more empathy for their parents' best intentions.

Grandparents and great-grandparents, with knowledge of 5 or more generations, are in a unique position to connect the younger generations with those that came before them through their personal recollections and stories. Grandparents and grandchildren may enjoy a special bond that is not complicated by the responsibilities, obligations, and conflicts in the parent–child relationship (Mueller & Elder, 2003). It is often said that grandparents and grandchildren get along so well because they have a common enemy. Such an alliance can be problematic if a grandchild is triangulated in a parent–grandparent conflict, as in the following case of an African American family.

After the death of her father, Sharleen, age 32, a single parent, and her son Shaun, age 6, moved in with her mother to consolidate limited resources. Shaun's misbehavior and disrespect toward Sharleen brought the family to therapy. At the first session, Shaun went to his grandmother for help in taking off his boots. She quickly took over the discussion while Sharleen shrank back. Shaun, sitting between them, glanced frequently to his grandmother for cues. Each time Sharleen and her mother started to argue, Shawn drew attention to himself. He ignored Sharleen's attempts to quiet him, but responded immediately to his grandmother.

The grandmother complained that she was overburdened by having to take care of "both children." Sharleen felt that her mother undercut her efforts to take more responsibility by criticizing everything she did as "not right," meaning not her way. We explored the impact of the grandfather's sudden death from a heart attack. The grandmother was devastated by the loss and uncertain how to go on with her life. Taking charge to help her daughter raise Shaun filled the void. Therapy focused first on the loss and changes for all three generations then directed attention to realigning relationships so that Sharleen could be a more effective mother with her son while honoring the grandmother's role as head of the household. Sharleen agreed to respect her mother's wishes about how she wanted her home kept as her mother agreed to respect Sharleen's ways of child-rearing and to support her parental leadership.

In poor, largely minority, communities with high rates of early pregnancy, grandparenting typically occurs early. Grandmothers, many in their 40s, provide care for the children, particularly when parents must work. In kinship care, many grandparents are assuming the primary role in raising their grandchildren (Engstrom, in press; see Garcia Preto, Ch. 15 in this volume). While this meets a crucial need for the youngsters, it can take a toll on their own health, especially when they are on a limited income and have other heavy responsibilities.

For many older adults, foster grandparenting can enrich later life, serve as a resource for single and working parents, and provide connectedness across the generations, especially where more informal contacts are lacking in age-segregated living arrangements. Seniors can also be encouraged to volunteer in child care centers and after-school tutoring and mentoring programs, contributing their knowledge and interest, helping children learn, and enhancing their development.

Chronic Illness and Family Caregiving

As our society ages, the number of people with chronic conditions is increasing dramatically and those impaired are living longer than ever before (Aldwin & Park, 2007). Even for those in good health, fears of loss of physical and mental functioning, chronic pain, and progressively degenerating conditions are common (Rolland, 1994; see Rolland, Ch. 23, this volume). Health problems and severity vary greatly. Among seniors age 65 to 84 arthritis, high blood pressure, and heart disease are most prevalent. Over age 85, the risks of cancer and extensive disabilities increase, combined with cognitive, visual, and hearing impairment. Physical and mental deterioration contribute to and are exacerbated by depression and anxiety. Suicide rates also increase with age, particularly for older White men.

Because our society lacks a coherent approach to care for people with disabling chronic conditions, too many live with deteriorated health and lack access to appropriate and affordable services. Families in poverty, largely in minority groups, are most vulnerable to environmental conditions that heighten the risk of serious illnesses, disabilities, and caregiver strain, as well as early mortality. Diseases such as asthma, diabetes, high blood pressure, and heart disease are most prevalent among the poor.

Family caregiving is a major concern for the increasing numbers of frail elderly (Qualls & Zarit, 2009). By 2020, it is expected that 14 million persons will need long-term care. In 1970, there were 21 potential caregivers (defined as people age 50 to 64) for each person 85 or older; by 2030, there are expected to be only 6 potential caregivers, severely straining intergenerational resources. As average family size decreases, fewer children are available for caregiving and sibling support. With more people having children later, many at midlife, the so-called sandwich generation—is caring simultaneously for their children and for aging parents, grandparents, and other relatives. Finances can be drained as children's college expenses collide with medical expenses for elders. Increasingly, adult children past retirement, with their own declining health and resources, assume care for their parents. The average age of caregivers is 57, but 25 percent are 65 to 74, and 10 percent are over 75. The role of primary caregiver has traditionally been assigned to women (nearly three in four), usually wives, daughters, and daughters-in-law. Now that the vast majority of women are in the workforce, with their income essential in most families, a juggling of work and family roles is required (Brody, 2004).

Elders with chronic conditions increasingly receive care at home. Only 5 percent of people over 65 reside in institutions, yet chronic health problems require frequent hospitalizations, medical costs, and intensive home-based care for daily functioning. Family and friends are the front lines of support. Nearly three quarters of disabled people rely exclusively on these informal caregivers. Prolonged caregiving takes a heavy toll. Eighty percent of caregivers provide help 7 days a week, averaging 4 hours daily. In addition to housekeeping, shopping, and meal preparation, two thirds assist with feeding, bathing, toilet, and dressing. The lack of useful management guidelines by most medical specialists adds to confusion and frustration. Some aspects of chronic illness are especially disruptive for families, such as sleep disturbance, incontinence, delusional ideas, and aggressive behavior. One symptom and consequence of family distress is elder abuse, which can occur in overwhelmed families, stretched beyond their means and tolerance, or in families with a history of substance abuse and violence.

Dementias: The Long Good-Bye

Progressive brain disorders are among the most difficult conditions for families. Alzheimer's disease, accounting for 60 percent of dementias, affects 1 in 10 people over 65—and nearly half of persons over 85. Alzheimer's has been aptly called "the long good-bye" because of the progressive losses of functioning, identity, family roles, and relationships. Such ambiguous loss complicates mourning processes (Boss, 1999, 2004). The irreversible course of this devastating disease can last from a few years to more than 20 years, becoming an agonizing psychosocial and financial dilemma for families. Over time, mental and physical capacities are stripped away in gradual memory loss, disorientation, impaired judgment, and loss of control over bodily functions. In early stages, family members, not understanding the disorder, often become frustrated when the individual repeatedly asks the same questions, forgets earlier answers, or prepares a meal and forgets to serve it. With impaired memory, judgment, and "sundowning," they may wander off, get lost, and forget who they are and where they live. They may make disastrous financial decisions. As the illness progresses, it is most painful for loved ones when they are not even recognized or are confused with others, even with those long deceased. Gentle humor can ease such situations, as in one case: At a weekly dinner with his parents, as David's mother cleared the table and went into the kitchen, his father leaned over to him and said: "Did you see that woman there? If I wasn't a married man I could really go for her!" David replied, "Dad, you are the luckiest man on earth because you ARE married to her—she's your wife!" They laughed together and his mother enjoyed the compliment.

With limited medical interventions for Alzeimer's disease, treatment primarily addresses symptom management and custodial care. Most families try to keep their loved one at home as long as possible. Part-time or full-time nurses or paid caregivers, extended family, and social support networks are crucial in coping with stresses, providing respite, and dealing with crisis situations. Adult daycare programs offer a therapeutic milieu, contact with others, and pleasurable activities for the impaired person as they relieve caregiver strain. Family psychoeducation provides useful illness-related information and management guidelines over the course of an illness, reduces caregiver anxiety and depression, and addresses functional and relational losses (Rolland, 1994).

Family Intervention Issues and Priorities

With all elder caregiving, family intervention priorities include 1) stress reduction; 2) information about the medical condition, functional abilities, limitations, and prognosis; 3) concrete guidelines for sustaining care, problem solving, and optimal functioning; and 4) links to supplementary services to support family efforts. To meet caregiving challenges, communities must support families through a range of services, from day programs to assisted living and commitment to active participation of elders, including those with disabilities, in community life.

Family dynamics may require attention. For couples, chronic illness and disability can skew the relationship between the impaired partner and caregiving spouse over time (Rolland, 1994; see also Chapter 23, this volume). It can deplete financial savings and dash plans for the golden years. Couple therapy can help partners to gain mutual empathy, address such issues as guilt and blame, and rebalance their relationship to live and love as fully as possible.

Intergenerational issues around autonomy and dependency come to the fore as aging parents lose functioning and control over their bodies and their lives. Meeting their increasing needs should not be seen as a parent–child role reversal, which can be infantilizing and shaming. Even when adult children give financial, practical, and emotional support to aging parents, they do not become parents to their parents. Despite frailties or childlike functioning, aged parents have had many decades of adult life experience and deserve respect as elders. Family thera-

pists can facilitate conversations about dependency issues with sensitivity and a realistic appraisal of strengths and limitations. Many elders worry about being a burden on loved ones. Giving children the power of attorney also involves a loss of self-determination. In many cases, adult children have to challenge a parent's judgment and take control of risky behavior. In our mobile society, driving a car is a symbol of independence and freedom. Older adults, especially men, often refuse to give up driving, even with seriously impaired vision, reflexes, and judgment, and may be unwilling to admit the danger. In one family, the sons had to take away the father's keys, only to find he had other keys hidden away. Next, they took the battery out of the car; the crafty father called a service station to install a new battery.

In some cases, an aging parent, losing control and functioning, can become overly dependent on adult children. One adult child may become overly responsible through anxiety or prior role functioning; others may distance themselves. A vicious cycle may ensue, with escalating neediness, burden, and resentment, as in the following case of an Italian American family:

Mrs. Zambrano, an 82-year-old widow, was hospitalized with multiple somatic problems and secondary symptoms of disorientation and confusion. She complained that her two sons, Vince, age 46, and Tony, 43, didn't care whether she lived or died. The sons reluctantly came for a family interview. Tony believed that his mother's hospitalization was merely a ploy for sympathy, to make him feel guilty for not being at her beck and call as Vince was. He said that he had learned to keep his distance. Vince was become increasingly frustrated: The more he did for his mother, the more helpless and critical she became. He felt drained by her neediness and complaints and was resentful toward Tony. This repeated a pattern in childhood: With the father often away on business, the mother had turned to Vince to meet her needs. The brothers were helped to realign their relationship to share responsibilities and to gain appreciation of their mother's losses, loneliness, and anxiety that her life was slipping out of her control. Raised to be "doers" and problem solvers, they felt helpless in the face of decline, death, and loss, no matter how much they did for her. They were encouraged to take turns visiting her and simply to be more fully present, sharing stories and reminiscences, which eased her anxiety, improved her functioning, and reassured her of their love.

From Designated Caregiver to Caregiving Team

In approaching all serious illness, we need to expand the traditional narrow focus on one individual who is designated as the caregiver to a collaborative approach to caregiving, involving all family members as a *caregiving team*. Too often, the designated caregiver becomes overburdened and other family members are on the sidelines, unsure how to be supportive. The sharing of responsibilities and challenges can become an opportunity to strengthen bonds and heal strained relationships. In families torn by past grievances, conflict, or estrangement, caregiving is likely to be more complicated. Life-and-death decisions can be emotionally fraught, as in the following case of a Euro-American family:

Joellen, 38, was deeply conflicted when her father, hospitalized for complications from chronic alcohol abuse, asked her to donate a kidney to save his life. She felt enraged to be asked to give up something so important when he had not been there for her as a father over the years. He had been a mean drunk, often absent and many times violent. She was also angry that he had brought on his deteriorated condition by his drinking and had refused to heed his family's repeated pleas to stop. Yet, a dutiful daughter and a compassionate Christian woman, she did not want her father to die because she denied him her kidney.

I broadened the dilemma to include her siblings, suggesting that she discuss it with them, but Joellen dismissed the idea, saying they were estranged and rarely in contact. I then encouraged her to talk with her mother, who informed her that the father had also asked her siblings for the kidney donation. Joellen was furious that old rivalries would be stirred up: who would be seen as the good giving child or the bad selfish ones. She now took initiative to get the siblings together. When they met, old rivalries melted as they began to grapple with the dilemma.

I widened the focus, suggesting that they begin to envision how they might collaborate to meet future challenges that might arise in caring for *both* aging parents. With this conversation, the eldest brother volunteered his kidney for their father. He was less conflicted because he remembered good times with the father before his problem drinking. The others offered to support him and agreed to keep in contact and to contribute to their parents' future well-being, forging a new solidarity.

Placement Planning

The point at which failing health requires consideration of extended-care placement can be a crisis for the whole family. Placement is usually turned to only as a last resort, when resources are stretched to the limit, and in later stages of mental or physical deterioration. Still, feelings of guilt and abandonment and stereotypes of institutionalization can make a placement decision highly stressful, as in this Indian American family:

Mrs. Gupta called for help, stating that she felt helpless to control her teenage son and feared that he needed to be "institutionalized." A family assessment revealed that the problems had developed over the past 8 months, since Mrs. Gupta's mother had been brought to live in their home. She wept as she described her mother's deteriorating Parkinson's condition, feeling unable to provide round-the-clock care. She couldn't sleep at night after finding her mother on the floor one morning. Her concerns about institutionalization concerned her mother: At her father's deathbed, a year earlier, he had asked her to promise that she would always care for her mother. She felt alone with her dilemma, with her husband preoccupied by his work.

This case underscores the importance of inquiry about elderly family members even when problems are presented elsewhere in the system. It is also crucial to explore a spouse's distancing and lack of support, in this case due to the husband's lingering guilt over having left the care of his dying mother to his sisters.

Family sessions, best done proactively, can enable members to assess needs and both kin and community resources and to share feelings, concerns, and mutual support in reaching a decision. Often, new solutions emerge that can support the elder's remaining in the community, with part-time or full-time in-home nursing care or in assisted living. Respite for caregivers is crucial to their well-being. When extended care placement is needed, therapists can help families to view it as the most viable way to provide adequate care and support their efforts in navigating the maze of options and coverage.

We must also revision chronic care beyond the narrow focus on medical services and nursing homes. A report commissioned by the Robert Wood Johnson Foundation over a decade ago (Institute for Health and Aging, 1996) advanced a broader view to address chronic care challenges for the twenty-first century. The report envisions a system of care: a spectrum of integrated services—medical, personal, social, and rehabilitative—to assist people with chronic conditions to live fuller lives. A continuum of care is needed to ensure that individuals and their families receive the level and type of care to fit their condition and changing needs over time and to support independent living, optimal functioning, and well-being.

Facing End-of-life Challenges, Widowhood, and Loss of Loved Ones

Dealing with terminal illness is among families' most painful challenges, complicated by agonizing end-of-life decisions. Most people hope for a natural death, but what is a natural death in our times? Medical technologies prolonging life and the dying process pose unprecedented family challenges. It is crucial to address elders' needs for dignity and control in their own dying process as well as palliative care for comfort and pain control. Clinicians need to work with families to reduce suffering and make the most of precious time together (Walsh, 2006).

Later life is a season of cumulative losses of loved ones, friends, and peers. Family adaptation to loss involves shared grieving and a reorganization of the family relationship system (Walsh & McGoldrick, 2004; see also McGoldrick & Walsh). Avoidance, silence, and secrecy complicate mourning. When patient and family hide knowledge of a terminal illness to protect one another's feelings, communication barriers create distance and misunderstanding, prevent preparatory grief, and deny opportunities to say good-byes. Therapists can assist family members

with feelings of helplessness, anger, loss of control, or guilt that they could not do more. It is usually easier for younger family members to accept the loss of elders whose time has come, than for elders to accept the loss—and their own survival—of siblings or their own children who die first. The death of the last member of the older generation is a family milestone, signifying that the next generation is now the oldest and the next to face death. It is important, also, to address the impact of an elder's death on grandchildren, often their first experience with death and loss.

Widowhood is a highly stressful transition, with a wide range of responses in adaptation. Women, with a longer life expectancy than men, and tending to be younger than their husbands, are more likely to be widowed and to lose their spouse at an earlier age with many years of life ahead. Women in traditional marriages, and more dependent on their husbands, tend to anticipate the prospect of widowhood (Neugarten, 1996). Men tend to be less prepared: The initial sense of loss, disorientation, and loneliness contributes to an increase in their death and suicide rates in the first 2 years (Lopata, 1996). Social contact is often more disrupted for men, since wives tend to link their husbands to family and social networks, especially after retirement. Yet the long-term hardships for widowed women tend to be greater, with more limited financial resources and remarriage prospects. Widows over age 75 are at highest risk of poverty.

The psychosocial tasks in the transition to widowhood involve grief over the loss and reinvestment in future functioning. Despite profound initial grief and challenges in daily living, most surviving spouses are quite resilient over time (Butler, 2008). Most widows view themselves as becoming more competent and independent, and take pride in coping well; only a small portion view the changes entirely negatively (Lopata, 1996). A realignment of relationships in the family system also occurs (Walsh & McGoldrick, 1991). The initial task is to take in the fact of death, transforming shared experiences into memories. Encouraging the expression of grief with family members and through meaningful rituals is most helpful. Attention must also turn to the reality demands of daily functioning and self-support. Wherever possible, clinicians and adult children should help both partners to anticipate and prepare for widowhood. Many need to acquire new skills for independent living, such as managing the household and finances, or returning to the job market. The adjustment to being physically alone, in itself, is difficult. With disabilities, housekeeping and caregiving arrangements may be needed.

Within 1 to 2 years, most widows regain interest in others and new activities. Reentry can be impeded if family and friends who have not faced their own grief, mortality, or possibility of widowhood distance. Further dislocation may occur if the family home is given up or if financial problems or illness block independent functioning. In such cases, many widows move in with adult children, siblings, or a very aged parent.

Remarriage is common for men but less so for women. Not only are there fewer available men, but also, many prefer not to remarry, especially if they have had heavy caregiving responsibilities for a spouse and are reluctant to take on that role again. Economic and legal constraints lead many older couples to live together as committed companions without formal marriage. Critical to the success of remarriage is the relationship with adult children and their approval of the union. Problems can arise when a child views remarriage as disloyal to the deceased parent. Adult children may be shocked by an aged parent's intimacy with a new partner—especially when they cannot conceive of the elderly as attractive or sexually active. Some assume that the new mate is interested only in money. Conflict over a will frequently arises, particularly if children view inheritance as compensation for earlier disappointments or as evidence that they are valued more than the new partner. Burial can be a contentious issue: whether with the deceased spouse and parent of children or with the new partner. Family therapists can facilitate important discussions and planning to avert later conflict.

Cross-Generational Interplay of Life Cycle Issues

In every family, the later life challenges of parents interact with salient developmental issues of their children at their concurrent life phases. With increasing diversity in family patterns and the tendency toward later marriage and child-rearing, different pressures and conflicts may arise. The issues that come to the fore between an older adult parent and young adult child will likely differ from those that arise between a parent and a middle-aged child. Tensions are heightened when developmental strivings are incompatible, as in the following case:

Julia, in her mid-20s, was beginning a social work career and engaged to be married when her 63-year-old mother, who lived 2,000 miles away, was diagnosed with congestive heart failure. Julia felt torn. Her love and sense of obligation were countered by reluctance to put her new job and marriage plans on hold indefinitely. The situation was complicated by issues of separation and identity, normative in early adulthood. She had always been close to her mother and dependent on her direction and support. The geographic distance from home in the life that she had established bolstered her self-reliance. Now, as she was on the threshold of adult commitments, her mother needed her most, and Julia feared losing her.

Phone contact became increasingly strained. Julia's mother saw her failure to return home as uncaring and selfish. Julia made a brief visit, feeling guilty and upset. The uncertain course of the illness made it difficult to know how long her mother would live or when to plan trips. Julia sent her mother gifts. One, picked with special care and affection, was a leather-bound book for her memoirs. On her next visit, Julia discovered the book, unopened, on a closet shelf. Deeply hurt, she screamed at her mother to explain. Her mother replied, "If I wrote my memoirs, I'd have to say how much you've let me down." Julia, very hurt, cut her visit short. Conflict escalated with her fiance, and the wedding plans were canceled. Deeply upset by the breakup, Julia phoned her parents for consolation. Her mother expressed her own disappointment at the canceled plans, saying that she now had nothing to live for. A few hours later, she had a stroke. Julia, too angry to respond, put off a trip home. Her mother died 2 weeks later. Julia scarcely grieved, throwing herself into her work and a new relationship. When that relationship broke up, delayed grief and remorse surfaced, bringing her for therapy. In learning more about her mother's life and losses, Julia found out that her mother's own mother had expressed disappointment in *her* as she was dying. In gaining compassion for her mother, she also reached out to her father, to know and appreciate him better while there was time.

In this case, the mother's developmental needs at the end of life occurred "off-time" from the perspective of the daughter's developmental readiness and out of sync with her age peers. Terminally ill, the mother needed to draw her family close and to feel that she had successfully fulfilled her role as a mother. The young adult daughter was threatened by the closeness and dependency at a time of impending loss, when she was not yet secure in her own life and felt her culture's pressure for autonomy. A transgenerational anniversary reaction complicated the situation as unresolved issues from the mother's estranged relationship with her own mother before her death were revived, adding fuel to the conflict, disappointment, and estrangement at her own life's end.

In our culture, young adults are emerging from the search for identity into issues of commitment and preoccupation with making initial choices, such as marriage, career, and residence, choices that define one's place in the adult world. Responding to caregiving needs and threatened loss of aging parents at this life stage may be fraught with conflict. Clinicians need to help young adults offset the cultural push for family disconnection and prioritize relationships with their elders approaching the end of life.

Successful Aging: Meaning and Connection

Abundant research, including recent neuroscience findings, reveals that the aging process is much more variable and malleable than was long believed (Butler, 2008; Cozolino, 2008). Elders can enhance their own development by actively approaching their challenges and making the most of their strengths and options (Baltes and Baltes, 1990). Studies of normal adult development and family functioning find that a variety of adaptive processes, rather than one single pattern, contribute to successful later-life adjustment (Bengtson, 1996; Birren & Schaie, 2006). This diversity reflects differences in family structures, individual personality styles, gender roles, and ethnic, social class, rural versus urban, and larger cultural influences. The development of new modes of response and aspects of life that were earlier constrained enables a greater role flexibility and adaptation that contribute to life satisfaction.

Betty Friedan's (1993) analysis of international studies on aging suggests that older adults may actually integrate problems at a higher level than the young, particularly in attending to ethical and contextual issues. In revealing "strengths that have no name," from studies of different populations, Friedan noted that many women who had experienced the most profound change and discontinuity were the most vital in later life. Those who were most frustrated, angry, and depressed had held on most rigidly to earlier constraining roles, or had repeated them in their relationships. What distinguished women who were vital was not which roles they played in earlier adulthood, but rather whether they had developed a quest, a sense of purpose, and structure for making life choices and decisions.

In contrast to the redefinition of self that many women move through with menopause, widowhood, or divorce, many aging men's identities continue to be invested in career success and sexual potency (Vaillant, 2002). Such culturally based "proofs" of masculinity generate anxiety, a sense of deficiency, and a void as these powers diminish. Vaillant found that meaningful relationships were the most important factor in men's successful aging. Intimacy can take many forms, deepening over time. It is important to challenge constraining views and explore possibilities for personal and relational fulfillment.

Similarly, successful family functioning in later life requires flexibility in structure, roles, and responses to new developmental priorities and challenges (Walsh, 2006). As patterns that may have been functional in earlier life phases no longer fit, new options can be explored. With the loss of functioning and death of significant family members, others are called upon to assume new roles, responsibilities, and meaningful connections. In doing so, they develop new competencies and enhanced sense of worth. Therapists can invite couples and families to reflect on the choices they have made in life and now wish to make for their remaining time, seeing their alternatives as both limited and extended by personal belief systems, ethnic and cultural identity, social and economic position, and gender. These choices are never simple; most often they are complex and intertwined with the needs and decisions of others.

As Lightfoot-Lawrence (2009) found, many older people from varied walks of life approach maturity with celebration, finding possibilities in aging for enrichment and unexpected pleasures. For her, the greatest reward of parenting has been delight in her fully grown progeny, considering them to be friends with an extra dimension of affection. She finds it powerfully reassuring at this time to think of life, and each day, as time to be fully savored. Many find it to be the best time of life, feeling freer to be themselves, reporting less conflict and more balance; better able to know and use their strengths; and surer of what counts in life.

The Wisdom and Spirit of the Elders

There is growing recognition that later years and relationships have a significance of their own. In Erikson's theory of human development, old age is seen as a critical period, when individuals review earlier life experiences and their meaning in the quest to achieve integration and overcome despair at the end of life's journey. In this process, new adaptive strengths and wisdom can be gained. The task of achieving integration is challenging, as older adults face the finiteness of life and awareness of past deficiencies, hurts, and disappointments. Vital involvement in the present is essential. Some look for models of aging in parents or grandparents; others look to friends, community members, and even media personalities. Such attributes as humor, compassion, curiosity, and commitment contribute to a sense of integrity. Interviews with octogenarians reveal many pathways for integration and reconciliation of earlier life issues (Erikson, Erikson, & Kivnick, 1986). For the most resilient aged people, past traumas and inescapable missteps are put into perspective. Even those who do not achieve integration are actively involved in meaning-making efforts to reach some acceptance of their lives.

A common thread in successful aging is the dynamic process as older people come to see themselves not as victims of life forces, defined by their limitations, but rather as resilient, with the capacity and initiative to shape as well as be shaped by events. Overcoming life's adversities involves the courage to reach out, seeing aging as a personal, relational, and spiritual evolution, seeking new horizons for learning, change, and growth. A priority for clinicians is to recognize and draw out sources of meaning and facilitate efforts by older adults and families to integrate the varied experiences of a lifetime into a coherent sense of self, relational integrity, and life's worth.

King & Wynne (2004) introduced the concept of *family integrity* as the achievement of older adults' developmental striving toward meaning, connection, and continuity within their multigenerational family system. It involves three competencies: 1) dynamic transformation of relationships over time responsive to members' changing life cycle needs; 2) resolution or acceptance of past conflicts and losses; and 3) shared creation of meaning by passing on individual and family legacies across generations. Gaining family integrity generates a deep and abiding sense of peace and satisfaction with past, present, and future family relationships.

Notable in this life phase is the search for life's transcendent meaning. Spiritual beliefs and practices come to the fore with aging, sustaining resilience for most elderly people (Schaie & Krouse, 2004; Walsh, 2009c). Research documents the power of personal faith and contemplative practices, such as prayer, meditation, and rituals, to strengthen well-being and healing by triggering positive emotions and brain activity and by strengthening immune and cardiovascular systems. For instance, a study of elderly patients after open-heart surgery found that those who were able to find hope, solace, and comfort in their religious outlook had a survival rate three times higher than those who did not. What matters most is the ability to draw on the power of faith to give meaning to precarious life challenges and to life itself.

The search for identity and meaning is a lifelong process. Individuals and their families organize, interpret, and connect experiences in many ways. We must be sensitive to the culture and time in which families and their members have lived and the contribution of critical events and structural sources of meaning. For some, religion is most salient; for others, it might be humanistic values, ethnic heritage, or their education that enabled them to rise out of poverty. Many elders show enormous potential for continual self-renewal as they forge new meaning and purpose in their later years (Weiss & Bass, 2001). Emerging research finds that older adults with a greater purpose in life have a reduced risk of Alzheimer's disease and mild cognitive impairment (Boyle, Buchman, Barnes, & Bennett, 2010).

The Significance of Relational Connections

We are relational beings. Companionate bonds, social ties, and community connections become increasingly valued with age (Sluzki, 2000). Research finds a strong link between social contact, support, and longevity. Elders who visit often with friends and family and maintain a thick network of diverse relationships are likely to live longer than those with few kin and social resources (Litwin, 1996). Baby boomers are creating "villages" of interdependence, so that they and their elders can live independently for as long as possible with community interaction, stimulating involvement, and access to needed services. Faith communities play an increasingly important role with aging, from shared communal values and rituals, involvement in congregational activities and community service, to practical, emotional, and spiritual support in times of need.

Longtime and childhood friends become increasingly valued; many reconnect at reunions and through Internet social networks. Old flames are sometimes rekindled in later life. Old friends connect us to our younger selves and offer perspective on our emerging lives. A woman in her mid-60s, anxious that her forgetfulness was an early sign of Alzheimer's, found humor and relief after her college roommate reminded her that she had always been absent minded.

Companion animals play a vital role for the well-being and resilience of many elderly (Baun, Johnson, & McCabe, 2006; Walsh, 2009a), especially those living alone. As one woman related, "My cats have been my constant companions and support— through marriage, divorce, remarriage and widowhood." Studies in nursing homes and dementia units find that animal-assisted therapy and weekly visits by volunteers with their pets significantly brighten mood, increase social interaction and appetite, and enhance the overall well-being of residents (Filan & Llewellyn-Jones, 2006). Clinicians should explore the meaning and significance of pets and their loss. Bereavement can be profound with the death of a cherished pet or with forced relinquishment when moving to a senior residence or nursing home that does not allow pets (Walsh, 2009b).

Clinical Challenges and Opportunities: A Resilience-Oriented Approach

A resilience-oriented approach to practice (Walsh, 2003a, 2006) engages elders collaboratively, affirms their personhood, and focuses on their strengths, resources, and potential. We show interest in their life journey, with compassion for their struggles, suffering, and losses, and with affirmation of their courage and endurance. We encourage their efforts for meaning, purpose, and connections, with conviction in their potential for personal and relational growth. We see their value in the lives of others and draw on kin and social networks to support their optimal functioning and well-being. In contrast, the traditional clinical focus on later life decline and deficits too often leads professionals to objectify the elderly, become unduly pessimistic, underestimate their resourcefulness, and make plans for them based on what professionals think best, as in the following case:

Rita, a 78-year-old widow, was admitted to a psychiatric unit, diagnosed with a confusional state and acute paranoia after an incident in which she accused her landlord of plotting to get rid of her. Rita's increasing visual impairment was making independent living more difficult and hazardous. Her apartment was in disarray. She was socially isolated, stubbornly refusing assistance from "strangers." Her only surviving family member, a sister, lived in another state. The hospital staff, doubting that Rita could continue to function independently, planned a nursing home placement for her. Rita vehemently objected, insisting on returning to her own apartment. Hospitalization was extended "to deal with her resistance."

A family therapist's strength-based interviews with Rita led to a new appreciation of her as a person and to a more collaborative plan. Asked what she valued about living alone, she replied, "I'm not alone; I live with my books and my birds." The therapist expressed interest in hearing more about her life. Rita had been a teacher, happily married without children until her husband's death 10 years earlier. Her beloved father died the following year. After those painful losses, she withdrew, determined never to become dependent on anyone again. Rita centered her life on her work; she was known as a "tough cookie," respected by colleagues for her perseverance with challenging students. Since retirement, she had immersed herself in her books, a vital source of her resilience, enhancing her cognitive functioning and pleasure, and transporting her beyond her immediate circumstances. Many books held special meaning, inherited from her father, a scholar. They revived her close childhood relationship with him, when he had spent countless hours reading to her. Now Rita's loss of vision was most distressing, cutting her off from her valued connections. She enjoyed the chattering and singing of her birds and did not want to give them up with a move.

Rita's strong identification with her father involved intense pride in his part-Native American heritage, a hardiness in adversity, and a will to survive and adapt. The therapist's visit to Rita's apartment revealed these strengths. At first glance, all appeared chaotic: piles of books, clothing, and food containers everywhere. However, at closer inspection, Rita had organized her environment in a system that made sense to adapt to her visual impairment. She had color-coded food containers with a magic marker; arranged clothes by function; and stacked books by subject, easily locating what she needed.

Rita's stubborn "resistance" had been viewed as pathological denial of dependency needs. Yet self-reliance had served Rita well over many years. It was the failing of her primary mode of adaptation—her vision—that brought confusion and anxiety. Her reluctance to become dependent made her reject any aid with one exception: She agreed to contact a religious organization that sent Brothers to read to her whenever she called. She could allow help when she took initiative and had some control in the relational boundaries. This positive experience became a model for building a resource network to support Rita's objective of independent living. She was encouraged to contact trusted neighbors and shopkeepers for occa-

sional assistance. She initiated weekly phone contact with her sister, which led to enjoyable visits with her niece, who loved hearing stories of her grandfather—Rita's beloved father.

Facilitating Family Healing and Resilience

Applying the concept of resilience to the family as a functional unit, a family-resilience approach affirms the potential in couples and families for healing and growth over the life course, tapping into their strengths and building resources as they confront later life challenges (Walsh, 2003b; 2006). Caregiving and end-of-life challenges also hold potential benefits, deepening and enriching relationships, if family members are encouraged to make the most of precious time. Because unresolved conflicts and cut offs may accompany children and grandchildren into their future relationships (Bowen, 1978), it is important to avert the fallout of hurt, misunderstanding, anger, alienation, sense of failure, and guilt. Strains can be prevented and repaired by helping family members to redefine and reintegrate their roles and relationships as they age and mature (King & Wynne, 2004).

A conjoint family life review expands the benefits of individual life-review sessions (Lewis & Butler, 1974) found to assist in the integration of earlier life stages, facilitating acceptance of one's life and approaching death. Sharing reminiscences can be a valuable experience for couples and family members, incorporating multiple perspectives and subjective experiences of their shared life over time. The process of sharing the varied perceptions of hopes and dreams, satisfactions and disappointments enlarges the family story, builds mutual empathy, and can heal old wounds. Earlier conflicts or hurts that led to cut offs or frozen images and expectations can be reconsidered from new vantage points (Fishbane, 2009). Misunderstandings and faulty assumptions about one another can be clarified. Successive life phases can be reviewed as relationships are brought up to date. People in later life are often able to be more open and honest about earlier transgressions or shame-laden family secrets. Past mistakes and hurts can be more readily acknowledged, opening possibilities for forgiveness (Hargrave & Hanna, 1997). At life's end, the simple words, "I'm truly sorry" and "I love you" mean more than ever. Family photos, scrapbooks, genealogies, reunions, and pilgrimages can assist this work. Stories of family history and precious end-of-life conversations can be videotaped and preserved. The transmission of family history to younger generations can be an additional bonus of such work.

Looking Ahead

Families should be encouraged to be proactive in considering and preparing for such challenges as transitional living arrangements and end-of-life decisions, discussions that are commonly avoided. Future-oriented questions can also open up new possibilities for later life fulfillment. One son worried about how each of his parents would manage alone on the family farm if widowed, but he dreaded talking with them about their death. Finally, on a visit home, he got up his courage. First he asked his mother, tentatively, whether she had ever thought about what she might do if Dad were the first to go. She replied, "Sure, I know exactly what I'd do: I'd sell the farm and move to Texas to be near our grandkids." Her husband shook his head and replied, "Well if that isn't the darnedest thing! I've thought a lot about it too, and if your mother weren't here, I'd sell the farm and move to Texas!" This conversation led the couple to sell the farm and move to Texas, where they enjoyed many happy years with their children and grandchildren.

Expanding Our Developmental Lens

Clinical literature and training programs tend to emphasize early developmental phases: young couples and families raising children. At launching of the young adults, attention follows the younger generation into their own couple and family formation, relegating the parent generation to the margins, as extended kin. The term "postparental" is unfortunate, as parents never cease to be parents, with lifelong concern for the well-being of their children. The term "family of origin" connotes an older generation left behind, with clinical inquiry about past influence. Because more people are living healthier and longer lives than in the past, we

lack role models for later-life family relations, just as we lack appropriate labels and role definitions. We need to expand our developmental lens to the full life course, addressing the assets, needs, and concerns of individuals, couples, and families in their later years. I once assigned a group of medical students to interview an older couple about their life course. The students looked stunned. One acknowledged that he had never had a real conversation with an older person, including his parents, and he had never considered what his own aging would look like. This led us to a valuable discussion of age segregation in our society and professional ageism stemming largely from our culture's preoccupation with youth and avoidance of the reality of aging, losses, and death.

As clinicians, we need to deepen awareness of our own apprehensions and biases, enlarge our perspective on the whole life course, and gain appreciation of what it is like to mature and become old, for relationships to evolve and grow stronger, and for new ones to develop, meeting emerging priorities. Our interface issues with our aging family members—and denial of our own aging process—may contribute to anxiety, avoidance, over-responsibility, or empathic difficulties. As we better appreciate the elders in our own families, attend to our own losses and grievances, and explore our own growing maturity, therapeutic work with individuals, couples, and families in later life will take on deeper meaning and possibilities for growth.

The complexity and diversity of family networks in later life require careful clinical assessment. Given the prevalent pattern of intimacy at a distance, we must look beyond the sharing of a household to identify significant relationships and potential bonds. Drawing a genogram with an elder can be useful in identifying those who are significant and could be drawn upon for support and companionship. Problems involving family relationships with elderly members are often hidden behind complaints of marital distress or child-focused symptoms. Older adults are more likely to present somatic complaints than emotional or relational problems. Family relationships can exacerbate or alleviate their suffering. The stressful impact of chronic illness on loved ones requires attention to family needs for support, information, caregiving guidelines, respite, and linkage to community resources. Families are our most valuable resources in providing not only caregiving, but also a sense of worth, lasting emotional ties, and human dignity in approaching life's end. We can strengthen their resilience by understanding their challenges and supporting them in our social policies and provision of health care.

The importance of prevention for healthy and satisfying later years cannot be overstressed (Weil, 2005). Efforts are needed to lower risk factors that diminish life expectance and well-being: the rampant increase of obesity, fast foods, sedentary life styles, and the loss of family ties, community participation, and productive employment or activity. Developmental models for understanding growth and change in later life need to include wisdom and integrative understanding of the values and meanings that are salient to elders. Clinical services must be flexible to fit the diversity of older people and their significant relationships and to support optimal functioning and integration in the community. It is important to engage in lifelong learning, keep active in meaningful pursuits, strengthen kinship bonds, rekindle old friendships, and make new ones.

This expansion of later life has been called the "aging revolution." What will we do with this gift of long life? How can we contribute to people's ability to live and to love with vitality into advanced old age? Important in the resilience of our society is a sense of pride in age, the value of history and life experience, and the capacity to adapt courageously to change. Elders can be encouraged to draw on their rich experience to inform both continuity and innovation, as society's historians and futurists. The wisdom of our elders, linked with the energy and new knowledge of the young, can be the basis for rich interchange and planning for the future.

Chapter 18

Death, Loss, and the Family Life Cycle

Monica McGoldrick & Froma Walsh

Death and loss are the most profound challenges families confront. They are transactional processes involving those who die and their survivors in a shared life cycle that acknowledges both the finality of death and the continuity of life. Yet, the dominant Anglo American culture long fostered a widespread tendency to deny death and to minimize the profound impact of loss (Becker, 1973). Indeed, the medical profession treated death as a failure to be avoided at all costs, and distanced from dying patients and their loved ones. More recently, developments in palliative care and hospice ease suffering and provide support and comfort to patients and families facing end-of-life challenges. We have transformed the funeral into a celebration of life alongside the sorrow of loss, with more active involvement of significant family members and others in sharing memories, stories, and grief and providing mutual support.

Still, insufficient attention has been given to the ramifications of loss for the family system and the immediate and long-term effects of death for siblings, parents, children, and extended kin. Legacies of loss touch all survivors' relationships, rippling throughout the family network, influencing many who have never even known the person who died. The meaning and consequences of loss vary depending on many factors, including the state of relationships, family functioning, and the particular phase of the life cycle at the time of loss (Walsh & McGoldrick, 2004). Whatever our therapeutic approach, a family life cycle perspective enables us to facilitate adaptation, which strengthens the whole family for future life passages.

Family Adaptation to Loss

Death poses shared adaptational challenges, involving both immediate and long-term family reorganization and changes in a family's identity and purpose (Shapiro, 1994). The ability to accept loss is at the heart of all strengths in healthy family functioning (Walsh, 2006). Adaptation does not mean resolution, but rather finding ways to put the loss in perspective and to move ahead with life. The multiple meanings of each death are transformed throughout the life cycle, as they are integrated with other life experiences, especially losses.

We must consider the tremendous diversity in cultural norms, religious traditions, and gender roles in approaching death, in funeral and burial or cremation rites, and in prescribed as well as proscribed mourning processes (Martin & Doka, 2000; Gamino & Ritter, 2009; Parkes, 2009; McGoldrick, Schlesinger, Hines, Lee, Chan, Almeida, Petkov, Garcia Preto, & Petry, 2004; Parkes, Laungani, & Young, 1997; Walsh, 2009a).

We also need to be mindful of the varied family structures and complex bonds in contemporary society and carefully assess the importance of relationships within and beyond a household (Walsh, 2003a). For instance, the loss of grandparents, generally expected in later life, can have profound meaning if the grandparents have played a central child-rearing role, as is common in many African American, immigrant, and single-parent families and in kinship care placements in cases of parental substance abuse, incarceration, child abuse, or neglect.

More complicated emotional ramifications are likely to flow down the system if the parent and grandparent had a troubled relationship, which remained unresolved at the time of the grandparent's death.

The bereavement field has matured from early expectations of fixed stages, sequences, or schedules in a presumed "normal" mourning process to recognize the wide variation, complexity, and diversity of family and individual coping styles and pacing in grief (Wortman & Silver, 1989). Attention commonly oscillates between preoccupation with grief and adaptive challenges ahead, reengaging in a world forever transformed by loss (Stroebe, Hansonn, Henk, & Stroebe, 2008). When profound loss is suffered, we should not expect resolution in the sense of some complete, "once-and-for-all" getting over it. Resilience should not be seen as simply "bouncing back," readily getting "closure" on the experience, and moving on (Walsh, 2003b). Recovery is a gradual process over time, usually lessening in intensity, yet often lasting a lifetime. Various facets of grief may reemerge with unexpected intensity, particularly with anniversaries and other nodal events. In traditional psychiatric approaches to grief work, mourning was thought to require letting go of lost attachments. Bereavement specialists now view adaptive mourning as best facilitated by transformation from physical presence of the loved one to continuing bonds through spiritual connections, memories, stories, deeds, and legacies to honor the life lost (Walsh & McGoldrick, 2004). Coming to terms with a significant loss involves making meaning of the loss, putting it in perspective, and weaving the experience of loss and recovery into the fabric of individual and collective identity and life passage.

While we must be mindful of the varied approaches to loss, there are crucial family adaptational challenges that, if not dealt with, heighten risk for individual and family dysfunction. Four major family tasks tend to promote immediate and long-term adaptation for family members and to strengthen the family as a functional unit.

1. SHARED ACKNOWLEDGMENT OF THE DEATH AND LOSS This is facilitated by direct contact with the dying person when possible and by clear information and open communication about the facts and circumstances of the death. Those unable to accept the reality of death tend to avoid contact or become angry with others who are grieving and moving on with life.

2. SHARED EXPERIENCE OF LOSS Funeral rituals and visits to the grave or memorial site provide opportunity to pay respects, to share grief, and to receive comfort. A climate of trust, empathic support, and tolerance for varied pathways in healing is crucial. Intense emotions can fuel reactivity, longstanding conflicts, and cut offs. Family efforts to make meaning of their loss experience involve gaining a meaningful perspective that fosters a sense of continuity with their belief system and life course, including future implications of the loss (Nadeau, 2001).

3. REORGANIZATION OF FAMILY SYSTEM Recovery from the disruptive impact of loss involves a realignment of relationships, redistribution of role functions to compensate for the loss, and restabilization in patterns of living, in order to promote adaptive cohesion and flexibility in the family system.

4. REINVESTMENT IN OTHER RELATIONSHIPS AND LIFE PURSUITS As time passes, survivors need to transform their lives and relationships to move forward, constructing new hopes and dreams, and revising life plans and aspirations.

Family Adaptation to Loss

The particular timing of a loss in the multigenerational family life cycle may pose a higher risk for dysfunction. In family assessment, a genogram and timeline are essential tools in tracking sequences and concurrences of nodal events over time in the multigenerational family system (McGoldrick, Gerson, & Petry, 2008; McGoldrick, 2010). When an individual in a family is symptomatic, we pay particular attention to unresolved past losses as well as recent and threatened losses. In cases of marital breakdown, we are especially careful to inquire about losses that occurred at the start of the relationship, as well as losses coinciding with problem onset. A number of factors influence the impact of loss.

UNTIMELY LOSSES Deaths that are premature in terms of chronological or social expectations, such as early widowhood, early parent loss, or death of a child, tend to be more painful for families. Many families struggle to find some meaning for a loss that seems unjust. Prolonged mourning is common. Survivor guilt can block life pursuits or satisfaction for spouses, siblings, and parents. The death of a child, which reverses the natural order of life, is the most painful loss of all.

PILE-UP OF MULTIPLE LOSSES AND OTHER MAJOR LIFE CHANGES When a loss coincides with other losses, developmental milestones, or major stress events, it may overload a family, posing incompatible demands. Extended kin and social support are crucial (McGoldrick & Walsh, 1983). We pay particular attention to the concurrence of death with the birth of a child, since preoccupation with grief may interfere with parenting. If grief is blocked, a child born at that time may assume a special replacement function, which can be the impetus for high achievement or dysfunction. Similarly, a marriage in the immediate wake of loss is likely to confound the two relationships, interfering with bereavement and/or investment in the new relationship in its own right.

TRANSGENERATIONAL PATTERNS AND TRAUMATIC LOSS Family patterns are often replicated in the next generation when a child reaches the same age or nodal point as the parent at the time of death or traumatic loss. One husband's extreme anger over his wife's desire to have a second child was only understood when genogram exploration revealed that his mother had died in giving birth to his younger sister. He had not realized his catastrophic fears of losing his beloved spouse.

With traumatic deaths, intense feelings are often cut off and may go underground, becoming encoded in covert family scripts that are enacted years later with dire consequences (Byng-Hall, 2004). When a child reaches the age at which a parent experienced a traumatic death, it is important to assess a risk of suicide or destructive behavior. In one chilling case, a 15-year-old youth stabbed an older stranger in the street in a dissociated episode, which was ignored by the family. Following a repeated stabbing offense

and psychiatric hospitalization, family assessment revealed that the father, at age 15, had witnessed the stabbing death of his own father by a stranger in the street. Study of such transgenerational anniversary patterns with traumatic loss is needed to more fully understand such systemic transmission processes. Clinical interventions should aim to help family members gain awareness of covert patterns and to differentiate present relationships from the past so that history need not repeat itself.

NATURE OF THE DEATH With *sudden death,* family members lack time to anticipate and prepare for the loss, to deal with unfinished business, or even to say their good-byes. Chronic conditions and a *prolonged dying process* can deplete family caregiving and financial resources and put needs of other members on hold. Relief at ending patient suffering and family strain is often guilt-laden (Ellison & Bradshaw, 2009). Moreover, with medical technology, families are increasingly confronted with excruciating *end-of-life dilemmas* over whether, and how long, to maintain life support efforts.

Ambiguity surrounding a loss can block mourning and produce anxiety and depression in family members (Boss, 2004). A loved one may be physically absent but psychologically present, such as an abducted child or a soldier missing in action. Uncertainty about whether they are dead or alive can be agonizing. Families may become consumed by desperate searches and attempts to get information to confirm the fate of their loved one. Serious conflict often arises as some members hold out hope when others have given up and are ready to move on with life. The inability to recover a body complicates grieving.

Violent deaths have a devastating impact. A senseless tragedy is especially hard to bear, such as a suicide or a death that is the result of deliberate harm or negligence, as in drunk driving. Clinicians should sensitively inquire about past traumatic loss, particularly in refugee experiences; in military service; and in communities impacted by high crime, drugs, and gangs. The witnessing of atrocities and the taking and loss of lives may haunt survivors for years to come. Body deformity or dismemberment may be a recurring image. Post-traumatic stress symptoms affect all family relationships (Figley, 1998). *Suicides* are the most anguishing deaths for families to come to terms with, as members struggle to comprehend the self-destructive act and whether they might have made a difference.

In *traumatic deaths,* research reveals that most survivors are resilient in recovery after initial deep distress (Bonnano, 2004; Walsh, 2007). However 15 to 30 percent suffer long-term symptoms of PTSD, depression, anxiety, substance abuse, relational conflict, and estrangement. Massive trauma or loss of hope and positive vision can fuel transmission of negative intergenerational patterns (Danieli, 1985), affecting those not yet born. Survivors blocked from healing may perpetuate suffering through self-destructive behavior or revenge and harm toward others. With murder, atrocities, and injustice, the impetus for retaliation to restore a sense of family or community honor can lead to cycles of mutual destruction. Family therapy, community support, and pastoral counseling can be valuable in facilitating possibilities for forgiveness, reconciliation, healing, and resilience (Walsh, 2007, 2009d).

ROLE FUNCTION AND STATE OF RELATIONSHIPS

The more important the person was in family life and the more central in family functioning (e.g., primary breadwinner or caregiver) the greater the loss. The death of an only child, or the only son or daughter, leaves a particular void. A death in highly conflictual or estranged relationships may be unexpectedly traumatic because it is too late to repair bonds. It is important to help families draw on their kin and social network to fill crucial role functions and to avoid precipitous replacement, such as a new partner or baby, sacrificing that individual's own needs and complicating that relationship.

Loss at Various Family Life Cycle Stages

Over the past century, the average life expectancy in the United States has increased dramatically from 47 years to nearly 80 years. Women die on average more than 5 years later than men, and Whites die, on average, more than 5 years later than African Americans (Hitti, 2010). Most Americans die in institutions. Those who die before middle age die mostly of accidents, homicide, or suicide, with firearms death a major factor (almost 30 percent) in death of adolescents and young adults (McIntosh, 1999). The expectable causes of death as well as the mourning process following it vary, depending on the phase of the family life cycle.

Young adult phase

We start the discussion at this phase, rather than at birth, because it begins a new systemic trajectory in life. Because of societal expectations for young adults to become independent from their families, the significance of loss may not be recognized and mourning may be more complicated. At launching, the family renegotiates intergenerational relationships to a more equal balance as adults to adults. Where relationships have been especially close or intensely conflictual, young adults may seek distance through physical or emotional cut off. Such pseudoautonomy tends to disintegrate upon contact with the family and leads to distancing in other relationships.

The death of a young adult is a tragedy for the entire family and may produce long-lasting grief (Rando, 1986, 1993). Many experience a sense of injustice in the ending of a life they have nurtured before it has reached its prime. Survivor guilt may block parents and siblings from continuing their own pursuits. Siblings may be expected to carry the torch and yet be blocked from realizing their own potential by prior sibling rivalry, survivor guilt, and conflicting family injunctions to replace, but not surpass, the lost child (Worden, 2008; McGoldrick, 2010, Chapter on siblings).

Brian (**Genogram 18.1**), age 29, sought therapy for a repeated cycle of setting grandiose career goals that he pursued at a fevered pitch, only to undermine himself each time he was on the brink of success. He felt extreme discomfort whenever he returned home, which his parents had made into a "shrine" to his older brother, who had been killed in military service at age 21. Pictures, medals, and plaques covered the walls. Brian felt a strong expectation from his parents to ful-

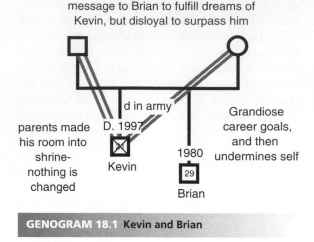

message to Brian to fulfill dreams of
Kevin, but disloyal to surpass him

d in army

parents made
his room into
shrine-
nothing is
changed

D. 1997

Kevin

1980

Grandiose
career goals,
and then
undermines self

Brian

GENOGRAM 18.1 Kevin and Brian

fill their dreams for their firstborn son—yet he sensed a
counter injunction that it would be disloyal to surpass his
brother. Therapy focused on shifting his triangulated position, helping him and his parents to unknot his bind.

The impact of parents' loss for young adults
may be seriously underestimated by them, their families, friends, and even therapists. A parent's terminal illness is particularly difficult for those who have
moved away and are invested in launching career or

relationship commitments and feel torn between
their own life pursuits and parental needs for care
(see Chapter 17 on Families in Later Life). Those
who are not yet secure on their own may also be
threatened by dependence and closeness. In a highly
fused relationship, a parent's dying may stir fears of
a loss of self. If the impact of parental loss is not
acknowledged, a young adult may distance from the
family and seek emotional replacement in a romantic
involvement or in having a baby.

In some cases, newly initiated adult life pursuits may need to be abandoned or put on hold. The
oldest son may be expected to become the head of
the family or carry on a family business. Daughters
are more likely expected to assume primary caregiving functions for the surviving parent, younger siblings, and aged grandparents. An adult child may
move back home or take in a widowed parent. In one
case, Jack (**Genogram 18.2**), the youngest son with
three older sisters from an Irish family, had lost his
mother to cancer when he was 16, the year before he
left home for college. All three sisters had been just
enough older that they had left home and married at
young ages within a year of the mother's death, in
what seemed an effort to distance from the pain of
her difficult last years, which the sisters and father
preferred to forget so they could think of her as a

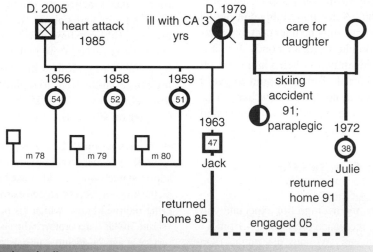

GENOGRAM 18.2 Jack and Julie

saint. While in college Jack tried to talk to his father who said God would forgive him for what he was saying about his mother's resentment and rages in her last years, but to Jack's surprise began dating the next week, for the first time in the 3 years since the mother's death. After Jack's graduation, he returned home to live with his father to whom he had become more attached and who suffered from a heart condition. While his career moved along, Jack could not find a relationship that worked until after his father's death—20 years later. It was only at that point, at age 42, that he fell in love for the first time and could focus on starting his own family. It is interesting that the partner he chose was a woman who had herself returned home at age 19, when her sister suffered brain damage in a skiing accident and became paraplegic, cared for at home. Caregiving responsibilities and both guilt and loyalty issues can block life cycle passage for years. Both the precipitous launching of Jack's older sisters, and his own delayed launching seemed to be precipitated by their mother's untimely death and the complex and negative legacy surrounding it. Jack's repair of his relationship with his father facilitated his eventual partnership with Julie—yet not until his death, The longterm complications might have been averted if the family had been able to work through their feelings about her in the wake of her painful death. However, the sisters had adamantly refused to meet with Jack, blaming him for his negative memories of their sainted mother.

Young couples: The joining of families through marriage

The untimeliness of widowhood in early marriage complicates bereavement for the surviving spouse (Parkes & Weiss, 1983; Parkes, 2009). Early widowhood can be a shocking and isolating experience without emotional preparation or social supports (Parkes 2001; Kastenbaum, 1998). Young widow(er)s, coping with spousal loss and the loss of shared dreams for the future, often find that peers distance to avoid confronting their own mortality or possible widowhood. Generally, widowed men receive more support than women; yet they are less likely to have intimate male friends for emotional sharing. Some confuse sexual intimacy with needs for comfort and dependency. Relationships with in-laws, strained at this time, often break off as the survivor moves on. Those who run precipitously into a new relationship to avoid the pain of loss most often carry along unaddressed mourning, which surfaces later. Men tend to move on more rapidly, expecting a new partner to be sympathetic toward their situation.

Infertility, miscarriage, and perinatal losses

Infertility, often a hidden loss, involves the loss of hopes and dreams (Werner-Lin & Moro, 2004). The impact of loss becomes more painful as each monthly cycle passes and as menopause approaches, especially when medical interventions repeatedly fail. When out of phase with siblings and friends, who are excited over their own pregnancies or newborns, distress is heightened and couples may avoid contact and discussion of their own situation. The incidence of infertility has been rising, associated, in part, with postponement of childbearing. Those who have pursued careers before starting a family are especially vulnerable to self-blame. It is crucial for clinicians to assuage feelings that adults have not progressed "normally" in the family life cycle without children and to help them find meaningful ways to express their generativity.

Losses in stillbirths, miscarriages, and abortion are often unknown, unacknowledged, or minimized by others, rendering the experience more painful and isolated (Doka, 2002; Werner-Lin, & Moro, 2004). A decision for abortion is not easily made and is fraught with moral, religious, and legal concerns. With perinatal losses, disappointment and sorrow may include the loss of a desired child and the fear of future pregnancy complications. Women, carrying the pregnancy, commonly feel the attachment and loss more deeply than their partners and are also more likely to be faulted or blame themselves. Well-intentioned relatives or friends may encourage couples to try immediately to conceive another child. Where there is social stigma or a lack of resources, partners may turn in on themselves, in a "two against the world" stance, or withdrawal and mutual blame for the inability to make up for each other's sense of loss. Since the loss of a child places a couple's relationship at risk, brief couples' intervention can facilitate the mourning process and mutual support (Oliver, 1999). It is crucial to help partners share their grief; typically, mothers attend perinatal loss groups for parents, but most fathers do not. Grief is facilitated by encouraging parents to name and have contact with and share photos of the newborn, hold a simple memorial service, and bury the child in a marked grave.

Parental illness or death

Parental illness or death may propel an individual into marriage, embedding residuals of unaddressed mourning in the new couple relationship (see Chapter 13 on couples). When young couples are focused on establishing their own lives, the sense of responsibility to parents may produce conflicts between loyalty to the family of origin and to the marriage. Increased attention, caregiving, or financial support to the dying or surviving parent or absorption in the grief process strains the couple relationship, especially if the grieving partner feels unsupported or the other partner feels neglected over an extended period of time. Disappointment and distancing may disrupt the intimate/sexual relationship (Paul & Paul, 1989). In cross-cultural marriages, a spouse expecting the marriage to come first may not understand that a partner, from a Latino culture, for example, is expected to place intergenerational bonds and obligations over spousal investment (Falicov, 1998). Encouraging mutual understanding and support facilitates mourning and strengthens relational resilience (Walsh, 2006).

Changes in adult sibling relationships are often brought on by the death of a parent. Sisters are more likely to be stressed by the cultural expectation for daughters to be primary parental caregivers (see Chapter 10 on Siblings). Brothers tend to shoulder more of the financial responsibilities but less of the day-to-day caregiving. Old sibling rivalries may erupt into conflict over who was more favored at the end, more burdencd, or more neglectful of the dying parent. Competitive struggles may ensue over succession issues where a family business is involved. In many cases, siblings develop better relations after parental death. Two brothers who had competed for their father's approval since childhood found their relationship freed from old rivalries after his death.

Families with young children

The loss of a mate at this life phase is complicated by financial and child-rearing obligations, which can interfere with the tasks of mourning. Children may cover their own grief and distract the bereaved parent from grieving out of anxiety of losing their only surviving parent (Fulmer, 1983). Support from extended family members and friends is essential to permit the surviving parent to grieve. Yet, well-intentioned family members or friends often encourage a survivor to rush into a new relationship, often to fill a missing parental role for children, but blocking their shared grief experience.

The death of a child is the most tragic of all untimely losses, reversing generational expectations (Worden, 2001). It is often said that, "When your parent dies, you have lost your past. When your child dies, you have lost your future." The sense of injustice in the death of a child can lead family members to the most profound questioning of the meaning of life, involving as it does the loss of parents' hopes and dreams. Most Americans turn toward their faith for comfort and new purpose in their lives (Walsh, 2009c). Some turn away, such as one father, who cried out, "I'm angry at God! How could a loving God take the life of an innocent child?" It was important to understand the tremendous significance of this child for the entire kin network: He was the firstborn son of the firstborn son in an Orthodox Greek extended family.

Of all losses, it is hardest not to idealize a child who has died. Grief tends to persist and may even intensify with the passage of time (Rando, 1986). A number of studies have documented the high distress of bereaved parents on such indicators as depression, anxiety, somatic symptoms, self-esteem, and sense of control in life. The couple relationship is particularly vulnerable after a child's death, with heightened risk of deterioration and divorce (Rando, 1986). Yet, couples that are helped to pull together and comfort each other can emerge with deepened relational bonds (Walsh, 2006; Oliver, 1999).

Particularly difficult are the death of the firstborn, an only child, the only son or daughter, a gifted child, or one with special needs. Because small children are so utterly dependent on parents for their safety and survival, parental guilt tends to be espe-

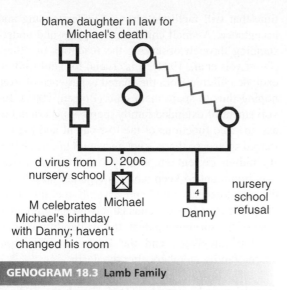

blame daughter in law for
Michael's death

d virus from
nursery school

D. 2006

M celebrates
Michael's birthday
with Danny; haven't
changed his room

Michael

Danny

nursery
school
refusal

GENOGRAM 18.3 Lamb Family

cially strong in accidental or ambiguous deaths, such as SIDS (sudden infant death syndrome). Blame is particularly likely to fall on mothers, who are expected to carry the primary responsibility for a child's well-being, even where paternal abuse or neglect are implicated. Parental difficulties with the loss of a child may be presented through symptomatic behavior of a sibling, as in the following case:

The Lamb family (**Genogram 18.3**: Lamb Family) came to therapy when their 4-year-old-son, Danny, refused to go to nursery school. In taking a family history, the therapist learned that an older brother, Michael, had died suddenly at the same age, 3 years earlier, after developing a high fever from a virus he had picked up at nursery school. Mr. Lamb—and his extended family—blamed the mother for the death and treated her coldly thereafter. Isolated in her grief, she kept Michael's room intact and continued to celebrate his birthdays with Danny, each year making a birthday cake with candles for the age he would have been.

Bereavement is eased when both parents have participated in taking care of a sick child prior to death and when they share a philosophy of life or strong religious beliefs that offer meaning and comfort (Walsh, 2009c). Multifamily groups can provide a valuable supportive network for dealing with the painful experience. Every effort should be made to involve both parents; too often only mothers participate in bereave-

ment groups or therapy. As noted above, the risk of divorce is high for parents who have lost a child. Strengthening their relationship is crucial at this vulnerable time (Oliver, 1999; Walsh, 2006).

The needs of siblings and other family members are too often neglected around the death of a child. Siblings may suffer silently on the sidelines. Along with their sibling's death, they may experience secondary parent loss through the parents' preoccupation with the dying process, funeral arrangements, and their own grieving. Some parents withdraw from surviving children to avoid ever being vulnerable to loss again. Others may become overprotective and vigilant and later have difficulty with separation and launching transitions.

Normal sibling rivalry may contribute to survival guilt that can block developmental strivings well into adulthood. A sibling may also be inducted into a replacement role for the family. Such response is not necessarily pathogenic. Investing energy in surviving children facilitates positive adjustment over time for parents (Videka-Sherman, 1982). However, the long-term consequences for the replacement child must be considered. Our clinical experience suggests that if the child's own needs and unique attributes are not affirmed, later attempts at separation and individuation may disrupt the family equilibrium and precipitate delayed grief responses in parents.

Children who lose a parent may suffer long-term effects, including illness, depression, and other emotional disturbances, as well as trouble forming intimate attachments or catastrophic fears of separation and abandonment (Boyd-Webb, 2002; Furman, 1974; Osterweis et al., 1984; Worden, 2008; Cook & Oltjenbruns, 1998). Later difficulty in parenting may emerge, particularly when another child reaches the age at which the family lost their first child. At that point, the relationship may become blocked, the parent may distance, and/or the child may become symptomatic.

Phil and Stacey Kronek (**Genogram 18.4**) had a stable if unhappy marriage for many years, both parents focusing their energies on their only daughter, Lisa. Phil, also an only child, was a successful lawyer involved in politics and community activities. He had had many affairs over the years and Stacey, who had herself come from an unhappy alcoholic family, had worked in his office but never asked too many questions about his many trips or hints she had of his affairs. She had finally initiated couples therapy only because her daughter was reacting to the tension between the parents; in the first session Phil announced that he wanted a separation. Within a month he introduced his daughter to his new girlfriend, Marti, whom he planned to marry, and insisted she call her "mom" although he was not even divorced. It took considerable effort to slow him down to explore the feelings behind his precipitous life changes. Lisa was just turning 15—his age when his own mother, also named Marty, had died of a sudden heart attack. His headlong rush to reconfigure his life seemed triggered by anxiety about his adolescent loss, which he still found intolerable to discuss.

Children's reactions to death will depend on their stage of emotional and cognitive development, on the way adults deal with them around the death, and on the degree of care they have lost. It is important for adults to recognize the limitations of a child's ability to understand what is happening and not to be alarmed by seemingly unemotional or "inappropriate" responses. It is important to keep communication open to the many conversations over

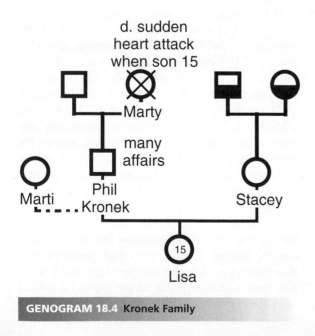

GENOGRAM 18.4 *Kronek Family*

time that will facilitate growing understanding and acceptance. A small child seeks support and understanding through observing the reactions of others (Osterweis et al., 1984). It is crucial for adults not to exclude children from the shared experience of loss, hoping thus to spare them pain (Bowen, 2004). Involvement of extended family members is crucial to assume role functions of the lost parent and the bereaved spouse so there is not a vacuum in caregiving. If children are sent temporarily to live with relatives, it is important to keep siblings together so they do not also lose that vital bond. Overall, a child's handling of parent loss depends largely on the emotional state of the surviving parent, the availability of other reliable caregivers, and the level of cooperation among family members after the death.

The loss of a grandparent is often a child's first experience in learning how to deal with the death of a significant family member. Children will be reassured by seeing that parents can cope with the loss. If the grandparent has suffered a prolonged illness with major caregiving demands, the parent will be stressed by pulls in two directions: toward the heavy responsibilities of caring for young children and toward filial obligations for the dying and surviving parent. In families where the grandmother had served a primary child-rearing role, her loss is more profound, because of both the emotional bond for children and the function she served in the family. Other major losses, which often go unrecognized for children, include loss of a nanny, housekeeper, godparent, or a cherished pet (Walsh, 2009b).

Families with adolescents

Death at this phase is complicated because the primary developmental tasks of adolescent separation and individuation conflict with the ability to acknowledge the significance of the lost bond and to give and receive emotional support. With life-threatening illnesses such as cancer, adolescent defiance often affects compliance with treatments, sparking battles with parents and heightening health risks. The most common adolescent deaths are from accidents, often complicated by impulsive, risk-taking, or self-destructive behavior, such as substance abuse and reckless driving, and from suicide and homicide

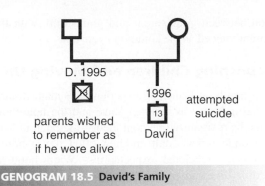

GENOGRAM 18.5 David's Family

(McIntosh, 1999). Family members commonly carry intense anger, frustration, sadness, and despair about the senseless loss of a young life. Lethal firearms have contributed to an alarming increase in homicides, particularly in neighborhoods where violence and drugs take a tragic toll of young lives. As Burton's (1995) research has shown, poor, minority adolescents in dangerous and blighted communities commonly have a foreshortened expectation of their life cycle and a sense of hopelessness about their future. The high risk of early violent death, especially for young males, fuels doubts about even reaching adulthood and contributes to a focus on immediate gratification, early sex and parenthood, and self-destructive drug abuse.

Any number of problems in living, fueled by the strong peer and media influences, contribute to an adolescent's self-destructive behavior, such as eating disorders, cutting, or an actual decision to commit suicide. When a suicide attempt occurs, the whole family should be convened, helped to understand and reconstruct meanings surrounding the experience, and helped to repair any family fragmentation from earlier adversities (Dunne & Dunne-Maxim, 2004). It is crucial to explore possible connections to other traumatic losses in the family system (Walsh & McGoldrick, 2004), especially other suicides, as in the following case.

David, age 13, (**Genogram 18.5**) was hospitalized following an attempted suicide. He and his family were at a loss to explain the episode and made no mention of an older brother, who had died shortly before David's birth. This event was revealed in doing the family genogram. In exploring this, David revealed that to relieve his parents'

sadness, he had grown up attempting to take his brother's place, wearing his handed down clothes and combing his hair to resemble photos of the brother he had never known. Now that he was turning 14, and changing physically, he didn't know how to be anymore, so he decided to join his brother in heaven. Family therapy focused on enabling David and his parents to relinquish his surrogate position and to encourage his own development.

Adolescents frequently retreat from family interaction following a death, may rebuff parents' initial attempts to engage them, and may talk to no one about the experience. Yet, studies find that most adolescents want to discuss core issues concerning the meaning of life, suggesting the importance of conversations that help them clarify their beliefs and feelings about death and loss (Walsh, 2009a). Such discussions will, of course, be attuned to each family's cultural and spiritual background and prior experience with loss.

Because our dominant culture encourages adolescents to push away from parental closeness, influence, and control, the death of a parent is likely to be complicated by mixed feelings and minimization of the significance of the loss. If the deceased parent is idealized by the family or community, a youth who experienced high conflict, abuse, or neglect may well feel disqualified and become alienated from the family, as in the case of Jack described above.

Adolescents who may have wished to be rid of parental control may feel considerable guilt if a parent actually dies. Such a loss at this phase may also be complicated by the pull of peer models, of acting-out behavior to escape pain, through stealing, drinking, drugs, sexual activity, or fighting, or they may withdraw socially. Girls often develop eating disorders, become sexually active or pregnant, or seek intimacy to comfort themselves and replace their loss. Adolescent acting-out behavior, in turn, stresses the family, and may involve school or juvenile authorities. Such larger systems tend to focus narrowly on the child's problem behavior. It is crucial to assess the context of behavior problems routinely and, where there are recent or impending losses, to assist the family, not only the symptomatic child, in addressing them. Weingarten (1996), drawing on her positive experience in sharing her battle with a life-threatening illness with her own teenage children, argues that maturity, relational connectedness, and empathy are fostered if adolescents are encouraged to stay connected to their parents and to understand their life struggles. Since adolescents may not approach parents, it's crucial for parents to encourage them to voice their concerns and to keep the door open as other concerns surface over time.

A single-parent called after finding her 13 year old daughter's letter to her camp counselor saying she wanted to die. The mother, who had been battling breast cancer for several years, had recently learned the cancer had spread and was no longer treatable. Trying to be cheerful, she kept the daughter busy with activities and avoided discussion of her terminal condition. The daughter, not wanting to burden her mother, showed no sign of distress and got straight A's at school. It was crucial to help them share the reality of her condition and anticipate the loss, so that they could prepare for the challenges ahead and make the most of precious time together.

Teenagers, as well as younger children, do worry about their own future. The daughter in this family, with heightened concern about her developing body at puberty, worried that she too would get breast cancer and die. With a heritable disease, offspring do carry risk of illness and death, and may suffer anticipatory loss (See Rolland, Chapter 23).

Adolescents are often less ambivalent and more openly expressive of sadness about the loss of a grandparent. Naturally, a parent can feel conflicted when having to cope simultaneously with the grandparent's death and the adolescent's separation. This experience may be intensified if the parent's own adolescence was troublesome and old relational conflicts are unresolved. Teens are frequently the barometer of family feelings, expressing the inexpressible and drawing needed attention to family problems. If parents cannot deal with their own emotional loss issues, an adolescent will often pick up parental feelings and, not knowing a better way to help, will draw fire by misbehavior. Mourning is likely to be complicated by longstanding intergenerational triangles, in which problems between parent and grandparent a generation earlier led to a coali-

tion between grandparent and grandchild, with the parent viewed as the common enemy.

Launching Children and Moving On

The family at launching experiences a major transitional upheaval as children leave and the household must be reorganized without them—although in hard economic times, adult children often return home, confusing relational expectations. Widowhood at midlife, like earlier widowhood, is much more difficult than in later life because it is off-time from social expectations and less commonly experienced by peers. At launching, couples hopefully reinvest energy in the marriage and make plans for their future together, with the anticipation of sharing activities that have been postponed while child-rearing consumed attention and financial resources. With the death of a partner, these dreams of a shared future are lost. Friends and other couples who are unready to confront their own mortality and survivorship may distance. The bereaved spouse may also be reluctant to burden recently launched children who are not yet established. We encourage widowed women and men to put their own lives in perspective: to consider how they will manage on their own, to develop meaningful pursuits, and to build a supportive social network for the years ahead.

Couples at launching are typically confronting losses on both sides: As their children are leaving home, their aging parents may be declining in health or dying. Most adults in their middle years are prepared to assume increased caregiving responsibilities for aging parents and to accept their deaths as a natural, inevitable occurrence in the life cycle (see Chapter 17 on Families in Later Life). Nevertheless, the clinician should be attentive to issues of caretaker burnout and resentments that may build up among siblings regarding caretaking. Interventions should focus on promoting collaboration among siblings as a caregiving team.

Caregiving and mourning processes are more complicated for the entire family if intergenerational tensions or cut offs have been longstanding. Clinically we move, wherever possible, to bridge cut offs and promote reconciliation, to strengthen the family in coping with loss and finding positive benefits through shared efforts. A conjoint family life review (see Chapter 12 on aging) can be valuable in structuring the sharing of memories to gain a more balanced, evolutionary perspective on family relationships over time. Members may have mellowed about past grievances, viewing them differently, with new opportunity for repair, or at least a more empathic understanding of differences and disappointments.

With the death of aging parents, adult children typically confront their own mortality and think more about the time that remains ahead of them. The death of the last surviving member of the older generation brings awareness that they are now the oldest generation and the next to die. Having—or anticipating—grandchildren commonly eases the acceptance of mortality, so there may be pressure on the recently launched generation to marry and start a family.

Families in Later Life

With expanded life expectancy, 4- and 5-generation families are becoming more common. Postretirement individuals and couples with declining resources are increasingly called upon to care for their very elderly and widowed parents. The central life cycle task of old age—accepting one's own mortality—becomes quite real with the deaths of siblings, spouses, and peers. Surviving the death of an adult child is especially painful. As the Chinese say, "White hair should never follow black [in death]." With so many losses common in later life, some older people withdraw and avoid funerals, so as not to face yet another painful loss and their own approaching death. Intergenerational family conflicts may erupt over issues of caregiving, dependency, loss of functioning and control as health declines (see Chapter 17 on Families in Later Life).

It is inevitable for couples that one partner will die before the other. Since women are more likely to outlive their husbands, more women over 65 are widowed whereas most older men are married, and tend to remarry younger partners. Many widowed women prefer not to remarry, with gendered role expectations to take care of another husband. If the prior marriage was deeply valued, many older widow(er)s prefer not to remarry. Widows from more traditional marriages often find themselves unprepared for the financial burdens and lack adequate retirement benefits of their own. Important areas for preventive intervention are to help men to attend to their own emotional process, and to help women become knowledgeable and empowered regarding their own economic security.

Widowers are at especially high risk of illness, death, and suicide in the first year of bereavement because of the initial sense of loss, disorientation, and loneliness and the loss of a wife's caretaking. While women generally have a higher rate of depression, men's risk of depression after spousal death is higher (Stroebe et al., 2008). For widowed men and women feelings of loneliness tend to predominate, even more than for other losses (Parkes, 2009). Husbands' vulnerability to loss may be greater because men are socialized to deny their dependency on their spouse. Death of widowers during the first 6 months of bereavement have been found to be 40 percent above the expected rate for married men of the same age.

The psychosocial tasks for widowhood, as for other losses, are twofold: to grieve the loss of the spouse and to reinvest in future functioning. Lopata (1996) has described the common tasks, which include loosening bonds to the spouse and acknowledging the fact of the death, transforming shared daily experiences into memories. Open expression of grief and loss is important. Typically within a year, attention turns to the demands of daily functioning, self-support, household management, and adjustment to being physically and emotionally alone. The challenge of widowhood is often compounded by other dislocations, particularly when the family home and social community are given up or when financial loss or illness reduce independent functioning. The label and identity of "widow" can be a constant reminder of the loss and may impede the process of reengagement. As one client recently put it, "It's so frustrating that everyone I meet wants either to fix me up, or they ignore me because I am alone. I wish no one even knew my situation because they refuse to just relate to me as myself."

Death in Divorced and Remarried Families

With current high rates of divorce, remarriage, and redivorce expected to continue, clinical inquiry must extend beyond the immediate household to the broader network of family relationships and not overlook deaths in prior marriages, stepfamilies, and committed partnerships. The death of a former spouse may bring a surprisingly strong grief reaction, even if the marriage ended years earlier.

Children's losses of kin or steprelations who have been important to them at some phase in their development should also be attended to. The death of the biological parent leaves the stepparent with no legal rights to continue a relationship with the children, even where they have formed a strong attachment and assumed financial and other responsibilities. In cases of remarriage where loyalty conflicts are strong, biological children may vehemently contest a will that favors a stepparent and/or stepchildren. Another consideration concerns decisions about burial or co-mingling of ashes: with which spouse and family? Old wishes may be rekindled by children who wish to reunite their parents for all time in their graves.

If the parents are divorced, the loss of the custodial parent may also set up problematic conflicts over who will take over raising the child. The loss of the noncustodial parent may be problematic because of residual feelings from the divorce, the child's lack of connection with the lost parent, and complex feelings between the custodial parent and the lost parent's extended family.

Varied Life Course Challenges: Hidden and Stigmatized Losses

To underscore our introductory remarks on the diversity of contemporary families, most lives today do not fit neatly into the categories and succession of stages described above. With many varied pathways through life, significant losses may be unrecognized. The loss of a committed partner may be felt as deeply as a marital spouse. Loss issues concerning infertility and miscarriage are not confined to early marriage and become more painful with the ticking of the biological clock. With remarriage in later years, the death of a newly wed spouse, although chronologically expectable, may, like in young couples, involve a shattering loss of hopes and dreams, without a shared history and memories to hold onto. Single individuals or couples, both gay and straight, who have chosen not to have children

may be assumed erroneously to be suffering, as in the label "childless," or compensating for loss if they prefer to live with companion animals. Indeed, the loss of a cherished pet is one of the most underappreciated losses. Too often the bond is belittled and bereavement is disqualified by others, who say "It's only an animal; you can get another one" (Walsh, 2009b). Meaningful rituals can be valuable in acknowledging and supporting the grief process.

Societal and religious attitudes and laws regarding sexual orientation complicate all losses in gay and lesbian relationships. For couples lacking the legal standing of marriage, the right to be at the hospital bedside of a dying partner may be denied, as well as death benefits. A death may be grieved in isolation when the relationship has been a secret or has been disapproved of by the family or faith community. In states where same-sex marriage is not recognized and a couple is raising children, the nonbiological parent must gain legal status through formal adoption or guardianship for parental rights after the death of the partner who is the biological parent. Laws and legal precedents in some states may even prevent these steps from being taken. In such cases, custody may be granted to relatives of the deceased biological parent, who may or may not provide the child access to the surviving partner/parent.

The epidemic of AIDS, which initially devastated the gay community, has increasingly affected heterosexual men, women, and their children in poor communities worldwide, with multiple losses throughout relationship networks. While treatment advances have brought new hope for many, tragically the high cost of drug regimens limit availability.

Diverse Cultural and Spiritual Beliefs and Practices

Helping family members face death and loss requires respect for their particular cultural traditions and spiritual orientation, which are intertwined (McGoldrick, Giordano, & Garcia Preto, 2005; McGoldrick et al., 2004; Walsh, 2008; 2009c). Religion and spirituality come to the fore with death and dying, from existential questions about the meaning of life to convictions about proper final rites and the mystery of afterlife. In Eastern and Native American spiritual belief systems, although death ends a life and brings sorrow for loved ones, it is seen as part of a larger life cycle, connecting all living beings.

It is crucial to explore ways that core beliefs may offer comfort, such as belief in reunion in heaven, or exacerbate suffering, such as the belief that infertility was God's punishment for the sin of infidelity. It is important to explore potential spiritual resources that fit client preferences. Research clearly documents the healing power of spiritual beliefs and practices: They offer transcendent values, meaning, and purpose and can provide solace and comfort through faith, prayer or meditation, congregational support, and connectedness to all of life (Walsh, 2009a).

Conclusion

At times of death, without mutual support the pain of loss is that much worse for those who grieve alone or not at all. When we foster relational connectedness in the face of loss, families and their members emerge strengthened and more resourceful in meeting future life challenges.

The uniqueness of each life course in its context needs to be appreciated in every assessment of the multigenerational family life cycle and in our understanding of the many meanings of loss. Our own personal, cultural, and spiritual beliefs and experiences surrounding loss need to be examined as they constrain or facilitate our efforts to help grieving families. By coming to accept death as part of life, we discover new possibilities for growth.

Chapter 19

Divorce: An Unscheduled Family Transition

Constance R. Ahrons

Although divorce is common in family life today, our culture clings to the view that it is deviant and the cause of many of society's social problems. In spite of greater social acceptance, divorce is still viewed as an abnormality that will go away if only we can find out how to make it do so. The reality is that divorce is a social institution in the same way that marriage is, and, as long as we continue to marry, we will continue to offer divorce as an optional safety valve for unsatisfactory marriages.

In this chapter, divorce will be examined from a normative perspective, and the process will be discussed as a multidimensional series of predictable transitions that affect families intergenerationally.* It is an *unscheduled* life transition that affects large numbers of families and alters their developmental life course. Although all divorces have some common denominators, the placement of divorce in the developmental life cycle will result in differential effects on family members. For example, parents who divorce when their children are young will face different issues and decisions, such as custody and living arrangements for children, than parents who divorce after their children are grown.

How divorce affects the family is also altered by diverse sociocultural factors. Ethnic and religious groups may differ in the way they perceive divorce, and these different perceptions influence how a family copes. In order to help families reorganize as healthy systems, clinicians need to understand the nature of the divorce process, the family's developmental stage, and the sociocultural background of the family.

The Context of Divorce: Historical and Legal Perspectives

On the rise for the past 3 centuries, divorce rates reached their peak in the late 1970s. Between 1965 and 1980—the prosperous years—divorce rates more than doubled. However, in the 1980s, the economy dipped, and the divorce rate declined slightly. Since then the rate has leveled off and has remained steady.

It is interesting to note that the first recorded divorce in America happened back in 1639, in a Puritan court in Massachusetts, when James Luxford's wife asked for a divorce because her husband already had a wife. The divorce was granted. Public and legal debates about the high divorce rates occurred as early as the late 1700s. These early debates were very similar in tone and content to the discussions we hear these days about whether we should make divorce laws more or less difficult. The pattern of liberalizing divorce laws and then tightening them, seesawing from honoring the individual to honoring the society and back again, is one that we have seen throughout Europe and the United States.

The latter part of the twentieth century was marked by major reforms. In 1969 to 1970, California became the first state to change divorce from an adversarial to a nonadversarial process. Other states followed and, although there is considerable variability in divorce laws from state to state, by 1985 every state had adopted some form of no-fault divorce law. As this less punitive approach to divorce evolved, waiting periods became shorter, and reconciliation counseling was no longer mandatory in most jurisdictions. Referred to as "the divorce revolution," this important symbolic shift continues to be a source of major debate in the United States, and controversy exists about its impact on divorce rates and societal family values (Adams & Coltrane, 2007).

Demographics and the Probability of Divorce

The probability of divorce is associated with a number of demographic factors. Age is the strongest predictor. Couples who are 20 years of age or younger when they marry have the highest likelihood of divorce. People with less income and education tend to divorce more than those with higher education and incomes. An important exception to this principle relates to women: Well-educated women (5 or more years of college) with good incomes have higher divorce rates than do women who are poorer and less educated.

Geographically, there are some differences as well. People in the Western part of the United States have higher divorce rates than those in the Northeast. This may be due partly to the fact that the average marriage age is lower in the West. Also, there is a higher concentration of Catholics in the Northeast.

There are also significant racial and ethnic differences. Divorce rates for the African American population are two times those of Whites or Hispanics. Although the explanations for the higher divorce rate among African Americans vary, socioeconomic differences seem to play a part. On the average, African Americans are less educated, poorer, and more often unemployed than European Americans. Latinos have a lower divorce rate; however, they appear to have higher rates of separation than other racial-ethnic groups. Asian Americans have the lowest rates of any racial-ethnic group (Demo & Fine, 2009).

Religion also plays a part. Catholics and Jews have a lower divorce rate than Protestants. Since Catholicism is the religion of traditional Hispanics, part of the explanation for the racial differences in divorce rates may be attributed to religious affiliation. Although Catholics have a lower divorce rate, their rates have risen just as rapidly as those of the general divorce population (Ahlburg & DeVita, 1992).

Cohabitation is increasingly accepted as an alternative to marriage, and this has affected both marriage and divorce rates. In some European countries, a recent decline in divorce rates can be attributed to the increase in informal cohabitation arrangements. In Sweden, for example, this increase in cohabitation has decreased the marriage rate as well as the divorce rate. Breakups of these informal unions, of course, are not included in the calculation of divorce rates.

At present, it is estimated that approximately 40 percent of first marriages in the United States end in divorce (Demo & Fine, 2009). Demographic trends suggest that the current divorce rates in the United States are now fairly stable. Demographers predict that 40 to 60 percent of all current marriages will eventually end in divorce. Those who predict the lower rates say that the divorce rate will decline as the baby boomers age; that boomers who wish to divorce have already done so, and those that haven't are past the stage of life when the odds of divorce are the highest (Glick, 1990). Those who predict an increase, whether large or small, say that women's and men's roles will continue to change. That change, plus the increasing financial independence of women—historically the less satisfied party in marriage—will continue to push the rates upward (Bumpass, 1990).

Ethnic and Life Cycle Variations

Although more studies are emerging on ethnic and racial populations, a serious weakness of the current state of divorce research is that most of the research is still based on White, middle-class samples. Our interest in divorce has been focused mainly on its effects on children, and most of the research has focused on young children and their mothers (Lamb et al., 1997). A growing body of research based on information collected from both parents, using court records rather than clinical data, is gradually beginning to provide important data on the entire family system (Ahrons, 1994; Hetherington, 1993; Maccoby & Mnookin, 1992; Stewart, Copeland, Chester, Malley, & Barenbaum, 1997). These studies tend to be small, in-depth studies based on in-person interviews, often conducted at two or three different time periods in the divorced family life cycle.

Larger studies, utilizing national samples, provide comparative information on divorced and married families. These studies usually focus on school-age children and their primary parent, most frequently the mother. These studies are often part of a larger study, and although they contribute greatly to our general knowledge of the effects of divorce, they provide less family interaction data than do the smaller, more intensive studies. There is also a paucity of research on divorce in midlife and later life and on the effects on older children and young adults.

Most of what is presented in this chapter is based on the existing research, with particular emphasis on the author's own longitudinal study.[*] When information is available in the literature on ethnic and life cycle variations, the findings will be noted.

The Social Context

Divorce is usually thought to be symptomatic of family instability and synonymous with family dissolution. This view is reflected in the terms used to describe the divorced family: "broken home," "disorganized," "fractured," "incomplete." Most research has been designed to search for problems created by divorce and often relies on clinical or problem-identified populations. Not only is divorce viewed that way in the professional literature, but it is also quite common to find divorce labeled in the media as the cause of all sorts of social problems, such as drugs, delinquency, and family violence.

The media is a powerful tool in defining how we view social issues. Unfortunately the media leans toward short, sound-bite answers, even to the most complex social questions. These sound-bites become polarized, and divorce is positioned as either good or bad; children are either doomed or saved. One day we hear divorce dooms children to lifelong problems; the next day we hear children are doing well. These extreme positions—of divorce as disaster and divorce as inconsequential—oversimplify the realities of our complex lives.

This view has given rise to a distorted perception of divorce, leading investigators and practitioners to focus primarily on pathology. For example, the term "single-parent family" implies that a family contains only one parent; however, in most divorced families, although mothers are usually the primary caregivers, both parents continue to function in parental roles (Stewart et al., 1997). Divorce creates new households with single parents, but it results in a single-parent family only when one of the parents, usually the father, has no further contact with the family and does not continue to perform a parental function. More appropriate terminology would distinguish between these two circumstances and would describe the former as a "one-parent household" (Ahrons, 1980a, 1980b).

Although the loss of the father–child relationship is an all too common outcome for many children in divorced families, innovative custody arrangements—such as joint custody and the increased involvement of fathers in child-rearing roles—have also created postdivorce family arrangements in which the children continue to be reared by both parents (Ahrons & Tanner, 2003). The majority of postdivorce families have evolved continuing and well-functioning relationships that do not appear to be at all pathological (Kelly, 2005; Lamb et al., 1997). In such cases, divorce has not terminated family relationships; rather, it has been a process whereby the form of these relationships has changed.

Divorce as a Multidimensional Process

From a legal and social status perspective, divorce is an event; it moves individuals from the condition of being legally married to that of being legally divorced. When the divorce decree is final, the partners are free to remarry. However, looked at from a family dynamics standpoint and not a legal standpoint, divorce is best regarded as a multidimensional process of family change. It has roots somewhere in the past, before the legal act transpired, and carries with it effects that extend into the future. Each family member will be profoundly affected by it; as members of a postdivorce family, individuals will be forced to learn new ways of coping and of relating to the society at large, as well as to each other.

The Binuclear Family

The process of divorcing culminates in a complex redefinition of relationships within the family. Although the structure of postdivorce families varies, some basic tasks must be accomplished in all separations. Once a family has established the ground rules for living separately (for example, where the children will reside or how visitation will be arranged), the family needs to clarify rules for relating within and across the various subsystems within the family system, for example, the parental subsystem or the parent–child subsystem.

Dual-household binuclear families

The multidimensional divorce process can be viewed as a series of transitions that mark the family's change from married to divorced status. This process involves disorganizing the nuclear family and reorganizing it into a binuclear family. The binuclear family consists of two households or subsystems, maternal and paternal, which then form the nuclei of the child's family of orientation (Ahrons, 1979, 1980a).

Binuclear families are similar to extended kin or quasi-kin relationships. In many families, for example, the marriage of a child marks the beginning of a quasi-kin relationship between the families of the newly married couple. In this quasi-kin structure, two families are bonded through the marriage of their children. Jewish families have institutionalized this nonblood familial relationship. The Yiddish term *machetunim* means "relatives through marriage," referring specifically to the relationship between the family of the bride and the family of the groom (Rosten, 1989). Many Jewish families frequently spend holidays and special events with their "machetunim." These two families may or may not like each other, but amicability is not the primary reason for their gathering. They gather not as intimates, but as "blood" relations.

The bonds created by families joined through marriage are similar to the bonds of the divorced family. In both types of families, a child gives rise to the continuing bond. In the family joined through marriage, the relationship between the two sets of in-laws usually determines the interrelationships within the extended family system. The style of relationship within the divorced family is usually based on the nature of the relationship between the divorced spouses.

Transitions of the Divorce Process

Transitions are turning points, uncomfortable periods that mark the beginning of something new while signifying the ending of something familiar. Although the changes may be anticipated with puzzlement and foreboding, they may also be approached with exhilaration. During transitional periods families are more personally vulnerable, but paradoxically these are also the times when personal growth is most likely to occur.

Usually, when we think of transitions, we think in terms of the biological developmental clock: adolescence, midlife, or aging. In defining biological developmental transitions, in outlining typical themes, common feelings, and experiences, we normalize situations that otherwise would feel, and appear to be, abnormal. When people know what to expect, it doesn't take away all the upheaval, but it does help them to cope better with the difficult changes that the transition inevitably brings. People experience great relief when they can place themselves within a natural progression that has a beginning and an end. Although we usually define transitions within developmental frameworks (e.g., birth of a first child, retirement), some life transitions are unrelated to developmental or social time clocks.

Unlike other transitions that occur more or less on predictable chronological timetables, divorce can occur at any time during the family life cycle. Unlike expected transitions in the life cycle, divorce has a greater potential to cause disequilibrium that can result in debilitating crises. And, unlike family crises of sudden onset, the divorce process begins long before the actual decision to obtain a legal divorce. Divorce is an internal crisis of relationship, a deliberate dissolution of the primary bond in the family, and the family's identity appears to be shattered. For most people, ending a marriage is the most traumatic decision of their lives. The usual ways of coping are unlikely to work. People often act in ways that no one around them can make sense of. Abigail Trafford (1982) refers to this period as "crazy time."

Stress, crisis, and adaptation are three concepts that are often used in understanding how families cope with life's distressful events, such as chronic illness, death of a loved one, and unemployment (Boss, 1987; Rodgers, 1986). Stress occurs when there is an imbalance (perceived or actual) between what is actually happening—the stressors—and what family members feel capable of handling. Crisis occurs when stress exceeds the ability of individuals in the family to effectively handle the stressors. All families have different levels of tolerance—breaking points—beyond which they are no longer able to cope with the situation. When too many things hit all at once, when stressors pile up, system overload sets in. When the family's reservoir of coping behaviors becomes depleted or outmoded and they do not know what to do they are in a crisis.

Divorce is ranked at the top of the list of stressful life events. Many stressors overlap in the divorce transitions. All of the normal coping abilities are taxed by complex personal and familial changes. Add the lack of adequate role models of good divorces, the absence of clear-cut rules or rituals for managing this new and unfamiliar stage of life, and the lack of external resources, such as community support and positive social sanctions, and crisis is certainly a predictable outcome.

Ambiguity is a big contributor to stress (Boss, 1983). For divorcing parents and their children, the knowledge that their family will continue to be a family, restructuring from a nuclear to a binuclear form, reduces some of the debilitating ambiguity associated with divorce. Understanding that divorce is a process with predictable transitions of disorganization followed by structured transitions of reorganization helps to at least reduce the intensity and duration of the crisis. When families have knowledge of what to expect with adequate role models to assist them, they can better identify which decisions need to be made—and when—and can then decide upon what kind of new rules need to be established. The knowledge and ability to plan facilitate their capacity to cope more effectively during the crisis and manage the mass of overwhelming feelings. In effect, they move the divorce process toward "normality."

The lack of adequate norms, knowledge, and role models has been detrimental for divorcing families. Clinicians working with them have also lacked the knowledge and skills to help these families move through the transitions and emerge as healthy binuclear families. New strategies for assisting families through the divorce process that incorporate normative models, such as mediation, psychoeducational workshops, co-parenting seminars, and collaborative law are emerging and creating healthier outcomes for families.

The Transitions Framework

Breaking down the very complex process of divorce into transitions—common developmental steps—allows us to then explore the ways people adapt at each of the stages. Developed from my longitudinal research on divorcing families, five overlapping transitions, each with distinct role changes and tasks, were identified (Ahrons, 1980a, 1994; Ahrons & Rodgers, 1987). The first three transitions—individual cognition, family metacognition, and systemic separation—form the core of the disorganizing emotional separation process. The last two transitions—systemic reorganization and systemic redefinition—form the family reorganization process.

Although they are presented sequentially in their ideal developmental order, the transitions usually overlap. Each transition includes social role transitions encompassing a complex interaction of overlapping experiences. There is no neat rule for when a particular transition will occur in a particular person or couple or for how long the transition will last. What we do know, from studies in the United States and from cross-national studies, regardless of cultural or national differences, is that it takes most people between one and a half and three years after the initial separation to stabilize their feelings (Cseh-Szombathy, Koch-Nielsen, Trost, & Weda, 1985). Each transition is heralded by increased stress. At the end of the transition, the stress tends to plateau or to decrease.

Individual Cognition: The Decision

The decision to end a marriage is usually far more difficult and prolonged than the decision to marry. The dread of negative repercussions, of an uncertain future, and of painful losses all combine to make the transition a wrenching and internally violent one. The first step toward divorce is rarely mutual. It begins within one person, often starting as a small, amorphous, nagging feeling of dissatisfaction. The feeling grows in spurts, sometimes gaining strength, sometimes retreating, flaring up, and again moving forward. For some people, this private simmering of unhappiness goes on for years. For others, a few months of depression may be more they can bear. The hallmark of this transition is ambivalence, accompanied by obsession, vacillation, and anguish. It is not uncommon for the individual in the throes of this process to have an affair and/or seek out a therapist.

When an individual begins to seriously question feelings for his or her mate, a passage of emotional leave-taking takes place. This "erosion of love" starts slowly and may be barely noticeable at first. Behaviors that were acceptable for years become annoying; habits that were tolerated become intolerable. More and more "evidence" is collected as a case is built to justify the decision to leave.

Characteristic of the coping mechanisms in this transition is the denial of marital problems. Spouses also resort to blaming to obtain respite from a situation that is perceived as intolerable. Marital conflicts usually escalate the search for fault in the other spouse and often result in his or her being labeled the culprit. This time can be a highly stressful one, especially for the children, who often become pawns in the marital strife. Conflict-habituated marriages are less threatening to some families than the uncertainty and change that accompany separation and divorce. In other families, instead of open conflict, there are a distancing and withdrawal of emotional investment, in the marriage and often in the family. In families with dependent children, it is not uncommon to make a decision—albeit often not adhered to—to stay in the marriage until the children are grown. The dissatisfied partner may decide to invest emotional energy in extramarital interests while attempting to maintain the facade of an intact family. These patterns usually result in family dysfunction. When marital relationships are highly conflictual or cold and distant, it is not unusual for a child living in that household to develop symptoms, which in turn may prompt the family to seek therapy. In this way, the "secret" may become exposed.

Another very common pattern that clinicians see is the couple who come in for therapy with two different—but not openly stated—agendas. Although both may come in for marriage counseling, one partner has already emotionally disengaged from the relationship and comes to therapy as a way to relieve his or her guilt. She or he can then say, "I've tried everything to make this marriage work, even marriage counseling." Or the disengaged partner, fearful of the other partner's reaction to the planned leave-taking, may seek out a therapist who can become the caretaker/rescuer of the soon-to-be left partner. In both cases, the therapist has the difficult task of trying to help the couple to honestly face their issues before any treatment contract can be arrived at.

Although a divorce often ends up being a mutual decision, at the early stages there is one person (the initiator or leaver) who harbors the secret desire to leave and one person who is initially unaware of that desire (the opposer or the left). In some cases, both partners may have had similar fantasies, but one person usually takes the first step and begins the process.

Leavers and lefts have very different feelings at the outset. The leaver has had the advantage early on of wrestling with his or her emotions, has already started grieving, and has already detached to some degree. The person being left is perceived to be the victim. This person's immediate reactions range from disbelief and shock to outrage and despair. The partners have unequal power at this point. The person being left is more vulnerable. Having had no time to prepare—to adapt to the overwhelming threat—the one being left is more likely to experience crisis at this point.

Who takes the role of leaver and who takes the role of left often relate to gender. In the United States and most European countries, it is estimated that two thirds to three quarters of all divorces are initiated by women. One of the biggest factors leading to this statistic is the increase in women's economic independence. It is not that women used to be happier in marriage than they are today, but they often believed that they could not survive outside of marriage without their husband's money. Even today, the lowest divorce rate occurs in traditional marriages with breadwinner husbands and full-time homemaker wives. Not only have women's economic opportunities expanded, so have their social opportunities. Even though we still live in a very coupled society, it is much easier today than it was even 20 years ago to live a full life as a single woman. Even so, many women say that they left because they had no choice. Stories of years of abuse, betrayal, or absenteeism by their husband are common.

Family Metacognition: The Announcement

Proclaiming one's desire to separate from one's partner is no easy task. But for some couples, the announcement is as far as their marital crisis will go. Sometimes, the moment of confrontation creates an opportunity to actually improve a marriage. For other couples, the announcement is the first step in a tangled escalating series of confrontations and reconciliations. For still others, one day they're married and the next day they're not; the announcement can also be a clear, direct, and sometimes almost instant path to separation and divorce.

Denial often follows any major shock. One common reaction is for the spouse to call the leaving partner's reasons frivolous. It is not uncommon, in the early phase right after the announcement occurs, to think that a few minor changes—becoming more attentive or more attractive—will help what seems to be an anomalous outburst to blow over. Although it is rare, sometimes a new wardrobe, flowers, extra telephone calls, and other efforts do help temporarily, especially when the potential leaver is still very ambivalent.

Leavers almost always portray a long, painful process of leave-taking. The one being left is coping not only with rejection but also with having to develop an account after the fact. In the first two phases of the process, the leaver commonly feels guilty; the left feels angry. Rarely is the process symmetrical, let alone rational or mutual.

In many cases, the announcement seems spontaneous, as much a dreadful surprise to the leaver as to the left. In these cases, the discomfort is often so severe that the leaver (either consciously or unconsciously) resorts to setting up a situation that will bring the issue into the open without anyone having

to accept responsibility. The leaver may get forgetful and leave a lover's letter on the dresser, stay out all night, or arrive home with the proverbial lipstick on the collar. Once discovered, the objects or events provoke a crisis, and it's over. Creating a crisis makes it possible to shift the blame. The couple can then fight about whatever issue got raised in the crisis, rather than dealing with the long-term issues of their distressing marital relationship.

Betrayal and blame

Statistics on extramarital affairs are very varied and highly unreliable, owing to the unwillingness of many people to disclose them (Brown, 1991; Spring, 1996), but they are quite common to marital separations. What is worse than the affair itself—more difficult to cope with—is the protective web of lies. As each lie gets uncovered or explodes during a battle about the affair, the betrayed spouse begins to question the entire history of the relationship. The betrayed person questions the betrayer closely, even obsessively, trying to separate truth from fiction. The betrayer and the betrayed rarely see eye to eye on how much talking is needed.

For a myriad of reasons, it is difficult for the betrayer to be truthful. Perhaps he or she wants to hold onto both the spouse and lover, wants to protect against possible legal ramifications, or does not want to inflict more pain. The betrayed senses that there is more and keeps pressing, trying to get to the bottom of things. The betrayer may comply for a while, then usually grows impatient with the constant focus and repetition. The betrayer thinks that the betrayed spouse is "carrying this too far." Blame then shifts to the betrayed spouse for not letting go (Brown, 1991; Lerner, 1993). This common and very predictable pattern, unfortunately, lays the groundwork for a highly acrimonious and destructive divorce process. If a clinician is brought into this process at this transition, she or he may be able to help the couple to sort out the issues and to understand the power struggle that pervades this process. However, all too often, the betrayer is unwilling to commit to therapy, and the issue of "the affair" pervades the rest of the divorce transitions. Although divorce is legally no-fault and adultery is no longer needed to show cause, blame often plays a big role in the emotional divorce process.

Rage, prejudicial myth making, depression, and impulsive desires to retaliate are normal reactions for the partner who is being left. Anger plays an important role when there is a bad blow to the ego. It temporarily shields the betrayed spouse from facing devastating emotions: grief, rejection, even self-hatred. If, over the course of the marriage, mutual anger has been buried, the anger can easily erupt in this transition. All the past injustices that were not confronted are replayed. Both the earlier denial and the current anger help the one who has been left to cope with a life that is swinging out of control.

Loss

Divorce is marked by severe losses. Not only are the losses related to the present life-style, but there are also losses of future plans and fantasies. Even for the couple in the early stages of marriage, there are powerful feelings of loss. Their whole dream of married life may be shattered; the children they had planned for and the house they were going to buy remain unrealized dreams. Couples with young children have to face that their future plans will never materialize: the wonderful skiing vacations they were planning to take in a couple of years or the camping trip to the Grand Canyon. The midlife couple who divorces after a long marriage may have had retirement plans that will never come to fruition: the long awaited trip to Europe after the children were grown or that secluded house at the lake.

Unresolved grieving for losses is a major deterrent to making a healthy adaptation to divorce. Clinicians need to be aware that when anger is the major coping mechanism of a divorcing spouse, uncovering the grief may need to be a very slow process. Otherwise, the depression may be so overwhelming that the spouse, especially if she or he is the primary parent, may not be able to function in the parental role.

This transition is key to the rest of the transitions. Family therapy at this time can be very productive. Sometimes even a few sessions can help to clarify how to deescalate the anger whenever it occurs during the divorce process. Additional sessions can help both children and adults to defuse their terror about the major changes that divorce brings; they can start to plan. To avert a serious crisis requires that both partners show considerable patience, maturity, and honesty. Leavers need to understand their partner's angry reaction and give him or her time to deal with it. Being able to talk about some of the changes that can be expected during the next transitions as the marriage is being dismantled is important, as frustrating and difficult as such talk may be. The more responsibly couples plan for a timely separation, the less likely it is to break down into debilitating crisis. For couples, being rational during such emotional times is often impossible without the help of a therapist.

Systemic Separation: Dismantling the Nuclear Family

Most people remember the day they separated—not the day their divorce was legally awarded—as the day their divorce began. Separation day is one of those marker events that divorced people never forget. For children, this is when they realize the enormity of what is going on, even though they may have suspected or feared the prospect for some time.

Some couples and children feel a great sense of relief at the separation transition, especially when the marriage had become highly stressful. Other families are overwhelmed with fear and anxiety. For still others, it is the worst crisis point of all. Everyone experiences this transition as a time of major disorganization, when the routines of daily life go up in smoke. It's a time of anomie—normlessness. Old roles disappear; new ones have yet to form. The future of the family is unknown.

There are no clear-cut rules for separating. Who moves out? How often should spouses continue to see one another? When (and what) should they tell family and friends? Who will attend the school conferences next week? Who will get the season tickets for the theater? Who will attend the wedding of a mutual friend next month? These types of questions, seemingly trivial but deeply resonant, plague newly separated people at all stages of the family life cycle.

Orderly and disorderly separations

Separations fall on a continuum from orderly to disorderly, from the anticipated to the utterly shocking. Orderly separations are the least destructive. They are most likely to occur if there has been time for some preparation and planning before the actual physical separation. Disorderly separations usually occur when the earlier crisis points have not been worked through. Separation involves major life changes, and it requires careful planning, especially when there are children. Children have the right to know what's going on, and they need to have adequate time to process it with both parents. Even couples with grown children need to prepare their adult offspring—and grandchildren—for the changes that separation entails.

Abrupt departures usually create severe crises for those left behind. It's the ultimate rejection—abandonment. The abandonment leaves one feeling totally helpless and frequently culminates in a severe debilitating family crisis, such as a suicide attempt by one partner or a major clinical depression requiring hospitalization. Abandoned children regress, get depressed, or act out. The rejection is too great and too sudden to cope with.

Orderly separations have two common factors: good management and firm relationship boundaries. Good management requires knowing about and preparing for the transitions of divorce, averting crises by defusing tension at marker points, and giving the process enough time for everyone to adjust.

Boundaries are simply rules for how separated spouses will interact—and not interact. To construct good boundaries, spouses need to recognize how their roles have changed. To keep the boundaries firm, new rules and rituals need to be developed.

For women in particular, the two roles of wife and mother traditionally provide a central core of identity. Often, the two roles become enmeshed. It is not unusual to hear an ex-wife say, "He left *us*." The more a woman's identity is tied to a combined wife/mother role, the more likely she is to experience this stress of role loss.

Men's role loss after divorce may seem less pronounced than women's. Even though gender roles are shifting, men are still more likely than women to define themselves by work and to define their roles as spouses more narrowly. The more demanding and compelling his work, the more a man can throw himself into it to fill his time and thoughts, thereby anesthetizing the pain of the separation.

Even for the couple that divorces in the early stages of marriage, the discomfort of role loss is felt. Losing the role of being coupled and returning to singleness are fraught with feelings of failure and loss of status. For couples married longer, the extent of the role losses are more complex and severe. Their lives have usually been defined by their married status: friends, neighbors, community, and family all view them as a couple. Returning to a single existence that they have not experienced for 20 or 30 years requires a totally new self-definition.

Rules are needed for any system to function. When one household becomes two, many of the rules that are built into the marital system become instantly obsolete. New rules will be needed to define a new relationship. Separated couples need to find ways to reduce the intimacy and appropriately increase their distance. Until the actual separation, a couple is usually unaware of how interdependent their lives have become. Trial and error may be necessary until they establish a new comfort level.

Rituals mark important transitions and events. They solidify, solemnize, and publicize our values. They also quell our anxiety by showing us how to behave in the face of the unknown (Imber-Black & Roberts, 1998). Although many rituals exist that help people to enter a marriage, welcome a newborn, start a new job, or retire from one, there are no socially accepted rituals to mark the end of a marriage, the announcement of a divorce, the construction of a binuclear family, or the acceptance of new and sometimes instant members into a family of remarriage. No rites of passage exist to help mourn the losses, to help healing, or to help solidify newly acquired roles. Unlike other important transitions, divorce lies in a zone of ritual ambiguity (see Chapter 12).

While leaving its participants in a void with respect to public rituals, divorce also affects the private rituals that are so central to family life. Daily rituals such as opening the mail together over coffee or walking together to get the newspaper are seamlessly woven into the texture of family life; the more elaborate rituals that many families construct around birthdays and holidays will also disappear or change, leaving gaping wounds. When the nuclear family is dismantled in the wake of divorce, it is also necessary to dismantle what seemed like a permanent point of view of a portion of the past, present, and future.

What roles, rules, and rituals each family chooses to establish will vary depending on individual preferences, sometimes on ethnic background, and certainly on the particular life stage of the family.

Reconciliations are common during the separation transition. The pain of separating, the continuing bonds of attachment, the distress of children and extended family, and the realities of divorce can cause couples to reunite. When the reconciliation is based on these reasons and not on a basic understanding and correction of the marital problems, it is likely to be brief. In some families, parents separate and reconcile briefly, perhaps several times, increasing and prolonging the stress of the separation. In the most common divorced family form, the mother and children remain as one unit while the father moves out and functions as a separate unit. The mother-headed household faces a dilemma: Should it reorganize and fill roles that had been enacted by the physically absent father, or should it maintain his psychological presence in the system by not reorganizing? If the mother–child subsystem tries to reassign roles, the father's return will be met with resistance. On the other hand, if they deal with him as psychologically present, they perpetuate family disequilibrium and stress. These children face a difficult and very stressful transition with the family in a constant state of disequilibrium characterized by boundary ambiguity (Boss, 1987) created by the father's intermittent exit and return. This "on again, off again" marital relationship often continues for years as the spouses resolve their ambivalence and make the transition to reorganization. This type of cyclical pattern is evidenced more in highly dysfunctional families, and family violence tends to be more prevalent in them (Kitson, 1992).

As the marital separation is shared with extended family, friends, and the community, the tasks of the economic and legal processes begin. These mediating factors can help or hinder the transitional process. The couple usually encounters the legal system at this time and faces additional stress as they confront economic hardship and child-focused realities. This may escalate the crisis, since spouses now need to divide what they had previously shared.

Legal issues

Although no-fault divorce legislation reflects changing social attitudes, the legal system still operates on an adversarial model. Based on a win–lose game, the legal divorce frequently escalates the spousal power struggle, adding additional stress to the already disorganized system. Today couples choosing to divorce have a variety of alternatives to address their differences in a less adversarial way. They may choose a *'pro se'* process in which they have no legal representation and write their own agreements. If they want some assistance in resolving their issues, they may choose mediation, a process that employs a neutral professional to help them resolve their differences in a nonadversarial manner (Katz, 2007). The newest model is collaborative divorce, a team approach that originated in 1990 and has steadily grown in societal acceptance. This is a "no-court model" in that the parties and the professionals agree not to pursue litigation to resolve the issues (Webb & Ousky, 2007). These alternative models encourage couples to be responsible for their own family decisions and teach the couple problem-solving techniques that will be useful throughout their postdivorce family life.

These first three turbulent transitions form the core of the emotional divorce process. The lingering feelings of attachment, ambivalence, and the ambiguity of the future combine in complex ways to make this a time of deep soul searching, anxious discomfort, and vacillating but intense desires. For couples with children, whether young or older, it is a process of letting go while still holding on. They have to begin the most difficult task of terminating their marital relationship while redefining their parental one.

Systemic Reorganization: The Binuclear Family

The presence of children, at any stage in the family life cycle process, requires that divorced parents restructure their lives in ways that allow children to continue their relationships with both parents. The nuclear family is now dissolved, and the highly complex and varied process of reorganizing needs to begin.

How a family reorganizes is crucial to the health and well-being of its members. Research clearly identifies several major factors that contribute to the healthy adjustment of children:

1. Children need to have their basic economic and psychological needs met.
2. They need support for maintaining the familial relationships in their lives that were important and meaningful to them before the divorce. That usually means not only parents but also extended family, such as grandparents.
3. They benefit when the relationship between their parents (whether married or divorced) is generally supportive and cooperative.

The reorganization into a binuclear family in which these three major factors are present provides children with the opportunity to survive divorce without long-term psychological damage (Ahrons, 2004; 2007). In most binuclear families, the children divide their living time—in a wide range of patterns—between two households. Some children divide their time fairly equally, either splitting the week or spending one week or longer in each household. Other children spend a majority of their time in one household, and still others alternate between households on a flexible, irregular pattern. The importance of the binuclear family model is that the family remains a family, although the structure is very different than it was before the divorce. Giving divorced families a name that acknowledges that families continue to be families even after divorce encourages the development of new, more functional role models for divorcing families. It also gives them a legitimate status and removes from them the stigma of social deviancy.

The former spouse relationship

To maximize the potential for these three factors requires a major transformation in the former spouse relationship. Each parent must find new ways of relating independently with the child while simultaneously developing new rules and behaviors with each other.

This co-parenting relationship is central to the functioning of the binuclear family in much the same way as the relationship between married spouses is central to the function of the nuclear family.

In the past, there was some disbelief that divorced partners could have an amicable relationship. The lack of language to describe the former spousal relationship, except in terms of a past relationship (e.g., "ex" or "former"), is an indication of the lack of acceptance of it as a viable form. The general distrust of a continuing relationship after divorce is reflected in the prevailing stereotype that former spouses must, of necessity, be antagonists; otherwise, why would they divorce? This stereotype is reinforced by a bias in the available clinical material. Clinicians tend to see only difficult or problematic former spousal relationships, while well-functioning divorced families are less apt to seek professional intervention.

Unlike the popular stereotype that former spouses are, of necessity, mortal enemies, the realities are that there is as much complexity and variation in these relationships as there is in married spouses' relationships. Former spouse relationships form a continuum with the very angry and hostile relationships at one end and the very friendly at the other. There are many relationship variations between the two extremes (Ahrons, 1981, 1994; Ahrons & Wallisch, 1986).

Co-parenting relationships

In analyzing the relationships between former spouses in the Binuclear Family Study, five typologies emerged: perfect pals, cooperative colleagues, angry associates, fiery foes, and dissolved duos. Perfect pals are a small group of divorced spouses who remain close friends. If they have children, they are almost always joint custody parents who, equitably sharing child-rearing responsibilities, are good problem solvers with few conflicts.

The cooperative colleagues are a larger group who would not call each other friends but who manage for the most part to have an amicable relationship. They are child-focused, and although they have conflicts, they are able to separate their marital from their parental roles, not allowing the former to contaminate the latter. When they are unable to resolve a conflict, they are likely to choose a mediator or thera-pist to help them rather than to resort to litigation. Some have shared custody; others elect to have a primary parent, but both fathers and mothers remain important and involved in their children's lives. A number of studies have found that about half the divorced parents fit into this broad category (Ahrons, 1994; Maccoby & Mnookin, 1992; Wallerstein & Kelly, 1980).

Angry associates are quite similar to coopera-tive colleagues in some ways; parents in these groups continue to interact and have involvement in their children's lives. The major difference between the cooperative colleagues and the angry associates is that the latter group cannot separate their parental and marital issues. When there is conflict about the children, it quickly fuses with an old marital fight. Power struggles are common to this group; their sep-aration and divorce battles often involved custody disputes and long legal battles over financial matters.

Fiery foes are hostile and angry all the time; the ex-spouse is the mortal enemy, and they are un-able to co-parent. Like conflict-habituated married couples, they are still very emotionally attached to each other, although they would be quick to deny it. Their divorces tended to have been highly litigious, involving extended family and friends, with legal battles continuing for many years after the divorce. With both angry associates and fiery foes as parents, children usually suffer from devastating loyalty con-flicts and often lose significant relationships with extended kin.

In the dissolved duos, ex-spouses have no fur-ther contact with one another, and one parent as-sumes totally responsibility for the children. Of the five groups, these families are the only ones that fit the "single-parent" category.

Establishing boundaries

While in the earlier transitions the absence of clear boundaries and the high ambiguity create most of the stress, in this reorganization transition, the clarifica-tion of the boundaries generates the distress. Bound-aries are hot issues in all intimate relationships, not just divorce. They touch off unresolved conflicts or crash into opposing strongly held values. Among ex-spouses, money and new loves often are the touchi-est issues, bound to set off escalating battles. Often, an old repetitive fight that the couple has engaged in for years continues, masked in the details of living separately. One major arena for these power strug-gles relates to the children.

All divorcing parents know how important it is to make decisions on the basis of their children's best interests. But the worst arguments can happen over what exactly these interests are. Which school John-ny should attend, although couched in an argument over his best interests, usually boils down to a pitched battle about which parent has more authority, more power, more control over Johnny's life. In reality, al-though "the best interests of the child" is a concept that is commonly accepted and heavily relied upon by judges, lawyers, mediators, and therapists, there is little consensus about the criteria (Kelly, 2007).

All parents, whether married or divorced, have parenting conflicts. How they affect children is de-termined by how the parents resolve their conflicts. In binuclear families, it is necessary to more specifi-cally construct firm boundaries—between house-holds, in each parent–child relationship, and between ex-spouses.

To co-parent effectively requires a contract that sets out the rules and roles in the binuclear family. This contract—what I call a limited partnership agree-ment—assumes that parents are partners, but the kinds of limits that are set on that partnership are determined by their relationship. Perfect pals can have a very flex-ible and often unwritten type of contract because they are able to negotiate easily. Most cooperative col-leagues find that they need to have a more structured agreement, outlining children's living schedules, how holidays will be spent, who goes to what meetings, who pay for what needs, and so on. Angry associates need an even more structured agreement, often stating specifics about what a parent can and cannot do with children. Fiery foes usually have everything possible written in a legal contractual form, although they are most likely to violate their contracts.

In the perfect pal and cooperative colleague families, ex-spouses often choose to spend some hol-idays together, attend children's events together, and share information about children's needs. In angry associate and fiery foe families, parallel parenting is the norm. They operate independently as parents, not sharing information or events.

Even midlife- and later-life couples with adult children need to have some agreement about how their postdivorce family will function. Will both parents attend the child's wedding? Will they sit at the same table for the celebration dinner? Will both grandparents attend their grandchild's birthday party or graduation? Establishing clear boundaries is important across all stages of the family life cycle.

Family Redefinition: The Aftermath

A process of family redefinition frequently includes remarriage and the introduction of stepparents into the postdivorce family. Remarriage creates a series of transitions that are beyond the scope of this chapter (see Chapter 25) but are part of the ongoing transitions of family redefinition. For some families, a potential remarriage partner or spouse-equivalent may become part of the family system before the legal divorce and at the early phases of the reorganization transition. Some unnamed (e.g., the relationships between mothers and stepmothers) and thus unsanctioned relationships within the binuclear family structure take on an importance in the redefinition process. They are kin or quasi-kin relationships in the context of the binuclear family (Ahrons & Wallisch, 1987).

Relationships between parents and stepparents in the binuclear family provide an important emotional continuity for both parents and children. They facilitate this transition by redefining the divorced family so that the amount of relationship loss experienced by children and parents is minimized.

Family values and structures of many African American families provide a helpful model for binuclear families. The African American family is centered on the children, the family unit often being defined as including all those involved in their nurturance and support. Encouraging extended family relationships for the benefit of the children allows for continued responsibility regardless of changes in marital relationships. Unlike the traditional family structure favored by most White American families, the African American family structure is less based

on the legal relationship between spouses; hence, divorce is less likely to interfere with the child's familial ties (Boyd-Franklin, 2003a; Crosbie-Burnett & Lewis, 1993). If the assumption of parental responsibility is not based on blood kin, then divorce is less likely to be as disruptive to the child's family relationships.

One important and frequently overlooked strength of many ethnic families is their bicultural socialization. Children in these families usually have to learn to live in two cultures simultaneously—that of their ethnic community and that of the wider society (Crosbie-Burnett & Lewis, 1993). This acculturation process could be a very helpful model for a child in learning to live in the two-household cultures of the binuclear family. If one parent remarries and there are children from another family (stepsiblings), being bicultural could facilitate their being better able to accommodate the different family cultures that ordinarily create considerable stress for stepfamilies.

Although we have little research data, it is likely that gay and lesbian families, who operate outside of the legal marital system, have kinship structures similar to those of African American families. For children, the family structures that incorporate extended family, fictive and quasi-kin, and family relationships by choice are more likely to remain intact if the primary love relationship wanes. Because family roles are more ambiguous in gay and lesbian families, they may also prepare children better to accept the ambiguity that is inherent when families change their structure.

Lesbians, who are socialized, as most women are, to value emotional connectedness, often try to remain friends or family after the breakup of a love relationship. Their subsequent connection may take various forms: focusing on co-parenting children, celebrating holidays or taking vacations together, or remaining friends within a close circle. As with postdivorce heterosexual couples, the transformation from lovers to friends takes a lot of work, but many women are committed to the process (Shumsky, 1997). In married and divorced heterosexual relationships, women tend to be the kinkeepers of the family, whether nuclear or binuclear. In the Binuclear Family Study, the findings show that the relationship between mothers and stepmothers was much more emotional and interactive than was the relationship between fathers and stepfathers (Ahrons & Wallisch, 1987).

Gay men, on the other hand, like many men, often lack the vocabulary or emotional access to their feelings of loss after a breakup. This is especially true of the sometimes ambiguous relationships that occur in gay male culture, in which open contracts may permit casual or transient affairs to co-exist with long-term relationships (Shernoff, 1997).

Of course, HIV and AIDS also have a profound effect on gay male relationships, in which there may be fear of a partner's HIV-positive status, guilt if one's own status is negative, or a tendency to stay together when both partners are negative, largely because it is safe (Remien, 1997). In all of these circumstances, it is extremely important for the therapist to help those who want to break up to do so in the least destructive and most caring way, helping them to remain connected if that is desirable. The gay community, Remien reminds us, is full of stories of ex-lovers who are at their ex-partners' bedside and who maintain a bond that nourishes them both.

The struggle to define all of these relationships and transitions for themselves—coupling, parenting, and breaking up—is made both more difficult and more creative by the fact that they exist outside of society's social and legal rules. Where children are concerned, however, the nonlegal standing of a non-biological, noncustodial parent can create devastation for someone who may for years have been a co-parent or even a primary parent of her or his partner's children (Sundquist, 1997). Interestingly, when a remarriage ends in a divorce, this same dilemma holds true for a stepparent, who has emotional but no legal, biological, or custodial ties to the child.

Clinical Overview

A model of divorce, characterizing it as a normative process rather than evidence of pathology or dysfunction, has been presented in this chapter. This is aimed at helping clinicians transcend prevalent stereotypes and myths, thereby creating clinical guidelines for treating families of divorce. Within this model, clinicians can recognize the transitions of the divorce process and help client families cope

more effectively during this very painful and complex process. They can then identify what differentiates divorces that are successful or "good" from those that are unsuccessful or "bad."

Quite simply, a good divorce has three major objectives: 1) The family remains a family; 2) the negative effects on children are minimized; and 3) both ex-spouses integrate the divorce into their lives in a healthy way. Although the structure of the family has been altered, parents continue to be parents who are responsible for socializing and attending to their children's emotional and economic needs. Bad divorces are those in which spouses are unable or unwilling to settle their marital conflicts without enmeshing the children in their divorce drama. Children in these divorces often lose a relationship with one parent (usually the father), are caught in painful loyalty conflicts about their parents, and suffer irreparable emotional damage (Ahrons, 1994, 2004).

By understanding the normal transitions of the divorce process, clinicians can help their clients to better understand and cope with the emotional, legal, and practical tasks they need to complete. By providing information and knowledge, clinicians can help divorcing couples to make decisions based on their children's best interests. And by learning and teaching important conflict reduction techniques, they can assist parents to make the many complex decisions that will need to be addressed.

Because divorce is a legal decision with economic repercussions, clinicians need to be aware of how the legal process works in their state. Even though all states now have no-fault legislation, many divorces continue to be adversarial. Learning which lawyers in your community are open to collaboration with a therapist and which lawyers' styles are more mediative than adversarial will be very helpful to the clinician's continuing work with the divorcing family. For the divorcing couple, as well as the therapist working with them, the impact of the legal system on the emotional process is complex and has the potential to be counterproductive to the therapist's goals. It is best to encourage the divorcing couple to make as many decisions together as possible before engaging the legal system. As was noted earlier, mediation is a very helpful way for divorcing couples to settle their differences in a mutual problem-solving approach.

The economics of divorce filter into every aspect of the divorce process. It is important for the clinician to understand how money was managed during the marriage. In a more traditional marriage, the wife frequently knows little about the financial picture. In such cases, the husband has more power in the discussion of finances. Although a therapist should never give financial advice or try to settle the overall economic distribution (unless formally trained and acting as a divorce mediator), it is important to have an understanding of how money is used in the negotiation of the divorce.

In marriages with dependent children, financial issues are entwined with custody decisions. When a wife has been the primary caretaker of the children and the husband has been the primary breadwinner, the most common scenario is that the children represent power for the mother and money represents power for the father. This gets played out in the emotional terrain, often in very subtle and complex ways.

In marriages with older or adult children, women often have less power in the negotiations than men do. These midlife divorces are frequently the ones that result in women becoming "displaced homemakers." The common situation is that of the wife, who either has left a job to take care of children and home or is less educated than her husband, finding herself at midlife having to seek a job without adequate experience, education, or training. Her earning potential is often much less than that of her husband. The law often does not provide adequate repayment to women for the years they devoted to caring for the family. A woman of 50 may find herself without retirement or Social Security benefits. Therapists need to be aware of these gender inequities and educate women about their rights.

Finally, it is important for the clinician to remember that divorce affects the entire family system. Parents and siblings of the divorcing couple usually become very involved in the process. When there are children, the grandparents, aunts, uncles, and cousins are all part of the kinship network. In good divorces, the kinship network continues satisfying relationships with the children and frequently with the divorcing in-law. In angry divorces, kin often take sides with their biological kin, creating breaches in relationships with the children as well. Clinicians would be wise to ask about extended family relationships and be open to bringing relatives into the sessions to help them sort out their issues.

Working with divorce requires a complex multi-level approach (Ahrons, 2007). Clinicians need to be aware of their own biases and stereotypes, and they need to correct for them by gaining adequate knowledge of the emotional, legal, and economic divorce processes. They need to look through a wide-angle lens and incorporate both spouses' families of origin. Ethnic, racial, and gender differences need to enter into the therapeutic equation, as do the family's developmental life cycle transitions. A therapist who chooses to work with divorcing families will need to tolerate a high level of conflicts and cope with complex painful emotions.

Therapy with divorcing families is a challenging and difficult process for both the therapist and the family. Working with a family and taking them through the process, helping them to emerge as a healthy, functioning binuclear family is a goal worth striving for.

Chapter 20

Single-Parent Families: Strengths, Vulnerabilities, and Interventions

Carol M. Anderson & Maria E. Anderson

When there is a commitment to living and loving together there is family.

From *The Single Mother's Book*, Joan Anderson, Peachtree Publishers.

Reprinted with permission.

Single–parent households make up an increasingly significant percentage of families in the population. They have grown in number, diversity, and acceptance across all income groups, from the very poor to the affluent and well educated (U. S. Census Bureau, 2006). In 2008, the Forum on Child and Family Statistics reported that 27 percent of children in the United States, between 0 and 17 years of age, lived with only a mother or a father (www.childstats.gov). The term "single parent" is defined by the U.S. Census Bureau (2006) as a parent who cares for one or more children under 18 without the assistance of another parent in the home. This broad umbrella encompasses a wide range of family types. There are postdivorce single parents, never-married teenagers with children, and an increasing number of both women and men who purposely choose single parenthood through adoption or donor insemination, or by raising a child who has been conceived in an uncommitted relationship. The varying pathways to becoming a single-parent household create different family characteristics that make it difficult to generalize the issues and problems involved.

All single parents and their children must find ways to deal with the loss on which they are founded, the risk of emotional and task overload resulting from the absence of two parents in the home, and most must work to create and nurture a network of support to make up for this absence. Beyond this, each category of single-parent family has a number of unique characteristics and needs. Low-income mothers, who remain the majority of single parents, often have little contact with their child's father and tend to struggle with finding ways to manage on public assistance (Barrett & Turner, 2005; Berger, 2007). Postdivorce households, even those with adequate financial and social resources, may need to cope with ongoing conflicts with ex-partners over child-rearing and custody arrangements (Furstenberg & Cherlin, 1991). Adoptive and alternative insemination single-parent households are likely to have educational and financial resources, but are likely to experience discrimination and have no other parent committed to their child's welfare (Groze, 1991). Understanding the impact of the pathways to becoming a single-parent household is complicated by the fact that this status often changes over time. Some will remain single-parent households for their entire family life cycle, while others will experience single parenthood as a transitional state, a way station between committed couple relationships (Park, 2005).

There is considerable disagreement about the impact of living in a single-parent household on the well-being of both parents and children. Compared to families with married parents, single parents work longer hours, face more stressful life changes, have more economic problems, and have less emotional support, so it shouldn't be surprising that some studies report more psychological problems in these parents and children (McClanahan & Sandefur, 1994). However, much of this research does not consider the comparative ongoing impact of living in a family with chronic conflict, violence, substance abuse, or poverty, all of which have a documented negative impact on child development (Afifi et al., 2006; Berger, 2007; Cain & Combs-Orme, 2005; Wen, 2008). We know that poverty in particular accounts for about half of the disadvantage in the lower achievement of children, and when its influence is factored out, the differences in the adjustment of children in one and two-parent families all but disappear (Barrett & Turner, 2005). Unfortunately the influence of poverty can't be factored out for the 75 percent of single parents who are largely minority and initially teen parents (U.S. Census, 2001). These lower-income parents also have less education and fewer resources, and live in more troubled communities, all conditions that correlate with high rates of parental depression, parenting overload, and a higher risk of child maltreatment (Berger 2007; Butterworth et al., 2007; Carlson, 2001; Ceballo & McLoyd, 2002; Zhan & Pandy, 2004). But single parenthood is not the culprit; most single-parent homes in all social classes are no more "broken" or troubled than those of comparative intact families. Single parents provide their children with structure and nurturance while finding ways to meet their own needs for intimacy, companionship, and community. They may make sacrifices, such as giving up a social life or a career to make time to provide the nurture and structure their children need, but they are not automatically dysfunctional. In fact, children in single-parent families appear to experience some benefits compared to those raised in two-parent households. They grow strong and make good use of their diverse experiences, assuming more responsibility, becoming more independent, and developing meaningful connections with extended family and friends. In fact, single-parent households appear to provide a better environment for some specific children, such as those adopted children who have disabilities, and their single parents describe the experience of raising them as transformative and empowering (Levine, 2009).

Surprisingly, despite the prevalence of single-parent households and the data supporting their viability, the culture continues to be ambivalent about accepting and supporting them (Thornton, 2009; Usdansky, 2009). The widely held idealized view of two-parent families seems to blind us to the strengths and accomplishments of this increasingly prevalent alternative family structure. For this reason, it is particularly important that clinicians who work with single-parent families understand their strengths and challenges and learn to use a wide-angle lens to see single parenthood in its current and historical context. In particular, clinicians need to be aware of how single parenthood influences each phase of the family life cycle in order to help these families to appreciate their own viability, meet the inevitable challenges of single-parent family life, and mobilize their ties to a supportive community.

Single Parents and the Family Life Cycle

Some children are born into single-parent families, some single-parent families are created mid-childhood through divorce or adoption. In fact, single-parent households can come into being at almost any stage of the family life cycle, superimposing the additional tasks of forming and maintaining a single-parent family on the usual issues of a particular family life cycle stage. All single-parent families have a shared present, but they may or may not have a shared past, and whatever structure they create may not continue if they make a future move to form a two-parent family. Single parents and their children build their families on a foundation of loss, whether the loss of a relationship, a two-parent family, or their traditional ideals. There is inevitable emotional baggage related to these losses that become a part of the single-parent family identity as it develops a blueprint for the future. The specifics of the structure created will depend on many factors, including the path taken to single parenthood, the ages of parent and child, the financial status of the family, the community/network context, and the extended family history and culture. Different cultures may be more or less accepting of the various pathways taken to single parenthood, but whatever pathway is taken at whatever stage of the life cycle, all single parents and their children will be initially working to create a sense of home, belonging, and safety along with establishing the flexibility to change and evolve over time. All of these factors contribute to the complexity and diversity of the tasks required of single-parent families as they also move through the stages of the traditional family life cycle. In fact, single-parent family life cycle tasks will complicate and sometimes even contradict normative developmental tasks, and accomplishing them without culturally prescribed single-parent family rituals can be particularly challenging. For instance, teens who have been moving toward independence may suddenly need help from their family; recently divorced single parents may require teenage children to sacrifice their normal time with peers to help with younger siblings; single parents by choice may need to give up their freedom in order to care for an infant, perhaps in the face of considerable disapproval from their family and friends.

New single-parent families with young children

The initial phase of establishing a single-parent household involves setting up a workable family structure that will provide children with consistent nurturance and limits, while insuring that parental needs are at least partially met. Single parents with a new child must make space for that child in their work and social network, realigning their own family relationships to allow their parents to play the role of grandparents. This whole process of adjustment requires that the single parent find ways to create a family identity they can be proud of, one that will nurture the child's development within the family, maintain contact with the missing parent if possible, and facilitate kin and friendship relationships to augment missing role models and overstretched resources. During this initial phase, single adoptive parents of children from different ethnic or racial groups must not only develop a family identity that incorporates potentially rich diverse racial and ethnic themes, but also one that accommodates parent–child racial differences and sometimes the negative reactions of their community to their family (Samuels, 2009). for those who live in traditional suburban communities of predominantly two-parent households, single parenthood, not to mention racial differences, may compound the marginalization of single-parent families. Single parents will then have to work to build bridges across cultural differences for their children's sake.

Creating a new family can be a stressful experience, and single fathers and mothers can become so preoccupied with the problems of their current reality that they fail to see the broader context that might provide support, solutions, or even just another perspective. The extended-family network may be particularly important for single-parent families as they go through their formative years and work to establish their new family identity (Jones et al., 2007). An increased awareness of the extended family life cycle context might reveal inspirational role models or other invisible resources. Mobilizing the rich knowledge and possible resources from these networks is especially important for the coping of single mothers who spend more time in child care than single fathers and yet receive less support from their extended family (Goldscheider & Kaufman, 2006; Hilton & Kopera-Frye, 2007; Hook & Chalasani, 2008).

As single-parent families form, both divorced and never-married teen mothers also have the challenge of finding ways to make a place for their child's father in their lives, because children in contact with their fathers do better. A solid relationship between child and father is more likely if it can be facilitated from the onset of the single-parent family life cycle. Unfortunately many fathers tend to lose contact with their children within a year of the divorce, and young minority fathers, many of whom become unemployed or incarcerated, also may fade quickly from their child's life (Devault et al., 2008; Dudley, 2007; Dyer, 2005; Forste, 2006; Swiss & Le Bourdais, 2009). Divorced single mothers almost always need support in allowing the father access to the child and tolerating the unfairness of those times when father is idealized and mother is blamed for his unpredictability (Fagan et al., 2009; Laakso, 2004). Rather than complaining about being single parents, many complain that they are not quite single enough. Teen mothers and their parents may need help in promoting continued father–child involvement, especially when the parents do not approve of their grandchild's father. (Cutrona et al., 1998; Roy & Dyson, 2005).

When teens begin to create their own single-parent families, they also confront the contradiction between their developmental need to move toward independence and their need for increased support from their parents to help with their child. It isn't easy for a teen to maintain her credibility as her child's parent when she must defer authority to her own parents. At the same time, her own parents must continue with the developmental life cycle task of launching and letting go, one that is more difficult if they feel their daughter seems irresponsible or needs continuing financial and emotional support.

310 Part 2 • Life Cycle Transitions and Phases

Finally, the practical daily challenges involved in starting a single-parent family are many, and parents may need help in sorting out routines and responsibilities. Managing the day-to-day tasks and chores alone is particularly complicated for those single parents living on limited incomes. Paying for decent child care is often impossible, leaving working single parents with young children having inadequate arrangements if potentially helpful relatives cannot be identified. If single-parent families are created at a time the children are slightly older, single parents have the daily pressures and stresses of maintaining a job while responding to the demands of their child's school and after school activities, not to mention the emergencies of child illnesses and parent–teacher conferences. For those working without benefits, responding to calls from the school about the common behavioral problems of children can mean missing a day's pay or even job loss, adding additional stress to family life (Carlson, 2001; Wen, 2008). One important barrier to managing these tasks for single parents of either gender is their assumption that they must be both mother and father to their child. Clinicians can be helpful by encouraging them to be 100 percent of the mother or father that they are and to talk with their child as needed about the absence of the parent who isn't there.

While most single parents are not at greater risk for mistreating their children, the relatively high percentage who are depressed are more likely to engage in poor parenting strategies unless they receive considerable support. Certainly many single parents are well connected with family and friends, but others can easily become isolated and overwhelmed and without the time and energy to maintain relationships or reach out for support. They feel the need to collapse on the couch after a trying day, and taking the initiative to connect may seem like just one more chore. Even in African American single-mother families who reportedly are more likely to have active family networks that provide frequent contact and mutual aid, it is often the single parents most in need of help who do not receive it (Butterworth et al., 2007; Ceballo & McLoyd, 2002; Caldwell, 1996; Thompson & Wilkins, 1992).

Some single parents attempt to gain additional support for family life by bringing a romantic partner into the household. If such a relationship can de-

velop into a loving, supportive, and lasting one, it can benefit single mothers and single fathers, as well as their children. In fact, such support has been noted to especially protect mothers from depression in the face of stressful life events (Brown & Harris, 1978). But live-in partners can be problematic in other ways. If there is no long-term commitment to the family, their entrances and exits can be disruptive and upsetting to children (Kamp-Dush, 2007). In addition, single parents of either gender can find themselves juggling conflicting loyalties between their children and their new partners, especially those partners who compete with children for the single parent's time and attention, undermine parental authority, or get intensely involved and then leave precipitously. Single mothers are left handling conflicts that arise when live-in boyfriends expect (because of their gender) to be in charge when they don't have parental credibility or a solid relationship with the child. Despite the risk of losing the support of someone they desperately need, mothers must be helped to make it clear to these partners that their role is not that of parent (see Chapter 19 in McGoldrick & Carter on the divorce cycle). In fact, they may need to protect their children from partners who do not have a biological bond to a child since these children are nearly 50 times more likely to die of injuries than children living with two biological parents (Schnitzer & Ewigman, 2005; Margolin, 1992).

Single-Parent families with older children and adolescents

As children in single-parent families become older, they are likely to take on and be granted more than usual authority over their younger siblings and household functioning. Getting help from so-called parental children is often essential for the survival of these families, only becoming a serious problem when children are encouraged to totally sacrifice their childhood to family chores and responsibilities. Most adolescents are given room to accomplish the developmental tasks of this life cycle stage, and most single parents manage to maintain their parental role in this process. The families they form have the advantages of becoming closer and less hierarchical as a result.

However, as children enter adolescence, many begin to challenge parental rules and values as they sort out their sense of self, and their parents are left tolerating their often rocky moves toward emancipation. Single parents of both genders encounter these challenges, although they are often more difficult for single mothers who tend to be less comfortable balancing reasonable rules with allowing age-appropriate freedoms. They need support for setting limits when teenage boys have behavioral problems or when teen daughters get depressed or over-involved in troubled romantic relationships that force them to make adult decisions before they are ready.

Fortunately, over time, the payoffs of being raised in a single-parent household become more obvious for children of both genders. The girls often mature earlier, developing earlier social skills and relationship abilities, and boys raised by single mothers become especially socially savvy, generous, and caring communicators while continuing to maintain their traditional masculine interests and traits (Drexler & Gross, 2005; Kimmel, 2008).

As teens actually begin to launch, all family structures must change in ways that allow them freedom to move out of the family and return for support as needed. The close relationship between single parent and teen may complicate this process with disagreements about who should perform various household tasks as the teen develops significant independent commitments to a life outside the family.

During these years the children of divorce may begin to question their role in the failure of their parents' marriage, and those who are adopted may begin to have questions about their biological history. Children in both of these categories may want to reconnect with the past, seeking more time with a divorced parent or seeking reunion with their birth mother (McNamara, 2009; Samuels, 2009). At the same time, single parents who have just begun to breathe a sigh of relief as their children gain increasing independence may find they need to provide care for their own parents who may be beginning to experience a number of sequential illnesses.

Single parenting in the post–child-rearing years

Eventually, the children of single parents grow up and leave just as all children do. As Lillian Rubin has said, most women, and we suggest most men also, respond to their children leaving home with a sense of

relief. But gracefully accomplishing this developmental task can be harder for single parents without the support or comfort of a partner to provide a continuing sense of belonging or family. The welcomed freedom, relief, and sense of accomplishment is counterbalanced by sadness that they are unable to share yet another of their child's developmental steps with a partner who cares as much as they do. Awareness of such parental anxieties can increase the child's guilt about becoming independent or stimulate anger if young adults feel smothered or constrained by the implicit demands of a parent's needs.

While most offspring eventually develop an adult–adult relationship with their parents it helps that children of single parents show an earlier appreciation of their parents as individuals with histories, strengths, and limitations of their own (Birditt et al., 2008; Fingerman et al., 2008). Those with stronger adult-to-adult relationships with their children can find them a comfort and a help in later years, making it easier for single parents to appreciate the successful adulthood and accomplishments of their progeny as they alter their own priorities to create an independent life. Single parents can then discover later-life opportunities to explore new roles on their own and in their children's lives, and many report great pleasure as they find ways to actively participate in the lives of their children's families, including the role of grandparent.

Yet there is the potential for several problems in the post child-rearing phase of the life cycle that can be challenges for single parents of either gender. Those who have not prepared for their child's independence by developing interests and networks of their own before their child has been launched are likely to have more difficulties. Most single parents appear to be able to make room for new relationships and interests during this phase, but those who do not, especially those who have concentrated only on child-rearing and work, may find themselves lonely and stymied about how to have meaning in their lives as they retire and are no longer needed by their children.

In addition, a sizable subset of aging single parents have financial difficulties, particularly those single mothers who have never had a strong employment history and/or the pension of an ex-partner to provide support. Compared to married women, single mothers are 55 percent more likely to be living in poverty after age 65 (Johnson & Favreault, 2004). For most single parents the eventual tasks of this life cycle stage involve finding ways to deal with health problems and possible diminished ability to function independently on their own without becoming a burden to their children.

When Single-Parent Families Seek Help

Single-parent families are likely to seek help as they deal with the fallout from life cycle transitions, those entrances and exits from the family such as birth, death, marriage, or divorce. Managing these life cycle events can stretch the already thinly spread coping resources of many single-parent families resulting in a range of emotional or behavioral problems for parent and/or child.

Most clinicians, especially those working in public agencies, are likely to see a disproportionate number of individuals living in single-parent families, contributing to the myth that all single parents and their children are dysfunctional. But while they may use mental health services more often than two-parent families (Crosier et al., 2007; Okun, 1996; Wang, 2004; Wen, 2008), their presenting complaints are probably generated less by clinical disorders than by life cycle transitions and interweaving of multiple life stresses (Wolfe, 2009).

For instance, single parents often initially seek care for a behaviorally disruptive or emotionally distressed child, but their requests for help in managing that child may be the result of parental coping mechanisms that have been compromised by experiences of cultural and racial prejudice, chronic financial problems, unresolved past losses or abuse, and the absence of adequate support from extended family and friends. These factors no doubt contribute to the high rates of distress in single parents, and in turn high rates of emotional or behavioral problems in their children.

Little data is available about the emotional well-being of single fathers, but there is considerable evidence that a high percentage of mothers, especially single mothers, bringing their children for care meet criteria for depression themselves (Afifi et al.,

2006; Anderson et al., 2006; Downey & Coyne, 1990; Swartz et al., 2006).

Taking a family systems/life cycle approach in responding to single parents who request help for their child has several advantages. A life cycle framework can be particularly helpful as they struggle to face the myriad inevitable issues that arise at various developmental stages and times of transition. Also, it provides a way to address the needs of distressed mothers, and perhaps fathers, since they tend not to seek help for themselves despite the interrelatedness of the problems of family members. Additionally, a contextual life cycle framework provides a wide-angle lens to locate these problems in the context of culture, time, history, and relationships, offering a view of values and patterns that help us understand single parents and their potential resources and opportunities, including the identification of possible role models from previous and current generations. Finally, it expands the concentrated and limited focus single parents often have on the current problem, a focus that can cause single parents under stress to be stuck in a present that does not provide solutions to their problems.

By definition, the formative stage of single-parent families is stressful, adding tasks to whatever stage of the family life cycle that is otherwise occurring. Becoming a single-parent family almost inevitably involves the reawakening of issues from earlier times that have not been resolved, and there are always echoes of loss of one sort or another. At the most basic level during these times, it is important to define the single parent as having the right to make the household rules.

Family stability and parental authority can be reinforced when the maintenance of family routines and rituals is supported. This practice helps to ensure predictability and structure. Some single parents with multiple responsibilities are so overwhelmed by day-to-day survival issues that they neglect the need for these routines and family rituals, forgetting the comfort, structure, and sense of continuity that they provide.

The single parent's ability to be in charge can also be complicated by the need to have older children take some responsibility for their younger siblings and household chores. In some families, single parents allow children to have so much authority that their own authority is compromised; they set limits that are too arbitrary, overly permissive; or they employ an unpredictable combination of the two based on the unpredictable stresses in their own lives. Finding solutions to these relationship issues is not always easy. Helping single parents to gain credibility and power with their children is a particularly difficult task for low-income teen parents with depression and low self-esteem and divorced women who have tended to rely on their spouses to provide discipline and limit setting. Maternal sanity can be better maintained in the long run by encouraging consistency. Helping single parents to effectively negotiate issues of power, rules, and responsibilities with their own parents, lovers, or the children themselves, is sometimes the most important task of therapy since it lays the groundwork for how everyone can live together and move through the life cycle. Therapists can help these parents to retain their status as ultimate authority and keep a direct line to each child even as they delegate more than the usual number of responsibilities to their older ones. It is helpful to both parents and children if they are encouraged to maintain structure, predictability, and family rituals during this stressful formative time, yet leave openings for the exploration of larger themes and stages of development.

At the same time, it is crucial to pay attention to the networks of both parent and child, along with the resources and stresses they might provide. Examining networks can lay the groundwork for reestablishing ties that have been weakened or disrupted by divorce, relocation, or disapproval of life choices. Some single parents lack the courage or skills to develop and maintain helpful relationships beyond the family. Their pride, fear of becoming a burden, fear of rejection, or even fear of loss of custody may make it hard to ask for help. Nurturing existing and potential contacts will facilitate a web of support, an interrelated archipelago of contacts that can provide a practical and emotional cushion for both parent and child. However, it may take a therapist, serving as a temporary cheerleader and coach, to help both parent and child to become embedded in a fabric of social support while simultaneously sorting out the problems in existing family relationships. If possible, therapists working with divorced families should

work to involve both parents and their networks as ongoing connections for their child. Even though we now know that divorce also has positive effects, a child's social network may be painfully disrupted in a divorce. It is important to strengthen the child's network by minimizing this loss of extended family members and family friends and increasing the involvement of community supports that can minimize the impact of losses that have occurred.

Cases of single-parent families seeking help

The following narratives provide examples of single parents, with dilemmas they have encountered. Each used therapy to come to terms with one or more of the common themes encountered during their life journeys as single parents.

Angela: Balancing a need for independence with the need for support

This first example is of a teen whose move toward independence became complicated by pregnancy, a cross-race relationship, and need for help from family. She struggled to maintain her dreams and a sense of herself as a competent adult in the face of increased parental involvement, while her own parents struggled with wanting to help her and their grandchild, but simultaneously wanting to promote their child's independence and personal development. Everyone tried to balance independence and parental credibility in the face of three generational dynamics.

Angela was an 18-year-old first-generation Mexican American living on campus in her freshmen year of college and dating Michael, a 19-year-old African American student. When she discovered she was pregnant Michael ended their relationship. She feared telling her parents not only because she didn't want to give up college life, but also because she knew they would be disappointed and upset that her baby would be biracial. When she eventually told them they were devastated but agreed to swallow their dreams for her success and encouraged her to move home so that they could look after her, and eventually her child. Angela, who valued her education, freedom, and the opportunity for a better life, insisted on first completing her second semester of college. When she did move home, the adjustment to her family's strict household rules/ structure was a difficult one, but being pregnant with no job, no money, and no other support left her with no alternative. She was thankful for their help, but she was used to making her own decisions in the months she had been on her own, and her family's negativity about Michael upset her. Trapped in her parent's home, she feared not only that she would never be able to finish college, but also that her biracial child would never be accepted by her family. Angela's family fell in love with their grandchild as soon as he was born, and they were eventually able to come to an agreement with Angela to try to work together to raise him. They developed a child care routine that allowed her to return to college at a school closer to home. Her parents struggled with just how much they should help to facilitate her participation in college life, and how much they should push her to be responsible for her child's care. Their concerns were exacerbated by requests from Michael to see his child even though he contributed no support, had dropped out of college, and no longer had a romantic relationship with Angela. They sought counseling for help with handling the ambiguities of Angela's parenting, issues fairly easily settled. Accepting Michael as their grandchild's parent was a much more difficult task. They blamed him for their daughter's pregnancy, the interruption of her college education, and his failure to work or contribute support. However as he and his parents continued to make efforts to be involved and provide occasional child care, they were gradually able to accept that he could play a positive role in their grandson's life. Angela, now 21, continues to hope to graduate from college and move out of her parent's home.

Daniel: A committed single-parent father against all odds

Daniel is just one of the increasing number of men who want or need to be the primary parent of their child. These men tend to receive less support for taking on the responsibilities of single parenting so they are often left to blaze their own trail. Daniel made a commitment to raise his young daughter despite the lack of support of his family and his network. He was a young African American college graduate in his early 20s, dating Pamela and leading a swinging social life when Pamela got pregnant. They married despite the disapproval of both sets of parents who each thought their child could have done better. Six

months later they had a daughter. A stormy 4-year marriage was followed by 4 years of conflict over child visitation. Eventually Pamela's drug use made it impossible for her to be an effective mother, and she offered Daniel custody. Aware that his daughter needed him, Daniel wanted to step up to the plate but was terrified of taking on sole responsibility for his daughter's well-being. Neither his single life style nor his own family history of generations of inadequate fathering had prepared him to have any idea of what it would take to be a good father, a fact that did not bode well for his chances of success. His father and grandfather, both now deceased, had failed to provide for their families either financially or emotionally. In the best of times, they had been neglectful and unavailable. Even Daniel's mother did not support his raising his child, saying men had no business raising daughters. Her opinions were at least in part based on the poor fathering she experienced in her own family and the lack of involvement of her husband with their four children. Paradoxically, however, she offered no help. Daniel also got little encouragement from his single friends who pointed out that becoming a full-time father would mean giving up his single life style. Determined to try, he sought counseling in hopes of gaining support for what he felt he had to do. He was coached to search for possible role models in his extended family and discovered a long-distant paternal uncle who not only expressed support and admiration for Daniel's desire to take responsibility for his child, but who was also willing to provide financial help. The sacrifices were considerable, and for several years Daniel's life was constrained by work and child care, which involved a lot of trial and error parenting. His social world gradually expanded as his daughter grew up and eventually went to college.

Mary: Divorced, overwhelmed, and in crisis

Some single parents live from crisis to crisis, losing sight of the impact of their culture, their extended family history, and the chance to understand and use the resources that might be available. Those who become overwhelmed and depressed may even abandon the most basic rules and important family rituals such as regular dinners, not to mention outings or birthday and other holiday celebrations (Kaplan et al., 2008). Some, like Mary, even deny the relevance of the rules and rituals they once maintained, viewing themselves as no longer a "real" family.

Mary was a 40-year-old recently divorced Polish American mother of three without much of an available network when she requested help for Stephan, her 8-year-old middle son, who had been acting out since his father abruptly left and moved to another state, now maintaining only occasional contact. Mary was not prepared to manage her children or a household without a husband. She never had enough money to meet her children's needs, much less provide them with the brand name clothes they claimed were essential for social survival. Worse yet, they blamed her for their father's absence. Frequently frazzled, exhausted, and feeling inadequate, her discipline was admittedly inconsistent, and the constant fighting and chaos in her home seemed to her to be par for the course. Despite these stresses that dominated her life, she would not have come to the mental health center if her son's teachers had not complained that he was underperforming and acting out in class. Getting her children together to come to counseling felt like just one more major and exhausting task, one that initially made the family's attendance at treatment sporadic. The turning point came when their counselor redefined the problem as the family being trapped in mourning their old family in ways that prevented them from creating a new one. She suggested they begin by addressing the pragmatics of defining a new single-parent household structure that provided a better chance of meeting everyone's needs. Together, Mary and her children used their sessions to work out a list of rules, chores, and consequences that made everyone's life a little less unpredictable. She successfully delegated increased responsibilities to her 12-year-old daughter for a few dinnertime and after-school chores and, somewhat less successfully, delegated to her sons the chore of cleaning their own room. They created a required regular Sunday family dinnertime to reinforce their sense of family. As the chaos diminished, Mary became less depressed and her children more comfortable. In treatment, the family turned to the issues of their anger at their absent father, how they could maintain some contact with him, and how they could find ways to make up for some of the losses they experienced after he left.

Kathleen: Independent with a vengeance

The issues that bring older single mothers by choice to treatment are quite different. Since they are usually better educated and have more resources, their daily life is usually easier to manage, and many even have hired help. But, as Kathleen's story demonstrates their lives have their own unique set of problems.

Kathleen was a 38-year-old woman who, as she said "had it all." An independent and successful financial advisor who owned her own home, she had a good relationship with her Irish American Catholic family of origin. She did not see herself as a woman waiting for her prince to come, having overtly rejected this message from the culture and the media. But as friend after friend married and began to have children, she increasingly felt she was a misfit. Her ticking biological clock eventually inspired her to become a single parent by donor insemination. Her family was shocked at this decision, and two of her siblings, embarrassed, cut off contact when she began to pursue this path. Without a partner, she did not have to make room for a child in a couple's relationship, but she did have to make room for a child in her very independent life. This task was not easy, but she worked hard to create a loving and predictable environment for her child. Motherhood was everything she hoped for, but she couldn't help feeling bad about the negative social reactions she occasionally experienced, not only for her route to single parenthood, but to her single parenthood itself. Her 38-year history of feeling accomplished and respected had not prepared her for being viewed as deviant or deficient. She struggled with coming to grips with who she was and eventually concluded she was okay. With the help of a coach, she eventually took on the task of repairing the close relationships she once had with her parents and siblings with the same determination she had always mobilized in her professional career. She began by reaching out to them in small ways, sending informal notes and photos of the baby. In search of role models, she also contacted an aunt who had successfully raised her children on her own after her husband died. Slowly other family members responded to her efforts to be a part of her family, and by her daughter's second birthday, nearly all came to the party and subsequently included her in other family events. Today, 10 years later, both Kathleen and her daughter are thriving. Kathleen defines her life as satisfying despite the fact that she rarely dates, claiming that between her work and parenting, she just hasn't the energy or the time.

Conclusion

The increased prevalence of single-parent families of all sorts has constituted a dramatic social change in recent years. Despite worries about the demise of the traditional nuclear family, this family form has gained increased acceptance, although many single parents continue to struggle to survive in a culture that defines them as deficient and provides little formal support.

The challenges of raising children solo are real, and not surprisingly a disproportionate number of single parents eventually seek help for themselves or their children, usually in traditional mental health and social service agencies. To have any chance to work effectively with single-parent families, clinicians in these community agencies must become sensitive to the challenges single parents encounter when they must raise children without the sanction of a marital relationship or in the aftermath of a marriage that was not viable. Because these issues may leave single parents unusually sensitive to criticism and more than a bit defensive, they are highly likely to become the treatment dropouts so frustrating to clinicians unless specific efforts are made to support and connect with them.

Engaging them is complicated by the fact that over-stretched single parents often experience the therapy they seek as just one more time-consuming burden. They also find that the required narrow focus on diagnosis and pathology required in public mental health systems often minimizes their strengths and fails to acknowledge the resources or patterns of the larger family system that play a role in the child's behavior and the single parent's needs.

Clinicians can effectively employ models of individual or family intervention if they counteract these negative forces by highlighting the factors contributing to successful single-family households. Particularly important factors are the stage of the single-parent family life cycle, the relationship with their extended family and social network, and the strategies they must develop to accommodate to the many daily realities of their unique lives.

In addition to adapting traditional therapy models to appropriately target the needs of single-parent families, a number of creative educational and supportive programs have emerged that allow single parents to receive help without being seen in the formal mental health services system. Just a few examples of creative programs include Internet interventions for single parents (Campbell-Grossman et al., 2009), single parent by choice support groups (Ben-Daniel et al., 2007), community programs in which low-income minority single mothers are paired with supportive older women (Roberts, 2006), and the Baby College that is part of the Harlem Children's Zone, helping low-income minority teen parents to become better parents while continuing to address their own needs (Tough, 2007). All of these programs could easily be disseminated to other communities to address the needs of various types of single parents.

Chapter 21

Families Transformed by the Divorce Cycle: Reconstituted, Multinuclear, Recoupled, and Remarried Families

Monica McGoldrick & Betty Carter

Divorce has become a normal life event in the United States, occurring in 50 percent of first marriages and over 60 percent of subsequent marriages. This chapter will discuss the divorce cycle, which describes families transforming and reconstituting themselves through marriage, divorce, remarriage, and re-divorce. Over the long haul, remarriage appears more stressful than divorce, especially the father's remarriage, which underscores the importance of taking a family life cycle perspective when working clinically to keep focus on the longitudinal course of family life (Ahrons, 2007).

Furthermore, many of the difficulties on the journey to couple happiness appear to result from our failure to redefine marriage to include gender equality, women's economic independence, and the economic viability of the man as well. So keeping our lens focused on gender and socioeconomic issues is essential. Unemployment and underemployment cause great stress on marriage. In addition, the lack of social support for an equal-partnership marriage is reflected in concrete obstacles such as the lack of affordable child care and inflexible workplace demands, as well as old, unrealistic, gendered expectations that men be breadwinners and women handle the second shift of housework, caretaking, and management of all relationships. This struggle to live out new roles while still playing by the old rules undermines marriage and remarriage and will continue to do so until we define and support new rules in emotional and concrete ways. We have found it useful to conceptualize divorce and its aftermath as an interruption or dislocation of the traditional family life cycle, which produces the kind of profound disequilibrium that is associated throughout the entire family life cycle with gains, losses, and shifts in family membership.

Although many conservative spokespersons, supported by a few researchers, still see divorce as a source of major family pathology (Coontz, Coleman, & Ganong, 2003; Wallerstein, 2001; Wolfinger, 2005; Popenoe, 2008) we agree with mainstream researchers and clinicians who have recognized that divorce is a transitional crisis that interrupts developmental tasks and requires readjustment of the family (Ahrons 1994; Hetherington, 1999, 2002, 2005, 2006). Because marital separation causes major practical as well as emotional readjustments, short-term distress is normal even when it is severe. As in other kinds of family crisis (e.g., migration, job loss, addiction, death, serious illness), the key that determines whether the crisis is transitional or has permanent crippling impact is whether it is handled adequately within the family system in spite of the general lack of social support offered by our society. If it is well-handled emotionally (and financially), family members, including children, may exhibit temporary symptoms and behavioral manifestations of anxiety over a period of months or a few years. But several years after the divorce, if the developmental tasks of divorcing and those of settling into the postdivorce transformed family are satisfactorily accomplished, there are few, if any, observable or testable differences due to having been part of a divorced family.

The transitional crisis of divorce has two overlapping phases: the separation and legal divorce and the settling into the so-called single-parent form in two households. For about one third of divorced women this stabilization after divorce becomes permanent. The once highly stigmatized household of mother and children has now become part of a growing variety of American family forms. Paradoxically, the stigma that was once associated with divorced mothers has now largely moved to unmarried mothers; being a divorced parent is no longer as stressful a label as it was in past generations. Most families will experience at least one more transitional crisis when either or both spouses remarry.

Thus, if we visualize a family traveling the road of life, moving from stage to stage in their developmental unfolding, we can see divorce as an interruption that puts the family on a new trajectory—an additional family life cycle stage—in which the physical and emotional losses and changes of divorce are put into effect and absorbed by the three-generational system. The family, now in two households, continues its forward developmental progress, though in a more complex form. When either spouse becomes involved with a new partner, a second detour occurs—a second additional family life cycle stage—in which the family must handle the stress of absorbing 2 or 3 generations of new members into the system and redefine their roles and relationships to existing family members. When this task of merging in mid-journey with another 3-generational system has been accomplished, the transformed family continues as a now much more complex system.

Gender Issues in Divorce

Until recently, women were socialized to invest their entire identity in marriage and were given the major responsibility for its success. Thus, regardless of the facts in the case, women may see divorce as a personal failure. It is crucial that the therapist not assume that remarriage is the chief solution to her problems, but rather help her connect to her strength, competence, and emotional ability to go it alone unless or until she chooses otherwise.

For divorcing men, there is the serious possibility that they will lose their children in one way or another. Unless fathers take concrete steps to stay connected with their children, most of the social and emotional forces that are at play during divorce and remarriage will increase the emotional distance between fathers and children. Men also need help in acknowledging the degree of their emotional dependence on their former wives before they can begin to mourn their losses, handle their guilt at leaving their children, and start to see what part they played in the marital breakup. It is urgent to explore the man's support network and counsel him to deal with the issues rather than escape to another intense relationship prematurely.

We believe that the crisis of divorce can be used in therapy for both women and men as an opportunity to do developmental work that was skipped in the earlier gendered socialization process. Thus, women should be helped to develop financial competence and to take responsibility for their lives and future, whether they remarry or not. Men need to learn the skills that will enable them to relate fully to their children, develop intimate friendships with men as well as women, and conduct their own emotional, domestic, and social life so that they need not remarry unless they choose to. Such goals require divorce therapy to be a resocialization process, which, of course, also requires coaching the client in work with the family of origin, as well as with the ex-spouse and children (see Chapter 27 on Coaching).

Time to Move Through This Life Cycle Phase

It takes a minimum of 2 or 3 years for a family to adjust to this transition—if there are no cut offs and if all the adults are working at it full tilt. Families in which the emotional issues of divorce are not adequately resolved can remain stuck emotionally for years, perhaps for generations.

The Divorce and Postdivorce Family Emotional Process

Our concept of the divorce and postdivorce emotional process can be visualized as a roller-coaster graph, with peaks of emotional tension at all transition points:

- At the time of the decision to separate or divorce
- When this decision is announced to family and friends

- When money and custody/visitation arrangements are discussed
- When the physical separation takes place
- When the actual legal divorce takes place
- When separated spouses or ex-spouses have contact about money or children
- As each child graduates, marries, has children, or becomes ill
- As each spouse forms a new couple relationship, remarries, moves, becomes ill, or dies

These emotional pressure points are found in all divorcing families—not necessarily in the above order—and many of them take place over and over again, for months or years. A more detailed depiction of the process appears in **Table 21.1**.

The emotions released during the process of divorce relate primarily to the work of emotional divorce, that is, the retrieval of self from the marriage. Each partner must retrieve the hopes, dreams, plans, and expectations that were invested in the spouse and in the marriage. This requires mourning what is lost and dealing with hurt, anger, blame, guilt, shame, and loss in oneself, in the spouse, in the children, and in the extended family.

Family emotional process at the transition to remarriage

The predictable peaks of emotional tension in the transition to remarriage occur at:

- The time of serious commitment to a new relationship
- The time a plan to remarry is announced to families and friends
- The time of the actual remarriage and formation of a stepfamily, which take place as the logistics of stepfamily life are put into practice.

The family emotional process at the transition to remarriage consists of struggling with fears about investment in a new marriage and a new family: one's own fears, the new spouse's fears, and the children's; dealing with hostile or upset reactions of the children, the extended families, and the ex-spouse; struggling with the ambiguity of the new family structure, roles, and relationships; re-arousal of intense parental guilt

and concerns about the welfare of children; and re-arousal of the old attachment to the ex-spouse (negative or positive). Our society offers stepfamilies two basic models, neither of which works: families that act like the Brady Bunch, where everybody lives together happily ever after, are glorified in the media; the alternative narrative involves the wicked stepparents of fairy tales. Thus, our first clinical step is to validate for stepfamilies the lack of societal role models and support in the paradigms of remarried families they are offered. The challenge is to help them be pioneers, inventing new and workable family structures, for which we recommend the following guidelines:

- Give up the old model of family and accept the complexity of a new form
- Maintain permeable boundaries to permit shifting of household memberships
- Work for open lines of communication between all parents, grandparents, children, and grandchildren

The residue of an angry and vengeful divorce can block stepfamily integration for years or forever. The re-arousal of the old emotional attachment to an ex-spouse, which characteristically surfaces at the time of remarriage and at subsequent life cycle transitions of children, is usually not understood as a predictable process and therefore leads to denial, misinterpretation, cut off, and assorted difficulties. As with adjustment to new family structures after divorce, stepfamily integration requires a minimum of 2 or 3 years to create a workable new structure that allows family members to move on emotionally.

Table 21.1 (the developmental steps required for remarried family formation, developed from the model of Ransom and co-workers, 1979), addresses the need to conceptualize and plan for the remarriage. While more advance planning would be helpful also in first marriages, it is an essential ingredient for successful remarriage. This is because a different conceptual model is required and because so many family relationships must be renegotiated at the same time: these include grandparents, in-laws, former in-laws, stepgrandparents and stepchildren, half-siblings, etc. (Whiteside, 2006). The presence of children from the beginning of the new relationship makes establishing

Table 21.1 Additional Stages of Family Life Cycle for Divorcing & Remarrying Families

Phase	Task	Emotional Process of Transition: Prerequisite Attitude	Developmental Issues
Divorce	**The decision to divorce**	Acceptance of inability to resolve marital problems sufficiently to continue relationship.	Acceptance of one's own part in the failure of the marriage.
	Planning breakup of the system	Supporting viable arrangements for all parts of the system.	a. Working cooperatively on problems of custody, visitation, and finances. b. Dealing with extended family about the divorce.
	Separation	a. Willingness to continue cooperative co-parental relationship and joint financial support of children. b. Working on resolution of attachment to spouse.	a. Mourning loss of intact family. b. Restructuring marital and parent–child relationships and finances; adaptation to living apart. c. Realignment of relationships with extended family; staying connected with spouse's extended family.
	The divorce	Working on emotional divorce: overcoming hurt, anger, guilt, etc.	a. Mourning loss of intact family; giving up fantasies of reunion. b. Retrieving hopes, dreams, expectations from the marriage. c. Staying connected with extended families.
Post-Divorce Family	**Single parent (custodial household or primary residence)**	Willingness to maintain financial responsibilities, continue parental contact with ex-spouse, and support contact of children with ex-spouse and his or her family.	a. Making flexible visitation arrangements with ex-spouse and family. b. Rebuilding own financial resources. c. Rebuilding own social network.
	Single parent (non-custodial)	Willingness to maintain financial responsibilities and parental contact with ex-spouse and to support custodial parent's relationship with children.	a. Finding ways to continue effective parenting. b. Maintaining financial responsibilities to ex-spouse and children. c. Rebuilding own social network.

Table 21.1 Additional Stages of Family Life Cycle for Divorcing & Remarrying Families *continued*

Phase	Task	Emotional Process of Transition: Prerequisite Attitude	Developmental Issues
Re-marriage	Entering new relationship	Recovery from loss of 1st marriage (adequate emotional divorce).	Recommitment to marriage and to forming a family with readiness to deal with the complexity and ambiguity.
	Conceptualizing and planning new marriage and family	Accepting one's own fears & those of new spouse and children about forming new family. Accepting need for time and patience for adjustment to complexity and ambiguity of 1. Multiple new roles. 2. Boundaries: space, time, membership, & authority. 3. Affective issues: guilt, loyalty conflicts, desire for mutuality, unresolvable past hurts.	a. Working on openness in the new relationships to avoid pseudomutuality. b. Planning for maintenance of cooperative financial and co-parental relationships with ex-spouses. c. Planning to help children deal with fears, loyalty conflicts and membership in two systems. d. Realignment of relationships with extended family to include new spouse and children. e. Planning maintenance of connections for children with extended family of ex-spouses.
	Remarriage & Reconstruction of Family	Resolution of attachment to previous spouse and ideal of "intact" family; Acceptance of different model of family with permeable boundaries.	a. Restructuring family boundaries to allow for inclusion of new spouse-stepparent. b. Realignment of relationships & financial arrangements to permit interweaving of several systems. c. Making room for relationships of all children with all parents, grandparents, and other extended family. d. Sharing memories & histories to enhance stepfamily integration.
	Renegotiation of Remarried Family at all future ife Cycle transitions	Accepting Evolving Relationships of Transformed Remarried Family.	a. Changes as each child graduates, marries, dies, or becomes ill. b. Changes as each spouse forms new couple relationship, remarries, moves, becomes ill, or dies.

an exclusive spouse-to-spouse relationship before undertaking parenthood impossible. So when there are children, the family is a "package deal," as it always is with in-laws, but not in such an immediate way!

The emotional tasks listed in column 2 of Table 21.1 are key attitudes that permit the family to work on the developmental issues of the transition process. If as clinicians, we find ourselves struggling with the family over developmental issues (column 3) before the prerequisite attitudes (column 2) have been adopted, we are probably wasting our efforts. For example, it is very hard for a parent to help children remain connected to ex-in-laws who were never close or supportive unless the parent has fully embraced the new model of family. Much education and discussion may be required before a client can put into effect ideas that may seem counterintuitive, aversive, or time-consuming.

As the first marriage signifies the joining of two families, so a second marriage involves the interweaving of three, four, or more families whose previous family life cycle courses have been disrupted by death or divorce. Like divorce, we consider forming a remarried family so complex that we view it as adding a whole extra phase to the family life cycle.

More than half of Americans today have been, are now, or will eventually be in one or more recoupled families during their lives. At the turn of the twenty-first century, families with stepchildren living in the household constituted about 13 percent of U.S. families (Teachman & Tedrow, 2004), although, of course this does not begin to convey the extent of re-coupled families, whether remarried or living together, and the number of children in multinuclear families who spend part of their time with stepsiblings. Indeed, stepfamilies are becoming the most common family form, and estimates are that there will soon be more multinuclear families than nuclear families in the United States (CDC, 2002). Estimates are that one third of children will live with a stepparent, usually a stepfather, before adulthood (Amato & Sobolewski, 2004). Half of the marriages that occur each year are remarriages. Almost 50 percent of first marriages are expected to end in divorce and approximately 70 percent of divorced individuals (more men than women) remarry. And even though stepfamily

relationships have been neglected in family research and are not generally as strong as first family ties, remarriage creates an enlarged pool of potential kin who may come to have very important family bonds.

Yet our society still does not recognize transformed and reconstituted families as part of the norm. Most family research has focused on intact first families. Only recently have norms for forming a remarried family begun to emerge. The built-in ambiguity of boundaries and membership defies simple definition, and our culture lacks any established language patterns or rituals to help us handle the complex relationships of acquired family members. The kinship terms we do have, such as "stepmother," "stepfather," and "stepchild," have such negative connotations that they may increase the difficulties for families trying to work out these relationships. Constance Ahrons (see Chapter 19 on Divorce) calls postdivorce families "binuclear," a term that is descriptive and nonstigmatizing. We have expanded this to refer to multinuclear families, because in remarriage there may at times be three or four or more households to consider at one time.

We originally chose to use the term "remarried" to emphasize that it is the marital bond that forms the basis for the complex rearrangement of several families in a new constellation, but increasingly reconstituted families are not actually marrying, or at least not marrying for a while. Still, it is the couple's bond that makes them take the trouble to go through the complexities of family reformation. So we sometimes refer to them as "re-coupled" families or "stepfamilies" to indicate the presence of children from past relationships as part of the remarried system.

A New Paradigm of Family

An entirely new paradigm of family is required for conceptualizing re-coupled families. Many difficulties these families experience can be attributed to attempts by the family or therapist to ignore their complexity and use the roles and rules of first marriage families as guidelines. Such attempts to replicate the "intact" nuclear family lead to serious problems. It is essential to acknowledge their actual relationships and empower them to move forward from those realities. In earlier times, when families lived in larger extended family and community enclaves, children had a whole network of adults who cared for them and helped to raise them. That is the model that helps here—not making choices about who is the better parent and then trying to ignore the broader complexities of connection.

Although it is extremely hard to give up the idea of the "nuclear family" by drawing a tight loyalty boundary around household members, excluding outside biological parents or children who reside elsewhere is neither realistic nor appropriate. Instead, families need to develop a system with permeable boundaries around the members of different households to allow children to belong in multiple homes, moving flexibly between households. Families need open lines of communication between ex-spouses and among children, their biological parents, their stepparents, grandparents, and other relatives. Indeed, extended family connections and outside connectedness may be even more important for children's well-being than they are in first families.

Because parent–child bonds predate the marital bond, often by many years, and are therefore initially stronger than the couple bond, stepparents may compete inappropriately with their stepchildren for primacy with their spouse, as if the couple and parent–child relationships were on the same hierarchical level, which, of course, they are not. Instead, remarried families must allow for the built-in ambiguity of roles and the differential ties based on historical connections. In particular, each parent needs to accept responsibility for his or her own children and not combat or compete with the other's parent–child attachments.

Forming a remarried family also requires a re-visioning of traditional gender roles. We must overturn completely the notion that the stepmother, just because she is a woman, should be in charge of the home, the children, or the emotional relationships of the system; such a view fails to respect the family's history, that is, that the parent with the historical relationship with the child is the only one who can really be the primary parent. Traditional gender roles, requiring women to take responsibility for the emotional well-being of the family, tend to pit stepmother and stepdaughter against each other and place the ex-wife and the new wife in adversarial positions, especially concerning the children. The old rules that called for women to rear children and men to earn and manage the finances do not work well in first-marriage families; they have no chance at all in a system in which some of the children are strangers to the wife and the finances include sources of income and expenditure that are not in the husband's power to generate or control (e.g., alimony, child support, and earnings of the ex-wife or current wife). These issues, in addition to the primacy of children's bonds to their biological parents, make stereotypical gender roles completely inadequate for remarried families.

Nontraditional families have much to teach us about adaptive strategies necessary in reconstituted families, especially about the complexity and ambiguity of roles and relationships and the permeability of household boundaries. Experience with nontraditional gender roles increases the flexibility necessary for stepfamily organization, and childhood experiences in a large family also help in dealing with the complexities.

Child-rearing responsibilities must be distributed in ways that validate the bond between biological parents and their children. Each spouse must take primary responsibility for raising and disciplining his or her own biological children. The relationship of the children and stepparent can only evolve over time as their connection develops and as an extension of the child's bond with the biological parent. Stepparents only gradually assume a role, hopefully friendly, as the partner of the child's parent. Unless the children are young at the time of the remarriage, the parent-and-child paradigm may never apply to the new parent. This is a life cycle reality, not a failure on anyone's part.

Ex-spouses are hopefully responsible adults who can learn to cooperate with each other for the sake of their children. New spouses hopefully begin as benign caretakers and build from there. Contraindications to postdivorce arrangements of joint or shared custody would obviously include the following:

- Mental illness in one or both parents
- A history of violence and/or child abuse or neglect
- Alcohol or drug abuse

Forming a remarried family is one of the most difficult developmental transitions for a family to negotiate. It is no wonder that unresolved losses of the previous families so often lead to premature closure resulting from the wish to end ambiguity and pain. In any case, earlier losses are very likely to be reactivated by the new family formation. Indeed, Montgomery, Anderson, Hetherington, and Clingempeel (1993) found in their longitudinal study that living together before remarriage provided a beneficial in-between stage of adjustment that reduced the trauma of remarriage. Much therapeutic effort must be directed toward educating families about the built-in complexities of the process so that families can work toward establishing a viable, flexible system that will allow them to get back on their developmental track for future life cycle phases.

It is easy to understand the wish for clear and quick resolution when one has been through the pain of a first family ending. But the instant intimacy that remarried families often hope for is impossible to achieve. The new relationships are harder to negotiate because they do not develop gradually, as first families do, but begin midstream, after another family's life cycle has been dislocated. Children's sibling position frequently changes, and they must cope with variable membership over several households. Naturally, second families carry the scars of first-marriage families. Neither parents, nor children, nor grandparents can forget the relationships that went before and that may still be more powerful than the new relationships. Children almost never give up their attachment to their first parent (biological or adoptive), no matter how negative that relationship was or is. Having the patience to tolerate the ambiguity of the situation and allowing each other the space and time for feelings about past relationships are crucial processes in forming a remarried family.

The most powerful clinical tool for helping families negotiate this complex transition is probably providing information that normalizes their experiences. Clinically useful research findings on remarried families come from the work of many authors: Duberman (1975); Hetherington, Clingempeel, and their colleagues (project results and citations summarized in Hetherington, (2002); Visher and Visher (1979, 1988, 1991, 1996); Ahrons and Rodgers (1987); Ahrons (1994); Cherlin, Furstenberg, and their colleagues (1994, 2009); Sager et al. (1983); Bernstein (1989, 1994, 1999); Bray & Easling (2005); Pasley and her colleagues (1995) and many others. The following trends and principles have been suggested by these researchers, as well as by our own clinical experience over the past 4 decades.

Predictable emotional issues in remarriage

The basic premise of family systems theory is that we all carry into our new relationships the emotional baggage of unresolved issues from important past relationships. This baggage makes us emotionally sensitive in the new relationships: We may put up barriers to intimacy, becoming self-protective, closed off, and afraid to make ourselves vulnerable to further hurt, or we may become expectant that the new relationships will make up for or erase past hurts. Either of these stances complicates new relationships. In first marriages, the baggage we bring is from our families of origin: our unresolved feelings about parents, siblings, and extended family. In remarriage, there are at least three sets of emotional baggage:

1. From the family of origin
2. From the first marriage
3. From the process and aftermath of separation, divorce, or death and the period between marriages

To the extent that either remarried partner expects the other to relieve him or her of this baggage, the new relationship will become problematic. On the other hand, to the extent that each spouse can resolve his or her own emotional issues with significant people from the past, the new relationship can proceed on its own merits.

The complexity of remarried families is reflected in our lack of positive language and kinship labels, the shifting of children's sibling positions in the new family, and society's failure to differentiate parenting from stepparenting functions. Boundary ambiguities and complexities include issues of membership, space, authority, and allocation of time. An additional boundary problem arises when instant incest taboos are called for, as when several previously unrelated teenagers are suddenly supposed to view each other as siblings.

The emotional issues of remarriage go back at least to the disintegration of the first marriage. The intensity of emotion unleashed by the life cycle disruption of divorce must be dealt with over and over again before the dislocated systems are restabilized. No amount of "dealing with" the emotional difficulties of divorce will finish off the process once and for all, although the more emotional work is done at each step, the less intense and disruptive the subsequent reactivations at later stages will be.

The most common mistakes parents make are

1. Preoccupation with themselves and neglect of their children's experience, which follows from the conflicting life cycle tasks: of parenting versus courtship
2. Treating the remarriage as an event, rather than a complex transformation of the family, which will take years
3. Trying to get children to resolve the ambiguities of multiple loyalties by cutting off one relationship to create clarity in another.

Failure to deal sufficiently with the process at each point may jam it enough to prevent remarried family stabilization from ever occurring, a problem that is reflected in the high rate of re-divorce.

AFFECTIVE PROBLEMS Predictable feelings include intense conflict, guilt, ambivalence, and anger about the previous spouse and children, denial of such feelings, and the wish to resolve the ambiguity.

PSEUDOMUTUALITY OR FUSION Remarried families are formed against a background of loss, hurt, and a sense of failure. Their "battle fatigue" often leads to a desire not to "rock the boat" this time, which suppresses doubt, conflicts, and differences that need to be dealt with, resulting in "pseudomutuality" that pretends total mutuality, covering over disagreements, and making current relationships all the more fragile in the long run.

LOYALTY CONFLICTS One of the hardest requirements on parents is to let their children have and express the full range of negative and positive feelings toward all of their parents, stepparents, and half- and stepsiblings. Often parents want the child's whole allegiance. Children feel caught, afraid that if they don't love a new stepparent, they will hurt and anger one parent, but if they do love the stepparent, they are disloyal and will hurt or lose the love of the other. Another loyalty conflict is the expectation for the new spouse to love the other's children as much as his or her own. Just because you fall in love with a person doesn't mean you automatically love their children, even though they are in this situation a "package deal."

PATTERNS OF COUPLING In as many as 70 percent of divorcing couples, at least one spouse is having an affair, but only a very small percent later marry this person. About one fourth re-divorce within the first 5 years, a rate much higher than that for first marriages. Men tend to remarry sooner and more often than women, and Whites sooner and more often than people of color. Whereas first wives are on the average 3 years younger than their husbands, second wives are on average 6 years younger than their husbands. The more income and education a woman has, the less likely she is to remarry. The reverse is true for men: The more income and education he has, the more likely he is to remarry, and the sooner.

PARENTAL RELATIONSHIPS The more effectively custodial parents can function and the less parental conflict children are exposed to, the better will be their children's adjustment. Cordial or courteous, low-intensity relationships with the ex-spouse and the ex-spouse's new marital partner work best. It helps if therapists think of all parental figures as potentially enriching the children's support network.

PARENT–CHILD RELATIONSHIPS AND VISITATION Children do better if they have regular contact with both parents, assuming neither parent is abusive, mentally ill, or involved in substance abuse. The more regularly children visit their noncustodial parents, the better will be their adjustment. Such contacts increase rather than decrease the likelihood that strong and positive relationships will develop between children and their stepparents. Serious discipline issues and visitation arrangements are best handled by the biological parent.

FAMILY CONNECTION/INTEGRATION VERSUS DISCONNECTION OR ABUSE Remarried family integration appears most likely when extended family approves of or accepts the remarriage, next best when they disapprove or are negative, and hardest when they are cut off or indifferent. The most complex remarried families, where both spouses bring children from previous relationships, tend to have the greatest difficulty establishing stability. All things being equal, it is also easiest if the previous spouse died, next easiest when the spouse is divorced, and hardest when the spouse has never been married. Integration is more likely when children are not left behind by either parent and when the new couple have a child together. The longer the new family has together as a unit, the more likely they are to have a sense of family integration. Developing a sense of belonging takes most family members 3 to 5 years, longer if there are adolescents.

DYSFUNCTION IN STEPFAMILIES Violence and abuse are vastly more common in stepfamilies than in first families, and many do not withstand the early stages of family reorganization. But the instability of remarried families should not be overstated. Remarried partners do not wait as long as partners in first families to leave an unhappy situation, and those who manage the early years have no greater likelihood of divorcing than in first marriages. Cut offs are more common with the paternal extended family, and connections are more often strong with maternal relatives, but extended family relationships are often difficult. While children are quite prepared to have multiple sets of grandparents, uncles, and aunts, the middle generation can get caught up in conflicts; and managing relationships with such a large network of kin is complicated.

STEPMOTHERS, STEPFATHERS, AND STEPCHILDREN The stereotypes of stepparents are deeply blaming. A stepmother's ambivalence about her parenting role is particularly acute when stepchildren are young and remain in the custody of her husband's ex-wife. In this common situation, stepmothers tend to feel less emotionally attached to the children and disrupted and exploited during their visits. Meanwhile the husband's co-parenting partnership may appear to be conducted more with his ex-spouse than with her. Stepfathers are frequently caught in the double bind of rescuer versus intruder, called upon to help discipline the stepchildren and then criticized by them and their mother for this intervention. Over-trying by the new parent is a major problem, often related to guilt about unresolved or unresolvable aspects of the system.

Most difficult of all is the role of stepmother. The problem for her is especially poignant, since she is usually the one most sensitive to the needs of others, and it will be extremely difficult for her to take a back seat while her husband struggles awkwardly with an uncomfortable situation. The fact is that she has no alternative. Women's tendency to take responsibility for family relationships, to believe that what goes wrong is their fault and that, if they just try hard enough, they can make things work out, are the major problem for them in remarried families, since the situation carries with it built-in structural ambiguities, loyalty conflicts, guilt, and membership problems. Societal expectations for stepmothers to love and care for their stepchildren are also stronger than for stepfathers. If stepfathers help out a bit financially and do a few administrative chores, they may get off the hook, not that that is a satisfying role! But the expectation for stepmothers is that they will make up to children for whatever losses they have experienced. Clinically it is important to relieve them of these expectations.

Overall, mothers, daughters, stepdaughters, and stepmothers experience more stress, less satisfaction, and more symptoms than fathers, sons, stepsons, and stepfathers. Stepmother–stepdaughter relationships tend to be the most difficult of all. Daughters, who are often closest to mothers in divorce, tend to have a lot of difficulty with stepfathers, no matter how hard the stepfather tries. Girls' stress probably reflects the fact that they feel more responsible for emotional relationships in a family and thus get caught between loyalty and protection of their biological mothers and conflicts with their stepmothers. While divorce appears to have more adverse effects for boys, remarriage is more disruptive for girls. Boys, who are often difficult for a single mother, may settle down after the entry of a stepfather. Conflicting role expectations set mothers and stepmothers into competitive struggles over child-rearing practices. It appears to be better for stepmothers to retain their work outside the home for their independence, emotional support, and validation. In addition to contributing needed money, it makes them less available at home for the impossible job of dealing with the husband's children.

Stepparents need to take a slow route to parenthood, first becoming friends with their stepchildren, and only gradually assuming an active role in parenting. It generally takes at least 2 years to become comanagers of their stepchildren with their spouses.

Along with finances, stepchildren are the major contributor to remarriage adjustment problems. Remarriage often leads to a renewal of custody difficulties in prior relationships. Families with stepchildren are much more complicated and twice as likely to divorce. Marital satisfaction is correlated with the stepparent's connection to stepchildren. Although the remarriage itself might be congenial, the presence of stepchildren often creates child-related problems that may lead the couple to separate. Some stepparents do not even consider their live-in stepchild as part of the family, and stepchildren are even more likely to discount their live-in stepparents. Stepchildren are much more likely to change residence or leave home early than biological children. Children in stepfamilies may appear to have more power than children in first families, although they experience less autonomy than in the single-parent phase, where they typically have more adult privileges and responsibilities.

FINANCES Finances are a major area of conflict in remarried families. Remarriage often leads to reopening of financial battles from the divorce and to children receiving less support from their biological fathers. Traditional gender roles run completely counter to contemporary economics and to the fact that both parents usually enter remarriage with significant financial obligations to the first family. Failure to pay or collect alimony or child support wreaks havoc in postdivorce families. A husband who is the sole wage earner in a remarried family often has to decide which set of children has top priority—his own or the stepchildren he lives with. These priorities are also influenced by his relation-

ship with his ex-wife; if it is bad, his visits and child support payments tend to lag or even cease. A new wife may complain about the money her husband gives to his children, particularly if she doesn't receive the child support owed for her own children. Overall children in intact first families tend to receive more from their parents than children whose parents remarry. In affluent families, problems also surface around wills and how much financial assistance should be given to which adult children. Where money is concerned, blood may suddenly seem thicker than relationship.

IMPACT OF REMARRIAGE ON CHILDREN AND EX-SPOUSES Remarriage of either spouse tends to decrease contact between fathers and their biological children. The level of contact between a divorced father and his children is likely to be much greater if he has not remarried and even greater if the mother has not remarried. If both parents have remarried, children are much less likely to have weekly contact with their fathers, compared with children when neither parent has remarried. Remarriage of a former spouse tends to reactivate feelings of depression, helplessness, anger, and anxiety, particularly for women. Men tend to be less upset by the remarriage of an ex-wife, possibly because it may release them from financial responsibility and because they are usually less central to the emotional system.

STEPFAMILY FORMATION FOLLOWING DEATH Different issues arise when stepfamilies are formed after the premature death of a parent. Gender differences are a key factor. A new stepfather may be perceived as rescuing the family from poverty after the death of the primary wage earner, whereas children tend to view their mother as completely irreplaceable and resent any efforts of another woman to function in her role. However, young children will eventually accept a stepparent, including a stepmother, if the remaining parent can help the children to grieve for their loss before confronting them with a stepmother. When the father does remarry, he must help the children to accept the new person in her own right rather than collude with the children in wanting the family to continue in the same way it did when their mother was alive. On the other hand, if insufficient attention is paid to the children's grief work, they may never accept a stepmother. (For a videotape with commentary of a family dealing with these issues, see McGoldrick, 1996.)

Although the fact that the ex-spouse is not around to "interfere" may be an advantage, ghosts can be even more powerful, especially given people's tendency to idealize a parent who is lost prematurely. It may be harder to recognize and deal with a triangle with a dead parent. Talking, remembering, and acknowledging the dead person's human failings and foibles help to exorcise the ghost, but none of this can be done without the active leadership of the remaining biological parent (see chapter 18 on Loss). Late adolescents or older children generally resist attempts to "replace" their dead parent, and the wise stepparent will honor that position.

GAYS AND LESBIANS IN STEPFAMILIES   A significant number of postdivorce families consist of a gay or lesbian couple with the children of one or both of them from a previous heterosexual marriage. These systems have all of the problems of heterosexual remarried systems in addition to the burdens of secrecy and isolation caused by the social stigma they have most likely experienced (Laird & Green, 1996).

In extreme cases, the adults may feel that they have to try to remain closeted, even to their children, for fear of repercussions in custody or employment. There is almost always anxiety about the consequences of coming out to family (LaSala, in press), the children's teachers and friends, co-workers, neighbors, and acquaintances. Therapists can be most helpful if, in addition to the usual therapy for remarried systems, they can acknowledge the societal stigma and help the couple sift through their various networks to dismantle the secrecy and isolation. Connection to supportive community groups and access to supportive literature are extremely important.

The Impact of Remarriage at Various Phases of the Family Life Cycle

In general, the wider the discrepancy in family life cycle experience between the new spouses, the greater the difficulty of transition will be and the longer it will take to integrate a workable new family, especially if they come from widely different cultural backgrounds, which always increases the bridge-building necessary for a couple. A father of late adolescent and/or young adult children with a new, young wife who was never previously married should expect a rather strenuous and lengthy period of adjustment, during which he will have to juggle his emotional and financial responsibilities toward the new marriage and toward his (probably upset) children. His wife, looking forward to the romantic aspects of a first marriage, will encounter instead the many stresses of dealing with adolescents who probably resent her, whether the children live with the couple or not.

If either spouse tries to pull the other into a lifestyle or attitude that denies or restricts the other spouse's family life cycle tasks or relationships with children from previous relationships, difficulties will expand into serious problems. If the husband expects his new wife to undertake immediately a major role in his children's lives or to be the one who always backs down gracefully when her interests and preferences clash with those of the children, there will be serious trouble in the new marriage, as the formation of the new couple bond is continuously given second priority.

On the other hand, if the new wife tries, overtly or covertly, to cut off or drastically loosen the tie between father and children or to take on the role of mother to them, or insists that her claims always have his prior attention, forcing him to choose between them, there will also be serious trouble. Variations in which the new wife claims to support her husband but embarks on a battle with his ex-wife as the source of the difficulties are equally dysfunctional.

Often the stepparent feels he or she knows what the other parent is doing wrong with his or her children and forcefully pushes these parenting ideas. Such efforts are doomed to failure and are very likely to jam the circuits for everyone—the new couple, the stepparent/stepchild relationships and extended family relationships where people get called upon to choose up sides.

Since it is not possible either to erase or to acquire emotional experience overnight, it is useful to conceptualize the joining of partners at two different life cycle phases as a process in which both spouses have to learn to function in several different life cycle phases simultaneously and out of their usual sequence.

The new wife will have to struggle with the role of stepmother to teenagers before becoming an experienced wife or mother herself. Her husband will have to re-traverse with her several phases that he has passed through before: the honeymoon, the new marriage with its emphasis on romance and social activities, and the birth and rearing of any new children of their own. Both need to be aware that a second passage through these phases automatically reactivates some of the intensity over issues that were problematic the first time. Attempts to "make up for" past mistakes or grievances may overload the new relationship. The focus needs to be on having the experiences again, not on undoing, redoing, or denying the past. With open discussion, mutual support, understanding, and a lot of thoughtful planning, this straddling of several phases simultaneously can provide rejuvenation for the older spouse and experience for the younger spouse that can enrich their lives. If the difficulties are not understood and dealt with, they will surface as conflict or emotional distance at each life cycle transition and subsystem of the remarried family.

Spouses at the Same Life Cycle Phase

When remarried spouses come together at the same phase of the family life cycle, their greatest difficulties generally relate to whether they are at a childbearing phase. Obviously, spouses with no children from previous marriages bring the least complexity to the new situation. Families with grown children and grandchildren on both sides have long and complex histories and will require careful thought to negotiate successfully. But neither of these circumstances provides nearly the degree of strain involved at phases including either young or adolescent children, in which the roles of active parenting and stepparenting must be included in the new family. Unfortunately, the advantage of having similar tasks, responsibilities, and experiences is frequently swamped in a competitive struggle that stems from the overload of these tasks and concerns (six children are not as easy to raise or support as three), the intense emotional investment in good parenting ("My methods are better than your methods"), and the need to include both ex-spouses in the many arrangements regarding the children ("Why do you let your ex dictate our lives?").

Stepfamilies and Young Children

Children's struggles with the predictable issues may surface as school or behavior problems, withdrawal from family and peers, or acting-out behavior, all of which complicate or even obstruct the process of family reorganization. Indications are that preschool children, if given some time and help in mourning their previous loss, adjust most easily to a new stepfamily while adjustment is most difficult for stepfamilies with teenagers. Latency age children seem to have the most difficulty resolving their feelings of divided loyalty and benefit from careful attention to their need for contact with both parents. Clearly, children of all ages suffer when there is intense conflict between their biological parents and benefit when their parents maintain civil, cooperative, co-parental relationships. If parents cannot be cooperative, tightly structuring the relationships is the next best alternative.

Stepfamilies With Adolescents

Since the difficulties that most American families have with adolescents are legendary, it is not surprising that early adolescence seems the most difficult time for both boys and girls to adjust to their parents' remarriage, and the additional complications of this phase in stepfamilies can push the stress level beyond manageable bonds. We have found the following issues common in stepfamilies at this phase.

1. Conflict between the remarried family's need to coalesce and the normal focus of adolescents on separation: Adolescents often resent the major shifts in their customary family patterns and resist learning new roles and relating to new family members when they are concerned with growing away from the family.
2. Stepparents get stuck if they attempt to discipline an adolescent.
3. Adolescents may attempt to resolve their divided loyalties by taking sides or actively playing one side against the other.
4. Sexual attraction may develop between stepsiblings or stepparent and stepchild, along with adolescent difficulty in accepting the biological parent's sexuality.

The Impact of Remarriage in Later Life Cycle Phases

Although there is not the daily strain of having to live together with stepchildren and stepparents, remarriage at a post–child-rearing phase of the life cycle requires significant readjustment of relationships throughout both family systems, which may now include in-laws and grandchildren. It is probable that grown children and grandchildren will accept a remarriage after a death of a parent more easily than after a late divorce. There is often great relief throughout the family if an older widowed parent finds a new partner and a new lease on life, whereas a later-life divorce usually arouses concern and dismay throughout the family. A frequent problem for older remarried couples is negotiating about money. The strength of children's reactivity to a parent's remarriage, even after they believe that they have long ago resolved the loss or divorce of the parent(s), may overwhelm them. They may need coaching to find a way to incorporate a parent's new partner into their lives.

Clinically, we find that the major factor in three-generational adjustment to remarriage in late middle or older age is the amount of acrimony or cooperation between the ex-spouses. When the relationship is cooperative enough to permit joint attendance at important family functions of children and grandchildren and when holiday arrangements can be jointly agreed upon, family acceptance of a new marriage tends to follow.

Clinical Intervention With Remarried Families

Whatever the presenting problem in a remarried family, it is essential to look laterally as well as back to previous generations and to evaluate the current and past relationships with previous spouses to determine the degree to which the family needs help to work out the patterns required by the new structure. Ongoing conflict or cut offs with ex-spouses, children, parents, and grandparents will tend to overload the relationships in the remarried family and make them problematic. We consider genograms particularly essential in work with remarried families, because the structural complexity so influences the predictable triangles of these situations (McGoldrick, 2010; McGoldrick, Gerson, & Petry, 2008).

We next describe several predictable triangles in remarried families. In first-marriage families, the major problematic triangles involve the parents with any or all of the children and each parent with his or her own parents and in-laws. In the more complex structures of remarried families, we have identified six of the most common triangles and interlocking triangles presenting in binuclear families. In no way do we mean to suggest by this focus that the triangles with the extended family and grandparental generation are unimportant to the understanding and the therapy of remarried families. In our clinical work with remarried families, coaching of the adults on further differentiation in relation to their families of origin proceeds in tandem with work on current family problems (see Chapter 27 on Coaching). Our experience indicates that families that are willing to work on relationships with their families of origin do better than those that are not.

Triangle between the new spouses and an ex-spouse

When a triangle focuses on conflict between new spouse and the old spouse and the partner in the middle, the usual issues are finances or sexual jealousy. Underneath, it is likely that the ex-spouses have not accomplished an emotional divorce. The first step in the tricky clinical work around this triangle is for the therapist to establish a working alliance with the new spouse who will otherwise sabotage efforts to focus on the first marriage. Efforts to work on the resolution of the divorce by seeing either the ex-spouses alone or all three in sessions together will probably create more anxiety than the system can handle. We have found that such work goes most smoothly when a spouse is coached in the presence of the new spouse to undertake steps outside of the therapy sessions that will change his or her relationship with the ex-spouse. Along the way, the new spouse will have to learn to acknowledge the importance of that past bond to his or her spouse and to accept the fact that some degree of caring will probably always remain in the relationship, depending on the length of time the first marriage lasted and whether there were children.

Triangle involving a pseudomutual remarried couple, an ex-spouse, and a child or children

In this triangle, the presenting problem is usually acting out or school problems with one or more children or perhaps a child's request to have custody shifted from one parent to another. The remarried couple presents itself as having no disagreements and blames either the child or the ex-spouse (or both) for the trouble. Although the request in therapy will be for help for the child or to manage the child's behavior, the background story will usually show intense conflict between the ex-spouses, the new spouse being totally supportive of his or her spouse in conflicts with that spouse's child. The first move in sorting out this triangle is to put the management of the child's behavior temporarily in the hands of the biological parent and get the new spouse to take a neutral position, rather than siding against the child. This move will probably calm things down, but they will usually not stay calm unless the pseudomutuality of the remarried couple is worked on, permitting differences and disagreements to be aired and resolved and permitting the child to have a relationship with his or her biological parent that does not automatically include the new spouse every step of the way. Finally, work will need to be done to end the battle with the ex-spouse and complete the emotional divorce, the lack of which is perpetuated by the intense conflict over the child or children.

Triangle involving a remarried couple in conflict over the child/children of one of them

The first of these triangles (stepmother, father, and his children), although not the most common household composition, is the most problematic because of the central role the stepmother is expected to play in the lives of live-in stepchildren. If the stepmother has never been married before, and if the children's mother is alive and has a less than ideal relationship with her ex-husband, it may be an almost impossible situation. The stepmother should be helped to pull back long enough to renegotiate with both her husband and the children regarding what her role can

realistically be. Rather than leave the stepmother and children to fight it out, the father will have to participate actively in making and enforcing whatever rules are agreed upon. When their immediate household is in order, the husband will have to work on establishing a cooperative co-parental relationship with his ex-wife, or else his conflict with her will set the children off again and inevitably reinvolve his new wife. If the first wife is dead, he may need to complete his mourning for her and help his children to do the same in order to let the past go and not see his second wife as a poor replacement of his first.

When a stepmother is involved, the father needs to deliver two messages to his children:

> Be courteous to my spouse (not "your" anything).
>
> You are answering to me. You haven't lost both your mother and me.

Triangle involving a pseudomutual remarried couple, his children, and her children

This triangle presents as a happily remarried couple with "no difficulties" except that their two sets of children fight constantly with each other. The children are usually fighting out the conflicts denied by the remarried couple either in the marriage or in the relationship with the ex-spouse(s). Since direct confrontation of the pseudomutuality stiffens resistance, and since the presenting request is made in regard to the children, it is wise to begin with an exploration of the triangles involving the children and ex-spouses, focusing on the welfare of the children.

Triangle involving a parent, the biological children, and the stepchildren

As in the previous situation, this triangle may present as simple household conflict with the parent caught in the middle between his or her biological children and stepchildren. It is, in fact, quite complex, always interlocking with the triangle involving the remarried couple (who may have either a pseudomutual or a conflictual relationship) and the triangles with both ex-spouses.

Triangle involving remarried spouses and the parents of either

This triangle features the in-laws as part of the presenting problem, but it should be remembered that relationships with the grandparents' generation are as crucial in remarried families as they are in all other families, and their exploration should be a routine part of any evaluation. The presentation of the older generation as part of the current problem is most likely to occur if they have disapproved of the divorce and remarriage or have been actively involved in caring for their grandchildren before or during the remarriage.

Clinical Guidelines

When there are child-focused problems, we routinely contact an ex-spouse and invite him or her to meet alone or with the children to hear our opinion of the children's problems that have been brought to our attention by the remarried family. When we inform the family of our intention to do this, we are frequently warned that the ex-spouse in question does not care, won't respond, or is crazy. Nevertheless, our phone calls frequently locate a concerned parent who is perfectly willing to come in, although warning us that our client is crazy. Ex-spouses can frequently be engaged in subsequent sessions alone or with the children.

Our general goal in working with remarried families is to establish an open system with workable boundaries and to revise traditional gender roles. This goal requires that the former spouses work through their emotional divorce, which we assume is not resolved if ex-spouses are not speaking or have continuous conflicts. The goal then is to create an open, working, co-parental relationship. The following guidelines summarize our clinical recommendations:

1. Take a three-generational genogram and outline previous marriages before plunging into current household problems.
2. Educate and normalize, normalize, normalize regarding the predictable patterns and processes in remarriage, keeping in mind particular difficulties related to:
   a. Family members being at different life cycle stages
   b. The emotionally central role of women in families and their special difficulties in moving into a new system where much is demanded of them
   c. Couples trying to maintain the myth of the intact nuclear family
3. Beware of families struggling with developmental tasks before they have adopted the prerequisite attitudes for remarriage: for example, a parent pushing a child and stepparent to be close without accepting that their relationship will take time to develop.
4. Help the family gain patience to tolerate the ambiguity and not "over-try" to make things work out. This includes accepting that family ties do not develop overnight. Encourage stepparents to understand that a child's negative reactions are not to be taken personally and help them tolerate guilt, conflicted feelings, ambivalence, divided loyalties, and so on.
5. Include the new spouse in sessions in which you coach the client to resolve his or her relationship with an ex-spouse, at least in the beginning—or you will increase the new spouse's paranoia about the old spouse—and take the frequent characterization of an ex-spouse as "crazy" with a grain of salt. The list of the ex-spouse's outrageous behaviors may reflect the client's provocations or retaliations.
6. When the remarriage ends a close single-parent/child relationship, the feelings of loss of that special closeness, especially for the child, have to be dealt with and will take time.
7. If the child is presented as the problem, try to involve all parents and stepparents as early as possible in therapy. If joint sessions are held, discussion should be directed toward cooperative work to resolve the child's difficulties, never about marital issues. Children should never have the power to decide on remarriage, custody, or visitation.
8. When problems involve child-focused uproar, put the biological parent in charge of the child temporarily. When the uproar subsides, coach the biological parent on ways to "move over" and include his or her spouse in the system—

first, as a spouse only. Warn the family that the shift to active stepparenting usually takes several years and will require the active support of the biological parent. In the case of older adolescents, it may be unrealistic to expect the shift to occur to any great degree at all.

9. Work to get parents to define predictable and adequate plans for visitation and to keep up relationships with the ex-spouse's extended family, and beware of the "hidden agenda" in any sudden proposals to rearrange custody, visitation, or financial arrangements.

10. Include work on the spouses' families of origin as early in treatment as possible.

CASE ILLUSTRATION

We conclude this chapter with a case meant to suggest some of the complexity of the divorce-remarriage cycle. This example illustrates a therapeutic relationship, which provided a wide net of support over a long period of the family's developmental journey.

When they came for marital therapy, Josh Steiner and Susan Watson (Genogram 21.1: Genogram of Josh and Susan) had been married for 14 years. They had a 12-year-old son, Sam, and a 10-year-old daughter, Karen. Susan's complaint was that Josh was a workaholic, like his father and hers, and now that Sam was approaching his teens, "he needs his father." Josh, a surgeon, and a senior administrator at the hospital, worked over 60 hours a week, often more. Susan, also a physician, had for years kept her hours strictly part-time to allow for child care. Their relationship had veered from distance to periods of conflict "about the kids and me, not about *us*," Josh said. As marital therapy seemed to go in circles, the therapist inquired closely into their past relationship and future commitment, causing Susan to admit that she had "given up on him" some years ago and "could not imagine growing old with him." She agreed to "try" to help put the marriage back together, but consistently "forgot" between-session assignments, "didn't notice" that Josh was coming home earlier, and so on. Both she and Josh resisted the therapist's suggestions that they put some energy into their family of origin relationships.

After 6 months of stalling, Susan admitted she wanted a divorce; she acknowledged that she had actually decided this years ago, had hoped to be able to postpone it until the children were older, but now could not tolerate the wait. Josh flew into a rage, quit therapy, hired an aggressive divorce lawyer, and told Susan that he planned to sue for custody of the

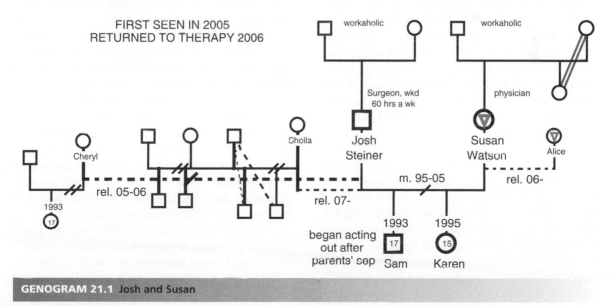

FIRST SEEN IN 2005
RETURNED TO THERAPY 2006

GENOGRAM 21.1 Josh and Susan

children. The therapist phoned Josh, convincing him to come back to therapy "for the sake of the children—whether it's marital or divorce therapy, they need you to rebuild or dismantle your marriage in an orderly way."

It was soon evident that it was to be divorce therapy, and although he was even further enraged, Josh made several steps "for the sake of the children": he stopped threatening to sue for custody and agreed to continue divorce therapy until the family was living separately and the separation agreement was signed. On her part, Susan agreed to forego any claims of alimony and let the lawyers negotiate about child support. She was interested in the therapist's suggestion that they go to divorce mediation, but Josh refused, and she decided not to press the point with him.

At this point, the therapist saw each of them separately for several sessions, inquiring in detail about Susan's financial plans, which she hadn't really thought about and Josh's plans for staying in close touch with his children ("You mean I should cancel my plan to get a studio apartment?"). For several months, the therapist saw Josh, Susan, and their two children separately and in various combinations as the couple first planned how to tell their children ("no blaming"), then told them, then arranged for the children to help Josh move to his new two-bedroom apartment, and put some of their things there. Along this path, the therapist helped each of them resist destructive suggestions from their lawyers (e.g., Josh should refuse to move out of the house; Susan should refuse to permit Sam's bar mitzvah plan to proceed). As the early logistics were put into place and family grieving over the changes came into focus, Josh suddenly fell in love and left therapy to make a new life, in spite of the therapist's warnings about timing.

Susan remained in therapy but wanted to focus on her reactions to Josh's girlfriend and her children's reactions to the other woman, who was divorced with a daughter Karen's age. Susan made several fairly superficial moves with her family of origin, mostly making more contact with her father and brother but couldn't think of specific issues with them except for a global sense of being the outsider. Susan was able to follow the therapist's coaching suggestions that she not get into conflict with Josh's girlfriend but rather tell Josh that she preferred to make visitation arrangements with him, not the girlfriend. She felt a huge sense of relief that the marriage was over and even acknowledged that Josh had not been a bad guy at all, except for always being away, "but then, I didn't really want him around all the time anyway." She recognized but couldn't identify the reasons for this ambivalence. When their separation agreement was declared satisfactory and signed by both of them, Susan expressed a mixture of sadness and relief and left therapy. She said that the kids were moody, but they had all survived Sam's bar mitzvah, which Josh had "ruined" by insisting on bringing along his now live-in girlfriend, even though Sam and even Josh's mother had objected. "But now it's almost over," Susan said as she thanked the therapist and left.

Less than a year later, Susan was back because of Sam's behavior at school—fights, failing grades, and disrespecting the teachers. He was now over 14 years old. Meanwhile, Josh and his girlfriend had broken up, and Josh was angrier and less available to the children than ever. Susan now had a housemate, an artist and writer, who "helps with the mortgage and helps with the kids. Karen loves her and Sam will too when he straightens out." After a few questions from the therapist, Susan burst into tears and acknowledged that the housemate was actually her lover. She said, "I *didn't* want to be gay; I *don't* want to be; but I never dreamed you could feel this way about someone." However, she said, no one else knew. "Can you imagine what Josh would do?" She told several stories of custody lost because of a parent's homosexuality and of gays and lesbians who had lost their careers and their families when their sexual orientation was discovered. As the discussion proceeded, she told the therapist that if this secret was behind Sam's bad behavior, she'd just have to give up her relationship with the woman she loved; she couldn't tell. The therapist urged her to go very slowly on any move, because society's attitude was a very big item here, and they should talk and think it through very carefully in therapy before she did anything. Susan agreed.

The first move the therapist suggested was that Susan locate a town in the area that had a legally established precedent of *not* changing custody because of a parent's homosexuality and that she keep that in mind as an "insurance policy" if

Josh or anyone threatened legal moves against her. Then, when Susan decided that, more than anything, she wanted to continue her relationship with her lover, Alice, she and the therapist worked out the following plan, which Susan put into effect over the next 2 years:

Susan told Alice to back off with the kids, not discipline them or act like a parent, but to spend some separate time occasionally with each, talking or doing something fun. Susan came out to her children, who were first upset, especially Sam ("You're more disgusting than Dad and Cheryl"), but then interested. They agreed to let their mother tell anyone else she decided to.

Therapy sessions then included various combinations of Susan, Alice, and the children to process the children's reactions and to help organize their family, which had the same structure as a heterosexual remarried household. They agreed to speak to the children's teachers and to participate in gay and lesbian social groups after Josh had been told so that they wouldn't have to live a secret life. Susan came out to Josh, who went into an uproar. Having predicted this and been coached not to react to it, Susan stayed calm and suggested that he return to therapy "for the sake of the children."

After this, Susan and Josh were seen separately—and occasionally together—for coaching in their families of origin and to review the marriage in light of their new situation. Josh had to get over his "wounded masculinity" because Susan had left him for a woman. He couldn't answer the therapist's question as to how it would feel better if she'd left him for another man. Slowly, their empathy for each other returned. Josh survived meeting Alice and even admitted that he rather liked her. Sam's acting out ceased, and both children became involved in their schoolwork and social activities, including those at a local center for gay and lesbian families.

Both did a little more work in their families of origin. Josh came to see that his position in his parental triangle, blaming his mother for the conflict with "poor dad," had set him up to repeat his father's pattern and be impatient with women's "demands."

Susan knew that she would never be able to know whether her feeling left out related to her unrecognized sexual orientation or her mother's favoritism toward her younger sister—or which came first. But she made sure she wasn't left out of current contact and gatherings.

Susan came out to her family, using it as an opportunity to deal differently with each member. Josh also used this revelation as an opportunity to open up to his family members and improve those relationships.

Susan told her closest associate at work and was relieved to find her colleague supportive.

Josh requested sessions for himself and a new, serious, woman friend, Sheila, because they were thinking of getting married but were concerned about the reaction of Sheila's two teenagers. They were also concerned that her ex-husband, who was extremely distant and paid only sporadic child support might use this opportunity to just cut off from his sons and invest his time and money in his own stepsons. Josh was also concerned about Sam and Karen's reactions to another major change.

This case shows the extreme complexity of the emotional and structural issues of reconstituted families. The divorce and remarriage issues interact with issues from the families of origin, issues from the family's current life cycle stage (e.g., adolescence), and issues created by social attitudes (e.g., homophobia). This family worked on their relationships over a period of more than 5 years before all the pieces fell into place. But when they did, the results were impressive: Susan, Alice, and the children all attended Josh's wedding, mingling pleasantly with the bride, her sons, and her family. And as Sam left for an excellent college, he said that he expected "all of my parents" to write, visit, and send goodies. Two years later, Karen graduated from high school with several honors at a ceremony attended by all of them.

What is most striking about their story are the many, many opportunities along the way to fall into conflict and cut offs, most of which, with the help of the therapist, they resisted, while setting a course aimed always at maintaining and improving their significant relationships.

Chapter 22

Migration and the Life Cycle

Celia J. Falicov

At the heart of the family life cycle construct is the notion that members of a family will most likely navigate interconnected life cycle events together. The experiences of migration pull exactly in the opposite direction by making it difficult to share these life cycle experiences. Indeed, most immigrants cannot plan a stable or predictable common future that involves family members, their communities, and cultures.

Migration alters in multiple ways how expected and unexpected life cycle events are lived. Immigrants endure, for better or for worse, the accumulation of several expected and unexpected transitions in the midst of a changed physical, social, and cultural landscape. Migration may be analogous to unexpected life events such as the adoption of children, divorce, remarriage, or early widowhood. The possibility of these events occurring was scarcely ever imagined in the immigrant's original life projections as her or his identity was being shaped from mid-childhood onwards. For non-normative events of this sort, there is little preparation, no celebratory rituals, few social frameworks for navigation, and only a few imagined new scenarios for development that could replace the old imagined maps of the future.

It is even possible to construct migration as a developmental process in itself, a process with its own stages and transitions, ranging from a preparatory stage, moving through periods of over-compensation or decompensation and ending with transgenerational impact (Sluzki, 1979). If migration itself is an evolutionary process, it follows that migration stages and transitions intersect with how other expected life cycle stages and transitions are experienced. Therefore, immigrants can be thought to be undergoing the experiences of migration as a developmental process in the context of undergoing the age-related natural or inevitable events of the life cycle.

Another distinctive feature of migration is the lifelong experience of ambiguous loss that most immigrants need to learn to live with (Boss, 1999; Falicov, 2001). To this already complex set of challenges, we must add the fact that immigrants like non-immigrants, cannot escape the eventuality of other unexpected transitions such as divorce, illness, or other losses.

This chapter will focus on how migration intersects with the life cycle of families. This focus requires first a brief historical social critique of the life cycle construct in family therapy. The issue of variation from the normative models is fundamental to an understanding of life cycle developments for immigrants. The age at the time of migration and contextual stressors such as poverty, discrimination, and undocumented status impact the life cycle of immigrants. Taking these variables into account, three topics are chosen for elaboration because they help therapists understand and frame life cycle issues when they engage in conversations with immigrant families. The three topics are family separations and reunifications, family reorganizations, and the impact of cultural change.

Although the majority of illustrations in this chapter come from my work with Latino immigrants, a significant portion of my clinical practice, the described processes of life cycle transformations apply to many other immigrant groups.

A Social Critique of Life Cycle Concepts in Family Therapy

The life cycle framework was first developed by family sociologists in the 1950s (Hill & Rogers, 1964; Duvall, 1957). At that time functionalist and universalistic ideals, informed by Talcott Parsons' model (1951) of traditional family roles in the nuclear family, were the prevailing models of family life and family development.

A very serious shortcoming of this foundational life cycle paradigm was the lack of attention paid to how life cycle experiences are inextricably tied to the socioeconomic and cultural-sociopolitical context of the family. Another shortcoming was that life cycle stages were regarded as predictable, normative, universal, and cumulative. Little room was made for the range of individual responses, the impact of gender or racial oppression, the cultural diversity patterns, and the unpredictable adaptations that we increasingly need to acknowledge today. A social constructionist viewpoint can potentially portray a more accurate picture of the family life cycle by acknowledging the impact of age and stage, cultural variation, social inequities, and individual uniqueness within a complex reality of multiple family forms (Erickson, 1998). The need for this new perspective of the life cycle is patently clear where a discussion about immigrant experiences is concerned, given that therapists must include cultural diversity, migration processes, and contextual stressors.

Age and Life Cycle Stage at the Time of Migration

The age at the time of migration, the stage of personal development, and the length of stay in the adopted country alter how migration is constructed and lived over time. Leaving one's country at a young age is significantly different than uprooting and new adaptations later in life. Migration is experienced differently by toddlers, school-age children, adolescents, young adults, and aging persons.

Migration is not necessarily easier or harder at one age or stage or another, but it is processed differently at the cognitive, emotional, and behavioral levels. During the first years of life, separation from the multiple caretakers that may have been present in the extended family may be a major loss. In middle childhood, the separation from the original school setting can be very confusing, even emotionally traumatic. The confusion may be accentuated by the differences in expectations between the culture of the old school and that of the new one.

In adolescence, separation from attachment to a country and a national identity may be dislocating

both at the cognitive and the emotional levels. Young adulthood may offer the felicitous coincidence of a need for an autonomous beginning in work or education and the openness to learning new language and customs. Growing old and anticipating death may alter an immigrant's view of the original wish to migrate and rekindle longings for a return to the homeland.

In sum, the level of flexibility to adaptation, the ability to learn a new language, the willingness to absorb new cultural values, the aim to obtain reasonable balances of continuity and change, and the ability to process transnational relationships will depend to some extent on one's age and life cycle stage at the time of migration. Even the possibility of raising the next generation in a binational, bilingual identity will depend to some extent on the age and the flexibility of the immigrant generations at the time of migration.

Contextual Stressors in the Life Cycle of Immigrants

Migration transforms individuals into the disadvantaged position of being members of a racial, cultural, socioeconomic, and citizenship minority. Even when they were people of color in their own country, they were not "others" in terms of culture and language. They were legitimate citizens of their nations. The stresses of racism are deleterious to health outcomes, intellectual performance, overall behavior, and family stability at all stages of the life cycle.

THE IMMIGRANT'S PARADOX Recent studies report that the generation of foreign-born immigrants has better physical and mental health than their children who are born and raised in this country. It appears that the higher the acculturation to American society in terms of language, citizenship, and self-identification, the poorer the mental health as expressed in depression or drug and alcohol abuse. Likewise, higher acculturation has been linked to health problems such as high blood pressure and diabetes and a variety of psychosomatic symptoms. This finding of decreasing physical and mental health with increased acculturation has been dubbed the immigrant's paradox (Vega et al., 1998; Organista, 2007; Alegria et al., 2008).

Thus, it appears that those immigrants who rapidly replace the values of their culture with those of the mainstream do worse than those who manage to retain significant family values. Efforts to be included through assimilation may be largely futile and rather than providing cultural and social protections they may result in further losses of the original cultural assets and social networks.

"DOUBLE CONSCIOUSNESS" Therapists need to be aware of the possible complex responses of families to their well-meaning interventions as these may unwittingly threaten the immigrant's dream of a better future, as the following example illustrates.

A family consisting of mother, father, and six children who had arrived in Southern California from Oaxaca, Mexico, 6 years ago was referred to therapy because a White upper-class neighbor had accused their 9-year-old son of "molesting" her 4-year-old daughter while the children played in the fields. The family had lived for 6 years in a home on the grounds of an estate belonging to their wealthy American employers. The father was employed as a ranch hand and the mother helped with household chores. As their story unfolded and I interviewed members individually, I began to suspect that the situation could easily be normalized within developmental limits. The little girl, the 9-year-old "alleged perpetrator," and his 6-year-old brother had been playing together outdoors. The three children agreed that the girl was wiggling and crossing her legs because she needed to urinate. The older Mexican boy pulled the girl's panties down, told her to spread her legs, and held her in the upright position because the toilet was too far to walk to make it on time. As the boy attempted to help the girl with her predicament, she got scared and started to scream. She then ran home to her mother, crying all the way. The agitated young mother took the girl to the pediatrician but a medical exam showed no evidence of genital bruising.

Racism was undoubtedly part of the negative interpretation of the boy's behavior. But it is also important to note that the White and economically privileged 32-year-old mother of the 4-year-old girl had just been diagnosed with a recurrence of leukemia. In her high state of emotional distress, fears about potential dangers to her daughter and worries that she might no longer be present to protect her rose to the fore. Certainly, this young mother was in the throes of an unexpected tragic turn of her own life cycle expectations. Through this and other similar experiences, I have come to believe that racism rears its ugly head even more intensely during times of stress than during stable times.

When I met with the Mexican family I offered my explanations for why the events may have been misinterpreted. The father, who had very dark skin and striking Mayan features, was usually a silent man. When he talked, a deep intelligence was revealed. He said, "I thank you very much for your efforts. We want to please ask you to do us a favor very important for us. We want you to tell "them" that in these sessions you have worked with our son and you think he is "cured" of whatever problems he had, and that in your professional opinion, no sexual transgressions will ever happen again." When I asked why he wanted me to go along with the accusation, he said, "Because, when they look at us, they think 'these Mexicans are good people because they work hard, le hacen la lucha' (they struggle hard), but if something goes wrong they suddenly see the faces that they believe were hiding under the surface, the faces of rapists and abusers."

I thought that his explanation was one of the best I had ever heard about "double consciousness" (Du Bois, 1903). This father knew who he was and how he was seen by others. He was painfully aware of the gross, racist preconceptions about Latino immigrants held by Whites.

He continued " and you cannot change that, or if you yourself want to take on that struggle, we will be hurt and we will lose what we gained. We miss our town very much but we can raise our family much better here. My wife has found a church for us, my oldest daughter may be able to go to medical school, my employer is buying a computer for my youngest boy who is very smart . . . you see . . . . I will keep an eye on this boy, I promise you, but please do not question their story, 'no vale la pena'(it is not worth the sorrow). It could cost us everything we worked for."

I think he was asking me not to rescue his family, because in doing so, I might be, like so many well-intentioned helping professionals, isolating elements of a complex social ecology without asking themselves or the families they treat if interventions meant to help at one level might cause problems at another. Perhaps this father's request would allow him to exercise some measure of protection for the collective life cycle needs of his large family (going to school, graduating, and getting a good career and livelihood). Choosing the greater good for the family at the expense of the individual could be understood as a cultural strategy of a collectivistic setting where so many interconnected people could lose a chance to a better future for the sake of defending one individual who is wrongly accused. The African American mother in the play *Doubt* (Shanley, 2007) elects to downplay or doubt the plausible sexual abuse of her son to avoid further stigmatization and hamper his already limited chances to succeed in life. Likewise, the Oaxacan father in my example, was electing to ignore or downplay the abuse being committed toward his own child because the consequences of defending him or pressing charges could be much more dire than accepting the injustice being perpetrated.

Fortunately for all involved, the accusing mother withdrew her complaint and the White employer collaborated with my view of the situation. I intervened also by asking the school to allow the boy to stay in an afternoon program that gave him more age-appropriate activities than playing with and rescuing younger children.

In this family, we can see the ambiguity of gains, losses, and dual visions of immigrants. Striving for the dream of stability in a new land is riddled with pressures to assimilate the dominant culture's story, which negatively judges dark-skinned, poor immigrants and deprives them of legal resources to fight unfair accusations. The social climate of structural exclusion and psychological violence suffered by immigrants and their children is not only detrimental to their participation in the opportunity structure, but it also affects the immigrant children's sense of self, through a process that Carola Suarez-Orozco (2002) aptly calls "social mirroring."

Although unspoken by this family and many others, another common burden that silences standing up for one's rights is the lack of legal residence documents. Many families are plagued with having to accept ignominies for the sake of continuous undercover residence, a situation that causes daily stress in the workplace and the neighborhood.

Unfortunately, economic stress and other forms of oppression that were the main motivator of the migration may continue to plague the immigrant in the new setting and affect life cycle outcomes in deleterious ways. Indeed, most immigrants and their children are aware of the hostilities and prejudice toward them and their barriers to full societal participation. From a psychological viewpoint this awareness may be debilitating when internalized or denied, but it may be empowering when it helps stimulate strategic social justice activism. Proponents of critical pedagogy emphasize that awareness of one's own marginal status is the first step toward empowerment (Trueba, 1999). Therapists must be able to discuss these topics to the extent that families are comfortable with them and have developed trust in the therapists' understanding of their complex predicaments.

Separations, Reunifications, and Life Cycle Consequences

Migration always involves *family separation* of one kind or another. Physical relocation separates individuals from the extended family or the nuclear family and at a minimum from the community and group of friends. The original family and social network would have experienced life cycle events together and would have helped shape, monitor, and support life transitions. Separations deprive immigrants from the possibility to continue to build shared life cycle narratives with loved ones.

The stages in the process of leaving one's home country begin with a prologue of thinking, planning, talking, and making concrete inquiries and moves. The time span for this prologue may vary from an impulsive individual decision to a prolonged mutual deliberation, but it always involves a powerful motivation full of doubts and certainties, hopes and regrets, choice points about who is to come, when, why, where, and what for, followed by interpersonal attributions of responsibility and most importantly the experience of ruptured attachments among family members.

There are multiple subjective consequences of these decisions upon the family that migrates and for those family members who remain behind. These consequences vary depending on the ages and life cycle stages of those who are planning to leave and those who are staying. Studies report a significant increase in anxiety about the safety and adaptation of the immigrants on the part of younger and older family members who have stayed in the country of origin (Gomez and Guzman, 2006). Depression is a common symptom among those who have left their home countries, regardless of their age.

The players in the drama of separation also vary. Separations and subsequent reunifications may take place between nuclear and extended family members when the nuclear family migrates together or between spouses or between a parent and the rest of the family when a man or a woman comes first with the thought of later reunification. Children who are left temporarily under kin care may be separated not only from parents but also from departing siblings. Of course, another separation will take place when the children leave the caretaker to be reunited with parents, causing difficult adaptations for all involved. The reverberations of separations and subsequent reunifications are felt during various life cycle stages. Here, I will focus primarily upon the significance of separations and reunions between parents and children.

Separations and reunions among parents and children

The most substantive ruptures of migration are those that involve primary systems of care; among these the most disruptive involve separations between parents and children, in particular those between mothers and children. Increasingly migrations around the globe involve separations between parents and children. Women, as well as men, leave their children with family caretakers to embark on a journey that could presumably remedy their economic poverty.

The family consequences of these often desperate decisions to separate vary depending on many factors. One factor is the preexistence of cultures of migration that support and legitimize leaving children behind and provide role models for these decisions in the history of the community. Other important elements are the quality of the relationship between caregiver and the biological parent as well the quality, frequency, and constancy of the transnational contacts over time. The ages of the children and possibly the length of the separation itself are

also fundamental aspects that shape the life cycle outcomes for the families involved (Suarez-Orozco, Todorova, & Louie, 2002).

The outcomes of these alterations depend to a large extent on the attributions of meaning made by those who left and those who stayed. A child can feel abandoned and neglected by a parent's absence or can regard the parent as a hero or heroine that has sacrificed his or her own comfort for the well-being of his or her children, depending on the family narratives that develop around the migration (Artico, 2003). For this reason, it is important for therapists to include inquiries about the meanings that each family member attributes to the separation.

Although many families navigate separations and reunifications successfully, those seen by clinicians present a more complex picture. Depending on the child's age, separations could injure attachments in profound ways and reunifications may be very laborious (Garcia-Coll & Magnuson, 1997). Current research about maternal depression after reunification reveals that encouraging communication about past experiences related to the separation has healing family effects (D'Angelo et al., 2009).

Children and adolescents may reject their parents. Parents in turn may feel discouraged, frustrated, and unprepared to deal with the unexpected poles of behavior. Children may display either regressive dependent behavior or the opposite, very independent and grown-up behavior after they have suffered separation. Adolescents that have been separated from their mothers and fathers manifest behavior problems, drug involvement, anxiety, and depression in clinical populations (Santisteban et al., 2009). School difficulties are also more frequent in children who have been separated (Suarez-Orozco, 2008). Unfortunately, many teachers lack information about the child's experiences of separation and reunification and are not able to utilize this knowledge to help the child's adaptation to school.

Separations add two new transitions to the expectable life cycle. One is the separation and the other is the reunification. Themes connected to the separation need to be integrated in therapy with immigrant families as these significant stressors alter many normative expectations about family life (Mitrani et al., 2004). The reverberations of the experience of separation may be painfully revisited at various life cycle stages for the main protagonists. Even in the case of older people, it is important to explore the history of separations and reunifications during migration.

The power of the past in the lives of immigrants may appear in full force in older age. A moderately successful 69-year-old farmer who had arrived in California from Mexico at the age of 16 requested psychotherapy for agitated depression. The focus of his ruminations is a debt of gratitude toward his long-deceased grandmother. Since his recent retirement, he has for the first time spontaneously reconnected with memories of those people in his life who demonstrated love and devotion toward him. At the top of his list is the gratitude he will never be able to express toward his grandmother.

Compounding his sense of loss is his current relationship with his five grown children. They do not value the many sacrifices he has made to provide an education for them. For example, the two younger children complain that he never went to their soccer games the way American fathers do.

In therapy two goals are outlined. One is to create bridges with the community his grandmother belonged to and explore concrete ways to honor her memory. The other goal is to spend time with his children and grandchildren to share his migratory narrative including the culture and class contexts in which he grew up. This both/and therapeutic approach is consonant with the lifelong need of many immigrants to be here and to be there at the same time.

TRUTH OR LIES The estrangement that often accompanies separations among family members is compounded by the tendency of those who left and those who stayed to alter the truth of their experiences in an effort to protect the listener from being exposed to difficult news such as unemployment, health issues, depression, or family conflicts that the listener cannot remedy or do anything about. Denial may play a further role in acknowledging the difficult realization that the sacrifices of migration may not have been worthwhile. This lack of transparency in long-distance immigrant communication may contribute to further emotional distance, rather than accomplishing the purpose of the call, which was to intensify or at least maintain the attachment bond.

Therapeutic techniques designed to make a bridge towards knowledge of events that took place in the lives of various family members, such as "catching-up" life narratives, are usually helpful at the time of reunification (Falicov, 1998, 2003).

A 33-year-old mother, Isabel, an immigrant from Manila, Philippines, was referred by a physician for multiple somatic complaints: aches and pains that traveled from place to place in her body (headaches, joints, heart palpitations) for which no medical cause could be found. Less than two years before Isabel had reunited with her now 13-year-old daughter, Violeta, from whom she had separated at age one and a half. The daughter had remained with the maternal grandmother for a decade with only one visit from her biological mother. The mother's plan to live together in the host country did not materialize into the expected panacea. It was as though strangers reunited with no shared history. Violeta was initially morose and uninterested in work or play and was doing poorly in school. The teenager only became more energized when she began to hang around with the " wrong crowd." Isabel had no authority over her, as the girl disrespected curfews and any directions that came from the mother.

It is not uncommon for parents and children to have idealized the thought of an eventual reunion only to find out that the harsh reality of the many losses incurred is very different than the fantasy everyone had imagined. Isabel had handled the ambiguities of migration, the separation, and her loss of physical and psychological home by postponing her grief, in the hopes of recovering a deep sense of home later, when she could reunite with her daughter. Now she awakened from her dream with a harsh reality of many losses. The daughter, of course, was experiencing multiple losses herself including the deep attachments to her grandmother, extended family, and peer group. She was now faced with her new marginal status as an immigrant in the United States and had become depressed. In fact, the costs of transnationalism on children may be manifested in the appearance of culturally specific depression-like disorders such as *nervios*, a syndrome of melancholy and anger that has been described in children in the Ecuadorian Andes separated from their fathers who migrate to the United States (Pribilsky, 2001).

Furthermore, during the years of separation and superficial contact, much of reality had not been shared. The mother protected the daughter from hearing about her loneliness and sadness and the employment instability and the many economic sacrifices she had to make to send money home. The daughter protected the mother by not sharing any of her feelings of being abandoned and not having a mother around when other children did. She did not tell her either about the teasing and exploitative behaviors she endured at the hands of her uncle and cousins who lived in the same household.

A catching-up life narrative technique was utilized in therapy. Both mother and daughter were asked to describe to each other the trajectory of their separated lives, including the homes they lived in, the school and work experiences, the joys and disappointments in friendships, the celebrations that stood out, the times when they missed each other and wanted to be together. The therapist took notes and asked them to bring photos, objects, mementos that symbolized those times in concrete and subjective ways. The notes and the objects were put inside a white cardboard box that was given to them with the project of decorating the box together. To the next session, Isabel and Violeta proudly brought the box that they had labeled as the "treasure box." Their first truly bonding experience had been to spend the weekend decorating top, bottom, and sides as a collage of cutouts of colorful magazine photos topped with paper flowers.

TRANSNATIONAL DIMENSIONS OF MIGRATION SEPARATIONS The life cycle of families acquires transnational dimensions when the transitions undergone by some members in one country may affect or be affected by transitions that other family members are undergoing in another country. Events that cannot be shared by those who left and those who stayed, such as growing old, illness, or death of a close relative intensify the ambiguities caused by the losses and gains of migration.

Immigrants today, unlike past immigrants, who could only maintain very occasional contact, can frequently utilize multiple technical means of communication to maintain fairly intense long-distance relationships (Falicov, 2007). Thus, many new immigrants believe that there will be time in the future to visit their home countries, renew old connections, and fulfill responsibilities to family. However, when these fantasized continuities come to a brutal halt with a discontinuous fatality, the emotional flooding can be overwhelming.

A 42-year-old woman, Ana Luisa had been married for 15 years and living in San Diego with her European American husband and their two daughters when she entered a marital crisis. She heard that her father has died suddenly in Honduras. Her husband does not understand the depth of her grief and is upset about her threats of divorce. He knows that she followed him back to America because she had fallen in love with him when he had met her in her country. For the first time she blames him now for her separation from her family. When she is inconsolable, her two young daughters and her husband can provide little comfort and sharing of memories because they hardly knew her father. Her own grief has become frozen and she is experiencing a great deal of confusion as to which family and which country she really belongs.

Therapeutic interventions include at-home and long-distance rituals that allowed for more collective participation in the life cycle transition. In therapy, the husband and children are asked if they would help Mom mourn her father and make preparations for a pretend wake or a funeral ceremony for her father. At their request, Ana Luisa's mother came to visit. She brought photos, records of her husband's favorite music, and some personal items of Grandpa's like a 1940s fedora hat that had made him look dapper. The five of them share nightly family meals and fireside chats with Grandfather's music in the background. They made a little altar over a small round table with these items, a photo, and candles. Sharing the threads of healing memories and stories never told before, they begin to weave a collective tapestry that envelops those who left and those who stayed with a common, transnational love. Ana Luisa reflects on her feelings of guilt, her realization that many years had passed when she was busy working and raising children, all the time counting that there would be a future time to reconnect more deeply with her father again, a truncated illusion that need to be reckoned with now.

Periods of grief and mourning may be capitalized on as an opportunity for renewal of the continuity of those family and social connections that are still possible to maintain with the communities of origin.

Family Reorganizations and Life Cycle Reverberations

Migration always precipitates family reorganization to cope with changed circumstances. Family organization and family functioning are altered because some family members compensate for the physical or emotional absence of others by assuming new roles and functions. These new makeshift family roles may precipitate or slow down the pace at which life cycle transitions, such as leaving home or getting married, occur.

The phenomena of the oldest child as the family helper and cultural intermediary (between parents and institutions, and even between parents and the younger children) has been widely reported in immigrant families. From an individualistic point of view, this family helper is sometimes regarded as overburdened and losing his or her chance to be free from responsibility in adolescence. However, he or she can also be regarded as performing a valuable family function that helps him or her to learn mature behaviors and increases self-esteem. Nevertheless, with increased age and acculturation the burdens of parentified status may begin to accrue, particularly when they interfere with other, new culturally patterned life cycle requirements. In these situations, we may observe that in some cases, the process of migration may have reversed generational hierarchies.

Mary Gonzales, a 32-year-old social worker of Mexican origin comes to therapy with her parents and her siblings. She wants to help them find a better way to deal with the discipline issues they are encountering with their youngest daughter, Gladys, who is 14 years old and defies her parents' authority. Twenty years ago, when the family arrived in California from Mexico bringing with them three children born there, the oldest child and only girl, Mary, became the translator and intermediary between the parents and the institutions of the new country. Gladys, one of three other children born in the United States, considers Mary to be the only person in the family who understands American culture and English well. Indeed, Mary has been the indefatigable translator of language and culture for her parents and her younger siblings.

Mary's first attempt to obtain more autonomy from her role as parentified daughter and sister took place when she married an American man of Scottish descent. However, in spite of this built-in cultural and language distance, she moved with her husband only as far as a lower floor in the apartment building where her parents and siblings lived and continued to perform the same intermediary role.

The second attempt toward greater autonomy from her family of origin appears during tragic circumstances when Mary anticipates her likely permanent absence from her family. The latter may be seen as the real motive for the current clinical consultation although the ostensible reason was Gladys's misbehavior. Recently, at age 32, Mary has received a diagnosis of fatal ovarian cancer. In the face of this unexpected life cycle tragedy, the rigid family organization that developed as an adaptation to migration must change to free Mary from parental tasks and to prepare her parents to take over those responsibilities. The therapeutic conversation is used to clarify that before the migration, the parents had been very capable parents who had raised three successful children, but had become debilitated in their authority toward their younger, American children because of the stresses of language and culture change (Falicov, 1997).

The intersection of gender and migration played a significant role in the reorganization of roles and functions of family members.

GENERATIONAL REORGANIZATIONS The developmental issues of adolescence involve fairly universally a striving toward greater personal autonomy, and this often implies testing parental limits. This process can be difficult in the face of high-risk conditions brought about by migration, poverty, and neighborhood dangers such as drugs, sex, and crime. Many immigrant parents exert their authority to protect their children from these dangers. The proverbial authoritarian parent imposes prohibitions on outings and peer relationships and dispenses harsh punishments when these rules are broken.

Freedoms can differ significantly for boys and girls within the same family. Many Latino parents will not let girls go out because of fear that they will get pregnant, and parents have biological arguments that designate girls as the "weaker sex."

A Mexican family in therapy for depression in the 19-year-old daughter, Consuelo, related that both the mother and the father controlled her behavior by having her boyfriend visit her in the home and sit and watch TV without touching even the side of their arms, because in their estimation the most minimal physical contact stimulated their temptations. In contrast, Consuelo's 18-year-old brother was allowed to come home late at night after drinking, going to dances, and spending time in the back of cars with girls. To add to the controls, this younger brother was supposed to supervise her activities in the street when boys were around. When Consuelo would express her emotional upset to her parents over the "double standard" implied, she would get a few slaps in the face for her disobedience and intimations that she was on the brink of becoming a woman of ill repute for wanting to go out alone with her boyfriend. Her depression needed to be seen in the context of immutable parental positions that were blocking her desires for greater age-appropriate autonomy.

"Lockdown" is an expression commonly used by second-generation adolescent girls referring to their parents' insistence that they stay home (Smith, 2006). Most likely, Latino parents exercise very high controls on girls because of their perception that the dangers are much greater for girls than for boys, even though boys are exposed to other dangers, such as drug abuse and gangs.

Zayas et al. (2005) have constructed a clinically useful model of why so many Latina teens attempt suicide, a model based on the notion that different cultural ideals of relatedness create internal conflicts for the immigrant family. The suicide attempt is seen as representing a major developmental internal conflict between the adolescent's need for autonomy and her deep respect for family unity and obedience that originated in her cultural socialization.

For other ethnic groups, such as Asian Americans, a similar generational dynamic takes place between adolescents and their parents. Strong cultural conflict with parents who exert their old cultural ideals rigidly and attempt to shelter their offspring against external dangers correlates with suicidal attempts in adolescent girls and boys following a disciplinary crisis (Lau et al., 2002).

Therapists must be cognizant of these dilemmas and not encourage cultural solutions that favor one generation over the other. New studies strongly suggest that families that embrace biculturalism (i.e. adolescents who attempt to maintain strong ties to their parents' cultures and have parents who reach out to learn the skills of the new culture) perform better academically, face less anxiety, and adjust more easily socially (Smokowski and Bacallao, 2009).

A new cultural scenario is brought about by global communication technologies that allow for transnational exposures and long-distance relationships in the lives of new immigrants (Falicov, 2007). A comparative study of adolescence in New York and in Ticuani, Mexico, by sociologist Robert Smith (2006) uncovers many interesting aspects of adolescence in transnational contexts. In New York, adolescent girls are locked down, parental controls are intense, and adolescence is experienced as a very constraining life stage. However, when the adolescents, girls and boys, go to Ticuani, their parents' hometown in Puebla, Mexico, it is like going to live in a better neighborhood. This is because parents and grandparents granted a lot more freedom to girls and boys during their summer visits. In Ticuani the adults experience a much greater sense of safety and familiarity than in New York. Thus, second-generation adolescents have to find a way to integrate these two sets of experiences and parental directives, complicating their life cycle predicaments between dependency and autonomy.

Contextual protections also play a role in that adolescents have more people around them in Ticuani than they do in New York, where their immigrant parents work more hours farther away and there is a less rich community of relatives and acquaintances to keep an eye on youth. So paradoxically, in their parents' country, adolescents have both more personal freedoms and more caring involvement from adults than in the United States.

GENDER REORGANIZATIONS IN MARITAL RELATIONSHIPS Tensions between tradition and modernity also affect relationships between husbands and wives. The economic opportunities open for women who migrate, the more liberal attitudes toward the control of fertility, and the legal protections against domestic violence that immigrant women encounter in the United States facilitate a desire for a more companionate, egalitarian model of marital relationships than the one envisioned or lived prior to the migration. Thus, immigrant women strive to develop a more modern type of marriage based on greater trust, intimacy, and sexual love. Marital conflict or marital growth may ensue, with men having a variety of reactions to these strivings, ranging from feeling threatened to sharing the dream of a different kind of intimacy (Hirsch, 2003). Of course, many couples around the world deal with similar issues due to the advent of women's liberation, but migration may intensify the conflict and precipitate divorce without the containing backdrop of extended family and community. These reorganizations intensified by migration have very real consequences for the life cycle development of men and women and for the cultural role models they pass on to the next generation.

Cultural Changes and Cultural Retention in the Family Life Cycle

A final topic for consideration is the notion that how the family life cycle is lived is affected by *cultural changes*. Cultural change is a theme that dominates the internal and external life of immigrants. Each society conditions the family to transmit rules that are adaptive to broad societal requirements. In turn, each family prepares its members to live in their own society and to speak the language of its people. The importance of taking into account cultural variations in conception and practices of the life cycle (Falicov, 1987, 1996, 1998) has been discussed before. Life cycle specifications about timing, markers, processes, and age and gender expectations are culturally and socially constructed and passed on through generations. A deep challenge for immigrants is how to fit into and conduct life cycle transitions in a different language and with different cultural ideals and norms than those acquired in the culture of origin. In the process, they must reconcile two different cultural codes.

When a family moves to another country, the cultural meanings attached to life cycle events may differ between the family and the dominant culture models. For example, the model of child-rearing in

an immigrant family is likely to be incongruent with the dominant culture's model, yet the original cultural views may continue to be reinforced by similar attitudes held by other immigrants living in the ethnic neighborhood or by repeated return trips to the country of origin. Normal developmental stresses may be intensified by cultural contrasts and dilemmas.

ACCULTURATIVE STRESSES If the family moves to a different country, they face linguistic and cultural incongruence with the new society. This incongruence has been described as a lack of reciprocity or lack of "fit" between the dominant society expectations and the immigrant family's ways (Minuchin, et al., 1967; Falicov, 1988). Patterns that are adaptive for individuals and families in a Guatemalan rural village do not function effectively in a New York urban ghetto. The values, norms, and behaviors learned in the home country become a source of stress when the family comes in contact with the institutions of the new culture. The immigrant parents' model of child-rearing and the developmental expectations may be "out of phase" with the dominant culture's model, as represented in the school, the peer group, or the health system. The discrepancy between the two models of child-rearing will become evident precisely at significant points in the family life cycle.

Normal developmental stresses are thus intensified by external cultural dissonance. In addition, the family needs to cope with inevitable developmental challenges that require shifts in boundaries, role functions, and family rules at a time when it is already taxed by its efforts to adapt to a new environment. For example, at the time of school entry, all families are faced with the developmental task of opening up their boundaries to share with the school the education of the child.

When immigrant families enter the school system, the cultural encounter with the school personnel may become stressful for all parties. Teachers do not understand the emotional reluctance of the immigrant parent who may be fearful to let go of their child to the unknown institution that represents the larger culture. Parents may not understand the teachers' insistence that they become more involved in their children's school tasks or in the school activities and may feel criticized by the implication that they should do things differently (Parra-Cardona et al., 2009). Parents may think they are doing their job by raising children in their home, and they believe that the teachers should do their work with the children without asking for the parents to help out, which of course is the opposite of what teachers believe in the U.S. today.

Growing up, leaving home, getting married, having children, and dying are universal experiences that depend on socially constructed and approved definitions. Grand narratives dominate public spheres and discourses, but at the local and individual level there are myriad variations in the timing, the tasks, the rituals for transition, the themes, coping mechanisms, and meaning attached to the different stages of the family life cycle. The dominant culture's age norms get internalized and translated into psychological expectations for self and others, lending a sense of being on time or off time, and of being early or late while undergoing life events. Remaining single until her late 20s would not lend an Irish woman a sense of being late or earn her the stigma of "spinster" as it would in many Latin American cultures. Reaching age 13 for an American Jewish boy provides a ritual demarcation for the family of his entrance into manhood, while the same age has no particular meaning for his Black classmate's family. Not only do the content and themes of the different stages vary with race, class, religion, and ethnicity, but also the developmental tasks and the mechanisms by which changes take place may differ.

Awareness by the clinician of cultural variations in the family life cycle and the cultural dissonances that immigrants often suffer in terms of how to navigate life cycle stages and transitions has implications relevant and even crucial to the treatment process, such as recognizing family crisis points, differentiating functional from dysfunctional behavior, and selecting treatment goals and interventions that are either culturally appropriate or take into account how to resolve cultural conflicts.

RITES AND RITUALS The application of rituals in therapy has been described extensively by Imber-Black et al. (2003), and the healing potential of these cultural continuities in the lives of immigrants needs to be considered in therapeutic interventions.

Many societies mark life cycle transitions with rituals of celebration and rites of passage that stress continuity over generations. Immigrant families may come from ethnicities that adhere to rituals and believe in their communal value. Questions about the cultural rituals and the adherence of each family to such rituals over the generations help us understand the meaning of the particular transition for each family.

SPONTANEOUS RITUALS I have described elsewhere (Falicov, 2002, 2003) that it is possible to discern a number of remembrance-oriented behaviors that acquire characteristics similar to rituals and that are inextricably connected to the processes of migration. Many immigrants create bridges to their families and hometowns by visiting and sending messages and remittances. They also recreate ethnic spaces in their current homes and neighborhoods that evoke the music, the sights, and flavors of their cultures. It is usual to preserve cultural rituals tied to the life cycle, such as birthdays, weddings, and funerals. An exploration of these rituals in therapy may give indications as to how culturally immersed or disengaged a family is and also provide possible potential therapeutic tools.

RELIGION AND SPIRITUALITY During cultural, developmental, and other life cycle transitions, immigrant families turn more intensely to the comfort and continuity of past traditions, such as prayer and local cures. The human tendency to search for stable meanings in the midst of change by revisiting cultural beliefs and rituals has been called "ideological ethnicity" (Harwood, 1981). This draw toward one's primary ethnicity can be used as a therapeutic resource to help immigrant families utilize practices that enhance continuity and belonging while propelling life forward. Even acculturated immigrants, who may have become disdainful or dismissive of indigenous practices or magical beliefs, may tend to tap into their ancestors' core beliefs when times are especially stressful.

Religion and spirituality have a powerful role in the navigation and demarcation of life cycle transitions through the performance of religious rituals. For immigrants, the practices of religion are the most transportable of all assets (Falicov, 2008). An interesting cultural phenomenon called *promesas* (promises) has been observed among the Mexican immigrants in New York who send their children every year to their hometown (Smith, 2006). A promesa usually involves a physical act like growing one's hair, running a race, or walking in a procession. This is a promise to perform certain acts to demonstrate devotion or gratitude to Jesus Christ or to the Virgin Mary for intervention on some issue. They are social, physical, and spiritual acts that enhance an adolescent's sense of competence while fostering love and respect for the traditions of the parents. Smith describes a mother and a daughter who had been estranged from each other because of the immigrant mother's grueling work schedule in New York. The mother attempted to find greater closeness by making a promise to walk in a religious procession in which they could both participate. A promesa can also be used to unite a family after separation and become a symbol of spiritual or religious gratitude tied to the reunification. The example of *promesas* also underscores the idea that cultural rituals that captivate the imagination and engagement of children and adolescents can be a form of preservation of identity for the next generation, not forced by or inherited from the parents, but rather part of their initiative and own experience. This is a wonderful example of flexible cultural retention that demonstrates the potential for biculturality.

Among Mexicans, the immigrant generation seems to have better overall physical and mental health and less depression and better school performance than the subsequent generations raised in the United States. Two large studies of Latino immigrant families, one in Michigan (Vega et al., 1991) and the other in Miami (Santisteban et al., 1999), suggest that flexible maintenance of traditions and cultural rituals creates a protective sense of "home" with a mix of the old and the new.

Nevertheless, adherence to traditional culture is not always protective. Among foreign-born Asian youth the rate of completed suicide is much higher than among U.S.-born Asian American youth. This may suggest that rapid family acculturation is more protective of depression and suicidality for Asians than for Latino adolescents. One of the theories for this finding is that acculturated youth have more support from their peer group. For the Asian families less acculturated to the U.S. life-style, intergenerational conflict may either threaten the very basis of their hierarchical value system or may isolate the adolescent without the supportive benefits of a peer group.

Thus, it may depend on the ethnic group whether it works better to have a low or high level of family acculturation, perhaps due to the fit between the original culture and the host culture. These ethnic-specific findings suggest that therapists need to adopt a careful and inquisitive stance in matters of acculturation and intergenerational conflict. At times, they could support families wishes to retain their language and cultures. In other instances, they may have to gently become agents of acculturation, depending on each family's wishes and needs and their particular blend of cultural continuity and cultural change.

Conclusion

Migration alters how expected and unexpected life cycle transformations evolve. The age and the stage of development at the time of migration affect the life cycle trajectory of individuals and families. Contextual stressors, such as poverty, discrimination, and uncertain citizenship status affect the lives of immigrants and limit their opportunities for growth. Three topics were chosen as central to an understanding of life cycle modifiers under conditions of migration. These are family separations and reunifications, family reorganizations, and the impact of culture change in the family life cycle of immigrants.

The dislocation of migration adds complexity and stresses to the developmental course. The successful adaptation to the multiple stresses involved will depend on favorable external circumstances and the family's flexibility and ability to adapt to new requirements while retaining important aspects of their cultural heritage. As migration increases everywhere, family adaptation to the inevitable life cycle progression will be greatly aided by the social justice extended to immigrants by institutions, communities, and individuals in the receiving country.

Chapter 23

Chronic Illness and the Life Cycle

John S. Rolland

When serious illness strikes, the dimension of time becomes a central reference point for families to successfully navigate the experience. The family and each of its members face the formidable challenge of focusing simultaneously on the present and future, mastering the practical and emotional tasks of the immediate situation while charting a course for dealing with the future complexities and uncertainties of their problem. Also, families draw on prior multigenerational experiences with illness and loss and core family beliefs to guide them.

Families and clinicians need an effective way to tap into the dimension of time both to comprehend issues of initial timing of an illness and to look toward the future in a more proactive manner. Placing the unfolding of chronic illness or disability into a multigenerational developmental framework facilitates this task. This requires understanding the intertwining of three evolutionary threads: illness, individual, and family development. To think systemically about the interface of these three developmental lines, we need a common language and set of concepts that can be applied to each yet permits consideration of all three simultaneously.

Two steps lay the foundation for such a model. First, we need a bridge between the biomedical and psychosocial worlds—a language that enables chronic disorders to be characterized in psychosocial and longitudinal terms, each condition having a particular personality and expected developmental life course. Second, we need to think simultaneously about the interaction of individual and family development. This is vividly demonstrated when we consider the impact of an illness on both a couple's relationship and each partner's individual development. The inherent skews that emerge between partners highlight the necessity to consider the interweaving of individual and family life cycle challenges (Rolland, 1994a, 1994b).

This chapter describes the Family Systems-Illness Model, a normative, preventive framework for assessment and intervention with families that are facing chronic and life-threatening conditions (Rolland, 1984, 1987, 1990, 1994a). This model is based on the systemic interaction between an illness and family that evolves over time. The goodness of fit between the psychosocial demands of the disorder and the family style of functioning and resources are prime determinants of successful versus dysfunctional coping and adaptation. The model distinguishes three dimensions

1. psychosocial types of disorders
2. major phases in their natural history
3. key family system variables

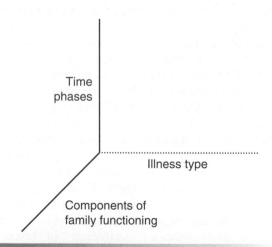

FIGURE 23.1 Three dimensional model: illness type, time phase, family functioning.

Excerpted from: Rolland, J. S., "Chronic Illness and the Life Cycle: a Conceptual Framework," *Family Process*, 26, no 2, 203–221, 1987. Reprinted with permission from Family Process.

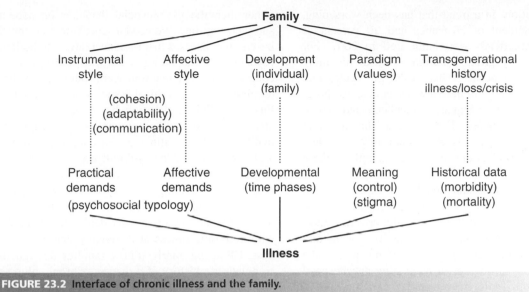

FIGURE 23.2 Interface of chronic illness and the family.
Excerpted from: Rolland, J. S. Family Systems and Chronic Illness. A Typological Model, *Journal of Psychotherapy and the Family,* vol 2, no 3, 143–168, 1987. Reprinted with permission from Family Systems Medicine.

A scheme of the systemic interaction between illness and family might look like the diagram in **Figure 23.2**: *Interface of chronic illness and the family.*

Family variables that are given particular emphasis include family and individual development, particularly in relation to the time phases of the disorder; multigenerational legacies related to illness and loss; and belief systems.

The first section of this chapter reviews a psychosocial typology and time phases of illness framework. Chronic illnesses are grouped according to key biological similarities and differences that pose distinct psychosocial demands for the ill individual and his or her family, and the prime developmental time phases in the natural evolution of chronic disease are identified. In the following section, integrating key concepts from family and individual developmental theory, the interface of disease with the individual and family life cycles will be described. Finally, multigenerational aspects of illness, loss, and crisis are considered.

The Social Context of Illness and Disabilities

It is important to state at the outset that families' experiences of illness and disability are enormously influenced by the dominant culture and the larger health systems embedded in this prevailing culture. Families from diverse minority and ethnic backgrounds and lower socioeconomic strata are disproportionately represented among the current 46 million uninsured and the additional 60 million underinsured people in the United States (U.S. Census Bureau, 2007e). For those with health coverage who are underinsured, a major illness often means financial ruin. Serious health problems represent the biggest cause of bankruptcies in the United States. For millions with disabilities, the assistance that would enable independent living is unobtainable. For these groups, a lack of access to adequate basic health care has major ramifications in terms of the incidence of illness, disease course, survival, quality of life, and a variety of forms of suffering caused by discrimination. In a trend that has been worsening, over 32 percent of Hispanics and 20 percent of African Americans were uninsured in 2007. For these minority groups, chronic diseases are more prevalent, will occur earlier in the life cycle, and, when they occur, will have a worse course and prognosis because of inadequate medical care and limited access to resources. Recent data showing that African Americans' life expectancy is 7 years less than that of Whites give a glaring example of these larger societal issues.

Dedicated mental health professionals work under severe constraints in helping affected families. In recent years, most forms of health coverage have severely limited mental health benefits. For the majority of families facing illness, this means that the longstanding difficulties of integrating psychosocial services with traditional biomedical care increase.

As the population of the United States ages, the current 133 million people with chronic conditions (Shin-Yi & Green, 2008) will balloon to over 170 million by the year 2030. With advances in technology, people are living longer with chronic illnesses, and the strain on families to provide adequate caregiving is unprecedented. For example, in 1970, there were 21 potential caregivers for each elderly person; by 2030, there will be only 6 such potential caregivers for each senior citizen (U.S. Census Bureau, 2007e). Many factors are involved, including decreasing birth rates; family networks that are getting smaller and more top-heavy, with more older than younger family members; geographic distance amongst family members; and women entering the workforce in increasing numbers and no longer being available for the traditional female role as unpaid family caregiver. These facts suggest that even the best family-centered systemic clinical models will be inadequate unless the United States develops a humane system of health care in which universal equitable care is a basic human right.

Psychosocial Typology of Illness

The standard disease classification is based on purely biological criteria that are clustered in ways to establish a medical diagnosis and treatment plan rather than the psychosocial demands on patients and their families. We need a schema to conceptualize chronic diseases that remains relevant to both the psychosocial and biological worlds and provides a common language that transforms our usual medical terminology. Two critical issues have hindered us. First, insufficient attention has been given to the areas of diversity and commonality that are inherent in different chronic illnesses. Second, there has been a glossing over of the different ways in which diseases manifest themselves over the course of an illness. Understanding the evolution of chronic diseases is hindered because clinicians often become involved in the care of an individual or family coping with a chronic illness at different points in the illness. Clinicians rarely follow families through the complete life history of a disease. Chronic illnesses need to be conceptualized in a manner that organizes these similarities and differences over the disease course so that the type and degree of demands relevant to clinical practice are highlighted in a more useful way.

The goal of this typology is to define clinically meaningful and useful categories with similar psychosocial demands for a wide array of chronic conditions affecting individuals across the life span. It conceptualizes broad distinctions of the pattern of onset, course, outcome, type and degree of disability, and level of uncertainty. Although each variable is in actuality a continuum, it will be described here in a categorical manner, selecting key anchor points.

Onset

Illnesses can be divided into those that either have an acute onset, such as strokes, or a gradual onset, such as Alzheimer's disease. For acute-onset illnesses, emotional and practical changes are compressed into a short time, requiring of the family to more rapidly mobilize their crisis management skills. Families that can tolerate highly charged affective states, exchange roles flexibly, problem solve efficiently, and utilize outside resources will have an advantage in managing acute-onset illnesses. Gradual-onset diseases, such as Parkinson's disease, allow a more gradual period of adjustment.

Course

The course of chronic diseases can take three general forms: progressive, constant, or relapsing/episodic. With a progressive disease such as Alzheimer's, the family is faced with a perpetually symptomatic member in whom disability worsens in a stepwise or gradual way. Periods of relief from the demands of the illness tend to be minimal. The family must live with the prospect of continual role change and adaptation as the disease progresses. Increasing strain on family caretakers is caused by exhaustion, with few periods of relief from the demands of the illness, and by new caretaking tasks over time. Family flexibility, in terms of both internal reorganization and willingness to use outside resources, is at a premium.

With a constant-course illness, the occurrence of an initial event is followed by a stable biological course. A single heart attack and spinal cord injury are examples. Typically, after an initial period of recovery, the chronic phase is characterized by some clear-cut deficit or limitation. Recurrences can occur, but the individual or family faces a semipermanent change that is stable and predictable over a considerable time span. The potential for family exhaustion exists without the strain of new role demands over time.

Relapsing or episodic course illnesses, such as disk problems and asthma, are distinguished by the alternation of stable low-symptom periods with periods of flare-up or exacerbation. Often, the family can carry on a normal routine. However, the specter of a recurrence hangs over their heads. Relapsing illnesses demand a somewhat different sort of family adaptability. Relative to progressive or constant-course illnesses, they may require less ongoing caretaking or role reallocation. The episodic nature of an illness may require a flexibility that permits movement back and forth between two forms of family organization. In a sense, the family is on call to enact a crisis structure to handle exacerbations of the illness. Families are strained by both the frequency of transitions between crisis and noncrisis and the ongoing uncertainty about when a crisis will next occur. The wide psychological discrepancy between low-symptom periods and flare-up is a particularly taxing feature unique to relapsing diseases.

Outcome

The extent to which an illness can be fatal or shorten one's life span has profound psychosocial impact. The most crucial factor is the initial expectation of whether a disease is likely to cause death. On one end of the continuum are illnesses that do not typically affect the life span, such as arthritis. At the other extreme are illnesses that are clearly progressive and usually fatal, such as metastatic cancer. An intermediate, more unpredictable category includes illnesses that shorten the life span, such as cystic fibrosis and heart disease, and those with the possibility of sudden death, such as hemophilia. A major difference between these kinds of outcome is the degree to which the family experiences anticipatory loss and its pervasive effects on family life (Rolland, 1990, 2004). The future expectation of loss can make it extremely difficult for a family to maintain a balanced perspective. Families are often caught between a desire for intimacy and a push to let go emotionally of the ill member. A torrent of emotions can distract a family from myriad practical tasks and problem solving that maintain family integrity. Also, the tendency to see the ill family member as practically in the coffin can set in motion maladaptive responses that divest the ill member of important responsibilities. The result can be the structural and emotional isolation of the ill person from family life. This kind of psychological alienation has been associated with poor medical outcome in life-threatening illness (Campbell , 2003; Weihs et al, 2002).

When loss is less imminent or certain, illnesses that may shorten life or cause sudden death provide a fertile ground for varied family perspectives. The "it could happen" nature of these illnesses creates a nidus for both overprotection by the family and powerful secondary gains for the ill member. This is particularly relevant to childhood illnesses such as hemophilia, juvenile-onset diabetes, and asthma (Minuchin, Rosman, & Baker, 1978).

Incapacitation

Disability can involve impairment of cognition (e.g., Alzheimer's disease), sensation (e.g., blindness), movement (e.g., stroke with paralysis), stamina (e.g., heart disease), disfigurement (e.g., mastectomy), and conditions associated with social stigma (e.g., AIDS) (Olkin, 1999). The extent, kind, and timing of disability imply sharp differences in the degree of family stress. For instance, the combined cognitive and motor deficits caused by a stroke necessitate greater family reorganization than does a spinal cord injury that leaves cognitive abilities unaffected. For some illnesses, such as stroke, disability is often worse at the beginning. For progressive diseases, such as Alzheimer's disease, disability looms as an increasing problem in later phases of the illness, allowing the family more time to discuss and prepare for anticipated changes and an opportunity for the ill member to participate in disease-related family planning while he or she is still cognitively able (Boss, 1999).

By combining the kinds of onset, course, outcome, and incapacitation into a grid format, we generate a typology that clusters illnesses according to similarities and differences in patterns that pose differing psychosocial demands (**Table 23.1**).

Uncertainty

The predictability of an illness and the degree of uncertainty about the specific way or rate at which it unfolds affects all the other variables. For highly unpredictable illnesses, such as multiple sclerosis, family coping and adaptation, especially future planning, are hindered by anticipatory anxiety and ambiguity about what the family will encounter. Families able to put long-term uncertainty into perspective and maintain hope are best prepared to avoid the risks of exhaustion and dysfunction.

Other important attributes that differentiate illnesses should be considered in a thorough, systemically oriented evaluation. These include the complexity, frequency, and efficacy of a treatment regimen; the amount of home versus hospital or clinic-based care required; and the frequency and intensity of symptoms, particularly those that involve pain and suffering.

Time Phases of Illness

Too often, discussions of "coping with cancer," managing disability, or dealing with life-threatening illness approach illness as a static state and fail to appreciate the dynamic unfolding of illness as a process over time. The concept of time phases provides a way for clinicians and families to think longitudinally and to understand chronic illness as an ongoing process with expectable landmarks, transitions, and changing demands. Each phase of an illness poses its own psychosocial demands and developmental tasks that require significantly different strengths, attitudes, or changes from a family. The core psychosocial themes in the natural history of chronic disease can be described as three major phases: crisis, chronic, and terminal (**Figure 23.3**: *Time line and phase of illness*).

The *crisis phase* includes any symptomatic period before diagnosis and the initial period of readjustment after a diagnosis and initial treatment plan. This period holds a number of key tasks for the ill member and family. Moos (1984) describes certain universal, practical, illness-related tasks, including

1. learning to cope with any symptoms or disability,
2. adapting to health care settings and treatments,
3. establishing and maintaining workable relationships with the health care team.

Also, there are critical tasks of a more general, existential nature. The family needs to

1. create a meaning for the illness that maximizes a sense of mastery and competency,
2. grieve for the loss of the life they knew before illness,
3. gradually accept the illness as permanent while maintaining a sense of continuity between their past and their future,
4. pull together to cope with the immediate crisis,
5. in the face of uncertainty, develop flexibility toward future goals.

The *chronic phase*, whether long or short, is the time span between the initial diagnosis/readjustment and the potential third phase when issues of death and terminal illness predominate. This phase can be marked by constancy, progression, or episodic change. It has been referred to as "the long haul" and "day-to-day living with chronic illness" phase. Often, the patient and family have come to grips psychologically and organizationally with permanent changes and have devised an ongoing coping strategy. The family's ability to maintain the semblance of a normal life with a chronic illness and heightened uncertainty is a key task of this period. If the illness is fatal, this is a time of living in limbo. For certain highly debilitating but not clearly fatal illnesses, such as a massive stroke or dementia, the family can feel saddled with an exhausting problem without end. Paradoxically, a family may feel that its only hope to resume a normal life can be realized after the death of their ill member. The maintenance of maximum autonomy for all family members in the face of protracted adversity helps to offset these trapped, helpless feelings.

In the *terminal phase*, the inevitability of death becomes apparent and dominates family life. The family must cope with issues of separation, death, mourning, and beginning the reorganization process needed for resumption of "normal" family life beyond the loss (Walsh & McGoldrick, 2004). Families that adapt best to this phase are able to shift their view of mastery from controlling the illness to a successful process of "letting go." Optimal coping involves emotional openness as well as dealing with the myriad practical tasks at hand. This includes seeing this phase as an opportunity to share precious time together, to acknowledge the impending loss, to deal with unfinished business, to say good-byes, and to begin the process of family reorganization. If they have not decided beforehand, the patient and key family members need to decide about such things as a living will; the extent of medical heroics desired; preferences about dying at home, in the hospital, or at hospice; and wishes about a funeral or memorial service and burial. For illnesses such as heart disease, in which death can occur at any time, or with progressive conditions that can increasingly impair mental functioning (e.g., Alzheimer's disease), it is vital that these conversations are encouraged much earlier in the illness.

Critical *transition periods* link the three time phases. These transitions present opportunities for families to reevaluate the appropriateness of their previous life structure in the face of new illness-related demands. Unfinished business from the previous phase can complicate or block movement through the transitions. Families or individuals can become permanently frozen in an adaptive structure that has outlived its usefulness (Penn, 1983). For

example, the usefulness of pulling together in the crisis phase can become maladaptive and stifling for all family members over a long chronic phase. Enmeshed families, because of their rigid and fused style, would have difficulty negotiating this delicate transition. Because high cohesion may be typical and not dysfunctional in some cultures, clinicians need to be cautious not to pathologize a normative cultural pattern. A family that is adept at handling the day-to-day practicalities of a long-term stable illness but limited in its emotional coping skills may encounter difficulty if their family member's disease becomes terminal. The relatively greater demand for affective coping skills in the terminal phase may create a crisis for a family navigating this transition.

The interaction of the time phases and typology of illness provides a framework for a normative psychosocial developmental model for chronic disease that resembles models for human development. The time phases (crisis, chronic, and terminal) can be considered broad developmental periods in the natural history of chronic disease. Each period has certain basic tasks independent of the type of illness. Each "type" of illness has specific supplementary tasks.

Clinical Implications

This model provides a framework for assessment and clinical intervention by facilitating an understanding of chronic illness and disability in psychosocial terms. Attention to features of onset, course, outcome, and incapacitation provide markers that focus clinical assessment and intervention with a family. For instance, acute-onset illnesses demand high levels of adaptability, problem solving, role reallocation, and balanced cohesion. In such circumstances, families' flexibility enables them to adapt more successfully.

An illness time line delineates psychosocial developmental phases of an illness, each phase with its own unique developmental tasks. It is important for families to address phase-related tasks in sequence to optimize successful adaptation over the long haul of a chronic disorder. Attention to time allows the clinician to assess family strengths and vulnerabilities in relation to the present and future phases of the illness.

Table 23.1 Categorization of Chronic Illnesses by Psychosocial Type

	Incapacitating		Nonincapacitating	
	Acute	**Gradual**	**Acute**	**Gradual**
Progressive F A T A L		Lung cancer with CNS metastases	Pancreatic cancer	
		Bone marrow failure		
		Amyotrophic lateral sclerosis	Metastatic cancer (e.g. breast, lung, liver)	
Relapsing			Incurable cancers in remission	
Progressive P O S S I B L Y S H O R T E N E D F A T A L L I F E S P A N		Parkinson's disease		Type 1 diabetes*
		Emphysema		Malignant hyper-tension
		Alzheimer's disease		
		Multi-infarct dementia		Insulin-dependent
		Multiple sclerosis late		Type 2 diabetes
		Chronic alcoholism		
		Huntington Disease		
		Scleroderma		
Relapsing	Angina	Early multiple sclerosis	Sickle cell disease*	Systemic lupus erythe-matosis*
		Episodic alcoholism	Hemophilia*	
Constant	Stroke	P.K.U. and other congenital errors of metabolism	Mild myocardial infarction	Hemodialysis treated renal failure
	Moderate severe myocardial infarction		Cardiac arrhythmia	Hodgkin's disease

Table 23.1 Categorization of Chronic Illnesses by Psychosocial Type
continued

| | Incapacitating | | Nonincapacitating | |
	Acute	*Gradual*	*Acute*	*Gradual*
Progressive		Rheumatoid arthritis Osteoarthritis		Noninsulin-dependent Type 2 diabetes
Relapsing	Lumbosacral disc disorder		Kidney stones Gout Migraine Seasonal allergy Asthma Epilepsy	Peptic ulcer Ulcerative colitis Chronic bronchitis Irritable bowel syndrome Psoriasis
Constant	Congenital malforma-tions Spinal cord injury Acute blindness Acute deafness Survived severe trauma & burns Posthypoxic syndrome	Nonprogressive mental retardation Cerebral paisy	Benign arrhythmia Congenital heart disease (mild)	Malabsorption syndromes (controlled) Hyper hypothy-roidism Pernicious anemia Controlled hyperten-sion Controlled glaucoma

(NONFATAL)

* = Early

Source: Revised and Reprinted from Rolland J. S. 1984. Toward a psychosocial typology of chronic and life-threatening illness. *Family Systems Medicine 2*, 245–62. Reprinted with permission of *Families, Systems, & Health*.

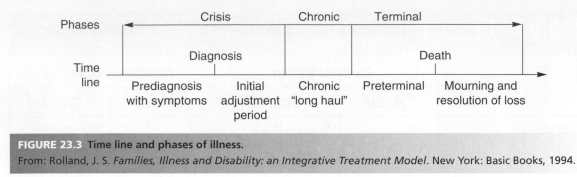

FIGURE 23.3 Time line and phases of illness.
From: Rolland, J. S. *Families, Illness and Disability: an Integrative Treatment Model.* New York: Basic Books, 1994.

The model clarifies treatment planning. Goal setting is guided by awareness of the components of family functioning that are most relevant to particular types or phases of an illness. Sharing this information with the family and deciding upon specific goals provide a better sense of control and realistic hope to the family. This process empowers families in their journey of living with a chronic disorder. Also, this knowledge educates the family about warning signs that should prompt them to request brief, goal-oriented treatment at the appropriate times.

The framework is useful for timing family psychosocial checkups to coincide with key transition points in the illness. Preventively oriented psychoeducational or support groups for patients and their families (Gonzales & Steinglass, 2002) can be designed to deal with different types of conditions (e.g., progressive, life-threatening, relapsing). Also, brief psychoeducational modules, timed for critical phases of particular types of diseases, enable families to digest manageable portions of a long-term coping process. Modules can be tailored to particular phases of the illness and family coping skills that are necessary to confront disease-related demands. This provides a cost-effective preventive service that also can identify high-risk families.

The model also informs evaluation of general functioning and illness-specific family dynamics. Other important components of an illness-oriented family assessment that are beyond the scope of this chapter include the family's belief system and process of meaning making (Rolland, 1998; Wright & Bell, 2009); medical crisis planning; capacity to perform home-based medical care; illness-oriented communication and problem solving; social support; and availability and use of community resources (see Rolland, 1994a).

Using this model, we can now address the interface of illness, individual, and family development.

Interface of the Illness, Individual, and Family Development

To place the unfolding of chronic disease into a developmental context, it is crucial to understand the intertwining of three evolutionary threads: illness, individual, and family development. A language is needed that bridges these developmental threads. Two overarching concepts are that of a *life cycle* and that of *life structure*.

Early life cycle frameworks assumed that there was a basic sequence and unfolding of the life course within which individual, family, or illness uniqueness occurs. More recent thinking has modified the notion of an invariant epigenetic process in light of the major influences of cultural, socioeconomic, gender, ethnic, and racial diversity. Illness, individual, and family development have in common the notion of phases, each with its own developmental tasks. Carter and McGoldrick have described six family life cycle phases, in which marker events (e.g., marriage, birth of first child, and last child leaving home) herald the transition from one phase to the next. Illness is a significant marker event that can both color the nature of a developmental phase and be colored by its timing in the individual and family life cycle.

Life structure refers to the core elements (e.g., work, child-rearing, religious affiliation, leisure, caregiving) of an individual's or family's life at any given point in the life cycle. Levinson (1978, 1986b), in his description of individual adult development, describes how life structures can move between periods of transition and building/maintaining. Transition periods are sometimes the most vulnerable because previous individual, family, and illness life structures are reappraised in light of new developmental tasks that may require significant change. The primary goal of a life structure-building/maintaining period is to form a life structure and enrich life within it on the basis of the key choices an individual/family made during the preceding transition period.

Different phases of the family life cycle coincide with shifts between family developmental tasks that require intense bonding or an inside-the-family focus, as in the "families with young children" child-rearing phase, versus phases such as "launching children and moving on" during which the external family boundary is loosened, often emphasizing personal identity and autonomy (Combrinck-Graham, 1985). In life cycle terms, this suggests a fit between family developmental tasks and the relative need for family members to direct their energies inside the family and work together to accomplish those tasks.

These unifying concepts provide a base to discuss the fit among illness, individual, and family development. Each phase in these three kinds of development poses tasks and challenges that move through periods of being more or less in sync with each other. It can be useful to distinguish

1. between child-rearing and non–child-rearing phases in the family life cycle,
2. the alternation of transition and life structure-building/maintaining periods in both individual and family development,
3. periods of higher and lower psychosocial demands over the course of a chronic condition.

Generally, illness and disability tend to push individual and family developmental processes toward transition and increased need for cohesion. Analogous to the addition of an infant member at the beginning of the child-rearing phase, the occurrence of chronic illness sets in motion an inside-the-family-focused process of socialization to illness. Symptoms, loss of function, demands of shifting or new illness-related roles, and the fear of loss through death all require a family to pull together. This inward pull of the disorder risks different normative strains depending on timing with the family's and individual members' phases of development. In clinical assessment, a basic question is "What is the fit between the psychosocial demands of a condition and family and individual life structures and developmental tasks at a particular point in time?" Also, how will this fit change as the illness unfolds in relation to the family life cycle and the development of each member?

Periods of Child-Rearing and Postlaunching

If illness onset coincides with the launching or post-launching phases of the family life cycle, it can derail a family's natural momentum. Illness or disability in a young adult may require a heightened dependency and return to the family of origin for disease-related caretaking. The autonomy and individuation of parents and child are in jeopardy, and separate interests and priorities may be relinquished or put on hold. Family dynamics as well as disease severity will influence whether the family's reversion to a child-rearing-like structure is a temporary detour or a permanent reversal. Since enmeshed families frequently face the transition to a more autonomous launching/postlaunching phase with trepidation, a serious illness provides a sanctioned reason to return to the "safety" of the child-rearing period.

When disease onset coincides with the child-rearing phases in the family life cycle, such as the "families with young children" phase, it can prolong this period. At worst, the family can become permanently stuck at that phase and enmeshed. When the inward pull of the illness and the phase of the life cycle coincide, there is a risk that they will amplify one another. In families that functioned marginally before an illness began, this kind of mutual reinforcement can trigger a runaway process leading to overt family dysfunction. This is particularly common with childhood-onset conditions (Weihs et al., 2002).

When a parent develops a chronic disease during the child-rearing phase, the family's ability to stay on course is most severely taxed. For more serious, debilitating conditions, the impact of the illness is like the addition of a new member, one with special needs that will compete with those of the real children for potentially scarce family resources. In psychosocially milder health problems, efficient reallocation of roles may suffice. A recent case of a family at the "family with young children" phase illustrates this point.

Scott and his wife Molly presented for treatment 6 months after Scott had sustained a severe burn injury that required skin grafting on both hands. A year of recuperation was necessary before Scott would be able to return to his job, which required physical labor and full use of his hands. Before this injury, Molly had been at home full time raising their two children, ages 3 and 5. In this case, although Scott was temporarily handicapped in terms of his career, he was physically fit to assume the role of househusband. Initially, both Scott and Molly remained at home, using his disability income to get by. When Molly expressed an interest in finding a job to lessen financial pressures, Scott resisted, and manageable marital strain caused by his injury flared into dysfunctional conflict.

Sufficient resources were available in the system to accommodate the illness and ongoing child-rearing tasks. Their definition of marriage lacked the necessary role flexibility to master the problem. Treatment focused on rethinking his masculine and monolithic definition of "family provider," a definition that had, in fact, emerged in full force during this phase of the family life cycle.

If the disease affecting a parent is severely debilitating (e.g., traumatic brain injury, cervical spinal cord injury), its impact on the child-rearing family is twofold: A "new" family member is added as a parent is "lost," analogous to becoming a single-parent family with an added special needs child. In acute-onset illnesses, both events can be simultaneous, in which case family resources may be inadequate to meet the combined child-rearing and caregiving demands. In this situation, families commonly turn to other children and extended kin to share responsibilities. This can become maladaptive for children to the extent to which they sacrifice their own developmental needs or a developmental detour for grandparents who must relinquish newly achieved freedom from parenting to resume child care. Yet we need to be cautious not to pathologize structural changes that may be necessary, for instance, in a single-parent household or may be culturally normative expressions of loyalty in some ethnic groups.

If we look at chronic diseases in a more refined way through the lens of the illness typology and time phases, it is apparent that the family inward pull increases with the level of disability or risk of death. With progressive diseases, the continuous addition of new caregiving demands keeps a family's energy focused inward on the illness. In contrast, after a family develops a functional adaptation, a constant-course disease (excluding those with severe disability) permits a family greater flexibility to enter or resume life cycle planning. As the following case in the postlaunching phase illustrates, the added inward pull exerted by a progressive disease increases the risk of reversing normal family disengagement or freezing a family into a permanently fused state.

Mr. L., a 54-year-old African American, had become increasingly depressed as a result of severe and progressive complications of his adult-onset diabetes over the past 5 years, including a leg amputation and renal failure that had recently required instituting home dialysis. For 20 years, Mr. L. had had an uncomplicated constant course, allowing him to lead a full, active life. He was an excellent athlete and engaged in a number of recreational group sports. Short- and long-term family planning had never focused on his illness. This optimistic attitude was reinforced by the fact that two people in Mrs. L.'s family of origin had had diabetes without complications. Their only child, a son (age 26), had uneventfully left home after high school and had recently married. Mr. and Mrs. L. had a stable marriage, in which both maintained many outside independent interests. In short, the family had moved smoothly into the postlaunching phase of the life cycle.

Mr. L.'s disease transformation to a progressive phase, coupled with the disabling and life-shortening nature of his complications, had reversed the normal postlaunching process for all family members. His advancing illness required his wife to take a second job, which necessitated giving up her many involvements with their church. Their son and his wife moved back home to help his mother take care of his father and the house. Mr. L., unable to work and deprived of his athletic social network, was isolated at home and spent his days watching television. He felt that he was a burden to everyone, was blocked in his own midlife development and future plans with his wife, and foresaw a future filled only with suffering.

The goal of family treatment centered on reversing some of the system's overreaction. For Mr. L., this meant both coming to terms with his losses and fears of suffering and death and identifying the abilities and possibilities that were still available to him. This involved reworking his life structure to accommodate his real limitations while maximizing his chances of remaining independent. For instance, although Mr. L could no longer participate on the playing field, he could remain involved in sports through coaching. For Mrs. L. and her son, this meant developing realistic expectations for Mr. L. that reestablished him as an active family member with a share of family responsibilities. This helped the mother and son to resume key aspects of their autonomy within an illness-family system.

Relapsing illnesses alternate between periods of drawing a family inward and periods of release from the immediate demands of disease. However, the on-call state of preparedness that many such illnesses require keeps some part of the family in a higher cohesion mode despite medically asymptomatic periods. Again, this may impede the natural flow of phases in the family life cycle.

One can think about illness time phases as moving from a crisis phase requiring intensified cohesion to a chronic phase often demanding less cohesion. A terminal phase forces most families back into being more inwardly focused and cohesive. In other words, the "illness life structure" that a family develops to accommodate each phase in the illness is influenced by the differing needs for cohesion dictated by each time phase. For example, in a family in which the onset of the illness has coincided with a postlaunching phase of development, the transition to the chronic phase permits a family to resume more of its momentum.

Life Cycle Transition Periods

Clinicians need to be mindful of the timing of illness-onset in relation to family and individual transitions. A diagnosis may force the family into a transition in which one of the family's main tasks is to accommodate the anticipation of further loss and possibly untimely death. When disease-onset coincides with an individual or family developmental transition, issues related to previous, current, and anticipated loss will often be magnified. Transition periods are often characterized by upheaval; rethinking of previous and future commitments; and openness to change. This poses a risk that the illness may become unnecessarily embedded or inappropriately ignored in plans for the next developmental phase. This can be a major precursor of family maladaptation. By adopting a longitudinal perspective, a clinician can stay attuned to future transitions, particularly overlaps in those of the illness, individual, and family development. Offering prevention-oriented family consultations at major transitions is very useful. The following example highlights this point.

In one Latino family, the father, a carpenter and primary financial provider, had a mild heart attack. He also suffered from emphysema. At first, his level of impairment was mild and stabilized. This allowed him to continue part-time work. Because their children were all teenagers, his wife was able to undertake part-time work to help maintain financial stability. The oldest son, age 15, seemed relatively unaffected. Two years later, the father experienced a second, more life-threatening heart attack and became totally disabled. His son, now 17, had dreams of going away to college. The specter of financial hardship and the perceived need for a "man in the family" created a serious dilemma of choice for the son and the family. This was additionally complicated for this family that had worked hard to move out of the housing projects and ensure that the children could get a good education for a better future.

This vignette demonstrates the potential collision between simultaneous transition periods: the illness transition to a more incapacitating and progressive course, the adolescent son's transition to early adulthood, and the family's transition from the "living with teenagers" to "launching young adults" phase. This example also illustrates the significance of the type of illness. An illness that was relapsing or less life-threatening and incapacitating (in contrast to one with a progressive or constant course) might have interfered less with this young man's individuation. If his father had an intermittently incapacitating illness, such as disc disease, the son might have moved out but tailored his choices to remain nearby and thus be available during acute flare-ups.

It is essential to situate these developmental issues in the context of cultural values, socioeconomic considerations, availability of family or community resources, and access to health care. In some cultures, such as this example of a Latino family, a strong emphasis on loyalty to family would normatively take priority over individual goals. This is especially true with a major illness or disability in the family. Also, the availability or lack of community resources and health care benefits can severely limit realistic family adaptation options. It is crucial for a clinician to be aware of his/her own cultural values about the relative balance between family loyalty and pursuit of individual life goals (here in the context of illness) and its relationship to those of the client family.

Life Structure-Maintaining Periods

Illness onset that coincides with a life structure-building/stable period in family or individual development presents a different challenge. These periods are characterized by the living out of choices that were made during the preceding transition period. Relative to transition periods, the cohesive bonds of the family and individual members are oriented to protect the family unit's and their own current life structures. Milder conditions (nonfatal, only mildly disabling) may require some life structure revision but not a radical restructuring that would necessitate a shift to a transitional phase of development. A severe condition will force families into a more complete developmental transition at a time when individual and family inertia is geared to preserve the momentum of a stable period. To successfully navigate this kind of crisis, family adaptability requires the ability to transform their entire life structure to a prolonged transitional state. For instance, in the previous example, the father's heart disease rapidly progressed while the oldest son was in a transition period in his own development. The nature of the strain in developmental terms would be quite different if his father's disease progression had occurred when this young man was 26, had already left home, had finished college and secured a first job, and had married and had his first child. In the latter scenario, the oldest son's life structure would be in an inwardly focused, highly cohesive, "families with young children" phase of the life cycle. Fully accommodating the needs of his family of origin could require a monumental shift of his developmental priorities, creating a potential crisis regarding his loyalty to his family of origin and his new nuclear family. When this illness crisis coincided with a developmental transition period (age 17), having made no permanent commitments, he might have felt very threatened about losing his status as a "single young adult" to a caregiving role that could become his life structure. Later, in his mid-20s, he would have made developmental choices and would have been in the process of living them out. Not only would he have made commitments, but also they would be more highly cohesive in nature, focused on his newly formed family. To serve the demands of an illness transition, the son might have needed to shift his previously stable life structure back to a transitional state. The shift would have happened out of phase with the flow of his individual and nuclear family's development. One complex way to resolve this dilemma of divided loyalties might be the merging of the two households.

This discussion raises several key clinical points. From a systems viewpoint, at the time of diagnosis, it is important to know the phase of the family life cycle and the phase of individual development of all family members, not just the ill member. Illness and disability in one family member can profoundly affect the developmental goals of another member. For instance, disability in an infant can be a serious roadblock to a mother's mastery of child-rearing, and a life-threatening illness in a married young adult can interfere with the well spouse's readiness to become a parent. Also, family members frequently do not adapt equally well to chronic illness. Each family member's ability to adapt and the rate at which he or she does so are directly related to the individual's own developmental phase and role in the family.

The timing of chronic illness in the life cycle can be normative or "off-time." Coping with chronic illness and death are considered normally anticipated tasks in late adulthood, whereas their occurrence earlier is out of phase and tends to be developmentally more disruptive (Neugarten, 1976). As untimely events, chronic diseases can severely disrupt the usual sense of continuity and rhythm of the life cycle. Chronic diseases that occur in the child-rearing period can be most devastating because of their potential impact on family financial and child-rearing responsibilities.

The notion of "out-of-phase" illnesses can be conceptualized in a more refined way that highlights patterns of strain over time. First, because diseases exert an inward pull on most families, they can be more developmentally disruptive to families in the "families with adolescents" or "launching children" phases of development. Second, the period of transition generated by the onset of a serious illness is particularly "out of phase" if it coincides with a stable, life structure-maintaining period in individual or family development. Third, if the particular illness is progressive, relapsing, increasingly incapacitating, and/or life-threatening, then the unfolding phases of the disease will be punctuated by numerous transitions. Under these conditions, a family will need to more frequently alter their life structure to accommodate shifting and increasing demands of the disease. This level of demand and uncertainty keeps the illness in the forefront of a family's consciousness, constantly impinging upon their attempts to get back in phase developmentally. Finally, the transition from the crisis to the chronic phase of the illness is often the key juncture at which the intensity of the family's socialization to living with chronic disease can be relaxed. In this sense, it offers a window of opportunity for the family to recover its developmental course.

Confronted by illness and disability, a family should aim, above all, to minimize family members' sacrifice of their own or the family's development as a system. It is important to determine whose life plans may be canceled, postponed, or altered and when plans put on hold and future developmental issues will be addressed. Families can be helped to strike a healthier balance with life plans as a way to minimize overall family strain and relationship skews between caregivers and the ill member. Clinicians can assist families to resolve feelings of guilt, over-responsibility, and hopelessness and to find family and external resources to enhance freedom both to pursue their own goals and to provide needed care for the ill member.

Early in the illness experience, families have particular difficulty appraising the need for temporary detours or permanent changes in life cycle plans. Once developmental plans are derailed, the inherent inertia of chronic conditions makes it more difficult to find one's original path. This underscores the importance of timely prevention-oriented psychoeducation for families. Also, the process by which life cycle decisions are reached is particularly important. Significant factors include gender-based or culturally defined beliefs about who should assume primary responsibility for caregiving. Cultures and families are quite diverse in their expectations about the relative priority of sacrifice for the family in time of need versus protecting personal goals and plans. A forward-thinking clinical philosophy that uses a developmental perspective as a way of gaining a positive sense of control and opportunity is vital for families dealing with chronic disorders.

Multigenerational Experiences With Illness, Loss, and Crisis

A family's current behavior, and therefore its response to illness, cannot be adequately comprehended apart from its history (Boszormenyi-Nagy, 1987; Bowen, 1978; Byng-Hall, 1995; Framo, 1992; Walsh & McGoldrick, 2004). This is particularly germane to families that face a chronic condition. A historical inquiry may help to explain and predict the family's current style of coping and adaptation and the creation of meaning about an illness. A multigenerational assessment helps to clarify areas of strength and vulnerability and identifies high-risk families who, burdened by unresolved issues and dysfunctional patterns transmitted across time, cannot absorb the challenges presented by a serious condition.

A chronic illness-oriented genogram focuses on how a family organized itself and adapted as an evolving system around previous illnesses and unexpected crises in the current and previous generations. Patterns of coping, replications, discontinuities, shifts in relationships (i.e., alliances, triangles, cut offs), and sense of competence are noted (McGoldrick, Gerson, & Petry, 2007). These patterns are transmitted across generations as family myths, taboos, catastrophic expectations, and belief systems (Seaburn, Lorenz, & Kaplan, 1992; Walsh & McGoldrick, 2004). A central goal is to bring to light areas of consensus and learned differences that are sources of resilience and conflict. Also, it is useful to inquire about other forms of loss (e.g., divorce, migration), crisis (e.g., lengthy unemployment; rape; a natural disaster, such as Hurricane Katrina), and protracted adversity (e.g., poverty, racism, war, political oppression). These experiences can provide sources of resilience and effective coping skills in the face of a serious health problem (Walsh, 2006).

Because ethnicity, race, and religion strongly influence how families approach health and illness, any multigenerational assessment should include inquiry into these areas (McGoldrick, Giordano, & Garcia Preto, 2005). As professionals, we need to be mindful of the cultural differences among the patient, the family, and ourselves. The different ethnic backgrounds of the adults in a family or among a family, professionals, and systems of health care may be primary reasons for discrepancies in beliefs that emerge at the time of a major illness. This is especially common for minority groups (e.g., African American, Asian, and Latino) that experience discrimination or marginalization from our prevailing White Anglo culture. Significant ethnic differences, particularly health beliefs, typically emerge in such areas as

1. beliefs about control,
2. the definition of the appropriate "sick role",
3. the kind and degree of openness in communication about the disease,
4. who should be included in the illness caretaking system (e.g., extended family, friends, professionals),
5. who the primary caretaker is (almost always women),
6. the kind of rituals that are viewed as normative at different phases of an illness (e.g., hospital bedside vigils, healing and funeral rituals) (Imber-Black, 2004).

Health and mental health professionals should become familiar with the belief systems of various ethnic, racial, and religious groups in their community, particularly as these translate into different behavior patterns during illness. For example, traditional Navajo culture holds that thought and language have the power to shape reality and control events (Carrese & Rhodes, 1995), that language can determine reality. From the Navajo worldview, discussing the potential complications of a serious illness with a newly diagnosed Navajo patient is harmful and strongly increases the likelihood that such complications will occur. This belief system clashes dramatically with those of health professionals (backed by powerful legal imperatives) that mandate explaining possible complications or promoting advance directives regarding the limits of medical care desired by the ill family member. Carrese and Rhodes, in their study of Navajo, give one example of a Navajo daughter describing how the risks of bypass surgery were explained to her father: "The surgeon told him that he may not wake up, that this is the risk of every surgery. For the surgeon it was very routine, but the way that my Dad received it, it was almost like a death sentence, and he never consented to the surgery" (p. 828).

Illness type and time phase issues

The illness type and time phases framework helps focus the clinician's multigenerational evaluation. Whereas a family may have certain standard ways of coping with any illness, there may be critical differences in their style and success in adaptation to different types of disorders. It is important to track prior family illnesses for sources of resilience and competence as well as areas of perceived failures or inexperience. A family may disregard the differences in demands related to different kinds of illnesses and thus may show a disparity in their level of coping with one disease versus another. Inquiry about experiences with different types of illness (e.g., life threatening versus non–life threatening) may find, for instance, that a family dealt successfully with non–life-threatening illnesses but reeled under the weight of the mother's metastatic breast cancer. Such a family might be well-equipped to deal with less severe conditions but may be particularly vulnerable to the occurrence of another life-threatening illness. Another family may have experienced only non-life-threatening illnesses and need psychoeducation to successfully cope with the uncertainties peculiar to life-threatening conditions. The following case consultation highlights the importance of family history in uncovering areas of inexperience.

Joe and his wife Ann, both of British-Scottish ancestry, and their three teenage children presented for a family evaluation 10 months after Joe's diagnosis with moderate-severe asthma. Joe (age 44) had been successfully employed for many years as a spray painter. Apparently, exposure to a new chemical in the paint triggered the onset of asthmatic attacks, which necessitated hospitalization and job disability. Initially, his physician told him that improvement would occur but remained noncommittal as to the level of chronicity. Although somewhat improved, Joe continued to have persistent and moderate respiratory symptoms. His continued breathing difficulties contributed to a depression, uncharacteristic angry outbursts, alcohol abuse, and family discord.

During the initial assessment, I inquired about the family's prior experience coping with chronic disease. This was the nuclear family's first encounter with chronic illness. In their families of origin, they had limited experience. Ann's father had died 7 years earlier of a sudden and unexpected heart attack. Joe's brother had died in an accidental drowning. Neither had had experience with disease as an ongoing process. Joe had assumed that improvement meant cure. Illness for both had meant either death or recovery. The physician and family system were not attuned to the hidden risks for this family going through the transition from the crisis to chronic phase of his asthma—the juncture at which the permanency of the disease needed to be addressed.

Another crucial issue was the onset of the father's disability during their children's adolescence and the looming launching phase of the family life cycle. In these situations, adolescents may become symptomatic (e.g., exhibiting acting-out behavior, school problems, or drug use) as a way of coping with their fears of loss of their father or con-

flicts about moving ahead with personal goals if family loyalty expectations require them to assume caregiving roles.

Tracking a family's coping capabilities in the crisis, chronic, and terminal phases of previous chronic illnesses can highlight both legacies of resilience and a history of difficulties at a specific time phase, which can alert a clinician to potentially vulnerable periods for a family with the current illness. A family that was seen in treatment illustrates the interplay of problems coping with a current illness that are fueled by unresolved issues related to disease experiences in one's family of origin. The type of illness and unresolved complications in the terminal phase are critical features of the following case.

Angela, her husband Bill, and their 8-year-old son Mark, an Italian Catholic, working-class family, presented for treatment 4 months after Angela had been injured in a life-threatening head-on auto collision. The driver of the other vehicle was at fault. Angela had sustained a serious concussion. Initially, the medical team was concerned that she might have suffered a cerebral hemorrhage. Ultimately, it was determined that this had not occurred. Over this time, Angela became increasingly depressed and, despite strong reassurance, continued to believe that she had a life-threatening condition and would die from a brain hemorrhage.

During the initial consultation, she revealed that she was experiencing vivid dreams of meeting her deceased father. Her father, with whom she had been extremely close, had died from a cerebral hemorrhage after a 4-year history of a progressive debilitating brain tumor. His illness had been marked by progressive and uncontrolled epileptic seizures. Angela was 14 at the time and was the "baby" in the family, her two siblings being more than 10 years her senior. The family had shielded her from his illness, culminating in her mother deciding to not have Angela attend either the wake or the funeral of her father. This event galvanized her position as the child in need of protection—a dynamic that carried over into her marriage. Despite her hurt, anger, and lack of acceptance of her father's death, she had avoided dealing with her feelings with her mother for over 20 years.

Other family history revealed that Angela's mother's brother had died from a sudden stroke, and her maternal grandfather had died of a stroke when her mother was 7 years old. Her mother had experienced an open casket wake for 3 days at home.

In this situation, Angela's own life-threatening head injury triggered a catastrophic reaction and dramatic resurfacing of previous unresolved traumatic losses involving similar types of illness and injury. In particular, her father's, uncle's, and grandfather's deaths by central nervous system disorders had sensitized her to this type of problem. The fact that she had witnessed the slow, agonizing, and terrifying downhill course of her father only heightened her catastrophic fears.

Therapy focused on a series of tasks that included Angela's initiating a series of conversations with her mother about her feelings of having been excluded from her father's funeral and about the pattern of mutual protection between mother and daughter over the years. Then, Angela wrote a good-bye letter to her father, experiencing the grief that she had bypassed for so many years. It was particularly important to include her husband throughout this phase of treatment because her grief directly stimulated his own anxiety about the looming loss of his own aging parents. The final phase of treatment involved a graveside ritual in which Angela, with her family of origin and nuclear family present, read her good-bye letter to her father.

Replication of system patterns

For any major health condition in an involved adult's family of origin, a clinician should try to get a picture of how the family organized itself to handle condition-related emotional and practical tasks. It is important for a clinician to find out what role each played in handling these tasks. Whether the parents (as children) were given too much responsibility (parentified) or were shielded from involvement is particularly important. What did they learn from those experiences that influences how they think about the current illness? Whether they emerge with a strong sense of competence or failure is essential information. By collecting the above information about each adult's family of origin, one can anticipate areas of conflict and consensus.

Evaluation of the system that existed and evolved around a prior illness includes assessment of the pattern of relationships within that system. In many families, relationship patterns are adaptive, flexible, and cohesively balanced. In other families, these relationships can be dysfunctionally skewed, rigid, enmeshed, disengaged, and/or triangulated. As Penn (1983) described, unresolved issues related to illness and loss frequently remain dormant and suddenly reemerge triggered by a chronic illness in the current nuclear family. Particular coalitions that emerge in the context of a chronic illness can be isomorphs of those that existed in each adult's family of origin. The following case is an example.

Mr. and Mrs. S. had been married for 9 years when their 6-year-old son Jeff developed Type 1 diabetes. Mrs. S. became very protective of her son and made frequent calls to their pediatrician expressing persistent concerns about Jeff's condition. This occurred despite Jeff's doing well medically and emotionally and frequent reassurances from the physician. At the same time, the previously close marital relationship became more distant, characterized by Mrs. S. arguing with her husband and Mr. S. actively distancing himself from his wife and son.

Mrs. S. had grown up with a tyrannical, alcoholic father. She had witnessed intense conflict between her parents. During her childhood and adolescence, Mrs. S. had tried to "rescue" her mother. To counterbalance her victimized mother, she tried to tend to her mother's needs and cheer her up. She talked frequently to her family physician about the situation at home. However, she felt that she had failed at this, since her mother continued over the years to be stuck and depressed.

Mr. S. grew up in a family in which his father had disabling heart disease. His mother devoted a great deal of time to taking care of his father. Not to further burden his parents, he raised himself, maintaining distance from the primary caretaking relationship between his parents. He stoically viewed this strategy as having been successful. He supported his mother's caregiving efforts by mostly taking care of his own needs.

With their son's illness, Mrs. S., burdened by feelings of guilt at being a failed rescuer, had a second chance to "do it right" and assuage her guilt. The diabetes gave her this opportunity, and it is a culturally sanctioned normative role for a parent, particularly a mother, to protect an ill child. These factors, her unresolved family of origin issues, and the culturally sanctioned roles promoted the enmeshment that developed with her son.

In this situation, Mr. S., though outwardly objecting to the coalition between his wife and son, honored that relationship, as if it would make up for the one he forfeited with his own mother. Further, despite his unmet needs as a child, he believed that the structure, and his role in it, had worked. Both Mr. and Mrs. S. replicated their particular positions in triangles from their families of origin. In a complementary way, Mrs. S. was a rescuer in a coalition and Mr. S. was in the distant position in the triangle they create with their son.

The roles of each person in this triangle fit traditional cultural norms. The mother was appropriately concerned and tending to her ill child. The father was in the more distant instrumental provider position. For this reason, it can be more difficult for a clinician to ferret out a traditional pattern from the beginnings of a dysfunctional reenactment of family of origin patterns developed around prior experiences with illness, crisis, or loss. Early assessment of multigenerational patterns such as these helps to distinguish normative from problematic responses. Further, it helps to identify the source and degree of commitment to gender-defined caregiving roles. Particularly in crisis situations such as illness onset, couples may fall back on traditional divisions of labor. The climate of fear and uncertainty itself is a powerful stimulus to seek the familiar, time-tested methods of coping. This is reinforced if traditional gender-defined roles worked well in prior illness or crisis situations. Or, as this case highlights, a sense of failure around a gender-based role can act as a powerful push toward reenactment in the current situation. In this case, Mrs. S. was driven to reenact the role of emotional rescuer, a typically female role that she felt she had failed with her mother in relation to her father's chronic alcoholism. Psychoeducational guidelines can help her to distinguish what forms and degree of responsiveness are appropriate from those that are excessive and unhelpful. Also, tasks for the husband and couple jointly would be useful to increase a more balanced, shared involvement in the burdens of a chronically ill child. This would counteract the peripheral position of the father.

In this case, early referral by the pediatrician was essential to prevent entrenchment of a long-term dysfunctional relationship pattern. At this early stage, the parents were able to reflect upon the situation, recognize the connection to family of origin issues, and disengage from a destructive path. If these kinds of cases are not detected early, they typically progress over a period of years to highly enmeshed intractable systems. Morbidity is high and may be expressed in a poor medical course and adherence issues, divorce, or child and adolescent behavioral problems. Reenactment of previous system configurations around an illness can occur largely as an unconscious, automatic process (Byng-Hall, 1995). Further, the dysfunctional complementarity that one sees in these families can emerge specifically within the context of a chronic disease. On detailed inquiry, couples will frequently reveal a tacit unspoken understanding that if an illness occurs they will reorganize to reenact unfinished business from their families of origin. Typically, the roles that are chosen represent a repetition or reactive opposite of roles that they or the same-sex parent in their family of origin played. This process resembles the unfolding of a genetic template that is activated only under particular biological conditions. It highlights the need for a clinician to distinguish between what constitutes functional family process with and without illness or disability. For families that present in this manner, placing a primary therapeutic emphasis on the resolution of family of origin issues might be the best approach to prevent or rectify an unhealthy triangle.

Distinct from families with dormant, encapsulated illness "time bombs" are those in which illnesses become imbedded within a web of pervasive and longstanding dysfunctional patterns. In this situation, clinicians may collude with a family's resistance to addressing preexisting problems by focusing excessively on the disease itself. If this occurs, a clinician becomes involved in a detouring triangle with the family and the patient, analogous to the dysfunctional triangles formed by parents with an ill child as a way to avert unresolved marital issues (Minuchin et al., 1978). When a chronic condition reinforces preexisting family dysfunction, the differences between the family's illness and non-illness patterns are less distinct. In the traditional sense of the term "psychosomatic," this kind of family displays a greater level of baseline reactivity; when an illness enters its system, this reactivity can get expressed somatically through a poor medical course and/or treatment adherence (Griffith & Griffith, 1994). Such families lack the foundation of a functional non-illness system that can serve as the metaphorical equivalent of a healthy ego in tackling family of origin patterns around disease. The initial focus of therapeutic intervention may need to be targeted more at current nuclear family processes than at multigenerational patterns.

Many families facing chronic conditions have not had dysfunctional multigenerational patterns of adaptation. Yet any family may falter in the face of multiple disease and nondisease stressors that affect it in a relatively short time. With progressive, incapacitating diseases or the concurrence of illnesses in several family members (e.g., families with aging parents), a pragmatic approach that expands the use of resources outside the family is most productive.

Life Cycle Coincidences Across Generations

A coincidence of dates across generations is often significant. We often hear statements such as "All the men in my family died of heart attacks by the age of 55." This is a multigenerational statement of biological vulnerability and a legacy and expectation of untimely death. In one case, a man who was vulnerable to stomach ulcers began to eat indiscriminately and drink alcohol excessively, despite medical warnings, when he reached the age of 43, precipitating a crisis requiring surgery. His failure to comply with treatment created a life-threatening situation. It was only after his recovery and upon his 44th birthday that he remarked that his own father had died tragically at age 43, and he had felt an overpowering conflict about surviving past that age.

Knowledge of such age-related multigenerational patterns can alert a clinician to risks of undiagnosable pain syndromes and somatization, adherence issues, blatantly self-destructive behaviors, and realistic fears that may emerge at the time of an illness diagnosis or a particular life cycle phase of the ill person or a family member. A brief intervention timed with an approaching multigenerational anniversary date is very useful preventively in this type of situation.

The New Era of Genetics

With the mapping of the human genome, there is burgeoning scientific knowledge that is rapidly increasing our understanding of the mechanisms, treatment, and prevention of disease. This has brought increased awareness that almost all diseases and conditions have a genetic component, not only in the cause of disease, but also disease susceptibility and resistance, prognosis and progression, and responses to illness and its treatments. The impact on the family system is enormous as members move through stages of information processing, decision making, and management of genetic conditions and genomic information over the life course (Miller, McDaniel, Rolland, Feetham, 2006).

The emerging field of genomic health presents new challenges for living with uncertainty and threatened loss (Rolland, 2006). Acquiring and living with genetic information and possible or likely future loss will increasingly become part of the fabric of our personal and family's lives. It will expand the meaning of health risk to include not only our nuclear but also our extended families, as well as future generations. And, it will increasingly impact present and future life cycle planning.

As with actual chronic disease, coping and adaptation to genetic risk information is an ongoing process that evolves over the life cycle. Clinicians can help family members become attuned to the ongoing interplay of genetic testing and risk information with individual and family development. Four key biological characteristics can guide such discussions: 1) likelihood of development of a condition based on genetic mutations; 2) expected clinical severity; 3) timing of expected onset in the life cycle; and 4) whether there exist effective treatments or preventive life-style options to modify symptom-onset and/or clinical progression (Rolland & Williams, 2005).

We can orient families to the value of prevention-oriented consultations at key future life cycle transitions, when the experience of genetic risk will likely be heightened. Concerns about loss may surface that family members had postponed or thought were "worked through." It is vital to prepare family members for the possibility that concerns about genetic risk and decisions about whether to pursue genetic-testing may be more activated with upcoming transitions, such as: 1) launching young adults, 2) marriage and partner commitments,

3) planning to have children, 4) relocation or retirement, and 5) divorce or remarriage. Also, such feelings can be reactivated by critical events such as genetic testing of another family member; diagnosis of any serious illness in immediate or extended families or friends; or death of a loved one. Clinicians can help family members decide about circumstances when further family discussion would be helpful, who would be appropriate to include, and how to discuss genetic risk with children or adolescents.

Conclusion

This chapter offers a conceptual base for thinking about the system created at the interface of chronic illness with the family and individual life cycles. A psychosocial typology and time phases of illness framework facilitate a common language for bridging the worlds of illness, individual, and family development. This developmental landscape is marked by periods of transition, periods of living out decisions and commitments, and periods of child-rearing and non–child-rearing. What emerges is the notion of three intertwined lines of development in which there is continual interplay of life structures to carry out individual, family, and illness phase-specific developmental tasks. Families' multigenerational paradigms related to chronic disease, crisis, and loss play upon these three interwoven developmental threads, adding their own texture and pattern.

Chapter 24

Alcohol Problems and the Life Cycle

Tracey A. Laszloffy

Classical views of alcoholism focus on the individual who is the drinker with less attention focused on the family life cycle context that alcoholism is always situated within. O'Farrell (1989) pointed out the myopia of this view by explaining that alcoholism impacts at least four persons in addition to the drinker. In all likelihood, this assessment is seriously underestimated because alcoholism affects family members well beyond the nuclear unit and across many generations. To assume a well-rounded approach to understanding and treating alcoholism it is necessary to employ a family systems perspective that illuminates how the addiction shapes the structure and functioning of families through the life cycle and how families shape the development and maintenance of the addiction (Steinglass, Bennett, Wolin, & Reiss, 1987). This chapter assumes that the best way to understand and address alcoholism clinically is by employing a family systems perspective that focuses on how life cycle issues and sociocultural factors shape the onset, evolution, effects, and efforts to treat this addiction.

Definitions of Alcoholism

Alcoholism, like other addictions, is difficult to define. A common misconception is that the quantity a person consumes determines whether she or he is an alcoholic. However, the quantity, regularity, and frequency of consumption culminating in alcoholism vary greatly from person to person. Mental health and substance abuse organizations tend to make a distinction between alcohol abuse and alcohol dependence. According to the DSM-IV, abuse involves repeated use despite recurrent adverse consequences, while dependence involves abuse combined with tolerance, withdrawal, and an uncontrollable drive to drink (American Psychiatric Association, 1994).

George Vaillant (1983) defined alcoholism as the point in a subject's life when he earned at least four points on the PDS (Problem Drinking Scale), and it ended when he spent a full year without any evidence of alcohol-related problems. His landmark longitudinal study is one of the best sources of data about how problem drinking changes over a lifetime. In spite of the limitation that most of his subjects were White males, Vaillant's work provides a unique view of alcoholism as a biopsychosocial condition that evolves over the course of the family life cycle and within a broader social context.

Steinglass, Wolin, Bennett, and Reiss (1987) expanded the definition of alcoholism to include the relationship between an individual drinker and her/his family system. They explained alcoholism as a systemic phenomenon, not just an individual one. However, they did draw a critical distinction between families that have an alcoholic member and alcoholic families where life is organized around alcohol. "Alcoholism becomes an inseparable component of the fabric of family life because their lives are organized around alcoholism, these families share unique developmental histories" (p. 9).

In this chapter, we define alcoholism as the persistent and excessive use of alcohol that results in physiological, psychological, and/or social impairment over the course of the life cycle (Vandenbos, 2007), and this behavior shapes and is shaped by family dynamics. Additionally, we refer to families with alcohol problems versus alcoholic families recognizing that the latter refers only to those systems where the structure and function of the family is organized around alcohol.

Scope of the Problem

In the United States, 17.6 million people abuse alcohol or qualify as alcohol dependent each year. Men have higher rates of alcoholism than women, although rates among women have increased over the last 30 years. Young adults between the ages of 18 and 29 have the highest rate of alcohol problems, while adults who are age 65 and older have the lowest. With respect to race and ethnicity, Whites have the highest rates of alcohol abuse in comparison to all other racial/ethnic groups. In terms of alcohol dependence, Native Americans have the highest rates, followed by Hispanics and then Whites. Mexican Americans have higher rates of alcoholism in comparison to other Hispanic groups, and acculturation to the United States is correlated with a rise in alcohol abuse. Puerto Ricans have higher rates of cocaine dependence (National Institute of Alcohol Abuse and Alcoholism, 2002, 2005). While rates of alcohol dependence are the lowest among Blacks and Asian Americans, problem drinking among Asian Americans is on the rise especially among Asian American women aged 18 to 29 (Johnston, O'Malley, & Bachman, 2001).

Risk Factors/Vulnerabilities

No single factor or known cluster of factor causes alcoholism. However, a variety of factors are correlated with an increased risk of developing alcohol abuse and/or dependence.

Biology and genetics

There is much controversy over the role that biology plays in the onset and progression of alcoholism. Relatively recent research has implicated a gene (D2 dopamine receptor gene) that, when inherited in a specific form, might increase a person's chance of developing alcoholism. Studies, including those conducted with adopted children and twins, demonstrate that children of alcoholics, especially males, are four times more likely to develop alcoholism than the general population (National Institute of Alcohol Abuse and Alcoholism, 2005), lending support to the genetic component of alcoholism. Yet, this figure should be interpreted cautiously because

it is difficult to discern how much of this correlation reflects biology and how much reflects the psychosocial effects of growing up in a family environment with a parent who displays negative alcoholic behaviors. For example, alcoholic parents are more likely to be separated from their children, and father absence in particular is correlated with the onset of alcoholism among adolescents, males in particular (Hoffmann, 2002).

A longitudinal study conducted at the University of California at San Diego demonstrated that men who had a high resistance to alcohol at age 20 were 2 to 3 times more likely to be alcoholic by age 30 or 40 in comparison to those who exhibited a low resistance to the effects of alcohol. This finding held up even when researchers controlled for factors such as family history, age of drinking onset, and the amount consumed. Investigators explained that resistance (or lack thereof) to the effects of alcohol is a hard-wired trait that affects the risk of alcoholism (Seppa, 2009).

Family of origin

Growing up in households characterized by a lack of parental support and monitoring, inconsistent and/or harsh discipline, and parental hostility or rejection also is associated with onset of alcoholism (Conger, 1994). Moreover, a history of physical or sexual abuse during childhood is a risk factor for developing alcoholism, especially for girls. In one study, 72 percent of women and 27 percent of men with substance abuse disorders reported physical or sexual abuse or both as children (Clark & Bukstein, 1998). Hence, it is always crucial when conducting a clinical assessment to explore family of origin experience with substance abuse and addiction to understand the potential influence of historical family patterns on the present.

Age

Age is a risk factor in several ways. First, the younger a person is when s/he begins drinking (e.g., age 14 or younger) the higher the risk of developing alcohol problems later in life compared to those who begin drinking at age 21 or after (Grant, Dawson, Stinson, Chou, Dufour, & Pickering, 2004). Second, the process of aging increases the risk of alcoholism. As people grow older alcohol affects their bodies with greater potency. Those who maintain the same drinking patterns they had at an earlier time in their lives are at increased risk of unwittingly developing alcohol dependency later in life. It takes fewer drinks to become intoxicated and older organs can be damaged by smaller amounts of alcohol (Thomas & Rockwood, 2001). Moreover, up to one half of the 100 most prescribed drugs for older people, especially those used for arthritis and pain management, react adversely with alcohol.

Attitudes and beliefs about alcohol

Personal, familial, and/or cultural beliefs that sanction the use of alcohol are a risk factor for alcoholism. Among adolescents in particular, peer acceptance of drinking and pressure to drink increase the probability of binge drinking, and teens and young adults who binge drink regularly are at a high risk of developing alcoholism (Hawkins & Fitzgibbons, 1993). Borsari and Carey (2001) reported that the influence peers exert over the decision to drink and the amount consumed is tied to the phenomenon of perceived social norms—or the belief that "everyone" is drinking, and drinking is acceptable.

Rates of alcoholism are also correlated with the extent to which specific ethnic and/or religious groups sanction or prohibit alcohol use. For example, Mormons, Orthodox Jews, and Muslims who have strong prohibitions against the use of alcohol manifest very low rates of alcoholism. The power such groups exert is observed by the fact that when members leave the group, their susceptibility to alcoholism increases exponentially.

Within various ethnic groups beliefs about the role that alcohol serves and attitudes toward consumption are strongly correlated with rates of alcoholism. For example Southern European and Mediterranean ethnic groups (e.g., Spanish, French, Portuguese, Italian, Greek) tend to have low rates of problem drinking. Attitudes and behaviors are such that children are introduced to alcohol as part of their regular family life and learn to drink moderate amounts while still young. Alcohol is commonly drunk with meals and is considered a natural and normal beverage. Drinking alcohol in moderation is encouraged, and abuse is met with disapproval. People drink for sociability rather than a means to achieve intoxication and there are no mixed feelings or uncertainties about alcohol (Hanson, 1995). While such groups may have high rates of alcohol-related diseases, such as cirrhosis of the liver, they consistently have lower rates of alcoholism and alcohol-induced accidents, fights, and homicides.

Conversely, cultural groups that encourage drinking that is not a part of eating or ritualized behaviors, and that view alcohol primarily as a way to escape from stress, achieve an altered state of consciousness, or demonstrate one's strength, are at higher risk of developing problems related to drinking (Heath, 1982). Also, cultural groups that have ambivalent relationships with alcohol are more likely to report higher rates of both abstinence and alcoholism (Room, 1976). Within Irish culture for instance, there is a strong dual message attached to alcohol. While drinking is deemed sinful and a sign of moral weakness, it also is strongly condoned and treated as central dimension of social and communal relating and bonding. This duality is reflected in Vaillant's (1983) finding that Irish Americans were seven times as likely to develop alcohol dependence as Italian Americans in spite of the fact that Irish Americans have a substantially higher abstinence rate.

The dual message that Irish culture transmits around alcohol also is reflected in dominant American culture. On one hand, a barrage of puritanical and restrictive messages are conveyed about alcohol, while on the other hand, drinking is portrayed as sophisticated, sexy, and cool, and often heavy drinking is regarded as a sign of strength and toughness. In the United States, alcohol is deemed to be so dangerous that people under the age of 21 are prohibited from consuming a single drink, even under parental supervision. Moreover, one might wonder how the United States prohibits any and all access to alcohol until the age of 21, but at the age of 18 young people can legally join the military where they can both kill and be killed. The contradictions that U.S. society reflects with regard to alcohol inevitably play a role in the fact that, as in Irish society, there are high rates of both abstinence and alcoholism (Room, 1976).

Psychiatric disorders

A correlation exists between alcoholism and psychiatric disorders such as depression and anxiety. Depression is found in about one third of all cases of alcoholism. The risk for heavy drinking in women who are depressed was 2.6 times greater than the risk in women who are not depressed. However, as pointed out by Vaillant (1983) alcoholism tends to be the *cause* of co-occurring depression and anxiety rather than a response to these conditions.

Social marginalization and devaluation

Membership in socially marginalized groups often results in social devaluation and trauma that can act as a risk factor for alcoholism. For example, Native Americans have the highest rate of alcoholism of all racial and ethnic groups. A study conducted by the Centers for Disease Control and Prevention between 2001 and 2005 found that nearly 12 percent of the deaths among Native Americans and Alaska Natives were alcohol related compared with 3.3 percent for the United States as a whole (Szlemko, Wood, Thurman, & Jumper, 2006). Genetic variation is often cited as an explanatory factor because Native Americans tend to manifest the alcohol-metabolizing enzyme, alcohol dehydrogenase that increases susceptibility to alcoholism (Herrick & Herrick, 2007). Yet the influence of social marginalization and devaluation also must be considered. The loss of ancestral homes; forced relocation to reservations; poverty and unemployment; a long history of aggression and exploitation at the hands of Whites; the loss of the Native American family unit as a part of a broader communal way of life; and feelings of dislocation, alienation, and hopelessness inevitably contribute to the devastating impact that alcoholism has had on native communities (Tafoya & Del Vecchio, 1996).

Bepko and Krestan (1985) pointed out that female alcoholism is often linked to gender oppression and the cultural devaluation of women. The nature of sexism is such that to be a "good woman" one is required to subjugate her needs to serve the needs of others, and to assume a pleasing, deferential posture in relation to patriarchal authority. At the same time, the role of a "good woman" is devalued by the broader culture. Women are socialized and pressured to serve and be pleasing although they are not respected and valued for this. In response to these conditions, women sometimes turn to substances like alcohol to help manage the frustrations and pressures. In this sense alcoholism is an adaptive strategy, an attempt to find a way to endure the unendurable.

Understanding Alcoholism From a Family Life Cycle Perspective

The expanded family life cycle framework guides us to recognize that families are not static units. Like individuals, families move through various life cycle stages characterized by the onset of developmental crises that involve exits from and entries into the family system that necessitate shifts in roles and relationships both within and between generational levels.

In healthy families, when a developmental crisis occurs (whether normative or non-normative, joyful or tragic) it creates pressure (in the forms of exits and/or entries) that demand that the system change and adapt by shifting roles and relationships. Healthy families are able to reorganize and then restabilize themselves in response to the pressure imposed by a crisis (Laszloffy, 2000). Unhealthy systems, like those organized around alcohol, resist change, striving to maintain a dysfunctional homeostasis at all costs. Within families organized around alcohol, family development is altered by the presence of alcoholism. "A careful review of the life history of the alcoholic family brings to light potential *distortions* in the customary life cycle introduced by the organization of family life around the alcoholic condition" (Steinglass, 1982, p. 143). In systems where alcoholism is present, families learn to organize themselves in such a way as to "blunt the destablizing impact of alcoholism, but it also acts to blunt *any* potentially destabilizing event in family life" (Steinglass, Bennett, Wolin, & Reiss, 1987, p. 83). Such systems merely make a series of compromises to ensure that things stay the same and "these compromises result in compromised lives" (p. 76). Therefore, when faced with developmental pressures, families struggling with alcohol resist necessary adaptations and shifts striving instead to maintain homeostasis.

A twofold relationship exists between alcoholism and family development. First, alcoholism can develop as a response to the pressures generated by a crisis. For example, in a family where a child has died, feelings of pain, anger, loss, and grief can provoke a family member to abuse alcohol. Hence, the crisis triggers the onset of the addiction. Second, when alcoholism is already a part of a family system, it influences how families respond to developmental crises, usually in maladaptive ways. Because families with alcohol problems are so organized around the addiction, most developmental demands are subjugated to the demands of the addiction. "Family regulatory behaviors are powerfully influenced by the invasion of alcohol and the shape of family growth and development may to a significant degree be responsive to the unique demands that alcoholism and alcohol related behaviors place on the family" (Steinglass, Bennett, Wolin, & Reiss, 1987, p. 98). Hence, families respond to developmental pressures in ways that defer to the needs of the alcohol.

Vaillant's (1995) study of 600 American males (who were not alcoholics at the start) from two research populations, an upper-middle-class college group and an inner-city group, demonstrated that alcoholism does not always follow a linear course over the life cycle. While his sample was all male and almost exclusively White, nevertheless following subjects from youth to old age provided key insights about the way that patterns of alcohol use, abuse, and dependence can shift dramatically over the course of a lifetime and not always in a single, linear progression. Vaillant's work provides important evidence of the need to understand alcoholism from a life cycle perspective.

The following section considers the various stages of the family lifecycle. It examines how developmental pressures may induce problem drinking, just as the presence of alcoholism in a family may affect the way the system negotiates changes associated with life cycle stages.

A Word About Contextual Factors

Understanding alcoholism across the family life cycle requires considering the influence of sociocultural factors. Gender, race, ethnicity, religion, age, socio-economic status, sexual orientation, and mental and physical abilities can shape the onset and progression of alcoholism. For example, experiences with marginalization and oppression can create a vulnerability to addictions of all kinds. Sociocultural factors can also influence how substance abuse issues are perceived and responded to by family members and by those outside of the family. For example, "African Americans drink less than their White counterparts, but they suffer more from health problems related to alcoholism, such as cirrhosis of the liver, alcohol-withdrawal delerium, esophageal cancer, and so forth" (Herrick & Herrick, 2007, p. 143), which underscore the impact of racism. Racial minorities, African Americans in particular, as well as those who are poor, are more frequently misdiagnosed as well as being disproportionately underserved in comparison those who are White and those who have middle or upper income (National Institute on Alcohol Abuse and Alcoholism (2002).

The launching and leaving phase

The transition from adolescence to young adulthood is marked by the launching/leaving home process. Children become young adults who leave home to attend college, get married/co-habit with a partner, or simply establish their independence by moving into their own residence and supporting themselves financially. This is a stage of life that is both exciting and painful for parents and their young adult children.

In healthy families, parents derive satisfaction from watching their young adult children step into their independence when they "leave the nest." This also frees parents in their middle years to focus more on their individual interests and intimate relationships, for better or worse. When young adult children leave home it is normal for their parents to feel anxious about having to face a partner they may have grown distant from while they were consumed with routine parenting responsibilities. It is also stressful to have to rediscover one's identity separate from the daily demands of parenting. For young adults the leaving home process is a characterized by exploration and experimentation. They are faced with making independent decisions and dealing with the consequences, struggling to succeed educationally and/or in new jobs, and striving to develop and sustain satisfying romantic and peer relationships. This exploration can be liberating and exciting, as well as overwhelming and scary.

Alcohol can exacerbate the normative stressors that arise during the launching/leaving home stage. For example, Wegsheider (1981) explained that it is not uncommon in families with alcohol problems for children to assume narrow and rigidly defined roles in response to the demands that alcoholism breeds. These roles include: 1) the caretaker, who subjugates her or his personal needs to serve those of other family members; 2) the hero, who compensates for the failures represented by the alcoholism through being successful and accomplished; 3) the scapegoat, whose problems become the excuse for everything that is wrong in the family; 4) the mascot/clown, who provides the distraction of comic relief and entertainment; and 5) the lost child, who disappears from the activity of the family and makes no demands.

The role one played as a child in an alcoholic system may complicate the leaving home process. For example, an individual who played a caretaker role in her family in response to a parent's alcoholism might feel pressures to not leave home. Alternatively, a person who served a hero role may be encouraged and feel compelled to leave but with the implicit condition that he is obligated to succeed at all costs to compensate for the family shame, and/or provide for the family financially. A person in the scapegoat role might leave in a manner that is disruptive and dramatic (e.g., running away or troubles with the law resulting in incarceration) thereby creating a distraction from the problems caused by the alcoholism. A young adult in the mascot or clown role is likely to appear unfocused and lacking in drive and direction thereby making leaving home unlikely. As such she or he can remain physically present and continue to provide distraction though comic relief. Finally, for a person in the lost child role, the leaving home process tends to be hard to detect. Since this role is defined by invisibility and making few demands, lost children tend to leave early and with minimal fanfare or support.

Another issue young adults may face is how much they will participate in drinking. Certainly, growing up in a family with an alcoholic parent is a risk factor. But one way or another, this stage of the life cycle is such that peers exert even a greater influence on drinking behaviors than do family. As young adults struggle to make friends in college or in new jobs they are vulnerable to perceived pressures to drink as a way of garnering approval. Moreover, young adults who tend to be impulsive, risk-takers, manifest antisocial traits, and are highly extroverted are more likely to drink heavily during this stage of life (Vaillant, 1995).

Where young people go when they are launched/leave home also shapes their vulnerability to alcohol. Those who attend college are confronted with intense academic, social, and psychological pressures. Many turn to alcohol to manage these pressures. The altered state of consciousness that alcohol provides is a welcome temporary relief from the insecurities and self-doubts that many young people face. All too often, one of the pressures young people face is peer pressure to drink. Yet because the drinking age is 21, few parents or colleges acknowledge and address the practical realities of underage drinking, hence few safeguards are in place to help young people cope effectively with the temptations they encounter.

Those who directly enter the workforce tend to drink more heavily than those who go to college, and it tends to take longer for them to phase out of heavy drinking (Galanter, 2005). Those who enter young adulthood and either get married, become parents, or both tend to show the lowest rates of alcohol consumption. It may be that assuming adult roles and responsibilities is correlated with limited drinking, and it also may be that young people who have already developed a serious problem drinking are less likely to gravitate toward these kinds of roles at an early age (Arnett, 2005). Those who enter the military early are more likely to drink heavily in comparison with those who enlist at an older age (Bray, Hourani, & Rae, 2003).

Race/ethnicity and gender also influence the extent to which alcohol will shape the launching/leaving home life cycle stage. During young adulthood rates of heavy drinking are higher for males than for females, and higher for Whites than for racial minorities. In fact, it is during this stage of life (between the ages of 19 and 22) that drinking among

Whites tends to peak while for Hispanics and African Americans it peaks much later and persists longer into adulthood (National Institute on Alcohol Abuse and Alcoholism, 2002). It may be that Whites see heavy drinking as part of a youthful life-style, whereas Hispanics tend to see heavy drinking as a "right" they earn when they reach maturity.

New couplehood

New couplehood is thought of as a euphoric period when people are under the spell of initial love and feeling good. For those with an established pattern of heavy drinking, the euphoria of new couplehood mixes with the euphoria of intoxication. The honeymoon phase of couple formation ends on average after about 9 months at which time couples begin to transition into a more reality-based perception of each other. This transition may be so disillusioning that it results in a parting of the ways, but if not, couples end up struggling to establish the (largely implicit) rules of their relationship in terms of power, money, sex, intimacy, communication, and the execution of instrumental tasks, at least until such time that other developmental crises occur and require further renegotiation.

    If one partner in a relationship is an alcoholic, and the nonalcoholic partner does not recognize and confront this person's drinking, the groundwork is laid for problematic dynamics. These include dysfunctional interaction patterns, skewed boundaries, poor communication, and imbalanced responsibilities, all of which undermine relationship quality and satisfaction over time.

Sober–intoxicated interaction patterns

When one partner is an alcoholic, couple interaction patterns shift based on whether that person is drunk or dry. This is known as the sobriety–intoxication pattern (Steinglass, 1981). Usually, these two patterns are oppositional in nature. For example, if a couple's interaction pattern in the intoxication phase is distance, it is likely to shift into greater closeness with the onset of the sobriety phase. Similarly, if a couple's intoxication pattern consists of a wife exerting high levels of authority and decision-making power while her husband is intoxicated, when he be-

comes sober their pattern is likely to shift in the other direction, whereby he assumes more authority and power and she relinquishes hers.

Skewed boundaries

Healthy boundaries are clear, meaning they are open enough to allow for a free flow of information, yet firm enough to distinguish the autonomy of each party. In alcoholic couple relationships, the constant cycling back and forth between the sober–intoxicated interaction pattern compromises boundaries such that spouses lean too heavily in one direction or the other. When a boundary is too rigid, partners are disconnected and do not adequately support each other. Often a crisis is required to pull them back into contact (Carruth & Mendenhall, 1989). Conversely, if the boundary is too diffuse, the nonalcoholic partner assumes too much responsibility for the relationship and for saving and "fixing" the alcoholic. In both cases, the drinking partner usually starts to drink more.

Poor communication and low problem solving

Alcoholic partners tend to use more negative communication consisting of criticizing, blaming, and contempt. They express more anger and show lower levels of warmth when trying to solve a problem than do nonalcoholic spouses. This kind of negative communication discourages the use of positive problem solving skills like brainstorming, open discussion, and encouragement. Nonalcoholic partners in such relationships may lose the desire to engage in problem solving and give up when alcohol is involved because they anticipate that the conversation will soon become negative.

Overfunctioning/underfunctioning

Alcoholic relationships are characterized by an overfunctioning/underfunctioning dynamic referred to as *co-dependency,* which is "an unconscious addiction to another person's abnormal behavior" (Wekesser, 1994, p. 168). In short, the relationship revolves around the alcoholic and alcohol-based crises. The nonalcoholic partner minimizes her or his needs and desires and focuses on trying to manage or cure the drinker. When "a person unknowingly helps the alcoholic by denying the drinking problem exists and helping the alcoholic to get out of troubles caused by his drinking" (Silverstein, 1990, p. 65) this is referred to as enabling. An enabling partner might clean up the alcoholic's vomit, bail the drinker out of jail, make excuses to employers or friends, avoid bringing outsiders to the home to hide problems caused by the alcoholism, and take on a disproportionate share of functional tasks. For example, nonalcoholic partners may singlehandedly assume the burdens of household chores, managing finances, communicating with extending family and friends, and child-rearing responsibilities. Over time this leads to exhaustion and burnout.

Gay and lesbian couples

Gay and lesbian couples face all of the same pressures and challenges as heterosexual couples, while also having to negotiate the strains imposed by heterosexism and homophobia. Alcohol abuse is often a response to the pain of rejection from family members, social marginalization and shaming, and subtle and overt forms of prejudice and discrimination. Alcoholism rates tend to be three times higher among gays and lesbians than among heterosexuals (Schafer, Evans, & Coleman, 1987). For those who are struggling to accept being gay, alcohol is both a disinhibitor and an anesthetic, a way of pressing down and numbing pain (Kus, 1989). For gay males in particular, "The traditional patriarchal tradition of underverbalizing vulnerable feelings such as sadness, fear, and loneliness can leave men trying to "anesthetize" these very feelings via alcohol or drugs" (Sanders, 2000, p. 249). In therapy with gay couples Sanders recommends encouraging clients to recognize how they may be "imprisoned" by the dominant society's pressure to silence emotions and affective communication, and part of the liberation process entails giving voice to feelings rather than burying them through substance use.

Due (1995) explained that until recently, gay and lesbian couples had few places to openly socialize that did not center around alcohol (e.g., bars, nightclubs, or discotheques). Hence a critical part of fostering nonsubstance-related coping strategies is by providing gays and lesbians, especially young people, with opportunities to socialize that do not revolve around alcohol.

Relationship violence

Alcohol abuse is frequently related to partner violence. Among battered wives, 40 to 60 percent reported that their husbands were heavy or problem drinkers. Among married men admitted to alcohol treatment centers, 50 to 70 percent reported participating in partner violence, with 20 to 30 percent of these men reporting having engaged in severe violence toward their spouses. Alcohol tends to make individuals more impulsive and to decrease their ability to restrain their aggression. This pattern is especially noticeable among spouses who are more aggressive even without alcohol. The more frequently men are intoxicated, the more likely they are to be verbally and physically violent toward their spouses and to inflict harm that is more severe and more likely to result in injury.

Pregnancy and new parenthood

Pregnancy is a life-altering developmental event. When adolescents become pregnant, often this event in unplanned and hence generates tension, anxiety, and conflict. But even when a pregnancy is planned, the transition that this event introduces is enormous. Once a person becomes pregnant, the most pressing change that is needed is the cessation of all drinking. In fact, most women stop using alcohol when they become pregnant, whether the pregnancy was planned or not and irrespective of their age (Bachman, Wadsworth, & O'Malley, 1997). Nevertheless, not all pregnant women cease drinking. In such cases, one of the most devastating consequences for the family life cycle is when the fetus suffers from the effects of alcohol exposure. Fetal alcohol syndrome (FAS) is the leading cause of birth defects resulting in craniofacial abnormalities, slow growth, nervous system impairments, and a range of learning and behavioral problems. A major factor influencing the risk of FAS is the timing of alcohol exposure during critical periods of development. Prenatal exposure to alcohol increases the risk of developing alcohol and other drug use disorder later in life.

Parenthood and young children

Becoming a parent is a major transitional event. Normal development requires that individuals and couples change and adapt in a number of key ways to accommodate the introduction of a new and totally dependent life. For those who are alcoholic prior to parenthood, a cessation of drinking is a necessary component of making a functional transition to the role of parenthood.

Teen mothers generally reduce their drinking when pregnant, yet their use of alcohol rises during the first year of parenthood in comparison with older new mothers (Kasier & Hays, 2005). Premature confrontation with the social responsibilities and pressures of early parenthood likely contributes to the rise in alcohol consumption after the parenthood transition. And, since children who grow up in alcoholic families are three time more likely to become alcoholic themselves, and because adolescent parents are more likely to abuse alcohol, adolescent parenthood is associated with a greater risk of intergenerational transmission of alcoholism (Johnson & Pickens, 2001). In comparison, those who delay parenthood until well into adulthood are more likely to manifest a decline in alcohol consumption when they become new parents, reflecting a functional adaptation to this new stage in the family life cycle.

Approaches to parenting

When couples become parents the interaction patterns that defined their couple subsystem shape how they approach parenting. In healthy couple relationships partners transfer functional interactional dynamics and clear boundaries to their role as parents. In relationships where alcoholism is present, "patterns of withdrawal and engagement first seen in the spousal subsystem, are conveyed to and utilized in the sibling subsystem" (Carruth & Mendenhall, 1989, p. 70). The constant cycling between sober–intoxicated interactions in the couple relationship creates an atmosphere of unpredictability and instability and a parenting style that reflects indecision and poor limit setting. When boundaries in the couple relationship lean toward too much rigidity, these tend to be mirrored in parenting thereby placing children at risk for emotional and/or behavioral neglect.

Conversely, when couple boundaries are too diffuse this tends to be reflected in an overinvolved and smothering approach to parenting.

Gender and alcoholism interact to influence approaches to parenting as well. Mothers who are alcoholic manifest high levels of guilt less commonly found among alcoholic fathers. Guilt tends to undermine feelings of self-worth and competence stimulating depression and leading to more hostile, disruptive, and rejecting approaches to parenting. Mothers who are alcoholics are more likely to have experienced dysfunctions in their family of origin leading to unresolved issues with parents and poor models for how to parent effectively (Whipple, Fitzgerald, & Zucker, 1995), all of which increase the probability of alcoholism and dysfunctional parenting. Fathers who are alcoholics tend to interact less frequently with their children, have less positive interactions, display more negative emotions, report higher levels of irritation, and are less attuned to and sensitive toward their children than nonalcoholic fathers (Watkins, O'Farrell, Suvak, Murphy, & Taft, 2009).

Effect of Alcoholism on Children

In healthy families life is child centered, but in alcoholic systems, family life is alcohol centered. Hence, children's needs often are subjugated to the demands imposed by the alcoholism. Emotional, cognitive, and behavioral problems often are symptomatic of living in an alcoholic system. In fact, children's symptoms are usually one of the first indicators of the presence of alcoholism in a family. Children of alcoholics, in contrast to children of nonalcoholics, experience more learning disabilities and lower scores on tests that measure cognitive and verbal skills. They also are more prone to psychiatric illnesses like anxiety and depression and are more likely to act out and display antisocial and aggressive behaviors (Hussong, Bauer, Huang, Chassin, Sher, & Zucker, 2008).

Children raised in alcoholic families are at greater risk for being abused and/or neglected, a situation that creates secondary emotional, cognitive, and behavioral problems. State child protective service agencies and state welfare records indicate that substance abuse is one of the two main problems exhibited by 81 percent of the families where child abuse has been reported. Research also suggests that alcoholism is more strongly related to child abuse than are other disorders, such as parental depression (Lung & Daro, 2006). Because of the strong association between alcoholism and violence, it is important for clinicians always to probe for one when the presence of the other has been determined.

Families with adolescents

Adolescence is the period between the ages of 12 and 17. This is a time of dramatic physical, psychological, and social change. Families with adolescents are teeming with the tension of separation and connection. On one hand teenagers exhibit a strong need to separate and become independent. At the same time they manifest a strong pull toward security and stability. Parents are routinely mystified by the mixed messages they get from their teenagers telling them to simultaneously "go away and also stay right here."

In healthy families, parents are able to contain both of the forces of "let go" and "hold on." They provide adolescents with opportunities for appropriate role experimentation and limit testing while at the same time fostering a safe, nurturing space. In families where alcoholism is present this kind of balanced energy is lacking. Instead, adolescents get either too much autonomy and not enough holding and nurturing, or they are held onto so tightly that they have little freedom to experiment and explore new roles and limits. Adolescents in alcoholic families often feel pressured to maintain the narrowly defined and rigid roles they adopted in response to the alcoholism (e.g., the caretaker, hero, mascot, scapegoat, or lost child) demonstrating how the needs of the alcoholism take precedence over normative developmental needs of individual members.

At the same time that adolescents may be grappling with a parent's alcoholism, many also find themselves struggling with the temptations of drinking. Adolescence is a life stage fraught with inner turmoil and conflict. Teens are confused about who they are and are plagued with insecurities and self-doubts. They tend to rely heavily on social approval from peers to establish a sense of meaning and worth. When all of these forces converge, the risk of using substances increases exponentially.

Whether or not teens drink, and if they do how much and under what conditions, is complicated by the mixed messages society conveys about alcohol. Parents or grandparents, religious leaders, and schools may send the message that drinking is dangerous and forbidden. At the same time, movies, television, music, and advertisements communicate that alcohol is cool, sexy, and sophisticated. Moreover, laws that prohibit alcohol consumption before the age of 21 enhance the seduction of drinking. Societies where it is common for parents to allow children to have a few sips of wine with dinner promote moderate and responsible drinking reflected in lower rates of teenage alcohol abuse and dependence. Conversely, in the United States where laws and social customs make consumption taboo before the age of 21, alcohol becomes a forbidden fruit that tempts teens into drinking excessively as soon as they have a taste of independence.

Experiences with social devaluation also can make some teens vulnerable to drinking. A study by Corliss and her colleagues (2008) found that sexual minority adolescents are prone to drink earlier than their heterosexual counterparts and to develop problems that persist into young adulthood at higher rates. This pattern must be understood within the context of the alienation, isolation, and oppression that sexual minorities are subjected to and that increase the vulnerability to substance abuse (Fifield, Latham, & Phillips, 1977).

Midlife Change

The middle years is a point in the life cycle when one experiences a significant shift in focus, attention, and direction related to the course of one's life. For some the shift is the traditional one of launching children and having to face the proverbial question: "what now?" —referred to as the "empty nest" syndrome. For others the middle years may involve making the decision to take on parenthood for the first time, after having delayed this to establish a career. For others the shift may involve changing career paths. And still yet, some combination of these or other issues may occur. In healthy families, whatever the particular directional change that arises, support and encouragement are present. In alcoholic families, since the fundamental energy of the system is focused around staying the same, the crisis of midlife change is often met with deep resistance. For example, a man in his 40s who is struggling with alcoholism may be bored in a career and desperate for a change of direction, yet his drinking may inhibit him from taking the steps that are required to pursue a new career.

Spouses of alcoholics, women in particular, may have hung in with the alcoholism for years out of a fear of being alone. The midlife years may be the point where many partners, women specifically, finally decide to take the risk of leaving the relationship and take their chances on their own. In such cases, support groups like Al Anon can play an important role in helping nonalcoholic partners find the inner resolve to free themselves from alcoholic relationships.

Divorce

Divorce has become so common in the United States that it can almost be considered a normative part of the family life cycle. Roughly 50 percent of all first marriages end in divorce and the rate for second marriages is even higher at around 67 percent. The fact that alcoholism is present in a third of the relationships that end in divorce speaks to the impact that this addiction has on marital stability and satisfaction.

Alcoholism is associated with a rise in aggression and partner violence, with less warmth and more blaming and contempt, poor communication, reduced sexual intimacy and desire, depleted finances spent on alcohol, and less time spent together, especially if the alcoholic frequently drinks away from home. Moreover, as alcohol abuse or addiction progresses, the nondrinking spouse often grows into a compulsive caretaking role, which generates feelings of resentment, self-pity, and exhaustion. At some point the nonalcoholic partner may reach her or his limit, leading to divorce.

Whether or not alcoholism is a factor, divorce tends to be hard on all members of a family. Even when a relationship is so deteriorated that divorce represents a relief from suffering, this life cycle stage is characterized by anger, grief and loss, guilt, and a sense of inadequacy and failure. The presence of alcoholism can exacerbate these emotions, especially for children who tend to blame themselves when parents divorce. Divorce may also compel children to cling more desperately to narrow roles they assumed

in relationship to the alcoholism. For example, a hero may attempt to save his parents' marriage. When divorce is imminent he may blame himself and try to overcompensate by excelling at various pursuits. Parents may unwittingly target a child who has been the scapegoat by blaming him or her for the failures of the marriage rather than dealing with the impact of the alcoholism. Those in a mascot role may try to distract parents and siblings from the pain of the divorce through humor. A lost child is likely to burrow more deeply into invisibility in an effort to not exacerbate already high levels of stress.

The trauma of divorce is also likely to trigger the onset of problem drinking. Divorced or separated men and women are three times more likely to be alcoholics or to have an alcohol problem than are married men and women. It is essential to assess alcohol use when people separate.

Aging and Later Life

As family members age they are faced with various life cycle transitions that include retirement, a decline in physical health and mobility, the death of a partner, and their own impending mortality. In healthy families, younger generations are able to provide support to help older family members adjust to these changes. Healthy families provide care as needed, while recognizing that older family members need to feel valued and have something to contribute. Allowing older generations to assume an active role as grandparents, to whatever extent this is feasible, is important. Providing physical care, while also honoring the need for autonomy, is crucial. And it is important to offer comfort when a loved one passes.

In families where alcoholism is present the capacity to provide support and care for older family members is compromised in various ways. Sometimes younger family members are too busy and occupied in their own lives to make time for older family members, especially if relationships are already strained. Adult children of increasingly frail and needy alcoholic parents may find it emotionally challenging to care for a parent who failed to be there for them while they were growing up. In situations where an adult child has been providing support to an alcoholic parent for a lifetime, sustaining this support when the parent is aging may be hard, especially as the parent grows increasing dysfunctional, weak, and needy. Adult children of alcoholics may simply be so exhausted from having provided decades of care that by the time their parents are elderly, they find themselves "surrendering" to the alcoholism, rather than continuing to fight it.

As adults age there is a risk of isolation. Reduced mobility and declining health make it hard to sustain contact with others, and if younger family members are not nearby or are otherwise estranged, the risk of isolation is heightened. As a result some turn to alcohol for comfort and distraction from loneliness. For others, a lifetime of alcoholism may be part of the reason that younger family members avoid and isolate them. Hence, alcoholism may be a response to, as well as a reason for, isolation. In some families, an aging alcoholic member may reside with family, and yet may live in isolation, confined by physical limitations to a room, and visited only for functional purposes, which in some cases include supplying alcohol. As one man admitted somewhat sheepishly, "My whole life I tried to get my dad to stop drinking, arguing with him, trying to protect him from himself. Now I look at him, this old man, and I think, it doesn't matter anymore. He got this far in spite of himself and he won't be here much longer. Now I just give him the damn bottle and leave him to enjoy the limited time he has left."

For most alcoholics consumption tends to decrease with the aging process, which may help to slow the demands placed on adult children. As the body ages it metabolizes alcohol more slowly; as a result, alcohol remains in the body longer. Those who continue to drink at the same rates they did at earlier ages may be more vulnerable to the effects of alcohol. They also are more likely to have health conditions that can be exacerbated by alcohol, including hypertension, strokes, memory loss, and mood disorders. Declining appetite is another challenge because the combination of alcohol with limited food intake exacerbates the effects alcohol. And for those who take medications there is the risk of interactions that can be dangerous or even life-threatening. All of this creates additional burdens for adult children who may already be exhausted from providing a lifetime of care to an alcoholic parent.

Whether or not an aging family member struggles with alcoholism, if her or his adult children are alcoholics, they may find it difficult to provide appropriate care and support for aging parents. In some cases, the burden falls upon the nonalcoholic partner who may find herself or himself taking care of a spouse's aging parent, because the spouse's alcoholism precludes him or her from doing so.

Implications for Treatment

Few families come to treatment acknowledging outright that alcohol is a problem. "Common presenting complaints often mask alcoholism, such as depression, marital discord, sexual dysfunction, sexual acting out, other compulsive disorders such as overeating or prescription drugs abuse, physical violence, incest, and school or behavioral problems in one of the children" (Bepko & Krestan, 1985, p. 79). Therefore therapists must look closely for signs of alcoholism. When families do not acknowledge that drinking is a problem, therapists should ask diagnostic questions such as: "Tell me about the role of alcohol in your family," or "What is the history of alcoholic drinking in your family?" or "Does anyone worry about anyone's drinking?" In families where alcohol is a problem these kinds of prompts are likely to arouse the three D's:

Defensiveness
Denial
Discomfort

Once an overt understanding exists that alcohol is present in the family and contributes to some of the family's challenges, there are additional factors therapists should assess including:

1. Who has the drinking problem? What is the frequency and quantity of consumption? How long has this person(s) been drinking?
2. What developmental issues are occurring within the family, and in particular, what life cycle phase is the drinker in?
3. How has alcoholism been manifest across multiple generations of the family system?
4. How is the family defined in terms of contextual factors, (e.g., what is the family's identity with regard to race, ethnicity, social class, religion, nationality/immigration status, and physical/mental ability)? What is the sexual orientation of each member? How does gender shape family dynamics?

5. What are the attitudes and beliefs about alcohol?
6. What role does each family member assume in relationship to the alcoholism?
7. What interaction patterns occur when the drinker is sober versus intoxicated?
8. What are the boundaries like?
9. What are the basic communication patterns that are employed?
10. What kinds of secretes has the alcoholism fueled?
11. Is the drinking an adaptive strategy (albeit a misguided one) in response to some other stressor? What does the family benefit as well as lose as a result of the drinking?

The answers to these questions will guide intervention. Each family is a unique case that requires interventions tailored to their specific situation that includes consideration of life cycle and contextual issues. For example, the interventions used with a single-parent family where a grandfather is an alcoholic and his adult daughter serves a caretaking role that interferes with parenting her three children would be different than those used with a new couple in their early 20s who both abuse alcohol and have just adopted a young child.

The first and pressing clinical focus must be on sobriety and toward that end the drinker must be willing to admit her or his problem with alcohol. Because denial is the hallmark of addictions, it is not uncommon for the alcoholic member to refuse to acknowledge dependence on alcohol. Treadway (1989) suggests that therapists use a contract to help the drinker recognize how little control she or he actually has over her or his consumption. The contract requires the individual to have exactly 2 drinks per day, no less and no more, for a period of two months. If the person is unable to comply with the terms of the contract exactly, this exposes the alcoholic's powerlessness over drinking making it easier to enlist that person in treatment.

When the alcoholism is acknowledged, therapists should encourage the drinker to attend AA and other family members attend Al Anon in conjunction with attending therapy. Bepko and Krestan (1985) warn that it is not uncommon for the drinker to resist attending AA, and the reasons offered for this resistance vary widely. They encourage therapists to avoid arguing with clients and to provide information that clarifies the purpose of AA and explains what a specific client might gain related to her or his unique situation.

One factor to be considered is the "goodness of fit" between the AA model and sociocultural issues. For example, a central AA concept involves accepting one's powerlessness over alcohol. Yet feminists have critiqued the use of this term on the grounds that it merely exacerbates the disempowerment that women and other marginalized groups experience. The term "surrender" has been proposed as a more oppression-sensitive alternative. Similarly, Native American communities have recognized the need to adapt AA to better fit with their values and orientation. The result has been the Wellbriety movement that adapts the twelve steps of AA to Native American culture (Inc. White Bison, 2002).

While the alcoholic may refuse to acknowledge her or his problem with alcohol, the family may accept and understand the addiction. In such cases therapists can work with the family of the alcoholic and require that they simultaneously attend Al Anon.

While specific approaches to clinical intervention vary widely, there are several guidelines therapists should follow irrespective of the family's life cycle stage. These include reorganizing the family system to achieve and sustain sobriety. Therapists strive to alter roles and interactional patterns to reduce overfunctioning/underfunctioning, increase use of clear, direct communication of thoughts and feelings, strengthen weak boundaries/soften rigid boundaries, and promote healthy skills for managing stress and conflict.

CASE STUDY

The Burton Family

The following case follows the Burton family through several phases of the family life cycle, tracking the influence of alcohol in each stage.

Peter, a White male, and Trisha, an African American female, met in their mid-20s while working as new attorneys in a New York law firm. Their relationship began passionately and they married

8 months later after Trisha became pregnant. Initially they both drank regularly as a part of the social dimension of their careers. After Trisha became pregnant she stopped drinking, but Peter continued to drink as an extension of his work activities, something Trisha missed. In addition to negotiating a new marriage and new baby, Amy, the Burtons faced extended family pressures related to race and class. Peter came from an upper-middle-class Long Island family. He was the eldest child and had a sister 3 years younger. Trisha grew up in a working-class family that became a single-parent family after her father left when she was 5. She was the middle child of three daughters.

While Peter's family outwardly embraced Trisha, she felt uncomfortable that Peter's father sometimes made off-handed racially insensitive comments. Peter acknowledged to her that his father's comments were awkward, yet he minimized Trisha's hurt by accusing her of being "overly sensitive." This fueled an underlying racial tension that the couple did not address directly but grew over the years.

Burton, Winn, Stevenson, and Clark (2004) have discussed the importance of the concept of "homeplace" as it relates to African Americans. The term refers to a location where one feels rooted, connected, and accepted, and where essential pieces of the Self are reflected and valued. For many African Americans, under the best of circumstances, families provide homeplace by serving as a source of strength and a site of resistance against devaluation and oppression. Under the worst of circumstances, homeplace is an unrealized dream and a source of conflict, loss, and grief. Many African Americans experience a deep sense of yearning related to homeplace that is tied to struggles with racial devaluation and discrimination. For Trisha, certainly there was such a yearning. The lack of a warm, loving family growing up and struggles to succeed within predominately White colleges undermined her sense of homeplace. Moreover, the White, New York corporate world where she and Peter met and worked was a place where Peter felt very much "at home," but certainly not Trisha. Her success there both reflected and intensified her lack of homeplace. Moreover, the cultural alienation she felt in relationship to her in-laws also heightened a yearning for "home."

Nearly 4 years after Trisha and Peter married, Mathew was born. At that point the couple decided Trisha would resign from the firm and devote herself full time to parenthood. Two years later, Trisha's mother died, which had a devastating impact. After Trisha's father left when she was 5, her mother grew increasingly dependent on alcohol to cope with her heartaches. This compromised her parenting. Trisha's older sister, Yvonne, assumed a caretaker role, while Trisha's younger sister, Lisa, became a scapegoat, frequently getting into trouble. Trisha functioned as a lost child, trying hard to be invisible and to need as little as possible. Trisha never felt close to her mother, yet upon her death she felt overwhelming grief. Shortly thereafter, she became pregnant with their third child, Rebecca. After Rebecca's birth Trisha struggled through a bleak postpartum depression. Eventually she recovered, but like her mother, she used alcohol to manage her frustration and pain.

Had Trisha's postpartum depression driven her to seek therapy, it is likely that she would not have named alcohol as a part of her problem. This is why it is critical for therapists to ask general questions about alcohol as part of every assessment. Also, with postpartum depression defined as the problem, it would be appropriate to ask what kinds of things Trisha was doing to help manage her difficulties, which would be another way of zeroing in on the role that alcohol was playing as a coping resource. Once Trisha's drinking was flagged, an opening would exist for the therapist to explore how alcohol was shaping family patterns and to confront the dangers of using alcohol as a coping. It also would be important for the therapist to explore sociocultural factors, and in particular, to consider how disruptions to Trisha's sense of homeplace contributed to her reliance on alcohol. This would inevitably lead to focused attention on how to repair her sense of homeplace (Burton, Winn, Stevenson, & Clark, 2004).

Including Peter and the children in the therapy would be important as well. It would elucidate how the children's needs were being neglected by virtue of Peter's over-involvement with work and by Trisha's depression and drinking. At this point, therapy would focus on restructuring interactions to get Peter more involved in parenting and to help Trisha mourn the losses related to the death of her mother. Moreover, it would be essential for the therapist to consider how issues of race, class, and gender intersected with Trisha's personal struggles, as well as the couple and family struggles.

As a couple, Peter and Trisha were emotionally estranged. Peter worked long hours leaving Trisha to handle family responsibilities without him. The combination of Trisha's drinking and the rigid boundaries between the parental and sibling subsystems meant the children's needs were often neglected. To compensate, Amy assumed a caretaking role. One unfortunate consequence of parental neglect was that the children received minimal healthy racial socialization. Amy's physical appearance was ambiguous and she struggled greatly with how to identify herself racially. She also noted that her siblings, who were both light-skinned, derived benefits from their lighter appearance that were denied to her. Unfortunately, her father lacked the racial insight to provide meaningful racial socialization, and he was rarely around, while her mother's alcoholism compromised what she had to offer. Consequently, Amy had to navigate the complexities of the racial landscape with minimal guidance.

Had the Burtons sought therapy at some point, perhaps in response to their marital estrangement, a thorough assessment would have exposed Trisha's drinking and how alcohol was shaping the couple and family dynamics. AA and Al Anon would have been encouraged in conjunction with therapy, and in addition to working with the couple unit it also would be important to meet with the whole family. Doing so would create an opening to challenge Amy's parentification in the face of her parent's neglect. Targeted attention would focus on both restructuring family interactions to reestablish healthier boundaries and allocation of responsibilities, as well as focusing on the couple relationship and exploring the underlying issues that had contributed to the strain and estrangement, including dynamics related to race, class, and gender, and how the strain was exacerbating Trisha's depressive symptoms and her reliance on alcohol as a coping strategy.

After their 17th anniversary, Peter revealed that he had fallen in love with another woman, who happened to be White, and he initiated a divorce.

One of the complaints he lodged against Trisha was her drinking, which infuriated her. She vehemently denied having a problem with alcohol. Trisha was crushed. Not only was her marriage ending, but also to add insult to injury, her husband was leaving her for a White woman and had accused her of being an alcoholic. Peter's leaving also replicated the abandonment she had felt as a little girl when her father left. With this, Trisha's drinking grew more severe.

The divorce took almost a year and was bitter and angry. Throughout Trisha wove in and out of sobriety and intoxication. When she was drunk Amy functioned as the adult in charge. During this period of time Amy also was applying to colleges. She was thrilled when she was accepted into Duke University in North Carolina. Yet, the family's regulatory behaviors required Amy's presence to caretake her younger siblings whose needs were being neglected in the face of Trisha's alcoholism and Peter's virtual abandonment.

Had Trisha sought therapy at this stage in the family life cycle, perhaps on the recommendation of her attorney or a good friend, as a routine part of assessment the therapist would have inquired about the role of alcohol, likely exposing Trisha's use. By including the children in the therapy, it would have been possible to better assess the impact of the divorce (and subsequently of Trisha's drinking) on interactional patterns. The therapist might help Trisha recognize the deleterious effects of alcohol on her emotional well-being and her capacity to parent and care for her children. Encouraging Trisha to attend AA meetings would be recommended, and the therapy process would provide a space for Trisha to express feelings of hurt and anger over Peter's betrayal and abandonment, to mourn loss, and to foster more constructive ways of channeling her emotions. The therapist also would restructure boundaries in the family so that Amy could be demoted from caretaking her mother and young siblings. This would require Trisha's cooperation because she would have to agree to assume greater parental responsibility, and give Amy explicit permission to leave to go to Duke. If possible, it also would be important to reach out to Peter to assess his openness to being a more active parent. This would require explaining that while Peter and Trisha are no longer a couple, nevertheless they always will be connected by virtue of conjoint parental responsibilities.

Amy sacrificed going to Duke so she could stay home to care for her younger siblings and mother. She attended a local community college and eventually became certified as a primary level educator, just as Rebecca was leaving home to attend college. Amy remained attached to her mother whose continued struggle with alcohol prevented her from using her middle years as an opportunity to grow in new ways. With the children grown and the divorce years behind her, she might have pursued a new career and started a new relationship. Instead, she lived in a small apartment that Amy paid for and continued to drink heavily.

At the age of 60 Trisha suffered a heart attack. At that point Amy was married with two young children but once again, she stepped forward to offer care. She moved her mother in with her family; however, by this time Amy was exhausted from caring for her mother. Eventually she began supplying her mother with alcohol to keep the peace. Amy also felt a lot of resentment toward her younger siblings who had never offered to share in the burdens of caring for their mother. The tension between Amy and Rebecca was especially high, which inevitably also reflected unspoken racial tensions that had existed between them for years.

At this stage in the family's life cycle, Amy might have contacted a therapist, possibly at the suggestion of a health care professional tending to Trisha after the heart attack. As part of a routine assessment the therapist would ask about the role of alcohol in the family system. The exhaustion from years of caretaking might have helped Amy to be open about her mother's alcoholism and the strains it had created. The therapist would educate the family about the dangers of alcohol, especially for an elderly woman who had just suffered a major health crisis, and would recognize the role that family patterns have played in sustaining Trisha's alcoholism. Therefore both AA and Al Anon would be suggested in addition to therapy.

Therapy would ideally create a place and space for family members to unpack stories of pain and struggle. Certainly Trisha's lifetime of abusing alcohol was a reflection of her experiences with devaluation, rejection, and loneliness. Similarly, Amy also has carried decades of hurt and pain related having made numerous sacrifices to care for her mother and siblings, often without acknowledgment or reward, and struggling alone with devaluation related to her racial identity. Hence, some part of the healing process would involve helping mother and daughter to speak unspoken truths, to express buried feelings of pain and rage, and to connect around shared struggles with racial and gender devaluation. At the same time, it would be critical to support Trisha in apologizing to Amy for the years she was unavailable and demanded more of Amy than was fair.

It would be useful to include Matt and Rebecca in the therapy to heal strains in the sibling relationships and to help more equitably distribute the burden of care for Trisha. It also would be wise for the therapist to introduce the issue of what will happen when Trisha passes away. Given her compromised health, it would benefit the family to talk about how they would like to relate as a family with the time they still have together.

As it happened, Trisha died a year after her heart attack. Had her children taken the opportunity to address their relationships in therapy prior to this, it is possible that the her death might have compelled one or all of them to enter therapy and talk openly for the first time about their mother's alcoholism and the ways it had impacted their family, their lives, and their relationships.

Conclusion

While alcoholism is highly treatable, it is essential for therapists to assume a systemic perspective that recognizes the salience of life cycle and contextual factors. Alcoholism is often a response to pain and hurt, and it always creates its fair share of pain and hurt. Families need to understand the dangers that alcoholism poses while also feeling that hope and recovery are possible, at any age and stage, and whatever an individual or family's particular circumstances and dynamics.

Chapter 25

Violence and the Life Cycle

Monica McGoldrick & Mary Anne Ross

The irony is that while Americans' greatest fear is of strangers in the streets, the greatest real danger is in one's own home at the hands of a loved one. We are more likely to be assaulted, beaten, or killed in our homes than anywhere else or by anyone else in our society. Unfortunately, violence is a widespread occurrence in families throughout the life cycle in our society as it is in all other patriarchal cultures. It is primarily directed toward women, children, and the elderly, which will be the focus of this chapter. Men are three times more than likely to kill their intimate partners as are women (Department of Justice, 2006), and 85 percent of victims of battering are female (Gosselin, 2010). While men experience violence throughout the life cycle, most of it occurs outside the home. The effect of this on the way men relate in intimate and familial relationships is an important and complex topic, unfortunately beyond the scope of this chapter (Barnett, Miller-Perrin, & Perrin, 2005). We know that as a culture we encourage male aggression and in some ways have made it a central part of male identity. Male violence is glorified in the media and intertwined with sports, such as football and boxing. Women are also violent at times, often abusing those most dependent on them. Lesbian partner violence is also a serious issue; it is grossly underreported and not acknowledged or adequately responded to by the criminal justice system (http://www.now.org/issues/violence/stats.html; Eaton, Kaufman, Fuhrel, Cain, Cherry, Pope, & Kalichman, 2008; Brown, 2008).

One of the most widespread forms of violence in the family is corporal punishment. Since ancient times children have been exploited, sold, treated as property, and beaten with religious fervor to exorcise evil and gain religious salvation (Crosson-Tower, 2010). The irony of corporal punishment is that it is almost invisible; it is seen as unremarkable, because almost everyone has been spanked or spanks (Straus, 2001). Loving parents regularly and deliberately

assault their children, when their children do not do what the parents want. For half of American children, being hit and spanked will be a regular part of their lives from the time they are infants until they are well into their teens (Straus, 2001). It is in the home, at the hands of those who love us the most, that we learn the moral rightness of violence.

Numerous suggestions have been made regarding children's rights, including a bill drafted by the New York State Youth Commission on Children's Rights (Crosson-Tower, 2010, p. 42). It asserts the right of every child to:

1. Affection, love, guidance and understanding from parents and teachers.
2. Adequate nutrition and medical care to aid mental, physical and social growth.
3. Free education to develop individual abilities and to become a useful member of society.
4. Special care if handicapped.
5. Opportunity for recreation in a wholesome, well-rounded environment.
6. An environment that reflects peace and mutual concern.
7. The opportunity for sound moral development.
8. Constructive discipline to help develop responsibility and character.
9. Good adult examples to follow.
10. A future commensurate with abilities and aspirations.
11. Enjoyment of all these rights, regardless of race, color, sex, religion, national or social origin.

But the U.S. has not been ready to pass a law prohibiting corporal punishment, as other countries like Sweden have done (Crosson-Tower, 2010). In fact in 21 states corporal punishment in schools is legal (Human Rights Watch, 2009).

To assess issues of abuse in any particular family at any life cycle stage or transition, it is essential to address the societal arrangements that foster oppression and violence by those with power against those with less power: men against women, dominant groups against gays and lesbians, and so forth. We must also assess the various forms of violence: physical, psychological verbal, and community victimization. Clinicians must be on guard to assess all couples for the ways in which power, intimidation, and threats of abuse as well as violence itself may organize a couple's relationship and, indeed, all the relationships in a family.

To understand both the context in which norms condone violence toward certain groups, especially women and children, we must of course always assess family violence in its cultural as well as its life cycle context (Lum, 2002 2003; McAdoo, 2006 2007; Webb & Lum 2001; Nguyen, 2005).

Violence in the family is not just aggression; it is abuse of power. The statistics show clearly that within families, it operates on the basis of the strongest victimizing the weakest. Thus, the greatest volume of abuse is directed against the weakest children, children under the age of 6. The most likely abuser is the more powerful parent: the father. The same is true of spouse abuse; the stronger tends to victimize the weaker (Finkelhor, 2008). In families in which the woman has less power by virtue of not being in the labor force or having less education, she is at higher risk of abuse. All forms of family abuse occur in the context of psychological abuse and exploitation, a process that victims sometimes describe as "brainwashing" (Finkelhor, 2008). Abuse is clearly associated with family isolation—lack of community ties, friendships, and organizational affiliations (Straus & Steinmetz, 2006).

Abuse has always been institutionally supported. For example, the dominant churches in the United States have encouraged the use of corporal punishment as an appropriate way of teaching children to "respect authority" (Ellison & Bradshaw, 2009). In assessing families throughout the life cycle, we must be careful to examine the hidden ways in which abuse, overt and dramatic, as well as subtle forms of intimidation and control, may be organizing family behavior. We must also be attuned to the patterns of violence in different contexts, depending on class, culture, gender, and life cycle phase. Families of color experience double jeopardy, being at once oppressed by both institutional racism and patriarchal oppression. Similarly, gay and lesbian relationships occur within a homophobic society in which their relationships are stigmatized, gay bashing is common, and no legal recognition or protection is offered. Traditional cultures and religions often condone a degree of marital violence. Having her own money and her own connections is highly protective for a woman against patriarchal abuse. Those without skills, status, money, or social connections generally have nowhere to go to avoid abuse (**Figure 25.1**).

A Family or Social Legacy

Abuse and the tolerance of abuse tend to be taught in families from generation to generation. But, like all gender and cultural inequalities, though transmitted through the family, they are generally social issues, not evolving at the interior of the family. Primary interventions with an abusive father must not relate to questions about his father. That would particularize issues of a social nature. Once the transgenerational patterns of violence are articulated in therapy with a couple in which the husband has abused his wife, treatment has tended to neutralize the husband's accountability, focusing on the couple's joint victimization. Although violence plays out in the interior of the family, it is not an intrafamilial issue. A man is not violent primarily because his father was violent toward him, but rather because we live in a society that condones violence. Women do not invite or enjoy abuse. Nor do they suffer from masochistic tendencies that force them to stay. Women often end up staying in abusive relationships because our society provides little support for them to leave.

While our interventions are obviously directed at changing intrafamilial behaviors, the primary understandings of these problems are social rather than familial. This is an important distinction. Many therapists have failed to relate their therapies sufficiently to the social dynamics of patriarchy, orienting themselves instead to intrapsychic issues or the family of origin as the source of primary understanding of a man's violent behavior and a woman's tolerance of it.

The primary context for helping men at all phases of the life cycle to understand and change their patterns of abuse requires placing them in the

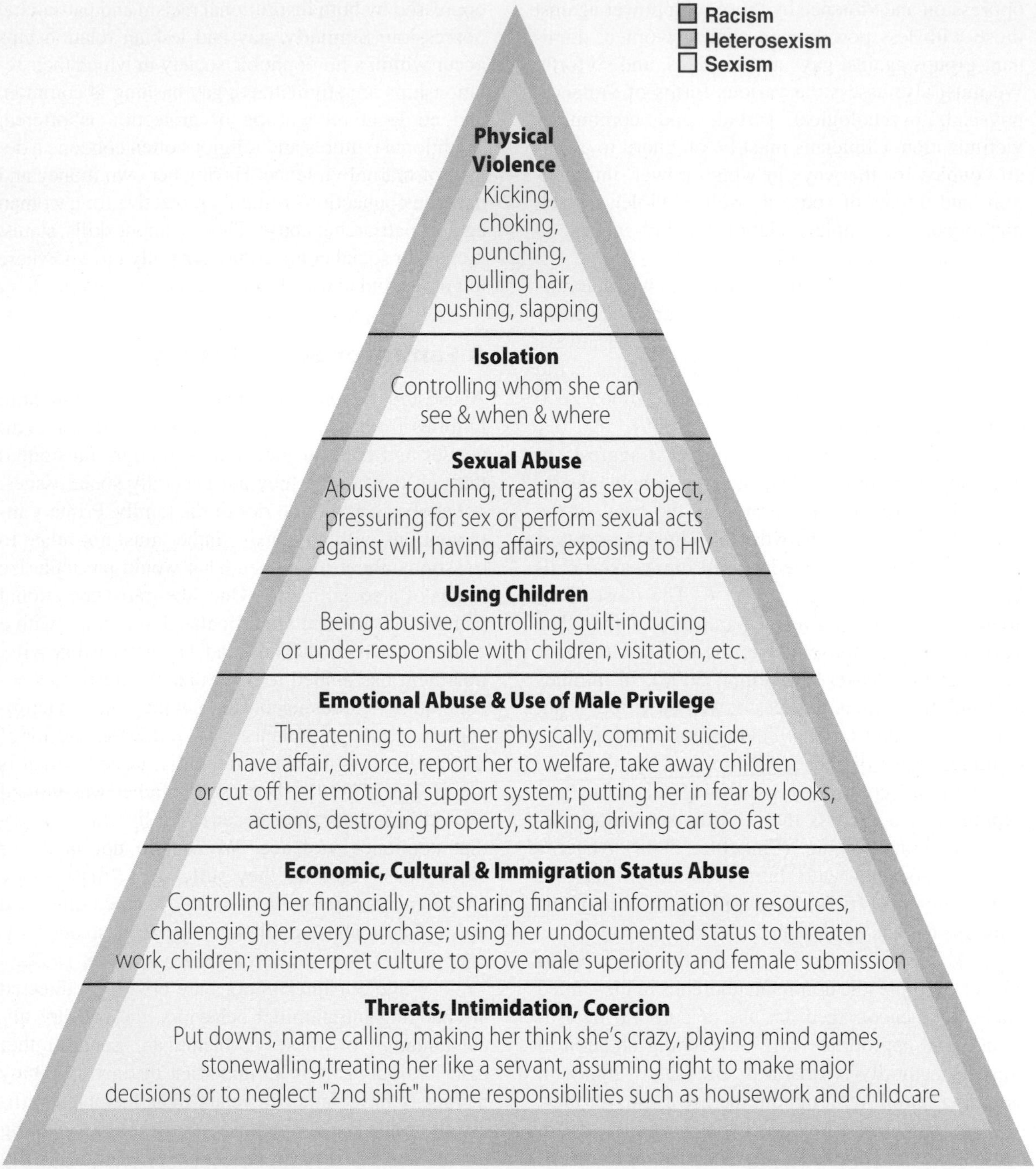

☐ Racism
☐ Heterosexism
☐ Sexism

Physical Violence
Kicking, choking, punching, pulling hair, pushing, slapping

Isolation
Controlling whom she can see & when & where

Sexual Abuse
Abusive touching, treating as sex object, pressuring for sex or perform sexual acts against will, having affairs, exposing to HIV

Using Children
Being abusive, controlling, guilt-inducing or under-responsible with children, visitation, etc.

Emotional Abuse & Use of Male Privilege
Threatening to hurt her physically, commit suicide, have affair, divorce, report her to welfare, take away children or cut off her emotional support system; putting her in fear by looks, actions, destroying property, stalking, driving car too fast

Economic, Cultural & Immigration Status Abuse
Controlling her financially, not sharing financial information or resources, challenging her every purchase; using her undocumented status to threaten work, children; misinterpret culture to prove male superiority and female submission

Threats, Intimidation, Coercion
Put downs, name calling, making her think she's crazy, playing mind games, stonewalling, treating her like a servant, assuming right to make major decisions or to neglect "2nd shift" home responsibilities such as housework and childcare

FIGURE 25.1 Power and control pyramid.*

* Expanded from maps of the Domestic Abuse Intervention Project (www.duluth-model.org) and Don Coyhis of the Wellbriety Movement (www.whitebison.org).

larger social context and offering them the opportunity to change their behavior in spite of all the societal forces that may support their abuse or pressure them not be accountable for their violence (Merry, 2009). For example, when others label them as "sissies," "wimps," or "fags" for being nonassertive, men are being covertly pressured to undervalue their mothers, sisters, wives, and children and to treat them with disrespect.

There are often wide discrepancies in estimates of family violence, which, until recently, was a well-hidden problem in the United States. Official estimates of family violence throughout the life cycle are shockingly high, but as we know, many incidents of abuse are never reported, and it is very difficult to get the full picture of its prevalence. Burton (2010) reports that in ethnographic family studies it took more than 6 months of in-depth interviewing for women to admit to sexual abuse or domestic violence, and in many cases it took a relationship of 2 years.

Throughout the life cycle, intimate relationships are much more dangerous for women than for men. Men are more often victimized by strangers, whereas most violence against women is perpetrated by family members, boyfriends, and acquaintances, and these acts usually occur in or near a women's home. Violence in the form of corporal punishment against children has been the norm and sexual abuse of children tragically widespread, while abuse of elders appears to be on the increase.

Young Adulthood

Almost 50 percent of college students have experienced intimate partner violence (IPV). Young women often do not identify dating violence as abuse and rarely report it to the police, though they frequently confide in friends. Indeed, women often feel that they are as responsible as their male partners, and men seem more than willing to have them take the blame. Women who have more traditional sex-role attitudes are more likely to stay in an abusive relationship. Therefore, it is important in working with young women to focus on how romantic ideals and acceptance of traditional gender roles may be influencing their tolerance of dating violence. This helps to make them conscious of the power dynamics in their relationships and the ways in which they may be controlled by their partner. Conflicts that frequently trigger violence such as jealousy, the use of alcohol, disagreements about sexual intimacy, and verbal abuse also reflect power inequities in couple relationships.

The term "sexual harassment" covers a wide range of behavior, from lewd remarks and dirty jokes to unwanted physical contact and rape. It takes place in the workplace, in schools, and in everyday social situations. An extremely high percentage of women will be harassed during their academic or working life. Women in traditionally male occupations suffer the most. Sexual harassment creates insecurity and a hostile, threatening work environment for women. Many are not sure how to respond and few file formal complaints. Clinical fallout includes self-blame, the loss of self-esteem, depression, and disempowerment. In practical terms, the therapist can act as a coach, rehearsing coping strategies and encouraging clients to get legal advice, learn about their companies' sexual harassment policies, and network with other women to empower themselves against the invalidation of such experiences.

One of the most insidious forms of sexual harassment that women encounter is date rape. The term "date rape" is truly a misnomer because it implies a romantic relationship between the assailant and the perpetrator. A more appropriate term might be "acquaintance rape." The most common assailants are male friends, boyfriends, neighbors, bosses, and fellow employees. We live in a rape-supportive culture. Many people think that in certain circumstances, it is okay for a man to force a women to have sex, for example, if they have been dating a long time, if they have had sex before, or if she has "led him on." Rape myths, such as that a woman "asked to be raped," liked it, or could have stopped it, are widely accepted and are reinforced in popular pornography. Formal and informal male social groups, such as fraternities, sports teams, or even the men at the local bar can reinforce the importance of sexual conquest and promote the objectification of women, creating an environment in which rape is acceptable for their members.

A survivor of acquaintance rape said, "Every day, I sat next to him in class. Every day I passed him in the hallway—the man who raped me. There was nothing I could do. He was a football hero, a hot catch. No one would ever believe me that I didn't want to have sex with him."

In response to the recent awareness of the epidemic proportions of acquaintance rape, many colleges have initiated rape prevention programs, but these changes are not enough, since the broader social attitudes that allow such behaviors have not changed. Many rapes nationwide occur in the workplace. Women often blame themselves and feel too ashamed to tell anyone. Because acquaintance rape is a betrayal by someone a woman trusts, it can be more psychologically damaging than stranger rape. Survivors frequently experience the symptoms associated with other severe traumas. These often go unrecognized by the survivor and those around her who do not know about the rape. Understandably, rape survivors frequently have difficulty trusting men and have problems with sexual intimacy, expressed by either a lack of interest in sex or compulsive sexual activity.

It is important to establish an emotionally safe environment in the wake of a rape. Medical issues and legal options should be explored. It is vital that those around the survivor believe her and not reinforce societal blaming of the victim. Parents, devastated by what has happened, often close down the issue of the rape trauma. Male relatives, intimates, and friends frequently respond in a stereotypical fashion, becoming outraged and preoccupied with thoughts of revenge. Family therapy provides an opportunity for those closest to the survivor to express their feelings and provide genuine support for the victim. Family therapy with the abuser, when possible, similarly expands the potential for social accountability.

A young man who had been arrested, but not convicted, for participating in a fraternity group rape of a woman at a college fraternity party was coached to have an accountability session with his parents, his siblings, and his wife regarding his participation in this behavior. His parents had initially minimized his actions and stopped discussing the assault as soon as the police backed off. He spoke to his family about his responsibility as a man to be different and to urge other men to be different so that his daughters, and other women would grow up in a different world.

Gay relationships are also plagued by courtship violence and acquaintance rape. This can be especially stressful because they occur within a homophobic environment that offers few resources and supports. Gay men and lesbians also suffer the added insult of being victimized by hate crime (NCAVP, 2008). The Anti-Violence Project (www.avp.org), a group that monitors such attacks, reports that there is an increase in hate crimes whenever the media or political groups focus on the gay community and that most of the victims of these crimes are young adults (see Figure 25.1).

Interventions with young adults can have a profound influence on the types of relationships they will form at this stage and other stages of their lives.

Marie O'Hara, who sought help for problems with her parents, gradually acknowledged that her father had been violent to her mother, herself, and her siblings throughout her childhood. Marie was now dating a man who was very jealous and had begun to shove her around. We made many interventions to increase her consciousness about the societal dimensions of abuse. Within a few months, she developed the courage to call for help when her boyfriend became belligerent in a public place, a courageous action that went very much against the grain of her Irish family background. The police came to the scene, and she left the boyfriend in their custody, finding her own way home.

Later, she became engaged to a very different sort of man. By this point, she had the courage to request of her father and her brother that they not participate in her fiancé's bachelor party if the activities became dehumanizing to women. Such a party did occur. Her fiancé left in protest, but her brother and father remained. Marie brought her father and brother into family therapy to confront them. Using the support of her sister and mother, she was able to hold them accountable and express how their actions had hurt and angered her. Her brother refused to accept responsibility and walked out of the session, but her father, with some coaching, was able to apologize to her for breaking his promise and to support her in her wish to have a very different type of relationship with men in the future. He also agreed to try to help his son understand the implications of his behavior.

Sexual harassment, courtship violence, and acquaintance rape are painful experiences that scar the psyches of their victims. They are experienced on a personal level but in a social environment that tolerates and even encourages their occurrence and denies the enormity of their impact. This promotes self-blame and erodes self-confidence, making it difficult for young people to accomplish the tasks intrinsic to young adulthood, that is, becoming independent and developing careers and intimate relationships.

Families With Young Children

Childhood is a scary and dangerous place for many of America's children. Almost all American children have been hit by their parents, often for many years. For at least one in five and perhaps almost half, hitting begins in infancy and continues until they leave home. The laws in every state allow parents to hit their children with hairbrush or belt as long as no serious injury results, and 28 percent of parents of children age 8 to 10 still hit their children with such instruments (Straus, 2001). Most homeless women and children are fleeing abuse (Tischler & Rademeyer, 2007). There are over 3 million referrals for child abuse every year. (U.S. Department of Health and Human Services, 2007). Almost five children die in the United States every day from abuse and neglect, most often children under 3 years of age (Gosselin, 2010).

The enormous responsibility of raising children changes a couple's relationship forever. If violence has already been a dynamic, it is likely to increase at this point. Indeed, it is quite common for men to begin abusing their wives during pregnancy. This may be because of the anticipated burdens of the child, because of the wife's new focus away from exclusive devotion to the husband, or perhaps because she is more dependent. Pregnancy also offers no protection from marital rape (Bergen, 1996; Russell, 1990). As their families grow, mothers may leave work because of the expense or lack of daycare, a situation that leaves them especially vulnerable. Women who do not work outside the home, who earn less than 25 percent of the family income, and who have young children at home are at highest risk of abuse (Kalmus & Straus, 1990).

Men who batter their wives may begin abusing their children. Sometimes, this serves as a turning point in the relationship; danger to the children is the most frequently cited reason battered women give for leaving their abuser (Hilton, 1992). Unfortunately, not being able to support those children independently is the most frequent reason women return (Gondolf & Fisher, 1988; Okun, 1986). Even if they are not the target, children who live in violent homes are at high risk of physical and psychological injury (Crosson-Tower, 2010). Children in violent homes tend to be exposed to various forms of psychological as well as physical violence several times a week (Graham-Berman, 2002). They often feel impelled to try to make peace between their parents or to protect whomever they perceive to be the victim. This puts them in the direct line of fire. The lives of children who witness marital violence are filled with fear. In a sense, they lose both parents. Their fathers are emotionally distant. Their mothers are often depressed, anxious, ill, and focused on the behavior of the abuser, with little emotional energy left for their children. It is estimated that up to 10 million children between the ages of 3 and 17 have witnessed parental violence (Straus & Steinmetz, 2006). Children who witness violence have been found to be more aggressive with peers and may go on to abuse their own children or partners. Not surprisingly, they have fewer friends, more learning problems, and more hyperactivity and anxiety (Crosson-Tower, 2010).

The relationship between parents and children is socially determined. Historically and culturally, there has been wide variety in what is considered an appropriate parent–child relationship. Children have been seen as a blessing, an obligation, or a burden. What is considered abuse in one setting is seen as good parenting in another. Male babies are more highly valued in many societies. Female infanticide has been a common practice in both European and Asian cultures. Little girls everywhere are raised differently from little boys, the most patriarchal cultures being the most oppressive of young girls' development. Child-rearing practices in the United States have always strongly endorsed corporal punishment. Study after study reveals that most Americans believe it's ok to spank a child. The most vocal advocates of corporal punishment at home and in school today are fundamentalist Christians (Ellison & Bradshaw, 2009). Corporal punishment is still legal and practiced in many school systems in the South and West. The states that have the strongest commitment to the use of force for morally legitimate purposes are among those with the highest rates of rape and child abuse. It is a serious issue: Violence conducted against children is carried out by morally righteous people (Straus, 2001). If we lower the amount of corporal punishment of those parents who routinely practice it, we could lower the level of child abuse dramatically. The more people have been hit by their parents in their early teens, the more likely they are to be depressed and think of suicide. Corporal punishment contributes to a sense of powerlessness and a lack of internalized moral standards. It also interferes with the likelihood of graduating from college or earning a good income and leads to more troubled child behavior in many dimensions (Straus, 2001). Straus in his extensive study demonstrates that not spanking is in many ways much more conducive to the goals parents hope to attain by spanking. Nonspanking parents are less likely to ignore misbehavior and better able to maintain strong bonds with their children (Straus 2001).

Child abuse occurs among all cultures, races, and economic groups. Sadly, the highest rates are among the youngest and poorest children and those who are disabled. Perpetrators of child abuse are usually parents or stepparents who are struggling with addictions, emotional problems, poverty, or other stresses (Crosson-Tower, 2010).

Sexual abuse is defined as interactions between a child and adult or an older child with the goal of the sexual gratification or stimulation of the perpetrator. This covers a wide range of behaviors such as intercourse, fondling, viewing pornography, or posing for pornographic pictures. Because of the secretive nature of sexual abuse, it is believed that most incidents go unreported. Children are vulnerable to sexual abuse from earliest childhood. The most common abusers are family members and others known to the family. The highest number of reports are about children between the ages of 9 and 11, but infants and toddlers are also abused. The rate for girls is at least three times higher than that for boys. Boys are even more reluctant to admit to sexual abuse than girls and are often perceived as being less damaged by the experience. They are less likely to receive counseling or be removed from their abusive homes (O'Leary & Barber 2008; Masho & Anderson, 2009). Most victims of sexual abuse do not become perpertrators of sexual abuse and violence. But almost all perpetrators do have a history of having been sexually abused themselves. Male perpetrators of sexual abuse tend to abuse a much higher number of boys over their life course than do men who abuse girls. Children are often threatened by their abuser or made to feel that they have caused the abuse themselves.

The long-term effects of sexual abuse include PTSD, depression, anxiety, juvenile delinquency, aggressive behavior, substance abuse, suicide, and problems with sexual relations. (Luthra, Abramovitz, Greenberg, Schoor, Newcorn, Schmeidl, Levine, Nomura, & Chemtob, 2009; Fullilove 2009). These problems may be exacerbated by the frequency of the abuse, the kind of sexual activity, the age at onset, the child–abuser relationship, the number of perpetrators, their gender, and whether or not the sexual abuse occurred within the context of other forms of abuse.

The role of the family at this stage in the life cycle is to provide a safe, supportive environment for the growth and nurturance of children. Violence and abuse are incongruent with these tasks. The primary goal of therapy is to help the family to create a safe environment for children by realigning and restructuring the power dynamics within the system. Roles are often reversed in violent homes, with children trying to protect their mother or siblings. Changes in these roles are often met with great resistance. Mothers need to be supported and empowered. Children in abusive homes are often impaired in their emotional and psychosocial development.

Assessment of children's safety is not always easy and requires a different set of skills and knowledge than those needed for work with adults. The therapist must be aware of the norms of development for young children. For example, certain behaviors, such as sexual play or victimization of other children, excessive masturbation, seductive behavior, and genital exposure, are associated with sexual abuse in both preschool and school-age children. Most mothers of incest victims take immediate steps to protect their children, often at great emotional cost to themselves. When there is sexual abuse, which is more often committed by fathers and even more by stepfathers, who play a central role in the emotional, financial, and psychological life of the family, children may feel that by seeking help, they are betraying someone they love and endangering the well-being of the entire family. Other family members may blame the child for talking. It is essential in treating incest that the positive aspects of the victim's and other family members' relationship with the abuser be acknowledged while holding the perpetrator responsible for the abuse and its impact on the child and family. For this reason, treatment programs require that the perpetrator admit to his behavior before relationships can continue. Since protection of the child is paramount, they also require that the offending parent not have unsupervised access to the children.

As our understanding of the development of the brain grows it becomes increasing clear that abuse and trauma have a detrimental impact on the physical development of the brain (Perry, 2009). Children who are being physically abused may have intellectual impairments, learning problems, difficulty concentrating in school, or developmental delays (Barnett et al., 2005). Children who experience or witness abuse at home often exhibit aggressive behavior, which interferes with both their school and social life (Crosson-Tower, 2010). Attention needs to be paid to emotional issues underlying these problem behaviors. Very young children may not be able to express themselves verbally; older children often do not respond well to direct questions. Story telling, family puppets, and the use of art and dolls can be effective in gathering information (Gil & Briere, 2006). Play therapy and group therapy help children to develop their social skills and deal with their fears, anxiety, depression, and shame.

Ideally, all family members, including the abuser, should be involved in treatment. This does not always happen, and participation in a program does not mean that the abuse will stop. Sometimes, it is necessary for a woman to end the relationship to keep the children safe. The maintenance of a safe home, acknowledging the importance of the abuser's relationships with all family members, and the separation of the abuser from the victim until it is certain that contact will not result in the revictimization of the child are guidelines that apply to work with physically and sexually abused children and those who witness domestic violence.

Therapists should have an understanding of a family's ethnic patterns, parenting beliefs, and stress levels. They should explore support systems, including extended family and friends, who might be incorporated into treatment plans. While legal definitions of child abuse vary from state to state, all have mandatory reporting laws requiring clinicians to notify the authorities if they suspect abuse. It is important for a clinician to understand these laws and to know what kind of services child protective agencies can offer in their area. Couples with young children need to know that disclosure of psychological, physical, or sexual abuse requires action on the part of the therapist.

Many parents feel that the use of physical punishment is an appropriate way of disciplining a child but are not aware of how dangerous this can be, especially with young children. Sometimes, parents have unrealistic expectations about how a child should behave. The clinician can coach parents on management of problem behaviors and help parents to develop a sense of competency in dealing with their children. Battered women often underestimate the amount of violence their children see. When helped to realize how it affects the children, they usually take steps to reduce their exposure.

Women with young children who try to leave their abuser may face seemingly insurmountable obstacles. Cultural norms pressure women not to break up the family, and the extended family, especially that of the abusive husband, may not be supportive of her decision to leave. Mothers do not always receive child support, and many are impoverished by divorce. Courts frequently refuse to consider spousal abuse an issue when considering custody. Fathers may try to manipulate the legal system to their advantage in custody, alimony, child support, and visitation negotiations. Finally, the woman's safety may be in great jeopardy when she separates. These times are, in fact, the most dangerous for women and are the periods when they are most at risk for increased violence and fatal assault. Harassment, threats, and abuse may continue in spite of divorce, separation, or restraining orders.

Families With Adolescents

For many years the primary focus on teenagers and violence was on the juvenile delinquent, but teenagers have the highest risk of any age group of being the victim of a violent crime. Many face abuse at home and violence in schools and their communities. One quarter of all cases of child abuse and neglect involve adolescents between the ages of 12 and 17. African American teenagers are twice as likely to be abused at home and five times more likely to be killed by a gun than White teens (National Council on Crime and Delinquency, 2002). Physical punishment remains more a part of teenage life than has been realized. Straus (2001) reports that one third of daughters and 43 percent of sons recall being hit more than six times a year during their adolescence.

As adolescents strive for independence, explore their sexuality, and begin to develop new identities, parents can no longer protect their children or themselves from the world outside their family and often have a difficult time as children rebel and question their authority. In family systems in which power and control are central dynamics, these conflicts easily escalate into violence. While fewer child abuse cases involve adolescents, reports of abuse for this age group are believed to be greatly underestimated. Perhaps this is because adolescents are perceived to be better able to defend themselves or to deserve the punishments they receive. The truth is that they and infants suffer the most severe injuries. Young people from violent homes often leave early, getting themselves into trouble because they left home to escape, rather than because they were ready to move on.

Eliana Gil (1994) distinguishes two different types of parental abuse experienced by adolescents: current abuse and cumulative abuse. Current abuse is rooted in conflicts connected to this particular stage of development, family crises, or inconsistent parenting. Young people who have grown up in a supportive environment up to this point but are now

experiencing abuse have a chance to master the developmental tasks of this stage through treatment focused on communication, limit setting, parenting skills, and boundaries. Adolescents who have experienced a lifelong history of cumulative abuse have different needs. They tend to suffer from depression, poor self-esteem, and anxiety and may have trouble developing social skills. In school, they are more likely to have behavioral and attention problems. Their frustration and pain are often expressed through acting-out behaviors. These youngsters are at greater risk for drug and alcohol abuse and have a higher rate of delinquency (Barnett et al., 2005).

Many young people experience violence in their educational and social environment as well as at home. The greatest health risk for teenage boys is violence from peers, while teenage girls are often abused by siblings and victimized by sexual harassment in school, leading them to experience high levels of depression, eating disorders, and suicide attempts. Teenage girl violence and arrest for assault has been on the rise for the past decade. Most girl violence was directed at same-sex peers. Girls are more likely to assault family members than are boys, who direct their aggression more at same-sex peers and outsiders.

Gang membership is an appealing option for many. Gangs serve as a pseudofamily, providing protection, power, status, and in some cases profit. Members usually share the same racial and ethnic background. This can reinforce cultural identity, especially in areas where the group is a minority. Though usually thought of as an inner-city problem, gangs are expanding in suburban and rural areas reflecting a widespread experience of disconnection among young people, which can only be understood or responded to by adults joining forces to offer meaningful pathways through life for every community (Hardy & Laszloffy, 2005).

Teenagers who live in high-crime areas are not only more frequently victimized, they also witness a great deal of violence, which can have severe psychological consequences. Very few inner-city families go through the adolescent phase without experiencing a violent death or injury up close (Perry, 2009; Cruz & Taylor 2008; Paradis, Reinherz, Giaconia, Beardslee, Ward, & Fitzmaurice, 2009).

Gay and lesbian adolescents have an especially difficult time during adolescence as they struggle with sexual identity. In a homophobic society, the first inkling of a homosexual orientation is cause for intense anxiety and denial. Those who do come out are ostracized and risk abandonment by their families and verbal and physical assault by their peers. Those that don't come out suffer in silence.

Adolescents can be defiant and resistant to therapy. Avoiding power plays with teens, giving them space to discuss their many thoughts and feelings without immediate challenge, and setting clear boundaries are approaches that can help them to develop trusting relationships. Nonverbal forms of therapy, such as art, music, drama, and group therapy can be especially helpful. Gil (1996) recommends establishing an alliance through individual work with the adolescent before beginning conjoint family therapy, which should be undertaken cautiously and only as the teen can handle the work and the family is ready to be accountable. Therapists who work with adolescent clients must not make assumptions about their sexual orientation. Instead, they should provide information about human sexuality in a supportive way. There is a large network of organizations and community programs designed to meet the special needs of young people. Clinicians can utilize these and incorporate them into treatment plans.

Families at Midlife

Intimate partner violence does not end as couples grown older. Women between the ages of 35 and 49 are more likely to be murdered by their partners than are any other age groups (U.S. Department of Justice, 2001). Middle age and older women who have been victims of domestic violence have a higher rate of overall mortality than those who have not (Baker, LaCroix, Wu, Cochrane, Wallace, & Woods, 2009).

Midlife is a time of major change. As children leave home, husbands and wives need to renegotiate their relationships with each other, their adult children, and their grandchildren. Men's careers are often at their peak. At the same time, women freed from child care responsibilities may begin to seriously develop their professional skills and interests. This is also a time of losses. Our culture's pairing of youth with beauty leaves little room for middle-aged women. This perceived loss of attractiveness is troublesome for those to whom it has been a prime source of self-esteem and power. The loss of children can be painful, especially for women whose sole focus was on the home and child-rearing and who fear being left alone in an abusive relationship. The incidence of physical assault often declines with age. Overt acts of violence may no longer be needed, as the husband's control is so well established. This does not mean that the relationship is no longer abusive. Often unrecognized is the spouse's ongoing verbal and psychological abuse. Threats, continuous criticism, outbursts of rage, and jealousy can all be used to keep a wife alert and focused on the needs of her husband. Such behavior is especially effective if it is combined with occasional expressions of love and if the victim is isolated from friends, family, and other sources of support (Schwartz, Anderson, Strasser, & Boulette, 2000). Psychological abuse is always present in physically abusive relationships, though physical assault may or may not be a part of psychological abuse. One particularly pathological form of psychological abuse has sometimes been referred to as "gaslighting," a reference to the classic movie *Gaslight*, in which the husband tries to drive his wife insane by telling her she is crazy any time she notices the things he is doing in their relationship to mystify her. This is often done by husbands who deny their affairs and call their wives "paranoid" for their suspicions. Years of psychological abuse take their toll. Women in abusive relationships often suffer from low self-esteem, feelings of powerlessness, major depression, anxiety, and posttraumatic stress.

An important part of work with women at this stage is identifying the abuse. The most widely held image of a battered woman is that of a young mother with small children. Professionals usually do not consider domestic violence and psychological abuse when assessing a woman at this stage. Doctors don't adequately question pat explanations of bruises and injuries. Clients themselves may have become so used to the way they are treated that they don't consider the relationship abusive. Those with traditional attitudes may consider it normal for a man to "lose his temper now and then." The power pyramid is again useful in detecting more subtle types of abuse. Not all women at this stage are in long-term relationships. Sometimes abuse starts in a second marriage. For many, though, their marriage represents an investment of 20 or 30 years. Divorce and separation can seem like a negation of everything they value. Groups are especially helpful for women struggling with these issues and for raising consciousness about the nature of psychological and physical dominance, while providing them the support and resources to confront it. Groups also combat isolation and build self-esteem.

A major concern for women at this stage is finances. They fear losing their home and health insurance. Abusive men often insist on maintaining total control of the family finances (Bureau of Justice, 2001). It is not unusual for wives not to know what the couple's financial assets are or even how to manage a checkbook. The therapist should assess what skills a wife will need to develop to have confidence in her ability to function independently from a husband who has fostered her dependence.

Relationships with adult children may be strained when midlife women decide to leave their marriage. Even children who have spent a lifetime watching their mother be victimized often become emotionally distant, in part fearing that she will now become dependent on them. They may feel that she deserves the abuse ("she's always nagging Dad"), or they may become abusive to their mother themselves. Although they may have urged their mother to leave for years, they can also have great difficulty letting her go or changing their perception of their parents' marriage. All of these issues need to be addressed if adult children are going to be able to support their mothers' efforts. Adult children will need to renegotiate their relationships with their fathers as well. Unfortunately, abusive men at this stage, as at other phases in the life cycle, often use their children to control and manipulate their wives, sometimes threatening them with emotional or financial abandonment.

Older Families

Women over 65 make up 21 percent of all domestic violence complaints, and it is estimated that 1 to 2 million people over the age of 65 have been abused by someone on whom they depended for care (NCEA, 2005).

"After all she survived all these years, things have got to be slowing down now that they are older." (Adult son, having trouble acknowledging that his 78-year-old mother was still being battered by her 82-year-old husband).

Several changes occur as people get older that make them more vulnerable to abuse. Older adults are systematically oppressed by ageism. Ageism is more than denigrating images portraying old people as feeble and helpless or as sweet little old ladies and men. It involves a lack of power—less opportunity for employment and lower income. It also involves the lack of resources and services to meet their changing medical and life-style needs.

As people live longer, more suffer from health problems that interfere with their ability to function independently The natural support system for older adults begins to deteriorate as people retire from their jobs and spouses and friends move away or pass away. Women who make up the greatest portion of this population tend to have relatively low retirement incomes and thus find themselves suddenly dependent on their adult children and on other family members for support.

Older adults may not recognize themselves as abuse victims, or they may fear institutionalization. The most common image of victims of domestic violence is a woman with young children. Older women often have trouble identifying with this. Those with chronic illnesses often fear that nursing home placement is their only other alternative to the suffering they experience at the hands of those who care for them.

Aging can be a difficult transition for both the elder adult and the entire family system. Earlier unresolved conflicts often erupt between parents and children or between siblings. As the parent's role changes from one of power and authority to one of dependence, there is a realignment of relationships among family members. The so-called role reversal involves a shift in roles for everyone in the family. Daughters or daughters-in-law usually become the primary caregivers and frequently find themselves torn between their jobs, their own families, and aging relatives. Many are seniors themselves and are beginning to have health problems of their own. A 63-year-old diabetic may be caring for her 85-year-old mother as well as her 65-year-old husband, who has a history of cardiac problems. For this reason, more than at any other stage of the life cycle, it is essential to work with the extended family.

This is especially important in working with older adults of different ethnic groups. A clear assessment of the cultural impact of issues on the family is vital. It is important to have a clear idea of the patient and their family's view of aging, sickness, caregiving, disclosure, and family roles. A well-made care plan worked out with the oldest daughter may be unworkable if the real power in the family lies with the son who lives 50 miles away. To assess family dynamics and understand the support network that is already in place, genograms should include all family members and those not connected by blood who are important in the everyday life of the older adult. This may include the pastor, the doctor, the next-door neighbor, and/or the home health aide who comes in 3 days a week.

Gay and lesbian elders grew up in a time when their sexual orientation was considered a crime, a sin, or a psychiatric illness. Because of this, many same-sex partners may refuse to identify themselves as a couple. Clinicians can respect this need for privacy and focus on the level of support partners can provide (Cook-Daniels, 1998; NCAVP, 2008). Gay seniors may have an extensive network of friends who act as family or they may be more isolated because that system has deteriorated or never existed.

Definitions of elder abuse vary from state to state and may include psychological ("If you don't stop wetting the bed you will end up in a nursing home") and verbal abuse ("You're useless. Why don't you die?"), as well as neglect and financial and physical abuse. While technically this term would encompass wives who are being hit by their husbands or adult children, the emphasis in the field has been on abuse that results from caregiver stress. The experience of domestic violence for older women was virtually ignored. Fortunately there is a new awareness of the needs of older women even if there are not enough shelters and services to cater to their special needs (Brandl, Herbert, Rozwadowki, & Spangler 2003).

In practice, the distinction between domestic violence and elder abuse can be difficult to discern. But making that distinction is vital, because treatment plans designed to reduce caregiver stress can actually end up blaming the victim ("She's so difficult to care for that I just lost my patience") and supporting the abuser.

Ironically, older women are at greatest risk from people who are dependent on them—such as adult children or spouses with a history of drug or alcohol abuse, mental illness, intellectual impairment, and economic problems (Malley-Morrison & Hines 2004).

Mrs. Foley was an 83-year-old widow with diabetes who lived alone in her small suburban home. Her grandson Tom relocated from another state and asked to live with her while he looked for a job. Tom was 44 and recently divorced. Initially, she welcomed Tom, but after a time his behavior raised suspicion that he was using drugs and alcohol. He was sloppy and offered no help around the house. He resented any criticism from his grandmother and would respond with a litany of complaints about how she had treated both him and his mother, Mrs. Foley's deceased daughter. By the time Mrs. Foley became aware that her grandson was stealing from her, she was too afraid and depressed to confront him. She spent more and more time alone in her room. She began to lose weight and would sometimes forget to take her medication. Her plight was discovered only after she fell and was hospitalized for a broken hip. At the time, she was also suffering from dehydration, and her blood sugar level was dangerously high. Her nurse observed how anxious she became before Tom's visits. When he showed up at the hospital drunk and was verbally abusive to his grandmother, the nurse called adult protective services. The worker interviewed Mrs. Foley, who denied any problems with Tom. The worker also met with Tom, who became quite defensive. He claimed that his grandmother was senile and that none of her statements could be believed. This made the social worker more suspicious. She interviewed Mrs. Foley's neighbors, who painted a clearer picture. They described Tom's comings and goings and expressed their concern about Mrs. Foley. The adult protective worker established rapport with Mrs. Foley during her recovery, and the older woman gradually confided her problems with Tom. She was given information about drug and alcohol addiction and made aware of her legal rights. Since she had no other children or grandchildren, a niece and nephew were contacted and brought into counseling. With their support, Mrs. Foley was able to confront her grandson and threatened to use legal measures unless he left her home, which he did. She continued to have a warm and supportive relationship with her sister's children and become more involved with their families.

Spousal mistreatment at earlier life cycle stages often foreshadows elder abuse, but the lack of such a history offers no assurance. A woman may remarry into an abusive relationship and be too embarrassed to discuss the situation with friends or family. Or events at this phase can increase tensions between a long-term couple. Retirement, health problems, and decline in sexual functioning can make men whose identity is rooted in power and control feel threatened. Unfortunately, one of the easiest ways for men to feel empowered is by abusing family members, particularly their wives (Spangler & Brandl, 2007).

Frequently, sudden behavioral changes are indicative of health problems. Therefore, all cases of late-onset abuse require a careful medical assessment to detect cognitive changes and the side effects of medication. The clinician should study the dynamics of the couple. Warning signs are similar to those at other stages of the life cycle: verbal abuse, possessiveness, control of finances, and reluctance to allow the partner to speak for herself or himself or to be interviewed separately. Unexplained bruises and injuries must be medically assessed, since older adults may take medications or have conditions to put them at higher risks for these signs.

Adult children and other family members may not be good informants. Many adult children seem embarrassed and ashamed of their parents' behavior and may not be aware of the abuse or really believe that their parent is in danger. They may blame the victim or be jaded after many previous attempts to intervene and resent suddenly being asked to be caregivers ("No matter how hard we tried she never left him before and we can't take care of her now if she does.")

For many older women, leaving a relationship may not be a viable option because of the economic realities they face and the traditional values they embrace. Therapy can empower women who stay by helping them to recognize that what they are experiencing is abuse and addressing its lifelong consequences. Clinicians can provide information about abuse in later life, help older women to identify their strengths, and validate the importance of their work as wives and mothers. They can also encourage them to make safety plans and provide referrals to local resources (Spangler & Brandl, 2007). Gays and lesbians may have difficulty using many of the services that are usually prescribed for older adults. Fearing the frequent prejudice in traditional social support systems, they may require special legal counseling, since their relationships are often not legally recognized (Cook-Daniels, 1998).

Older adults suffering from dementia are at greater risk for abuse, especially those who are aggressive toward their caregivers (Coyne, Reichman, & Berbig, 1993). Dementia raises particularly thorny problems in assessment because patients may not be able to remember incidents of abuse, or they may suffer from paranoid delusions that focus on mistreatment at the hands of a family member. They may refuse to eat or bathe, putting the caregiver in the position of forcing them to cooperate or risk being charged with neglect. Episodes of sudden belligerence may require physical intervention and restraints that can result in bruises, which may give the appearance of physical abuse. Behavioral or personality changes, suspiciousness, withdrawal from previous activities, difficulty managing finances, getting lost, minor automobile accidents, neglect of personal hygiene, and other changes in daily activities may be the early signs of dementia. Often, family members do not recognize the significance of such changes and will make excuses or deny the extent of the deterioration. Sometimes, they will interpret the older person's inability to function as willful and become angry and accuse him or her of being stubborn and spiteful. This is particularly difficult if the caregiver has previously had a conflicted relationship with the older person. The professional can sometimes fall into the same trap and may label an elder as uncooperative and unwilling to be helped when, in fact, the person's judgment may be too impaired to understand the need for help. An assessment and planning session with as many family members as possible can be important, not only for clarifying the situation but also for supporting all family members in their shared responsibility and concern for the aging person.

The experience of caring for someone with dementia can be overwhelming and incredibly sad for family members. Husbands may not recognize their wives; mothers may not recognize their children. Basic skills such as bathing, reading, or writing are lost. Communication becomes more difficult as language skills become impaired. Piece by piece, the personality of the person with dementia seems to disappear; yet he or she is still there and requires an ever-increasing level of care. The continued decline of a family member despite the best efforts of those caring for the person causes feelings of inadequacy, helplessness, and anger. Validating the sadness, anger, frustration, and fear that caregivers often feel helps to counter their burnout and frustration. It is important to normalize and reframe the patient's behavior. For example, a patient with Alzheimer's repeatedly accused his 83-year-old spouse of having an affair. His wife was greatly relieved to learn that delusions of infidelity are common in people with dementia and that her husband hadn't secretly harbored doubts about her throughout their 50-year marriage. In family counseling, caregiving tasks can be redistributed among family members. Options for the immediate situation and long-term care can be presented to everyone at the same time, and conflicts and concerns can be discussed openly. This helps the family to move forward as a whole and to keep the needs of an aging parent from becoming the point of contention among feuding relatives. Such approaches can actually help to prevent abuse by relieving family and caregiver stress before it escalates.

Interventions and treatment goals with abused elders may be different from those at other stages of the life cycle. Home visits and extensive telephone work are important tools in providing care. Clinicians must work with their clients' natural support system. This may mean contacting the family doctor to understand health problems and the side effects of medication or asking a neighbor to provide respite. It may also mean advocating with community agencies, especially those that provide concrete services such as transportation or meals on wheels. Family work will focus on realigning relationships with adult children and the abuser, dealing with concerns about health and death, and providing concrete services. Older woman have tended not to use battered women's services, which are often neither accessible to them nor designed to meet their needs. But they do use programs tailored especially for them. Abuse is a crime. Many states have mandatory reporting laws and agencies to which incidents must be reported. The clinician must be aware of these and work within those guidelines.

Conclusion

The study of family violence is relatively new, as is the very concept that it is a social problem. When we address the societal arrangements that foster violence and oppression throughout the life cycle, we are confronting norms and beliefs that are deeply rooted in the dominant culture. These inequities have been formalized in law and by religious institutions as if they were sanctioned by God. They have become so widely accepted that they have rarely been noticed, much less questioned.

Victims of violence have more often been stigmatized than supported. They have little legal recourse, and they often receive little support or understanding even from their families and social circle. When we understand that violence is the abuse of power, we are able to recognize it in all its forms—physical abuse, psychological abuse, sexual abuse, and economic, political, and social oppression. We call on family therapists not to focus solely on the particular emotional and psychological dynamics of individual relationships and family systems, because this denies the impact of broader social forces on our clients throughout the life cycle that may encourage violence. We must enlarge our focus so that we can work together to support families to stop violence, develop nonviolent ways of resolving conflicts, and challenge the values that have promoted and allowed violence to continue in our society.

Chapter 26

Psychiatric Illness and the Life Cycle

Ellen Berman & Alison Heru

Psychiatric illness disrupts the individual's ability to navigate the world, and can disrupt family and community relationships throughout the life cycle. In milder forms of illnesses, people may function well, although they may be in distress. Some illnesses have their onset during a particular period of life and then disappear (e.g. postpartum depression). Some long-term disorders, such as attention deficit disorder (ADD) in adulthood or obsessive compulsive disorder, leave many areas of good functioning, but some symptoms may prove difficult within the family. For example, a disorganized person with ADD may be a loving parent but unable to manage a child's school and sleep schedule.

However, when persistent psychiatric illness seriously impairs the basic tasks of social/family life and work, family members struggle with grief, become caregivers, deal with stigma, and navigate a fragmented mental health system. Parents grieve for their son's or daughter's pain and the loss of their own dreams of the child's future; parents and grandparents often become depressed themselves. Partners and children cope with confusing and unpredictable behavior. In the active phases of the illness, individuals become fundamentally different from their pre-illness selves, so that family relationships change radically. Families are, however, a critical source of care and healing, and often the best guarantee that the person with psychiatric illness has a fulfilling life.

Psychiatric conditions are common across the world, and are among the leading causes of disability in all regions. (Global Burden of Disease, 2004 report). Most psychiatric illnesses have their onset in adolescence or early adulthood, and many are chronic or relapsing, producing difficulties in each life cycle stage. A young person, just becoming ill, stresses the resources of parents and grandparents and takes needed attention from siblings. An ill parent changes the dynamics of child-rearing in the family. Long-term illness in later stages of the life cycle may cause hostility, estrangement, or serious caregiver burden in spouses or grown children. Normal family life cycle transitions may worsen psychiatric symptoms. Conversely, psychiatric illness may make transitions more stressful or derail them completely. Understanding the generational position of the ill person (child, parent, elder) and the family's life cycle stage is vital to supporting the family. Many psychiatric illnesses have a genetic component, and more than one person in a 3-generation system may be symptomatic, increasing the family's burden.

The family's ability to support the ill family member(s) and maintain functional family life depends on its ability to access and utilize resources within the family, the community, and the mental health system. Women carry a disproportionate share of the caretaking burden. Cultural beliefs about illness, its treatment, and the family's responsibilities strongly influence the family's choices of treatment, the family's coping mechanisms, and the ability of the person to live independently. Some communities have the resources to provide consistent and compassionate care, but many do not.

Identifying, treating, and caring for ill members at different points in the life cycle. Anna, now 60 years old, a schoolteacher of German heritage, was initially referred for depressive symptoms at age 35. At that time her husband Ron, also of German ancestry, was 36 years old and worked as a salesman. They had three young children. As part of the evaluation, the psychiatrist requested a couples session, during which the therapist realized that Ron had symptoms of bipolar I (manic depressive) disorder. Anna,

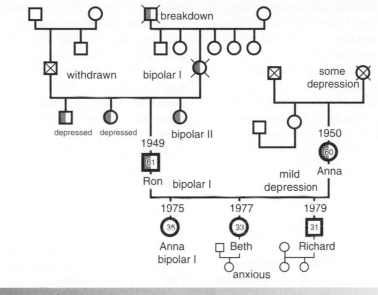

GENOGRAM 26.1 Anna and Ron

warm but stoic, a product of her German roots in small-town Nebraska, had soothed Ron during depressions and kept him from risky behavior during his periods of ebullient, expansive moods. This took great effort, and she often felt overburdened. Neither of them had identified his behavior as an illness, because the symptoms were relatively mild. They had not sought help until Anna became depressed. Ron's mood swings had not prevented him from working in sales; he was highly effective when hypomanic, and able to work, although with difficulty, when depressed. However, his symptoms severely taxed the family in the early stages of child-rearing. In fact, the timing of his entering treatment was determined by Anna's stress, not his. Their children, and Anna's mother, had all been ill over the last several months, and Anna became exhausted and depressed from trying to cope with everything.

Rather than begin Anna on antidepressants, the psychiatrist started Ron on lithium, which stabilized his mood cycle. The couple was given psychoeducational material regarding bipolar disorder, including information on how to identify illness episodes early so they could be treated quickly. They learned to separate bipolar symptoms, which lasted for weeks, included euphoria, decreased sleep need, increased sexuality, and overspending (in hypomania) and sadness and decreased ability to function (in depression), from everyday moods, which were evanes-

cent, linked to events of the day, and did not include behavioral changes. They were encouraged to call their doctor immediately if symptoms were not controlled with medication. Ron took more responsibility for his own care and that of the children. Anna's depression ended as she felt support and Ron's moods stabilized.

The psychiatrist reviewed their families of origin. Anna's family was close and generally functioned well. Ron's mother had had severe, and untreated, bipolar disorder, which severely impacted her parenting abilities. His father, an engineer, unable to tolerate her behavior and from a culture that demanded stoicism and avoidance of illness, immersed himself in his work. Ron and his siblings cared for themselves, tried to care for their mother when she was depressed, and managed her unpredictability when manic, throughout their childhood. His mother's illness and father's refusal to step in had serious implications for their children. As adults, two of Ron's siblings were depressed from parental neglect, and the third had bipolar disorder. His mother had died of cancer when Ron was 30. The therapist met with Ron and his father to discuss Ron's childhood experiences. His father acknowledged and apologized for his unavailability, and they left with a sense of greater connection.

Anna's parents were also told about Anna's depression and Ron's bipolar disorder. Anna's mother had been worried about them, and she took time away from home to help Anna with the children. This troubled Anna's father, who had recently retired and wanted his wife home, which briefly destabilized their later-life transition.

Anna and Ron were encouraged to tell their children in simple language that their Dad had a problem sometimes being extra happy or extra sad, that it was not about them, and that he was taking medication to keep his moods even. As the children reached school age, Ron was encouraged to label the problem and talk about it. Understanding that children's concerns change over time, the entire family was seen for a consult when the children were school age; the children seemed developmentally on track and comfortable with both parents.

The couple attended follow-up sessions frequently over the years to discuss life stage transitions and medication management. Ron continued to have mild but manageable mood changes. The children generally did well during childhood and adolescence, but during the young adult/launching period, each of them developed issues related to Ron's illness. The oldest developed severe depression during her first year in college. Since bipolar disorder has a large genetic component, she was immediately seen by their psychiatrist, who diagnosed bipolar disorder based on her history of previous mood fluctuations and her current symptoms. With rapid treatment with a mood stabilizer, she was functioning well within a few weeks, unlike her grandmother's and father's experiences. Her sister requested help for anxiety symptoms soon after marriage, related to concerns about men's ability to be consistently available, and was referred for therapy. Her brother had fears about dating, concerned about sharing his family history. Two family consultation sessions were held at this time.

Ron's mood became unstable again at retirement as his sense of self-worth decreased and his days became unstructured. Medication changes and a discussion of how to structure his time and think of himself as an "elder" were helpful. At age 60, with a 30 year marriage, Anna reports that she is "getting tired" of helping Ron manage his moods, and worries about her children's health. She has reduced her own stress by working less and practicing yoga. Their married children watch their own children anxiously for signs of mood disorder. The family's genetic history will be part of its ongoing story.

Treatment of psychiatric illness includes supporting the individual and the family in managing the tasks of their particular life stage. A family life cycle approach allows the therapist to anticipate stressors, such as college or retirement, that are likely to increase symptoms, and pay attention to family tasks that might be affected by the illness. Anna and Ron's psychiatrist knew, for example, that the process of launching would be stressful for all family members and brought the young adults in rapidly when problems occurred, thus preventing months of confusion and difficulty.

Anna and Ron are middle class, able to access therapy and medication and deal with the medical care system. They have had the same psychiatrist for 25 years, a major support in long-term illness. Anna's culturally learned stoicism has helped anchor the family. While bipolar disorder has affected each life stage and each generation, their resilience, knowledge, and willingness to confront the problems has eased the impact of illness on the next generation.

The Concept of Psychiatric Illness

The concept of psychiatric illness has a complex history in the popular imagination and the therapeutic community. Opinions have ranged from "it doesn't exist" to "it's due to bad parenting" to "it's purely biological." These differing opinions are confusing for families and make collaboration difficult for therapists. A multifactorial, systemic view of mental functioning is finally beginning to develop.

In recent years we have learned more about how the brain and the family/social system interact. Much of the brain's function is social in nature: it is designed to connect with others and to change from that interaction. While genetics set the boundaries of what is possible, the brain changes throughout the life cycle in response to environmental stimuli by increasing or decreasing neural connections, growing neurons, and changing patterns of neurotransmitters (epigenetics). The changed brain then interacts differently with the environment (Siegel, 2006). Nature and nurture are a true, connected system. This is why both medications and psychotherapy work, although they may target somewhat different symptoms, and both may be needed for symptom relief.

A stress-vulnerability model of psychiatric illness assumes that a person inherits a high or low vulnerability to environmental events. For example, a genetic predisposition to depression in response to loss will manifest when there is sufficient loss to produce problems. However, if the stress is high enough, depression, in particular, is more likely to occur regardless of genetic predisposition. Symptoms of schizophrenia and bipolar illness, which have a high genetic component, may occur at what would be low stress levels for most people. Family life cycle transitions, especially members entering or leaving a family, are particular relational stressors and often trigger psychiatric events.

The Evolving Nature of Diagnosis

Psychiatric illness is a nonspecific term for a variety of problems in thinking, feeling, and behavior that cause distress or disability. Because there are as yet no consistent biological markers for psychiatric diagnosis, the Diagnostic and Statistical Manual of Mental Disorders of the American Psychiatric Association is a classification system that divides mental disorders into types based on criteria sets. It was designed so that researchers, or therapists sharing cases, could be reasonably sure they are speaking about the same problem. As our knowledge of brain functioning increases, many of these diagnostic categories evolve and change. DSM IV TR states clearly that these are not exact categories with clear boundaries, and that the line between normal and ill is not always clear. (DSM IV TR, 2000, p. xxxi) The DSM is based only on individual diagnosis. There is as yet no agreed-upon method for categorizing relationship difficulties.

The diagnosis given to a person may change as symptoms shift with age. It may also vary with the skill of the interviewer and the behavior of the person at the time of interview. However, diagnosis matters because psychiatric treatment is, to the best of our ability, based on diagnosis. Getting a diagnosis also changes the perception of the self and how the person is seen in the family. For example, a teenager staying in bed all day may be called lazy, but if he is given a diagnosis of depression, he will be seen as "ill" and treated differently. The teenager and family may be relieved by having a label for the problem or frightened by the idea of an illness or both.

Different cultures express symptoms in different ways, making diagnosis more complex. In societies where depression is shameful, patients may present with physical symptoms rather than sadness. Misdiagnosis can occur when the doctor is not familiar with cultural norms. For example, culturally appropriate intense expressions of emotions by Latinos may be interpreted as pathological in New England. Distrust of the White medical establishment by African Americans, based on historical events and current treatment disparities, may be interpreted as paranoia. In some cultures, illness is seen as caused by supernatural forces, which complicates traditional Western treatment. Cultural competence leading to more accurate diagnosis is a major focus in many training programs and requires the mental health providers to understand their own culture, assumptions, and how different cultural groups understand emotion, illness, and appropriate care.

Diagnostic uncertainty is a frequent concern, given our incomplete knowledge. People change over time, and diagnostic categories change over time. Depending on the circumstances and the person's point in the life cycle, the same person may have his or her diagnosis changed several times over a lifetime. This process is confusing, even if a new diagnosis suggests more effective treatment. However, continued attention to this issue is important, because the longer the period between symptom onset and correct treatment, the more likely that the patient will be slow to meet normal developmental milestones and that family life cycle functioning will be altered.

Diagnostic changes over several life cycle stages. John (**Genogram 26.2**) is the oldest child of two Anglo-Saxon Protestant, highly successful lawyers. In 1985, when John was in his 20s, an unattached young adult in his first job, he saw a psychiatrist because of an inability to finish tasks, depression, and low self-esteem, persisting from childhood. He was diagnosed with major depressive disorder and treated with antidepressants, but had very little symptom change. Although creative, he struggled with work, being fired at least twice for angry outbursts and disorganization. His parents were annoyed with him and

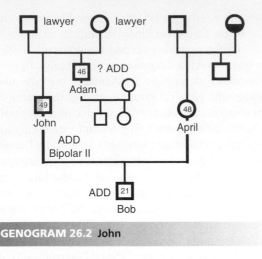

GENOGRAM 26.2 John

unsupportive, unable to understand why he didn't "pull himself together." They were bothered by his emotionality, which was a bad fit with their cultural assumption of early independence and emotional control. The launching process was fraught with conflict, which increased his symptoms.

He did marry, but his marriage was troubled by his unreliability and volatile moods. When they became parents this worsened, and his wife became an overwhelmed caretaker with little patience for their difficult son. Over the next 10 years, as John went to other therapists, he was also called passive–aggressive and diagnosed with narcissistic personality disorder, because he seemed so self-involved.

In 2003, when he was 43, his now 15-year-old son was diagnosed with ADD, having struggled for years with impulsivity, disorganization, and lack of focus at school. During a family meeting scheduled to discuss parenting strategies for ADD, the therapist and John realized that John had the same symptoms. While in 1985 it was frequently assumed that ADD symptoms disappeared by adulthood, by 2003 it was recognized that symptoms usually continued throughout life and that ADD was highly heritable. As a result of the constant struggle to focus or complete tasks, and their frequent mistakes, many ADD adults become depressed or appear narcissistic. They are often first diagnosed correctly when their children are treated.

Treatment for John in 2003, in midlife, included medication for his ADD, an anger management program, and help developing strategies to build on his creativity

without sacrificing organization and timeliness. John felt better and his work functioning improved. Couples sessions helped his wife to understand that John's lateness and distractibility were related to his diagnosis, not a lack of caring for her or passive–aggressiveness. This improved their couple functioning. As the emotional climate improved at home, their son became less oppositional, agreeing to take medication and work on organization "like my dad."

Nevertheless, John continued to have periods of depression. In 2009, as Bob is launched, he is being assessed for bipolar II disorder, which we now know is frequently associated with ADD, and which requires additional medication. He is, career-wise, considerably behind where he might have been, making the post child-rearing phase more difficult as he works to pay for his son's college and maintain the respect of his parents and wife. At this point in the life cycle, John's therapist must work with him and his wife to let go of past hurts and move forward effectively with family life.

Psychiatric Illness and the Family System

Psychiatric illness often affects the ability to read social situations accurately and empathize with and nurture others. Psychiatric illness increases the likelihood of troubled relationships (Whisman 2006). Conversely, family conflict can cause illness, depression and anxiety in one or more family members; approximately 50 percent of troubled marriages have at least one depressed member. With severe and persistent psychiatric illness, there may be an inability to perform normal tasks, to parent effectively, or to maintain an income. In addition, people with serious psychiatric illness often refuse to admit that they are ill, to accept responsibility for problems, or to take medication, making the situation even more difficult.

The ability of families to maintain a warm emotional climate is stressed by the difficulties and unhappiness of any family member. In families that have high rates of criticism, hostility, and emotional overinvolvement toward the patient, relapse is more frequent than in families with less intensity. This behavioral constellation, first described by Brown and Rutter (1966) is labeled high expressed emotion, and is a stressor for those with psychiatric disorders, as in the case of John, just described. (Wearden et al., 2000). The pattern is bidirectional: expressed emotion increases in families as the individual's symptoms increase and time of illness lengthens (Miklowitz, 2008). This does not suggest that these families are pathological, but that the ill member's behavior is a stress for family members trying to cope. In order to assess expressed emotion, it is important to take into account the community and family's cultural norms before making assessments of the family environment. Treatment that includes communications training will decrease the emotional intensity in the family and result in lower levels of expressed emotion. Understanding that many symptoms are not under the patient's control is helpful in reducing criticism (Miklowitz 2004). A more complete review of interventions to decrease family stress when there is a psychiatric disorder can be found in Solomon (2009).

The process of treatment may also stress the family. There may be disagreement among doctors and family members about the diagnosis, what kind of family support is appropriate, or who, if anyone, is "to blame." Providers may insist on remaining out of contact with the family, or require family therapy in which all family members are seen as needing to change, rather than offering education and support. Medications, although often necessary, can cause difficulties for the family. Many patients have difficulty agreeing to remain on medication over long periods of time, and family conflict may result if symptoms return. Family opinions about whether the person "really needs" medication, who is in charge of compliance, or what the family should do in the face of medication refusal, may become the focus of power struggles between parents and ill adult children, between spouses, and adult children with their ill parents. Medication side effects such as sleepiness, weight gain, decrease in libido, as well as the possibility of overdose may affect couple and family dynamics.

Caregiving in psychiatric illness includes both the subjective burden of managing difficult behavior and the objective burden of handling practical issues, such as wage earning or dealing with the mental health system. Families must decide how much of their resources to devote to an ill member, who, if anyone, is responsible for active caregiving, and what the boundaries are between providing appropriate caregiving and supporting overly dependent behavior. Family members may take on tasks unusual for the family life stage. For example, a grandmother or an oldest child may become the primary parent, or a teen may become the family wage earner. Cross-generational alliances are common.

Over the course of the life cycle, if the person has periods of good functioning and remains committed to treatment, the family adjusts. If the ill person who is past young adulthood, refuses to admit to or deal with their illness, the family may extrude them, or one member may remain completely focused on the ill person (most often the mother) well into old age, while other family members give up. Sometimes the ill person cuts off all family contact.

While some illnesses remit quickly with appropriate treatment, for others, improvement of symptoms may be measured in months or years. In long-term illness the goal is to support the family without expecting full recovery. Differences in level of function are less about the diagnosis and more about the level of symptom severity. For example, someone with well controlled symptoms of bipolar disorder, may cause less stress on the family than a highly anxious person who constantly demands attention and reassurance.

Caregiving is not all negative. Many families report that through weathering a crisis together, their relationships are enriched and more loving than they might otherwise have been. The assessment and support of strengths is an important key part of the clinician's work (Marsh & Lefley 1996). The family's resilience may vary at different points in the life cycle and the position of the ill person in the family. For example, if the family breadwinner becomes too ill to work, the struggle to survive economically may strain the family's resources to the breaking point, while caring for an elderly parent when there are enough people to share the burden may be a source of strength. If the family cannot manage the ill person, he or she may become the community's responsibility. Such persons may become homeless, or cared for in hospitals or small community settings.

Culture and Psychiatric Illness

Cultural issues impact both diagnosis and treatment of psychiatric illness. Major mental health disorders like schizophrenia, bipolar disorder, depression, and panic disorder are found worldwide across all racial and ethnic groups. In the United States, the annual prevalence of all psychiatric disorders is about 21 percent. The Surgeon General's supplement, 2001, states:

> *Racial and ethnic minorities collectively experience a greater disability burden from mental illness than do whites, This stems from minorities receiving less care and poorer quality of care, rather than from their illnesses being inherently more severe or prevalent within the community. . . . (http://www.surgeongeneral.gov/library/ mental-health/cre/execsummary-2.html).*

In addition to having less access to care, treatment may be delayed for patients living in poverty because their stressed families have less energy to deal with psychiatric problems until a crisis occurs.

Culture and class profoundly influence caregiving in many different ways. In the United States ill persons who are ethnic minorities are more likely to live with family members. According to studies, rates are about 75 to 85 percent for Latinos, 66 percent for African Americans, and 40 percent for Whites (Lefley, 2009). However, family members living separately may also spend much time and energy caring for and worrying about ill relatives. Midlife and older siblings or parents, living alone and refusing medical or psychiatric help, are particularly painful problems for their siblings and children.

Gender also influences both illness diagnosis and caretaking. Rates of schizophrenia and bipolar illness are the same for men and women, but women are twice as likely to be depressed, beginning at mid-puberty and persisting through adult life (Piccinelli & Wilkinson, 2000). Possible causes include hormonal changes, learned behaviors of caring for others before caring for self, and the subordinate position of women in society.

Women represent the majority of caregivers, as mothers, daughters, wives, or sisters. They shoulder more of the emotional burden and organize much of the interaction with the health care system, whether in the work force or not, as illustrated by our cases. Women caregivers tend to fare worse than men, reporting higher levels of depression and anxiety and lower levels of subjective well-being, life satisfaction, and physical health (McGuire et al., 2007).

Maintaining good connections and a functioning family life requires support from the extended family and community. Due to the stigma surrounding mental illness, neighbors and extended family may avoid the family, uncertain how to help. If the family feels ashamed and closes its boundaries to outside help, normal developmental transitions, especially the movement of children toward adulthood, may be more difficult.

Psychiatric Illness and the Family Life Cycle

Adolescence and the launching process

Most psychiatric illnesses first manifest themselves when the individual is between 17 and 30 years old, but peculiar thinking and behavior may occur much earlier. Adolescence is a period of rapid change and teen, parents, and therapist may be confused about the meaning of the symptoms. Adolescents who are depressed or pre-psychotic may withdraw, become involved with alcohol and drugs, or have difficulty socializing, but these are behaviors that are common in high school. They are often reluctant to admit to suicidal or "crazy" thoughts, or to talk to a therapist. Underdiagnosis and overdiagnosis are frequent.

Hospitalization, for suicidal or dangerous behaviors, is less dependent on diagnosis than on the family's ability to manage the situation, and the availability of affordable outpatient care. If the family is already in crisis from divorce, death, or other losses, parents will be less available and the adolescent's symptoms are likely to increase. In these situations, it is particularly difficult to tell if there is a biologically based illness, or if the problems are embedded in the family crisis and will remit with attention to the family system. Grandparents often become involved, offering financial help for therapy or giving helpful or contradictory advice. It is not unusual for grandparents as well as parents to become depressed if the child is severely acting out or hospitalized. Inclusion of the extended family in evaluation or education sessions is often useful.

Even with a correct diagnosis, the treatment plan and prognosis are often unclear because individual strengths and weaknesses are not fully known. If John has barely finished high school, does not want to attend college, and insists he needs to stay home in bed, should the family accommodate him or push him to work? If he wants to live by himself, is it safe? Should Alice, who is been hospitalized once for anorexia, go to college far away, or should she stay close to the family and her therapist? Parental disagreement over these decisions will produce more stress. If Alice needs constant care, her mother, who has been organizing her treatment, may become anxious, her younger brother may try to be the good child and the peacemaker, and her father may become angry or withdrawn. Family therapists must help the parents and extended family system make the best decisions they can, while understanding that there are no definitive answers. It is helpful to remember that many adolescents who go through serious emotional crises, and a prolonged and complicated launching period, recover during early adulthood and function well.

Unattached young adults

For the unattached young adult, any psychiatric illness compounds the difficulties of developing an adult relational system outside the family. Odd behavior makes friendship and dating more difficult. Sexual side effects from medications make sexual experimentation difficult. Even if the person's social skills are intact, rejection is always a possibility, resulting in social withdrawal and symptom worsening in fragile people. Alcohol and drugs are common ways to cope. Suicide attempts in this age group can be precipitated by the breakup of a relationship compounded by alcohol abuse. Nevertheless, the majority of people who are reasonably functional eventually marry.

Seriously ill young people who cannot manage either college or work may be unable to take the most basic steps toward independence. Development may be slowed or completely halted, so that they live outside of normal developmental time, preoccupied by illness. If the child remains symptomatic over years, parents must grieve the loss of their dreams for the future of their child. The task of launching other children may be compromised by financial strain, parental distraction, or the siblings' belief that they are needed at home. If the child lives at home, the parents may never reach the post childrearing stage. Few long-term alternatives to home care exist. For single parents, the stress of providing home care for the ill child may be overwhelming. Seriously ill young adults may never complete the tasks of young adulthood, keeping the family from moving forward, as in the following case.

Family development halted by illness

Bill (**Genogram 26.3**) is a 30-year-old African American man with schizophrenia, who lives at home with his mother Joan, a 65 year-old, secretary. Bill's father, Ted, developed symptoms of schizophrenia soon after Bill was born. After a tumultuous 8 years, his mother divorced Ted, leaving her with full-time care of Bill and his younger brother Jim. Ted was unable to contribute financially to child care. He maintained contact with the children, but these contacts were highly disturbing for Bill. Ted's father, Bill's grandfather, also suffers from schizophrenia, and is a source of worry for the family. Joan's sister and mother live nearby and often visit her and the children.

Bill was an "odd" and difficult child. In adolescence his behavior became more volatile, with rages and serious suicide attempts. Bill attacked his mother and brother during one episode. His younger brother Jim, unable to handle the conflict, and becoming depressed himself, went to live with an aunt at age 16. Bill became acutely psychotic at age 18, hallucinating and delusional, and was diagnosed with schizophrenia. Without the funds for private hospitalization, he was treated in a large urban hospital and discharged quickly

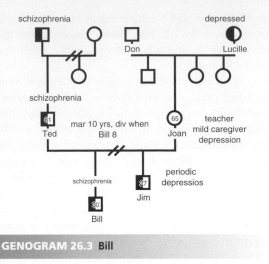

schizophrenia   depressed

Don   Lucille

schizophrenia

Ted   mar 10 yrs, div when   Joan   teacher
       Bill 8   mild caregiver
                                       depression

schizophrenia   periodic
                             depressios

Bill   Jim

GENOGRAM 26.3 Bill

to a community mental health center with a long waiting list. The admission was frightening for everyone. Little attention, advice, or education was given to the relatives who came to visit. Between 18 and 24 years of age, he was hospitalized three further times, once for a serious suicide attempt. Although Bill has never been arrested, his family has been constantly afraid that, as an African American man, any threatening behavior outside the home might produce a police response. Over the last 12 years he has seen approximately 20 outpatient therapists, due to high turnover in the mental health clinic. Due to medication side effects, he is on his eighth medication regimen. Sometimes Bill goes off his medications and psychotic symptoms recur; he is taken to the emergency room, where he is medicated, occasionally kept for 24 hours, and discharged. His current therapist has raised the question of independent living for him, given that he is long past the normal launching age, but everyone feels that he is safest at home, and there are few good alternatives.

Bill has remained highly sensitive to any stress and been unable to hold a steady job, although he is willing to do odd jobs in the neighborhood. He is overweight from lack of activity and drinks excessively. At a point when he would normally be launched and his mother dealing with retirement issues, Joan is still working to support them both, and wondering what will happen to Bill when she dies. Jim has moved to another state and is not involved with the family. Although basically a cheerful person, Joan has become depressed as caregiver burden increases and

she realizes that Bill, like his father, will probably always be ill. She has joined a local NAMI (National Alliance on Mental Illness (NAMI.org)) chapter, which has helped her find resources and a support group; she also is deeply involved with her church group.

FAMILY RESPONSE TO ILLNESS EPISODES AND HOSPITALIZATION As with Bill, personality changes may begin long before a full-blown episode of psychiatric illness (McFarlane, 2002). Family members may subliminally be aware that something is wrong, but unless they have previous experience with illness, problems may progress to the point of a dramatic event, such as a suicide attempt, before help is sought. Fear, relief, shame, grief, and shock are common reactions to a diagnosis of psychiatric disorder. The family's response in crisis mode is similar to that for physical illness (see Chapter 23 on Chronic Illness) for both practical and emotional tasks.

Hospitalizations occur when the family cannot handle the situation at home. They are particularly likely early in an illness when treatment has not begun, or if the person has dropped out of treatment. In today's mental health system, most hospitalizations are brief. Unlike physical illness, where the ill person usually accepts hospitalization, many psychiatrically ill individuals resist hospitalization. Family members may feel that they are betraying the person by insisting on hospitalization, especially with an involuntary commitment. If the ill person is psychotic but refuses treatment and does not present a "danger to self or others" the hospital may refuse to admit them involuntarily, or may discharge them after 72 hours, leaving the family to deal with an acutely ill, resistant person. With short hospital stays, like Bill's, the person is likely to return home still symptomatic, and the aftermath of a hospitalization can be a time of "family wide form of post traumatic stress" (Miklowitz, 2008). Family anxiety increases if a previously functional, emancipated adult returns to his or her parents' home to recuperate. With young people, especially, there may be a "revolving door" with multiple brief hospitalizations before stabilization occurs.

Hospitalization can be particularly confusing if the culture of the patient and the hospital staff differ. Cultural differences between the physician and the patient and the family may cause problems. For example, a quiet respectful stance in an Asian father may be incorrectly interpreted as understanding and agreement. The outpouring of emotion in a West Indian family may be misinterpreted as anger or depression.

THE FAMILY AND THE MENTAL HEALTH SYSTEM

Hospitalization and subsequent outpatient referral expose the patient and family to the complexities of the mental health system. Community mental health centers are mostly underfunded, and rural psychiatric services may be unobtainable. These centers tend to provide a disproportionate level of care to minorities and the lack of funding enhances disparity in mental health care. We know that psychoeducation and family support increase family and patient functioning (Anderson et al., 1986; McFarlane, 2002; Micklowitz, 2008) but unfortunately, the mental health system may not provide education, alliance, and support, thus leaving families feeling helpless and anxious. Although the system is changing, there are still programs that see the family as the cause of the patient's problems, or believe that involving families violates the patient's autonomy. When patients are aged 21 or older, their consent is needed for the doctor to speak to the family, and many physicians are reluctant to explain the need for family involvement and obtain consent. A caregiving family needs contact with the adult child's therapist in order to support a treatment plan and react well in emergencies.

Most families with a member who has serious psychiatric illness will deal with 5 to 50 mental health professionals of varying degrees, beliefs, and skill sets over a lifetime. This is particularly true for poor families, who are treated in facilities where staff turnover is high. Even when families can afford private care, psychiatrists are often limited by insurance companies to medication management, while therapy is done by nonmedical therapists. Therefore, families will likely be working with at least two professionals at once,

professionals who may not communicate adequately. If more than one family member is in treatment, multiple therapists are part of the system. It is then up to the family to insist on information, education, and communication between providers. Families who have dealt with mental health problems for years face different problems later in the life cycle; they are likely to know more about the illness and previous treatment than the mental health professionals assigned to them and be exhausted and financially drained by the constant difficulties.

Self-help organizations such as NAMI and DBSA (Depression and Bipolar Support Alliance dbsalliance.org) fill some of the gaps in support and education and provide crucial emotional support. These organizations however, tend to be disconnected from the rest of the mental health system.

Illness and the couple

A happy relationship is one of the best predictors of psychological health. A calm, affectionate relationship mitigates everyday stress, and a troubled marriage is in itself stressful. The relationship between psychological disorders and couplehood is bidirectional. Sometimes relational conflict causes psychiatric symptoms, especially anxiety and depression, sometimes psychiatric symptoms cause couple conflict; in many cases it is impossible to determine if one preceded the other. In couples with a family history of abuse and alcoholism, a combination of untreated mental illness, alcohol, and anger may produce marital violence.

MATE SELECTION Many people with more severe mental illness do not marry, or marry during periods of relative health. Often they choose partners with severe problems who can tolerate and understand their behavior. An alternative pattern is that of a caregiver (often the resilient adult child of an ill parent) who chooses an ill person to rescue, hoping this time they can "do it right." The marriage rate for schizophrenia is lower than that for other psychiatric problems. Patients who are hypomanic or borderline often appear romantic and exciting during courtship; their problems may not be obvious until later.

ILLNESS DEVELOPING AFTER MARRIAGE After the glow of early couplehood wears off, problems occur even in well-functioning relationships, as the partners discover that the relationship does not help them solve their problems. People with a history of childhood trauma and loss may function well until marital losses, such as an affair or work-related separation, precipitate a depression. If a serious psychiatric disorder develops, the partner may feel deeply disillusioned. The therapist's task is to support the couple and find areas of strength. Good communication is particularly important, and basic psychoeducation and communications training are helpful for couples beginning a life together.

Many couples, however, function well in the face of illness. Functional couples are those in which there is affection and support, little demand for perfection, and patients who are generally compliant with the treatment regimen and willing to accept responsibility for handling their problems, as Ron did in the first example. Community and extended family support are important in keeping the couple part of the larger world. Even so, over time, as with Anna and Ron, caregiver burden and disaffection may become overwhelming.

The Family With Young and Adolescent Children

Couples with a heavy genetic loading for serious mental illness must consider whether or not to have children. For most couples, the drive to create a family wins out over the possible risks. Care providers should do their best to give couples all the information available, help them weigh risk and benefits, and support whatever decision they make.

Parental illness

Postpartum depression is a psychiatric emergency that demands immediate attention; the possibility of suicide or harm to the child can occur quickly. Even if there is no physical harm, children of mothers with untreated postpartum depression and no social supports are at developmental risk (Murray & Cooper, 1997).

Parents with serious psychiatric illness are likely to have difficulties parenting due to volatile moods and irritability, difficulty mirroring the child, or inability to provide consistent limits and reality testing. If the main family wage earner becomes ill, the family's financial security may be at risk. Social supports may be lost if the family drops down a social class. Alcohol and drug use may increase, further decreasing parenting ability. Seriously ill parents, especially if poor and single, may lose their children to foster care if there are no family supports.

Parenting alone as a working parent is a particularly high-stress situation. Single-parent mothers have a higher incidence of depression, due to the constant demands and increased financial burden.

Children have varied responses to parental illness. They may be buffered by siblings, depending on birth order. Some hyper-resilient children, most often the oldest, become lifetime caretakers of their parents, younger sibs, or as adults, with spouses. Other children may have difficulty with emotional regulation or become oppositional and may be misdiagnosed with psychiatric illness because no one has understood the chaos at home. Adolescents often leave the house precipitously to escape the family difficulties. Mediating adults such as the other parent or grandparents can provide relief if they are available, supportive, and able to help the child understand and manage the situation.

While local educational resources for children of ill parents are still in early development in this country, there are excellent books (e.g., Sherman, 2006; Holloway, 2006) and Web sites (e.g., Children of Parents with Mental Illness http://www.aicafmha.net.au/copmi/) available, and support groups in some areas.

PSYCHIATRIC ILLNESS IN THE CHILD Children are highly reactive to family stress. It is often difficult to determine diagnosis (if any) and to develop a treatment plan for children, who are changing rapidly. Parental disagreement over the need for and type of treatment, especially with difficult younger children, can become the focus of serious marital conflict. Undiagnosed, untreated depression in adolescents frequently leads to substance abuse and suicide attempts. When children are seen by therapists, parents must be involved in the treatment plan. For children with odd behavior in adolescence and family histories of schizophrenia, early intervention may delay the onset of illness (McFarlane, 2002).

Psychiatric illness at midlife

It is less common for a serious psychiatric illness, other than depression or dementia, to manifest itself for the first time after age 40. Midlife depression may occur in response to losses in income, a deep sense of life failure, poor health, or loss of a relationship, such as a parent. Such depressions are often successfully treated. Couples with a previously well functioning relationship usually weather the crisis.

Long-term psychiatric problems may change in midlife. In many people with schizophrenia, psychiatric symptomatology becomes less intense in midlife and older adulthood, and some demonstrate relatively complete remission, although the lost years of development can never be completely made up. Recurrent depressions, however, tend to worsen over time if inadequately treated.

Relationships may become more comfortable, particularly after children launch. However, if the illness has been persistent, and the person difficult to live with, compassion fatigue may develop in the partner. Sometimes the better functioning spouse begins an affair and/or leaves the marriage when the children reach late high school or college age. Divorce affects these couples in unpredictable ways. The more dysfunctional ex-partner may get better or worse; the more functioning partner may become depressed rather than relieved. The grown children in this situation may have been encouraging the more functioning spouse to leave for years, or may feel a desperate need to care for the less functioning one. Often these roles are split between siblings. Enmeshed adult children who become the caretakers of the "left behind" parent often develop anger, anxiety, and depression.

The ability and willingness of the family to provide care alters over time; a parent may be more willing to invest time, energy, and money into a 25-year old than a 45-year old with multiple hospitaliza-tions and poor medication compliance. After a parental death, midlife siblings may not be as available to an ill sibling as their parents were.

Working with families at this life stage involves an examination of the situation to determine what could be changed and what must be accepted. Family members must balance loyalty to ill family members against their own and the rest of the family's needs and find ways to deal with guilt and split loyalties.

SINGLE AND ILL AT MIDLIFE Single, ill midlife adults usually remain part of a family system, although they are likely to live alone. Parents, siblings, or adult children commonly provide emotional or financial support. Parents with an ill, midlife adult child may find their marriage still organized around worry for the child. While they might be less willing to support the child completely, most parents do not give up emotionally unless there has been violence, substance abuse, or unbearable personal hostility.

Boundary issues—such as how much care, time, and money the ill person should receive—are common family systems issues. In larger, extended families with a culture of caregiving, there may be more psychological space available for care. In scattered nuclear families where there is less of a tradition of caregiving, it is more common for the burden of care to fall on one relative, most often a daughter, or for the person to fall off the family map.

A fair number of chronically ill adults outlast their welcome with any family member or choose to cut themselves off from the family. An increasing number are incarcerated for odd behavior; many live in halfway houses or small apartments supported by welfare, SSI, or family members. Some become homeless, especially if they are substance abusers, and may refuse all contact with family members until a health crisis occurs.

Deaths among persons with mental illness are more likely to occur when the person is living alone, over 40, and cut off from family. Rather than suicide, they are likely to die from untreated medical illness from lack of self-care, smoking, drinking, and refusal to seek or follow medical advice.

Older adults with acute or chronic illness

In older adults, late onset depression is often associated with increasing physical infirmity, a loss of purpose after retirement, or the loss of loved ones. In the United States, ageism may contribute to depression or paranoia. Throughout the world, suicide rates are highest among the elderly. The risk factors for suicide include psychiatric illness and substance abuse, male gender, divorce, prior suicide attempt, family history of psychiatric disorder or suicide, a firearm in the home, and a recent, severely stressful life event (Moscicki, 1995). Dementia is a common issue of aging, and it is often difficult to distinguish from mental confusion due to depression, overmedication, or systemic illness. The effort required for correct diagnosis and treatment is often exhausting for everyone in the family. For older adults with chronic psychiatric illness, social withdrawal and years of poor functioning often leave them with a limited social network, and they have to navigate the aging process alone.

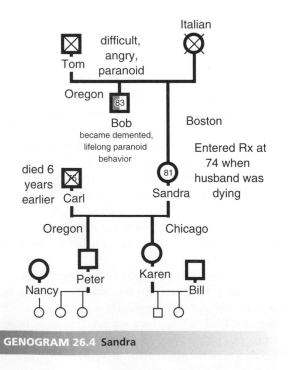

GENOGRAM 26.4 Sandra

Caregiving, loss, depression, and dementia in an older family system

Sandra, (**Genogram 26.4**) of European Jewish descent, now age 81, and living in Boston, originally entered therapy at 74 when her husband was dying. Sandra and Carl have two grown children, Karen, married and living in Chicago, and Peter, married and living in Oregon. Sandra had had previous mild depressions, but Carl's illness precipitated a severe episode. In therapy, the couple reviewed longstanding marital issues, their love for each other, and their grief over his illness and impending death. They were encouraged to involve their children in connecting with Carl and talking openly to him. The therapist's focus on the family's life cycle needs for life review and closure, and connection during the dying process, allowed Sandra's depression to be placed in context and family members to take care of each other. Sandra grieved after his death, but with support from her therapist, her children, and her friends, recovered from her depression and was able to function well.

She returned to therapy 6 years later when her older brother, Bob, developed dementia. Bob lived in Oregon, alone, and had a lifelong history of odd and paranoid behavior. He had supported himself and managed his life, although with almost no social network. He had had only phone contact with Sandra for years. Now an acquaintance of his called her, because Bob was found wandering in the street. She was angry at her brother, who had been no help to her at any point in her life, but there was no one else left in her family of origin. Sandra's family included a number of Holocaust survivors, and the idea that she would abandon a family member was unbearable. Alone in Boston, 81 years old, she became depressed and panicked about how to handle the situation. Realistically at this life stage she could not handle the situation alone, and needed help from her adult children. With support from her therapist, Sandra enlisted her children, especially Peter, who lived in the same city as his uncle, although he had not seen him for years. Their previous family work had made it easier for them to work together. Sandra and Peter found a care manager to help plan for Bob's care. Following the pattern of women caretakers, Peter's wife, Nancy, became heavily involved as well, which took some time away from her school age children. With a great deal of effort, they arranged for his admission to a nursing home and were able to persuade him to go. Sandra, Peter, and his wife were highly stressed by the experience; it took Sandra some months to recover from her anxiety. Still, Sandra's determination and resilience, and Peter and Nancy's unselfish help, got Bob to a safe place and allowed Sandra to continue her life.

Conclusion

Psychiatric illnesses are complex and ongoing stressors for families and have impact across generations. Their impact depends on the life cycle stage of the family, the duration of illness and level of function of the ill person, and the ability of all to maintain connection and hope. Particularly difficult periods include illness during the young adult stage, which decreases the ability to form a functional life structure, illness during parenting, which impacts children, and illness during elder years without fam-

ily support. Poverty, racial disparities, stigma, and poorly funded psychiatric services increase difficulties in treatment. Caregivers are more likely to be women, and many become depressed at points in the process. Support from members of extended family, community, and professionals allow families to access their strengths and support the person's best functioning. Assessment of the entire network, including family members, community, and mental health providers, is critical to helping the family. Family psychoeducation and support is crucial. Traditional family therapy can also be useful at different points in the process. Coping with illness requires family and individual resilience and commitment from everyone, including all the professionals involved in care.

Chapter 27

Coaching at Various Stages of the Life Cycle

Monica McGoldrick & Betty Carter

All clients have very specific issues and triangles related to their stage of the family life cycle and to the particular history and circumstances of their families of origin. This chapter will outline Bowen's method of coaching and discuss common triangles and coaching interventions to suggest a way to orient clinically to individuals and families throughout the life cycle. We summarize the process of "coaching" individuals in their efforts to change themselves in the context of their nuclear and parental family systems at various points throughout the life cycle. We consider this theoretical framework to be powerful for assessing and intervening with families at each point through life. This multigenerational and multicontextual life cycle "coaching" framework helps clients define themselves proactively in relationship to others in their family throughout their lives, without emotionally cutting off or giving in. Coaching is a method of therapy based on the theoretical concepts of Dr. Murray Bowen (1978; Papero, 1990; Kerr & Bowen, 1988) and elaborated by his students Carter, Fogarty, Friedman, Guerin, Kerr, Lerner, McGoldrick, Titleman, and others. The term "coaching" refers to the therapist's being like a coach, on the sidelines of a game, keeping the big picture in mind, advising on strategy, and noting reactions, strengths, and weaknesses. The coach cheers players on, but the work and the responsibility to reach the goal remain with the players. The word "coach" also, of course, describes a teacher or mentor helping a student to master a difficult task.

Bowen family systems is based on the idea that if one person changes, all others in emotional contact with him or her will have to make compensatory changes. This approach focuses on overall patterns of relationships rather than just an individual's intrapsychic processes. It focuses on the most motivated and functional family member, rather than the "sickest," because this is the person who is most able to take action to change his or her part in the family process. The emphasis in coaching is on the who, what, when, where, and how of family patterns and themes, rather than on the why of individual motivation. The most of the work is conducted outside of therapy sessions in the relationships with actual family members, rather than during sessions in the relationship with the therapist. Teaching, thinking, planning, and other intellectual processes leading up to actual relationship change are given priority over interpretation and insight, which may otherwise substitute for action, or emotional catharsis and support, which might eliminate the anxiety that drives motivation to change. Emotional functioning is viewed in the context of universal reciprocal processes that vary in degree from family to family. Feelings are addressed as related to family emotional patterns, rather than being dealt with primarily in the therapeutic relationship. The therapist encourages the development of a calm atmosphere and to diminish emotional intensity, as the best context for the therapeutic endeavor.

Coaching begins by training clients to become observers and researchers of their own role in the family patterns of behavior over the family life cycle. Coaching then moves to help them bring their behavior more in line with their deepest beliefs, even if this means upsetting family members by disobeying family "rules," which it usually does.

The ultimate goal of family systems work is to get a person-to-person relationship with each living person in your current nuclear and extended family. The process of working out personal relationships occurs at different levels from monitoring internal anxiety to tracking intimate conversations to doing genealogical research, and the work on each level depends on the client's internal clock.

The basic idea of coaching is that if you can change the part you play in your family problems and hold it despite the family's reaction, while keeping in emotional contact with family members, you maximize the likelihood of changing not just your own role, but also the dynamics of the family overall. Family relationships tend to be highly reciprocal, patterned, and repetitive, and to have circular, rather than linear, motion. Thinking, which asks "why?" tends to blame someone for the problem, however unwittingly, and is viewed as not as useful as identifying patterns and tracing their flow. This is because family patterns, once established, tend to be perpetuated by everyone involved, even though not all family members have equal power or influence on family processes. The key clinical point is that, although there is a reciprocal aspect to all relationships, a person's individual participation in any system is all he or she can change.

If a person changes his or her predictable emotional input, reactions also change, interrupting the previous flow of interactions in the system. Other family members will be jarred out of their own unthinking responses, and, in the automatic move toward homeostasis inherent in all systems, will tend to react by trying to get the disrupter back into place again. In two-person subsystems, the reciprocity of emotional functioning can be striking, as in the marriage of the dreamer and the doer, the optimist and the pessimist, or the intergenerational involvement between the nagging parent and the dawdling child. This is not to say that the power of both partners to change a relationship is equal. Women and children in families embedded in a patriarchal social system have decidedly less power to influence the structure than do men, and people of color, the poor, and homosexuals are highly disadvantaged in their leverage to change existing social structures. Thus, the analysis of the system must include analysis of the unequal power distribution among members of a system. Thus, men have more power than women to define and determine the relationships in a system; parents have more power than children; and people who are more privileged because of their race,

culture, class, or sexual orientation have more power than those with less privilege. Even so, relationships are reciprocal; though, one must also factor in the dimension of power in order to think clearly about how to change patterns in a system.

Fusion and Differentiation

Emotional anxiety tends to lead to a kind of fusion, or "stuck togetherness," of family members within a system. They may attempt to control or dominate others, fail to develop themselves, or give up part or most of their identity out of fear that they will lose the love of other family members. Indeed, women in our society have for centuries been raised to give up self in this way. Emotional maturity is a measure of the extent to which individuals are able to follow their own values and self-directed life course, while being emotionally present with others, rather than living reactively by the cues of those close to them. They do not have to spend their life energy on winning approval, attacking others, intellectualizing, keeping themselves emotionally walled off, or maneuvering in relationships to obtain control or emotional comfort. They can move freely from emotional closeness in person-to-person relationships to work on their personal life goals and back. They can freely take "I positions,"—calm statements of their beliefs or feelings—without having to attack others or defend themselves. In their personal relationships they can relate warmly and openly without needing to focus on others or on activities or impersonal things in order to find common ground.

In cultures that focus on family and/or team functioning rather than on the individual, relationships will look different than in Anglo-European families. For example, reactions of Anglo-European young adults launching from the parental home in early adulthood, couples living far from their parents, and grandparents moving to Florida as they age may be very different from such life cycle patterns of intergenerational connection for Latino, African, or Asian families. Nevertheless, every culture will have its own norms for appropriate levels of connection at each life cycle phase. Ignoring such cultural differences leads to errors, such as an Anglo therapist thinking that daily phone calls in a Latino or Jewish family indicates fusion in the same way they might in an Anglo family. Or perhaps a client from the younger generation is angrily and defiantly adopting mainstream American norms over the objections of immigrant parents. In this case, a coach needs to help the client understand where the parents are coming from and try to find culturally respectful ways of disagreeing, if at all possible.

Distancing and Cut Off

While patterns of relating differ from culture to culture, the concepts of fusion and reactive distance or cut off exist in all cultures and are central to Bowen systems theory. The pull for togetherness in a relationship can be pictured as exerting a force like that of two magnets. When the pull becomes too strong and threatens to engulf individuality and blur separateness, there will be a reactive pulling away on the part of one or both. Analyzing families at different life cycle stages in terms of their fusion, distancing, and cut off is essential for tracking systemic process. Much of the emotional interaction between spouses and between parents and children consists of the jockeying of each for an optimal position in relation to the other, in which the emotional bond will be felt as comfortable, rather than too close or too distant. Because each is highly likely to have a different comfort range, the shifting back and forth is continuous. When the emotional intensity in the system is too great, and the pull toward fusion too strong, family members may cut off the relationship entirely.

Cutting off a relationship by physical or emotional distance does not end the emotional process; in fact, it intensifies it. If one cuts off relationships with parents or siblings, the emotional sensitivities and yearnings from these relationships tend to push into one's other relationships, (e.g., relationships with a spouse or with children), becoming all the more intense in the displacement. The new relationships will tend to become problematic under this pressure and lead to further distancing and cut offs.

Triangles

Forming a triangle is a typical way for two-person systems under stress to stabilize themselves (Bowen, 1974, 1975; Caplow, 1968; Fogarty, 1975; Guerin,

Fogarty, Fay, & Kautto, 1996). Few people can relate as a dyad for very long before running into some issue that makes one or both anxious, at which point it is common to "triangle" in a third person or thing (e.g., TV, the Internet, or alcohol) as a way of diverting the anxiety from the relationship of the twosome. Triangles are dysfunctional in that they offer stabilization through diversion, rather than through resolution of the issue in the twosome's relationship. They are also harmful to those who are pulled into the middle or to one side of a conflict. Thus, a couple under stress may focus on a child because his or her misbehavior gives them a focus on which to join together. Repeated over time, triangulation becomes a chronic dysfunctional pattern, preventing resolution of differences in the couple and making one or more of the three vulnerable to physical or emotional symptoms. Such dysfunctional stabilization, although problematic, may be experienced as preferable to change.

In a healthy triad, each relationship is independent of the other two. In a triangle, the three relationships are interdependent; they are not three separate person-to-person dyads. Any dyad in a triangle functions in relation to the relationship of the other two. The more distance there is between spouses, the closer one spouse will be to the third point of the triangle (e.g., a child or a grandparent). The closer one parent and one child are to each other, the more distant both will be from the other parent. Attempts to change this by moving toward the distant person will disturb the equilibrium with the close person as well as that person's relationship with the distant person.

Detriangulation is the process whereby the client frees him- or herself from the enmeshment of the triangle and develops separate person-to-person relationships with each of the other two. Involvement in triangles and interlocking triangles is one of the key mechanisms whereby patterns of relating and functioning are transmitted over the generations in a family.

Differentiation

Bowen's (1978) concept of differentiation describes a state of self-knowledge and self-definition that does not rely on the acceptance of others for one's beliefs but rather encourages one to be emotionally connected to others without the need to defend oneself or attack the other. Bowen's term "differentiation," which he equated with "maturity," is commonly misused and misquoted as if it meant autonomy, separateness, or disconnectedness. Differentiation does not in any way mean suppressing authentic and appropriate emotional expressiveness, which is part of the primary goal of Bowen therapy (Papero, 1990). Grounding oneself emotionally and learning to connect emotionally by developing a personal relationship with every member of one's family are the "blueprints" for all subsequent emotional connections.

This process must acknowledge the disparities of opportunity and power that exist within our society; disparities mystify those who are in an oppressive, inequitable situation. Women have long been expected to put the needs of others before their own. Even to define their own values, wishes, or opinions has generally been seen as selfishness. People of color have been required to be deferential to Whites and to accept the privileges that Whites have in this society. They must fight harder for any opportunities they get and stifle their resentments for insults and slights on an everyday basis. Gays and lesbians are also pressured by social attitudes and laws not to tell who they are. A heterosexual White male who tries to differentiate will generally be responded to with respect; a woman, gay person, or person of color who tries to differentiate may be penalized, ostracized, or even harmed by the family or community. Thus, our assessment of a person's differentiation must include assessment of social obstacles to accomplishing the tasks that lead to maturity.

Most problematic issues and triangles in minority-group families will be directly influenced by their lack of power and stigmatized status in the larger society. The most important clinical intervention is to help family members to get on the same side against the social problem instead of letting it divide them. It is essential to evaluate carefully the consequences for such clients of changing their role in any system, emotional or social, and to incorporate these caveats in the planning. Disadvantaged social status reduces the options available for personal change. The difficulties of changing in the face of social obstacles and stigma

should not be attributed to lack of client motivation or maturity.

It is useful to help the client conceptualize the presenting problem in terms of triangles; and understanding how family forces may maintain the problem or exacerbate its stress. A family that presents with an Alzheimer's patient, for example, will probably have both an overburdened caretaker (usually female) and other family members trying to escape the emotional turmoil by distancing. A client can be taught how triangles operate and then coached to change his or her input into the triangles of the presenting problems as a way of untying the knot that brought him or her into therapy. Once this initial work has brought some relief, the therapist reviews with the client the ways in which his or her emotional reactivity may be connected to triangles and issues in the family of origin or larger social context and suggests that the client work on these. The decision to proceed is up to the client, with the option to continue in the future if the client decides not to proceed at present.

However, a person may become enmeshed in many intense triangles in the original family, the nuclear family, or the current relationship system at work, with friends, or in the community. Coaching may require dealing with any of these. Once the immediate crisis that brought a person into therapy is put in perspective, coaching generally focuses on helping the client to define him- or herself in the family of origin and in the current family in life cycle terms.

In this framework, family relationships are forever, and it never makes sense to write off a family member once and for all. The exception would be couple relationships, the only "optional" relationships in a family—the only ones that we choose and that we may decide to end. Even here, we cannot end our ongoing connections to a former partner if we have had children together. In other words, one can be an ex-spouse but not an ex-co-parent, an ex-father, ex-mother, or ex-child. If one partner really changes and the other remains inaccessible or unchanging, it means that the couple system is not viable, and the first partner probably has no option but to move on. Thus, if the wife of an alcoholic differentiates, it may precipitate her husband into AA, or she may learn that her husband is too caught up in his addiction to respond, no matter what she does. If he chooses his addiction over the marriage, her only real choice may be to leave. The difference between this and a relationship with an alcoholic parent or sibling is that in those relationships, the mature family member remains open to the possibility of a transformation of the relationship, however unlikely. A person's ability to change his or her emotional functioning will depend, of course, on a number of factors, starting with life cycle stage and position. Children and people of any age who are not financially independent will have limited ability to take a position of emotional independence in a family.

Reversals and Detriangling

Detriangling involves shifting the motion of a triangle and unlocking the compulsory loyalties so that three dyadic relationships can emerge from the enmeshed threesome. A reversal is essentially an attempt to change a habitual pattern of relating by saying or doing the opposite of what you usually say or do in response to someone else. Reversals use the recurring pattern in the triangle but place the client in a different position in it. Although a client may at first call this "lying," the reversal actually expresses the unspoken and unacknowledged other side of an issue and tends to break up rigid, predictable, repetitive communication patterns. A wife who ordinarily gets angry when her husband gets sick and calls him a hypochondriac reverses her pattern and plays Florence Nightingale; a man who usually cannot talk to his father because he is so dictatorial asks for advice. A son who has an overly involved relationship with his mother and a distant relationship with his father might begin to detriangle by going to his father with the confidences his mother has inappropriately shared with him, saying, "Mom seems terribly upset, I don't know how to help out, but I'm sure you will be able to help her out. I don't know why, but she came to me with her worries and said . . ." To prevent a "two-step," where the mother would get angry and accuse the son of betraying her, the plan would have to include a way to deal with mother's anger and sense of betrayal when father confronts her with the son's report. He might do this by telling the mother,

when she confronts him, that he was so distressed by her upset that he felt he had to share it with his father to help her out.

Opening Up a Closed System

In trying to open up important but buried issues, there are several ways to proceed. Sometimes, it can be done merely by contacting family members who have been cut off from the family or by carefully raising emotionally loaded issues with various family members. A more complex operation for a system that is not in current crisis is what Bowen called setting up "a tempest in a teapot;" magnifying small emotional issues in such a way that old dormant triangles are activated and can be dealt within a new manner. Family members may be stuck emotionally in the same life cycle phase as when the family got derailed in previous generations, and opening up these issues may promote healing and change. Tactics that stir up an emotional system that is not currently in a state of tension, without attacking, are necessary because emotional patterns tend not to be clear when the system is calm. At such times triangles and other dysfunctional patterns tend to be dormant, until the next family crisis.

Engagement and System Mapping

At this stage, we find it useful to broaden the perspective on the presenting problem or the central relationships by asking about similar issues at earlier life cycle phases and at the same phase in earlier generations, inquiring about various members' views of central issues, and gradually introducing systems concepts such as triangles and automatic reactive processes into the discussion.

Planning: Learning About the System and One's Own Role in It

The first real step in coaching is to ask the person to draw a genogram (McGoldrick, 2010; McGoldrick, Gerson, & Petry, 2008), showing factual and relationship information for the family over at least 3 generations—names, births, deaths, marriages, divorces, geographical location, and all significant physical, social, and psychological changes or dysfunction. This includes the biological, legal, and "kinship type" relationships with godparents, foster parents, or close friends and the sociocultural and migration history of the family (Congress, 1994; Hardy & Laszloffy, 1995; McGoldrick, Giordano, & Garcia Preto, 2005). Family history is mapped through discussion of the genogram, which should not be treated as a form to fill out, but rather as a framework for understanding family patterns. Questions or comments from the coach that highlight the connection between the presenting problem and the family system will, hopefully, enhance the client's engagement.

We also ask for a family chronology, which is like a time map, as the genogram is a structure map. It shows in chronological order the major family events and stresses, and it is especially useful for understanding the motion of family patterns over time and the intersection of the client's life and symptoms with these patterns. This is important because the connections among major family events tend to be obscured by the anxiety that these events generate.

During the initial phase of engagement and history taking, it is important for the coach to set a calm, matter-of-fact tone to help defuse the intensity of emotion that is aroused by a current crisis or by opening up anxiety-producing material. It is also useful to introduce family systems concepts as soon as the anxiety is low enough for them to be heard, including ideas about emotional interaction, reciprocity, triangles, changing self, effects of sibling position on relationships, and the transmission of relationship patterns from one generation to the next.

Gaps in the genogram or family chronology are obvious places to start. The assumption is that the more information you have, the better position you are in to evaluate what has happened in your family and, thus, to understand your own position and to change it if you wish. In terms of gaining a preliminary focus on family patterns, for example, one could look at the similarity between the central triangles over 3 generations: self, mother, father, and each parent with his or her parents; the effects of sibling position on the family process (McGoldrick, 1995; Sulloway, 1996; Toman, 1976) and triangling in each generation; and the stress on the family at crucial points in the family history, such as just

before the marriage and around the birth of each child. Other patterns that may be examined are the reciprocity in the marriages in the family: Who overfunctions and who underfunctions? Who tends to move in and who tends to move out? What toxic issues in the family tend to be avoided? All of these are of primary importance. When a client is too caught up in a current crisis to sit still for "history," it is useful to take the crisis theme and the red-hot triangle in which it is embedded and track this theme and triangle (e.g., parents and a child who is acting out; a couple with wife and mother-in-law conflict, etc.) through the extended family and past generations. This will give access to the necessary historical information, while reassuring the client that his or her current problem is being addressed.

We favor holding off on concrete moves in a family at least long enough for the person to get a general notion of how the emotional system operates, what the central issues are, and what the client's own agenda and motivations are. If one wants to make someone else happy, save someone, change someone, tell someone off, get someone's approval, or justify and explain oneself, the effort will likely fail. In any case, it will not be worth the struggle, because it will either present no change, or it may even reverse positions, as when the victim becomes the bully.

When the coachee's anxiety has diminished to the point at which she or he can discuss how personal thoughts and feelings fit into family patterns and give some consideration to possible changes and their effects, coaching can really begin. The person may ask, "If I were to try to get to know my father better, how would I go about it and how would that help me with my current problem?" Understated questions from the coach that are designed to elicit in detail the tone and history of this relationship and the main triangles in which it is embedded are better at this point than suggestions for concrete actions, which may increase anxiety again. However, gathering genogram information and the very process of looking at the family in this way shift the focus from guilt and blame to a more objective "researcher" position. As the coachee begins to observe and listen at a family gathering, instead of participating as usual, shifts in thinking and relating may occur; these should be carefully noted and incorporated into the planning.

If the person is involved in a conflictual win/lose relationship with a parent and the issue has been displaced onto some specific concrete explosion, such as a falling out over some long-past insult or onto some abstract issue such as religion or politics, we frequently recommend as a first step that the person "let go of the rope" in this tug-of-war so that the personal emotional issues can have a chance to emerge. By this, we mean not only stopping the argument or cut off but actually acknowledging the parent's point of view in some way so that the relationship can move on to more important personal matters.

John Martin, a fourth-year medical student, sought coaching with M. M. after hearing a lecture on systems ideas. He had been cut off from his father since beginning medical school because his father, a widower who had recently remarried, had, unbeknownst to John, taken all John's savings for medical school and used it for his own honeymoon. John had been so outraged that he had refused to speak to his father since that time., Now felt challenged and intrigued by the idea of bridging cut offs.

John's mother had died of cancer when he was 16, leaving behind two younger children as well, Peter (age 14) and Susan (age 12). John's father had maintained great distance from all three children, burying himself in his work and leaving them with one housekeeper after another. John became the functional parent to both younger siblings, went to the local state university, and worked hard each summer. He saved his money because his father had told him that 4 years of college was all he could afford to pay for. He was totally shocked when he went to take out money for his first medical school payment to discover that his father had cleaned out the account for a honeymoon to Hawaii. He managed somehow to begin medical school anyway, without missing a beat, and was now a 4th-year student. The coaching task was to help John see himself as powerful enough to forgive his father and set himself free. The therapist suggested that the father sounded like he was operating under the delusion that he was the child and John the adult, or else he would never have done such an absurd thing as to steal his son's money for his own enjoyment. It was suggested that there seemed to be a grain of truth in this, since John had in fact managed much more successfully and maturely than the father for many years. The therapist suggested that he could forgive his father and let him know that he was looking for a connection and would welcome a reconciliation because he needed a father and was missing him. John rose to the occasion and wrote his father a most touching letter about his love for him, how much he missed his mother, how happy he was for his father that he had found love again, and his hopes for his brother and sister. His father's response was positive, though not apologetic, and John felt, when seen later that year, that he had "gotten a father back."

Guidelines to Teach Clients

We have found the following guidelines useful in our coaching of clients.

1. Keep your own counsel. Do not try to share efforts with others in the family. At times there is a strong pull to "differentiate together," with a spouse, for example, or a favorite sibling; but differentiation is an individual process and talking about it with others in the family may raise their anxiety and lead to efforts to get you to stop or at least do it their way.

2. Keep clearly in mind that your changes are for yourself. The work cannot be undertaken for the coach, for a partner, or for anyone else but yourself. Nor can it be an effort to change others in the family, although that is often the initial motivation.

3. Don't underestimate the family's reaction to your efforts. Your family's reactiveness is likely to be intense and will take you off guard if you are not prepared.

4. Have a plan. Schematizing and hypothesizing ahead of time, as well as thinking out very clearly who you want to be and what you want to do, will be help you avoid becoming reactive to your family rather than relating the way you want to. Your most useful mantra will be "Don't attack; don't defend; don't placate; and don't shut down."

5. Use strong feelings of anger or hurt as signals. When you start to see villains or victims in the family or to feel that you are one yourself, question your own feelings to get a better perspective on their place in the circular processes of the system.

6. Distinguish carefully between planned and reactive distance. It is often useful to distance

from an intense emotional field in order to gain objectivity. In particular, it is useful for people who tend to move toward others to plan instead to back off. However, it is important that this move be intentional and based on flexibility, so that when the other starts moving in, you are free to come back also, rather than keeping the distance fixed.

7. Expand the context. When anxiety is high, it is often useful, to bring up the problem with members of the larger family system in order to increase the realm in which it can be managed and absorbed.

8. Keep family visits time limited in order to maintain your focus. Never stay with your family longer than you can afford to be generous. Once you lose your generosity, you are better off not being there.

9. Take up serious issues with people individually, rather than at large, ritualized family gatherings.

10. If someone is blocking the way to a distant family member, it is usually futile to try to get around such interference. It makes much more sense to develop a relationship with the person who is blocking, even though he or she may seem peripheral to your efforts. If, for instance, your sister-in-law monitors all your efforts to deal directly with your brother, you will need to commit yourself to developing a relationship with her as a necessary part of getting connected with him because you are unlikely to be able to go around her to get to him.

11. Writing letters that are not attacking or defensive is a useful way to open difficult emotional issues without having to deal immediately with the reactivity of the system. By predicting the response in the letter itself, some of the intensity can also be deflected. In general, writing individual letters, and taking up only one emotional issue in each letter, may help to focus your efforts.

The following sections discuss some typical triangles and coaching suggestions for various life cycle phases.

The Single Young Adult

The basic triangle at this phase is usually with parents, though the presenting problem may be about uncertainties in relationships with boyfriend or girlfriend or anxiety about educational or occupational decisions. Asking the question "What do your parents think about this?" will usually elicit the problematic triangle.

All theories of adult development, including ours, view this as the stage in which the young person leaves childhood dependency behind and begins to build his or her own life, distinct from that of the family of origin. Nevertheless, this process is context bound and varies considerably, depending on the larger society.

Parents now in their 50s and 60s remember leaving the parental home shortly after high school or college to work and live on their own if they were male or to marry if they were female. They think that something is wrong with a son or daughter who remains or returns home. Yet adult children are doing that in record numbers, more males than females. They may move out and then back again; they may move from job to job or be unable to find any suitable job; they may move in with a boyfriend or girlfriend; or they may go to graduate school through their late 20s. Above all, they do not marry until much later than the previous generation. Parents often don't realize that contemporary society, with its economic uncertainty, its requirement of protracted education and skill training, and the acceptability of late or no marriage or childbearing, tends to keep the young in an adolescent or barely post adolescent mode until they are in their 30s.

Financial dependence breeds emotional dependence, and the level of emotional dependency must be carefully assessed in planning the therapy of a single young adult. Certainly, emotional issues with the family of origin are paramount, because the basic task of this phase is to get a good start on the process of differentiation. However, this can be a difficult idea for young Americans who imagine that the past is unimportant and they can invent themselves by willpower or through geography—moving far away from the family.

A further complication at this stage is the widespread belief, often shared by therapists, that autonomy is the major goal. Emotional connected-ness is largely overlooked, if not openly rejected, al-though it might be more tolerated for young females. It is extremely important for clinicians to realize that both autonomy and emotional connectedness are necessary characteristics for maturity in both males and females and that being separate does not mean being disconnected; it means being self-directed, self-supporting, and able to choose and pursue one's course through life. Young women of recent genera-tions have begun to insist on their right to autonomy, but few voices clamor for men's right to learn the skills of connecting emotionally (Silverstein & Raushbaum, 1994).

Some young adults may be mature enough to be coached in the same way as older adults. For those who are not ready there are useful adaptations, such as coaching young adults in groups, which can be an excellent way to engage and motivate them. When the therapist brings several single young adults together for coaching, there is almost always someone who begins to do the tasks with his or her family and reports progress and exhilaration to the group, inspiring others to try. Therapists using this approach see it as the method of choice for clients in their 20s. There is one caveat: Coaching is not group therapy. The therapist must resist the pull of group process and work with the clients one at a time in the group, limiting comment from the group regarding anyone else's work.

If a group is not available or feasible, we gen-erally work with the young adult clients alone through the engagement and planning phases. How-ever, if the client seems to be unwilling or unable to carry out tasks with parents, we suggest bringing one or both parents into the session and doing the tasks directly. It is made clear that the young adult will have to take the lead in bringing up whatever issue she or he has planned in a nonattacking, non-defensive way. This forestalls the experience we have all had of young clients introducing their par-ents to us and then sitting back and waiting for us to do the work for them. The therapist's role in this ses-sion is to monitor the traffic and block attacks or counterattacks from anyone.

After a family session, the therapist can meet again with the young adult alone to debrief and to absorb the lessons of the joint session and to plan for the next issue or the next family member to be invit-ed to a session.

The positive aspect of this format is that it allows a young client to take personal responsibility and still feel supported as she or he learns to speak about difficult issues with parents. It doesn't push the client back into an adolescent position, which would happen if all sessions were family sessions. It also demonstrates the importance of family emotion-al issues, which the young client might deny if all sessions were individual sessions.

The young couple

Typical triangles at this phase involve spouses and in-laws; spouses and partners or friends from previ-ous days; and spouses and work, money, division of labor, how to spend leisure time, etc. Couple prob-lems in this life cycle phase as at other phases typi-cally lead back to each partner and his or her family of origin. Couple problems are never solely dyadic problems. Conceptualizing or treating them as such tends to intensify the couple's negative fusion or lead to the wife's feeling more responsible for the problem.

In coaching work with couples, it is usually advantageous to see them together as each works on his or her own family. Seeing a spouse so vividly in the context of the family of origin and hearing the details of the spouse's socialization and struggle to surmount the inevitable problems with parents not only increase a partner's understanding and empathy toward the spouses, but also help significantly to di-minish blame for current marital problems. If spous-es are so locked in bitter conflict that they harden their hearts against the other's struggle, or if they use information revealed to buttress their own accusa-tions or interrupt with unhelpful comments, then they should be seen separately for coaching, in this or any phase of the life cycle.

As in the previous stage, the influence of is-sues from the family of origin is extremely important but will tend to be minimized by the couple, usually focused on their disappointments with each other and may see family of origin work as irrelevant to their specific problems.

With young couples, the therapist can alternate the focus between their relationship and their families of origin in any given session. It is essential that the therapist track the presenting complaints through both families of origin early on to provide evidence that connects the complaints to longstanding family issues and triangles. It is not enough to point out these connections in one genogram session. The therapist must refer to the connections frequently to expand the couple's focus from themselves. This process of making connections also tends to reduce blame as problems are expanded beyond the spouse's personal ill-will. Tacking up a large genogram in the therapy room or handing out copies of each partner's genogram in sessions may help to keep the whole family system in everyone's minds.

An important clinical question is asking how each member of the couple left home. Did they leave in a calm, planned way and spend enough time alone to become a functioning self? Or did they explode out in conflict, distance themselves from the family, or marry immediately? Leaving home is like a fingerprint or footprint, providing an indication of the degree of differentiation (i.e., maturity) that each partner achieved personally before their coupling. Current relationships with parents also indicate the relationship issues that sooner or later will play out in the couple relationship.

Given the growing number of unmarried couples who live together, it is important to give some thought to the clinical implications of this phenomenon. When there is no permanent commitment, couples therapy tends to focus on superficial complaints and disappointments or the argument about whether to marry or not.

We believe that a couple's failure to make a public commitment to each other has meaning, and the therapy format should reflect the fact that they are as much singles as they are a couple. We may set up a format whereby we see each partner individually in succeeding weeks and then, in the third week, see them as a couple. This gives ample space for each to consider calmly whether to stay in the relationship or leave and to work on their own part of the problem without losing face. This also gives the therapist an opportunity to try to engage each partner in the family of origin work, which usually reveals

and helps to resolve the couple impasse, if you can get them to do it.

Because of its connection to power and to love, analyzing how a family deals with money is an important issue in coaching. If a young person (or a traditional wife) has no access to the money necessary for survival, he or she remains functionally dependent on others which will certainly affect his or her ability to freely disagree or differentiate from those who control the means of survival. It is important to ask who controls the money; whether there have been conflicts regarding wills; and whether the family believes in financially assisting grown children.

The therapist should look for gender differences in handling money because if a husband controls a couple's money, they will not be able to negotiate as equals.

Families with young children

Typical triangles involve 1) each spouse and a child (or the children as a group); 2) either or both spouses, a child, and a grandparent or grandparents; 3) in-law triangles; 4) each spouse and the husband's work; or 5) each spouse and an affair. This stage has a very high divorce rate. If the couple doesn't present with marital problems, the state of the marriage should be explored and evaluated in connection with any or all of the above triangles.

If the presenting problem concerns a child, as it often does, it is important to attend to that problem to some degree before attempting to engage the parents in family of origin work. Once the crisis has receded, both parents should be engaged in coaching if possible. The motivation of clients in this stage of life is noticeably better than that in previous stages. Becoming parents usually allows the younger generation finally to see the relevance of family. Also, parents are often willing to do things for the sake of their children that they might not undertake for themselves. Although this motivation will need to shift to the self, doing it for the children's sake is a reason to begin.

Including the couple's marital work, concerns about children, and the families of origin of both spouses in the process of therapy requires therapist flexibility in shifting focus and the ability to keep track of the couple and larger system levels. If the client is an unmarried or postdivorce single parent, there are some special areas of focus and other typical triangles in coaching work, which we will consider below.

Families with adolescents

Because of the major physical, social, and psychological changes that adolescents go through, the most common triangles at this phase concern the adolescent and his or her peer group. Parents may become polarized in response to adolescent behavior, or adolescents may act out in response to parental triangles involving work, affairs, or grandparents.

Clients at this stage may present with marital crises or concerns about adolescent acting out. Again, the acute crisis should be dealt with before full-scale coaching begins, but a carefully elaborated genogram will undoubtedly shed much light on the antecedents of the couple's or adolescent's problems.

Parents at this phase of the life cycle, usually in their 40s, may be the most highly motivated coaching clients of all. They usually understand quite well the importance of emotional connectedness to the family of origin and may feel guilty themselves about their teenagers' problems. Their parents are getting older and perhaps ill, and they know that they don't have forever to resolve their own issues with them.

The couple at or past the launching stage

Couple problems at this stage usually reflect long-standing marital conflict or distance and are likely to be embedded in multiple interlocking triangles of the couple and their parents, siblings, children, work, affairs, or visions of the future.

At the launching stage, the intergenerational balance of power shifts, and the relationship between parents and their launched or launching young adult children is no longer mostly in the hands of the parents. At this stage, coaching involves helping parents deal with the increased independence of the generation below as well as the growing dependence of that above. The parents of these parents are either elderly and quite possibly in failing health or are already deceased. Nevertheless, clients at this stage of life can often be rather easily engaged in discussion of the intergenerational issues. The usual objection to actually raising difficult issues with elderly parents is that they are "too old" to upset. Our experience is that parents are never too old or even too ill to benefit from whatever their adult children want to communicate, assuming that it is communicated in a nonattacking manner. After all, it is the elderly person's developmental task to bring closure to life's storms, and when the family system is not too rigid, efforts by their adult children are usually accepted in this framework.

We have encouraged midlife adults to speak to dead parents at their gravesites; to write letters to dead parents; to say "I love you" or "I want to forgive you" to elderly parents who are drunk, drugged, or in a coma; or to say, "Tell me that you love me" to a senile parent. These dramatic moves are the culmination of the work conducted in discussion with surviving or unimpaired family members who knew the parent and by genealogical exploration, which usually reveals issues, triangles, and ghosts that shed light on current generations.

Even a formerly abusive, now ill elderly parent can be sent a letter about the abuse that is not attacking: "I used to think I could never forgive you for the abuse, which had such a lasting negative impact on my life, but now I am trying to believe that these actions on your part were the result of something terribly wrong in your own life. I want to believe that you didn't mean to harm me to such a degree, but that you were swept up in some emotional storm that you didn't know how to control," and so on. The letter should be followed up by a visit or phone call in which the topic is pursued, assuming always that the parent is not mentally ill or addicted.

In terms of their own launched or launching young adults, parents should be coached to shift gears from "boss" to "fellow adult." Parents not only need to let go, but also to conduct their half of a changed adult-to-adult relationship with their grown children. This may mean ceasing or curtailing financial support, accepting the young adult's choices regarding work or mate, changing inputs into their lives from directive to suggestive, maintaining a flexible pattern of visits and phone calls in both directions, and, most of all, being willing to conduct open discussions, stripped of the need to shield "the children" from the parents' real concerns, and expressing interest but not intrusion in their lives.

Remembering the old adage "A son is a son till he gets him a wife, but a daughter's a daughter for all of her life," therapists should pay extra attention to parents' expectations of and relationships with their grown sons. This is especially important for mothers of sons, whose relationships are socially invalidated (Silverstein & Rashbaumsp, 1994). The older generation should be coached to avoid conflict with their children-in-law, to take up issues or problems that arise between families with their own child, and to give up blaming difficulties on the in-law. Needless to say, "problem grandparenting" is something grandparents can be helped with in coaching and, if feasible, in joint sessions with their adult child (initially without the child's spouse). At issue here are the unarticulated expectations of all concerned about the proper degree of involvement of grandparents. These differences are usually quite negotiable once automatic reactivity is stopped.

If grown children are involved in ongoing conflict with their parents, it is wise to suggest inviting the younger generation to participate in therapy, since they have most of the power. Because you will be seen as the parents' therapist, it is a good idea to see the younger ones alone first to hear their uncensored version of events and to assure them by word or deed of your generational neutrality. The best outcome would be for one or more of them to be willing to be coached to assume responsibility for their part of the problem and to use the power they have to restore the relationship.

If members of the younger generation are already in their own therapy and want the parents to see their therapist, we agree to this as long as they are seeing a family therapist. If they agree to join the parents' therapy, we see the various individuals, couples, and generations both separately and together, depending on issues and clinical timing. In general, joint sessions accomplish less if neither generation has been coached to present a changed position, but they do provide the therapist with an invaluable picture of the family's approach to handling differences for evaluation purposes.

When grown children use extreme distance or cut off to try to deal with parents, parents can do a lot of wrong things but can't end the cut off until the adult child is ready to do so. Helping parents to see the cut off as multigenerational process instead of the child's personal meanness is a first step. Then all

the details of the issue that caused the final rupture must be discussed so that the therapist can put himself or herself into the child's position and guess his or her probable feelings and interpretations of parental words and actions. Finally, the parents should be coached to communicate carefully worded messages to the child. Such letters may convey a change of position or apology, if those seem appropriate, or may simply express the parents' desolation at the loss of contact. The therapy consists largely of getting parents to the point of readiness to write such letters. Each parent should write separately to eliminate the typical problem of presenting themselves and being reacted to as a unit instead of as two separate people.

Elderly clients

The most common triangles at this phase are between the elderly couple and a middle-aged child; an elderly woman, her daughter, and her grandchild; or an elderly parent, his or her doctor, and the middle-aged children.

In private practice, we are more likely to hear about elderly parents or grandparents than to meet them. However, they should always be present in the therapist's mind, because they are often the key to nodal events of the past, as well as the gateway to change for the next generation, as described in the previous section.

Many therapists do direct clinical work with the elderly through agency outreach or in nursing homes. The majority of such clients are women, because women live longer and because they rarely give up their concern about relationships. If the family relationships are in poor shape or, in the case of older men if they feel they didn't succeed at work, depression can be a problem. Men mellow as they age and as they leave their competitive struggles behind them. This natural process can make the most belligerent man into a more empathic, relationship-oriented person. Consider the remarkable turnaround of Governor George Wallace of Alabama; the deathbed apology of Lee Atwater, the publicist who was responsible for the racist "Willy Horton" political ads; the end-of-life admission by French Premier Valéry Giscard d'Estaing of his Nazi connections; and the apparently agonizing quest by Robert McNamara, former Secretary of Defense, to understand and acknowledge his role in the Vietnam War.

We recommend encouraging the elderly in their life review, urging them to approach the task with compassion for self and to share their story with family members. It is the family task at this phase to care for the elderly and to receive their story and their wisdom. If family members don't seem to be doing their part of the job, we recommend getting in touch and, again, proceeding with both individual and joint sessions as needed, coaching both generations to resolve their issues with the other.

Coaching Single Parents

The most common triangles involve a single mother, her child, and her parents or the mother, her child, and the child's father. With such clients, it is important to learn the family's reaction to the woman's parenthood. A woman's unmarried pregnancy carries more stigma than a single-parent adoption, although concerns will also exist about that situation because of our society's devotion to the traditional family as the "correct" one. It is extremely important in this, as in any other controversial situation, that the client understand and accept her parents' disapproval as almost inevitable in our society before she initiates conversation with them about it.

In all situations that involve strong parental disapproval, it is necessary to coach the client, first to try to understand the source of the disapproval apart from parental ill will and second to realize that to become a mature adult, it is necessary to give up the need for parental approval, although most people never give up wanting it.

In addition to coaching single parents in the context of their families of origin, it is extremely important to coach them toward creating a meaningful community for themselves. An isolated parent and child are at risk; a single parent and child connected to a caring group at church or temple, or a close-knit group of friends, can be expected to thrive.

Divorcing and Postdivorce Parents

The most common triangles involve divorced or divorcing spouses and each of their children; a divorced spouse, his or her children, and the parents

and family of the ex-spouse; the divorced spouses and a new love interest of either; or the interlocking triangles of a divorced spouse, the ex-spouse, the new love interest, and the children.

At the time of divorce, coaching can play an invaluable role in the current situation. We recommend the fulling guidelines:

- See each parent separately if possible, and coach each to minimize destructive, vengeance-seeking behavior. If only one parent will come to coaching, help that one to understand the rewards to self and children of "unilateral disarmament," refusing to respond in kind to the partner's provocations.

- Help each or either parent to understand the importance of keeping the children out of the battle.

- Focus on money and financial matters with the wife, helping her to plan a return to work if necessary or feasible.

- Focus on the children with the husband, helping him to gain the skills necessary to conduct his own relationship with his children and to abide by his financial commitments to them.

- To rework the relationship of the ex-spouses into one of co-parental cooperation, the client must be helped to stop blaming the divorce or failed marriage on the exspouse and examine closely his or her own role, however large or small, in the debacle. This is the work of the "emotional divorce," which requires giving up as finished the hopes and dreams invested in the marriage, and reinvesting in one's own future course. If the divorce is in the past and most of the above has not occurred smoothly (and it usually hasn't), coaching can help either parent to undo his or her part in the ensuing conflict or cut off with the ex-spouse.

- The clinician must, of course, also track the issues of the failed marriage and divorce in relation to the extended family from very early in therapy. The client is coached to discuss the divorce in some meaningful way with parents and to deal with their reactions to the divorce.

As the current struggle with the ex-spouse or focus on adaptation to postdivorce realities recedes to the point at which something other than the divorce can be attended to, coaching shifts to other multigenerational themes, issues, and triangles. At the stage at which the client is able to look to the future, the coaching becomes like a resocialization process, usually helping men to develop their relationship skills and women their autonomy and self-sufficiency.

At the close of this work, the client should be free to have a cooperative co-parental relationship with the ex-spouse (assuming that the ex-spouse is sane and not violent or addicted). The client should also feel free to pursue a single life until such time as he or she may choose to remarry, and then with the expectation of forming a different kind of marriage.

Coaching Remarried Family Members

In addition to tracking the issues in the family of origin of a spouse in a remarried family, it is necessary to get information on the family of the ex-spouse or the deceased spouse. It is also important to get the details of the divorce or the death to determine whether they were handled adequately or are unresolved and intruding into the current family. If they are unresolved, the client should be coached to redo the mourning or the emotional divorce. In either case, it is important to include the second spouse in the sessions in which a client is being coached to resolve the death or the divorce. If left out of these sessions, the second spouse has a tendency to become paranoid, wondering whether the therapy will undermine the second marriage. When included, the second spouse tends to become a staunch ally of the therapist, understanding that unresolved issues from a first marriage take up emotional space in the present.

Both the biological parent and the stepparent usually need help in distinguishing their roles (see Chapter 21 on The Divorce Cycle). If the stepparent and stepchildren are in an uproar, with the biological parent caught in the middle, direct coaching of the couple to detriangle will be necessary.

Special attention should be given to the situation of the stepmother in a remarried family; she is usually in the most vulnerable position. Coaching in the families of origin helps to strengthen both partners for a most complex family situation. It is also important to coach a biological parent to maintain contact with the family of the deceased or divorced spouse, because these are the children's grandparents.

The Main Work

Once clients have begun to think about themselves and their families in systems terms and to make initial moves to shift their position, they may begin to put a lot of thought and effort into the endeavor, often focusing at first on the family themes that seem most relevant to their current lives.

At this point, the coach must pay very careful attention to the details of relationship interaction so that what exactly the client needs to change in word and deed to promote positive change becomes clear. It is very important to get a grasp here of the family's cultural norms, which are influenced by their race, ethnicity, religion, education, income, gender attitudes, and life stages. "Too involved" is a totally different concept in Jewish, Scandinavian, and African American families. Almost no client complaints can be understood or addressed apart from their socioeconomic context, including clearly universal issues, such as violence. Even addictions and mental illness are construed differently in different cultures. All of this becomes particularly intricate when coach and client are from different cultures.

Because this work is about changing relationships, which in turn affects the themes and patterns that will be transmitted to the next generation, it is important for the coach to be aware of the typical triangles and issues at each stage of family life. For example, coaching a stepfather in a remarried family about how to position himself with an adolescent stepson (as benign and casual friend and mentor) in relation to the son's biological mother, who must play the role of limit setting, is completely different from coaching a biological father about how to deal with his teenage son (as caring, but limit-setting parent) in relation to his wife, who is co-parent. Coaching parents once their children have left home and become self-supporting is again different, and these life cycle stage differences must always be taken into account.

Follow Through

The length of time that people will devote to intensive work with their family of origin varies with the degree of motivation and the felt impact of the results on their lives. Once a person has decided to engage in coaching, there is often a period of considerable enthusiasm. People tend to begin work around some central problematic focus—with a parent or a spouse, a significant family secret, or a cut off. Sometimes, during work on a relationship that mistakenly ignores an important triangle in which the dyad is imbedded, the intensity of the third person's reaction is seen as a new and startling problem that may confuse and overwhelm the client. This is particularly likely to occur when a sibling has not been taken into account in the planning of work with a parent.

In our experience, clients tend to work in phases interspersed with periods of inactivity and to vary in the ability to work at certain levels. For example, some work very well for a time in the nuclear family but have great difficulty moving into the extended family. Others will work well and hard in the parental generation but have great difficulty understanding how symptoms are related to a spouse or an ex-spouse. At times, a coach may recommend shifting some particular issues to another level of work as a way around an impasse at the immediate level. Those who work in a systemic way over an extended period of time can have very positive results in the form of relief of immediate stress and an ability to deal differently with future stress.

Coaching sessions may begin at regular weekly or biweekly intervals, but these intervals will usually be lengthened as the focus shifts from learning and planning to doing the work. A systems therapist rarely terminates a case in the traditional sense of a mutual decision that the work is finished. Rather, appointments gradually become spaced at longer intervals, and even when it is agreed that a major piece of work is accomplished, there is usually the understanding that the person will continue on his or her own trying to apply the principles in family, work, and social relationships and that further appointments with the therapist can be sought if s/he gets stuck or sees a potential crisis ahead. It is not uncommon for a client, after 1 or 2 years' absence, to request a few appointments to get back on course.

Money and the Family

Analyzing how a family deals with money is an important task in coaching: Among the questions to ask are:

Who handles it?

Who controls it?

Have there been conflicts or cut offs over wills?

How do siblings in different financial positions deal with these differences? (This is really a question about how class issues play out for different siblings.)

What are the family's beliefs about children's rights to support, help for education, inheritance, buying a home, and so on?

How are financial arrangements made for the care of any disabled family member and how does this interact with emotional caretaking?

What have been the gender differences regarding the control or managing of money?

The handling of money issues in coaching is a complex issue. Here we can only allude to a few of the common problems. Where a family business or a will has left family money unequally divided among siblings, relationships are likely to be impaired or even cut off, often for generations. Coaching family members about undoing such arrangements before they happen or after they happen for the benefit of their relationships may be the best way around such difficulties. In addition, family members who are held hostage by threats of being cut off and losing their inheritance if they contact a "forbidden" relative or marry someone from another race, may be encouraged to "let go of the rope" in order to free themselves emotionally. If they are not prepared to lose the inheritance, they can never free themselves emotionally.

Gender Issues in Coaching

Women are typically the carriers of family heritage in certain ways. They often feel more responsible for the family, for those in need, for dealing with the pain of family secrets, and for injustices done to family members. Men may disconnect more easily, given society's support for the "independent" male. Older sisters may be particularly accessible and helpful in promoting family reconnections because they are likely to feel so responsible for family well-being. Because of our society's rules for male and female socialization, men may fit into the stereotypes of being less accessible, less willing to acknowledge their vulnerability, and less aware of the emotional process in the family. However, if the coach keeps a life cycle perspective, he or she can be on the lookout for moments when male clients may become more open, especially during times of transition and loss. As with race or any other issue of injustice in relationships, a sister will have to come to terms with the unfairness before she will become free to move toward a new equilibrium and attempt to change oppressive family rules of over-responsibility for daughters and glory for sons.

Guidelines for the Therapist (Coach)

1. Expect intense resistance to the idea of dealing directly with parents and family members in real life about troubling issues instead of complaining in private to an understanding therapist. Discuss the advantages for the client in doing so. The client must be helped to see that the goal is to create change in the actual family relationships, not simply in the client's feelings about them. We often encounter clients whose years in psychodynamically oriented therapy have produced little or no change in their family interactions. They may have tried to initiate change, but were then unprepared for family resistance—"the two step."

2. Clients often come in crisis, but the coach works to create a calm, thoughtful atmosphere for the sessions, which are about thinking and planning regarding the whole life cycle, not emotional catharsis. When the coach shows interest in the client's reports and information about the family through comments and questions and does not encourage or support emotional reactivity, the client's anxiety level, it is hoped, goes down enough for him or her to be able to hear the coach's ideas about the situation. Now the coach can start to explain systems concepts, tell stories about others or his or her own family, and suggest readings that are relevant to the client's situation. In addition to material written for the general public, many clients also benefit from reading professional books and papers, if the material relates to their problem or circumstances, or to their ethnicity, race, gender, class, sexual orientation, or culture.

3. Advise the client to expect a surge of anxiety symptoms with each new move, and normalize this. We sometimes ask what symptoms the client experienced during adolescence as a way of indicating the intensity of the emotional reactions that are ahead.

4. Once the client has agreed to work, emphasize the need for planned, not reactive or impulsive, moves in the family system.

5. Resist the pull to see the individual as the unit of dysfunction or treatment. Resist the pull to accept the client's descriptions of family members and their motivations as "truth." Keep the multigenerational family and its cultural context in mind as the client speaks. Put yourself mentally in the position of various family members the client is complaining about.

6. Be prepared to help the client to prioritize and strategize throughout the work, without getting ahead of the client in investment in the work. Encourage the client's curiosity and research interest in family patterns by asking questions about family process. Keep in mind the gender, sexual orientation, racial, and cultural context of the client and family when making suggestions.

7. Keep monitoring your own family, gender, life cycle, class, race, and cultural issues.

8. Remember that a coach also cheers from the sidelines and provides encouragement and appreciation. This is not the same as being a source of emotional support, approval, reassurance, or pity, all of which may be condescending or disabling to the client because they increase the transference phenomena, focusing the client's attention and emotions on the therapist instead of on his or her own family. Convey the belief that clients can deal with their families, a basic premise of this approach.

9. If you have not worked on differentiating yourself in your own family, you will probably be prone to misjudge the intensity of systemic

reaction to your client's moves and to accept the client's resistance.

10. When clients are concurrently in another type of therapy, suggest that they put one of you on hold until the other therapy is completed because this orientation goes counter to most other therapies.

11. Resist clients' tendencies, to try to make you the "good parent" or intensify the emotional climate between you. Explain openly that coaching is focused on dealing with family-of-origin relationships directly, rather than through replacement relationships with the therapist.

12. If the client is of a different race, ethnicity, religion, gender, sexual orientation, or social class, you have a responsibility to educate yourself about the issues involved for that client.

Conclusion

Although the contextualization of problems goes counter to the quick-fix orientation of today's managed care pressures, coaching can be a practical format to use when there are time constraints on therapy. This approach generally requires far fewer sessions than other therapies and emphasizes clients' work on their own between sessions. Reading, doing homework tasks with the family, making notes after each family move, and making an occasional telephone call to the therapist in a crisis easily carry the motivated client from session to session. This model places much less clinical strain on the therapist, since clients are encouraged to turn to their natural resources for support, a situation that can enhance therapist attentiveness, interest, and learning. The method does require that therapists have a sophisticated understanding of their own issues as well as a comprehensive appreciation for the patterns that make all families tick. The hopeful and expansive orientation of this approach in its focus on the connectedness of all systems tends to encourage therapists to help clients find the strengths and resources in their history and in their present that will empower them for their future. This orientation toward individual and family resilience (Walsh, 2007) is an extremely useful approach in this era when health care is being so strenuously limited.

Chapter 28

Creating Meaningful Rituals for New Life Cycle Transitions

Evan Imber-Black

Every culture makes rituals. Anchoring us with the past and where each of us comes from, while simultaneously moving us into the future, rituals capture and express the duality of continuity and change and constancy and transformation, required for families and cultures.

The capacity of rituals to both make and mark transitions makes them especially salient for life cycle changes. Life cycle events and transitions such as birth, marriage, and death are most frequently marked with familiar rituals. Many religious and ethnic groups also have rituals to mark young adult development (e.g., bar mitzvah, confirmation, or quincinera), or such development may be marked by secular rituals such as graduation. These rituals, while often seen as discrete events, such as *the* wedding, and *the* christening or baby naming, are in actuality processes that occur over time, involving advance preparation and reflection afterward. Choices about who participates in the planning and execution of a life cycle ritual reflect family relationship patterns. Negotiations that occur during the preparation for life cycle rituals may be opportunities to change such patterns. Thus, such rituals may be seen as the visible and condensed drama of the life cycle transitions that they mark.

Relying on symbols, metaphors, and actions that may have multiple meanings, life cycle rituals function to reduce anxiety about change. According to Schwartzman (1982), rituals make change manageable, as members experience change as part of their system rather than as a threat to it. Similarly, Wolin and Bennett (1984) suggest that rituals contribute to a family's identity and its sense of itself over time, facilitating the elaboration of roles, boundaries, and rules. Imber-Black and Roberts (1992) have delineated how rituals define family and

group membership; heal losses; maintain and/or change individual, family, and cultural identity; express core beliefs; and facilitate the celebration of life. Rituals enable us to hold and express contradictions. Thus, a wedding marks the loss of particular roles in the families of origin while at the same time marking the beginnings of the new couple and in-law relationships. Since the ritual event is time and space bounded, a safe and manageable context for the expression of strong emotions is created. Rituals marking life cycle transitions function at many levels, enabling individual change (e.g., from adolescent to young adult, from single adult to married adult), relationship change (e.g., from parent–child to two adults, from dating couple to married couple), family system change (e.g., expansion through the addition of members or contraction through members leaving), and family–community change (e.g., graduation marks not only a child's leaving school, but also a change in the family's relationship to larger systems; a retirement party marks not only a person's ending work, but also a change in the family's relationship to the outside world). Rituals may connect a family with previous generations, providing a sense of history and rootedness, while simultaneously implying future relationships. The performance of and participation in such rituals link a family to the wider community through the repetition of familiar rites.

The critical importance of rituals in our lives is evident in the responses of oppressed people when rituals are forbidden to them. African Americans held in slavery were not permitted to marry. They created their own secret wedding ceremony, "jumping the broom," to mark a committed relationship. Jewish women in Nazi concentration camps turned conversations with each other into remembering rituals and wrote out recipes for rich and delicious food in the midst of forced starvation. In so doing, they proclaimed connections to their villages, their faith, and their families (DeSilva, 1996).

Creating Rituals as a Developmental Task for Couples

Among the many developmental tasks facing any new couple is creating rituals. Coming from different families of origin, members of a couple often encounter differences in preferred and familiar rituals of everyday life, such as meals or greeting each other at the end of a busy day, family traditions such as birthdays or anniversaries, and holiday celebrations. Struggles over how to perform rituals are a lens through which couples can learn about each other's family of origin. Such struggles are particularly challenging for couples coming from different religions, ethnic groups, or social classes. While a couple may be able to create an interfaith wedding, they may discover that rituals that mark the birth of children, celebrate religious holidays, or remember the dead with an interfaith funeral become the crucible for working out loyalties to extended family and current differentiated beliefs and identities.

Gay and lesbian couples may face unique challenges where rituals are concerned. While legal marriage has begun in a few states, most gay and lesbian couples still must create innovative rituals to mark a committed relationship. Many gay and lesbian couples find that they have acceptance and support from the extended family of one partner but not the other, leading them to adopt the rituals of only one partner while the other partner's legacy gets lost. Therapy with gay and lesbian couples should include conversations about meaningful rituals starting from the premise that each is bringing an encyclopedia of rituals from which to choose ways to make new meaning together.

Jerry Corbell and Stan Best had lived together for 15 years. Since Jerry's family had rejected him, all of Stan and Jerry's holidays were celebrated only with Stan's family. Jerry felt so much pain over his family's cut off that he abandoned all familiar rituals from his own childhood, leaving him with the double loss of family relationships and family rituals.

The rituals with Stan's family, while warm and caring, were at the same time a sharp reminder of his losses. In our therapy, I suggested that Jerry's parents' rejection did not mean that Jerry needed to lose meaningful rituals that belonged to him. Rather, he needed to reclaim and alter those rituals to fit his life now. Jerry began by unpacking key symbolic objects that he had hidden away—his grandmother's candlesticks from Eastern Europe, Christmas ornaments that his aunt had given him every year as a child, a card file of recipes of his favorite dishes from his family of origin. Over time, Jerry and Stan integrated these special symbols into their ritual life together.

Many couples seeking therapy today come with multiple differences in religion, ethnicity, race, and social class. Often, the couple has not identified these differences as a source of difficulty, yet their struggles and conflicts over rituals will mirror these. Nonconfrontational conversation about each one's ritual life is often an excellent entry point, enabling couples to see the power of their own heritage in the present. Any therapy with bicultural couples must spend time helping the couple to examine each one's history with rituals and negotiate meaningful rituals for their lives together.

Contemporary Life Cycle Transitions

While all individuals and families experience some normative life cycle transitions and participate in rituals that facilitate these transitions, many individuals and families are faced with life cycle transitions that are new or novel. The seemingly different or unusual nature of these transitions often means they are not marked by rituals or may have rituals that simply don't fit the circumstances and need to be adapted. For instance, when Sherry and Bruce Callahan had their first baby, they planned a christening that was exactly like all such rituals, with the addition of one aspect. Their baby had been conceived through assisted insemination with donor sperm. They decided well before their baby's birth that they did not want their use of new birth technologies to be a secret that part of their family knew and others did not know. They also wanted to be able to speak about this easily with their child when the time came and not allow it to be a taboo subject. In our therapy, we talked of ways to adapt the christening ritual to include the fact of donor insemination. They decided that after the christening, Bruce would speak to all assembled, publicly thanking their anonymous donor for helping them to have the precious gift of their baby. Bruce told me later, "I was so scared to say those words, but when I did, any shame I had previously felt just lifted and flew out of the church" (Imber-Black & Roberts, 1998).

New life cycle transitions may include bicultural marriage; gay or lesbian marriage; families formed by adoption, especially when there is overt or covert nonsupport from family members; families formed by new birth technologies; the birth of a handicapped child; the birth or adoption of a child by an unmarried mother or father; pregnancy loss; forced separation through hospitalization, imprisonment, or terror; reunion after such forced separations; migration; living together relationships; the end of nonmarried relationships; foster placement and the reunion after foster placement; sudden, unexpected, or violent death, including suicide; the leaving home of a mentally or physically handicapped young adult, especially when this leaving has not been anticipated; and chronic, incapacitating illness. This list, which is intended to be suggestive rather than exhaustive, is shaped by broad social processes that may change over time and may differ with various cultural and socioeconomic groups. For example, pregnancy outside of a legal marriage may or may not be an idiosyncratic life cycle event with all of the aspects described below attendant to it, depending on the norms of the family, the family's reference group, and the response of the wider community. While the list above may seem an unusual combination, all have several elements in common:

Familiar, repetitive, and widely accepted rituals do not exist to facilitate required changes and to link individual, family, and community.

All require complex reworking of relationships, similar to normative life cycle transitions, but lack the available maps that attend to more expected transitions.

Contextual support from family of origin, the community, and the wider culture is often

lacking. Individual and family events and processes are not confirmed by family of origin, larger systems, and the community.

A balance of being both like others (e.g., a family with a severely handicapped member shares many features with other families) and being unlike others (e.g., a family with a severely handicapped member has certain aspects of their functioning that are different from those of other families) is often difficult to achieve, resulting in a skewed sense of either denying the differences or maximizing them to the exclusion of a sense of connectedness with others.

A sense of stigma is often experienced because of prejudice from the wider community. This, in turn, may lead to the emergence of secrets and conspiracies of silence that constrain relationship possibilities.

Involvement with larger systems is often problematic. Families with handicapped members, hospitalized members, imprisoned members, or fostered members are required to deal with larger systems in ways that alter family boundaries and relationships, often over many years. Families experiencing forced migration or migration for economic necessity are often involved with intimidating larger systems. Because family identity and sense of competency include reflections from larger systems with whom they interact, families with any of the idiosyncratic life cycle events and transitions listed above may be at greater risk of incorporating negative images.

The family may abandon or interrupt familiar rituals that contribute to its sense of itself, especially if these elicit painful memories. For instance, after the loss of a member through sudden death, hospitalization, or imprisonment, members may avoid family rituals. Families that are unable to accept members' gay relationships or nonmarried heterosexual relationships may restrict participation in rituals. Paradoxically, such ritual abandonment or interruption prevents healing and relationship development.

El Salvador and the Bronx

When the Torres family arrived in the Bronx from El Salvador, Mrs. Torres, her son Manuel, age 13, and her daughter Maria, age 11, were coping with the recent death of their husband and father in the Salvadoran civil war and recovering from their own terrifying wartime experiences. They remained very close for the first 2 years but abandoned many familiar rituals from their culture. Since most of their rituals were communal or religious and depended on people from their own country, they struggled with little success to find ways to develop meaningful rituals. Simply meeting the demands of daily life in the Bronx took precedence.

The children quickly learned English in school. Mrs. Torres became worried that they would forget Spanish and forget that they were Salvadoran. She spoke to them in Spanish at home, but they insisted on responding in English. In a fairly typical pattern among parents and adolescents who have migrated, they were soon struggling, as Mrs. Torres wanted to talk about "home," while her children insisted that home was in the Bronx.

When I met the Torres family in family therapy, I suggested that they bring symbols to our next session—symbols of El Salvador and the Bronx. Mrs. Torres was very surprised to see that Manuel and Maria brought symbols of El Salvador that showed how connected they still were to their original home. The teens brought toys and photographs that their mother didn't know they had kept. They talked with their mother about their memories, letting her know that they were involved with their homeland in deeply emotional ways. Their symbols from the Bronx included a music tape and a poster from a concert. Mrs. Torres listened respectfully to them describe what this music meant to them, replacing their usual arguments about North American music. Mrs. Torres brought food for both of her symbols, including her wonderful Salvadoran cooking and a small pizza to symbolize the Bronx and the arguments they had been having when her children wanted pizza instead of her ethnic dishes. The family and I sat and ate both foods together.

Following this ritual that enabled the holding and expressing of past and present, their prior life and their current life, their losses and their surviving, the Torres family agreed to hold a weekly storytelling session at home to include Mrs. Torres' stories of El Salvador and Manuel and Maria's stories of the Bronx. Over time, the children also shared memories of El Salvador, and Mrs. Torres began to tell stories of her daily life in the Bronx. This ritual enabled the family to express their deep sense of loss and sadness connected to their forced migration while providing healing as the ritual anchored them in a new life that could include elements of both El Salvador and the Bronx (Imber-Black & Roberts, 1998).

The Emergence of Symptoms

Family life cycle theorists (Carter & McGoldrick, 1980; Haley, 1973) have described the connection between life cycle derailment and the emergence of symptoms in individuals and families. Families who are experiencing idiosyncratic life cycle events and processes may be at particular risk for the development of symptoms in members. The convergence of lack of social support, intergenerational cut offs and isolation, stigma, secrecy, sense of shame in one or more members, and frequently stressful relationships with larger systems with whom the family must interact may be mirrored by a paucity of rituals to mark developmental change. Rigid and repetitive symptoms and interactions of family members in response to symptoms metaphorically express the family's stuck position. The clinician who searches for normative life cycle issues to hypothesize about the emergence of symptoms may find that idiosyncratic and often hidden life cycle processes are salient.

The house-cooling party

Candice Meyers first contacted me for therapy because she was depressed. Her family physician had prescribed antidepressant medication, but she wanted to try therapy first. In our first meeting, she told me through her tears that her husband, Brent, had left her for another woman 6 months earlier. Married for 6 years, they had been talking about starting a family. Brent had been secretly planning to leave for over a year.

After their separation, Candace became isolated from family and friends. She stopped participating in any family rituals, giving the excuse that she was exhausted and had frequent headaches. It was clear to me that Candace was suffering from many unacknowledged and unritualized losses—of her marriage, her hoped-for first child, and all of her relationships with family and friends. Her many symptoms—sleeplessness, headaches, weight loss, hopelessness—were directly related to her unanticipated divorce.

Candace felt very ashamed that she had been left by her husband. She stopped inviting anyone to her home, since hosting people alone seemed to emphasize her abandonment. This was in marked contrast to her earlier married life when her home had been the center for all of the holidays and other rituals with her extended family and friends. She called her house her "loneliness and her memories." I suggested that she might want to begin her healing by replacing some of the familiar and jointly owned items in her home with some new things that represented her individual tastes. As Candace began to put together a house that suited her, the acute depressive symptoms abated.

But for a long while, Candace was still unable to invite anyone to her home. "I feel like a strange sort of prisoner in my own home. But I'm not locked in—other people are locked out," Candace told me.

I was intrigued with her metaphor of the lock. I wondered with Candace what effect a new lock on her door might have. Candace agreed to buy a new lock and to simply sit with it each day and ask herself, "What would it take to put this new lock on my door—a lock that I could open to my family and friends?"

During that week, Candace went through many emotions—sadness, anger, a sense of betrayal. By the end of the week, she felt ready to reclaim her life. She decided to make a special ritual, a "house-cooling party." She told me, "People usually have house-warming parties when they move to a new home, I'd like to mark my divorce with some humor and have a "house-cooling party." She designed an invitation that read: "Please come to my house-cooling party. Please do bring gifts appropriate for the lovely home of a single woman—I need to replace the 'his and her' stuff!" Just before the party, Candace had the new lock put on her front door, symbolizing that she was now in charge of her life (Imber-Black & Roberts, 1998).

Therapeutic Rituals

Many clinicians have described the efficacy of therapeutic rituals in facilitating systemic change (Imber-Black, 1986a, 1986b; Imber-Coppersmith, 1983, 1985; O'Connor, 1984; O'Connor & Horwitz, 1984; Palazzolli, Boscolo, Cecchin & Prata, 1977; Papp, 1984; Seltzer & Seltzer, 1983; van der Hart, 1983). Differing from simple tasks whose intent is to target the behavioral level and that the therapist expects to be performed as prescribed, rituals are intended to affect the behavioral, cognitive, and affective

levels. The family or individual is expected to improvise to tailor the ritual to particular and personal circumstances. Rather than relying only on concrete instructions, rituals utilize symbols and symbolic actions that may have multiple meanings.

Therapeutic rituals draw on elements attendant to normative life cycle rituals to highlight similarities to others, while including unusual elements that are capable of affirming differences rather than hiding them. Thus, Candace's house-cooling party began with the new lock as a powerful symbol of her autonomy after divorce. Many rituals include documents. Candace's invitation became a document to announce her divorce, and the party allowed her to ask others for support. Friends and family gathered to witness and celebrate her life cycle transition, just as they would with any other life cycle ritual.

Although there are several categories of rituals that may be useful in therapy, three categories are particularly beneficial for idiosyncratic life cycle events and processes. These include transition rituals, healing rituals, and identity redefinition rituals. Transition rituals have been described extensively by van der Hart (1983), primarily in reference to normative life cycle transitions. Such rituals mark and facilitate transitions of specific members and of membership in the family, altering boundaries and making new relationship options available. The transitions in idiosyncratic life cycle events and processes often have no rituals. Indeed, the family may not have anticipated the transition and all of the relationship changes attendant on it.

The giving of gifts

A physician referred a family to me for therapy for what was identified as depression in the mother. The family consisted of two parents, Mr. and Mrs. Berry, and two young adult children, Karen, age 22, and Andrew, age 20. Karen was diagnosed as severely mentally retarded shortly after her birth. Karen's pediatrician advised Mrs. Berry to quit her job and remain at home to care for Karen. Extended family supported this advice and visited often while Karen and Andrew were small. The parents were told that Karen would never function on her own and would always remain "like a child." Eventually, Karen went to a special school, but the parents were never counseled in ways to prepare for Karen's adolescence or adulthood. Karen developed language and self-care skills. The family functioned well during Karen and Andrew's childhood. However, as both children became teenagers, severe difficulties arose. No one in the nuclear or extended family knew how to cope with Karen as an emerging young woman. Fearful that Karen might be exploited sexually, the family became increasingly protective of her. Andrew was required to spend most of his free time taking Karen to any outside events that were scheduled by her special school, and he grew increasingly resentful and withdrawn. His own plans to go away to college seemed impossible to him. Karen became rebellious and difficult for the family to be with, and the parents felt that they had failed her and needed to try harder. At the same time, Karen's school began to push the family to put Karen in a group home. This option had not existed at the time of Karen's birth and had never been anticipated by the family. For a period of 2 years, the parents and the school struggled over Karen's future. The parents were unable to articulate their fears to the school personnel, who saw them as overinvolved with Karen. Consequently, adequate explanations of what the group home could offer Karen and her family were not forthcoming. During this time, everyone in the family deteriorated emotionally and functionally, culminating in the referral for family therapy by the mother's physician.

Through the course of a therapy in which I helped the family to anticipate the life cycle change of Karen's eventually leaving home, and that richly credited the family for their contributions to Karen, the family became able to ask for and receive adequate information from the group home about Karen's future there. As the leaving home was normalized, the parents were able to articulate expectations about visiting and holiday time together that would mark the relationship of most young adults and their families. Andrew became freer to live his own life and made plans for going away to college in 4 months, after Karen was to go to the group home. The family was preparing itself for many changes. However, as Karen began to visit the group home, first for dinners and then for brief overnights stays, conflicts began to break out between Karen and her parents. Mr. and Mrs. Berry became alarmed that Karen was not as ready to move out as they had thought. In a session alone with the therapist, they cried and said that they feared for Karen's future.

Since the family had made so many changes in the direction of Karen's leaving home and were on the verge of completing the actual leaving when the arguments emerged, the therapist decided that a ritual to mark

Karen's leaving home was needed. The Berrys had stated frequently that they "didn't think we had given Karen enough in order to equip her for life in the outside community." This sense of not having given her enough was intensified by the school's criticism of the family. Their phrase "given her enough" was used to construct a leaving home ritual that would confirm Karen's young adulthood, would promote the family's confidence in her and themselves, and would highlight ongoing connectedness among the members.

I asked the parents and Andrew each to select a gift for Karen for her to take to her new home. I suggested that they choose a gift that would remind Karen of them and would also ease her way in her new setting. Karen, in turn, was asked to select a gift for each member, that would remain with them when she left. The family members were told not to buy these gifts, but rather to choose something of their own or to make something. They were asked to bring these gifts to the next session and not to tell anyone else in the family about their gift before the session.

When the family arrived, they appeared very excited and happy in a way that had not been seen before during therapy. They had not shared their gifts before the session but had decided during the 2 weeks to wrap them and put them in a large bag, which Karen carried into the meeting. Mrs. Berry began by saying that during that week, they had decided on a definite date for Karen to move out, which they had not been able to do previously. Karen had gone for several visits to the group home. She also said that there had been a lot of secretive laughter during the 2 weeks, as people prepared their gifts, and no fighting!

I suggested a format for the exchange of gifts that was simple and largely nonverbal, which involved each member giving their gift, with a brief explanation if needed, and the recipient simply saying "thank you," other discussion being reserved for after the gift exchange. This was done to highlight the family as a group together and to facilitate equal participation, since Karen often fell silent when verbal discussions became rapid. Mr. Berry began the ceremony. He reached into the bag and gave Karen an unusual-shaped package, which turned out to be his favorite frying pan. Traditionally, Mr. Berry made Sunday breakfast. Because Karen was learning some simple cooking skills in school, she always wanted to use this frying pan, but her father had been afraid that she would ruin it and so had not let her use it. Karen beamed and said, "Thank you." Mrs. Berry's package was small, and she shyly handed it to Karen. It contained an almost full bottle of perfume and a pair of earrings. Mrs. Berry related briefly that she had often scolded Karen for using her perfume and had never allowed her to wear earrings. She looked at Karen and said, "I think you're grown up enough for these—they belonged to my mother and she gave them to me and now I'm giving them to you." With tears in her eyes, Karen said, "Thank you."

The mood changed profoundly when it was Andrew's turn. He remarked that he couldn't bring his whole gift to the session, but that Karen would understand. She opened his package to find a partially used box of birdseed. Leaving for school meant that Andrew would have to leave his parakeet. He had been allowed various pets at home, and had been responsible for them, while Karen had not. He explained that he had called Karen's group home, and they would allow her to bring the bird. He said that he would teach her to care for it before she moved out. Karen said, "Thank you," and Mrs. Berry expressed relief that the parakeet was leaving home too.

Karen then gave her gifts. To her mother, Karen gave her favorite stuffed animal, which she had had since early childhood and with which she still slept. She said to her mother, "I can't sleep with this in my new home—please keep it." To her father, she gave a photograph of her that had been taken during one of her visits at the group home. The photograph showed her sitting with several young men and women, and she said to her father, "These are my new friends." To Andrew, she gave her clock radio. This was a prized possession that had been a Christmas present. She gave it to Andrew and said, "Don't be late for school!"

Two weeks after this session, Karen moved into the group home, and a month later, Andrew left for college. The family ended therapy. At their 1-year follow-up, the family reported that both children had adjusted well to their new settings and were visiting home for holidays. Mrs. Berry had also returned to school to train for paid employment.

Discussion of the Ritual

This leaving-home ritual functioned in a number of ways. Through the course of the family therapy, the family had been preparing for Karen's leaving home but seemed to get stuck just on the verge of her actual leaving. Like many normative life cycle rituals, the therapeutic ritual worked to confirm a process that was already in motion and was not simply a discrete event. The ritual symbolically affirmed and made simultaneous the contradictions of separation and ongoing connectedness that are involved when any child leaves home. The family members, in their giving of gifts, were able both to give permission for separation and affirm their ongoing but changing relationships.

The ritual was designed to introduce symmetry into a system that had been primarily marked by complementary relationships. Thus, all members participated in the giving and receiving of gifts and in the planning and thoughtfulness that went into gift selection, altering the previous pattern in the family whereby the parents and Andrew were seen to be the "givers," the "providers," the "protectors," and Karen was seen to be the recipient of care, advice, and protection.

The ritual was also designed to confirm individual boundaries as each member was individually responsible for his or her own planning and selection of gifts. Individuation was promoted through the instruction of secret planning by each member. Dyadic relationships between Karen and every member were also confirmed, in a family that had previously operated with triads involving Karen as their primary mode of relationship. Finally, each member's contribution to the ritual was highlighted as important to the entire process, thus symbolically celebrating the whole family unit. Various aspects of the ritual functioned to introduce differences in pattern to the family system.

By asking the family to bring their gifts to the therapy session, I was able to serve as witness to the process. Witnesses are frequently a part of normative life cycle rituals. Here, the therapist also may be seen to symbolically represent an outside helping system in a celebratory stance with a family that had been used to criticism and disparagement from outside systems.

Healing Rituals

Every culture has rituals to mark profound losses, deal with the grief of survivors, and facilitate ongoing life after such loss. There are many creative contemporary examples of cultural healing rituals. The Vietnam War Memorial in Washington, DC, is visited by families and friends who lost men and women in the war and make pilgrimages to the memorial, during which they search for their loved one's name, perhaps leave items that have special meaning, and often make rubbings to carry back home. Public grieving for a war that held so much secrecy and shame is facilitated by this repeated ritual.

The AIDS quilt, consisting of several thousand hand-sewn patches, each memorializing a person who has died of AIDS, is displayed with a powerful ceremony in which all of the names of the dead are read aloud as the quilt is unfolded in planned, repetitive motions of connection and uplift. A quilt is often a community endeavor. The AIDS quilt connects a community of mourners with a symbol of warmth and care.

The Clothesline Project is a women's ritual devoted to recovery from abuse. A growing collection of hand-painted T-shirts is hung on a clothesline. This community ritual includes the ringing of gongs and bells and blowing of horns to symbolize how often a woman is assaulted, raped, and murdered. The marvelous contradiction of regaining power in the face of servitude is clearly contained in these hand-painted depictions of violence hung ironically on a clothesline for all to see.

More recently, we witnessed the powerful healing rituals created in the wake of 9/11. The association of Black Firefighters in New York and their wives and families—the Vulcans and Vulcanettes—created sustaining rituals to mark their losses. Beginning with the universal ritual of storytelling, they gathered to speak of those they lost. Family elders lit candles, while the youngest in each family participated in a procession to proclaim there would be a future. Since there were no images of the lost Black firefighters on television or in the newspapers, they created a special memorial flag consisting of 12 small helmets and the names of their heroes who died in 9/11 trying to save others. When New York City stated it was removing firefighters from the 9/11 site, the Vulcans created a series of emotional, spiritual, and political rituals and thereby fought the edict. In a public ceremony, surviving Black firefighters made commitments of care to the children who had lost fathers, stating, "The needs your father might have met, we will meet them" (Imber-Black, 2003).

Healing may also be necessary for losses sustained through the breakup of relationships, for the reconciliation of relationships after painful revelations such as affairs, for unresolved grief when normative healing rituals have not occurred or have not succeeded, for losses of bodily parts and functions due to illness, and for the often attendant loss of roles, life expectations, and dreams (see Imber-Coppersmith, 1985, for case examples of healing rituals). Therapeutic healing rituals are particularly useful when normative healing rituals do not exist or are not sufficient for the magnitude of the loss.

Setting fire to the past

Alice Jeffers, age 35, requested therapy, saying that she was depressed and unable to live her life normally. Alice was single and lived alone. She was a trained and practicing veterinarian. In the first session, she described to me an 8-year-long relationship with a man. The relationship, which had included periods of living together, had been very stormy and had finally ended 2 years previously at his insistence. Alice's family had not approved of the relationship. They were relieved when it ended but seemed unable to extend any support to Alice for the pain she felt. Friends told her that she was well rid of him. Over the 2 years, Alice grew increasingly isolated, and by the time she came to therapy, she did not go out with any friends, spent all her free time thinking about her former lover, dreamed about him nightly, had gained a lot of weight, and felt that her work was being affected. Her family and friends' inability to confirm her pain and loss seemed to contribute to her own need to do nothing else but think about him and feel sad. She said she felt that if she had been married and divorced, people would have been more supportive of her, as they had been of her sister in such circumstances.

I began with simple confirmation of Alice's loss and grief and highlighted that, indeed, there are no agreed-upon processes for the end of a nonmarried relationship. I asked Alice to perform a task that would allow her both to grieve and to begin to get on with other aspects of her life. For 1 hour a day, Alice was told to do nothing but review memories of the relationship, since this was something that obviously still needed to be completed. I suggested that she write these memories out on separate index cards and bring them to the next session. Outside of the hour a day, I urged Alice to do other things. Alice returned with a stack of index cards, which she had creatively color-coded, using purple for "mellow" memories, green for "jealous" memories, and blue for "sad" memories. With laughter, she stated, "And, of course, my angry ones are RED!" As the therapy session focused on the cards and their meanings, Alice stated that she had felt much better during the three weeks, that she began to find that an hour a day was too much time, and that she had stopped dreaming about her former love. I asked her whether there were cards she felt ready to let go of, and she said that there were. She was asked to take the cards home and sort them out, differentiating between those she still wanted to hang on to and those she felt ready to let go of.

Alice arrived 2 weeks later, dressed more brightly than before and eager to talk. She had started to go out with friends a bit and had looked into an aerobics class. After reporting this, she took out two stacks of cards. She said she had decided she wanted to keep the purple "mellow" memories, as these were a part of her that she wanted to maintain. She felt the good parts of the relationship had changed her in positive ways, and she said she wanted to carry this into any new relationship she might have. This was the first mention of a sense of future. She also wanted to keep most of the red "anger" memories, as these helped her to remember how shabbily she had been treated many times and thus kept her from romanticizing the past. However she was very ready to let go of the green "jealousy" memories, which often made her feel bad about herself, and the blue "sad" memories, as she felt that she had been sad long enough. At that point, I left the room and returned with a ceramic bowl and a book of matches, which I silently offered to Alice, who smiled and said, "Oh, we should burn them!" It is important to note that she saw the burning as a joint endeavor by herself and me. I handed the cards back to Alice, who put them in a pile in the bowl and lit them. She used several matches to get a good fire going and then sat silently for several moments watching the flames. At one point, she said, "It's so final, but it's good." A few minutes later, she joked, "We should toast marshmallows—that would be the final irony," referring to the fact that her boyfriend had often criticized her body and her weight and yet brought her treats. Toward the end, she said, "This is good—my final memory is of warmth."

In sessions after to the burning ritual, Alice dealt with many family of origin issues that had previously been unavailable because of her stuck position vis-a-vis her boyfriend. She was able to renegotiate several family relationships, began going out more with friends, and joined a scuba class. When therapy ended, she was beginning flying lessons, an apt metaphor for her new beginnings.

Identity Redefinition Rituals

Identity redefinition rituals function to remove labels and stigma from individuals, couples, and families and often realign relationships between the family and larger systems. This is especially necessary when the larger systems have held negative points of view toward a family. A reworking of an earlier idiosyncratic life cycle transition that went awry may be accomplished. New relationship options, previously unavailable because of the constraints of labels, become available (see Imber-Coppersmith, 1983). A balance of being both similar to others and different from others becomes achievable.

A mutual adoption celebration

I met Bob Simmons, a 37-year-old single gay man, about a year and a half after he had adopted his 9-year-old son, Alan. "We're definitely a new sort of family," Bob told me in our first therapy session. "I don't have to tell you that as a gay man, I had to look all over the country to find an agency that would let me adopt a child. It took me four years, but I finally succeeded," Bob reflected proudly.

Bob had found an agency across the country that let him make a home for Alan, a biracial child with many special educational and emotional needs. Alan had been in six foster homes after his crack-addicted mother abandoned him when he was 2 years old. He had been severely abused, both in his biological family and in at least three of his foster homes. Now, living with Bob, Alan showed many of the signs of an abused and neglected child. Alan had learned to survive by drawing into himself, allowing little contact with others. Bob came to family therapy to help his son, to build their relationship, and to learn parenting strategies.

As I met with Bob and his young son, Alan refused to talk to me. No doubt, having met many professionals whose jobs had been to move him from one place to another, Alan was not about to take any risks with me. As Bob described his frustrations learning to parent, Alan sank lower and lower in his chair. My many attempts to reach him were met with shrugs and a cap pulled farther and farther over his eyes. "Tell me something," I said to Alan, "he adopted you, right?" "Right," Alan whispered in return. "Have you adopted him?" I asked. Alan's cap flew off, and his eyes grew as big as saucers. He rose up in his seat. "Oh, how could I do that?" his voice boomed. "I don't know," I replied. "How do *you* think you could do that?" "I would have to go to court and get some papers," Alan replied. "I think you've hit on something important here," Bob said.

For the rest of the session, we talked about how Bob adopted Alan. As a gay man, he was made to feel stigmatized everywhere he turned to realize his dream of being a father. When he finally adopted Alan, he didn't make a celebration. There was no ritual to mark and help make this critical transition. Most of Bob's friends couldn't understand his decision to be a single father. His sister yelled at him over the phone that he had no right to be a parent. When Bob and Alan began to live together as father and son, Bob was unprepared for how difficult parenting a boy who had been so abused would be. He often told Alan how lucky he was to be in a nice home. Without meaning to, Bob made Alan feel that he was in a very unbalanced situation. When I asked Alan whether he had adopted Bob, I struck an important chord of mutuality, one that excited Alan with its possibilities.

I met alone with Alan and told him that he wouldn't need to go to court to adopt Bob. He would just need to write out his own document on his computer at home. We agreed to keep this private between us as he worked on a "certificate to adopt my dad."

The therapy contained many other elements, including helping Bob to set appropriate limits for Alan, reconnecting Bob to his own mother, who wanted to be a loving grandmother for Alan, and aiding Bob in finding other single dads, both gay and straight. When our therapy concluded, Bob and Alan invited Bob's mother and some new and supportive friends over for a special ritual, a mutual adoption ceremony, in which Alan and Bob openly adopted one another.

Designing and Implementing Rituals for New Life Cycle Transitions

Designing and implementing rituals such as those discussed in this chapter, is a learnable skill. Several guidelines will enhance this process.

Just as normative rituals are processes, rather than discrete events, so therapeutic rituals are part of a larger therapeutic process. Their efficacy relies on planning, careful assessment, especially regarding life cycle phases and idiosyncratic life cycle events, and respect and rapport between family and therapist. The rituals are not games or tricks, but rather rise out of a relational context that appreciates the ritualizing tendency of human beings and the need for meaning in human relationships.

The family and therapist search for the appropriate symbols and symbolic acts of the individual, family, ethnic group, and cultural group, which represent the possibility of relationship development. Such symbols and metaphorical action should connect the family with the familiar, while also being capable of leading to the unfamiliar.

The family and therapist design the ritual with a focus on special time and special space. Thus, rituals may occur at a particular time or over time. Time may be used to draw particular distinctions or to highlight simultaneity. A sense of connection to past, present, and future is made. The ritual may occur in the therapy session, at home, or at some other agreed-upon place, such as by a body of water, in the woods, or in a cemetery. If the ritual requires a witness, then the therapy session is often the preferred time and space, or the therapist may accompany the family to an agreed-upon place.

The therapist attends to alternations in order to incorporate contradictions. Thus, holding on may be alternated with letting go in a single ritual, or a ritual of termination or separation may be followed by a ritual of renewal or celebration.

The therapist looks for ways to involve the family in co-designing the ritual to facilitate imagination that may lead to problem solving and enhanced functioning. A sense of humor and playfulness are used when appropriate.

Therapeutic rituals for idiosyncratic life cycle events borrow heavily from normative rituals, yet utilize symbols and symbolic actions that are relevant to the particular life cycle transition.

The therapist remains open to the family's development of the ritual, including their choice to not perform the ritual. Therapeutic rituals should not be hollow events, practiced simply because someone said to do it. Rather, they are opportunities for the confirmation of existing relationships and for the beginnings of relationship change. Family readiness must be carefully gauged and respected. In successful therapeutic rituals, the ritual and its outcome ultimately belong to the family.

Conclusion

New life cycle events and transitions pose particular difficulties for individuals and families. Lacking available maps that fit their situation and without wider contextual support and confirmation, complex feedback processes may be set in motion, resulting in symptoms and a high level of distress and isolation. Since rituals have the capacity to hold and express differences rather than homogenize them, they are particularly powerful resources for any life cycle transition that differs from the conventional. Therapy needs to include conversations about meaningful rituals. Creatively and sensitively crafted rituals, which both borrow richly from established life cycle rituals and are simultaneously brand new, facilitate necessary transitions and the expansion of relationship possibilities.

Chapter 29

The Therapist and the Family: The Intersection of Life Cycles

Steve Lerner

The family life cycle model developed by Carter and McGoldrick (this book in all editions) provides a richly contextualized, multidimensional framework for understanding the movement of the family through time. This framework helps us to locate the points at which the chronic background anxiety in a family is likely to coincide with the acute stress of navigating a current life cycle transition. These are the times in family life when symptoms and dysfunction are most likely to emerge, in both our own and our clients' families.

These crucial transitions in family life are viewed as being inextricably linked to the sociocultural context in which family life is embedded. Factors such as gender, race, class, ethnicity, and sexual orientation shape the nature of the playing field on which life cycle transitions are negotiated.

In this chapter, I focus on the intersection between the therapist's life cycle stage and that of the family in treatment—a key dimension of the fit between therapist and family as the clinical process unfolds (Simon, 1988). More specifically, I propose that when the therapist brings unresolved issues from a past or current life cycle stage into the clinical work with a family that is struggling to navigate that same life cycle stage, predictable problems may emerge.

Some therapists zoom in zealously to remake the client in the image of their own wished-for but unachieved resolution of a particular life cycle issue, overfunctioning for the client's family as they continue to underfunction in their own. Others will become ineffective, fuzzy thinkers, underfunctioning for both themselves and the family. A therapist may become overly aloof and distant or, alternatively, may end up in a power struggle with the family. Whatever the error tendency of a particular therapist,

it is useful to examine one's functioning through the wide-angle lens of the family life cycle model. For example, what unresolved life cycle struggle of the therapist's may now be interacting with that of the family, fueling a therapeutic impasse? How might anxiety from other similarities and differences add to the problem in the therapy? Can the therapeutic problem serve as a signal that, when heeded, may result in renewed growth for both the therapist and the clinical family?

Many therapists have studied their own families of origin as part of their professional training. They have worked to identify and modify their part in multigenerational patterns, with an eye toward navigating family relationships and life cycle transitions with greater clarity, objectivity, and calm. Those of us who have worked diligently on our own families may mistakenly believe that we have "done that" and can now focus single-mindedly on the family life cycle of the families we work with. Often, we will be reminded that we cannot leave ourselves out of the picture when we encounter pronounced similarities or differences between our own lives and those of our clients.

Dimensions of Similarity Between Therapist and Client

Figure 29.1 lists the family life cycle stage as one of many important dimensions on which the therapist and client will be more or less similar—or out of sync. When life cycle stages intersect for the therapist and the clinical family, the therapist can be at the same stage, an earlier stage, or a later stage than the family. The details of a particular stage in the therapist's life and that of the family (say, the birth or the launching of children) may be very similar or

Multigenerational history
Unresolved emotional issues with significant others
Typical ways of managing stress
Other family patterns and legacies
Sibling position
Family life cycle
Age
Current life events
Health
Culture
Gender
Race
Class
Ethnicity
Sexual orientation
Religion
Politics
Community, work system, friendship circle

FIGURE 29.1 Interfacing dimensions between therapist and family

very different. The match between the therapist and the clinical family on variables such as race, ethnicity, gender, class, sibling position, and sexual orientation will also influence the degree to which the life cycle issues become emotionally loaded in therapy. For example, a young White therapist, herself the youngest in her own family, finds herself dealing with an older Mexican American couple, both first-borns, who are caring for their aging parents. The therapist might suffer from an overwhelming sense of "juniority" in the therapy process as her age, ethnicity, birth order, and lack of life experience combine to foster feelings of incompetence, both real and imagined.

Brief Scenarios: Complex Therapist–Family Life Cycle Interactions

The potential complexity of therapist–family life cycle interactions is further illustrated by the following vignettes.

Ann, a middle-aged White therapist, recently came out to her family after entering her first serious live-in relationship with a woman. Her father has not yet accepted her sexual orientation and has refused to meet her partner. This situation is very painful for Ann, who worries that she could lose her relationship with her father, who is in failing health. She also feels responsible for the escalating tensions in her parents' marriage as they become increasingly polarized around the issue of accepting her lesbianism.

Ann is now working with a White client who is seriously dating an African American man. Her client wants to tell her parents about this relationship but fears that her father, in particular, will not get past his racist response. The client's family is replete with cut offs as a patterned way of managing conflict and differences. How might Ann's own issues and anxieties about the coming-out process influence her work with this client?

Don, a White therapist in his 20s, is the youngest child in his upper-middle-class family. His father initiated a divorce when Don was 15, following the discovery of his wife's affair. Don began living with his father after the separation and has never truly modified his angry, distant relationship with his mother. He is now seeing a working-class African American couple contemplating separation, after the wife's affair came out into the open. Their youngest son has just turned 15. What obstacles might Don face as he not only deals with the gulf posed by racial, class, and life cycle differences, but also is confronted head-on with all that is evoked from his own past?

Kathy, an Irish American therapist in her 50s, lost her mother in a car wreck when she was 12 and is now the same age that her mother was when she died. Kathy and her older brother were "protected" from the facts about the accident, which was shrouded in layers of secrecy. Her mother had been intoxicated and caused the crash, which also killed a young child in another car. Almost from the moment Kathy's mother's funeral ended, her memory was gradually erased because of the family's shame about her alcoholism and its terrible cost. Their father remarried within the year, and the children were instructed to call their new stepmother "Mom."

Now Kathy is beginning work with an Italian American family in which the mother is dying of complications of diabetes. The parents are grief-stricken and worried about their depressed children but are very reluctant to permit an outsider to help them with the enormous tragedy they face. How can Kathy find a way to connect with this family and help them open up their reactions to this upcoming loss of a mother, and how might Kathy's regrets and anxiety about her own past influence her work? How might Kathy's ethnicity and that of the clinical family interact to make this therapy process more difficult (McGoldrick, Giordano, & Preto, 2004).

Families With Young Children: A Complex Intersection

A life cycle stage that is particularly challenging is that of the family with young children (see Chapter 15). With the birth of the first child, a profound realignment of family relationships occurs. The whole family diagram shifts one notch upward, and every family member gets a new name: husband and wife become father and mother; siblings become uncles or aunts; parents become grandparents; grandparents become great-grandparents.

The marital couple faces the largest challenge as they adjust to their new roles. Many equal partnerships succumb to the powerful tidal pull of the previous generation's far less equitable gender roles and expectations (Lerner, 1998). Even the most pioneering of couples will struggle with the enormous challenges of this stage and are often left with unresolved dissatisfaction stemming from the compromises and accommodations that began after the first child was born. The marital relationship becomes the crucible in which the seeds of inequality and disillusionment grow, resulting in early divorce or the later dissolution of the marriage when the children are adolescents or have been launched. Therapists who are not actively examining the pervasive impact of gender on their own and their parents' marriages—or who deny the enormous impact of gender on every aspect of personal and work life—will be limited in helping families to navigate the complexities of life with young children and the marital renegotiations that are required to make things work.

She Nurtures/He Earns: The Therapist's Transition Gets in the Way

The following case was presented by a therapist in a small supervision group that met twice monthly. The contract was that supervisees presented clinical cases and their families of origin. My theoretical framework as the supervisor was Bowen family systems theory, informed by feminist theory, and the family life cycle model of Carter and McGoldrick (this book, all editions).

Alan, the therapist, was seeing a married woman with two young children who had sought help after a period of increasing depression. She was distressed about an upcoming move to another city precipitated by her husband's transfer to the headquarters of his company, which was to take place in 6 months. She was upset about the prospect of leaving her circle of close women friends and her parents and sisters, who lived nearby. Before having children, she had worked full-time, and she remembered those years with nostalgia as a time when she felt free to pursue her dreams. Currently, she had a part-time job that she enjoyed and had found an excellent child care situation that would be impossible to duplicate, since it included her mother caring for her children two afternoons a week. She had tentative plans to pursue more education but had put her career goals on hold since the children arrived.

Alan empathized with her sadness and asked some good questions: What did she know about the new city? Had she visited there with her husband and researched the work and educational opportunities and child care options? But in the therapist's mind, the move was a given, which was precisely how his depressed client saw it. So there were certain questions Alan did not ask.

He did *not* ask: How was the decision to move negotiated between the couple? What impact did her husband's income and earning power (he earned 90 percent of the family's income) have on the decision process? How did she understand the fact that she has acted as though she had no option but to reflexively go along with the move, which she called a "fait accompli"?

Supervision

In supervision, I asked Alan to consider the similarities and differences between the clinical couple's way of navigating their current life cycle transition and the way in which he and his wife handled their own.

Alan and his wife, both first-borns, had one 2-year-old child. His wife had cut back from a full-time position at a magazine to do freelance work when their baby was born. At the current time, she had decided to go back to work, as her old job has been offered to her. The couple had been arguing over how to divide household and child care responsibilities if she took the position, and Alan just didn't see how it could work. Before having a child, Alan believed in shared parenting, but now he did not want his child "raised by a stranger." Also, he made $90 an hour, while his wife would make only $16 an hour in her new position. He said, "Given the high cost of child care, and the reality of how little her job pays, I really wish she'd stay with the freelance work for a few more years." Alan admitted that he felt anxious and defensive when his wife talked about resuming full-time work.

Alan's own parents followed the traditional path: His mother nurtured and his father earned. Their family moved four times because of his father's career, and to his knowledge, his mother never objected. Alan had no idea whether either of them had ever considered another arrangement or how the traditional path suited them.

Supervisory feedback

In response to Alan's presentation of his clinical case, a female supervisee commented that he had quickly conveyed the underlying message that the move could not, and should not, be questioned. It was as if he were saying, "Cheer up, it's not that bad, and besides, with a little elbow grease, you'll have almost as good a situation in the new city." I added that he also did not locate the client's depression, or the move itself, in any larger context: her marriage, her family of origin, or her life cycle stage.

I suggested that Alan's current life cycle issues (i.e., the marital tension surrounding his wife's decision to resume full-time work) were interfacing with his client's in a way that was impeding his objectivity. To move toward a clearer frame of reference on his own life cycle transition and that of the client, I encouraged Alan to open up a discussion with each of his parents about the way in which decisions were made in their own relationship, with particular reference to the four career moves.

Family of origin data

Alan's father told him that there had never been any question but that the family would move when his job changed. Like his father before him, he had seen himself as the provider for the family. "That's just the way life was back then," his father said. "Your mother and I never questioned it."

When Alan talked to his mother, he learned that she *had* questioned the moves—but only to herself. The moves had been extremely difficult for her. "I started to feel like a refugee, like my grandmother from Poland, but I didn't see any alternative." She revealed that she had become quite depressed when the fourth move took the family sufficiently far from her hometown that she could no longer easily visit her own parents. Her mother had also been upset to lose her close connection to her grandchildren. At that point, Alan's mother had thought of staying behind, but for a number of reasons it had seemed like an impossible choice. By the time retirement came along, she had become more assertive in the marriage. She had been working outside of the home for several years, which she continued to do after her husband retired. Over time, largely as a result of her growing independence and her husband's mellowing in later life, the decision-making process had shifted to much more of a partnership than it had been before. In a later conversation, she said to Alan, "I might have considered divorce at the time of the fourth move if it had been as common as it is today. But on the other hand, I never really protested or fought it out with your father. Maybe he would have put me before his career—I guess I'll never really know for sure."

Alan reported that the discussions with his parents had gotten him thinking about his own marriage and whether he was putting it in jeopardy by "following in my father's footsteps where work is concerned—I never wanted to do that!" I commented, "So, Alan, I guess the challenge for you is whether you want to wait until retirement to figure out how to become an equal partner with your wife, or whether you want to try to do that now?" Alan smiled and wryly observed, "If I don't do it now, we won't be together at retirement—my wife is much more outspoken than my mother!" He later reported that he had started to initiate talks with his wife about how they could work together to make room for both of their careers, including the option of his cutting back some on his practice, despite the financial sacrifice, and his spending more time parenting.

In the client's therapy, he began to ask questions about the decision-making process about the planned move. He suggested that his client invite her husband to join her in the sessions, and through further questioning, he helped the couple to explore the pluses and minuses of the move for each of them, their children, and their extended-family relationships. The work that Alan did in his own family paid off. He was now a clearer and more effective questioner who helped the couple to explore a wider range of options because Alan could now see these options himself. Alan was also better able to help the couple examine their own families of origin and life cycle issues as a result of his work on his own.

The Long-Term View: Working With One Family Over Successive Life Cycle Stages

As successive life cycle stages bring new challenges, a family may return to the same therapist over decades. Seeing the same family navigate successive life cycle stages offers a unique learning experience for both the therapist and the clinical family. For the therapist, long-term contact can provide direct longitudinal experience with a family other than one's own. For the clinical family, there is the knowledge that they have a coach they can return to—a known quantity who has the background information to help them meet another life challenge. In such a long-term process, it becomes far more likely that particular issues in the therapist's life will coincide with the clinical family's, as was the case in my work with the Vintons, which spanned a period of 25 years.

The Vintons initially came to see me with their three children because of the parents' concern about Jane, their oldest child. A 1-year therapy ended with decreased symptoms and Jane's successful departure for college. Five years later, with their second child now also out of the home, the couple came back to work on marital issues that

had emerged as Sheila went back to work. She was starting something new, while Jack felt stuck in a demanding and ungratifying job. Work on their respective families of origin, in which men were the sole breadwinners and women stayed at home, helped each of them to achieve a more tolerant, less reactive position with each other, as they saw their own struggles as part of a larger family and cultural legacy.

Four years later, the couple returned for additional marital work. They had now launched their youngest son, and the older two children were married. Sheila complained that Jack was unavailable for intimacy, while Jack felt increasingly worn out by his management job, which required frequent travel. This phase of therapy lasted for 6 months, and when it concluded, Sheila was less focused on Jack. When he was unavailable to do things with her, she made her own plans. For his part, Jack was gradually able to see his irritability and frustration as being related to the pattern of men and work in his family; typically, men worked incredibly hard in thankless jobs that they saw as tickets to a comfortable retirement in their "golden years." Then many of them died before or just after retiring, never having enjoyed what they had worked so hard to achieve.

During this phase of therapy, I was diagnosed with a malignant melanoma at the age of 41. In the face of this personal crisis, I had to cancel and reschedule several sessions. I chose to tell Jack and Sheila about my diagnosis because in our small community they were likely to hear about it from others. They asked me a number of questions, including my prognosis, which by that time was guardedly positive and later was upgraded to excellent. They appreciated hearing directly from me about my illness, and my disclosure seemed to facilitate their work on their own issues in therapy (Gerson, 1996).

Several years later, Jack, now 57, came in again for individual consultations. He was now eager for retirement and dreamed of opening a small specialty bookstore in a nearby university town. In the midst of this phase of therapy, however, he was diagnosed with lung cancer. His wife joined our sessions at that time.

Jack asked me what had helped me to deal with my cancer diagnosis, and I told him that I had found self-regulation training helpful. During the period after my diagnosis, I had learned biofeedback techniques for anxiety management and immune system mobilization. Later, under supervision, I worked with several clients who were struggling with physical illness. Jack asked whether I could teach him biofeedback, and I agreed. I also arranged for him to meet with my supervisor, Pat Norris, an international expert in the use of biofeedback with cancer patients. Jack became proficient with thermal and muscle biofeedback and found it very helpful. He asked me more about my own experience with cancer, and although he knew that my prognosis had been much better than his, he nevertheless saw my survival as a hopeful sign. "You've been there—you know what I'm up against," he said.

During the next 2 years, I continued to see Jack as he learned to be his own advocate in the medical system and struggled to regain his strength. He was determined to live long enough to dance at the wedding of his youngest son, which he succeeded in doing. A few days later, I received a call from Jane, the original identified patient, telling me that Jack was dying and the family would like me to come to the hospital. I arrived at his room, where his entire family was assembled, just as he died.

Some weeks after his funeral, which I attended, Sheila resumed therapy to focus on her grief and to help the children cope with their loss. Then, several years later, now a grandmother four times over, she returned to treatment, this time to focus on her new live-in relationship with Elliot, who was divorced with four grown children of his own. Her choice to live with her new partner had elicited strong reactions from her children, who had thought nothing of living with their own lovers before marriage but did not see this as permissible for their mother. In particular, she wanted to work on paving the way for her upcoming marriage to Elliot, which was planned for the following year. We worked together on finding a role for her three children in the wedding, which she carried out beautifully. She mentioned Jack during the ceremony, saying that she felt he would support her moving ahead with her life. She terminated therapy after her remarriage, saying, "You know me. I'll probably be back someday."

My thinking as a family therapist evolved during the many years I worked with the Vinton family. Sharing some aspects of my experience with cancer had deepened my relationship with them and contributed to my ability to work closely with them throughout Jack's illness and dying process. Later, when Sheila contemplated remarriage, both she and I were aware that I brought a very different perspective into the therapy regarding her new relationship with Elliot than I had had in the earlier marital work

with Sheila and Jack. This was particularly evident as I helped her to think through the loaded issues of money, power, decision making, and who was responsible for dealing with their respective children as they formed a remarried family. Sheila knew that she and her family had helped to "train" me and "bring me up" as a therapist. As a result, she (and Jack earlier) felt a certain well-earned pride, which I reciprocated, about our ability to work well together.

Working With Loss: A Link Between Life Cycle Stages

When I was 20, my mother, age 49, died of breast cancer 10 years after her initial diagnosis. For a variety of reasons, her illness and subsequent death were underprocessed in my family; indeed, for some years after her death, my mother was rarely discussed. Over the years, I worked on the impact of her death and tried to modify my part in the silence surrounding it. Some of the payoff from this earlier work was reflected in the way my siblings and I recently rallied to my father's side when he became critically ill and nearly died. Also, during the same time frame, I became a partner with my wife in caring for her elderly parents, who had moved to Topeka to be near us. Going through these experiences brought home the fact that I would not be caring for my mother in her old age. This was a life cycle transition that I would miss, and I felt the loss especially acutely during the crisis with my father and my ongoing involvement in caring for my elderly in-laws.

Not coincidentally, it was during this time that I began to work one day a week in a nursing home in a small Kansas town. The work began when I saw an elderly stroke victim in a rural hospital where I consult. Later, she was transferred to the nursing home, where I continued to see her weekly, first with her daughter and then also with her son. The administrator of the nursing home, impressed with her response to therapy, asked me to start a group for those residents—women mostly in their 80s—who were capable of conversing. Group work seemed especially fitting because these residents, most of whom had known each other throughout their lives in the small town, tended to avoid socializing, retreating to their rooms as soon as meals were over.

I run the group using a multiple family model and do a genogram for each member. Visiting relatives are also invited to attend. Molly, a stroke victim who also suffered from severe gastrointestinal problems, was admitted when her husband Morris could no longer care for her in the home. Her siblings were dead, and Morris was all she had. Molly was quite agitated and periodically during the group sessions would shout, "I want to go home; I want to go home!" Morris, who attended several sessions with her, would become frustrated, guilty, and depressed and try to exhort her to settle down. Then, two months after her admission, he suddenly died of a heart attack.

In a session following Morris's death, Molly dozed off for the first part of the group and then suddenly woke up and shouted, "I have no one! I'm all alone! I have to go home!" I asked Georgia, Maxine, Violet, and Elizabeth, the other group members, what their reactions were to Molly's situation and what they wanted to say to her when she shouted out that she had no one. Georgia, a woman with severe physical problems of her own, said in a clear, strong voice, "Molly, I know you miss Morris. He was a fine man. Would you like me to be your sister? I'd like to be your sister, why, we all would. You're not alone, Molly. Would you like me to be your sister?" Molly nodded. One by one, each other group member voiced her willingness to be a sister to Molly. Then there was a silence, and the women all looked at me. I turned to Molly and said, "Molly, I'm only here on Thursday afternoons, and I can't be your sister. But I'd be glad to be your younger brother." Molly smiled, and the other members laughed.

I think that my investment in these women and my interest in working in a context in which past, current, and impending loss is a constant feature of their lives relate to my current life cycle position, in which I have begun to help the previous generation in their old age. This work enriches my life because the untimely death of my mother precluded the possibility of my being available to her as she aged. I mentioned to the group recently that they were teaching me a great deal about life. Georgia turned to me and said, "If you ever need to go into a nursing home, you'll know just what to expect."

Conclusion

The interaction between therapist and family life cycle stages offers both pitfalls and opportunities during the conduct of family therapy. When we get off track by confusing our unresolved issues at a particular stage with those of the clinical family, revisiting how we have been navigating the transitions confronting us and identifying where we are stuck will usually help us to find a more creative direction to take in the therapy. This shift in focus typically requires a review of our own family history and the patterns in which we participate and a renewed effort to modify our part in them. This may involve the opening up of topics that have not been spoken about before or a return to issues that we dealt with in the past but then too quickly dropped.

The experience that we gain from negotiating life cycle transitions also facilitates our work with families, enabling us to point out options that anxious family members may have overlooked and to ask questions and understand our clients in ways that we might not have been able to do had we not been through similar struggles in our own lives.

Our work with families, perhaps especially when they are most like us or most different from us, requires us to examine our own attitudes, beliefs, stereotypes, relationships, and life choices through many lenses, including our own position in the family life cycle vis-à-vis that of our clients. As one therapist that I talked to recently observed, "You mean I have to keep *that* in mind, too?" I am afraid that we do if we plan to continue growing as people and therapists. In the end, this is the beauty of this rather impossible profession we have chosen.

APPENDIX

A Multicontextual Life Cycle Framework for Clinical Assessment

Monica McGoldrick, Betty Carter, and Nydia Garcia Preto

This appendix offers the reader a format for a multicontextual assessment to help clinicians think of assessment and intervention within both a cultural and longitudinal framework. We urge clinicians to go beyond the clients' presenting problems to discuss their values, dreams, and strengths and vulnerabilities in the context of their personal, familial, community, and cultural heritage. The dominant Western therapeutic interventions involve "talking it out" in individualized therapy, which emphasizes confidentiality above connectedness. In other cultural contexts the essentials of healing include restoring social supports and relationships. In these contexts song, dance, and storytelling are often what clients experience as most comforting, supportive, and natural (Dacey & Travers, 2004). Toward that goal we have provided examples of questions to amplify both the context and possibilities for intervention.

The information for this assessment can be gathered in a structured interview or as it emerges over several sessions, but obviously it is important to do it sooner rather than later. We advocate using a **genogram** and **a family chronology** or time line as basic tools, for this assessment framework. We begin by focusing on:

- What is the presenting problem and for whom in the family?
- Why now?
- Who is making the referral and what is that person's stake in the problem?
- What are the life cycle stage or transition issues for the family at this time?

The following outline offers a map for gathering information on clients' problems within a multicontextual family life cycle framework.

A Multicontextual Assessment

I. ASSESSING INDIVIDUAL LIFE CYCLE DEVELOPMENT AND STRESSORS (BODY, MIND, AND SPIRIT)

A. **Age and Life Cycle Stage:** Is there an appropriate level of intergenerational and same-generation interdependence for life cycle stage and circumstances? For instance, is the client involved in spousal, parental, and other caretaking of family members? Is a middle-aged adult living as a dependent with his aging parents, or are young teenagers expected to handle parental responsibilities for toddlers?

B. **Biological and Psychological Factors**
- *Individual Development:* Is there appropriate development of cognitive, physical, emotional and social functioning? What are the client's assets, strengths and disabilities: intelligence? Strong self-direction? Musical, artistic, or other talents? Learning disorder? Developmental lag? Have symptoms developed such as sleep or mood disorders, behavioral disturbances, addictions to drugs, alcohol, food, sex, gambling, spending, etc.?
- *Life Cycle Stressors:* Have there been life stressors such as births, loss of work, immigration or other moves, divorce, separation, a history of chronic physical or mental illness, genetic problems, trauma, untimely, unresolved or recent losses, physical or sexual abuse, war or crime?
- *Temperament:* Is the client shy? Passive? Outgoing? Affiliative? Aggressive? etc.?

C. Life Skills
- *Autonomy skills:* Can the client function independently? Does the client believe that his or her ideas and wishes are heard?
- *Education:* What is the client's level of education, skill, and development of his or her talents?
- *Work Patterns:* What are the client's competencies, experiences, frustrations, and problems with work? Does s/he view work as meaningful or insignificant? What is the history of layoffs, hopelessness about finding meaningful work? Is the client a workaholic?
- *Financial Competence:* What is the client's yearly income and from what sources? How much control does the client have over income? Are there child support payments? What is the level of debt? How many people does the client support? What are the savings, expected inheritance, or trust funds?
- *Allocation of Time:* How much time does the client spend at work? School? With family? On childcare? Housework? Leisure? Taking care of others? Taking care of self or of own desires?

D. Social and Cultural Factors
- *Race and Ethnicity:* Does the client relate to his or her sociocultural heritage with pride, discomfort, or indifference? How does s/he handle negativity of the larger society toward his or her group? How may societal prejudices be influencing client's current situation? How acculturated or alienated does the client feel in relation to the dominant culture?
- *Gender Roles and Sexual Orientation:* What is the client's sexual orientation and general attitude about gender roles? How do the client's attitudes fit with those of his or her family and community?
- *Social Class:* How may the education, financial resources, and social status of the client and of his or her spouse be influencing the current situation? How may class mobility have influenced family relationships, created unacknowledged tensions, or led to isolation or loss for family members? What is the client's social location in relation to that of others in the family and community?
- *Religious, Philosophical, and Spiritual Values, Hopes and Dreams:* What are the client's beliefs about God and about the meaning of life, death, and life after death? What are his or her concerns about those who are less fortunate? Does s/he believe in something larger than him or herself? Does the client belong to a faith community? Does s/he feel at home there?
- *Sense of Belonging, Social Participation, and Friendship Networks:* Does the client have a sense of "home" or of comfort and belonging in his or her family? Community? Nation? Friendship network? Work system, etc.? Explore the client's social network, his or her confidants and friends. What is the client's connection to community organizations and social groups? Does the client initiate social contacts or share doubts and dreams with anyone? How developed is his or her ability to feel empathy? What is the client's ability to work collaboratively as well as independently?
- *Power and Privilege:* What is the client's sense of psychological power, physical strength, and financial resources in relation to his or her life needs? The needs of family members or community? Are there any indications of abuse or oppression at home, work, school, or in the community? Any such indications should be assessed immediately.

E. Hopes and Dreams:
What are the client's hopes and dreams for him or herself, family, community, as well as for future generations? To what degree do they pursue their fulfillment?

II. ASSESSING THE FAMILY: IMMEDIATE AND EXTENDED FAMILY SYSTEM
Assessment of families should include consideration of multigenerational issues that may be influencing the immediate situation. Gathering information about the extended family is

essential to understand the present emotional system in families. The relevance of the extended family is not limited to the past. This is a current and supremely significant emotional system, whether or not family members acknowledge that, and even if they are not speaking to each other. Assessment includes exploration of the following:

A. **Family Life Cycle Stage:** Assess how family members are engaging in normative tasks at their specific life stage.

B. **Family Structure:** Assess for special pressures on single-parent families and on single adults. Special attention should be paid to the person's friendships and community connections. If the a client has been divorced or remarried, attention should be paid to communication and relationships with the ex-spouse and with his or her family, especially if there are children.

C. **Emotional and Relational Patterns:** The emotional climate may be intimate, disorganized, unpredictable, emotional, tense, angry, cold, or distant. How do family members communicate with each other and set boundaries? What triangles are operating? Are there secrets such as births out of wedlock, suicides, affairs, myths, legacies, taboos, or important themes in the family? Are there skills, talents, strengths, vulnerabilities, disabilities, or dysfunctions that are affecting the family's structure? Does the family have appropriate interdependence for their life cycle circumstances?

- *Boundaries and Relationship Patterns:* Are there cut-offs, conflicts, triangles, fusion, or is there enmeshment in marital, parent/child, and sibling relationships, as well as those with other family members or caretakers?
- *Communication Patterns:* Assess communication patterns including decision making (authoritarian, egalitarian, casual, rigid), negotiation skills, and ability to share intimately with each other.
- *Strengths and Vulnerabilities or Dysfunctions:* Does the family show brilliance, artistic and musical talent, success, talent for relationships or for transforming bad situations? Or on the other side, do they have learning, developmental, and physical disabilities, addictions, violence, chronic illness, and mental illness?

D. **Socioeconomic and Cultural Issues:** Inquire about ethnicity, race, sex, gender identity, sexual orientation, social class, migration history and cultural change, religious and spiritual values, income, education, work, finances, sense of belonging, friendships, and community connections, power/privilege, or powerlessness/vulnerabilities.

E. **Loss and Trauma:** Is there a history of chronic physical or mental illness, genetic problems, traumatic, untimely, unresolved, or recent losses, physical or sexual abuse, war, crime, immigration?

F. **Values, Beliefs, Rituals, and Practices:** What are the family's beliefs about the meaning of life and relationships, from "The family is everything" to "Upward mobility is essential," or "Money can get in the way of spiritual peace." Be sure to inquire about beliefs and values related to the current symptoms. Are they God's punishment, or the result of someone being a "bad seed," or putting a spell on another?

III. ASSESSING THE SOCIAL AND CULTURAL CONTEXT

Families often belong to formal or informal groupings, which meet for mutual activity and support. Such groups connect them to the larger society and buffer them from its stress. They may enhance spirituality, by connectedness and by fostering interests and purposes larger than one's own. They may mitigate the impact of social inequities, provide information, meaning, enrichment, mutual support, and foster joint action. The powerful healing quality of such networks is probably a main reason Alcoholics Anonymous and other community-based self-help groups that have sprung from informal networking systems have developed worldwide standing as effective treatment interventions.

Assessing families' connections to work, friends, and their broader community is essential to understanding their problems and to developing strategies for intervention. Very often, interventions need to involve helping families increase their contextual supports. This is especially important for populations that tend to be isolated, such as divorced men, widowed elderly, single parents, and newly arrived immigrant families. Families cannot be successful in a vacuum or without positive linkages to the wider social system. Areas to assess include:

A. **The Individual and Family's History of Sense of Belonging, Safety, and Homeplace.**
B. **Connection to Community, Religious, Political, Ethnic, and Social Groups, Clubs, and Fraternities.**
C. **Privilege and Oppression in Relation to**
   - **Culture**
   - **Race**
   - **Gender**
   - **Class**
   - **Religion**
   - **Age**
   - **Sexual Orientation**
   - **Access to Political and Economic Power**
   - **Family Structure**
   - **Abilities and Disabilities**

Assessing Families' Multiple Contexts:

The framework behind this multicontextual assessment and all the suggested questions offered in this Appendix are aimed at helping clinicians view clients as belonging to history, to their present context, and to the future. Therapists need to be as attuned to immigration stresses and ethnic identity conflicts as they are to other stresses of a family's life. Assessing such factors is crucial for determining whether a family's dysfunction is a "normal" reaction to a high degree of cultural stress, or whether it goes beyond the bounds of transitional stress. The following questions are designed to help clients and their families locate themselves in their cultural context, and to explore and identify values in their heritage that are sources of strength and resilience, and that can help them transform their lives, and their ability to work toward long-range goals that fit with their cultural values.

Questions to Help Clients Think About Their Family's Migration and Cultural Heritage in a Multicontextual Life Cycle Perspective:

- Why did you and/or your family migrate to this country? What were they leaving behind? What was their experience when they arrived in this country? How old were family members when migration occurred?
- How did their age at migration influence family members?
- What ethnic groups, religious traditions, nations, racial groups, trades, professions, communities, and other groups do you consider yourself a part of?
- How old were the family members who remained in the homeland? Do they still have contact with family members in their country of origin?
- How did the life cycle phase at the time of migration influence the family's adaptation? Was there a reversal of the parents' hierarchy, because parents were less able to negotiate the new culture than their children were? Were certain children drawn into adult status because they learned English faster than the parents, or because the family had no resources to treat them as children?

- Did they (do you) feel secure about your status in the United States? Did they (do you) have a green card?
- What language did they (do you) speak at home? In the community? In your family of origin? Were grandparents limited by their inability to learn English?
- Has immigration changed family members' education or social status, or sense of belonging and confidence?
- What do you think have been the most stressful experiences your family members have had in the United States?
- What wounds has your racial or ethnic group experienced? What burden does your ethnic or racial group carry for injuries to other groups? How have you been affected by the wounds your group has committed or that have been committed against your group? What would reparations entail?
- To whom do family members in your culture turn when in need of help? What helps them when they are down?
- What are your culture's values regarding male and female roles? Education? Work and success? Family connectedness? Family caretaking? Religious practices? Have these values changed in your family over time?
- What do you feel about your culture(s) of origin? Do you feel you belong to the dominant U.S. culture?

Questions to help clients look beyond the stress of their current situation and access the strengths of their heritage:

- How might your grandfather, who dreamed of your immigration but never made it himself, think about the problem you are having with your children?
- What do you think are the strengths you got from these ancestors that may help you in dealing with your problem?
- How do you think your Italian roots and your wife's Irish roots may influence the way you handle conflicts?
- Your ancestors must have survived the Middle Passage and slavery for hundreds of years because of their great strength and courage. What do you think made them able to survive?
- Your great-grandmother immigrated at 21 and became a pieceworker in a sweat shop but managed to support her six children and had great strength. What do you think were her dreams for you, her daughter's daughter's daughter? What do you think she would want you to do now about your current problem?
- Your father died of his alcoholism, but when he came to this country at age 18, he undoubtedly had dreams of his future. What do you think he cared about? How do you think he felt about the parents he left behind? What do you think he would want for you now?
- Are there some Latino political groups in your town that could help you fight for the resources you and your group have deserved from the United States for 150 years?

Questions About Values

We encourage clients to reflect about their real lives as they are actually leading them by asking questions such as:

- What would my grandmother want me to do now?
- What would my unborn grandchildren want me to do now?
- Do my relationships work?
- Am I teaching my children what they need to know?
- Do I like my work?

- Do I care about money too much or not enough?
- Is the balance of my life working for me?
- Do I have caring connections to my family and to others? Am I contributing to anyone else's life?
- Do I belong to a place that feels like home?
- What do I stand for?

Questions About Privilege and Oppression

The following can help raise issues of privilege and oppression with couples and families:

- Ask routinely exactly how much income each spouse earns or has access to. Inquire what effect a large disparity in income has on a couple's overall decision-making process. Ask who manages the money, who has veto power, how financial decisions are made, whose name is on their assets. Find out the family's level of debt, exact number of credit cards, and number of people they support or expect to support in later years.
- Challenge the expectation of middle- and upper-class women that they will be supported financially for life by their husbands.
- Question a wife who plans to stay home with her children as to whether she is "economically viable"—that is, has enough money or skills to risk not being a money earner in a society with a 46 percent divorce rate, in which women are often left with inadequate resources to care for themselves.
- Explore the wife's work or career plans and the husband's fathering. Challenge the notions that work prevents greater involvement in the family or that a wife must be the primary parent or she is not a "good mother."
- Inquire about each spouse's ethnicity. If they are of different races or ethnic backgrounds, ask what issues arise for them, their children, and their families of origin because of the differences. Ask—or think about—what impact their and your racial or ethnic values have on the presenting problem and on the therapy.
- Be aware that gender, race, class, and sexual orientation connect people to a more powerful or less powerful place in the operating hierarchies. Be alert to the ways in which racism, sexism, elitism, and homophobia may be played out as couple or family problems.
- When working with gay and lesbian clients, be aware of society's intense homophobia. Explore the impact of social stigma on gay and lesbian relationships and evaluate the wisdom or consequences of coming out in different contexts: work, family, church, mosque, or temple.
- Be aware of the different value systems held by the various socioeconomic classes in the United States. For example, they have different approaches to gender roles, education, religion, and work. Be aware of the influence of your own class background on your value system when discussing these value-laden issues with the couple.
- Ask how much time each parent spends with the children and how much time the partners has alone together. Explore their satisfaction with their sexual relationship and their method of negotiating differences of all kinds.
- Ask specifically how child care and housework chores are divided between the partners and among the children. Note and comment when appropriate on whether these tasks are allocated according to traditional gender roles. Ask whether both spouses find involvement with children and task allocation fair and satisfactory.
- Ask how much time each parent spends at work, how secure and satisfactory their work is, whether they control their own time at work, and whether they need to work as many hours as they do to support the family adequately.

- Inform couples struggling with marital or divorce issues what the facts and statistics are in the larger society regarding alimony allocation, child support collection, contact between fathers and children, the divorce rate for first and subsequent marriages, and other factors relevant to their situation.
- Ask routinely about clients' friendships and their neighborhood and community connections and include such.
- Help clients to think about the meaning of spirituality in their lives and what values make their lives meaningful. Encourage clients to consider changes that help them live according to their own values.
- Help clients connect the above sociocultural issues to the presenting problem by exploring their emotional relevance in the client's family of origin.
- The more we deal with these issues in our own lives, the easier it will be to notice and deal with them in clients' lives.

Tools for Assessment

We recommend that clinicians use a **genogram** and **time line** as basic tools for conducting a multicontextual family life cycle assessment.

The Genogram

The genogram is the basic and most important tool for recording information about a client. It helps us contextualize our kinship network in terms of culture, class, race, gender, religion, family process, and migration history because all of these are noted on the genogram. When we ask people to identify themselves ethnically, we are asking them to highlight themes of cultural continuity and cultural identity to make them more apparent. Genograms help clinicians to quickly conceptualize individuals in context within the growing diversity of family forms and patterns in our society and to see their life cycle in context—which parts of the family are going through which phases—launching, adolescence, migration, separation or divorce, recoupling, retirement, or chronic illness. Using the genogram to collect historical and contextual assessment information is a collaborative, client-centered therapeutic process. By its nature the process involves the telling of stories and emphasizes respect for the client's perspectives, while encouraging the multiple views of different family members. The genogram helps clinicians map the basic information essential to a multicontextual assessment:

- *Who?* Who is in the family? Names, ages, gender, class, race, sexual orientation, dates of birth, marriage, separation, divorce, illness, or death. Who is presenting the problem? Who is defining the problem, if that is different? Who is the identified patient (Index Person or IP)? How do others in the family or context view this problem? Who is the referrer? What is their relationship to the family and the problem? Might any triangles develop with them?
- *What?* What is the problem as defined by whom? Does the IP share the definition? Does anyone not share the definition?
- *When?* What life cycle phase is the family in now? Are there life cycle tasks the family has not realized they need to focus on? Have there been stresses in previous generations at this life cycle phase?
- *Why now?* What may be precipitating stresses? Are there concurrent pressures on the family? Moves, losses (illness, job loss, or important person who left home or area), life cycle transitions (launching, retirement, remarriage, divorce, or death)
- *History of Presenting Problem:* What do they see as a problem? What response do they want for the problem? What are the family's cultural strengths for dealing with this problem?

- *Life Cycle Stage and Dates of Entry and Exit of Key Members of the Family's Network:* What has been the timing of births, deaths, moves in or out of the household, school, or job change indicative of life cycle transition (entry into high school, retirement, etc.)?
- *Physical and Mental Health History:* What has been the timing of illnesses in the family and what kind of relationship have they had with professional helpers and self-help support?
- *Socioeconomic Information:* What is the family's history with education, occupation, income, work, and financial stress?
- *Cultural Heritage:* What is the ethnic and racial background of family members and what has been the impact of racism on them? Have they lived in an ethnic enclave or community or in a community in which they were viewed as outsiders? Have their spiritual and religious beliefs supported or minimized their acknowledgment of their ethnic heritage? What is their social location and have clients changed social class from other members of their family? On the other hand, have certain other members of the system changed their social location creating rifts, distance, or conflicts?
- *Belief Systems, Religion, and Spiritual Beliefs:* What are the primary beliefs that organize the family? What is their general worldview, and are they organized by particular myths, rules, spiritual beliefs, or family secrets? What is the family members' history of religious beliefs and practices, including changes in belief? What has been the impact of intrafamily differences in belief as well as differences between the family and community in belief?
- *Language Skill and Acculturation of Family Members:* Family members vary in how quickly they adapt, how much of their heritage they retain, and the rate at which they learn English. Knowing and speaking the language of the country of origin will serve to preserve its culture. What language(s) were spoken while the children in the family were growing up? Are there differences in language skills and acculturation within the family, which may have led to conflicts, power imbalances, and role reversals, especially where children are forced to translate for their parents?

Family chronology or time line

Listing the events of family history in chronological order is essential to tracking the evolution of family history over time. This tool enables the clinician to track stressors in relation to family life cycle events, particularly the entry and exit of family members and changes in the functioning or relationships of family members. We have found that utilizing this tool with individuals and families helps them remember events and to make connections that clarify and change their perspective about the present situation, often in a positive way.

The therapist should track the antecedents of the presenting problems by asking dynamic relationship-oriented questions such as: How did your parents react when you adopted a child of a different race? What attitudes have they expressed about African Americans? Is anyone else in the family interracially married or adopted? Did they know that you had fertility problems? How did daughters and mothers get along in the family? Did your mother ever have similar conflicts with her mother? How did her sisters get along with their mother? How did sons and fathers get along? How did your father and mother react when you came out as gay? Are there other gay family members, and what roles do they play in the family?

The underlying reason for this multicontextual longitudinal assessment and all the suggested questions offered here is to look at clients as belonging to history, to the present context, and to the future.

Standard Symbols for Genograms

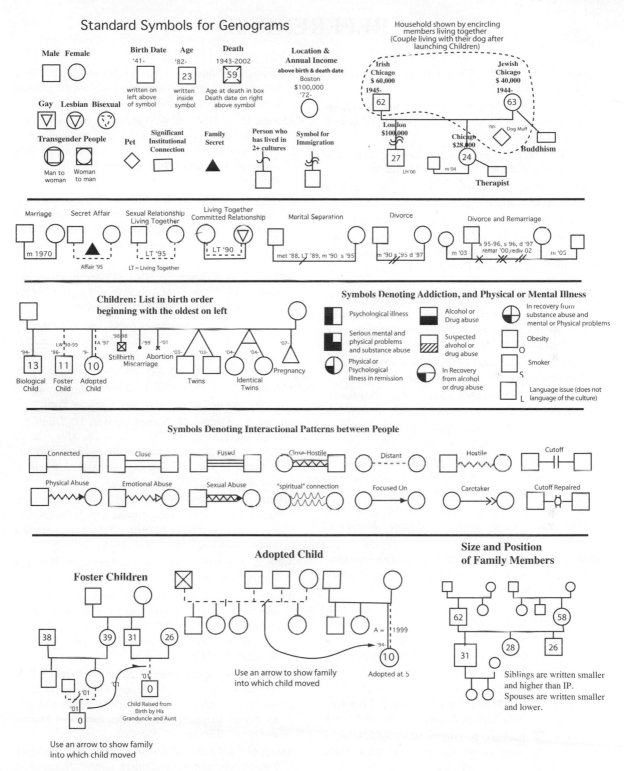

REFERENCES

Adams, B. N. (1968). *Kinship in an urban setting.* Chicago: Markham.

Adams, M., & Coltrane, S. (2007). Framing divorce reform: Media, morality, and the politics of family. *Family Process, 46,* 17–34.

Adler, A. (1959). *The practice and theory of individual psychology.* Patterson, NJ: Littlefield, Adams.

Adler, A. (1979). *Superiority and social interest.* New York: W. W. Norton.

Afifi, T. O., Coz, B. J., & Enns, M. W. (2006). Mental health profiles among married, never-married and separated/divorced mothers in a nationally representative sample. *Social Psychiatry and Psychiatric Epidemiology, 41,* 122–129.

Agency for Healthcare Research and Quality (2003). *National healthcare disparities report: 2003.* Rockville, MD: Author. Retrieved (6/28/10) from www.ahrq.gov/qual/nhdr03/ nhdr03.htm

Ahlburg, D., & DeVita, C. (1992). New realities of the American family. *Population Bulletin, 47,* 15.

Ahrons, C. (1979). The binuclear family: Two households, one family. *Alternative Lifestyles, 2,* 499–515.

Ahrons, C. (1980a). Divorce: A crisis of family transition and change. *Family Relations, 29,* 533–540.

Ahrons, C. (1980b). Redefining the divorced family: A conceptual framework for postdivorce family systems reorganization. *Social Work, 25,* 437–441.

Ahrons, C. (1981). The continuing coparental relationship between divorced spouses. *American Journal of Orthopsychiatry, 51,* 315–328.

Ahrons, C. (1994). *The good divorce: Keeping your family together when your marriage comes apart.* New York: HarperCollins.

Ahrons, C. (1996). *Making divorce work: A clinical approach to the binuclear family* [videotape]. New York: Guilford Press.

Ahrons, C. (2004). *We're still family: What grown children have to say about their parents' divorce.* New York: HarperCollins.

Ahrons, C. (2007). Family ties after divorce: Long-term implications for children. *Family Process, 46,* 53–65.

Ahrons, C., & Rodgers, R. (1987). *Divorced families: A multidisciplinary developmental view.* New York: W. W. Norton.

Ahrons, C., & Tanner, J. (2003). Adult children and their fathers: Relationship changes 20 years after a parental divorce. *Family Relations, 52,* 340–351.

Ahrons, C., & Wallisch, L. (1986). The relationship between former spouses. In S. Duck & D. Perlman (Eds.), *Close relationships: Development, dynamics, and deterioration* (pp. 269–296). Beverly Hills, CA: Sage Publications.

Ahrons, C., & Wallisch, L. (1987). Parenting in the binuclear family: Relationships between biological and stepparents. In K. Pasley & M. Ihinger-Tallman (Eds.), *Remarriage and stepfamilies* (pp. 225–256). New York: Guilford Press.

Akhtar, S., & Kramer, S. (Eds.). (1999). *Brothers and sisters: Developmental, dynamic and aspects of the sibling relationship.* New York: Jason Aronson.

Akinyela, M. (2008). Once they come: Testimony therapy and healing questions for African American couples. In M. McGoldrick & K. Hardy (Eds.), *Re-visioning family therapy* (2nd ed., pp. 356–366). New York: Guilford.

Aldwin, C. M., & Park, C. L. (2007). *Handbook of health psychology and aging.* New York: Guilford Press.

Alegria, M., Canino, G., Shrout, P., Wee, M., Duan, N., Vila, D., Torres, M., Chen, C. N., & Meng, X. L. (2008). Prevalence of mental illness in immigrant and non-immigrant groups. *American Journal of Psychiatry, 165,* 359–369.

Alksnis, C., Desmarais, S., & Curtis, J. (2008). Workforce segregation and the gender wage gap: Is "women's" work valued as highly as "men's"? *Journal of Applied Social Psychology, 38*(6), 1416–1441.

Allen, K. R. (1989). *Single women; family ties.* Newbury Park, CA: Sage.

Amato, P. R., & Sobolewski, J. M. (2004). The effects of divorce on fathers and children: Nonresidential fathers and stepfathers. In M. E. Lamb (Ed.), *The role of the father in child development* (4th ed., pp. 341–367). Hoboken, NJ: Wiley.

Amburg, S. M., van, Barber, C. E., & Zimmerman, T. S. (1996). Aging and family therapy: Prevalence of aging issues and later family life concerns in marital and family therapy literature (1986–1993). *Journal of Marital and Family Therapy, 22,* 195–203.

American Civil Liberties Union Lesbian, Gay, Bisexual, Transgender and AIDS Project. (2009). *Transgender people and the law*. Retrieved August 7, 2009, from www.aclu.org/lgbt/transgender/kyr_transgender.html

American Psychiatric Association. (2000). *Diagnostic and statistical manual of mental disorders* (4th ed., text revision). Washington, DC: Author.

American Psychological Association. (2002). *Ethical principles of psychologists and code of conduct*. Retrieved (4/12/10) from www.apa.org/ethics/code2002.html

Anderson, C., Reiss, D., & Hogarty, G. (1986). *Schizophrenia and the family: A practitioner's guide to psychoeducation and management*. New York: Guilford Press.

Anderson, C. M., Robins, C., Cahalane, H., Greeno, C., Carr, G., Copeland V., & Andrews, R. M. (2006). Why low-income mothers do not engage with the formal mental health care system: Preliminary findings from an ethnographic study. *Qualitative Health Research, 16*(7), 926–943.

Anderson, C. M., Stewart, S., & Dimidjian, S. (1994). *Flying solo*. New York: Norton.

Anderson, E. (2000). *Code of the street: Decency, violence, and the moral life of the inner city*. New York: W. W. Norton.

Anderson, T. (1984). Widowhood as a life transition: Its impact on kinship ties. *Journal of Marriage and the Family, 46*(1), 105–114.

Angelou, M. (1981). *The heart of a woman*. New York: Random House.

Angelou, M. (1986). *All God's children need traveling shoes*. New York: Vintage.

Angier, N. (2002, November 5). Weighing the grandma factor. *New York Times*, pp. S1, S4.

Ano, G. G., & Vasconceles, E. B. (2005). Religious coping and psychological adjustment to stress: A meta-analysis. *Journal of Clinical Psychology, 61,* 461–480.

Antonucci, T. C. (1994). A life span view of women's social relationships. In B. F. Turner & L. E. Troll (Eds.), *Women growing older* (pp. 239–269). Thousand Oaks, CA: Sage.

Aponte, H. J. (1994). *Bread and spirit: Therapy with the new poor*. New York: W. W. Norton.

Aponte, H. J. (2009). The stresses of poverty and the comfort of spirituality. In F. Walsh (Ed.), *Spiritual resources in family therapy* (2nd ed., pp. 125–140). New York: Guilford.

Apter, T., (1985). *Why women don't have wives*. New York: Schoken Books.

Apter, T. (1995) *Secret paths: Women in the new midlife*. New York: W. W. Norton.

Aries, P. (1962). *Centuries of childhood: A social history of family life*. New York: Vintage.

Arnett, J. J. (2000). Emerging adulthood: A theory of development from the late teens through the twenties. *American Psychologist, 55*(5), 469–480.

Arnett, J. J. (2004). *Emerging adulthood: The winding road from the late teens through the twenties*. New York: Oxford.

Arnett, J. J. (2005). The developmental context of substance use in emerging adulthood. *Journal of Drug Issues, 35,* 235–253.

Arnett, J. J. (2007). The long and leisurely route: Coming of age in Europe today. *A Journal of Contemporary World Affairs, 106,* 130–136.

Arnett J. J., & Galambos, N. J. (2003). Conceptions of the transition to adulthood among emerging adults in American ethnic groups. In J. J. Arnett & N. J. Galambos (Eds.). *Exploring cultural conceptions of the transition to adulthood: New directions for child and adolescent development* (pp. 63–75). San Francisco: Jossey-Bass.

Arnetz, B. B., Wasserman, J., Petrini, B., & Brenner, S. (1987). Immune function in unemployed women. *Psychosomatic medicine. 49*(1), 3–12.

Artico, C. I. (2003). *Latino families broken by immigration: The adolescents' perceptions*. New York: LFB Scholarly Publishing LLC.

Atkins, D. C., Jacobson, N. S., & Baucom, D. H. (2001). Understanding infidelity: Correlates in a national random sample. *Journal of Family Psychology, 15,* 735–749.

Ault-Riche, M. (1994). Sex, money and laundry: Sharing responsibilities in intimate relationships. *Journal of Feminist Family Therapy, 6*(1), 69–87.

Avis, J. (1985). The politics of functional family therapy: A feminist critique. *Journal of Marital and Family Therapy, 11*(2), 127–138.

Bachman, J. G., Wadsworth, K. N., & O'Malley, P. M. (1997). *Smoking, drinking, and drug use in young adulthood: The impacts of new freedoms and new responsibilities*. Mahwah, NJ: Lawrence Erlbaum Associates.

Badinter, E. (1996). *XY. On masculine identity*. New York: Columbia University Press.

Baker, M., LaCroix, A., Wu, C., Cochrane, B., Wallace, R., & Woods, N. (2009). Mortality risk associated with physical and verbal abuse in women aged 50 to 79. *Journal of the American Geriatrics Society, 57*(10), 1799–1809.

Baldwin, J. My Dungeon Shook: A letter to my nephew on the one hundredth anniversary of the emancipation. Retrieved April 6, 2010, from www.thenagain.info/Classes/Sources/Baldwin.html

Baltes, P. B., & *Baltes, M. M.* (1990). Psychological perspectives on successful aging: The model of selective optimization with compensation. In P. B. Baltes & M. M. Baltes (Eds.), *Successful aging: Perspectives from the behavioral sciences* (pp. 1–34). New York: Cambridge University Press.

Bank, S. P., & *Kahn, M. D.* (2008). *The sibling bond.* New York: Basic Books.

Barker, G. T. (2005). *Dying to be men: Youth, masculinity and social exclusion.* New York: Routledge, Taylor & Francis.

Barnett, R. C., & *Gareis, K. C.* (2008). Community: the critical missing link in work-family research. In A. Marcus-Neuhall, D. F. Halpern, & S. J. Tan (Eds.). *The changing realities of work and family* (pp. 71–84). New York: Wiley-Blackwell.

Barnet, B., *Liu, J.*, & *DeVoe, M.* (2008). Double jeopardy: Depressive symptoms and rapid subsequent pregnancy in adolescent mothers. *Archives of Pediatrics & Adolescent Medicine, 162*(3), 246–252.

Barnett, O. W., *Miller-Perrin, C. L.*, & *Perrin, R. D.* (1997). *Family violence across the lifespan.* Thousand Oaks, CA: Sage.

Barnett, O. W., *Miller-Perrin, C. L.*, & *Perrin, R. D.* (2005). *Family violence across the lifespan, 2nd ed.* Thousand Oaks, CA: Sage.

Barnett, R. C., & *Gareis, K. C.* (2008). Community: the critical missing link in work-family research. In A. Marcus-Neuhall, D. F. Halpern, & S. J. Tan (Eds.), *The changing realities of work and family.* (pp. 71–84). New York: Wiley-Blackwell.

Barnett, R. C., & *Rivers, C.* (1996). *She works/he works: How two-income families are happier, healthier, and better-off.* San Francisco: Harper.

Barnett, R. C., & *Rivers, C.* (2004). *Same difference: How gender myths are hurting our relationships, our children, and our jobs.* New York: Basic Books.

Barrett, A. E., & *Turner, R. J.* (2005) Family structure and mental health: The mediating effects of socioeconomic status, family process and social stress. *Journal of Health and Social Behavior, 46,* 156–169.

Barrett, M. J. (2009). Healing from relational trauma: The quest for spirituality. In F. Walsh (Ed.), *Spiritual resources in family therapy* (2nd ed., pp. 267–285). New York: Guilford.

Bass, D. M., & *Bowman, K.* (1990). Transition from caregiving to bereavement: The relationship of care-related strain and adjustment to death. *The Gerontologist, 30,* 135–142.

Basson, R. (2000). The female sexual response: A different model. *Journal of Sex and Marital Therapy, 26,* 51–65.

Basu, M. (2009, May 19). *Survey delves into high birthrate for young Latinas.* Retrieved (4/14/10) from www.cnn.com/2009/HEALTH/05/19/latinas.pregnancy.rate/index.html

Bateson, C. (2001). *Composing a life.* New York: Grove Press.

Bateson, M. C. (1994). *Peripheral visions.* New York: HarperCollins.

Baun, M., *Johnson, R.*, & *McCabe, B.* (2006). Human-animal interaction and successful aging. In A. Fine (Ed.), *Handbook on animal-assisted therapy* (2nd ed., pp. 287–302). San Diego, CA: Academic Press.

Bearman, P., & *Bruckner, H.* (2001). Promising the future: Virginity pledges and first intercourse. *American Journal of Sociology, 106(4),* 859–912.

Beck, M. (1994). The infertility trap, *Newsweek, 123,* 30–31.

Becker, E. (1973). *The denial of death.* New York: Free Press.

Bedford, V. H. (1989). Understanding the value of siblings in old age. *American Behavioral Scientist, 33,* 33–44.

Bedford, V. H. (2005). Theorizing about sibling relationships when parents become frail. In V. L. Bengston, A. C. Acock, K. R. Allen, P. Dilworth-Anderson, & D. M. Klein (Eds.), *Sourcebook of family theory & research* (pp. 173–174). Thousand Oaks, CA: Sage Publications.

Belenky, M. F., *Clinchy, B. M.*, *Goldberger, N. R.*, & *Tarule, J. M.* (1986). *Women's ways of knowing.* New York: Basic Books.

Belkin, L. (2008, September 8). When mom and dad share it all: Adventures in equal parenting. *New York Times,* p. 4.

Belsky, J., & *Kelly, J.* (1994). *The transition to parenthood.* New York: Dell.

Ben-Daniel, N., *Rokach, R.*, *Filtzer L.*, & *Feldman, R.* (2007). When two are a family: Looking backward and looking forward in a group intervention with single-by-choice mothers. *Journal of Family Therapy, 29*(3), 249–266.

Bengtson, V. (2001). Beyond the nuclear family: The increasing importance of multigenerational bonds. *Journal of Marriage and the Family, 64*(1), 7–17.

Bengtson, V., & Lowenstein, A. (Eds.). (2003). *Global aging and challenges to families.* New York: Aldine de Gruyter.

Benjamin. J. (1988). *The bonds of love: Psychoanalysis, feminism, and the problem of domination.* New York: Pantheon.

Bennett, M. D. (2007). Racial socialization and ethnic identity: Do they offer protection against problem behaviors for African American youth? *Journal of Human Behavior in the Social Environment, 15*(2–3), 137–161.

Benshorn, S. (2008) *A qualitative examination of the ecological systems that promote sexual identity comfort among European American and African American lesbian youths.* Unpublished Doctoral Dissertation, DePaul University.

Bepko, C., & Krestan, J. A. (1985). *The responsibility trap: A blueprint for treating alcoholic families.* New York: Free Press.

Bergen, R. K. (1996). *Wife rape: Understanding the response of survivors and service providers.* Thousand Oaks, CA: Sage.

Berger L. M. (2007) Socioeconomic factors and substandard parenting. *Social Service Review, 8*(3), 485–522.

Bergman, S. (1991). *Men's psychological development: A relational perspective.* Wellesley, MA: Stone Center Press.

Bergner, R., & Bridges, A. (2002). The significance of heavy pornography involvement for romantic partners: Research and clinical implications. *Journal of Sex & Marital Therapy, 28,* 193–206.

Bergquist, W. H., Greenberg, E. M., & Klaum, G. A. (1993). *In our fifties: Voices of men and women reinventing their lives.* San Francisco: Jossey-Bass.

Berkowitz, G. (2002). *UCLA study on friendship among women: An alternative to fight or flight.* Retrieved from (4/14/10) www.anapsid.org/cnd/gender/tendfend.html

Berman, E. (1999). Gender, sexuality, and love genograms. In R. DeMaria, G. Weeks, & L. Hof (Eds.), *Focused genograms: Intergenerational assessment of individuals, couples, and families* (pp. 145–176). Philadelphia, PA: Brunner/Mazel.

Bernard, J. (1982). *The future of marriage.* New Haven, CT: Yale University Press.

Bernikow, L. (1980). *Among women.* New York: Harper & Row.

Bernstein, A. C. (1999). Reconstructing the Brothers Grimm: New tales for stepfamily life. *Family Process, 38,* 415–429.

Bernstein, A. C. (1989). *Yours, mine, and ours: How families change when remarried parents have a child together.* New York: Norton.

Bernstein, A. C. (1994). Women in stepfamilies: The fairy godmother, the wicked witch, and Cinderella reconstructed. In M. P. Mirkin (Ed.), *Women in context: Toward a feminist reconstruction of psychotherapy* (pp. 188–216). New York: Guilford Press.

Bersamin, M., Fisher, D., Walker, S., Hill, D., & Grube, J. (2007). Defining virginity and abstinence: Adolescents' interpretations of sexual behaviors. *Journal of Adolescent Health, 41,* 182–188.

Bertrand, M., Luttmer, E., & Mullainathan, S. (2000). Network effects and welfare cultures. *Quarterly Journal of Economics, 115,* 3, 1019–1025.

Berzoff, J., & Silverman, P. R. (2004). *Living with dying: A handbook for end-of-life healthcare practitioners.* New York: Columbia University Press.

Biaggio, M., Coin, S., Adams, W. (2002). Couples therapy for lesbians: Understanding merger and the impact of homophobia. *Journal of Lesbian Studies, 6*(1), 129–138.

Bieschke, K. J., Perez, R. M., & DeBord, K. A. (2007). *Handbook of counseling and psychotherapy with lesbian, gay, bisexual, and transgender clients* (2nd ed.). Washington DC: American Psychological Association.

Bigner, J. (1996). Working with gay fathers: Developmental, postdivorce parenting, and therapeutic issues. In J. Laird & R. J. Green (Eds.), *Lesbians and gays in couples and families: A handbook for therapists* (pp. 370–403). San Francisco: Jossey-Bass.

Billingsley, A. (1992). *Climbing Jacob's ladder: The enduring legacy of African-American families.* New York: Simon & Schuster.

Birditt, K. S., Fingerman, K. L., Lefkowitz, E. S., Kamp Dush, C. M. (2008). Parents perceived as peers: Filial maturity in adulthood. *Journal of Adult Development, 15*(1), 1–12.

Birkenmaier, J., Behrman, G., & Berg-Weger, M. (2005). Integrating curriculum and practice with students and their field supervisors: Reflections on spirituality and the aging (ROSA) model. *Educational Gerontology, 31,* 745–763.

Birren, J., & *Schaie, K. W.* (Eds.). (2006). *Handbook of the psychology of aging* (6th ed.). San Diego: Academic Press.

Bitzer, J., & *Alder, J.* (2000). Sexuality during pregnancy and the postpartum period. *Journal of Sex Education & Therapy, 25*(1), 49–58.

Blenkner, M. (1965). Social work and family relationships in later life with some thoughts on filial maturity. In E. Shanas & G. Strieb (Eds.), *Social structure and the family: Generational relations* (pp. 46–59). Englewood Cliffs, NJ: Prentice-Hall.

Blumstein, P., & *Schwartz, P.* (1983). *American couples: Money, work and sex.* New York: William Morrow & Company.

Blumstein, P., & *Schwartz, P.* (1991). Money and ideology: Their impact on power and the division of household labor. In P. Blumberg & R. Lesser (Eds.), *Gender, family and economy: The triple overlap* (pp. 261–288). New York: Sage.

Bogle, K. A. (2008). *Hooking up: Sex, dating and relationships on campus.* New York: New York University.

Bonanno, G. A. (2004). Loss, trauma, and human resilience. *American Psychologist, 59,* 20–28.

Borsari, B., & *Carey, K. B.* (2001). Peer influences on college drinking: A review of the research. *Journal of Substance Abuse, 1*(4), 391–424.

Borysenko, J. (1996). *A woman's book of life: The biology, psychology and spirituality of the feminine life cycle.* New York: Riverhead Books.

Boss, P. (1983). Family separation and boundary ambiguity. *The International Journal of Mass Emergencies and Disasters, 1,* 63–72.

Boss, P. (1987). *Family stress.* Beverly Hills, CA: Sage.

Boss. P. (1999). *Ambiguous loss: Learning to live with unresolved grief.* Boston: Harvard University Press.

Boss, P. (2004). Ambiguous loss. In F. Walsh & M. McGoldrick (Eds.), *Living beyond loss* (2nd ed., pp. 237–246). New York: Norton.

Boss, P., & *Greenberg, J.* (1984). Family boundary ambiguity: A new variable in family stress theory. *Family Process, 24,* 535–546.

Boszormenyi-Nagy, I. (1987). *Foundations of contextual therapy: Collected papers of Ivan Boszormenyi-Nagy, MD.* New York: Brunner/Mazel.

Bowen, M. (1974). Bowen on triangles, Part I. *The Family, 1*(2), 45–49.

Bowen, M. (1975). Bowen on triangles, Part II. *The Family, 2*(1), 35–38.

Bowen, M. (1978). *Family therapy in clinical practice.* New York: Aronson.

Bowen, M. (2004). Family reaction to death. In F. Walsh & M. McGoldrick, (Eds.), *Living beyond loss* (pp. 79–92). New York: W. W. Norton.

Bowerman, C. E., & *Dobash, R. M.* (1974). Structural variations in inter-sibling affect. *Journal of Marriage and the Family, 36,* 48–54.

Bowleg, L. (2008). When Black + lesbian + woman ≠ Black lesbian woman: The methodological challenges of qualitative and quantitative intersectionality research. *Sex Roles, 59,* 312–325.

Bowleg, L., Burkholder, G., Teti, M., & *Craig, M. L.* (2008). The complexities of outness: Psychosocial predictors of coming out to others among Black lesbian and bisexual women. *Journal of LGBT Health Research, 4*(4), 153–166.

Boyce, G. C., & *Barnett, W. S.* (1993). Siblings of persons with mental retardation: A historical perspective and recent findings. In Z. Stoneman & P. W. Berman (Eds.), *The effects of mental retardation, disability, and illness on sibling relationships: Research issues and challenges (pp. 145–184).* Baltimore: Paul H. Brookes.

Boyd-Franklin, N. (1989) Black Families in Therapy: A multisystems approach. New York: Guilford.

Boyd-Franklin, N. (2003a). *Black families in therapy: Understanding the African American experience* (2nd ed.). New York: Guilford Press.

Boyd-Franklin, N. (2003b). Race, class, and poverty. In F. Walsh (Ed.), *Normal family processes: Growing diversity and complexity* (3rd ed., pp. 260–279). New York: Guilford Press.

Boyd-Franklin, N., Franklin, A. J., with *Toussaint, P.* (2000). *Boys into men: Raising our African American teenage sons.* New York: Dutton/Penguin Books.

Boyd-Franklin, N., & *Lockwood, T.* (2009). Spirituality and religion: Implications for psychotherapy with African American families. In F. Walsh (Ed.), *Spiritual resources in family therapy* (2nd ed., pp. 141–155). New York: Guilford.

Boyd-Webb, N. (Ed.). (2002). *Helping bereaved children: A handbook for practitioners* (2nd ed.). New York: Guilford Press.

Boyle, P. A., Buchman, A. S., Barnes, L. L., & *Bennett, D. A.* (2010). Effect of a purpose in life on risk of incident Alzheimer disease and mild cognitive impairment in community-dwelling older persons. *Archives of General Psychiatry, 67*(3), 304–310.

Bradford, M. (2004a). The bisexual experience: Living in a dichotomous culture. *Journal of bisexuality, 4*(1/2), 7–23.

Bradford, M. (2004b). Bisexual issues in same-sex couple therapy. In J. J. Bigner & J. L. Wetchler (Eds.), *Relationship therapy with same-sex couples* (pp. 43–52). New York: Haworth Press.

Brady, E. M., & *Noberini, M. R.* (1987, August). *Sibling support in the context of a model of sibling solidarity.* Paper presented at the annual meeting of the American Psychological Association, New York, New York.

Bramlett, M. D., & *Mosher, W. D.* (2002). *Cohabitation, marriage, divorce, and remarriage in the United States.* National Center for Health Statistics. *Vital Health Statistics, 23(22).* Retrieved (6/16/10) from www.cdc.gov/nchs/data/series/sr_23/sr23_022.pdf

Brandl, B., Hebert, M., Rozwadowski, J., & *Spangler, D.* (2003). Feeling safe, feeling strong: Support groups for older abused women. *Violence Against Women, 9*(12), 1490–1503.

Bray, J. H., & *Easling, I.* (2005). Remarriage and stepfamilies. In W. M. Pinsof & J. L. Lebow (Eds.), *Family psychology: The art of the science* (pp. 267–294). New York: Oxford University Press.

Bray, R. M., Hourani, L. L. & *Rae, K. L.* (2003). *Department of defense survey of health-related behaviors among military personnel.* Research Triangle Park, NC: RTI International.

Britz, J. D. (2006, March 23). To all the girls I've rejected [Letter to the Editor]. *New York Times,* p. 23.

Brody, E. (1985). Parent care as normative family stress. *Gerontologist, 25,* 19–29.

Brody, E. (2004). *Women in the middle: Their parent-care years.* New York: Springer.

Brody, J. (1998, January 28). Genetic ties may be a factor in violence in stepfamilies. *New York Times,* pp. C1, C4.

Brody, L. R., & *Hall, J. A.* (1993). Gender and emotion. In M. Lewis & J. Haviland (Eds.), *Handbook of emotions* (pp. 442–460). New York: Guilford.

Brown, C. (2008). Gender-role implications on same-sex intimate partner abuse. *Journal of Family Violence, 23,* 457–462.

Brown, E. (1991). *Patterns of infidelity and their treatment.* New York: Brunner/Mazel.

Brown G. & *Harris T.* (1978). Social origins of depression: A study of psychiatric disorder in women. London: Tavistock Press.

Brown, G. W. & *Rutter, M.* (1966). The measurement of family activities and relationships: A methodological study. *Human Relations,* 19:241–63.

Brown, T. N., & *Lesane-Brown, C. L.* (2006). Race socialization messages across historical time. *Social Psychology Quarterly, 69*(2), 201–213.

Bullard, S. (1997). *Teaching tolerance.* St. Charles, MO: Main Street Books.

Bumpass, L. (1990). What's happening to the family? Interactions between demographic and institutional change. *Demography, 27,* 483–498.

Burchinal, M. R., Roberts, J. E., Zeisel, S. A., & *Rowley, S. J.* (2008). Social risk and protective factors for African American children's academic achievement and adjustment during the transition to middle school. *Developmental Psychology, 44*(1), 286–292.

Bureau of Labor Statistics. (2007). *American time use survey* (DC USDL 08-0859). Washington DC: U. S. Government Printing Office.

Burton, L. M. (2010). Uncovering hidden facts that matter in interpreting individuals' behaviors: An ethnographic lens. In B. J. Risman (Ed.), *Families as they really are* (pp. 20–23). New York: W. W. Norton.

Burton, L. M., & *Lawson, C. S.* (2005). Homeplace and housing in the lives of low-income urban African American families. In McLoyd, V., Hill, N., & Dodge, K. (Eds.), *African American family life. Ecological and cultural diversity* (pp. 166–188). New York: Guilford Press.

Burton, L. M. (1995). Intergenerational patterns of providing care in African-American families with teenage childbearers: Emergent patterns in an ethnographic study. In V. L. Bengtson, K. W. Schale, & L. M. Burton (Eds.), *Adult intergenerational relations: Effects of societal change,* (pp. 79–125). New York: Springer.

Burton, L. M. (1996a). Age norms, the timing of family role transitions and intergenerational caregiving among aging African American women. *Gerontologist, 36*(2), 199–208.

Burton, L. M. (1996b). The timing of childbearing, family structure and the role responsibilities of aging Black women. In E. M. Hetherington & E. A. Blechman (Eds.), *Stress, coping and resiliency in children and*

families (pp. 155–172). Mahwah, NJ: Lawrence Erlbaum Associates.

Burton, L. M., Hurt, T. R., Eline, C., & Matthews, S. (2001, October). *The yellow brick road: Neighborhoods, the homeplace, and life course development in economically disadvantaged families.* Keynote address presented at the second biennial meeting of the Society for the Study of Human Development, Ann Arbor, MI.

Burton, L. M., Obeidallah, D. A., & Allison, K. (1996). Ethnographic insights on social context and adolescent development among inner-city African-American teens. In R. Jessor, A. Colby, & R. Shweder (Eds.), *Essays on ethnography and human development* (pp. 395–418). Chicago: University of Chicago Press.

Burton, L. M., Winn, D. M., Stevenson, H., & Clark, S. L. (2004). Working with African American clients: Considering the "homeplace" in marriage and family therapy practices. *Journal of Marital and Family Therapy, 30*(4), 397–410.

Burton, L., Obeidallah, D. A., & Allison, K. (1996) p. 406. Ethnographic insights on social context and adolescent development among inner-city African-American teens. In R. Jessor, A. Colby, & R. Shweder (Eds.), *Essays on ethnography and human development.* Chicago: University of Chicago Press.

Butler, R. (2008). *The longevity revolution: The benefits and challenges of living a long life.* New York: Perseus Books.

Butterworth, P., Crosier, T., & Rodgers, B. (2007). Mental health problems among single and partnered mothers: The role of financial hardship and social support. *Social Psychiatry and Psychiatric Epidemiology, 42,* 6–13.

Byng-Hall, J. (1995). *Rewriting family scripts.* New York: Guilford Press.

Byng-Hall, J. (2004). Loss and family scripts. In F. Walsh & M. McGoldrick (Eds.), *Living beyond loss* (pp. 85–98). New York: Norton.

Cain, D. S., & Combs-Orme, T. (2005) Family structure effects on parenting stress and practices in the African American family. *Journal of Sociology and Social Welfare, 32*(2), 19–40.

Cain, V., Johannes, C., Avis, N., Mohr, B., Schocken, M., & Ory, M. (2003). Sexual functioning and practices in a multi-ethnic study of midlife women: Baseline results from SWAN. *Journal of Sex Research, 40(3),* 266–276.

Caldwell, C. H. (1996). Predisposing, enabling and need factors related to patterns of help-seeking among African American women. In H. W. Neighbors & J. S. Jackson (Eds.), *Mental health in Black America* (pp. 146–160). Thousand Oaks. CA: Sage.

California Newsreel. (2008). *Unnatural causes…is inequality making us sick?* Retrieved (4/14/10) www.unnaturalcauses.org/press_reaction.php

Campbell, T. L. (2003). The effectiveness of family interventions for physical disorders. *Journal of Marital and Family Therapy, 29*(2), 263–281.

Campbell-Grossman, C. K., Hudson, D. B., Keating-Lefler, R., & Heusinkvelt, S. (2009). The provision of social support to single, low-income, African American mothers via e-mail messages. *Journal of Family Nursing, 15*(2), 220–236.

Canada, G. (1996). *Fist stick knife gun: A personal history of violence in America.* Boston: Beacon.

Canada, G. (1998). *Reaching up for manhood: Transforming the lives of boys in America.* Boston: Beacon.

Canino, I., & Spurlock, J. (1994). *Culturally diverse children and adolescents: Assessment, diagnosis and treatment.* New York: Guilford Press.

Caplan, P. J. (1996, October). Take the blame off mother. *Psychology Today.*

Caplow, T. (1968). *Two against one: Coalitions in triads.* Englewood Cliffs, NJ: Prentice Hall.

Carlson, M. J. (2001). Family structure and children's behavioral and cognitive outcomes. *Journal of Marriage and Family, 63,* 779–792.

Carnegie Council on Adolescent Development. (1995). *Great transitions: Preparing adolescents for a new century.* New York: Carnegie Corporation.

Carrese, J., & Rhodes, L. (1995). Western bioethics on the Navajo reservation: Benefit or harm. *Journal of the American Medical Association, 274,* 826–829.

Carruth, B., & Mendenhall, W. (1989). *Co-dependency: Issues in treatment and recovery.* Binghamton, NY: Haworth Press.

Carstensen, L. L., Gottman, J. M., & Levenson, R. W. (1995). Emotional behavior in long-term marriage. *Psychology and Aging, 10*(1), 140–149.

Carter B. (1991). Death in the therapist's own family. In F. Walsh & M. McGoldrick (Eds.), *Living beyond loss: Death in the family* (pp. 273–283). New York: Norton.

Carter, B. (1993). *Clinical dilemmas in marriage: The search for equal partnership.* [Videotape produced by Steve Lerner]. New York: Guilford Press.

Carter, B., & McGoldrick, M. (1999). *The expanded family life cycle: Individual, family and social perspectives* (3rd ed.). Boston: MA: Allyn & Bacon.

Carter, B., & Peters, J. (1996). *Love, honor and negotiate: Building partnerships that last a lifetime.* New York: Pocket Books.

Carter, E. A. (1978). Transgenerational scripts and nuclear family stress: Theory and clinical implications. In R. R. Sager (Ed.), *Georgetown Family Symposium: Vol. 3, 1975–76.* Washington, DC: Georgetown University.

Carter, E. A., & Lerner, S. (1997a). *Clinical dilemmas in marriage: The search for equal partnership* [Video]. New York: Guilford Publications.

Carter, E. A., & Lerner, S. (1997b). *Addressing economic inequality in marriage: A new therapeutic approach* [Video]. New York: Guilford Publications.

Carter, E. A., & Lerner, S. (1997c). *Who's in the kitchen: Helping men move toward the center of family life* [Video]. New York: Guilford Publications.

Carter, E. A., McGoldrick, M., & Orfanidis, M. (1976). Family therapy with one person and the family therapist's own family. In P. J. Guerin (Ed.), *Family therapy* (pp. 193–219). New York: Gardner.

Carter, E. A., & McGoldrick, M. (1980). The family life cycle and family therapy. In E. A. Carter & M. McGoldrick (Eds.), *The family life cycle: A framework for family therapy* (pp. 3–20). New York: Gardner Press.

Cass, V. C. (1979). Homosexual identity formation: A theoretical model. *Journal of Homosexuality, 4*(3), 219–237.

Cass, V. C. (1998). Sexual orientation identity formation: A Western phenomenon. In R.J. Cabal & T. S. Stein (Eds.), *Textbook of homosexuality and mental health* (pp. 227–251). Washington, DC: APA.

CBS News (2009). *Survey: U.S. spends but child welfare lags.* Retrieved from www.cbsnews.com/stories/2009/09/01/national/main5280103.shtml

Ceballo, R., & McLloyd, V. C. (2002). Social support and parenting in poor, dangerous neighborhoods, *Child Development, 73*(4), 1310–1321.

Centers for Disease Control. (2008). *Births, marriages, divorces and deaths: Provisional data for 2007.* National Vital Statistics Report, 56(16). Retrieved (4/14/10) from www.cdc.gov/nchs/products/nvsr.htm

Centers for Disease Control and Prevention. (2006). *Understanding intimate partner violence. Fact sheet.* Retrieved (6/16/10) from http://www.cdc.gov/ncipc/dvp/ipv_factsheet.pdf

Centers for Disease Control and Prevention, National Center for Injury Prevention and Control. (2008). *Web-based Injury Statistics Query and Reporting System (WISQARS)* [online].

Chandler, K. (1995). *Passages of pride: True stories of lesbian and gay teenagers.* Los Angeles: Alyson Books.

Chantrill, C. (2009). *U.S. Education spending 1791–2014 – Charts.* Retrieved (4/14/10) from www.usgovernmentspending.com/

Chapman, A. (2007). In search of love and commitment: Dealing with the challenging odds of finding romance. In H. McAdoo (Ed.), *Black families* (pp. 282–296). Thousand Oaks, CA: Sage.

Chaudhury, S. R., & Miller, L. (2008). Religions identify formation among Bangladeshi American Muslim adolescents. *Journal of Adolescent Research, 23*(4), 383–410.

Cherlin, A. J. (1992). *Marriage, divorce, remarriage* (rev. and enlarged ed.). Cambridge, MA: Harvard University Press.

Cherlin, A. J. (2005). American marriage in the early twenty-first century. *The Future of Children, 15*(2) 33–55.

Cherlin, A. J. (2009a). American marriage in the early twenty-first century. In A. S. Skolnick & J. H. Skolnick (Eds.). *Families in transition,* (pp. 171–191). Boston: Allyn & Bacon.

Cherlin, A. J. (2009b). *The marriage-go-round: The state of marriage and family in America today.* New York: Knopf.

Cherlin, A. J., & Furstenberg, F. F. (1994). Stepfamilies in the United States: A reconsideration. *Annual Review of Sociology, 20,* 359–381.

Cherry, K. E., Galea, S., & Silva, J. L. (2007). *Successful aging in very old adults: Resiliency in the face of natural disaster.* In M. Hersen & A. M. Gross (Eds.), *Handbook of clinical psychology, Vol. 1: Adults* (pp. 800–803). Hoboken, NJ: Wiley.

Chodorow, N. (1974a). Family structure and feminine personality. In M. Z. Rosaldo & L. Lamphere (Eds.), *Woman, culture and society* (pp. 43–66). Stanford, CA.: Stanford University Press.

Chodorow, N. (1978). *The reproduction of mothering: Psychoanalysis and the sociology of gender*. Berkley: University of California Press.

Chodorow, N., with Contratto, S. (1991). The fantasy of the perfect mother. In N. J. Chodorow: *Feminism and psychoanalytic theory* (pp. 79–96). New Haven: Yale University Press.

Chugh, D., & Brief, A. P. (2008). 1964 was not that long ago: A story of gateways and pathways. In A. P. Brief (Ed.), *Diversity at work* (pp. 318–340). New York: Cambridge University Press.

Cicirelli, V. G. (1982). Sibling influence throughout the life span. In M. E. Lamb & B. Sutton-Smith (Eds.), *Sibling relationships: Their nature and significance across the lifespan* (pp. 267–284). Hillsdale, NJ: Lawrence Erlbaum Associates.

Cicirelli, V. G. (1983). Adult children's attachment and helping behavior to elderly parents: A path model. *Journal of Marriage and the Family, 45*, 815–825.

Cicirelli, V. G. (1985). Sibling relationships throughout the life cycle. In L. L'Abate (Ed.), *The handbook of family psychology and therapy* (pp. 177–214). Homewood, IL: Dorsey Press.

Cicirelli, V. G. (1989). Feelings of attachment to siblings and well-being in later life. *Psychology and Aging, 4*, 211–216.

Cicirelli, V. G. (1994). The longest bond: The sibling life cycle. In L. L'Abate (Ed.), *Handbook of developmental family psychology and psychopathology* (pp. 27–43). New York: Wiley.

Cicirelli, V. G. (1995). *Sibling relationships across the life span*. New York: Plenum Press.

Cicirelli, V. G. (2006). *Older adults' views of death*. New York: Springer.

Clark, D. B., & Bukstein, O. G. (1998). Traumas and other adverse life events in adolescents with alcohol abuse and dependence. *Journal of the American Academy of Child and Adolescent Psychiatry, 22*(2), 117–121.

Clearfield, M. W., & Nelson, N. M. (2006). Sex differences in mothers' speech and play behavior with 6-, 9-, and 14-month-old infants. *Sex roles, 54*(1–2), 127–137.

Cochran, S.V. (2005). Psychotherapy with men navigating the life terrain. In G. E. Good and G. R. Brooks (Eds.), *The new handbook of psychotherapy and counseling with men* (pp. 186–200). San Francisco, CA: Jossey-Bass.

Cohen, G. D. (2005). *The Mature Mind: The positive power of the aging brain*. New York: Basic Books.

Cohen, J., & Sandy, S. (2007). The social, emotional and education of children: Theories, goals, methods and assessments. In R. Bar-On, J. G. Maree & M. J. Elias (Eds.), *Educating people to be emotionally intelligent* (pp. 63–77). Westport, CN: Praeger.

Cohler, B., & Beeler, J. (1996) Schizophrenia and the life course: Implications for family relations and caregiving. *Psychiatric Annals, 26*(12), 745–756.

Cohler, B., Hosteler, A. J., & Boxer, A. (1998). Generativity, social context and lived experience: Narratives of gay men in middle adulthood. In D. McAdams & E. de St. Aubin (Eds.), *Generativity and adult development. Psychosocial perspective on caring and contributing to the next generation*. Washington, DC: American Psychological Association Press.

Cohler, B. J., & R. Galatzer-Levy, R. (2000). *The course of gay and lesbian lives: social and psychoanalytic perspectives*. Chicago: The University of Chicago.

Cole, D. (2009, July 2). The same-sex future. *New York Review of Books*, pp. 12–16.

Cole, E. (2009). Intersectionality and research in psychology. *American Psychologist, 64*(3), 170–180.

Cole, E., & Rothblum, E. (1990). Commentary on "sexuality and the midlife woman." *Psychology of Women Quarterly, 14*, 509–512.

Cole, J. B. (1996). Community, family and the healing power of responsibility. In E. Dinwiddie-Boyd (Ed.), *In our own words*. New York: Avon Books.

Coll, C. G., & Szalacha, L. A. (2004). The multiple contexts of middle childhood. *The Future of Children, 14*(2), 81–97.

Collins, P. H. (1998). *Fighting words: Black women and the search for justice*. Minneapolis: University of Minnesota Press.

Coltrane, S. (1996). *Family man: Fatherhood, housework, and gender equity*. New York: Oxford.

Combrinck-Graham, L. (1985). A developmental model for family systems. *Family Process, 24*, 139–150.

Comer, J. P. (2008). Promoting well-being among at-risk children: Restoring a sense of community and support for development. In K. K. Kline (Ed.), *Authoritative communities: The scientific case for nurturing the whole child* (pp. 305–321). New York: Springer.

Comer, J. P. (2009). *What I learned in school: Reflections on race, child development and school reform*. New York: Jossey-Bass.

Comer, J. P., Joyner, E. T., & Ben-Avie, M. (2004). *Six pathways to healthy child development and academic success: Field guide to Comer schools in action.* Thousand Oaks, CA: Corwin Press.

Comer, J. P., & Poussaint, A. F. (1992). *Raising Black children.* New York: Penguin.

Conger, R. D. (1994). The family context of adolescent vulnerability and resilience to alcohol use and abuse. *Sociological Studies of Children, 6,* 55–86.

Congress, E. P. (1994). The use of culturagrams to assess and empower culturally diverse families. *Families in Society, 75*(9) 531–540.

Conley, D. (2005). *The pecking order.* New York: Vintage.

Connell, R. (1987). *Gender and power: Society, the person and sexual politics.* Stanford, CA: Stanford University Press.

Connidis, I. A. (2001). *Family ties and aging.* Thousand Oaks, CA: Sage.

Connidis, I. A., & Kemp, C. (2008). Negotiating actual and anticipated parental support: Multiple sibling voices in three-generation families. *Journal of Aging Studies, 22*(3), 220–238.

Connolly, C. M. (2004a). A process of change. *Journal of GLBT Family Studies, 1*(1), 5–20.

Connolly, C. M. (2004b). Clinical issues with same-sex couples: A review of the literature. In J. J. Bigner & J. L. Wetchler (Eds.), *Relationship therapy with same-sex couples* (pp. 3–12). New York: Haworth Press.

Cook, A. S., & Oltjenbruns, K. A. (1998). *Dying and grieving: Life cycle and family perspectives.* Orlando, FL: Harcourt, Brace & Co.

Cook-Daniels, L. (1998). Lesbian, gay male, bisexual and transgendered elders: Elder abuse and neglect issues. *Journal of Elder Abuse and Neglect, 9*(2), 35–50.

Coontz, S. (1992). *The way we never were: American families and the nostalgia trap.* New York: Basic Books.

Coontz, S. (1998). *The way we really are.* New York: Basic Books.

Coontz, S. (2000). Historical perspectives on family studies. *Journal of Marriage & the Family, 62*(2), 283–297.

Coontz, S. (2005). *Marriage: A history.* New York: Viking.

Coontz, S. (2009, February 5). Till children do us part. *New York Times,* p. A 31.

Coontz, S., Coleman, M., & Ganong, L. (2003). *Divorce reality. Points & counterpoints: Controversial relationships and family issues in the 21st century (an anthology).* Los Angeles: CA: Roxbury Publishing Co.

COPMI (Children of Parents with Mental Illness) website: www.aicafmha.net.au/copmi/

Corliss, H. C., Rosario, M., Wypij, D., Fisher, L. B., & Austin, B. S. (2008). Sexual orientation disparities in longitudinal alcohol use patterns among adolescents: Findings from the growing up today study. *Archives of Pediatric Adolescent Medicine, 162*(11), 1071–1078.

Cose, E. (1995). *A man's world: How real is male privilege–and how high is its price?* New York: Harper Collins.

Costello, C. B., Wight, V. R., & Stone, A. J. (2003). *The American woman: 2003–2004.* New York: Macmillan.

Cote, J. (2000). *Arrested adulthood: The changing nature of maturity and identity.* New York: New York University.

Cowan, C., & Cowan P. (1992). *When partners become parents: The big life change for couples.* New York: Basic Books.

Cowan, C. P., Cowan, P. A., Heming, G., & Miller, N. B. (1991). Becoming a family: marriage, parenting, and child development. In P. A. Cowan & M. Hetherington (Eds.). *Family transitions* (pp. 79–109). Hillsdale, NJ: Lawrence Erlbaum.

Coyne, A., Reichman, W., & Berbig, L. (1993). The relationship between elder abuse and dementia. *American Journal of Psychiatry, 1*(50), 643–646.

Cozolino, L. (2008). *The healthy aging brain: Sustaining attachment, attaining wisdom.* New York: Norton.

Cramer, D. W., & Roach, A. J. (1988). Coming out to mom and dad: A study of gay males and their relationship with their parents. *Journal of Homosexuality, 15*(3/4), 79–91.

Crohn, J. (1995). Mixed matches: How to create successful interracial, interethnic and interfaith relationships. New York: Ballantine Books.

Crosbie-Burnett, M., & Lewis, E. (1993). Use of African-American family structures and functioning to address the challenges of European-American postdivorce families. *Family Relations, 42,* 243–248.

Crosier, T., Butterworth, P., Rodgers, B. (2007). Mental health problems among single and partnered mothers: The role of financial hardship and social support. *Social Psychiatry and Psychiatric Epidemiology, 42*(1), 6–13.

Crosson-Tower, C. (2010). *Understanding child abuse and neglect* (8th ed). Boston: Allyn & Bacon.

Cruz, M., & Taylor, D. (2008). Inner-city violence in the United States: What pediatricians can do to make a difference. *International Journal of Child and Adolescent Health, 2*(1), 3–12.

Cseh-Szombathy, L., Koch-Nielsen, I., Trost, J., & Weda, I. (Eds.). (1985). *The aftermath of divorce—*

Coping with family change: An investigation in eight countries. Budapest, Hungary: Akademiai Kiado.

Cutrona, C. E., Hessling, R. M., Bacon, P. L., & Russell, D. W. (1998). Predictors and correlates of continuing involvement with the baby's father among adolescent mothers. *Journal of Family Psychology, 12*(3), 369–387.

Dacey, J. S. & Travers, J. E. (2004). *Human development across the lifespan* (5th ed.). Boston: McGraw Hill.

D'Angelo, E., Llerena-Quinn, R., Colon, F., Shapiro, R., Rodriguez, P., Gallagher, K. (2009). Adaptation of the preventive intervention program for depression for use with Latino families. *Family Process, 48,* 269–291.

Danieli, Y. (1985). The treatment and prevention of long-term effects and intergenerational transmission of victimization: A lesson from Holocaust survivors and their children. In C. R. Figley (Ed.), *Trauma and its wake* (pp. 295–313). New York: Bruner/Mazel.

D'Augelli, A. R., Grossman, A. H., & Starks, M. T. (2006). Childhood gender atypicality, victimization, and PTSD among lesbian, gay, and bisexual youth. *Journal of Interpersonal Violence, 21,* 1462–1482.

D'Augelli, A. R., Hershberger, S. L., & Pilkington, N. W. (2001). Suicidality patterns and sexual orientation-related factors among lesbian, gay and bisexual youths. *Suicide and Life-Threatening Behavior, 31,* 250–265.

Day, R. D., Lewis, C., O'Brien, M., & Lamb, M. (2004). Fatherhood and father involvement: Emerging constructs and theoretical orientations. In V. Bengsten, A. Acock, K. Allen, P. Dilworth-Anderson, & D. Klein (Eds.), *Sourcebook of family theory & research* (pp. 341–351). Thousand Oaks, CA: Sage Publishers.

DeFrain, J. (1991). Learning about grief from normal families: SIDS, stillbirth, and miscarriage. *Journal of Marital and Family Therapy, 17,* 215–232.

Delahunty-Britz, J. (2006, March 23). To all the girls I've rejected [Letter to the Editor]. *New York Times,* p. 24.

Delany, S., & Delany A. E. (1993). *Having our say: The Delany sisters' first 100 years.* New York: Dell.

Demo, D., & Fine, M. (2009). *Beyond the average divorce.* Los Angeles: Sage.

Denizet-Lewis, B. (2009, September 27). Junior high: Coming out in middle school. *New York Times Magazine,* p. 36.

DePaulo, B. (2006). *Singled out: How singles are stereotyped, stigmatized, and ignored, and still live happily ever after.* New York: St. Martins' Press.

DeSilva, C. (Ed.). (1996). *In memory's kitchen: A legacy from the women of Terezin.* New York: Jason Aronson.

Deutsch, B. (2010). The male privilege checklist. In M. S. Kimmel & M. A. Messner (Eds.), *Men's lives.* Boston: Allyn & Bacon.

Devault, A., Milcent, M., Ouellet, F., Laurin, I., Jauron, M., & Lacharite, C. (2008). Life stories of young fathers in contexts of vulnerability. *Fathering, 6*(3), 226–248.

Diamond, L., & Butterworth, M. (2008). The close relationships of sexual minorities: partners, friends and family. In M.C. Smith & T.G. Reio (Eds.), *Handbook of research on adult development and learning* (pp. 348–375). Mahwah NJ: Lawrence Erlbaum.

Diener, M. L., Isabella, R. A., Behunin, M. G., & Wong, M. S. (2008). Attachment to mothers and fathers during middle childhood: Associations with child gender, grade, and competence. *Social Development, 17*(1), 84–100.

Dillon, S. (2009, April 22). Large urban-suburban gap seen in graduation rates. *New York Times,* p. A14.

Dilworth-Anderson, P., Burton, L., & Johnson, L. B. (1993). Reframing theories for understanding race, ethnicity and families. In P. G. Boss, W. J. Doherty, R. LaRossa, W. R. Schumm, & S. K. Steinmetz (Eds.), *Sourcebook of family theories and methods: A contextual approach* (pp. 627–646). New York: Plenum.

Diner, H. (1983). *Erin's daughters in America: Immigrant women in the 19th century.* Baltimore: Johns Hopkins Press.

Dinnerstein, D. (1976). *The mermaid and the minotaur.* New York: Harper & Row.

Doka, K. (1996). *Living with grief after sudden loss.* Washington, DC: Taylor & Francis.

Doka, K. (2002). *Disenfranchised grief.* Champaign, IL: Research Press.

Domhoff, W. (2006). *Wealth, power, and income: Who Rules America?* Retrieved (4/14/10) from sociology.ucsc.edu/whorulesamerica/power/wealth.html

Dooley, C., & Fedele, N. M. (2004). Mothers and sons: Raising relational boys. In Jordan. J.V., Walker, M., & Hartling L. M. (Eds.). *The complexity of connection: Writings from the Stone Center's Jean Baker Miller Training Institute* (pp. 220–249). New York: Guilford.

Dowling, C. (1996). *Red hot mamas: Coming into our own at fifty.* New York: Bantam Books.

Downey, G., & *Coyne, J. C.* (1990). Children of depressed parents: An integrative review. *Psychological Bulletin, 108,* 50–76.

Doyle, J. A., & *Paludi, M.* (1998). *Sex and gender: The human experience.* Boston: McGraw-Hill.

Draut, T. (2007). *Strapped: Why America's 20-and-30-somethings can't get ahead.* New York: Anchor.

Drew, L. M., & *Silverstein, M.* (2004). Intergenerational role investments of great-grandparents: Consequences for psychological well-being. *Ageing and Society, 24(1),* 95–111.

Drexler P., & *Gross I.* (2005). *Raising boys without men: How maverick moms are creating the next generation of exceptional men.* Emmaus, PA: Rodale Press.

Driscoll, E. (2008, June/July). Bisexual species: Unorthodox sex in the animal kingdom. *Scientific American Mind,* 69–77.

DSM-IV-TR 4th Edition Text Revision. (2000). American Psychiatric Press Inc.

Du Bois, W. E. B. (1903). *The souls of black folk.* Chicago: McClurg.

Duberman, L. (1975). *The reconstituted family: A study of remarried couples and their children.* Chicago: Nelson-Hall.

Dudley, J. R. (2007). Helping nonresidential fathers: The case for teen and adult unmarried fathers. *Families in Society, 88*(2), 171–181.

Due, L. (1995). *Joining the tribe: Growing up gay & lesbian in the '90s.* New York: Anchor Books.

Dunne, E., & *Dunne-Maxim, K.* (2004). The aftermath of suicide. In F. Walsh & M. McGoldrick (Eds.), *Living beyond loss* (2nd ed., pp. 272–284). New York: Norton.

Durby, D. D. (1994). Gay, lesbian and bisexual youth. In T. DeCrescenzo (Ed.), *Helping gay and lesbian youth: New policies, new programs, new practices.* Binghamton, NY: Harrington Park Press.

Duvall, E. M. (1957). *Family development.* Philadelphia: Lippincott.

Duvall, E. M. (1977). *Marriage and family development* (5th ed.). Philadelphia: Lippincott.

Dye, J. L. (2008). *Participation of mothers in government assistance programs: 2004. Current Population Reports, (pp. 70–116).* Washington DC: U.S. Bureau of the Census.

Dyer, W. J. (2005). Prison, fathers, and identity: A theory of how incarceration affects men's paternal identity. *Fathering, 3*(3), 201–219.

Eaton, L., *Kaufman, M.*, *Fuhrel, A.*, *Cain, D.*, *Cherry, C.*, *Pope, H.*, & *Kalichman, S. C.* (2008). Examining factors co-existing with interpersonal violence in lesbian relationships. *Journal of Family Violence, 23,* 607–705.

Edin, K., & *Kefalas, M.* (2005). *Promises I can keep: Why poor women put motherhood before marriage.* Berkeley: University of California.

Edwards, T. (2009, October 1). Stay-at-home moms are more likely younger, Hispanic and foreign-born than other mothers. *U. S. Census Bureau News,* pp. CB09–132.

Ehrenreich, B. (1989). *Fear of falling: The inner life of the middle class.* New York: HarperCollins.

Elder, G. (1992). Life course. In E. Borgatta & M. Borgatta (Eds.), *Encyclopedia of sociology* (Vol. 3, pp. 1120–1130). New York: Macmillan.

Elder, G. (1999). *Children of the great depression: Social change in life experience* (25th anniversary ed.). Boulder, CO: Westview Press.

Elder, G. H., & *Johnson, M. M.* (2002). Perspectives on human development in context. In C. von Hofsten & L. Backman (Eds.), *Psychology at the turn of the millennium* (Vol 2: Social, developmental and clinical perspectives, pp. 153–177). Florence, KY: Taylor & Frances/Routledge.

Elder, G. H., & *Shanahan, M. J.* (2006). The life course and human development. In R. M. Lerner & W. Damon (Eds.), *Handbook of child psychology* (Vol. 1, 6th ed., pp. 665–715). Hoboken, NJ: John Wiley & Sons.

Ellison, C., & *Bradshaw, M.* (2009). Religious beliefs, sociopolitical ideology, and attitudes toward corporal punishment. *Journal of Family Issues, 30*(3), 320–340.

Encyclopedia of World Biography (2010). Ruth Bader Ginsberg. www.notablebiographies.com/Gi-He/Ginsburg-Ruth-Bader.html (Retrieved 6/7/10).

Engle, P. (1997). The role of men in families: Achieving gender equity and supporting children. *Gender and Development, 5,* 31–40.

Engstrom, M. (in press). Kinship care families. In F. Walsh (Ed.), *Normal family processes* (4th ed.). New York: Guilford Press.

Entwistle, D. R., & *Doering, S. G.* (1981). *The first birth.* Baltimore: Johns Hopkins Press.

Erera, P. I. (2002). *Family diversity: Continuity and change in the contemporary family.* Thousand Oaks, CA: Sage Publications.

Erikson, E. (1963). *Childhood and society* (2nd ed.). New York: W. W. Norton.

Erikson, E. (1968). *Identity: Youth and crisis.* New York: Norton.

Erikson, E. (1982). *The life cycle completed.* New York: Norton.

Erikson, E. (1994). *Identity and the life cycle.* New York: W. W. Norton.

Erikson, E. (1997). *The life cycle completed.* New York: Norton & Company.

Erikson, E. H., Erikson, J. M., & Kivnick, H. (1986). *Vital involvement in old age: The experience of old age in our time.* New York: Norton.

Erickson, M. (1998). Re-visioning the family life cycle theory and paradigm in marriage and family therapy. *American Journal of Family Therapy, 26*(4), 341–353.

Erikson-Boland, S. (2005). *In the shadow of fame: A memoir by the daughter of Erik H. Erikson.* New York: Viking.

Fagan, J., Palkovitz, R., Roy, K., & Farrie, D. (2009). Pathways to paternal engagement: Longitudinal effects of risk and resilience on nonresident fathers. *Developmental Psychology, 45*(5), 1389–1405.

Falicov, C. J. (1988). Family sociology and family therapy contributions to the family development framework: A comparative analysis and thoughts on future trends. In C. J. Falicov (Ed.), *Family transitions: Continuity and change over the life cycle* (pp. 3–51). New York: Guilford Press.

Falicov, C. J. (1997). So they don't need me anymore: Weaving migration, illness and coping. In S. Daniel, J. Hepworth, & W. Doherty (Eds.), *The shared experience of illness: Stories about patients, families and their therapists* (pp. 48–57). New York: Basic Books.

Falicov, C. J. (1998). *Latino families in therapy: A guide to multicultural practice.* New York: Guilford Press.

Falicov, C. J. (2002). Ambiguous loss: Risk and resilience in Latino families. In M. Suarez-Orozco & M. Paez (Eds.), *Latinos: Remaking America* (pp. 274–288). Berkeley: University of California Press.

Falicov, C. J. (2003). Immigrant family processes. In F. Walsh (Ed.), *Normal family processes* (pp. 280–300). New York: Guilford Press.

Falicov, C. J. (2005). Mexican families. In M. McGoldrick, J. Giordano, & Garcia Preto. *Ethnicity and family therapy* (3rd ed., pp. 229–242). New York: Guilford Press.

Falicov, C. (2005a). Emotional transnationalism and family identities. *Family Process, 44*(4), 399–406.

Falicov, C. J. (2007). Working with transnational immigrants: Expanding meanings of family, community and culture. *Family Process, 46,* 157–172.

Falicov, C. J. (2008). Religion and spiritual traditions in immigrant families: Significance for Latino health and mental health. In F. Walsh (Ed.), *Spiritual resources in family therapy* (2nd ed., pp. 156–173). New York: Guilford Press.

Falicov, C. (2009). Commentary: On the wisdom and challenges of culturally attuned treatments for Latinos. *Family Process, 48,* 2.

Falicov, C. J., & Brudner-White, L. (1983). The shifting family triangle: The issue of cultural and contextual relativity. In C. J. Falicov (Ed.), *Cultural perspectives in family therapy* (pp. 51–67). Rockville, MD: Aspen.

Falk, W. (2009, December 29). Should old articles be forgot. *New York Times,* p. A31.

Faludi, S. (1991). *Backlash: The undeclared war against American women.* New York: Crown Publishers.

FBI (2008) Hate Crime Statistics. Table 1: Incidents, Offenses, Victims and Known Offenders. Retrieved 4/14/10 www.realcourage.org/2009/11/fbi-releases-2008-hate-crime-statistics/

Fernandez, R., Fogli, A., & Olivetti, C. (2004). Mothers and sons: Preference formation and female labor force dynamics. *Quarterly Journal of Economics, 119*(4), 1249–1300.

Fifield, L., Latham, J. & Phillips, C. (1977). *Alcoholism in the gay community: The price of alienation, isolation, and oppression.* The Gay Community Services Center.

Figley, C. (1998). *The traumatology of grieving.* San Francisco: Jossey-Bass.

Filan, S., & Llewellyn-Jones, R. (2006). Animal assisted therapy for dementia: A review of the literature. *International Psychogeriatrics, 18*(4), 597–611.

Fingerman, K. L., Pitzer, L., Lefkowitz, E. S., Birditt, K.S., & Mroczek, D. (2008). Ambivalent relationship qualities between adults and their parents: Implications for the well-being of both parties. *The Journals of Gerontology: Series B: Psychological Sciences and Social Sciences, 63B*(6), 362–371.

Finkelhor, D. (2008). *Childhood victimization: Violence: Crime and abuse in the lives of young people (Interpersonal violence).* New York: Oxford University Press.

Fishbane, M. D. (2007). Wired to connect: Neuroscience, relationships, and therapy. *Family Process, 46*(3), 395–412.

Fishbane, M. D. (2009). Honor your father and your mother: Intergenerational values and Jewish tradition. In F. Walsh (Ed.), *Spiritual resources in family therapy* (2nd ed., pp. 174–193). New York: Guilford.

Fishel, E. (1979). *Sisters: Love and rivalry inside the family and beyond.* New York: William Morrow.

Fisher, H. (2004). *Why we love: The nature and chemistry of romantic love.* New York: Henry Holt.

Fishman, C. (manuscript in preparation). *Power of culture: Capitalism and its discontents.*

Flouri, E. (2004, September). Mothers' nonauthoritarian child-rearing attitudes in early childhood and children's adult values. *European Psychologist, 9*(3), 154–162.

Fogarty, T. (1975). Triangles. *The Family, 2,* 11–20.

Fong-Torres, 1994. The rice room: Growing up Chinese-American, from number two son to rock 'n' roll. New York: Penguin Books.

Ford, A., & *Van Dyk, D.* (2009, October 16). Then & now: A statistical look back from the 1970s to today. *Time Magazine, 174*(16), p. 27.

Forste, R., (2006) Maybe someday: Marriage and cohabitation among low income fathers. In L. Kowaleski-Jones & N. H. Wolfinger. *Fragile Families and the Marriage* Agenda (pp. 189–209). New York: Springer Science and Business Media.

Forste, R., Bartkowski, J. P., & *Jackson, R. A.* (2009). Just be there for them: Perceptions of fathering among single, low-income men. *Fathering, 7*(1), 49–69.

Fosse, N. E. (in press). Doubt, duty, destiny: The cultural logics of infidelity among the urban poor. *The Annals of the American Academy of Political and Social Science.*

Fosse, N. E. (2010) The repertoire of infidelity among low-income men: Doubt, duty, and destiny. The Annals of the American Academy of Political and Social Science, 629, pp. 125–143.

Framingham Heart Study Press Releases. (2008, May 21). *Smokers quit together and flock together: Social networks exert key influences on decisions to quit smoking.* Retrieved (6/16/10) from www.framingham-heartstudy.org/participants/pr/08_0521.html

Framo, J. L. (1992). *Family-of-origin therapy: An intergenerational approach.* New York: Brunner/Mazel.

Francese, P. (2003, November 1). Well enough alone. *American Demographics.* Retrieved February 27, 2010, from findarticles.com/p/articles/mi_m4021/is_9_25/ai_109384501/?tag=content;col1.

Franklin, A. J. (2004). *From brotherhood to manhood: How Black men rescue their dreams and relationships from the invisibility syndrome.* Hoboken, NJ: Wiley.

Franklin, J. H. (1988). A historical note on Black families. In H. P. McAdoo (Ed.), *Black families* (2nd ed., pp. 23–26). Newbury Park, CA: Sage.

Freire, P. (2000). *Pedagogy of the oppressed.* London: Continuum.

Friedan, B. (1993). *The fountain of age.* New York: Simon & Schuster.

Friedman, F. B. (2003, April). Siblings of a certain age: The impact of aging parents on adult sibling relationships. *Dissertation Abstracts: 2003-95007-127. International Section A: Humanities & Social Sciences, 63*(10-A), p. 3727.

Friedman, L. J. (1999). *Identity's architect.* New York: Scribner.

Friend, R. (1991). Older lesbian and gay people: A theory of successful aging. In J. A. Lee (Ed.), *Gay midlife and maturity* (pp. 99–118). New York: Haworth Press.

Fullilove, M. (2004). *Root shock: How tearing up our neighborhoods hurts America and what we can do about it.* New York: Ballantine.

Fullilove, M. (2009). Toxic sequelae of childhood sexual abuse. *American Journal of Psychiatry, 166*(10), 1090–1092.

Fulmer, R. H. (1983). A structural approach to unresolved mourning in single parent family systems. *Journal of Marital and Family Therapy, 9*(3), 259–270.

Fulmer, R. H. (2006). From law to love: Young adulthood in Milton's *Paradise Lost. American Imago, 63*(1) 25–56.

Fulmer, R. H. (2008). 'Don't Save Her'-Sigmund Freud meets Project Pat: The rescue motif in hip-hop. *The International Journal of Psychoanalysis, 89*(4) 727–742.

Furman, E. (1974). *A child's parent dies: Studies in childhood bereavement.* New Haven, state: Yale University Press.

Furstenberg, F. F. (2007). *Destinies of the disadvantaged: The politics of teen childbearing.* New York: Russell Sage Foundation.

Furstenberg, F. F., & *Cherlin, A. J.* (1994). *Divided families: What happens to children when parents part.* Cambridge, MA: Harvard University Press.

Furstenberg, F. F., Jr., *Kennedy, S.*, *McCloyd, V.*, *Rumbaut, R.*, & *Settersten, R., Jr.* (2003, July 29). Between adolescence and adulthood: Expectations about the timing of adulthood. *Network on transitions to adulthood and public policy, research network Working Paper, 1.* Retrieved 4/14/10 from www.transad.pop.upenn.edu/news/betweeen.pdf

Galanter, M. (Ed.). (2005). *Recent developments in alcoholism, Vol. 17: Alcohol problems in adolescents and young adults.* New York: Springer.

Galderisi, S. & *Mucci, A.* (2000). Emotions, brain development, and psychopathologic vulnerability. *CNS Spectrums. 5*(8), 44–88.

Gallagher, W. (1993, May). Midlife myths. *The Atlantic Monthly,* pp. 551–568.

Gallup, G. H., Jr. (2002). *The Gallup Poll: Public Opinion 2001.* Washington, DC: Scholarly Resources.

Gallup, G. H., Jr., & *Lindsay, D. M.* (1999). *Surveying the religions landscape: Trends in U.S. beliefs.* Harrisburg, PA: Morehouse.

Gamino, L. A., & *Ritter, R. H.* (2009). *Ethical practice in grief counseling.* New York: Springer.

Gannon, L. R. (1999). *Women and aging.* Oxford, UK: Routledge.

Garcia-Coll, C., *Cook-Nobles, R.*, & *Surrey, J.* (1997). Building connection through diversity. In J. Jordan (Ed.), *Women's growth in diversity: More writings from the Stone Center* (pp. 176–198). New York: Guilford Press.

Garcia-Coll, C., & *Magnuson, K.* (1997). The psychological experience of immigration: A developmental perspective. In A. Booth, A. C. Crouter, & N. Landale (Eds.), *Immigration and the family: Research and policy on U.S. immigrants* (pp. 105–134). Mahwah, NJ: Lawrence Erlbaum Associates.

Gardner, H. (2006). *Multiple intelligences.* New York: Basic Books.

Gartrell, N., *Banks, A.*, *Hamilton, J.*, *Reed, N.*, *Bishop, H.*, & *Rodas, C.* (2000). Interviews with mothers of five-year-olds. *American Journal of Orthopsychiatry, 70*(4). *Retrieved February 27, 2010 from* www.nllfs.org/publications/fiveyearolds.htm

Gay Lesbian Straight Education Network. (2009). Retrieved (4/14/10) from Gay Lesbian Straight Eduction Network. (2009).

Geronimus, A. (1992). The weathering hypotheses and the health of African-American women and infants: Evidence and speculations. *Ethnicity and Disease, 2*(3) 207–221.

Gerson, B. (Ed.). (1996). *The therapist as a person: Life crises, life choices, life experiences, and their effects on treatment.* Hillsdale, NJ: Analytic Press.

Gerson, K. (1993). *No man's land: Men's changing commitments to family and work.* New York: Basic Books.

Gerstel, N., & *Sarkisian, N.* (2006). Marriage, the good, the bad and the greedy. *Contexts, 5*(4), 16–21.

Gerstel, N., & *Sarkisian, N.* (2007a). Marriage reduces social ties. Discussion paper for the *Council on Contemporary Families.* Retrieved 4/14/10 from www.prospects.org/cs/articles?article=marriage_poverty_ and_ public_policy

Gerstel, N., & *Sarkisian, N.* (2007b). Adult children's relationship to their parents: The greediness of marriage. In J. Suiter & T. Owens (Eds.), *Interpersonal relations across the life course. Advances in the life course Research* (Vol. 12, pp. 153–190). London: Elsevier Science.

Giamatti, B. (1998). Take time for paradise. In D. Halberstam & K. S. Robson (Eds.), *A great and glorious game: Baseball writings of A. Bartlett Giamatti* (pp. 87–116). Chapel Hill, NC: Algonquin Books.

Gil, E. (1994). *Play in family therapy.* New York: Guilford.

Gil, E. (1996). *Treating abused adolescents.* New York: Guilford.

Gil, E., & *Briere, J.* (2006). *Helping abused and traumatized children: Integrating directive and nondirective approaches.* New York: Guilford.

Gilbert, S. (1997, September 10). Youth study elevates family's role. *New York Times,* p. C10.

Giles, H., *Noels, K. A.*, *Williams, A.*, *Ota, H.*, *Lim, T. S.*, & *Ng, S. H.*, (2003). Intergenerational communication across cultures: Young peoples' perceptions of conversations with family elders, non-family elders, and same-age peers. *Journal of Cross-cultural Gerontology, 18*(1), 1–32.

Gilles-Donovan, J. (1991, Summer). Common misunderstandings. *American Family Therapy Academy Newsletter, 44,* pp. 7–14.

Gilligan, C. (1991). Women's psychological development: Implications for psychotherapy. In C. Gilligan, A. Rogers, & D. Tilman (Eds.), *Women, girls and psychotherapy: Reframing resistance* (pp. 5–32). New York: Haworth.

Gilligan, C. (1993). *In a different voice.* Cambridge, MA: Harvard University Press.

Gilligan, C., Lyons, N. P., & Hanmer, T. (1990). *Making connections.* Cambridge, MA: Harvard University Press.

Gillis, J. (1996). *A world of their own making: Myth, ritual, and the quest for family values,* New York: Basic Books.

Gilman, L. (1992). *The adoption resource book* (3rd ed.). New York: HarperCollins.

Gilmore, D. (1990). *Manhood in the making: Cultural concepts of masculinity.* New Haven: Yale University Press.

Ginsberg, T., Pomerantz, S., & Kramer-Feeley, V. (2005). Sexuality in older adults: Behaviors and preferences. *Age and Aging, 34*(5), 475–480.

Gladwell, M. (2008). *Outliers: The story of success.* Boston: Little Brown.

Glick, I. O., Parkes, C. M., & Weiss, R. (1975). *The first year of bereavement.* New York: Basic Books.

Glick, P. (1990). American families: As they are, and were. *Sociology and Social Research, 74,* 139–145.

Gold, D. T. (1987). Siblings in old age. Something special. *Canadian Journal on Aging, 6,* 199–215.

Gold, D. T. (1989). Sibling relationships in old age: A typology. *International Journal of Aging and Human Development, 28,* 37–51.

Goldberg, C. (1996, December 5). Gain for same-sex parents, at least. *New York Times,* p. B 16.

Goldenberg, H., & Goldenberg, I. (1998). *Counseling today's families* (3rd ed.). California: Brooks/Cole.

Goldner, V. (1985). Feminism and family therapy. *Family Process. 24*(1), 31–48.

Goldner, V. (1988). Generation and gender: Normative and covert hierarchies. *Family Process, 27,* 17–31.

Goldscheider, F. & Kaufman, G. (2006) Single parenthood and the double standard, *Fathering, 4*(2), 191–208.

Goldstein, S., & Brooks, R. B. (Eds.). (2005). *Handbook of resilience in children.* New York: Kluwer Academic/ Plenum Publishers.

Goleman, D. (1986, April 1). Two views of marriage explored: His and hers. *New York Times,* p. 19.

Goleman, D. (2006). *Emotional intelligence, 10th Anniversary Edition, Why it can matter more than IQ.* New York: Bantam.

Goleman, D. (2007). *Social intelligence.* New York. Bantam.

Gomez de Leon del Rio, J., & Vicencio Guzman, J.V. (2006). The impact of absence: Families, migration and family therapy in Ocotepec, Mexico [Monograph]. *American Family Therapy Academy, 2*(1): 34–43.

Gondolf, E. W., & Fisher, E. R. (1988). *Battered women as survivors: An alternative to treating learned helplessness.* Lexington, MA: Lexington.

Gonzalez, S., & Steinglass, P. (2002). Application of multifamily groups in chronic medical disorders. In W. F. McFarlane (Ed.), *Multifamily groups in the treatment of severe psychiatric disorders* (pp. 315–341). New York: Guilford Press.

Good, C. (2002). Girls and boys. On *The Young and the Hopeless* [CD]. Epic Records.

Good, G. E. & Brooks, G. (2005). *The new handbook of psychotherapy and counseling with men.* San Francisco: Wiley & Sons.

Goode, W. (1993). *World changes in divorce patterns.* New Haven, CT: Yale University Press.

Gorbaty, L. (2008). *Family reintegration of reserve service members following a wartime deployment: A qualitative exploration of wives' experience.* Unpublished doctoral dissertation. Boston: The Massachusetts School of Professional Psychology.

Gorina, Y., Hoyert, D., Lentzner, H., Goulding, M. Trends in causes of death among older persons in the United States. National Center for Health Statistics 2005. U.S. Dept. of Health and Human Services. Retrieved from www.cdc.gov/nchs/data/ahcd/agingtrends/06old-erpersons.pdf

Gosselin, D. K. (2010). *Heavy hands: An introduction to the crime of intimate family violence* (4th ed.). Englewood Cliffs, NJ: Prentice Hall.

Gottfried, A. E., & Gottfried, A. W. (2008). The upside of maternal and dual-earner employment: A focus on positive family adaptations, home environments and child development in the Fullerton Longitudinal Study. In A. Marcus-Neuhall, D. F. Halpern, & S. J. Tan (Eds.), *The changing realities of work and family* (pp. 25–42). New York: Wiley-Blackwell.

Gottman, J. (1993). The roles of conflict engagement, escalation, and avoidance in marital interaction: A longitudinal view of five types of couples. *Journal of Counseling and Clinical Psychology, 61*(1), 6–15.

Gottman, J. (1994). *Why marriages succeed or fail.* New York: Simon & Schuster.

Graham-Berman, S. A. (2002). Child abuse in the context of domestic violence. In J. E. B. Myers, L. Berliner,

J. Briere, C. T. Hendrix, C. Jenny, & T. A. Reid (Eds.), *APSAC handbook on child maltreatment* (pp. 119–129). Thousand Oaks, CA: Sage.

Grant, B. F., Dawson, D. A., Stinson, F. S., Chou, P. S., Dufour, M. C., & Pickering, R. P. (2004). The 12-month prevalence and trends in DSM-IV alcohol abuse and dependence: United States, 1991–1992 and 2001–2002. *Drug and Alcohol Dependence, 74*(3), 223–234.

Green, R. J. (1998). Traditional norms of male development. In R. Almeida (Ed.), *Transforming gender and race* (pp. 81–84). New York: Harrington Park Press.

Green, R. J., Bettinger, M., & Zacks, E. (1996). Are lesbian couples fused and gay male couples disengaged? Questioning gender straitjackets. In J. Laird & R.-J. Green (Eds.), *Lesbians and gays in couples and families: A handbook for therapists* (pp. 185–230). San Francisco: Jossey-Bass.

Green, R. J., & Mitchell, V. (2008). *Gay and lesbian couples in therapy: Homophobia, relational ambiguity and social support.* In A. S. Gurman & N. S. Jacobson (Eds.), *Clinical handbook of couple therapy* (4th ed., pp. 662–680). New York: Guilford.

Greene, B. (1998). Family, ethnic identity and sexual orientation: African American lesbians and gay men. In C. J. Patterson & A. R. D'Augelli (Eds.), *Lesbian, gay, and bisexual identities in families: Psychological perspectives* (pp. 40–52). New York: Oxford University Press.

Greene, B. & Boyd-Franklin, N. (1996). African American lesbians: Issues in couples therapy. In J. Laird & R. J. Green (Eds.), *Lesbians and gays in couples and families: A handbook for therapists* (pp. 420– 437). San Francisco: Jossey-Bass.

Griffin, C. W., Wirth, M. J., & Wirth, A. G. (1986). *Beyond acceptance: Parents of lesbians and gays talk about their experiences.* Englewood Cliffs, NJ: Prentice-Hall.

Griffith, J., & Griffith, M. (1994). *The body speaks.* New York: Basic Books.

Groze, V. (1991). Adoption and single parents: A review. *Child Welfare, 70*(3), 321–332.

Guerin, P., Fogarty, T., Fay, L., & Kautto, J. G. (1996). *Working with relationship triangles: The one-two-three of psychotherapy.* New York: Guilford.

Gunn-Allen, P. (1992). Angry women are building: Issues and struggles facing American Indian women today. In M. L. Anderson & P. H. Collins (Eds.), *Race, class, and gender* (pp. 42–46). Belmont, CA: Wadsworth.

Hadley, T., Jacob, T., Milliones, J., Caplan, J., & Spitz, D. (1974). The relationship between family developmental crises and the appearance of symptoms in a family member. *Family Process, 13,* 207–214.

Hale, J. E., Bailey, W. A., & Franklin, V. P. (2001). *Learning while Black: Educational excellence for African American children.* Baltimore: Johns Hopkins University Press.

Hale-Benson, J. E. (1986). *Black children: Their roots, culture and learning styles.* Baltimore: Johns Hopkins University Press.

Haley, J. (1973). *Uncommon therapy: The psychiatric techniques of Milton H. Erickson.* New York: Norton.

Haley, J. (1980). *Leaving home: The therapy of disturbed young people.* New York: McGraw-Hill.

Hall, R. L., & Greene, B. (1994). Cultural competence in feminist family therapy: An ethical mandate. *Journal of Feminist Family Therapy, 6*(3), 5–28.

Hankin, B. L., Mermelstein, R., & Roesch, L. (2007). Sex differences in adolescent depression: Stress exposure and reactivity models. *Child development, 78*/1, pp. 279–295.

Hansberry, L. (1969). *To be young, gifted and Black.* New York: Signet.

Hanson, D. J. (1995). The United States of America. In D. B. Heath, D.B. (Ed.), *International Handbook on Alcohol and Culture* (pp. 300–315), Westport, CT: Greenwood Press.

Harden, B. (2007, March 4). Numbers drop for the married with children; institution becoming the choice of the educated, affluent. *Washingtonpost.com.* Retrieved (4/14/10) from www/washingtonpost.com/wp-dyn/content/article/2007/03/03/Ar2007030300841.html

Hardy, K. V., & Laszloffy, T. A. (1995). The cultural genogram: Key to training culturally competent family therapists. *Journal of Marital and Family Therapy, 21,* 227–237.

Hardy, K. V., & Laszloffy, T. A. (2005). *Teens who hurt: Clinical interventions for breaking the cycle of adolescent violence.* New York: Guilford.

Hardy, K. V., & Laszloffy, T. A. (2008). The dynamics of a pro-racist ideology: Implications for training family therapists. In M. McGoldrick & K. V. Hardy (Eds.), *Re-visioning family therapy: Race, culture and gender in clinical practice* (pp. 225–237). New York: Guilford Press.

Hare-Mustin, R. T. (1991). Sex, lies and headaches: The problem of power. *Journal of Feminist Family Therapy, 3/1*, 63–84.

Hargrave, T. D., & **Hanna, S. M.** (1997). *The aging family: New visions of theory, practice, and reality.* New York: Brunner/Mazel.

Harwood, A. (1981). *Ethnicity and medical care.* Cambridge, MA: Harvard University Press.

Hart, T. (2006). Spiritual capacities of children and youth. In E. C. Roehlkepartain, P.E. King, L.Wagener, & P.L. Benson, *The Handbook of Spiritual Development in Childhood and Adolescence.* Thousand Oaks, CA: Sage Publications, Inc.

Hartman, A. (1987). Personal communication.

Hartman, A. (1993). Secrecy in adoption. In E. Imber-Black (Ed.), *Secrets in families and family therapy* (pp. 86–105). New York: Norton.

Hartman, A. (1996). Social policy as a context for lesbian and gay families: The political is personal. In J. Laird & R.-J. Green (Eds.), *Lesbians and gays in couples and families (pp. 69 -86).* San Francisco: Jossey-Bass.

Hassin, D. S., Goodwin, R. D., Stinson, F. S., & **Grant, B. F.** (2005). Epidemiology of major depressive disorders: Results from the national epidemiologic survey on alcoholism and related conditions. *Archives of General Psychiatry, 62*(1), 1097–1106.

Hastings, P. D., McShane, K. E., Parker, R., & **Ladha, F.** (2007). Ready to make nice: Parental socialization of young sons' and daughters' prosocial behaviors with peers. *Journal of Genetic Psychology, 168*(2), 177–299.

Hatfield, E., & **Rapson, R.** (2006). Passionate love, sexual desire and mate selection: Cross cultural and historical perspectives. In P. Noller and J. Feeney (Eds.), *Close relationships: Functions, forms, and processes* (pp. 227 -243). Hove, England: Psychology Press/Taylor Francis.

Hawkins, J. D., & **Fitzgibbon, J. J.** (1993). Risk factors and risk behaviors in the prevention of adolescent substance abuse. *Adolescent Medicine: State of the Art Reviews, 4*, 249–262.

Heath, D. B. (1982). Sociocultural variants in alcoholism. In E. M. Pattison & E. Kaufman (Eds.), *Encyclopedic handbook of alcoholism* (pp. 426–440). New York: Gardner Press.

Heilbrun, C. G. (1979). *Reinventing womanhood.* New York: Norton.

Heilbrun, C. G. (1988). *Writing a woman's life.* New York: Norton.

Heilbrun, C. G. (1997). *The last gift of time: Life beyond sixty.* New York: Dial Press.

Heiss, J. (1988). Women's values regarding marriage and the family. In H. P. McAdoo (Ed.), *Black Families* (2nd ed., pp. 201–214). Newbury Park, CA: Sage.

Henderson, L. (2009). *Religious coping and subjective well-being: African Americans' experiences of surviving Hurricane Katrina.* Unpublished doctoral dissertation. Boston: Massachusetts School of Professional Psychology.

Hennig, M., & **Jardim, A.** (1977). *The managerial woman.* Garden City: Anchor/Doubleday.

Herdt, G., & **Beeler, J.** (1998). Older gay men and lesbians in families. In C. J. Patterson & A. R. D'Augelli (Eds.), *Lesbian, gay, and bisexual identities in families: Psychological perspectives* (pp. 177–196). New York: Oxford University Press.

Herman-Giddens, M. E., Slora, E. J., & **Wasserman, R. C.,** (1997). Secondary sexual characteristics and menses in young girls seen in office practice: A study from the pediatric research in office settings network. *Pediatrics, 99*, 505–512.

Heron, M. (2007, November). Deaths: Leading causes for 2004, (5), pp. 1–96.

Heron, M. (2007). *Deaths: Leading causes for 2004. National vital statistics report, 56* (5). Retrieved (6/16/10) from www.cdc.gov/nchs/data/nvsr/nvsr56/nvsr56_05.pdf

Herrick, C., & **Herrick, C.** (2007). *100 answers and questions about alcoholism.* Indianapolis: Jones & Barrett Publishers.

Hertlein, K., Weeks, G., & **Gambescia, N.** (Eds.). (2008). *Systemic sex therapy.* New York, : Routledge.

Hess, B. B., & **Waring, J. M.** (1984). Changing patterns of aging and family bonds in later life. *The Family Coordinator, 27*(4), 303–314.

Hetherington, E. M. (1993). An overview of the Virginia Longitudinal Study of Divorce and Remarriage with a focus on early adolescence. *Journal of Family Psychology, 7*, 39–56.

Hetherington, E. M. (Ed.). (1999). *Coping with divorce, single-parenting and remarriage: A risk and resiliency perspective.* Hillsdale, NJ: Lawrence Erlbaum.

Hetherington, E. M. (2002). *For better or for worse: Divorce reconsidered.* New York: W. W. Norton.

Hetherington, E. M. (2005). The adjustment of children in divorced and remarried families. In V. L. Bengston, A. C. Acock, K. R. Allen, P. Dilworth-Anderson, & D.

M. Klein (Eds.). *Sourcebook of family theory and research* (pp. 137–139). Thousand Oaks, CA: Sage.

Hetherington, E. M. (2006). The influence of conflict, marital problem solving and parenting on children's adjustment in nondivorced, divorced and remarried families. In A. Clarke-Stewart & J. Dunn (Eds.), *Families count: Effects on children and adolescent development* (pp. 203–237). New York: Cambridge University Press.

Hewlett, S. A. (2002). *Creating a life: Professional women and the quest for children.* New York: Talk Miramax Books.

Heyn, D. (1997). *Marriage shock: The transformation of women into wives.* New York: Villard.

Higginbotham, E., & Weber, L. (1995). Moving up with kin and community: Upward social mobility for Black and White women. In M. L. Anderson & P. H. Collins (Eds.), *Race, class & gender: An anthology* (2nd ed., pp. 134–147). Belmont, CA: Wadsworth.

Hill R., & Rodgers R. (1964). The developmental approach. In H. Christensen (Ed.), *Handbook of marriage and family* (pp. 171–211). Chicago: Rand McNally.

Hill, R. B. (1999). *The strengths of Black families: Twenty-five years later.* Lanham, MD: University Press of America.

Hillman, J. (2008). Sexual issues and aging within the context of work with older patients. *Professional Psychology: Research and Practice, 39*(3), 290–297.

Hilton, J. M., Kopera-Frye, K. (2007). Differences in resources provided by grandparents in single and married parent families. *Journal of Divorce & Remarriage, 47*(1–2), 33–54.

Hilton, Z. (1992). Battered women's concerns about their children witnessing wife assault. *Journal of Interpersonal Violence, 7*(1), 77–86.

Hines, P., (2008). Climbing up the rough side of the mountain. In M. McGoldrick & K. V. Hardy (Eds.), *Revisioning family therapy: Race, culture and gender in clinical practice* (2nd ed., pp. 367–377). New York: Guilford Press.

Hines, P., & Boyd-Franklin, N. (2005). African American families. In M. McGoldrick, J. Giordano, & N. Garcia Preto (Eds.), *Ethnicity and family therapy* (3rd ed., pp. 87–100). New York: Guilford Press.

Hines, P., Richman, D., Hays, H., & Maxim, K. (1989). Multi-impact family therapy: An approach to working with multi-problem families. *Journal of Psychotherapy and the Family, 6,* 161–175.

Hines, P., & Sutton, C. (1998). *SANKOFA: A violence prevention curriculum.* Piscataway: University of Medicine & Dentistry of New Jersey.

Hirsch, J. (2003). *A courtship after marriage: Sexuality and love in Mexican transnational families.* Los Angeles: University of California Press.

Hitti, M. (2010). New record for U. S. life expectancy. WebMD Health News. Retrieved April 9, 2010, from www.webmd.com/healthy-aging/news/20060419/record-us-life-expectancy

Hochschild, A. (1997). *Time binds: When work becomes home and home becomes work.* New York: Metropolitan Books.

Hochschild, A. (2003). *The second shift: Working parents and the revolution at home.* New York: Viking.

Hodge, D. R. (2004). *Spiritual assessment: Handbook for helping professionals.* North American Association of Christian Social Workers.

Hoffmann, J. P. (2002). The community context of family structure and adolescent drug use. *Journal of Marriage and Family, 64,* 314–330.

Hoffman, L. W. (1972). Early childhood experiences and women's achievement motives. *Journal of Social Issues 28*(2), 261–278.

Hoffman, L. W. (1989). Effects of maternal employment in the two-parent family. *American Psychologist, 44,* 283–292.

Holland, B. (1992). *One's company.* New York: Ballantine.

Holloway, A. 2006. The bipolar Bear family: when a parent has bipolar disorder. Bloomington, Indiana: AuthorHouse.

Hook J. L., & Chalasani, S. (2008) Gendered expectations? Reconsidering single fathers' child-care time. *Journal of Marriage and Family 70*(4), 978–990.

hooks, b. (1999). *Yearning: Race, gender, and cultural politics.* Boston: South End Press.

Hudson, J. I., Hiripi, E., Pope, H. G., Kessler, R. C. (2007). The prevalence and correlates of eating disorders in the national comorbidity survey replication. *Biological Psychiatry, 61*(3) 348–358.

Hughes, E. M., & O'Rand, A. M. (2004). The lives and times of the Baby Boomers. In Harley, R., Haaga, J. (2005). *The American people census 2000.* New York: Russell Sage Foundation.

Hughes, J. M., Bigler, R. S., & Levy, S. R. (2007). Consequences of learning about historical racism among European American and African American children. *Child development, 78*(6), 1698–1705.

Human Rights Watch. (2009). Impairing Education. Retrieved (4/14/10) from http://www.hrw.org/en/reports/2009/08/11/impairing-education-0.

Hunter, J., & *Mallon, G. P.* (2000). Lesbian, gay, and bisexual adolescent development. In B. Green and G. L. Croom (Eds.), *Education, research, and practice in lesbian, gay, bisexual, and transgendered psychology—A research manual. Psychological perspectives on lesbian and gay issues* (Vol. 5, pp. 226–243). Thousands Oaks; CA: Sage Publication.

Hunter, S. (2005). *Midlife and older LGBT adults: Knowledge and affirmative practice for the social services.* New York: Routledge.

Hunter, S., Sundel, S. S., Sundel, Martin (2002). *Women at midlife: Life experience and implications for the helping professions.* Washington: National Association of Social Workers.

Hussong, A. M., Bauer, D. J., Huang, W., Chassin, L., Sher, K. J., & *Zucker, R. A.* (2008). Characterizing the life stressors of children of alcoholic parents. *Journal of Family Psychology, 22,* 819–832.

Imber-Black, E. (1986a). Odysseys of a learner. In D. Efron (Ed.), *Journeys: Expansion of the strategic-systemic therapies (_ -).* New York: Brunner/Mazel.

Imber-Black, E. (1986b). Towards a resource model in systemic family therapy. In M. Karpel (Ed.), *Family resources* (pp. 148–174). New York: Guilford Press.

Imber-Black, E. (2003). September 11th: Rituals of healing and transformation. In E. Imber-Black, J. Roberts, & R. Whiting (Eds.), *Rituals in families and family therapy* (2nd ed., pp. 333–344). New York: W. W. Norton.

Imber-Black, E. (2004). Rituals and the healing process. In F. Walsh & M. McGoldrick (Eds.), *Living beyond loss: Death in the family* (pp. 340–357). New York: W. W. Norton.

Imber-Black, E., & *Roberts, J.* (1998). *Rituals for our times: Celebrating, healing and changing our lives and our relationships.* New York: Jason Aronson.

Imber-Black, E., Roberts, J. & *Whiting, R. A.* (2003). *Rituals in families and family therapy.* New York: Norton.

Imber-Coppersmith, E. (1983). From hyperactive to normal but naughty: A multisystem partnership in delabel-ing. *International Journal of Family Psychiatry, 3*(2), 131–144.

Imber-Coppersmith, E. (1985). We've got a secret: A non-marital marital therapy. In A. Gurman (Ed.), *Casebook of marital therapy* (pp. 369–386). New York: Guilford Press.

Institute for Health & Aging, University of California, San Francisco. (1996). *Chronic care in America: A 21st century challenge.* Princeton, NJ: Robert Wood Johnson Foundation.

Institute for Women's Policy Research (2008, September). *The gender wage gap: 2008, # C350.* Retrieved (4/14/10) from www.iwpr.org/pdf/C350.pdf

Israel, B. (1996, January). Happiness and the single woman: What's good and what's not about being unattached in America. *Mirabella,* 68–73.

Israel, G., (2004). Supporting transgender and sex reassignment issues: Couple and family dynamics. In J. J. Bigner & J. L. Wetchler (Eds.), *Relationship therapy with same-sex couples* (pp. 53–64). New York: Haworth Press.

Jayson, S. (2007). Free as a bird and loving it: Being single has its benefits. *USA Today.com.*

Joint Commission on Accreditation of Healthcare Organizations. (2008). Retrieved (6/16/10) from www.jointcommission.org

Johnson, A. G. (1997). *The gender knot.* Philadelphia: Temple University Press.

Johnson, C. L. (1982). Sibling solidarity: Its origin and functioning in Italian-American families. *Journal of Marriage and the Family, 44,* 155–67.

Johnson, E. O., & *Pickens, R. W.* (2001). Familial transmission of alcoholism among nonalcoholics and mild, severe, and dyssocial subtypes of alcoholism. *Alcoholism: Clinical and Experimental Research, 25,* 661–666.

Johnson, M. K., Foley, K. L., & *Elder, G. H.* (2004). Women's community service, 1940–1960: Insights from a cohort of gifted American women. *Sociological Quarterly, 45*(1), pp. 45–66.

Johnson, R. W., & *Favreault, M. M.* (2004) Economic status in later life among women who raised children outside of marriage. *Journal of Gerontology: Series B: Psychological Sciences and Social Sciences, 59B,* 6, S315–S323.

Johnson, T. W. (1992). Predicting parental response to a son or daughter's homosexuality (Doctoral dissertation, Rutgers University, 1992). *Dissertation Abstracts*

International, 54 (9-B) 4901. New Jersey: Rutgers University Press.

Johnson, T. W., & **Colucci, P.** (2005). Lesbians, gay men, and the family life cycle. In B. Carter and M. McGoldrick (Eds.), *The expanded family life cycle* (3rd ed., pp.346–361). Boston: Allyn & Bacon.

Johnson, T. W., & **Keren, M. S.** (1996). Creating and maintaining boundaries in male couples. In J. Laird & R. J. Green (Eds.), *Lesbians and gays in couples and families: A handbook for therapists* (pp. 231–250). San Francisco: Jossey-Bass.

Johnson, W. (2007). Working with marginalized and minority men. In M. Flood, J. Gardiner, B. Pease, & K. Pringle (Eds.), *International encyclopedia of men and masculinities* (Vol. 1). London: Routledge.

Johnston, L. D., O'Malley, P. M., & **Bachman, J. G.** (2001). *Monitoring the Future: National Survey Results on Drug Use, 1975–2000. Volume 1: Secondary School Students.* (NIH Pub. No. 014924). Bethesda, MD: National Institute on Drug Abuse.

Jones, D. J., Zalot, A. A, Foster, S. E., Sterrett, E., & **Chester, C.** (2007). A review of childrearing in African American single mother families: The relevance of a coparenting framework. *Journal of Child and Family Studies, 16*(5), 671–683.

Jones, J. V. (2006, March 26). Marriage is for White people. *Washington Post,* p. B 1.

Jordan, J. V. *(Ed.).* (1997). *Women's growth in diversity: More writings from the Stone Center.* New York: Guilford Press.

Jordan, J. V., Kaplan, A. G., Miller, J. B., Stiver, I. P., & **Surrey, J. L.,** Eds. (1991). *Women's growth in connection.* New York: Guilford.

Jordan, J. V., Kraus, D. R., & **Ware, E. S.** (1993). Observations on loss and family development. *Family Process, 32,* 425–440.

Jordan, J. V., Walker, M., & **Hartling, L. M.** (Eds.). (2004). *The complexity of connection: Writings from the Stone Center's Jean Baker Miller Training Institute.* New York: Guilford.

Josephson, G., & **Whiffen, V. E.** (2007). An integrated model of depressive symptoms in gay men. *American Journal of Men's Health, 1,* 60–72.

Kagan, J., & **Moss, H.** (1962). *Birth to maturity.* New York: Wiley.

Kahn, M. D., & **Lewis, K. G.** (Eds.). (1988). *Siblings in therapy. Life span and clinical issues.* New York: Norton.

Kaiser, M. M., & **Hays, B. J.** (2005). Health-risk behaviors in a sample of first-time pregnant adolescents. *Public Health Nursing. 22,* 483–493.

Kalmus, D., & **Straus, M. A.** (1990). Wife's marital dependency and wife abuse. In M. A. Straus & R. J. Gelles (Eds.), *Physical violence in American families: Risk factors and adaptations to violence in 8,145 families* (pp. 369–382). New Brunswick, NJ: Transaction Books.

Kamenetz, A. (2007). *Generation debt: How our future was sold out for student loans, credit cards, bad jobs, no benefits, and tax cuts for rich geezers—and how to fight back.* New York: Riverhead.

Kamp-Dush, C. M. (2009). The association between family of origin structure and instability and mental health across the transition to adulthood. In H. E. Peters & C. M. Kamp-Dush (Eds.), *Marriage and family: Complexities and perspectives* (225–243). New York: Columbia University Press.

Kamya, H. (2005). African immigrant families. In M. McGoldrick, J. Giordano, & N. Garcia Preto (Eds.), *Ethnicity and family therapy* (3rd ed., pp. 101–116). New York: Guilford.

Kamya, H. (2009). Healing from refugee trauma: The significance of spiritual beliefs, faith community and faith-based services. In F. Walsh (Ed.) *Spiritual resources in family therapy* (2nd ed., pp. 286–300). New York: Guilford.

Kaplan, R., McLoyd, V. C., Toyokawa, T. (2008). Work demands, work-family conflict, and child adjustment in African American families: The mediating role of family routines. *Journal of Family Issues, 29*(10), 1247–1267.

Karenga, M. (1988). *The African American holiday of Kwanzaa: A celebration of family, community and culture.* Los Angeles: University of Sankore Press.

Kastenbaum, R. J. (1998). Death, society and human experience (6th ed.). Boston: Allyn & Bacon.

Katz, E. (2007). A family therapy perspective on mediation. *Family Process, 46,* 93–107.

Keel, P. K., Dorer, J., Eddy, K.T., & **Franko, D.** (2003). Predictors of mortality in eating disorders. *Archives of General Psychiatry, 60*(2) 179–183.

Kehoe, M. (1989). *Lesbians over sixty speak for themselves.* New York: Haworth Press.

Kelcourse, F. B. (2004). *Human development and faith: Life-cycle stages of body, mind, and soul.* St. Louis: Chalice Press.

Kelley, M. L., and *Fitzsimons, V. M.* (2000). *Understanding cultural diversity*. Sudbury, MA: Jones and Bartlett.

Kelly, J. (2007). Children's living arrangements following separation and divorce: Insights from empirical and clinical research. *Family Process, 46*, 35–52.

Kelly, J. B. (2005). Developing beneficial parenting plan models for children following separation and divorce. *Journal of American Academy of Matrimonial Lawyers, 19*(2), 101–118.

Kerr, B. (1994). *Smart girls: A new psychology of girls, women and giftedness* (Rev. ed.). Scottsdale, AZ: Gifted Psychology Press.

Kerr, M. & Bowen, M. (1988). *Family Evaluation*. New York: W. W. Norton.

Khazan, I., *Mchale, P.*, & *Decourcey W.* (2008). Violated wishes about division of childcare labor predict coparenting process during stressful and non stressful family evaluation. *Infant Mental Health Journal, 29*, 343–361.

Kilmartin, C. (1994). *The masculine self*. New York: Macmillan.

Kim, Bok-Lim, C. & Ryu, E. (2005). Korean families. In M. McGoldrick, J. Giordano, & N. Garcia Preto (Eds.), *Ethnicity and family therapy* (3rd ed., pp. 349–362). New York: Guilford Press.

Kimmel, D. C., & *Sang, B. E.* (1995). Lesbians and gay men in midlife. In A. R. D'Augelli & C. J. Patterson (Eds.), *Lesbian, gay, and bisexual identities over the lifespan: Psychological perspectives* (pp. 190–214). New York: Oxford University Press.

Kimmel, M. (1996). *Manhood in America: A cultural history*. New York: Free Press.

Kimmel, M. S. (2000). *The gendered society*. New York: Oxford Press.

Kimmel, M. S. (2005). *Manhood in America: A cultural history* (2nd ed.). New York: Free Press.

Kimmel, M. S. (2008). *The gendered society* (3rd ed.). New York: Oxford University Press.

Kimmel, M. S. (2009). *Guyland: The perilous world where boys become men*. New York: Harper/Collins.

Kimmel, M. S., & *Messner, M. A.* (2008). *Men's lives* (8th ed.). Needham Heights: MA: Allyn & Bacon.

King, D. A., & *Wynne, L. C.* (2004). The emergence of "family integrity" in later life. *Family Process, 43*(1), 7–21.

Kinsella, K., & *He, W.* (2009). *An aging world: 2008. International Population reports*. U.S. Census Bureau. Washington, DC: US Government Printing Office. Retrieved (6/16/10) from www.census.gov/prod/2009pubs/p95-09-1.pdf

Kinsey Institute for Research in Sex, Gender, and Reproduction (2008). *Frequently asked sexuality questions to The Kinsey Institute*. Retrieved September 15, 2008, from www.kinseyinstitute.org/resources/FAQ.html#Age

Kitson, G. (1992). Portrait of divorce: Adjustment to marital breakdown. New York: The Guilford Press.

Kivel, P. (2002, February 10). Affirmative action for White men? *Motion Magazine*, Retrieved February 27, 2010 from www.inmotionmagazine.com/pkivel4.html

Kivel, P. (2010). The act-like-a-man box. In M. S. Kimmel & M. A. Messner (Eds.), *Men's lives* (pp. 83–85). Boston: Allyn & Bacon.

Kliman, J. (1998). Social class as a relationship: Implications for family therapy. In. M. McGoldrick (Ed.). *Re-visioning family therapy: Race, culture, and gender in clinical practice* (pp. 50–61). New York: Guilford Press.

Kliman, J. (2005). Many differences, many voices. In M. P. Mirkin, K. L. Suyemoto, & B. F. Okun (Eds.), *Psychotherapy with women: Exploring diverse contexts and identities* (pp. 42–63). New York: Guilford Press.

Kliman, J. (2010). Intersections of social privilege and marginalization: A visual teaching tool. *Theory, Expanding Our Social Justice Practices: Advances in Theory and Practice*. [special issue.] *AFTA Monograph Series: A Publication of the American Family Therapy Academy (*Winter, 2010), 39–48.

Kliman, J., & *Madsen, W.* (2005) Social class and the family life cycle. In B. Carter & M. McGoldrick (Eds.), *The expanded family life cycle: Individual, family, and social perspectives* (3rd ed., pp. 88–123). Boston: Allyn & Bacon.

Knepper, P. (2008). Rethinking the racialisation of crime: The significance of African American "firsts." *Ethnic and Racial Studies, 31*(3), 503–523.

Kochanska, G., & *Aksan, N.* (2007). Conscience in childhood: Past, present, and future. In G. W. Ladd (Ed.), *Appraising the human developmental sciences: Essays in honor of Merrill-Palmer quarterly* (pp. 238–249). Detroit: Wayne State University Press.

Koestner, R., Franz, C., & *Weinberger, J.* (1990). The family origins of empathic concern: A 26-year longitudinal study. *Journal of Personality and Social Psychology, 58*(4), 709–717.

Kolata, G. (2007, January 3). A surprising secret to a long life: Stay in school. *New York Times,* pp. 1, 29.

Korin, E., McGoldrick, M., & *Watson, M.* (1996). Individual and family life cycle. In M. Mengel & W. L. Holleman (Eds.), *Principles of clinical practice: Vol. 1,* Patient, doctor and society, (pp. 21–46). New York: Plenum.

Korin, E. C., & *Petry, S. S.* (2005). Brazilian families. In M. McGoldrick, J. Giordano, & N. Garcia Preto (Eds.), *Ethnicity and family therapy* (3rd ed., pp. 166–177). New York: Guilford Press.

Kposowa, A. (2000). Marital status and suicide in the national longitudinal study. *Journal of Epidemiology and Community Health, 54,* 254–261.

Kreider, R. (2007) *Living arrangements of children: 2004. Current Population Reports.* Washington DC: U.S. Census Bureau.

Krestan, J., & *Bepko, C.* (1980). The problem of fusion in the lesbian relationship. *Family Process, 19*(3), 277–289.

Kruger, D. J. & *Nesse, R. M.* (2006). An evolutionary life-history framework for understanding sex differences in human mortality rates. *Human Nature, 17,* 74–97.

Kunjufu, J. (1995). *Countering the conspiracy to destroy Black boys* (Vol. 4). Chicago: African American Images.

Kunjufu, J. (2005). *Keeping Black boys out of special education.* Chicago: African American Images.

Kupers, T. (1993). *Revisioning men's lives: Gender, intimacy, and power.* New York: Guilford Press.

Kus, R. J. (1989). Alcoholism and non acceptance of gay self: The critical link. *Journal of Homosexuality, 15,* 25–41.

Kuvalanka, K. A., McClintock-Comeaux, M., & *Leslie, L. A.* (2004). Children with lesbian, gay, bisexual, and transgender parents: Current research, legislation, and resources available for family professionals. In P. Amato & N. Gonzalez (Eds.). *Vision 2004: What is the Future of Marriage.* 3, 53–59. Minneapolis, MN: National Council on Family Relations.

Laakso J. (2004). Key determinants of mothers' decisions to allow visits with non-custodial fathers. *Fathering, 2*(2), 131–145.

Laird, J. (1993). Lesbian and gay families. In F. Walsh (Ed.), *Normal family processes* (4th ed., pp. 282–328). New York: Guilford Press.

Laird, J. (1996). Invisible ties: Lesbians and their families of origin. In J. Laird & R. J. Green (Eds.), *Lesbians and gays in couples and families: A handbook for therapists* (pp. 89–122). New York: Jossey-Bass.

Laird, J., & *Green, R. J.* (1996). *Lesbians and gays in couples and families.* New York: Jossey-Bass.

Lamb, M. E., & *Sutton-Smith, B.* (1982). *Sibling relationships: Their nature and significance across the lifespan.* Hillsdale, NJ: Erbaum.

Lamb, M., Sternberg, K., & *Thompson, R.* (1997). The effects of divorce and custody arrangements on children's behavior, development, and adjustment. *Family and Conciliation Courts Review, 35,* 393–404.

Lamb, S. (2006). *Sex, therapy, and kids: Addressing their concerns through talk and play.* New York: W. W. Norton & Company.

Lane, S. D., Keefe, R. H., Rubinstein, R. A., Levandowski, B. A., Freedman, M., Rosenthal, A. Cibula, D. A., & *Czerwinski, M.* (2004). Marriage promotion and missing men: African American women in a demographic double bind?. *Medical Anthropology Quarterly, New Series, 18*(4), 405–428.

Lareau, A. (2010). Briefing paper: Unequal childhoods. In B. J. Risman (Ed.), *Families as they really are* (pp. 295–298). New York: W. W. Norton.

La Sala, M. (2010). *Coming out, coming home.* New York: Columbia University Press.

Laszloffy, T. A. (2000). The systemic model of family development. *Family Relations, 51*(3), 206–215.

Lau, A. S., Jernewall, N. M., Zane, N., & *Myers, H. F.* (2002). Correlates of suicidal behaviors among Asian-American outpatient youths. *Cultural Diversity and Ethnic Minority Psychology, 8,* 199–213.

Laumann, E., & *Michael, R.* (Eds.). (2001). *Sex, love and health in America: Private choices and public policies.* Chicago: University of Chicago Press.

Laumann, E., Michael, R., & *Gagnon, J.* (1994) *The social organization of sexuality: Sexual practices in the United States.* Chicago: University of Chicago Press.

Laumann, E., Paik, A., Glasser, D., Kang, J. H., Wang, T., & *Levinson, B. et al.* (2006). A cross-national study of subjective sexual well-being among older women and men: Findings from the global study of sexual attitudes and behaviors. *Archives of Sexual Behavior, 35*(2), 145–161.

Lawrence-Lightfoot, S. (2009). *The third chapter: Passion, risk, and adventure in the 25 years past fifty.* New York: Farrar, Straus, & Giroux.

Lazar, K. (2008, November 13). Concern over safety soaring in Hub area: Study finds link between health, fear of violence. *The Boston Globe.* Retrieved (6/16/10) from www.boston.com/news/local/massachusetts/articles/20 08/11/13/concern_over_safety_soaring_in_hub_area/?p age=full

Le, H., Ceballo, R., Chao, R., Hill, N. E., Murry, V. M., & *Pinderhughes, E. E.* (2008). Excavating culture: Disentangling ethnic differences from contextual influences in parenting. *Applied Developmental Science, 12*(4), 163–175.

LeBlanc, A. (2004). *Random family: Love, drugs, trouble, and coming of age in the Bronx.* New York: Scribner.

Leder, J. M. (1991). *Brothers and sisters: How they stage our lives.* New York: Ballantine.

Lee, E., & *Mock, M.* (2007). Asian families: An overview. In M. McGoldrick, J. Giordano, & N. Garcia Preto (Eds.), *Ethnicity and family therapy* (3rd ed., pp. 469–489). New York: Guilford Press.

Lee, M. Y., & *Mjelde-Mossey, L.* (2004). Cultural dissonance among generations: A solution-focused approach among elders and their families. *Journal of Marital & Family Therapy, 30*(4), 497–513.

Lefley, H. (2009). *Family psychoeducation for serious mental illness.* New York: Oxford.

Leiblum, S. (1990). Sexuality and the midlife woman. *Psychology of Women Quarterly, 14,* 495–508.

Leiblum, S. (2003). *Getting the sex you want: A woman's guide to becoming proud, passionate, and pleased in bed.* New York: ASJA Press.

Leiblum, S. (Ed.). (2006). *Principles and practice of sex therapy* (4th ed.). New York: Guilford Press.

Leiblum, S., & *Brezsnyak, M.* (2006). Sexual chemistry: Theoretical elaboration and clinical implications. *Sexual and Relationship Therapy, 21*(1), 55–69.

Lerner, H. (1993). *The dance of deception: Pretending and truth-telling in women's lives.* New York: HarperCollins.

Lerner, H. (1998). *The mother dance: What children do to your life.* New York: HarperCollins.

Lerner, M. (1995, November/December). The oppression of singles. *Tikkun, 10*(6), pp. 9–11.

Lev, A. (2004). *Transgender emergence: Therapeutic guidelines for working with gender-variant people and their families.* New York: Haworth Press.

Levant, R. F. (2005). The crisis of boyhood. In G. Good & G. Brooks (Eds.), *The new handbook of psychotherapy and counseling with men* (pp. 161–171). San Francisco: Wiley & Sons.

Levant, R. F., & *Kopecky, G.* (1995). *Masculinity reconstructed.* New York: Dutton.

Levant, R. F., & *Pollack, W. S.* (Eds.). (1995). *A new psychology of men.* New York: Basic Books.

Levine, K. A. (2009). Against all odds: Resilience in single mothers of children with disabilities. *Social Work in Health Care, 48*(4), 402–419.

Levine, J., Murphy, D., & *Wilson, S.* (1993.) *Getting men involved: Strategies for early childhood programs.* New York: Scholastic.

Levine, M. (2003). *The myth of laziness.* New York: Simon and Schuster.

Levinson, D. J. (1986a). *The seasons of a man's life.* New York: Ballantine Books.

Levinson, D. J. (1986b). A conception of adult development. *American Psychologist, 41,* 3–13.

Levinson, D. J. (1996). *The seasons of a woman's life.* New York: Knopf.

Levinson, D. J., Darrow, C., Klein, E., Levinson, M., & *McKee, B.* (1978). *The seasons of a man's life.* New York: Knopf.

Lewin, T. (1997a, September 5). Equal pay for equal work is no. 1 goal of women. *New York Times,* p. A20.

Lewin, T. (1997b, September 15). Women losing ground to men in widening income difference. *New York Times,* p. A1.

Lewin, T. (2006, July 9). The new gender divide: At colleges, women are leaving men in the dust. *New York Times.* Retrieved February 27, 2010, from www.nytimes.com/2006/07/09/education/09college.html

Lewis, M., Feiring, C., & *Kotsonis, M.* (1984). The social network of the young child. In M. Lewis (Ed.), *Beyond the dyad: The genesis of behavior series* (Vol. 4, pp, 129–160). New York: Plenum.

Lewis, M. I., & *Butler, R. N.* (1974). Life review therapy. *Geriatrics, 29,* 165–173.

Lewis, M. J., Edwards, A.C., & *Burton, M.* (2009). Coping with retirement: Well-being, health, and religion. *The Journal of Psychology, 143*(4), 427–448.

Lieberman, D., & Hatfield, E. (2006). Passionate love, sexual desire, and mate selection: Evolutionary and cross-cultural perspectives. In P. Noller and J. Feeney (Eds.), *Close relationships: Functions, forms, and processes* (pp. 227–244). New York: Psychology Press.

Liebow, E. (1967). *Talley's corner*. London: Little, Brown.

Lifton, R. J. (1975). Preface. In A. Mitscherlich & M. Mitscherlich (Eds.), *The inability to mourn* (pp. vii–xiv). New York: Grove.

Lifton, R. J. (1979). *The broken connection: On death and the continuity of life*. New York: Simon & Schuster.

Litwin, H. (1996). *The social networks of older people: A cross-national analysis*. Greenwood, CT: Praeger.

Liu, F. (2006). School culture and gender. In C. Skelton, B. Francis, & L. Smulyan (Eds.), *The Sage handbook of gender and education* (pp. 425–438). Thousand Oaks: CA: Sage.

Liu, H., & Umberson, D. J. (2008). The times they are a changin': Marital status and health differentials from 1972 to 2003. *Journal of Health and Social Behavior, 49*(3), 239–253.

Lopata, H. (1996). *Current widowhood: Myths and realities*. Thousand Oaks, CA: Sage.

Lopata, H. Z. (1979). *Women as widows: Support systems*. New York: Elsevier.

Lorde, A. (1984a). Our difference is our strength. In A. Lorde (Ed.), *Sister outsider* (pp. 64–71). Freedom, CA: The Crossing Press (as cited in Walters & Old Person, 2008).

Lorde, A. (1984b). *Sister outsider*. Freedom, CA: The Crossing Press.

Losoff, M. M. (1974). Fathers and autonomy in women. In R. B. Kundsin (Ed.), *Women and success: The anatomy of achievement* (pp. 103–109). New York: William Morrow.

Lott, B. (1994). *Women's lives* (2nd ed.). Pacific Grove, CA: Brooks/Cole.

Lowis, M. J., Edwards, A. C., & Burton, M. (2009). Coping with retirement: Well-being, health, and religion. *The Journal of Psychology, 143*(4), 427–448.

Lukes, C. A., & Land, H. (1990). Biculturality and homosexuality. *Social Work, 35,* 155–161.

Lum, D. (2003). *Social work practice and people of color*. Monterey, CA: Brooks Cole.

Lung, C. T., & Daro, D. (2006). *Current trends in child abuse reporting and fatalities: The results of the 2006 annual fifty state survey*. Chicago: Prevent Child Abuse America.

Luthra, R., Abramovitz, R., Greenberg, R., Schoor, A., Newcorn, J., Schmeidl, J., Levine, P., Nomura, Y. & Chemtob, C. (2009). Relationship between type of trauma exposure and posttraumatic stress disorder among urban children and adolescents. *Journal of Interpersonal Violence, 24*(11), 1919. Retrieved December 26, 2009, from ProQuest Social Science Journals. (Document ID: 1870505741).

MacCallum, F., & Golombok, S. (2004). Children raised in fatherless families from infancy: A follow-up of children of lesbian and single heterosexual mothers at early adolescence. *Journal of Psychology and Psychiatry, 45*(8), 1407–1419.

Maccoby, E. E. (1990). Gender and relationships: A developmental account. *American Psychologist, 45,* (4), 513–520.

Maccoby, E. E. (1999). *The two sexes: Growing up apart: Coming together (The family and public policy)*. Boston: Belknap Press.

Maccoby, E. E., & Mnookin, R. (1992). *Dividing the child: Social and legal dilemmas of custody*. Cambridge, MA: Harvard University Press.

Madsen, W. (2007). *Collaborative therapy with multistressed families* (2nd edition). New York: Guilford.

Mahony, R. (1995). *Kidding ourselves: Breadwinning, babies and bargaining power*. New York: Basic Books.

Malley-Morrison, K., & Hines, D. A. (2004). *Family violence in a cultural perspective*. Thousand Oaks, CA: Sage.

Mallon, G. P. (2004). *Gay men choosing parenthood*. New York: Columbia University Press.

Mallon, G.P. (2008a). Social work practice with lesbian, gay, bisexual, and transgender people within families. In G. Mallon (Ed.), *Social work practice with lesbian, gay, bisexual, and transgender people* (2nd ed., pp. 241–268).

Mallon, G. P. (2008b). Social work practice with LGBT parents. In G. Mallon (Ed.), *Social work practice with lesbian, gay, bisexual, and transgender people* (2nd ed., pp. 269–312). New York: Routledge.

Malpas, J. (2006). From otherness to alliance: Transgender couples in therapy. *Journal of GLBT family studies, 2*(3/4), 183–206.

Maltz, W., & Maltz, L. (2008). *The porn trap: Overcoming problems caused by pornography*. New York: Collins/HarperCollins.

Malveaux, J. (2005) Affirmative action for men? *Black issues in higher education,* May 5.

Mann, J. (1996). *The difference: Discovering the hidden ways we silence girls—Finding alternatives that can give them a voice.* New York: Warner Books.

Marcus-Newhall, A., Halpern, D. F., & *Tan, S. J.* (Eds.). (2008). *The changing realities of work and family.* New York: Wiley-Blackwell.

Margolin, L. (1992). Child abuse by mothers' boyfriends: Why the overrepresentation? *Child Abuse & Neglect 16*(4), 541–551.

Marsh D. T. & *Lefley H. P.* 1996 The family experience of mental illness: Evidence for resilience. Psychiatric Rehabilitation Journal 20(2) 3–12.

Marsh, D. T. & *Lefley, H. P.* (1996). The family experience of mental illness: Evidence for resilience. *Psychiatric Rehabilitation Journal, 20*(2), 3–12.

Marshak, L., Seligman, M., & *Prezant, F.* (Eds.). (1999). *Disability and the family life cycle: Recognizing and treating developmental challenges.* New York: Basic Books.

Marsiglia, F. F., Parsai, M., Kulis, S., & *Nieri, T.* (2005). God forbid! Substance use among religious and nonreligious youth. *American Journal of Orthopsychiatry, 75*(4), 585–598.

Martin, A. (1993). *The lesbian and gay parenting handbook.* New York: HarperCollins.

Martin, E., Taft, E., & *Resick, P. A.* (2007). A review of marital rape. *Aggression and Violent Behavior, 12*(3), 329–347.

Martin, R. M., & *Green, J. A.* (2005). The use of emotional explanations by mothers: Relation to preschoolers' gender and understanding of emotions. *Social Development, 14*(2), 229–249.

Martin, T. L., & *Doka, K. J.* (2000). *Men don't cry . . . women do: Transcending gender stereotypes of grief.* New York: Brunner/Mazel.

Masho, S. W., & *Anderson L.* (2009) Sexual assault in men: A population-based study of Virginia. *Violence and Victims, 24*(1), 98–110.

Mass General Hospital for Children. (n.d.). *Puberty.* Retrieved September 14, 2008, from www.mass-general.org/children/adolescenthealth/articles/aa_puberty.aspx

Mathias, B. (1992). *Between sisters: Secret rivals, intimate friends.* New York: Delacorte Press.

Mathias, B., & *French, M. A.* (1996). *Forty ways to raise a nonracist child.* New York: Harper.

Matthews, T. J., Menacker, F., & *MacDorman, M.* (2002). *Infant mortality statistics from the 2000 period: Linked birth/infant death data set. National Vital Statistics Report, 50(12).* Centers for Disease Control. Retrieved (4/14/10) from www.cdc.gov/nchs/data/nvsr/nvsr57/nvsr57_02.pdf

Mazama, A. (Ed.). (2003). *The Afrocentric paradigm.* Trenton, NJ: Africa World Press.

Mbiti, J. S. (1970). *African religions and philosophies.* New York: Anchor.

McAdoo, H. P. (2007). *Black families.* Thousand Oaks, CA.: Sage Publications.

McBride, J. (1996). *The color of water: A Black man's tribute to his White mother.* New York: Riverhead Books.

McCarthy, I. C. (1994). Abusing norms: Welfare families and a fifth province stance. In I. C. McCarthy (Ed.), *Poverty and social exclusion, a special issue of human systems, 5*(3–4), 229–239.

McConnell, K. M., Pargament, K., Ellison, C. G., & *Flanell, K. J.* (2006). Examining the links between spiritual struggles and symptoms of psychopathology in a national sample. *Journal of Clinical Psychology, 62*(12), 1469–1484.

McCubbin, H., & *Patterson, J.* (1983). The family stress process: The double ABCX model of adjustment and adaptation. In H. McCubbin, M. Sussman, & J. Patterson (Eds.), *Social stress and the family: Advances and developments in family stress theory and research* (pp. 7–37). New York: Haworth Press.

McFarlane, W. (2002). *Multifamily groups in the treatment of severe psychiatric disorders.* New York: Guilford Press.

McGhee, J. L. (1985). The effects of siblings on the life satisfaction of the rural elderly. *Journal of Marriage and the Family, 41,* 703–714.

McGill, D., & *Pearce, J. K.* (2005). American families with English ancestors from the colonial era: Anglo Americans. In M. McGoldrick, J. Giordano, & N. Garcia Preto (Eds.), *Ethnicity and family therapy* (pp. 520–533). New York: Guilford Press.

McGoldrick, M. (1977). *Some data on death and cancer in schizophrenic families.* Presentation at Georgetown Presymposium, Washington, DC.

McGoldrick, M. (1987). On reaching mid-career without a wife. *The Family Therapy Networker, 11*(3), 32–39.

McGoldrick, M. (1989a) Irish women. In M. McGoldrick, C. Anderson, & F. Walsh (Eds.), *Women in families* (pp. 169–200). Norton: New York.

McGoldrick, M. (1989b). Sisters. In M. McGoldrick, C. Anderson, & F. Walsh (Eds.), *Women in families* (pp. 244–266). Norton: New York.

McGoldrick, M. (1996). *Living beyond loss* [Videotape]. New York: Newbridge Communications, available through www.psychotherapy.net

McGoldrick, M. (1998). Belonging and liberation: Finding a place called "home." In M. McGoldrick (Ed.), *Re-visioning family therapy: Race, culture and gender in clinical practice* (pp. 215–228). New York: Guilford Press.

McGoldrick, M. (2005). Irish families. In M. McGoldrick, J. Giordano, & Garcia Preto (Eds.), *Ethnicity and family therapy* (3rd ed., pp. 544–566). New York: Guilford Press.

McGoldrick, M. (2011). The Genogram Journey. New York: Norton. (1st ed: *You can go home again: Reconnecting with your family.* New York: Norton.)

McGoldrick, M., & Carter, B. (2001). Advances in coaching: Family therapy with one person. *Journal of Marital and Family Therapy, 27*(3), 281–300.

McGoldrick, M., Gerson, R., & Petry, S. (2008). *Genograms: Assessment and intervention.* (3rd ed.). New York: W. W. Norton.

McGoldrick, M., Giordano, J., & Garcia Preto, N. (2005). *Ethnicity and family therapy* (3rd ed.). New York: Guilford Press.

McGoldrick, M., & Hardy, K.V. (2008). *Re-visioning family therapy: Race, culture, and gender in clinical practice.* (2nd edition). New York: Guilford Press.

McGoldrick, M., Loonan, R., & Wohlsifer, D. (2006). Sexuality and culture. In S. Leiblum (Ed.), Principles and practice of sex therapy (4th ed., pp. 416-441). NY: Guilford Press.

McGoldrick, M. & Preto, N. G. (1984). Ethnic intermarriage: Implications for therapy. *Family Process, 23*(3), 347–363.

McGoldrick, M., Schlesinger, J. M., Hines. P. M., Lee, E., Chan, J., Almeida, R., Petkov, B. et al. (2004). Mourning in different cultures: English, Irish, African American, Chinese, Asian Indian, Jewish, Latino, and Brazilian. In F. Walsh & M. McGoldrick (Eds.), *Living beyond loss: Death in the family* (2nd ed., pp. 119–160). New York: Norton.

McGoldrick, M., & Walsh, F. (1983). A systemic view of family history and loss. In M. Aronson & D. Wolberg (Eds.), *Group and family therapy 1983* (pp. 252–272). New York: Brunner/Mazel.

McGuire, L.C., Anderson, L.A., Talley, R.C., & Crews, J. E. (2007). Supportive care needs of Americans: A major issue for women as both recipients and providers. Journal of Womens Health (Larchmont, NY). (July-August) *16*(6), 784–789.

McHale, S. M., & Crouter, C. A. (2005). Sibling relationships in childhood: Implications for life-course study. In V. L. Bengston, A. C. Acock, K. R. Allen, P. Dilworth-Anderson, & D. M. Klein (Eds.), *Sourcebook of family theory & research* (pp. 184–190). Thousand Oaks, CA: Sage Publications.

McIntosh, J. L. (1999). Death and dying across the life span. In T. L. Whitman, T. V. Merluzzi (Ed.), *Life-span perspectives on health and illness* (pp. 249–274), London: Psychology Press.

McIntosh, P. (1985). *On feeling like a fraud.* (Work in Progress Working Paper Series, 18). Wellesley, MA: The Stone Center.

McIntosh, P. (1988). *Working paper: White privilege and male privilege: A personal account of coming to see correspondences through work in women's studies.* Wellesley College Center for Research on Women, Wellesley, MA.

McIntosh, P. (1989). *On feeling like a fraud,* (Part 2). (Work in Progress Working Paper Series, 37). Wellesley, MA: The Stone Center.

McKay, V., & Caverly, S. (2004). The nature of family relationships between and within generations: Relations between grandparents, grandchildren, and siblings in later life. In J. Nussbaum & J. Coupland (Eds.), *Handbook of communication and aging research* (2nd ed., pp. 251–272). Mahwah, NJ: Lawrence Erlbaum Associates Publishers.

McKelvey, C., & Stevens, J. (1994). *Adoption crisis.* Golden, CO: Fulcrum.

McKinnon, J. (2003). The Black population in the United States: March 2002. *Current Population Reports, Series P20–541.* Washington, DC: U.S. Bureau of the Census.

McLanahan, S. S., & Sandefur, G. (1994). *Growing up with a single parent.* Cambridge, MA: Harvard University Press.

McLaughlin, C. (2008). Emotional well-being and its relationship to schools and classroom: A critical reflection. *British Journal of Guidance and Counselling, 36*(4), 355–366.

McLoyd, V., & Enchautegui-de-Jesūs, N. (2005). Work and African American family life. In V. McLoyd, N. Hill, & K. Dodge (Eds.), *African American family life. Ecological and cultural diversity* (pp. 135–161). New York: Guilford Press.

McManus, M. (2006, July 23). Life without children. *The Washington Times*. Retrieved (4/14/10) from www.washingtontimes.com/news/2006/jul/22/2006 0722-112056-7424r/

McNamara P. M., (2009) Review of "In search of belonging: Reflections by transracially adopted people." *Australian Social Work, 62*, 1, 121–123.

McQuaide, S. (1998). Women at midlife. *Social Work, 43*(1), 21–31.

McWhirter, D. P., & Mattison, A. M. (1984). *The male couple: How relationships develop*. Englewood Cliffs, NJ: Prentice-Hall.

Mead, M. (1972). *Blackberry winter*. New York: William Morrow.

Meeker, M. (2008). *Boys should be boys: 7 secrets to raising healthy sons*. Washington DC: Regnery Publishing.

Meinhold, J. (2006). The influence of life transition statuses on sibling intimacy and contact in early adulthood. (Doctoral dissertation, Oregon St. Univ., 2006). *Dissertation Abstracts International Section A: Humanities and Social Sciences, 67*(30), 1107.

Merrell, S. S. (1995). *The accidental bond: The power of sibling relationships*. New York: Times Books.

Merrill, D. M. (1996). Conflict and cooperation among adult siblings during transition to the role of filial caregiver. *Journal of Social and Personal Relationships, 13*(3), 339–413.

Merry, S. E. (2009). *Gender violence: A cultural perspective*. New York: Wiley-Blackwell.

Meth, R., & Pasick, R. (1990). *Men in therapy: The challenge of change*. New York: Guilford Press.

Meyers, M., Diamond, R., Kezur, D., Scharf, C., Weinshel, M., & Rait, D. (1995). An infertility primer for family therapists: Medical, social and psychological dimensions. *Family Process, 34*, 219–229.

Miedzian, M. (2002). *Boys will be boys: Breaking the link between masculinity and violence*. New York: Doubleday.

Miklowitz, D. (2004). The role of family systems in severe and recurrent psychiatric disorders: A developmental psychopathology view. *Development and Psychopathology, 16*, 667–688.

Miklowitz, D. (2008). *Bipolar disorder: A family focused treatment approach*. New York: Guilford Press.

Miller, J. B. (1976) *Toward a new psychology of women*. Boston: Beacon.

Miller, S., McDaniel, S., Rolland, J., & Feetham, S. (Eds.). (2006). *Individuals, families, and the new era of genetics: Biopsychosocial perspectives*. New York: W. W. Norton.

Mintz, S. (2010). American childhood as a social and cultural construct. In B. J. Risman (Ed.), *Families as they really are* (pp. 48–62). New York: W. W. Norton.

Minuchin, S., Montalvo, B., Guerney, B., Rosman, B., & Schumer, F. (1967). *Families of the slums: An exploration of their structure and treatment*. New York: Basic Books.

Minuchin, S., Rosman, B. L., & Baker, L. (1978). *Psychosomatic families: Anorexia nervosa in context*. Cambridge, MA: Harvard University Press.

Mitchell, S. (2002). *Can love last?* New York: W. W. Norton.

Mitchell, V. (1995). Two moms: Contribution of the planned lesbian family to the deconstruction of gendered parenting. *Journal of Feminist Family Therapy, 7*(4) 47–63.

Mitchell, V., & Helson, R. (1990). Women's prime of life: Is it the 50's? *Psychology of Women Quarterly, 14*, 451–470.

Mitrani, V. B., Muir, J. A., & Santisteban, D. A. (2004). Addressing Immigration-related separations in Hispanic families with a behavior-problem adolescent. *American Journal of Orthopsychiatry, 74*(3), 219–229.

Mock, M. (1998). Clinical reflections on refugee families: Transforming crises into opportunities. In M. McGoldrick & K. V. Hardy? (Eds?.), *Re-visioning family therapy: Race, culture, and gender in clinical practice* (pp. 347–359). New York: Guilford Press.

Mock, M. (2008). Visioning social justice: Narratives of diversity, social location and personal compassion. In M. McGoldrick & K. V. Hardy (Eds.), *Re-visioning family therapy: Race, culture and gender in clinical practice* (2nd ed., pp. 425–441). New York: Guilford Press.

Modell, J., & Elder, G. H. (2002). Children develop in history: So what's new? In W. Hartup & R. A. Weinberg (Eds.), *Child psychology in retrospect and prospect: In celebration of the 75th anniversary of the Institute of Child Development* (pp. 173–205). Mahwah, NJ, Lawrence Erlbaum Associates.

Money, J. (1986). *Venuses, penises: Sexology, sexosophy, and exigency theory.* New York: Prometheus Books.

Monteiro, M. B., de Franca, D. X., & Rodrigues, R. (2009). The development of intergroup bias in childhood: How social norms can shape children's racial behaviors. *International Journal of Psychology, 44*(1), 29–39.

Montgomery, M. J., Anderson, E. R., Hetherington, E. M., & Clingempeel, W. G. (1993). Patterns of courtship for remarriage: Implications for child development and parent-child relationships. *Journal of Marriage and the Family, 54,* 686–698.

Moore-Thomas, C., & Day-Vines, N. L. (2008). Culturally competent counseling for religious and spiritual African American adolescents. *Professional School Counseling, 11,* 159–165.

Moos, R. (Ed.). (1984). *Coping with physical illness: Vol. 2, New perspectives.* New York: Plenum Press.

Morales, E. S., (1989). Ethnic minority families and minority gays and lesbians. *Marriage and Family Review, 14,* 217–239.

Moscicki, E. K. (1995). Epidemiology of suicide. *International Psychogeriatrics, 7*(2), 137–148.

Mueller, M. M., & Elder, G. H., Jr. (2003). Family contingencies across the generations. Grandparent-grandchild relationships in holistic perspective. *Journal of Marriage and the Family, 65*(2), 404–417.

Mueller, M. M., Wilhelm, B., & Elder, G. H. (2002). Variations in grandparenting. *Research on aging, 24*(3), 360–388.

Mueller, P. S., & McGoldrick-Orfanidis, M. (1976). A method of co-therapy for schizophrenic families. *Family Process, 15,* 179–192.

Murray L. & Cooper, P. (1977). Effects of postnatal depression on infant development. Archives of Disease in Childhood Aug:77 (2) 99–101.

Murray, L., & Cooper, P. (1997). *Postpartum depression and child development.* New York: Guilford Press.

Murry, V. M., & Brody, G. H. (2002). Racial socialization processes in single-mother families. Linking maternal racial identity, parenting and racial socialization in rural, single-mother families with child self-worth and self-regulation. In H. P. McAdoo (Ed.), *Black children: Social, educational and parental environments* (2nd ed., pp. 97–115). Thousand Oaks, CA: Sage Publications.

Musil, C., & Standing, T. (2006). Grandmothers' diaries: a glimpse at daily lives. In B. Hayslip, Jr., & J. Hicks Patrick (Eds.), *Custodial grandparenting. Individual, cultural, and ethnic diversity* (pp. 89–104). New York: Springer Publishing Company.

Myerhoff, B. (1992). *Remembered lives: The work of ritual, storytelling, and growing older.* Ann Arbor: University of Michigan Press.

Myers, S. (2006). Religious homogamy and marital quality: Historical and generational patterns. *Journal of Marriage and the Family, 68*(2), 292–304.

Nadeau, J. W. (2001). Family construction of meaning. In R. Neimeyer (Ed.), *Meaning reconstruction and the experience of loss* (pp. 95–111). Washington, DC: American Psychological Association.

NASW (2008). *Code of ethics of the National Association of Social Workers.* Retrieved (6/16/10) from www.socialworkers.org/pubs/code/code.asp

National Center for Health Statistics. (2009). *Health, United States, 2008 with chart book.* Hyattsville, MD.: U.S. Government Printing Office.

National Center for Lesbian Rights. (2009). *Legal recognition of LGBT families.* Retrieved August 8, 2009, from www.nclrights.org/site/DocServer/Legal_Recognition_of_LGBT_Families.pdf?docID=2861 Nclrights.org

National Center for Health Statistics. (2009). *Health, United States, 2008.* Washington, DC: Government Printing Office.

National Coalition Against Elder Abuse (NCEA). (2005). *Elder abuse incidence and prevalence fact sheet, U.S. Administration on Aging.* Washington DC: Government Printing Office. Retrieved (4/14/10) from www.ncea.aoa.gov/ncearoot/Main_Site/pdf/publication/FinalStatistics050331.pdf

National Coalition of Anti-Violence Programs (NCAVP). (2008). *Lesbian, gay, bisexual and transgender domestic violence in the United States in 2007.* Retrieved (8/8/09) from www.avp.org/documents/2007NCAVPDVREPORT.pdf

National Coalition for the Homeless. (2006). *Education of homeless children and youth. Fact Sheet # 10.* Retrieved (4/14/10) from www.ucdenver.edu/academics/colleges/ArchitecturePlanning/discover/centers/CYE/Publications/Documents/education-homeless.pdf

National Council on Crime and Delinquency (2002). Our vulnerable teenagers. Retrieved April 26, 2010, from www.nccd-crc.org

National Gay and Lesbian Task Force. (2009a). *Relationship recognition for same-sex couples in the U.S.*

Retrieved August 7, 2009, from www.thetaskforce.org/ issues/marriage_and_partnership_recognition

National Gay and Lesbian Task Force. (2009b). *State laws prohibiting recognition of same-sex relationships.* Retrieved August 7, 2009, from www.thetaskforce.org/ downloads/reports/issue_maps/samesex_relationships_ 7_09.pdf

National Institute on Alcohol Abuse and Alcoholism (2002). *Alcohol alert no. 55: Alcohol and minorities: An update.* Retrieved September 2, 2009, from pubs. niaaa.nih.gov/publications/aa55.htm

National Institute of Alcohol Abuse and Alcoholism. (2005). *A family history of alcoholism: Are you at risk?* Retrieved September 2, 2009, from http://pubs.niaaa. nih.gov/publications/FamilyHistory/famhist.htm

National Institute of Mental Health. (2009a). *Suicide in the U.S.: Statistics and prevention.* Washington DC: Government Printing Office.

National Institute of Mental Health. (2009b). *The numbers count: Mental disorders in America.* Washington DC: Government Printing Office.

National Library of Medicine and National Institutes of Health (n.d.) *Medline Plus: Medical encyclopedia.* Retrieved (4/14/10) from www.nlm.nih.gov/medline-plus/ encyclopedia.htm

National Organization of Women (2009). *Violence against women in the United States: Statistics.* Retrieved (4/14/10) from www.now.org/issues/ violence/stats.html

National Vital Statistics. (2009). *American community survey reports, 57*(7).

Neblett, E. W., Jr., White, R. L., Ford, K. R., Philip, C. L., Nguyen, N., Hoa X., & Sellers, R. M. (2008). Patterns of racial socialization and psychological adjustment: Can parental communications about race reduce the impact of racial discrimination? *Journal of Research on Adolescence, 8*(3), 477–515.

Neugarten, B. (1968). The awareness of middle age. In B. Neugarten (Ed.), *Middle age and aging: A reader in social psychology* (pp. 93–98). Chicago: University of Chicago Press.

Neugarten, B. (1976). Adaptation and the life cycle. *The Counseling Psychologist, 6,* 16–20.

Neugarten, B. (1979). Time, age and the life cycle. *American Journal of Psychiatry, 136,* 887–894.

Neugarten, B. (Ed.). (1996). *The meanings of age: Selected papers of Bernice L. Neugarten.* Chicago: University of Chicago Press.

Neustifter, R. (2008). Common concerns faced by lesbian elders: An essential context for couple's therapy. *Journal of Feminist Family Therapy, 20*(3), 251–267.

Nguyen, T. D. (2005). *Domestic violence in Asian American communities.* Lanham, MD: Rowan & Littlefield.

Nicholas, G., Helms J. E., Jernigan, M. M., Sass, T., Skrzypek, A., & De Silva, A. (2008). A conceptual framework for understanding the strengths of Black youths. *Journal of Black Psychology, 34*(3), 261–280.

Nitsche, N., & Brueckner, H. (2009, August). *Opting out of the family? Social change in racial inequality in family formation patterns and marriage outcomes among highly educated women.* Paper presented at the American Sociological Association 104th Annual Meeting, San Francisco.

Noberini, M. R., Brady, E. M., & Mosatche, H. S. (in press). *Personality and adult sibling relationships: A preliminary study.*

Nobles, W. W. (2004). African philosophy: foundations for Black psychology. In R. Jones (Ed.), *Black psychology* (4th ed., pp. 18–32). New York: Harper & Row.

Norris, J. E., & Tindale, J. A. (1994). *Among generations: The cycle of adult relationships.* New York: W. H. Freeman & Company.

North American Council on Adoptable Children (2009). *Claiming the federal adoption tax credit for special needs adoptions.* Retrieved (4/14/10) from www.nacac. org/postadopt/taxcredit.html

Nuckolls, C. W. (1993). *Siblings in South Asia: Brothers and sisters in cultural context.* New York: Guilford Press.

Obama, B. (2004). *Dreams from my father: A story of race and inheritance.* New York: Three Rivers Press.

O'Connor, J. (1984). The resurrection of a magical reality: Treatment of functional migraine in a child. *Family Process, 23*(4), 501–509.

O'Connor, J., & Horwitz, A. N. (1984). The bogeyman cometh: A strategic approach for difficult adolescents. *Family Process, 23*(2), 237–249.

O'Farrell T., J. (1989). Marital and family therapy in alcoholism treatment. *Journal of Substance Abuse Treatment, 6*(1), 23–9.

Ogbu, J. U. (1990). Cultural mores, identity, and literacy. In J. W. Stigler, R. A. Shweder, & G. H. Herdt (Eds.), *Cultural psychology: Essays on comparative human development* (pp. 520–541). New York: Cambridge University Press.

Okun, B. F. (1996). *Understanding diverse families: What practitioners need to know.* New York: Guilford Press.

Okun, L. (1986). *Woman abuse: Facts replacing myths.* Albany: State University of New York Press.

O'Leary, P. J., & **Barber J.** (2008) Gender differences in silencing following childhood sexual abuse. *Journal of Child Sexual Abuse, 17*(2), 133–143.

Oliver, L. E. (1999). Effects of a child's death on the marital relationship. A review. *Omega, 39*(3), 197–227.

Olkin, R. (1999). *What psychotherapists should know about disability.* New York: Guilford Press.

Organista, K. (2007). *Solving Latino psychosocial and health problems: Theory, practice and populations.* New York: John Wiley and Sons.

Osherson, S. (1986). *Finding our fathers: How a man's life is shaped by his relationship with his father.* New York: Fawcett Columbine.

Osterweis, M., **Solomon, F.**, & **Green, M.** (Eds.). (1984). *Bereavement: Reactions, consequences, and care.* Washington, DC: National Academy Press.

Pachankis, J. (2009). The use of cognitive behavioral therapy to promote authenticity. *Pragmatic Case Studies in Psychotherapy, 5*(4) 28–38.

Padan, D. (1965). *Intergenerational mobility of women: A two-step process of status mobility in a context of a value conflict.* Tel Aviv, Israel: Publication of Tel Aviv University.

Palazzoli, M., **Boscolo, L.**, **Cecchin, G.**, & **Prata, G.** (1977). Family rituals: A powerful tool in family therapy. *Family Process, 16*(4), 445–454.

Papero, D. (1990). *Bowen family systems theory.* Boston: Allyn & Bacon.

Papp, P. (1984). The links between clinical and artistic creativity. *The Family Therapy Networker, 8*(5), 20–29.

Paradis, A., **Reinherz, H.**, **Giaconia, R.**, **Beardslee, W.**, **Ward, K.**, & **Fitzmaurice, G.** (2009). Long-term impact of family arguments and physical violence on adult functioning at age 30 years: Findings from the Simmons longitudinal study. *Journal of the American Academy of Child & Adolescent Psychiatry, 48*(3), 290–298.

Park, J. M. (2005). The roles of living arrangements and household resources in single mothers' employment. *Journal of Social Service Research, 31*(3), 46–67.

Parker, P. (1985). *Jonestown & other madness.* Ithaca, NY: Firebrand Books.

Parker, R. (2005, August 12). *A review of gay, lesbian, bisexual and transgender adolescent research.* Paper presented at Annual Meeting. American Sociological Association, Philadelphia, PA.

Parker-Pope, T. (April 20, 2009). What are friends for? A longer life. *New York Times,* Section D.

Parkes, C. M. (2001). *Bereavement: Studies of grief in adult life.* London, Routledge.

Parkes, C. M. (2009). *Love and loss: The roots of grief and its complications.* New York: Routledge.

Parkes, C. M., **Laungani, P.**, & **Young, B.** (1997). *Death and bereavement across cultures.* New York: Routledge.

Parkes, C. M., & **Weiss, R. S.** (1983) *Recovery from bereavement.* New York: Basic Books.

Parks, M. (2009). *Authentic happiness and religious coping for displaced African Americans three years after Hurricane Katrina.* Unpublished doctoral dissertation. Boston: Massachusetts School of Professional Psychology.

Parra-Cardona J. P., **Holtrop, K.**, **Córdova D. Jr.**, **Escobar-Chew, A. R.**, **Horsford, S.**, **Tams L. et al.**, (2009). Queremos aprender: Latino immigrants' call to integrate cultural adaptation with best practice knowledge in a parenting intervention. *Family Process, 48*(2), 211–231.

Parsons, T. (1951). *The social system.* Glencoe, Ill: Free Press.

Paschal, A. (2006). *Voices of African-American teen fathers: "I'm doing what I got to do."* New York: Haworth Press.

Pasick, R. (1992). *Awakening from the deep sleep: A powerful guide for courageous men.* New York: Harper Collins.

Pasley, K., & **Ihinger-Tallman, M.**, Eds. (1994). *Stepparenting: Issues in theory, research and practice.* Westport, CT: Praeger.

Patrick, L. (2002). Eating disorders: A review of the literature with emphasis on medical complications and clinical nutrition. *Alternative Medicine Review, 7*(3), 184–202.

Patterson, C. J. (1992). Children of lesbian and gay parents. *Child Development, 63,* 1025–1042.

Patterson, C. J. (1996). Lesbian mothers and their children: Findings from the Bay Area Families Study. In J. Laird & R. J. Green (Eds.), *Lesbians and gays in couples and families: A handbook for therapists,* (pp. 420–437). San Francisco: Jossey-Bass.

Paul, N., & **Paul, B.** (1989). *A marital puzzle.* New York: Norton.

Pear, R. (2008, March 23). Gap in life expectancy widens for the nation. *New York Times,* p. 19.

Penn, P. (1983). Coalitions and binding interactions in families with chronic illness. *Family Systems Medicine, 1*(2), 16–25.

Penner, A. M., Paret, M. (2008). Gender differences in mathematics achievement: Exploring the early grades and extremes. *Social Science Research. 37. 1. 239–263.*

Perel, E. (2006). *Mating in captivity: Unlocking erotic intelligence.* New York: Harper Collins.

Perry, B. (2009) Examining child maltreatment through a neurodevelopmental lens: Clinical applications of the neurosequential model of therapeutics. *Journal of Loss and Trauma, 14*(4), 240–255.

Perry, B. D. (2002). Childhood experience and the expression of genetic potential: What childhood neglect tells us about nature and nurture. *Brain & Mind, 3*(1), 79–100.

Petry, S. S. (2004). Bereavement customs of Brazil—Mourning in different cultures. In F. Walsh & M. McGoldrick (Eds.). *Living beyond loss: Death and the family* (2nd ed., pp. 119–160). New York: W. W. Norton.

Pew Forum on Religion & Public Life. (2008, February). *U.S. religious landscape survey: Religious affiliation diverse and dynamic.* Retreived (4/14/10) from religions.pewforum.org/pdf/report-religious-land scape-study-full.pdf

Pew Forum on Religion & Public Life (2009, December). *Many Americans mix multiple faiths: Eastern, new age beliefs widespread.* Retrieved (4/14/10) from http:// pewforum.org/newassets/images/reports/multiple faiths/multiplefaiths.pdf

Phillips, F. B. (1990). N. T. U. psychotherapy: An Afrocentric approach. *Journal of Black Psychology, 71*(1), 55–74.

Piaget, J. (1973). *The child and reality.* New York: Viking.

Piccinelli, M., & **Wilkinson, G.** (2000). Gender differences in depression: Critical review. *British Journal of Psychiatry, 177,* 486–492.

Pinderhughes, E. (1982). Afro-American families and the victim system. In M. McGoldrick, J. Pearce, & J. Giordano (Eds.), *Ethnicity and family therapy* (pp. 108–122). New York: Guilford Press.

Pinderhughes, E. (1989). *Understanding race, ethnicity and power.* New York: Free Press.

Pipher, M. (1994). *Reviving Ophelia.* New York: Ballantine Books.

Pittman, F. (1994). *Man enough: Fathers, sons and the search for masculinity.* New York: Perigree Books.

Pleck, J. H. (1981). *The myth of masculinity.* Cambridge, MA: MIT Press.

Poe-Yamagata, E., & **Jones, M.** (1998). *And justice for some.* San Francisco: Youth Law Center.

Pogrebin, L. C. (1996). *Getting over getting older.* New York: Berkley Books.

Pollack, W. (1999). *Real boys: Rescuing our sons from the myths of boyhood.* New York: Owl Publishing Company.

Pollitt, K. (2006, March 23). Affirmative action for men. *The Nation,* Retrieved 6/28/10: www.insidehighered. com/news/2006/03/27/admit.

Popenoe, D. (2008). *War over the family.* Piscataway, NJ: Transaction Publishers.

Porter, N. (2002). Contextual and developmental frameworks in diagnosing children and adolescents. In M. Ballou & L. Brown (Eds.), *Rethinking mental health and disorder: Feminist perspectives* (pp. 262–278). New York: Guilford.

Powell-Johnson, G. (1983). *The psychosocial development of minority group children.* New York: Bruner/Mazel Publishers.

Pribilsky, J. (2001). Nervios and modern childhood: Migration and shifting contexts of child life in the Ecuadorean Andes. *Childhood: A global journal of child research, 8*(2), 251–273.

Project on Student Debt. (2009). Retrieved (4/14/10) from www.projectonstudentdebt.org/

Pruchno, R., & **Rosenbaum, J.** (2003). Social relationships in adulthood and old age. In R. M. Lerner, M. A. Easterbrooks, J. Mistry, & I. B. Weiner (Eds.), *Handbook of psychology: Developmental psychology* (Vol. 6, pp. 487–511). Hoboken, NJ: John Wiley and Sons.

Pruett, K. (2001). *Father need: Why father care is as essential as mother care for your child.* New York: Broadway.

Qualls, S. H., & **Zarit, S. H.,** Eds. (2009). *Aging families and caregiving.* New York: Wiley.

Quintana, S. (2008). Racial perspective taking ability: Developmental, theoretical and empirical trends. In S. Quitana & C. McKowan (Eds.), *Handbook of race, racism and the developing child* (pp. 16–30). Hoboken, NJ: John Wiley.

Rabina, T. (2009). *Disaster relief workers: Growth and meaning making after Hurricane Katrina.* Unpublished doctoral dissertation. Boston: Massachusetts School of Professional Psychology.

Rampage, C. (2004). Working with gender in couple therapy. In A. Gurman & N. Jacobson (Eds.), *Clinical*

handbook of couple therapy (3rd ed., pp. 533–545). New York: Guilford Press.

Rand Corporation Center for the Study of Aging: Research Brief (1998). Health, marriage, and longer life for men. *Center for the Study of Aging.* Retrieved February 26, 2010, from www.rand.org/pubs/research_briefs/RB5018/index1.html

Rando, T., Ed. (1986). *The parental loss of a child.* Champaign, IL.: Research Press.

Rando, T. (1993). *Treatment of complicated mourning.* Champaign, IL: Research Press.

Ransom, J. W., Schlesinger, S., & Derdeyn, A. (1979). A stepfamily in formation. *American Journal of Orthopsychiatry, 49*(1).

Regan, P., & Berscheid, E. (1999). *Lust: What we know about human desire.* Thousand Oaks, CA: Sage Publications.

Reid, J. D. (1995). Development in late life: Older lesbian and gay lives. In A. R. D'Augeli & C. J. Patterson (Eds.), *Lesbian, gay and bisexual identities over the lifespan: Psychological perspectives* (pp. 215–242). New York: Oxford University Press.

Remien, R. (1997). Three portraits of how HIV and AIDS can complicate a break-up. *In the Family,* 3, 18–19.

Rennison, C. M. (2001). *Intimate partner violence and age of victim* October 28, 2001 (NCJ 187635). U.S. Department of Justice (2001). Bureau of Justice Statistics. Retrieved (4/14/10) from www.legis.state.wi.us/assembly/asm76/news/PDF%20files/intimate%20partner%20violence.pdf

Rennison, C. M. (2001). *Intimate partner violence and age of victim* (NCJ 187635). U.S. Bureau of Justice. Retrieved (4/14/10) from new.abanet.org/domesticviolence/ Pages/Statistics.aspx

Rilke, R. M. (1954), Letters to a young poet. Translated by D. M. Hester, New York: W. W. Norton.

Ritter, K. Y., & Terndrup, A. I. (2002). *Handbook of affirmative psychotherapy with lesbians and gay men.* New York: Guilford Press.

Robbins, M. S., Szapocznik, J., Mayorga, C. C., Dillon, F. R., Burns, M., & Feaster, D. J. (2007). The impact of family functioning on family racial socialization processes. *Cultural diversity and ethnic minority psychology, 13*(4), 313–320.

Roberts, S. (2006). Creating an intergenerational support system in an African American church. *Dissertation Abstracts International Section A: Humanities and Social Sciences, 67*(6A), 2193.

Roberts, S. (2008, February 21). Most children still live in two-parent homes. *New York Times,* p. A 14.

Robinson, B. E., Walters, L. H., & Skeen, P. (1989). Response to learning that their child is homosexual and concern over AIDS: A national study. In F. W. Bozett (Ed.), *Homosexuality and the family* (pp. 59–80). Binghamton, NY: Harrington Park Press.

Rochlen, A., Suizzo, M., McKelley, R., & Scaringi, V. (2008). "I'm just providing for my family": A qualitative study of stay-at-home-fathers. *Psychology of Men and Masculinity, 9,* 193–206.

Rodgers, R. (1986). Postmarital reorganization of family relationships: A prepositional theory. In S. Duck, & D. Perlman (Eds.), *Close relationships: Development, dynamics, and deterioration* (pp. 239–268). Beverly Hills, CA: Sage.

Roehlkepartain, E. C., King, P. E., Wagener, L., & Benson, P. L. (2006). *The handbook of spiritual development in childhood and adolescence.* Thousand Oaks, CA: Sage Publications, Inc.

Rolland, J. R. (1994). *Families, illness, and disability.* New York: Basic Books.

Rolland, J. S. (1984). Toward a psychosocial typology of chronic and life-threatening illness. *Family Systems Medicine, 2,* 245–263.

Rolland, J. S. (1987). Chronic illness and the life cycle: A conceptual framework. *Family Process, 26*(2), 203–221.

Rolland, J. S. (1990). Anticipatory loss: A family systems developmental framework. *Family Process, 29*(3), 229–244.

Rolland, J. S. (1994a). *Families, illness, and disability: An integrative treatment model.* New York: Basic Books.

Rolland, J. S. (1994b). In sickness and in health: The impact of illness on couples' relationships. *Journal of Marital and Family Therapy, 20*(4), 327–349.

Rolland, J. S. (1998). Beliefs and collaboration in illness: Evolution over time. *Families, Systems & Health, 16,* 7–25.

Rolland, J. S. (2004). Helping families with anticipatory loss and terminal illness. In F. Walsh & M. McGoldrick, (Eds.), *Living beyond loss: Death in the family* (2nd ed., pp. 213–236). New York: Norton.

Rolland, J. S. (2006). Living with anticipatory loss in the new era of genetics: A life cycle perspective. In S. Miller, S. McDaniel, J. Rolland, & S. Feetham (Eds.), *Individuals, families, and the new era of genetics:*

Biopsychosocial perspectives (pp. 139–172). New York: Norton.

Rolland, J. S., & Williams, J. K. (2005). Toward a biopsychosocial model for 21st century genetics. *Family Process, 44*(1), 3–24.

Romer, N. (1981). *The sex-role cycle: Socialization from infancy to old age.* New York: McGraw-Hill.

Room, R. (1976). Ambivalence as a sociological explanation: The case of cultural explanations of alcohol problems. *American Sociological Review, 41,* 1047–1065.

Rosario, M., Scrimshaw, E., & Hunter, J. (2004). Ethnic/racial differences in the coming-out process of lesbian, gay and bisexual youths: A comparison of sexual identity development over time. *Cultural Diversity and Ethnic Minority Psychology, 10* (3) 215–228.

Rosario, M., Schrimshaw, E., & Hunter, J. (2008). Butch/femme differences in substance use and abuse among young lesbian and bisexual women: Examination and potential explanations. *Substance Use & Misuse, 43*(8) 1002–1015.

Rosario, M., Scrimshaw, E., Hunter, J., & Braun, L. (2006). Sexual identity development among lesbian, gay, and bisexual youths: Consistency and change over time. *Journal of Sex Research, 43*(1), 46–58.

Rosen, E. (1998). *Families facing death* (2nd ed.). San Francisco: Jossey-Bass.

Rosen, E., & Weltman, S. F. (2005). Jewish families: An overview. In In M. McGoldrick, J. Giordano, & N. Garcia Preto (Eds.), *Ethnicity and family therapy* (3rd ed., pp. 667–679), New York: Guilford Press.

Rosen, R. (2006). Erectile dysfunction: Integration of medical and psychological approaches. In S. Leiblum (Ed.), *Principles and practice of sex therapy* (4th ed., pp. 277–312). New York: Guilford Press.

Rosten, L. (1989). *The joys of Yinglish.* New York: Penguin Books.

Rowe, D., & Grills, C. (1993). African centered drug treatment: An alternative conceptual paradigm for drug counseling with African-American clients. *Journal of Psychoactive Drugs, 25*(1), 21–33.

Roy, K. M., & Dyson, O. L. (2005) Gatekeeping in context: Babymama drama and the involvement of incarcerated fathers. *Fathering, 3*(3), 289–310.

Rubin, L. (1993). *Just friends: The role of friendship in our lives.* New York: Harper Collins.

Russell, D. E. H. (1990). *Rape in marriage.* Indianapolis, IN: Indiana University Press.

Ryan C., Huebner, D., Diaz, R.M., & Sanchez, J. (2009). Family rejection as a predictor of negative health outcomes in White and Latino lesbian, gay, and bisexual young adults. *Pediatrics, 123*(1) 2007–3524.

Ryding, E. L. (1984). Sexuality during and after pregnancy. *Atca Obstetricia et Gynecologica Scandinavica, 63,* 679–682.

Sack, K. (2008, August 13). Health benefits inspire rush to marry or divorce. *New York Times,* p. A1.

Sager, C. J., Brown, H. S., Crohn, H., Engel, T., Rodstein, E., & Walker, L. (1983). *Treating the remarried family.* New York: Brunner/Mazel.

Salovey, P. (2007). Integrative summary. In R. Bar-On, J. G. Maree, & M. J. Elias (Eds.), *Educating people to be emotionally intelligent* (pp. 291–298). Westport, CT: Praeger / Greenwood Press.

Saltzman, A. (1991). *Down-shifting: Reinventing success on a slower track.* New York: Harper Perennial.

Saluter, A. (1996). Marital status and living arrangements, March, 1995. *Current Population Reports,* (pp. 20–491). Washington DC: U.S. Census Bureau.

Samuels, G. M. (2009). "Being raised by White people": Navigating racial difference among adopted multiracial adults. *Journal of Marriage and Family, 71*(1), 80–94.

Sanders, G. L. (2000). Men together: Working with gay male couples in contemporary times. In P. Papp (Ed.), *Couples on the fault line: New directions for therapists* (pp. 222–256). New York: Guilford Press.

Sanders, G. L., & Kroll, I. T. (2000). Generating stories of resilience: Helping gay and lesbian youth and their families. *Journal of Marital and Family Therapy, 26*(4), 433–442.

Sandmaier, M. (1994). *Original kin: The search for connection among adult sisters and brothers.* New York: Plume.

Sandmaier, M. (1996, May/June.). More than love. *The Family Networker,* 21–33.

Santisteban, D. A., & Mena, M. P. (2009). Culturally informed family therapy for adolescents: A tailored and integrative treatment for Hispanic youth. *Family Process, 48*(2), 253–268.

Santisteban, D.A., Tejeda, M., Dominicis, C., Szapocznik, J. (1999). An efficient tool for screening for maladaptive family functioning in adolescent drug abusers: The problem oriented screening instrument for teenagers. *American Journal of Drug and Alcohol Abuse , 25*(2) 197–206.

Savin-Williams, R. C. (1996). Self-labeling and disclosure among gay, lesbian, and bisexual youths. In J. Laird & R.-J. Green (Eds.), *Lesbians and gays in couples and families: A handbook for therapists* (pp. 153–182). San Francisco: Jossey-Bass.

Savin-Williams, R. C. (2005). *The new gay teenager.* Cambridge MA: Harvard.

Sayer, L., Bianchi. S., & Robison, J. (2004). Are parents investing less in children? Trends in mother's and father's time with children. *American Journal of Sociology, 110,* 1–43.

Schachter-Shalomi, Z. (1995). *From age-ing to sage-ing: A profound new vision of growing older.* New York: Warner Books.

Schaefer, S., Evans, S., & Coleman, E. (1987). Sexual orientation concerns among chemically dependent individuals. *Journal of Chemical Dependency Treatment, 1,* 121–140.

Schaie, K. W., & Krouse, N. (Eds.). (2004). *Religious influences on health and well-being in the elderly.* New York: Springer.

Schaie, K. W., & Willis, S. L. (1986). *Adult development and aging.* Boston: Little, Brown & Company.

Schaie, W., & Elder, G. (Eds.). (2005). Historical influences on lives and aging. In *Societal impact on aging series.* New York: Springer.

Scharlach, A. E., & Fredricksen, K. (1993). Reactions to the death of a parent during midlife. *Omega, 27,* 307–319.

Schnarch, D. (2010). *Intimacy and desire.* New York: Beaufort Books.

Schnitzer P. G. & Ewigman, B. G. (2005). Child deaths resulting from inflicted injuries: Household risk factors and perpetrator characteristics, *Pediatrics, 116,* 687–693.

Schultz, G. (2007, January 17). Married couples are a minority in U.S. households. *Census Report.* Retrieved (4/14/10) from www.lifesitenews.com/ldn/2007/jan/07011703.htm

Schulz, A. J., & Mullings, L. (Eds.). (2006). *Gender, race, class & health: Intersectional approaches.* San Francisco: Jossey-Bass.

Schwartz, A., Anderson, S., Strasser, T. J., & Boulette, T. (2000). Psychological maltreatment of spouses. In M. Hersen & R. Ammerman (Eds.), *Case studies in family violence* (pp. 349–374). New York: Plenum Press.

Schwartz, P. (1994). *Peer marriage: How love between equals really works.* New York: Free Press.

Schwartzberg, N., Berliner, K., & Jacob, D. (1995). *Single in a married world.* New York: W. W. Norton.

Schwartzman, J. (1982). Symptoms and rituals: Paradoxical modes and social organization. *Ethos, 10*(1), 3–23.

Schwartzman, J. (1983). Family ethnography: A tool for clinicians. In C. J. Falicov (Ed.), *Cultural perspectives in family therapy* (pp. 137–149). Rockville, MD: Aspen Systems Corporation.

Schydlowsky, B. M. (1983). *Friendships among women in midlife.* Unpublished doctoral dissertation, University of Michigan.

Schwartzberg, N., Berliner, K., & Jacob, D. (1995). *Single in a married world.* New York: W. W. Norton.

Scott, A. O. (2009, April 15). Directors in their magic hour. *New York Times,* p. AR1.

Scrivner, R., & Elderidge, N. S. (1995). Lesbian and gay family psychology. In R. H. Miskell, D. Lusterman, & S. H. McDaniel (Eds.), *Integrating family therapy: Handbook of family psychology and systems theory* (pp. 327–344). Washington, DC: American Psychological Association.

Seaburn, D., Lorenz, A., & Kaplan, D. (1992). The transgenerational development of chronic illness meanings. *Family Systems Medicine, 10*(4), 385–395.

Seltzer, W., & Seltzer, M. (1983). Magic, material and myth. *Family Process, 22*(1), 3–14.

Senge, P. (2006). *The fifth discipline: The art and practice of the learning organization.* New York: Doubleday.

Seo, J. (2007). The long-term influence of father involvement on emerging adults' psychological well-being. *Dissertation Abstracts International Section A: Humanities and Social Sciences, 68*(5-A), 2191.

Seppa, N. (2009, May 22). Sensitivity to alcohol connected with alcoholism risk: An imperviousness to alcohol's effects may not be so good. *Science News.* Retrieved August 31, 2009, from www.sciencenews.org/view/generic/id/44037/title/High_tolerance_connected_with_increased_alcoholism_risk

Sew, J. W. (2006). Review of multiple intelligences reconsidered. *Discourse and Society, 17*(4), 554–557.

Shaffer, C., & Amundsen, K. (1993). *Creating community anywhere: Finding support and connection in a fragmented world.* New York: Tarcher/Perigee Books.

Shanahan, M. J., & Elder, G. H. (2002). History, agency and the life course. In L. J. Crocket (Ed.), *Agency, motivation and the life course* (pp. 145–186). Lincoln, NE: University of Nebraska Press.

Shanas, E., & **Streib, G. F.** (1965). *Social structure and the family.* Englewood Cliffs, NJ: Prentice-Hall.

Shanley, J. P. (2007). *Doubt: A parable.* New York: Dramatist Play Service.

Shapiro, E. (1994). *Grief as a family process.* New York: Guilford.

Shapiro, P. G. (1996). *My turn: Women's search for self after children leave.* Princeton, NJ: Peterson's.

Sheehy, G. (1977). *Passages.* New York: Bantam.

Sheehy, G. (1995). *New passages.* New York: Ballantine Books.

Sherman, M. & **Sherman, D. A.** (2006). I'm Not Alone: A teen's guide to living with a parent who has a mental illness. MN: Beavers Pond Press.

Shernoff, M. (1997). Unexamined loss: An expanded view of gay break-ups. *In the Family,* 10–13.

Shin-Yi, Wu, & **Green, A.** (2008). Projection of chronic illness prevalence and cost inflation. RAND Corporation.

Shinn, M., & **Yoshikawa, H.,** Eds. (2008). *Toward positive youth development: Transforming schools and community programs.* New York: Oxford University Press.

Shippy, R. A., Cantor, M. H., & **Brennan, M.** (2004). Social networks of aging gay men. *Journal of Men's Studies, 13*(1), 107–120.

Shufro, C. (2008). Findings: The daughter effect. *Yale Alumni Magazine, LXXI*(6), 30.

Shumsky, E. (1997). Making up the rules: Lesbian ex-lover relationships. *In the Family,* 14–15.

Siegal, D. J. (1999). *The developing mind: How relationships and the brain interact to shape who we are.* New York: Guilford Press.

Siegal, M. (1987). Are sons and daughters treated more differently by fathers than by mothers? *Developmental Review, 7,* 183–209.

Siegel, D. (2006). An interpersonal neurobiology approach to psychotherapy. *Psychiatric Annals 36*(4), 248–256.

Silvana, G., & **Armida, M.** (2000). Emotions, brain development, and psychopathologic vulnerability. *CNS Spectrums, 5*(8), 44–88.

Silverstein, H. (1990). *Alcoholism.* New York: Franklin Watts.

Silverstein, O., & **Rashbaum, B.** (1994). *The courage to raise good men.* New York: Penguin Books.

Simms, M., Fortuny, K., & **Henderson, E.** (August, 2009). Racial and ethnic disparities among low-income families. *Urban Institute LIWF Fact Sheet.*

Simon, R. M. (1988). Family life cycle issues in the therapy system. In M. McGoldrick & E. A. Carter (Eds.), *The changing family life cycle: A framework for family therapy* (2nd ed., pp. 107–118). New York: Gardner Press.

Sisk, J. (2006). Sexuality in nursing homes: Preserving rights, promoting well-being. *Social Work Today, 6,* 17–20.

Skolnick, A. (2009). The life course revolution. In A S. Skolnick & J. H. Skolnick (Eds.). *Family in transition* (15th ed., pp. 31–39). Boston: Allyn & Bacon.

Slater, S. (1995). *The lesbian family life cyle.* New York: Free Press.

Sluzki, C. (2000). Social networks and the elderly: Conceptual and clinical issues, and a family consultation. *Family Process, 39*(3), 271–284.

Sluzki, C. (2008). Migration and disruption of the social network. In M. McGoldrick & K. V. Hardy (Eds.), *Re-visioning family therapy: Race, culture and gender in clinical practice* (2nd ed., pp. 39–47). New York: Guilford.

Sluzki, C. F. (1979). Migration and family conflict. *Family Process, 18*(1), 379–392.

Smith, A. L., & **Harkness, J.** (2002). Spirituality and meaning: A qualitative inquiry with caregivers of Alzheimer's disease. *Journal of Family Psychotherapy, 13*(1–2), 87–108.

Smith, J. A. (2009). *The daddy shift.* Boston: Beacon Press.

Smith, R. C. (2006) *Mexican New York: Transnational lives of new Immigrants.* Berkeley: University of California Press.

Smith, S. (2007). *Lone pursuit: Distrust and defensive individualism among the Black poor.* New York: Sage Foundation.

Smokowski, P., & **Bacallao, M.** (2009). Entre dos mundos/between two worlds: Youth violence prevention for acculturating Latino families. *Research on Social Work Practice 19,* 165–178.

Snarch, D. (2010). *Intimacy & desire.* New York: Beaufort Books.

Society for the Study of Emerging Adulthood. (2008). *Emerging Adulthood Publications.* Retrieved (4/14/10) from www.ssea.org/resources/publishing_publications.htm

Solnit, R. (2009). *A paradise built in Hell: The extraordinary communities that arise in disaster.* New York: Viking.

Solomon, P. (2009). Family interventions. In P. Corrigan, K. Mueser, R. Drake, & P. Solomon (Eds.), *Principles*

and practices of psychiatric rehabilitation: An empirical perspective (pp. 234–262). New York: Guilford.

Spangler, D., & Brandl, B. (2007). Abuse in later life: Power and control dynamics and a victim-centered response. *Journal of the American Psychiatric Nurses Association, 12*(6), 322–331.

Spark, G. (1974). Grandparents and intergenerational family therapy. *Family Process, 13,* 225–238.

Spark, G., & Brody, E. M. (1970). The aged are family members. *Family Process, 9,* 195–210.

Speck, R. & Attneave, C. (1973). Family Networks. New York: Pantheon Books.

Spock, B. (1997, May). Take charge parenting. *Parenting,* p. 123.

Stacey, J. (1996). *In the name of the family: Rethinking family values.* Boston: Beacon.

Stack, C., & Burton, L. (1993). Kinscripts. *Journal of Comparative Family Studies, 24*(2), 157–170.

Staples, R. (1988). An overview of race and marital status. In H. P. McAdoo (Ed.), *Black families.* (2nd ed., pp. 187–189). Newbury Park, CA: Sage.

Staples, R. (2007). An overview of race and marital status. In H. McAdoo (Ed.), *Black families* (4th ed. pp. 281–284). Thousand Oaks, CA: Sage.

Staples, R., & Johnson, L. B. (1993). *Black families at the crossroad: Challenges and prospects.* San Francisco: Jossey-Bass.

Stavridou, F., & Kakana, D. (2008). Graphic abilities in relation to mathematical and scientific ability in adolescents. *Educational research, 50*(1), 75–93.

Stein, P. (1981). Understanding single adulthood. In P. Stein (Ed.), *Single life: Unmarried adults in social contexts* (pp. 9–20). New York: St. Martin's Press.

Steinglass, P. (1981). The alcoholic family at home: Patterns of interaction in dry, wet, and transitional stages of alcoholism. *Archives of General Psychiatry, 38*(5), 578–584.

Steinglass, P. (1982). The role of alcohol in family systems. In J. Orford & J. Harwin (Eds.), *Alcohol and the family* (pp. 127–150). London: AEC Publishing.

Steinglass, P., Bennett, L. A., Wolin, S. J., & Reiss, D. (1987). *The alcoholic family.* New York: Basic Books.

Steinhauer, J. (1995, April 10). Big benefits in marriage, studies say. *New York Times,* p. A 10.

Stevens, M., Golombok, S., & Beveridge, M. (2002). Does father absence influence children's gender development? Findings from a general population study of preschool children. *Parenting: Science & Practice, 2*(1), 47–60.

Stevenson, H., Winn, D-M., Coard, S., & Walker-Barnes, C. (2003, May). Towards a culturally relevant framework for interventions with African-American families. Presentation made at the Emerging Issues in African-American Family Life: Context, Adaptation, and Policy Conference, Duke University, Durham, NC.

Stevenson, R., & Elliot, S. (2006). Sexuality and illness. In S. Leiblum (Ed.), *Principles and practice of sex therapy* (4th ed., pp. 313–349). New York: Guilford Press.

Stewart, A., Copeland, A., Chester, N., Malley, J., & Barenbaum, N. (1997). *Separating together: How divorce transforms families.* New York: Guilford Press.

Stierlin, H. (1977). *Psychoanalysis and family therapy.* New York: Jason Aronson.

Stiver, I. P., & Miller, J. B., (1998). The healing connection. Boston: Beacon Press.

Stone, B. (2009, March 29). "Is Facebook growing up too fast"? *New York Times,* p. BU1.

Straus, M. A. (2001). *Beating the devil out of them: Corporal punishment in American families.* Edison, NJ: Transaction Publishers.

Straus, M. A., & Steinmetz, S. (2006). *Behind closed doors: Violence in the American family.* Edison, NJ: Transaction Publishers.

Stroebe, M., Hansonn, R., & Henk, S. & Stroebe, W. (2008). *Handbook of bereavement research and practice: Advances in theory and intervention.* Washington, DC: American Psychological Association.

Suárez-Orozco, C., & Suárez-Orozco, M. (2001). *Children of immigration.* Cambridge: MA: Harvard University Press.

Suárez-Orozco, C., Suárez-Orozco, M., & Todorova, I. (2008). *Learning a new land: Immigrant students in American society.* Cambridge, MA: Harvard University Press.

Suárez-Orozco, C., Todorova, I., & Louie, J. (2002) Making up for lost time: The experience of separation and reunification among immigrant families. *Family Process 41*(4), 625–644.

Sue, D. W., & Sue, D. (2008). *Counseling the culturally diverse: Theory and practice.* Hoboken, NJ: Wiley & Sons.

Suizo, M. N., Robinson, C., & Pahlke, E. M., 2008. African American mothers' socialization, beliefs, and goals with young children: themes of history, education, and collective independence. *Journal of Family issues.* 29(3), pp. 287-316.

Sulloway, F. J. (1996). *Born to rebel: Sibling relationships, family dynamics and creative lives.* New York: Pantheon.

Sundquist, K. (1997). She gets the kids: Becoming an every-third-weekend and -Tuesday ex-co-mom. *In the Family, 20,* 21–27.

Sutton-Smith, B., & Rosenberg, B. G. (1970). *The sibling.* New York: Holt, Rinehart & Winston.

Swartz, H. A., Shear, M. K., Wren, F. J., Greeno, C. G., Sales, E., Sullivan, B. K., & Ludewig, D. P. (2006). Depression and anxiety among mothers who bring their children to a pediatric mental health clinic. *Psychiatric Services, 56*(9), 1077–1083.

Swiss, L., & Le Bourdais, C. (2009). Father-child contact after separation: The influence of living arrangements. *Journal of Family Issues, 30*(5), 623–652.

Szlemko, W. J., Wood, J., Thurman, W. & Jumper, P. (2006). Native Americans and alcohol: Past, present, and future. *Journal of General Psychology, 133*(4), 435–451.

Taffel, R. (2005). *Breaking through to teens. Psychotherapy for the new adolescence.* New York: Guilford.

Taffel, R. (2009). *Childhood unbound: Saving our kids' best selves—Confident parenting in a world of change.* New York: Free Press.

Taffel, R., & Blau, M. (2001). *The second family: How adolescent power is challenging the American family.* New York: St. Martin's Press.

Taffel, R., & Blau, M. (2002). *Parenting by heart: How to stay connected to your child in a disconnected world.* Cambridge, MA: Da Capo Press.

Taffel, R., with Israeloff, R. (1994). *Why parents disagree: How women and men parent differently and how we can work together.* New York: William Morrow.

Tafoya, N., & Del Vecchio, A. (2005). Back to the future: An examination of the Native American holocaust experience. In M. McGoldrick, J. Giordano, & N. Garcia Preto (Eds.), *Ethnicity and family therapy* (3rd ed., pp. 55–63). New York: Guilford Press.

Tatum, B. (1997). *"Why are all the black kids sitting together in the cafeteria?" And other conversations about race.* New York: Basic Books.

Taylor, M. F., Clark, N., & Newton, E. (2008). Counseling Australian Baby Boomers: Examining the loss and grief issues facing aging distance-separated

sibling dyads. *British Journal of Guidance & Counselling, 36*(2), 189–204.

Taylor, S. E. (2002). *The tending instinct.* New York: Henry Holt.

Taylor, S. E., Klein, L. C., Lewis, B. P., Gruenewald, T. L., Gurung, R. A. R., & Updegraff, J. A. (2000). Female responses to stress: Tend and befriend, not fight or flight. *Psychological Review, 107*(3), 41–429.

Teachman, J. & Tedrow, L. (2004). The demography of stepfamilies in the United States. In J. Pryor (Ed.), *The international handbook of stepfamilies* (pp. 3–29). New York: Wiley.

Teicher, M. (2002). Scars that won't heal: The neurobiology of child abuse. *Scientific American, 286 (3),* 68 75.

Thomas, N. (2006). What's missing from the weathering hypothesis? *American Journal of Public Health, 955*(96), 6.

Thomas V. S., & Rockwood, K. J. (2001). Alcohol abuse, cognitive impairment, and mortality among older people. *Journal of American Geriatric Society, 49,* 415–20.

Thompson, M. S., & Wilkins W. P. (1992). The impact of formal, informal, and societal support networks on the psychological well-being of Black adolescent mothers. *Social Work, 37*(4), 322–328.

Thompson, R. A. (2006). Nurturing developing brains, minds, and hearts. In R. Lally & P. Mangione (Eds.), *Concepts of care: 20 essays on infant/toddler development and learning* (pp. 47–52). Sausalito, CA: WestEnd.

Thompson, R. A., Goodvin, R., & Meyer, S. (2006). Social development: Psychological understanding, self-understanding, and relationships. In J. Luby (Ed.), *Handbook of preschool mental health: Development, disorders and treatment* (pp. 3–22). New York: Guilford.

Thorne, B. (1993). *Gender play: Girls and boys at school.* New Brunswick, NJ: Rutgers University Press.

Thornton, A. (2009) Framework for interpreting long-term trends in values and beliefs concerning single-parent families. *Journal of Marriage and Family, 71*(2), 230–234.

Tindale, J. (1999). Variance in the meaning of time by family cycle, period, social context, and ethnicity. In W. Pentland, A. Harvey, M. Lawton, & M. McCall (Eds.), *Time use research in the social sciences* (pp. 155–168). Dordrecht, Netherlands: Kluwer Academic Publishers.

Tischler, V., & **Rademeyer, A.** (2007). Mothers experiencing homelessness: Mental health, support and social care needs. *Health & Social Care in the Community, 15*(3), 246–253.

Toman, W. (1976). *Family constellation* (3rd ed.). New York: Springer.

Tough, P. (2007). *Whatever it takes: Geoffrey Canada's quest to change Harlem and America.* New York: Houghton Mifflin.

Townsend, P. (1957). *The family life of older people.* London: Routledge and Kegan Paul.

Trafford, A. (1982). *Crazy time.* New York: Harper & Row.

Treadway, D. (1989). *Before it's too late: Working with substance abuse in the family.* New York: W. W Norton.

Treas, J. (2002). How cohorts, education, and ideology shaped a new sexual revolution on American attitudes toward nonmarital sex, 1972–1998, *Sociological Perspectives, 45*(3), 267–283.

Troll, L. (1994). Family connectedness of old women: Attachments in later life. In B. F. Turner, & L. E. Troll (Eds.), *Women growing older* (pp. 169–201). Thousand Oaks, CA: Sage.

Troll, L. E., & **Smith, J.** (1976). Attachment through the life span: Some questions about dyadic bonds among adults. *Human Development, 19*, 156–170.

Trueba, E. T. (1999). *Latinos Unidos: From cultural diversity to the politics of solidarity.* Lanham, MD: Rowman & Littlefield.

Tully, C. T. (1989). Caregiving: What do midlife lesbians view as important*? Journal of Gay and Lesbian Psychotherapy, 1*, 87–103.

Tunnell, G., & **Greenan, D. E.** (2004). Clinical Issues with gay male couples. In J. J. Bigner & J. L. Wetchler (Eds.), *Relationship therapy with same-sex couples* (pp. 13 – 26). New York: Haworth Press.

Twaite, J., & **Lampert, D. T.** (1997). Outcomes of mandated preventive services programs for homeless and truant children: A follow-up study. *Social Work, 42*(1), 11–18.

Upchurch, D., **Levy-Storms, L.**, **Sucoff, C.**, & **Aneshensel, C.** (1998). Gender and ethnic differences in the timing of first intercourse [Electronic version]. *Family Planning Perspective, 30(3).* Retreived on January 4, 2009, from www.guttmacher.org/pubs/journals/3012198.html

U.S. Bureau of Labor. (2009). *Employment rates for African Americans.* Washington, DC: U.S. Government Printing Office.

U.S. Census Bureau. (2000). *Statistical abstract of the United States.* Washington, DC: U.S. Government Printing Office.

U.S. Census Bureau. (2001). *Gender: 2000 Census brief report.* Washington DC: U.S. Department of Commerce.

U.S. Census Bureau. (2005). *We the people: Women and men in the United States* (Census 2000 special reports). Washington: U.S. Department of Commerce.

U.S. Census Bureau. (2006–2008). *American community survey.* Washington, DC: U.S. Government Printing Office.

U.S. Census Bureau. (2006a). *Educational attainment by selected characteristic: 2006.* Retrieved (4/14/10) from www.census.gov/population/www/socdemo/educ-attn.html

U.S. Census Bureau. (2006b). *Mean earnings by highest degree earned: 2006.* Retrieved (4/14/10) from www.census.gov/Press-Release/www/releases/archives/education/007660.html

U.S. Census Bureau. (2007a). *Income, poverty, and health insurance coverage in the United States: 2007.* Washington DC: U.S. Department of Commerce.

U.S. Census Bureau. (2007b). *Use of mammography for women 40 years old and over by patient characteristics: 1990–2005.* Retrieved (4/14/10) from www.census.gov/compendia.statab/2008/cats/health_nutrition.html

U.S. Census Bureau. (2007c). *Facts for features: Women's history month* (CB07-FF.03). Washington DC; U. S. Census Bureau.

U.S. Census Bureau. (2007d). *Income, poverty, and health insurance coverage in the United States.* Washington, D.C.: U.S. Government Printing Office.

U.S. Census Bureau. (2007e). *Statistical abstract of the United States.* Washington, DC: U.S. Government Printing Office.

U.S. Census Bureau. (2008). *Families and living arrangements.* Retrieved (4/14/10) from www.census.gov

U.S. Department of Health and Human Services. (2007). *Child Maltreatment, 2007.* Retrieved (4/14/10) from www.acf.hhs.gov/programs/cb/pubs/cm07/

U.S. Department of Health and Human Services/Agency for Healthcare Research and Quality. (2007). *National healthcare disparities report.* Rockville, MD: Retrieved (4/14/10) from www.ahrq.gov/qual/nhdr07/nhdr07.pdf

U.S. Department of Justice. (2000). *Extent, nature, and consequences of intimate partner violence: Findings from the national violence against women survey.* (NCJ

181867). Retrieved (4/14/10) from www.ncjrs.gov/App/abstractdb/AbstractDBDetails.aspx?id=181867

U.S. Department of Justice. (2000, July). *Sexual assault of young children as reported to law enforcement: Victim, incident, and offender characteristics* (NCJ 182990). Retrieved (4/14/10) from www.jrsa.org/dvsa-drc/bibliography/bibliography-sa.shtml

U.S. Department of Justice. (2006a). *Bureau of justice statistics.* Retrieved (4/14/10) from http://www.ojp.usdoj.gov/BIA/grant/jag.html

U.S. Department of Justice. (2006b). *Prison and jail inmates midyear 2005.* Retrieved (4/14/10) from http://www.publicsafety.ohio.gov/links/ocjs prison andjailinmatesmidyear2005.pdf

U.S. Department of Justice-Bureau of Justice Statistics. (2006) Prison and jail inmates midyear 2005. [retrieved from http://www.ojp.usdoj.gov/bjs/abstract/pjim05.htm]

U.S. Department of Justice, Bureau of Justice Statistics. (2006) *Homicide trends in the United States.* Retrieved August 28, 2009, from www.ojp.usdoj.gov/bjs/homicide/intimates.htm

U.S. Department of Justice. (2008, May). *Violence by teenage girls: Trends and context. Girls Study Group.* Retrieved (4/14/10) from www.ncjrs.gov/pdffiles1/ojjdp/218905.pdf

Usdansky, M. L. (2009). A weak embrace. Popular and scholarly depictions of single-parent families 1900–1998. *Journal of Marriage and Family, 71*(2), 209–225.

Vadasy, P. F., Fewell, R. R., Meyer, D. J., & *Schell, G.* (1984). Siblings of handicapped children: A developmental perspective on family interactions. *Family Relations, 33*(1), 155–167.

Vaillant, G. E. (1977). *Adaptation to life.* Boston: Little, Brown and Company.

Vaillant, G. E. (1983). *The natural history of alcoholism.* Cambridge, MA: Harvard University Press.

Vaillant, G. E. (1995). *The natural history of alcoholism revisited: Causes, patterns, and paths to recovery.* Cambridge, MA: Harvard University Press.

Vaillant, G. (2002). *Aging well: Surprising guideposts to a happier life.* Boston: Little, Brown and Company.

Van der Hart, O. (1983). *Rituals in psychotherapy: Transition and continuity.* New York: Irvington Publishers.

van Gennep, A., (1960). *The rites of passage.* Chicago: University of Chicago Press.

Vandello, J., Bosson, J., Cohen, D., Burnaford, R., & *Weaver, J.* (2008). Precarious manhood. *Journal of Personality and Social Psychology, 95*(6) 1325–1339.

Vandenbos, G. R., Ed. (2007). *APA dictionary of psychology* (1st ed.). Washington, D.C.: American Psychological Association.

Vega, W. A., Kolody, B., Aguilar-Gaxiola, S., Alderete, E., Catalano, R., & *Caraveo-Anduaga, J.* (1998). Lifetime prevalence of DSM-III-R psychiatric disorders among urban and rural Mexican American in California. *Archives of General Psychiatry, 55,* 771–782.

Vega, W. A., Kolody, B., Valle, R. & *Weir, J.* (1991). Social networks, social support, and their relationship to depression among immigrant Mexican women. *Human Organization, 50,* 154–162.

Venkatesh, S. (2006). *Off the books: The underground economy of the urban poor.* Cambridge, MA: Harvard University Press.

Videka-Sherman, L. (1982). Coping with the death of a child: A study over time. *American Journal of Orthopsychiatry, 52,* 688–698.

Visher, E. B., & *Visher, J. S.* (1979). *Stepfamilies: A guide to working with stepparents and stepchild.* New York: Brunner/Mazel.

Visher, E. B., & *Visher, J. S.* (1988). *Old loyalties, new ties: Therapeutic strategies with stepfamilies.* New York: Brunner/Mazel.

Visher, E. B., & *Visher, J.* (1991). *How to win as a stepfamily* (2nd ed.). New York: Brunner/Mazel.

Visher, E. B., & *Visher, J. S.* (1996). *Therapy with stepfamilies.* New York: Brunner/Mazel.

von Sydow, K. (1999). Sexuality during pregnancy and after childbirth: A metacontent analysis of 59 studies. *Journal of Psychosomatic Research, 47*(1), 27–49.

Waite, L. (1995). Does marriage matter? *Demography, 32*(4), 483–507.

Walker, A. J., Allen, K. R., & *Connidis, I. A.* (2005). Theorizing and studying sibling ties in adulthood. In V. L. Bengston, A. C. Acock, K. R. Allen, P. Dilworth-Anderson, & D. M. Klein (Eds.), *Sourcebook of family theory and research* (pp. 167–173). Thousand Oaks, CA: Sage Publications.

Wallerstein, J. (2001). *The unexpected legacy of divorce.* New York: Hyperion Books.

Wallerstein, J., & *Kelly, J.* (1980). *Surviving the breakup: How children and parents cope with divorce.* New York: Basic Books.

Walsh, F. (1978). Concurrent grandparent death and birth of schizophrenic offspring: An intriguing finding. *Family Process, 17,* 457–463.

Walsh, F. (1983). The timing of symptoms and critical events in the family life cycle. In H. Liddle (Ed.), *Clinical implications of the family life cycle* (pp. 120–132). Rockville, MD: Aspen.

Walsh, F. (2003a). Changing families in a changing world. In F. Walsh (Ed.), *Normal family processes* (3rd. ed., pp. 3–26). New York: Guilford Publications.

Walsh, F. (2003b). Family resilience: A framework for clinical practice. *Family Process, 35,* 261–281.

Walsh, F., Ed. (2003c). *Normal family processes: Growing diversity and complexity,* (3rd ed.). New York: Guilford Press.

Walsh, F. (2006). *Strengthening family resilience* (2nd ed.). New York: Guilford Press.

Walsh, F. (2007). Traumatic loss and major disasters: Strengthening family and community resilience. *Family Process, 46,* 207–227.

Walsh, F. (2008). Spirituality, healing and resilience. In M. McGoldrick, & K. V. Hardy (Eds.), *Re-Visioning family therapy: Race, culture and gender in clinical practice* (2nd ed., pp. 61–75). New York: Guilford.

Walsh, F. (2009a). Human–animal bonds: I. The relational significance of companion animals. Special section, *Family Process, 48*(4), 462–480.

Walsh, F. (2009b). Human–animal bonds: The role of pets in family systems and family therapy. *Family Process, 48*(4), 481–499.

Walsh, F. (Ed.). (2009c). *Spiritual resources in family therapy* (2nd ed.). New York: Guilford Press.

Walsh, F. (2009d). Spiritual resources in family adaptation to death and loss. In F. Walsh (Ed.), *Spiritual resources in family therapy* (2nd ed., pp. 3–30). New York: Guilford.

Walsh, F., & *McGoldrick, M.* (2004). *Living beyond loss: Death in the family* (2nd ed.). New York: Norton.

Walsh, J. (2007, November 28). *Are women initiating divorce?* Retrieved December 29, 2009, from ezinearticles.com/?Are—Women—Initiating—Divorce?&id=855366

Walters, K. L., Old Person, R. L., Jr. (2008). Lesbians, gays, bisexuals and transgender people of color: Reconciling divided selves and communities. In G. Mallon (Ed.), *Social work practice with lesbian, gay, bisexual, and transgender people* (2nd ed., pp. 41–68). New York: Routledge.

Walzlawick, P. (1978). *The language of change: Elements of therapeutic communication.* New York: Basic Books.

Wang, J. L. (2004). The difference between single and married mothers in the 12-month prevalence of major depressive syndrome, associated factors and mental health service utilization. *Social Psychiatry and Psychiatric Epidemiology, 39*(1), 26–32.

Washington, E. L. (2007). Female socialization: How daughters affect their legislator fathers' voting on women's issues. *American Economic Review, 86*(3), 425–441.

Watkins, L. E., O'Farrell, T. J., Suvak, M. K., Murphy, C. M., & *Taft, C. T.* (2009). Parenting satisfaction among fathers with alcoholism. *Addictive Behaviors, 34*(6/7), 610–612.

Watson, M. (1998). African American siblings. In M. McGoldrick (Ed.), *Re-visioning family therapy* (1st ed., pp. 282–294). New York: Guilford Press.

Watts-Jones, D. (1997) Toward an African American genogram. *Family Process, 36,* 375–383.

Wearden, A. J., Tarrier, N., Barrowclough, C., Zastowny, T., & *Rahill, A. A.* (2000). *A review of expressed emotion research in health care. Clinical Psychology Review, 20*(5), 633–666.

Webb, F. J. (2005). The new demographics of families. In V. Bengston, A. C. Acock, K. R. Allen, P. Dilworth-Anderson, & D. M. Klein (Eds.), *Sourcebook of family therapy and Research* (p. 101). *Thousand Oaks,* CA: Sage.

Webb, N. B., & *Lum, D.,* Eds. (2001). *Culturally diverse parent-child and family relationships.* New York: Columbia University Press.

Webb, S., & *Ousky, R.* (2007). *The collaborative way to divorce.* New York: Plume.

Weber, G., & *Heffern, K. T.* (2008). Social work practice with bisexual people. In G. Mallon (Ed.), *Social work practice with lesbian, gay, bisexual, and transgender people,* (2nd ed., pp. 69–82). New York: Routledge

Wegscheider, S. (1981). *Another chance.* Palo Alto: Science and Behavior Books.

Weihs, K., Fisher, L., & *Baird, M.* (2002). Families, health, and behavior. *Families, Systems, and Health, 20*(1), 7–47.

Weil, A. (2005). *Healthy aging.* New York: Alfred A. Knopf.

Weinberg, M. S., Williams, C. J., & Pryor, D. W. (1994). *Dual attraction: Understanding bisexuality.* New York: Oxford University Press.

Weingarten, K. (1996). The mother's voice: Strengthening intimacy in families. New York: Guilford Press.

Weiss, R. S. & Bass, S. A. (Eds.) (2001). *Challenges of the third age: Meaning and purpose in later life.* New York: Oxford University Press.

Wekesser, C. (1994). *Alcoholism.* San Diego: Greenhaven Press.

Wellman, B. L. (1979). The community question: The intimate networks of East Yorkers. *American Journal of Sociology, 84*(5), 1201–1231.

Welsh, M. (2008). *A phenomenological exploration of adolescents raised by same-sex parents.* Unpublished doctoral dissertation, Massachusetts School of Professional Psychology, Boston: MA.

Wen, M. (2008). Family structure and children's health and behavior. *Journal of Family Issues, 29*(11), 1492–1519.

Werner, L. A., & Moro, T. (2004). Unacknowledged and stigmatized losses. In F. Walsh & M. McGoldrick (Eds.), *Living beyond loss* (pp. 247–271). New York: Norton.

Western, B. (2006). *Punishment and inequality in America.* New York: Sage Foundation.

Weston, K. (1991). *Families we choose: Lesbians, gays, kinship.* New York: Columbia University Press.

Whipple, E., Fitzgerald, H., & Zucker, R. (1995). Parent-child interactions in alcoholic and nonalcoholic families. *American Journal of Orthopsychiatry, 65,*153–159.

Whisman, M. (2006). Role of couples relationships in understanding and treating mental disorders. In S. Beach, M. Wambolt, & N. Kaslow (Eds.), *Relational processes and DSM-V, neuroscience, assessment, prevention and treatment* (pp. 225–238). APPI Press.

Whisman, M. A., & Uebelacker, L.A. (2006). Impairment and distress associated with relationship discord in a national sample of married or cohabiting adults. *Journal of Family Psychology 20,* 369–377.

White Bison, Inc. (2002). *The red road to wellbriety: In the Native American way.* Colorado Springs, CO: Coyhis Publishing.

White, L., & Edwards, J. N. (1993). Emptying the nest and parental well-being: An analysis of national panel data. *American Sociological Review, 55,* 235–242.

White, L. K., & Riedman, A. (1992a). Ties among siblings. *Social Forces, 71*(1), 85–102.

White, L. K., & Riedmun, A. (1992b). When the Brady Bunch grows up: Step/half-and full-sibling relationships in adulthood. *Journal of Marriage and the family, 54,* 197–208.

White, M. (2007). *Maps of narrative practice.* New York: Norton.

Whiteside, M. F. (2006). Remarried systems. In L. Combrinck-Graham, (Ed.), *Children in family contexts: Perspectives on treatment* (pp. 163–189). New York: Guilford Press.

Williams, C. (1992). *No hiding place: Empowerment and recovery for our troubled communities.* San Francisco: Harper.

Williams, D. R., Neighbors, H. W., & Jackson, J. S. (2003). Racial/ethnic discrimination and health: Findings from community studies. *American Journal of Public Health, 903,* 200–208.

Williams, W. L. (1998). Social acceptance of same-sex relationships in families. Models from other cultures. In C. J. Patterson & A.R. D'Augelli (Eds.), *Lesbian, gay, and bisexual identities in families: Psychological perspectives* (pp. 53 – 74). New York: Oxford University Press.

Wilson, W. J. (1997). *When work disappears: The world of the new urban poor.* New York: Vintage.

Wilson, W. J. (2009). *More than just race: Being Black and poor in the inner city.* New York: W. W. Norton.

Wink, P., & Dillon, M. (2002). Spiritual development across the adult life course: Findings from a longitudinal study. *Journal of Adult Development, 9*(1), 79–94.

Woehrer, C. (1982). The influence of ethnic families on intergenerational relationships and later life transitions. *Annals of American Academy, 464,* 65–78.

Wolf, A. E. (2001). *Get out of my life but first could you drive me and Cheryl to the mall?* New York: Noonday Press.

Wolf, S. J. (2009, June). What makes us happy. *Atlantic,* 8–16.

Wolfe, D. L. (2009). Review of single by chance, mothers by choice: How women are choosing parenthood without marriage and creating the new American family. *American Journal of Sociology, 114*(5), 1568–1570.

Wolfer, L. T., & Moen, P. (1996). Staying in school: Maternal employment and the timing of Black and White daughters' school exit. *Journal of Family Issues, 17*(4), 540–560.

Wolfinger, N. H. (2005). *Understanding the divorce cycle.* New York: Cambridge University Press.

Wolin, S. J., & *Bennett, S. A.* (1984). Family rituals. *Family Process, 23*(3), 401–420.

Wong, G. (2005). Ka-ching! Wedding price tag nears $30K. *CNN/Money.* Retrieved May 20, from www. CNNmoney.com

Wong, L., & *Mock, M. R.* (1997). Asian American young adults. In E. Lee (Ed.), *Working with Asian Americans: A guide for clinicians* (pp. 196–207). New York: Guilford Press.

Woods N., & *Mitchell, E.* (2006). Depressed mood symptoms during the menopausal transition: Observations from the Seattle Midlife Women's Health Study. *American Sociological Review, 55,* p. 235–242.

Worden, J. W. (2001). *Children and grief: When a parent dies.* New York: Guilford.

Worden, J. W. (2008). *Grief counseling and grief therapy* (4th ed). New York: Springer.

Worden, J. W., Davies, B., & *McCown, D.* (1999). Comparing parent loss with sibling loss. *Death Studies, 23,* 1–15.

Wortman, C., & *Silver, R.* (1989). The myths of coping with loss. *Journal of Counseling and Clinical Psychology, 57,* 349–357.

Wright, L., & *Bell, J.* (2009). *Beliefs and illness: A model for healing.* Calgary, Alberta, Canada: 4th Floor Press.

Yurgelun-Todd, D. A., & *Killgore, W. D. S.* (2006). Fear-related activity in the prefrontal cortex increases with age during adolescence: A preliminary fMRI study. *Neuroscience Letters, 406,* 194–199.

Zahn, M., & *Pandy, S.* (2004). Economic well-being of single mothers: Work first or post-secondary education? *Journal of Sociology and Social Welfare, 31*(3), 87–112.

Zayas, L. (2006). Introduction to the Conference on Developing Interventions for Latino Children, Youth and Families, Washington University St. Louis, MO.

Zayas, L. H., Lester, R. J., Cabassa, L. J., & *Fortuna, L. R.* (2005). Why do so many Latina teens attempt suicide? A conceptual model for research. *American Journal of Orthopsychiatry, 75*(2), 275–287.

Zayas, L. H., & *Pilat, A. M.* (2008). Suicidal behavior in Latinas: Explanatory cultural factors and implications for intervention. *Suicide and Life-Threatening Behavior, 38,* 334–342.

Zernike, K. (2007, January 21). Why are there so many single Americans. *New York Times,* p. D2.

Zezima, K. (2008, August 20). More women than ever are childless, census finds. *New York Times,* p. A12.

Zukow, P. G. (Ed.). (1989). *Sibling interaction across cultures.* New York: Springer-Verlag.

Zuniga, M. (1991). Transracial adoption: Educating the parents. *Journal of Multicultural Social Work, 1*(2), 17–31.

NAME INDEX

SUBJECT INDEX